P9-EEL-733

131545

# BEACON
## BIBLE COMMENTARY

THIRD PRINTING, 1967

COPYRIGHT 1964 BY
BEACON HILL PRESS OF KANSAS CITY
KANSAS CITY, MO.

LIBRARY OF CONGRESS
CARD NUMBER 64-22906

Printed in the United States of America

# BEACON
## BIBLE COMMENTARY

*In Ten Volumes*

## Volume VI

**MATTHEW**

. *Ralph Earle, B.D., M.A., Th.D.*

**MARK**
*A. Elwood Sanner, M.A., D.D.*

**LUKE**
*Charles L. Childers, B.D., M.A., Ph.D.*

BEACON HILL PRESS OF KANSAS CITY
Kansas City, Missouri

# BEACON BIBLE COMMENTARY

## In Ten Volumes

Volume

I. Genesis; Exodus; Leviticus; Numbers; Deuteronomy

II. Joshua; Judges; Ruth; I and II Samuel; I and II Kings;
I and II Chronicles; Ezra; Nehemiah; Esther

III. Job; Psalms; Proverbs; Ecclesiastes; Song of Solomon

IV. Isaiah; Jeremiah; Lamentations; Ezekiel; Daniel

V. Hosea; Joel; Amos; Obadiah; Jonah; Micah; Nahum; Habakkuk; Zephaniah; Haggai; Zechariah; Malachi

VI. Matthew; Mark; Luke

VII. John; Acts

VIII. Romans; I and II Corinthians

IX. Galatians; Ephesians; Philippians; Colossians; I and II
Thessalonians; I and II Timothy; Titus; Philemon

X. Hebrews; James; I and II Peter; I, II, and III John; Jude;
Revelation

# Preface

"All scripture is given by inspiration of God, and is profitable for doctrine, for reproof, for correction, for instruction in righteousness: that the man of God may be perfect, throughly furnished unto all good works" (II Tim. 3:16-17).

We believe in the plenary inspiration of the Bible. God speaks to men through His Word. He hath spoken unto us by His Son. But without the inscripted Word how would we know the Word which was made flesh? He does speak to us by His Spirit, but the Spirit uses the written Word as the vehicle of His revelation, for He is the true Author of the Holy Scriptures. What the Spirit reveals is in agreement with the Word.

The Christian faith derives from the Bible. It is the Foundation for faith, for salvation, and sanctification. It is the Guide for Christian character and conduct. "Thy word is a lamp unto my feet, and a light unto my path" (Ps. 119:105).

The revelation of God and His will for men is adequate and complete in the Bible. The great task of the Church, therefore, is to communicate the knowledge of the Word, to enlighten the eyes of their understanding, and to awaken and to illuminate the conscience that men may learn "to live soberly, righteously, and godly, in this present world." This leads to the possession of that "inheritance [that is] incorruptible, and undefiled, and that fadeth not away, reserved in heaven."

When we consider the translation and interpretation of the Bible, we admit we are guided by men who are not inspired. Human limitation, as well as the plain fact that no scripture is of private or single interpretation, allows variation in the exegesis and exposition of the Bible.

The *Beacon Bible Commentary* is offered in ten volumes with becoming modesty. It does not supplant others. Neither does it purport to be exhaustive or final. The task is colossal. Assignments have been made to thirty-three of the ablest writers available. They are trained men with serious purpose, deep dedication, and supreme devotion. It is candidly admitted that this is a commentary written from the viewpoint of Wesleyan-Arminian theology. Nevertheless, it is hoped that it will have value to all who seek to know the truth as it is in Jesus. The sponsors and publishers, as well as the contributors, earnestly pray that this new offering among Bible commentaries will be helpful to preachers, teachers, and laymen in discovering the deeper meaning of God's Word and in unfolding its message to all who hear them.

We, the Board of General Superintendents of the Church of the Nazarene, recommend the *Beacon Bible Commentary* for general usage to all who love and desire better to know "the word of God, which liveth and abideth for ever."

—G. B. WILLIAMSON

# Acknowledgments

The writers and editors wish to acknowledge indebtedness to all whose works have been consulted and quoted. Permission to quote from copyrighted material has been received as follows:

Abingdon Press: *The Interpreter's Bible; Interpreter's Dictionary of the Bible.*

"Christianity Today": a poem, "As in Thy Sight."

Concordia Publishing House: *Follow Me: Discipleship According to St. Matthew.*

William B. Eerdmans Publishing Company: *The Gospel According to St. Matthew.* "Tyndale New Testament Commentaries."

Harper and Row: *A Commentary on the Gospel According to St. Matthew.* "Harper's New Testament Commentaries."

Herder and Herder: *New Testament Introduction.*

John Knox Press: *The Gospel According to St. Matthew.* "The Layman's Bible Commentary."

Macmillan and Company: *The Names of Jesus.*

University of Chicago Press: *A Greek-English Lexicon of the New Testament and Other Early Christian Literature.*

Scripture quotations have been used from the following sources:

*The Amplified New Testament.* Copyright 1958, The Lockman Foundation, La Habra, California.

*The Berkeley Version in Modern English.* Copyright 1958, 1959, Zondervan Publishing House.

*The Bible: A New Translation,* James Moffatt. Copyright 1950, 1952, 1953, 1954, by James A. R. Moffatt. Used by permission of Harper and Row.

*The Bible: An American Translation,* J. M. Powis Smith, Edgar J. Goodspeed. Copyright 1923, 1927, 1948 by The University of Chicago Press.

*New American Standard Version.* Copyright 1960, 1962, 1963, The Lockman Foundation, La Habra, California.

*The New English Bible.* © The Delegates of the Oxford University Press and the Syndics of the Cambridge University Press, 1961.

We acknowledge our debt to the many unnamed persons who have given time and counsel in planning for the *Beacon Bible Commentary.* Special appreciation is due Dr. Richard S. Taylor for assistance to the editors in the preparation of this first volume to be released in the series.

# *How to Use the Beacon Bible Commentary*

The Bible is a Book to be read, to be understood, to be obeyed, and to be shared with others. The *Beacon Bible Commentary* is planned to help at the points of understanding and sharing.

For the most part, the Bible is its own best interpreter. He who reads it with an open mind and receptive spirit will again and again become aware that through its pages God is speaking *to him*. A commentary serves as a valuable resource when the meaning of a passage is not clear even to the thoughtful reader. Also after one has seen his own meaning in a passage from the Bible, it is rewarding to discover what truth others have found in the same place. Sometimes, too, this will correct possible misconceptions the reader may have formed.

*Beacon Bible Commentary* has been written to be used with your Bible in hand. Most major commentaries print the text of the Bible at the top of the commentary page. The editors decided against this practice, believing that the average user comes to his commentary from his Bible and hence has in mind the passage in which he is interested. He also has his Bible at his elbow for any necessary reference to the text. To have printed the full text of the Bible in a work of this size would have occupied approximately one-third of the space available. The planners decided to give this space to additional resources for the reader. At the same time, writers have woven into their comments sufficient quotations from the passages under discussion that the reader maintains easy and constant thought contact with the words of the Bible. These quoted words are printed in boldface type for quick identification.

## ILLUMINATION FROM RELATED PASSAGES

The Bible is its own best interpreter when a given chapter or a longer section is read to find out what it says. This book is also its own best interpreter when the reader knows what the Bible says in other places about the subject under consideration. The writers and editors of *Beacon Bible Commentary* have constantly striven to give maximum help at this point. Related and carefully chosen cross-references have been included in order that the reader may thus find the Bible interpreted and illustrated by the Bible itself.

## PARAGRAPH TREATMENT

The truth of the Bible is best understood when we grasp the thought of the writer in its sequence and connections. The verse divisions with which we are familiar came into the Bible late (the sixteenth century for the New Testament and the seventeenth century for the Old). They were done hurriedly and sometimes missed the thought pattern of the inspired writers. The same is true of the chapter divisions. Most translations today arrange the words of the sacred writers under our more familiar paragraph structure.

It is under this paragraph arrangement that our commentary writers have approached their task. They have tried always to answer the question, What was the inspired writer saying in this passage? Verse numbers have been retained for easy identification but basic meanings have been outlined and interpreted in the larger and more complete thought forms.

## INTRODUCTIONS TO BIBLE BOOKS

The Bible is an open Book to him who reads it thoughtfully. But it opens wider when we gain increased understanding of its human origins. Who wrote this book? Where was it written? When did the writer live? What were the circumstances that caused him to write? Answers to these questions always throw added light on the words of the Scripture.

These answers are given in the Introductions. There also you will find an outline of each book. The Introduction has been written to give an overview of the whole book; to provide you with a dependable road map before you start your trip—and to give you a place of reference when you are uncertain as to which way to turn. Don't ignore the flagman when he waves his warning sign, "See Introduction." At the close of the commentary on each book you will find a bibliography for further study.

## MAPS AND CHARTS

The Bible was written about people who lived in lands that are foreign and strange to most English-speaking readers. Often better understanding of the Bible depends on better knowledge of Bible geography. When the flagman waves his other sign, "See map," you should turn to the map for a clearer understanding of locations, distances, and related timing of the experiences of the men with whom God was dealing.

This knowledge of Bible geography will help you to be a better Bible preacher and teacher. Even in the more formal presentation of the sermon it helps the congregation to know that the flight into Egypt was "a journey on foot, some 200 miles to the southwest." In the less formal and smaller groups such as Sunday school classes and prayer meeting Bible study, a large classroom map enables the group to see the locations as well as to hear them mentioned. When you have seen these places on your commentary maps, you are better prepared to share the information with those whom you lead in Bible study.

Charts which list Bible facts in tabular form often make clear historical relationships in the same way that maps help with understanding geography. To see listed in order the kings of Judah or the Resurrection appearances of Jesus often gives clearer understanding of a particular item in the series. These charts are a part of the resources offered in this set.

*Beacon Bible Commentary* has been written for the newcomer to Bible study and also for those long familiar with the written Word. The writers and editors have probed each chapter, each verse, every clause, phrase, and word in the familiar King James Version. We have probed with the question, What do these words mean? If the answer is not self-evident, we have charged ourselves to give the best explanation known to us. How well we have succeeded the reader must judge, but we invite you to explore these words or passages that puzzle you when you are reading God's written Word.

## EXEGESIS AND EXPOSITION

Bible commentators often use these words to describe two ways of making clear the meaning of a passage in the Scriptures. *Exegesis* is a study of the original Greek or Hebrew words to understand what meanings those words had when they were used by men and women in Bible times. To know the meaning of the separate words, as well as their grammatical relationship to each other, is one way to understand more clearly what the inspired writer meant to say. You will often find this kind of enriching help in the commentary. But word studies alone do not always give true meaning.

*Exposition* is a commentator's effort to point out the meaning of a passage as it is affected by any one of several facts known to the writer but perhaps not familiar to the reader. These facts may be (1) the context (the surrounding verses or chapters), (2) the historical background, (3) the related teachings from other parts of the Bible, (4) the significance of these messages from God as they relate to universal facts of human life, (5) the relevance of these truths to unique contemporary human situations. The commentator thus seeks to explain the full meaning of a Bible passage in the light of his own best understanding of God, man, and the world in which we live.

Some commentaries separate the exegesis from this broader basis of explanation. In *Beacon Bible Commentary* writers have combined the exegesis and exposition. Accurate word studies are indispensable to a correct understanding of the Bible. But such careful studies are today so thoroughly reflected in a number of modern English translations that they are often not necessary except to enhance the understanding of the theological meaning of a passage. The writers and editors seek to reflect a true and accurate exegesis at every point, but specific exegetical discussions are introduced chiefly to throw added light on the meaning of a passage, rather than to engage in scholarly discussion.

The Bible is a practical Book. We believe that God inspired holy men of old to declare these truths in order that the readers might better understand and do the will of God. *Beacon Bible Commentary* has been undertaken only for the purpose of helping men to find more effectively God's will for them as revealed in the Scripture—to find that will and to act upon that knowledge.

## Helps for Bible Preaching and Teaching

We have said that the Bible is a Book to be shared. Christian preachers and teachers since the first century have sought to convey the gospel message by reading and explaining selected passages of Scripture. The *Beacon Bible Commentary* seeks to encourage this kind of expository preaching and teaching. The set contains more than a thousand brief expository outlines that have been used by outstanding Bible teachers and preachers. It is hoped that these outlines will suggest ways in which the reader will want to try to open the Word of God to his class or congregation. Some of these analyses of preachable passages have been contributed by our contemporaries. When the outlines have appeared in print, authors and references are given in order that the reader may go to the original source for further help.

In the Bible we find truth of the highest order. Here is given to us, by divine inspiration, the will of God for our lives. Here we have sure guidance in all things necessary to our relationships to God and under Him to our fellowman. Because these eternal truths come to us in human language and through human minds, they need to be put into fresh words as languages change and as thought patterns are modified. In *Beacon Bible Commentary* we have sought to help make the Bible a more effective Lamp to the paths of men who journey in the twentieth century.

A. F. HARPER

# Table of Contents

## VOLUME VI

**MATTHEW**

| | |
|---|---|
| Introduction | 19 |
| Commentary | 27 |
| Bibliography | 255 |

**MARK**

| | |
|---|---|
| Introduction | 263 |
| Commentary | 269 |
| Bibliography | 415 |

**LUKE**

| | |
|---|---|
| Introduction | 419 |
| Commentary | 425 |
| Bibliography | 620 |

**MAPS AND CHARTS**

| | |
|---|---|
| Mark's Chronology of Holy Week | 366 |
| Temple Floor Plan | 622 |
| Palestine During the Ministry of Jesus | 623 |

# Abbreviations and Explanations

## The Books of the Bible

| | | |
|---|---|---|
| Gen. | Isa. | Luke |
| Exod. | Jer. | John |
| Lev. | Lam. | Acts |
| Num. | Ezek. | Rom. |
| Deut. | Dan. | I or II Cor. |
| Josh. | Hos. | Gal. |
| Judg. | Joel | Eph. |
| Ruth | Amos | Phil. |
| I or II Sam. | Obad. | Col. |
| I or II Kings | Jonah | I or II Thess. |
| I or II Chron. | Mic. | I or II Tim. |
| Ezra | Nah. | Titus |
| Neh. | Hab. | Philem. |
| Esther | Zeph. | Heb. |
| Job | Hag. | Jas. |
| Ps. | Zech. | I or II Pet. |
| Prov. | Mal. | I, II, or III John |
| Eccles. | Matt. | Jude |
| Song of Sol. | Mark | Rev. |

| | |
|---|---|
| Vulg. | The Vulgate |
| LXX | The Septuagint |
| ASV | American Standard Revised Version |
| ERV | English Revised Version |
| RSV | Revised Standard Version |
| Amplified NT | Amplified New Testament |
| NASB | New American Standard Bible |
| NEB | New English Bible |
| c. | chapter |
| cc. | chapters |
| v. | verse |
| vv. | verses |
| OT | Old Testament |
| NT | New Testament |
| Heb. | Hebrew |
| Gk. | Greek |

## Quotations and References

Boldface type in the exposition indicates a quotation from the King James Version of the passage under discussion. Readings from other versions are put in quotation marks and the version is indicated.

In scripture references a letter (*a, b,* etc.) indicates a clause within a verse. When no book is named, the book under discussion is understood.

Bibliographical data on a work cited by a writer may be found by consulting the first reference to the work by that writer, or by turning to the bibliography.

*The Gospel According to*

# MATTHEW

**Ralph Earle**

# *Introduction*

## A. IMPORTANCE

The great French critic Renan has often been quoted in his famous statement that the Gospel of Matthew is "the most important book which has ever been written." It is doubtful if that assertion will be seriously challenged. It was the leading Gospel in the Early Church and has a large place today. Zahn says: "In greatness of conception, and in the power with which a mass of material is subordinated to great ideas, no writing in either Testament, dealing with a historical theme, is to be compared with Matthew."[1] It stands on the threshold of the New Testament, linking it with the Old.

## B. AUTHORSHIP

All four Gospels are anonymous; they bear no author's names. However, the tradition of the Early Church assigns them respectively to Matthew, Mark, Luke, and John.

Papias, who wrote about A.D. 140 is the earliest witness on the subject of authorship. He said that Matthew composed the discourses or sayings (*logia*) "in the Hebrew dialect" (Aramaic), and "every one translated it as he was able."[2]

The anti-Marcionite prologue to Matthew has been lost. But the one to Luke says that Matthew wrote his Gospel in Judea.[3] Irenaeus (*ca.* A.D. 185) says: "Matthew, indeed, produced his gospel among the Hebrews in their own dialect whilst Peter and Paul proclaimed the gospel and founded the church at Rome."[4] Origen (*ca.* A.D. 220) says of the Gospels: "The first is according to Matthew, the same that was once a publican, but afterwards an apostle of Jesus Christ, who having published it for the Jewish converts, wrote it in the Hebrew."[5] The fact that this Gospel was written for Jews is well supported by the nature of its contents. Eusebius' own comment is this: "Matthew also having first pro-

---

[1]Theodor Zahn, *Introduction to the New Testament* (Grand Rapids: Kregel Publications, 1953 [reprint]), II, 556.

[2]Eusebius *Ecclesiastical History*, trans. C. F. Cruse (Grand Rapids: Baker Book House, 1955 [reprint]), III. 39 (p. 127).

[3]Alfred Wikenhauser, *New Testament Introduction*, trans. Joseph Cunningham (New York: Herder and Herder, 1958), p. 181.

[4]Eusebius, *op. cit.*, V. 8 (p. 187).

[5]*Ibid.*, VI. 25 (p. 245).

claimed the gospel in Hebrew, when on the point of going also to other nations, committed it to writing in his native tongue, and thus supplied the want of his presence to them, by his writings."[6]

The earliest testimony, then, cites an Aramaic collection of "sayings." Is our present Gospel of Matthew a translation of this? Wikenhauser writes: "It may be taken as certain that an Aramaic original of the Gospel of St. Matthew can be defended only if we regard Greek Matthew not as a literal translation of the Aramaic, but as a thorough revision made with frequent use of the Gospel of St. Mark."[7]

Tasker, who is professor emeritus of New Testament exegesis in the University of London, interprets the early tradition thus: "It is conceivable that Matthew, who was in all probability bilingual, himself translated his original work or republished it in an enlarged Greek edition."[8] He also says: "Of all the apostles whose previous occupations are known to us, Matthew would appear to be the most qualified to undertake the composition of the kind of narratives that we find embedded in the 'first' Gospel."[9]

Matthew is listed by that name in all four of the lists of the twelve apostles (Matt. 10:3; Mark 3:18; Luke 6:15; Acts 1:13), but only in Matthew's list is he identified as "the publican" (i.e., "tax collector"). The only other place in the New Testament where the name Matthew occurs is in connection with his call to follow Jesus, as recorded by Matthew (9:9). In the other two accounts of this call he is designated as "Levi" (Mark 2:14; Luke 5:27, 29). It appears that this apostle, in keeping with numbers of other men in the New Testament, was known by two different names (cf. John Mark; Saul, Paul). The refusal of many scholars today to identify Matthew with Levi is unreasonable.

The current arguments against the Matthean authorship of the first Gospel are unconvincing. Recently one of the leading New Testament scholars in America has written a vigorous exposition and defense of the traditional view that Matthew the

[6]*Ibid.*, III. 24 (p. 108).

[7]*Op. cit.*, p. 195.

[8]R. V. G. Tasker, *The Gospel According to St. Matthew* ("Tyndale New Testament Commentaries"; Grand Rapids: Wm. B. Eerdmans Publishing Co., 1961), p. 15.

[9]*Ibid.*, p. 14.

apostle was the writer of this Gospel.[10] Of course, it should be realized that, since the four Gospels are anonymous, one is not bound to accept any theory of authorship. But the tradition of the Early Church should not be dismissed lightly. There must have been some historical basis for the universal assignment of the names Matthew, Mark, Luke, and John to these four books. So we take the position that Matthew the apostle wrote the Gospel which bears his name.

### C. Date

As in the case of most of the books of the New Testament, the date is uncertain. Older writers assigned Matthew to about A.D. 60. Most scholars today prefer 80 or 85. Streeter favors the latter.[11] The matter is not of vital importance, though we prefer the earlier date.

### D. Place of Writing

Again there are two main views. The traditional one is that Matthew was written in Palestine (cf. "Judea," above). Streeter says the place was Syrian Antioch,[12] and he is followed by the majority of scholars today. Perhaps the Aramaic collection of sayings was written in Palestine and the Greek Gospel in Antioch.

### E. Purpose

It is evident that Matthew wrote his Gospel for the Jews, to present Jesus as the Messiah. When the Gospel was written the nation had already rejected Him, and was soon—if Matthew was written in the sixties—to suffer severe judgment for it in the destruction of Jerusalem (A.D. 70). Hayes says: "The first Gospel had something of the character of an official ultimatum. It was a last call of Jehovah to his people."[13]

### F. Sources

It is the general consensus of scholarship today that Matthew (as also Luke) used Mark as the main source for his historical framework, and a collection of "Sayings" (Q, or the Logia) for the teachings of Jesus. Matthew often summarizes Mark's narra-

---

[10]Edgar J. Goodspeed, *Matthew, Apostle and Evangelist* (Philadelphia: John C. Winston Co., 1959), pp. 77-98. The title of the book indicates its thesis.

[11]B. H. Streeter, *The Four Gospels* (rev. ed.; London: Macmillan and Co., 1930), pp. 523-24.

[12]*Ibid.*, pp. 500-507.

[13]D. A. Hayes, *The Synoptic Gospels and the Book of Acts* (New York: Methodist Book Concern, 1919), p. 90.

tives and is usually less vivid in his descriptions. Over 90 percent of the material in Mark is found also in Matthew. But Mark does not seem to be an abridgement of Matthew, as Augustine held, because its style and presentation are fresher and more vigorous.

Streeter has postulated another source, called M, to account for the material found only in Matthew.[14] But Tasker has a good answer for this. He says: "The difference between Matthew and Mark may equally well be explained on the supposition that the Gospel of Matthew retains details originally handed down by the apostle of that name, and that the Gospel of Mark often draws upon Peter's reminiscences."[15] We would go one step further than Tasker and say that the details were *written down* by Matthew in the composition of his Gospel.

### G. CHARACTER

The Gospel of Matthew is the most *Jewish* of the Gospels. Its Jewish genealogy of Jesus goes back only to Abraham, and is placed at the beginning of the Gospel. This was because the Jews' first question would be about a man's ancestry. Luke does not give his genealogy of Jesus until the third chapter, and he takes it back to Adam. Jesus is described in the very first verse of Matthew as "the son of David, the son of Abraham." Matthew does not explain Jewish customs and terms, as Mark and Luke do, for his readers would understand them. He makes more reference to the law of Moses than do the others (cf. c. 5). He gives more fulfillments of Old Testament prophecy than the others do. Phrases such as "that it might be fulfilled which was spoken" occur thirteen times in Matthew and never in Mark or Luke (six times in John). Matthew emphasizes "righteousness" more than all the other Gospels put together. This was the central idea of Jewish religion. The word "kingdom" occurs more often here (fifty-six times) than in any other Gospel, and the phrase "the kingdom of heaven" is found only in Matthew (thirty-three times) in the entire New Testament.

Jesus is presented to the Jews not only as their Messiah, but as their King. At the very beginning the genealogy gives the royal line, proving Jesus' right to the throne of David. The wise men asked for "the King of the Jews" (only in Matthew). There is more emphasis on Jesus as King than in the other Gospels.

---

[14]*Op. cit.*, p. 150. See also G. D. Kilpatrick, *The Origins of the Gospel According to St. Matthew* (Oxford: Clarendon Press, 1946), p. 9.

[15]*Op. cit.*, p. 14.

The other outstanding characteristic of this Gospel (besides its Jewishness) is its *systematic arrangement.* Matthew had probably received some business training, and had to keep books as a tax collector. He presents his material in systematic order. He has seven (perfect number) parables of the Kingdom in chapter thirteen. In chapters eight and nine he groups together ten miracles of Jesus. Three and seven are both prominent numbers in his Gospel, and here he adds them together.

The most obvious example of this characteristic is Matthew's arrangement of the teachings of Jesus into five great discourses. These are: (1) the Sermon on the Mount, cc. 5—7; (2) Instructions to the Twelve, c. 10; (3) Seven Parables of the Kingdom, c. 13; (4) The Christian Community, c. 18; (5) the Olivet Discourse, cc. 24—25. Each one concludes with the formula: "And it came to pass, when Jesus had ended."

The main impression one receives as he reads this Gospel is that a Jewish writer is presenting Jesus to Jews as their Messiah. D. A. Hayes says that the Gospel of Matthew is "almost a manual of Messianic prophecy."[16]

[16]*Op. cit.,* p. 44.

# Outline

I.   The Preparation of the Messiah, 1:1—4:25
    A.  The Genealogy of Jesus, 1:1-17
    B.  The Birth of Jesus, 1:18-25
    C.  The Childhood of Jesus, 2:1-23
    D.  The Ministry of John the Baptist, 3:1-12
    E.  The Baptism of Jesus, 3:13-17
    F.  The Temptation of Jesus, 4:1-11
    G.  The Beginnings in Galilee, 4:12-25

II.  First Discourse: Sermon on the Mount, 5:1—7:29
    A.  The Setting of the Sermon, 5:1-2
    B.  The Nature of the Disciples, 5:3-16
    C.  The Righteousness of the Disciples, 5:17-48
    D.  The Religion of the Disciples, 6:1-34
    E.  The Life of the Disciples, 7:1-29

III. Narrative Resumed: A Ministry of Miracles, 8:1—9:34
    A.  Three Healing Miracles, 8:1-17
    B.  The Cost of Discipleship, 8:18-22
    C.  Three More Miracles, 8:23—9:8
    D.  Mercy, Not Sacrifice, 9:9-17
    E.  Third Group of Miracles, 9:18-34

IV.  Second Discourse: Instructions to the Twelve, 9:35—10:42
    A.  The Need for Laborers, 9:35-38
    B.  The Mission of the Twelve, 10:1-42

V.   Narrative Resumed: Rejection of the Messiah, 11:1—12:50
    A.  Jesus and John the Baptist, 11:1-19
    B.  Jesus and the Cities, 11:20-24
    C.  Jesus and the Simple, 11:25-30
    D.  Jesus and the Pharisees, 12:1-45
    E.  Jesus and His Family, 12:46-50

VI.  Third Discourse: Parables of the Kingdom, 13:1-52
    A.  The Setting, 13:1-2
    B.  The Seven Parables, 13:3-50
    C.  The Sequel, 13:51-52

VII. Narrative Resumed: Journeys of Jesus, 13:53—17:27
    A.  Jesus and John Rejected, 13:53—14:12
    B.  Further Miracles, 14:13-36
    C.  Ceremonial vs. Moral Defilement, 15:1-20
    D.  More Miracles, 15:21-39

       E. Blind Pharisees and Seeing Disciples, 16: 1—17: 27

VIII. Fourth Discourse: The Christian Community, 18:1-35
       A. The Christian and Children, 18:1-14
       B. The Christian and His Brother, 18:15-35

  IX. Narrative Resumed: Discipleship and Controversy, 19:1—23:39
       A. Discipleship, 19:1—20:34
       B. Controversy, 21:1—23:39

   X. Fifth Discourse: Olivet Discourse, 24:1—25:46
       A. The End of the Age, 24:1-51
       B. Three Parables on Preparedness, 25:1-46

  XI. The Passion, 26:1—27:66
       A. Preparation for Death, 26:1—27:31
       B. Death and Burial, 27:32-66

  XII. The Resurrection, 28:1-20
       A. The Day of the Resurrection, 28:1-15
       B. The Great Commission, 28:16-20

# Section I The Preparation of the Messiah

## A. THE GENEALOGY OF JESUS, 1:1-17

### 1. Who Jesus Was (1:1)

As noted in the Introduction, Matthew wrote his Gospel especially for the Jews. It is very natural, therefore, that it should begin with a genealogy. Particularly after the Babylonian captivity the Jews put a great deal of emphasis on proper genealogical records. This is highlighted in the long lists of generations in the first nine chapters of I Chronicles. The Book of Nehemiah tells how some Levites were put out of the priesthood because they could not produce their genealogies (Neh. 7:63-65). Obviously, Jesus would not be accepted as the Jewish Messiah unless it could be proved by the genealogical records that He was the son of David, for the Jews believed that their Messiah would come from the royal line of Israel's greatest king and that He would be born in David's hometown of Bethlehem (see 2:4-6).

Jesus is first identified as **Christ.** This is from the Greek *christos,* which is the equivalent of the Hebrew *mashiah* (Messiah). Both mean the "anointed one." **Jesus** is the Greek equivalent of the Hebrew *yehoshua* (Joshua) in its later form *yeshua.* The name means "Jehovah will save." Thus the Supreme Person of this Gospel is identified as the Saviour-Messiah. But by the time the Gospel of Matthew was written **Jesus Christ** had come to be used as a proper name.

The Subject of this book is identified in the second place as **the son of David.** That is, He was the lawful Heir to the throne of David. Also this was a Messianic title. Vincent Taylor writes: "Like the name 'Christ', 'the Son of David' is a Messianic title; it describes the Messiah as a human figure, a national deliverer, under whose leadership, it was hoped, the ancient promises of God for Israel would be fulfilled."[1]

In the third place Jesus is identified as **the son of Abraham.** That asserts that He was a true Jew. This fact was all-important,

[1]Vincent Taylor, *The Names of Jesus* (London: Macmillan & Co., 1953), p. 24.

for no Gentile would be acceptable to the Jews as a religious leader.

The Greek word for **generation** is *genesis*. It means "origin, lineage."[2] Arndt and Gingrich say: "The expression *biblos geneseos* Matt. 1:1 is from the Old Testament: Gen. 2:4; 5:1; in the former of these two passages it equals *history of the origin,* which would be a fitting heading for Matt. 1, while in the latter it equals *genealogy,* which describes the contents of Matt. 1:1-17."[3] Zahn thinks that the first verse was intended to be the title for the entire book. He says of the author of Matthew's Gospel: "He gave his writing the title 'Book of the History of Jesus.' "[4] Other scholars take the first verse as constituting the heading for the genealogy alone (1:2-17).

## 2. *From Abraham to David* (1:2-6a)

Most of the recent versions (RSV, NEB) and private translations (e.g., Weymouth, Moffatt, Goodspeed, Verkuyl, Williams) have "Abraham was the father of Isaac" (which is more up-to-date language), and so on down through the entire genealogical table. But the Greek says quite clearly and simply: **Abraham begat Isaac (2).**

In the first paragraph of the genealogy we find the names of three women, and a fourth is mentioned in verse 6b. This is a strange phenomenon, to say the least. And doubly surprising is the character of these four women. Two were Gentiles—**Rachab** and **Ruth** (5). While the other two were Israelites, their names are sullied. **Tamar** (3) was guilty of incest (Gen. 38:13-18) and **the wife of Urias** was (6) a partner in adultery (II Sam. 11:2-5).

The presence of such persons in the genealogy of Jesus illuminates His mission as Saviour and furnishes a marvelous display of the grace of God. Not only outwardly righteous Jews, but foreigners and sinners as well, were to be offered an entrance into the kingdom of Heaven. This is what makes the gospel Good News for all mankind.

Then too, Jesus must be truly human as well as divine if He was to be the Saviour of humanity. The Incarnation meant

[2]G. Abbott-Smith, *A Manual Greek Lexicon of the New Testament* (2d ed.; Edinburgh: T. & T. Clark, 1923), p. 90.

[3]*A Greek-English Lexicon of the New Testament and Other Early Christian Literature* (Chicago: University of Chicago Press, 1957), p. 154.

[4]Theodor Zahn, *Introduction to the New Testament* (Grand Rapids: Kregel Publications, 1953 [reprint]), II, 532.

that He must be a part of the human race, which involved inevitably His having sinful ancestors.

### 3. *From David to the Captivity* (1:6b-11)

This is the kingdom period. Following Solomon the names of the kings of Judah are given, for it was David's dynasty that ruled the southern kingdom. Strangely, four kings are omitted from the list, as a comparison with the Old Testament Books of Kings will show. Ahaziah, Joash, and Amaziah are omitted after **Joram** (8), and Jehoiakim after **Josiah** (11). The only reason, apparently, that can be assigned for this is that Matthew wished to preserve his systematic arrangement of the genealogy into three groups of fourteen each.

### 4. *From the Captivity to Christ* (1:12-16)

This is largely the period between the Old and New Testaments. Hence the names are unfamiliar.

The exact wording of the sixteenth verse is exceedingly significant. The writer changes from the active **begat** to the passive **was born** (16). Thus he protects the fact of the Virgin Birth, soon to be described. Joseph was the foster-father of Jesus, but not His physical father. But Mary was actually His mother.

On the meaning of the word *begat* in this chapter M'Neile has this to say: "The nature of the genealogy shows that *egennesen* throughout denotes legal, not necessarily physical, descent," but the passive, *egennethe,* **was born,** "denotes physical birth."[5]

### 5. *Summary of the Genealogy* (1:17)

Why does Matthew use the threefold enumeration of **fourteen** (17)? Tasker says: "It has been suggested, with considerable probability, that the significance he found in the number *fourteen* is that the numerical value of the Hebrew consonants in the word *David* add up to that number."[6]

It should be noted that the three periods pointed up here stand out in bold relief. The first was that of the patriarchs and judges, the second that of the kings, the third that of Gentile domination (except for the brief time of Maccabean independence).

[5]Alan H. M'Neile, *The Gospel According to St. Matthew* (London: Macmillan & Co., 1915), p. 4.

[6]R. V. G. Tasker, *The Gospel According to St. Matthew* ("The Tyndale New Testament Commentaries"; Grand Rapids: Wm. B. Eerdmans Publishing Co., 1961), pp. 31-32.

**Unto Christ** is literally "unto the Christ." Morison makes this apt observation: "And thus the evangelist passes from the use of the word *Christ* as a mere proper name to its use as an appellative, *until the Messiah,* until, that is to say, the preeminently Anointed One, the highest of all kings, and the most priestly of all priests, as well as the most inspiring and inspired of all who have ever been prophets or spokesmen for God."[7]

## B. THE BIRTH OF JESUS, 1:18-25

The so-called Infancy Narratives are found in Matthew 1:18—2:23 and Luke 1:5—2:52. The two accounts are almost entirely different. But they do not contradict each other. Plummer comments: "The two accounts agree, not only as to the main fact of the Virgin-birth, but also as to the manner of it,— that it took place through the agency of the Holy Spirit." He goes on to enumerate four other points of agreement which are "further signs of historical reality": (1) when the divine will was made known to Joseph and Mary they were espoused to each other; (2) Christ was to be called "Jesus"; (3) He was born at Bethlehem; (4) He was brought up at Nazareth.[8]

The story of the birth of Jesus is told with great beauty and delicacy. Mary was **espoused** to Joseph (18). Perhaps "betrothed" (RSV) or "engaged" (Berkeley) would seem a bit more up-to-date. The Greek verb is used only here and in Luke 1:27; 2:5. It means "to promise in marriage, betroth."[9] Arndt and Gingrich say that in the passive it denotes "be betrothed, become engaged."[10] But it must be remembered that among the Jews the breaking of a betrothal required a formal divorce. Edersheim says the relationship of betrothed young people was so sacred that "any breach of it would be treated as adultery; nor could the bond be dissolved except, as after marriage, by regular divorce."[11]

Before they were married or had any marriage relationship, Mary **was found with child of the Holy Ghost.** Thus does

[7]James Morison, *A Practical Commentary on the Gospel According to St. Matthew* (London: Hodder and Stoughton, 1899), pp. 7-8.

[8]Alfred Plummer, *An Exegetical Commentary on the Gospel According to St. Matthew* (London: Elliot Stock, 1909), p. 4.

[9]Abbott-Smith, *op. cit.,* p. 295.

[10]*Op. cit.,* p. 527.

[11]Alfred Edersheim, *The Life and Times of Jesus the Messiah* (8th ed.; New York: Longmans, Green, and Co., 1903), I, 150.

Matthew confirm Luke's fuller account (Luke 1:35). This posed a serious problem for Joseph. Being a just or "righteous" (ASV) man, he did not feel that he could go through with their plans for marriage. But being a merciful man, and one who loved Mary deeply, he was **not willing to make her a publick example (19)**; that is, expose her to shame. So he decided to divorce her quietly **(privily)**. All that was required was the presence of two witnesses. No court case was needed.

It may seem strange that Joseph should be called **her husband**. But M'Neile explains it thus: "After betrothal, therefore, but before marriage, the man was legally 'husband' (cf. Gen. xxix.21; Dt. xxii. 23 f.); hence an informal cancelling of betrothal was impossible: the man must give to the woman a writ, and pay a fine."[12]

While Joseph was pondering over his problem "an angel" (not **the angel**) appeared to him **in a dream**. The heavenly messenger addressed him as **Joseph, thou son of David (20)**. This is what gave Jesus legal right to the throne of David. Joseph was assured that he need not be afraid to take Mary as his wife, for her conception was **of the Holy Ghost**. Thus was the annunciation made to Joseph, as well as to Mary. She needed it to save her from terrifying perplexity over her coming condition. He needed it to save him from feeling that Mary had been unfaithful to him.

Joseph was informed that the Son to be born was to be named **JESUS** ("Jehovah is salvation"), for He would **save his people from their sins (21)**. Salvation was first for the Jews **(his people)**, and then for the whole world (cf. Luke 2:32). Our Lord's mission was not primarily social, political, or physical, but moral and spiritual. He came to "put away sin" (Heb. 9:26). He came to save *from* sin, not *in* sin.

For those who have been saved through His grace, this name holds special charm and sweetness. Vincent Taylor well says: "Of all names none is more precious in Christian ears than the name of 'Jesus.' "[13]

One of the outstanding characteristics of Matthew's Gospel, written for the Jews, is its frequent quotation from the Old Testament. The divine inspiration and authority of the Scriptures are emphasized by the form of the introduction: **that it**

[12]*Op. cit.*, p. 7.
[13]*Op. cit.*, p. 5.

**might be fulfilled which was spoken of the Lord by the prophet** (22). There follows a quotation from Isa. 7:14. The Hebrew name **Emmanuel** is interpreted as meaning **God with us** (23).

Joseph obeyed the angel's command. He took Mary into his house as his wife. But he had no marriage relations with her until after the birth of the promised Child. The significance of the language here is well pointed out by Plummer. He asserts that the use of the imperfect tense is "against the tradition of the perpetual virginity of Mary"; that while the use of the aorist "would have implied that she subsequently had children by him," yet "the imperfect implies this more strongly."[14] This is a reasonable view of the matter.

G. Campbell Morgan finds in this paragraph two prophetic words: (1) the hope—**they shall call his name Emmanuel, which being interpreted is, God with us,** and (2) the realization—**thou shalt call his name JESUS: for he shall save his people from their sins.**

## C. THE CHILDHOOD OF JESUS, 2:1-23

### 1. *The Visit of the Wise Men* (2:1-12)

**Jesus** was born in **Bethlehem of Judaea** (1). This was David's hometown, located about five or six miles south of Jerusalem, on the road to Hebron. The name means "house of bread"—a very appropriate designation for the village where the Bread of Life (John 6:35) was to appear among men. It is identified as being of **Judaea,** to differentiate it from a town with the same name in the territory of Zebulun (Josh. 19:15), near Nazareth. Also this designation of **Judaea** emphasized the fact that Jesus was of the royal line of David; He must be of the tribe of Judah.

Christ was born **in the days of Herod the king.** Herod the Great, as he is known in history, was an Idumean (Edomite), the son of Antipater—who was appointed by Julius Caesar in 47 B.C. as procurator of Judea. The Idumeans, who during the Babylonian captivity had taken over the southern part of the territory of Judah, were compelled to be circumcised by John Hyrcanus in 125 B.C. So they were nominally Jews. But Herod's religion, at best, was only "skin-deep." He was a cruel man, almost without a conscience.

[14]*Op. cit.,* p. 9.

Herod the Great's reign is sometimes spoken of as beginning in 40 B.C., sometimes in 37 B.C. This is due to the fact that, though the senate at Rome gave Herod the title "king of the Jews" in 40 B.C., it was 37 B.C. before he gained the throne after two years of intensive fighting.

The statement here that Jesus was born in the days of Herod, coupled with the fact that Herod the Great died in 4 B.C., indicates that our calendar is at least four years in error. Actually Jesus was probably born in 5 B.C.[15] and died in A.D. 30 (some say 29).

**From the east** came **wise men** to Jerusalem. The Greek term *magoi* (Magi) "originally denoted the priestly caste among the Persians and Babylonians (cf. Dan. 2:2, 48; 4:6-7; 5:7)."[16] It is used in Acts 13:6 for "sorcerer." But here "Matthew uses the term in the better sense to designate honorable men from an Eastern religion."[17] It is not certain from which country they came. Atkinson says, "They probably came from Mesopotamia."[18] That is as good a guess as any. Beare asserts categorically that they were "Chaldean astrologers."[19]

The question of the wise men (2) shows that they had had some definite intimation that a great **King of the Jews** (2) was born. Logically they expected to find Him in the nation's capital. Whether the star was a natural or supernatural phenomenon is a question that no one can answer but it gave divine guidance to these foreigners. It perhaps should be noted that **in the east** probably means "at its rising." At any rate, the star was

[15]The present method of dating events A.D. (*Anno Domini:* "in the year of our Lord") was introduced by Dionysius the Little about A.D. 530 and came into general use during the reign of Charlemagne (768-814). Dionysius placed the birth of Jesus on December 25, 754 A.U.C. (*Anno urbis conditate:* "in the year of the founding of the city [of Rome]"). But Edersheim has calculated that Christ was born in 749 A.U.C. (corresponding to 5 B.C. on Dionysius' calendar) and scholars are agreed that Edersheim's calculation is substantially correct. Thus Dionysius' mistake accounts for the dating of Jesus' birth from 6 to 4 B.C. (Edersheim, *op. cit.*, I, 187, 212-13).

[16]Homer A. Kent, Jr., "Matthew," *Wycliffe Bible Commentary*, ed. Charles F. Pfeiffer and Everett F. Harrison (Chicago: Moody Press, 1962), p. 932.

[17]*Ibid.*

[18]Basil F. C. Atkinson, "Gospel According to Matthew," *New Bible Commentary* (2d ed.; Grand Rapids: Wm. B. Eerdmans Publishing Co., 1954), p. 775.

[19]F. W. Beare, *The Earliest Records of Jesus* (New York: Abingdon Press, 1962), p. 31.

a type of Christ (Num. 24:17). The wise men were so greatly impressed by it that they trekked for many weary months to come and **worship him.**

Herod was greatly **troubled** (3) by this turn of events. The one thing he feared above all else was a threat to his throne. He had three of his own sons put to death because he thought they were becoming too eager to succeed him. Augustus Caesar is said to have made this pun: "It is better to be Herod's swine than his son."[20] The Greek word for "pig" is *hus,* for "son" *huios.*

Not only was Herod **troubled,** but **all Jerusalem with him.** The Roman government allowed considerable religious freedom to the people of the various nations it governed. Specifically, the Jews were permitted by the idolatrous Romans to carry on their worship of the one true God. But a "King of the Jews"? This sounded like revolution. In the eyes of the emperor this was the sin par excellence. Rome always had its ear to the ground to hear any rumblings of a revolution. The Jewish leaders feared severe reprisals if it was known that another ruler of their nation had appeared.

The worried king called together the **chief priests and scribes** (4). These were the two main groups in the Great Sanhedrin at Jerusalem, the religious governing body of the Jews. The chief priests were Sadducees, the scribes mainly Pharisees. **Scribes** is *grammateis*—literally, "writers." It was the responsibility of these men to copy the sacred Scriptures and to teach them to the people.

Herod demanded of these men **where Christ should be born.** The Greek says "the Christ"; that is, the Messiah. This shows that the king was familiar with the Jewish Messianic expectations. He doubtless had heard the Old Testament prophecies read and had a superstitious fear of what the fulfillment of them might mean to his throne and to his wicked life.

The Jewish leaders were ready with an answer. They replied, **In Bethlehem of Judaea** (5). As support for this answer they quoted from their Scriptures. The quotation from Mic. 5:2 differs somewhat from both the Hebrew text and the Septuagint (Greek) version of this passage, and perhaps borrows from II Sam. 5:2. Filson says: "It freely blends O.T. materials in a way which the Essene commentaries of the Dead Sea Scrolls show was current

---

[20]*Ibid.,* p. 32.

in first-century Judaism, and gives the material a Messianic interpretation."[21] There is also the possibility that Matthew used a Greek version of the Old Testament which varied from the Septuagint, or he may have adopted "a free translation from the Hebrew."[22]

The implications of this narrative are well stated by Plummer. He says:

> Pagans, who had nothing to guide them but smatterings of science mingled with much superstition, nevertheless are so kindled with enthusiasm by the signs which God, by means of these imperfect instruments, had granted to them, that they take a long journey and make careful investigations, in order to pay due reverence to the new Ruler who has been sent into the world. But the Jewish hierarchy, with the Pentateuch and Prophets in their hands, are so far from being elated at this report of the fulfillment of types and prophecies, that they do not care so much as to verify it.[23]

Herod called the wise men **privily (7)**. This is an older English term for "privately" (cf. 1:19). The Greek word means "secretly." One of the main characteristics of Herod was craftiness. He was very deceitful himself, and he did not trust anybody else. He asked the wise men exactly what time the star appeared. Then he sent them on to Bethlehem with orders to search **diligently (8)**—"with exactness, carefully"—for the newborn Child. They were to report to him, **that I may come and worship him also.** Subsequent events proved that his real purpose in seeking this information was something far different. He intended to have the Child assassinated, and so to eliminate the possibility of a political rival.

When the wise men started out on the last short lap of their long journey, they discovered again divine guidance in the star shining overhead. It led them to the place where the young Child was **(9)**. The sight of the star filled them with **exceeding great joy (10)**. They knew now that their quest would be satisfied.

Is there an implication here that the wise men lost sight of the star while they were consulting with Herod and the Jewish

---

[21]Floyd V. Filson, *A Commentary on the Gospel According to St. Matthew* ("Harper's New Testament Commentaries"; New York: Harper & Brothers, 1960), p. 58.

[22]Plummer, *op. cit.*, p. 14.

[23]*Ibid.*, pp. 13-14.

leaders in Jerusalem? If they had only paid attention to the star, instead of seeking human guidance, would they have been led on to Bethlehem? In that event, would the horrible massacre of the infant children have been avoided? Do we sometimes get ourselves and others into trouble because we seek human advice from the wrong people when we should be depending on divine guidance?

When they came into the **house** they saw the **young child** (11). This is something different from the shepherds finding the baby Jesus in a manger the night He was born (Luke 2:16). The **child** was probably about a year old and the family had a settled residence in Bethlehem. Pictures or plays showing the wise men kneeling at a manger are thus not scripturally accurate.

The wise men **fell down, and worshipped him.** Quite clearly they believed Jesus to be worthy of adoration. Then they presented to Him royal gifts: **gold, and frankincense, and myrrh.** These were products of south Arabia, but were sold widely and would be accessible in the Chaldean country.

Barclay has beautifully pointed out the symbolical significance of the three gifts.[24] He notes Seneca's statement that in Parthia one could approach the king only if he brought a gift. **Gold** was the most appropriate present for a *king*—and so for the One who was born to be the King of Kings. **Frankincense** was the gift for a *priest*, since the priests offered it in the Temple. So it was a fitting present to give Him who would be the great High Priest. **Myrrh** was the gift for one who would die. It was used for embalming. And so it was particularly appropriate for the Son of God, who came to die on the Cross. These three gifts "foretold that He was to be the true King, the perfect High Priest, and in the end the supreme Saviour of men."[25]

The biblical account gives no indication as to how many wise men came to see Jesus. Probably because three kinds of gifts are mentioned, the legend sprang up that there were three visitors. Finally they were designated "kings"—perhaps because of the royal gifts they brought—and names have been assigned to them: Caspar, Melchior, and Balthasar. But all this is purely legendary.

[24]William Barclay, *The Gospel of Matthew*, I (2d ed.; "The Daily Study Bible"; Philadelphia: Westminster Press, 1958), pp. 22-24.
[25]*Ibid.*, p. 24.

When the wise men were **warned of God in a dream that they should not return to Herod,** they went back home by another route (12). The devout attitude of these learned astrologers from the East is thus described by one commentator: "There, at the threshold of the Gospel, we see the true relation of science and religion.

> 'Let knowledge grow from more to more,
> But more of reverence in us dwell;
> That mind and soul, according well,
> May make one music as before.' "[26]

The visit of the wise men suggests a sort of firstfruits of the Gentiles who would come to Christ for salvation. The Gospel of Matthew closes with the Great Commission to evangelize the world.

Alexander Maclaren has a good outline on "The First Fruits of the Gentiles." He notes (1) Heathen wisdom led by God to the cradle of Christ (1-2); (2) The alarm of His own people at the whisper of His name (3); (3) The council of the theologians (4-6); (4) Herod's crafty counsel (7-8); (5) The discovery of the King (9-11); (6) Adoration and offering follow discovery (11).

### 2. *The Flight into Egypt* (2:13-15)

After the departure of the wise men, **the angel of the Lord appeareth to Joseph in a dream,** telling him to take **the young child and his mother, and flee into Egypt** because Herod would try to destroy Jesus (13). Leaving **by night** (14), so as to avoid detection, Joseph carried the family safely to Egypt. This was a trip of some two hundred miles. The traditional picture of Joseph walking beside the donkey, on which Mary is riding with the Child in her arms, is very probably true to life.

The family stayed in Egypt **until the death of Herod** (15). This was in 4 B.C. In keeping with his usual custom, Matthew quotes from the Old Testament again—this time from Hos. 11:1. Originally the words referred to Israel, God's **son.** Here they are applied to Christ, the unique Son of God, who also represented Israel. As in verse 6, Matthew does not quote the Septuagint. Plummer says, "He gives an independent translation of the Hebrew, which he may or may not have made for himself"; and

---

[26]John M. Gibson, *The Gospel of St. Matthew* ("The Expositor's Bible"; New York: A. C. Armstrong & Son, n.d.), p. 20.

adds in a footnote to this: "Only in a few cases are the quotations in Matthew taken from the Septuagint."[27]

### 3. *The Slaughter of the Innocents* (2:16-18)

The fact that Herod slew all the boys in Bethlehem and its "neighborhood" (NEB), **from two years old and under, according to the time which he had diligently inquired of the wise men** (16), indicates that "it was now almost two years since the star had appeared."[28] It would seem that Christ was somewhere around a year old when visited by the wise men.

Again Matthew cites an Old Testament prophecy as having been fulfilled. This was from Jer. 31:15. **Rama** (18) was five miles north of Jerusalem. But the tomb of **Rachel** was on the road to Bethlehem (Gen. 35:19). The traditional site, shown today, is about a mile north of Bethlehem. The passage in Jeremiah related primarily to the captives from Jerusalem as they were led past Ramah on their way to Babylonia in 586 B.C.

While there is no record in secular history of this wanton massacre of the innocent babes of Bethlehem, it fits perfectly the character of Herod. As already noted (cf. comments on 2:3), this cruel, wicked king had three of his sons put to death. He also killed his favorite wife, Mariamne, and her mother. Josephus tells how Herod, when he knew he was dying, sent for "all the principal men of the entire Jewish nation" to come to him at Jericho, on penalty of death for disobedience. There he ordered them shut up in the hippodrome. Fearful that he would die without being lamented, he gave orders to his sister Salome that when he died, and before public announcement of his death was made, all the Jewish leaders in the hippodrome were to be slain. Thus he would have "the honour of a memorable mourning at his funeral."[29]

### 4. *The Return to Nazareth* (2:19-23)

When Herod the Great had died, **an angel of the Lord appeareth in a dream to Joseph** (19) and instructed him to return to **the land of Israel** (20). This is the third time that mention is made of an angel appearing to Joseph in a dream (cf. 1:20; 2:13).

---

[27]*Op. cit.*, p. 17.

[28]Frederick C. Grant, "Matthew," *Nelson's Bible Commentary* (New York: Thomas Nelson & Sons, 1962), VI, 32.

[29]Josephus *Antiquities* XVII. 6. 5.

The phrase **in a dream** occurs altogether five times in these first two chapters (cf. 2:12, 22).

As Joseph came to the borders of Palestine he learned that Archelaus was reigning in Judea as successor to his father. This made him afraid to settle there. For Archelaus was the worst of the sons of Herod the Great, notorious for his wickedness and cruelty. Josephus says that right after his accession to the throne this savage monster massacred three thousand people.[30]

It would seem that Joseph had intended to return to Bethlehem and locate there. This would be a natural thing for him to do in the light of the angel's annunciation to him (1:20-21). Since Jesus was in a unique way "the son of David" (cf. 1:1), it would seem most fitting for Him to be brought up in Bethlehem.

But such was not to be the case. Warned once more **in a dream** (22), Joseph **turned aside into the parts of Galilee.** Probably he went down the Jericho Road, crossed the Jordan River, and went up the east side of the valley, recrossing the river south of the Lake of Galilee. The territory he thus traversed was ruled by Herod Antipas—the "Herod" of the Gospels. Though a son of Herod the Great, he was not as cruel as his brother in Judea. So the refugees would be safer here. They settled down in their former hometown of Nazareth (cf. Luke 1:26; 2:4). This village was located eighty miles north of Jerusalem and about halfway between the Mediterranean and the Sea of Galilee. It was obviously a rather small and obscure town, for it is not mentioned in the Old Testament, Josephus, or the Talmud. The attitude toward it on the part of the Jews in Jesus' day is clearly shown in John 1:46—"Can there any good thing come out of Nazareth?"

One of the most problematical passages in this Gospel is found in the quotation, **He shall be called a Nazarene** (23). All scholars are agreed that there is no such statement in the Old Testament. Green, for instance, declares: "There is no prophecy in the Old Testament remotely resembling it."[31]

The thing that should be noted is that Matthew does not assign this quotation to any specific prophet; it was **spoken by the prophets.** So it could be taken as a general presentation of an important truth. Morison puts the case well when he says:

[30]*Ibid.,* XVII. 9. 3; *War,* II. 6. 2.

[31]F. W. Green, *The Gospel According to Saint Matthew* ("The Clarendon Bible"; Oxford: Clarendon Press, 1936), pp. 112-13.

"It indicates that the evangelist is not referring to any one prediction in particular; he is rather gathering together several
prophetic statements, and translating their import into the peculiarly significant phraseology of his own time and locality."[32] Then
he adds by way of explanation: "To be called a Nazarene was to
be spoken of as despicable."[33]

Some have tried to find a connection of Nazarene with
"Nazirite." This view was propounded by Tertullian and Jerome
in the Early Church, and held by Erasmus, Calvin, Beza, and
Grotius in the Reformation period.[34] But the theory suffers from
two fatal defects: (1) the Hebrew roots of the two words are
very different; (2) Jesus did not claim to be a Nazirite, nor did
He live that kind of life. So this idea must be rejected.

A more plausible connection is with the Hebrew word for
"Branch," or "Shoot," which is found in several passages in the
prophetic books of the Old Testament. Lange writes: "The conclusion at which we have arrived is, that the title Nazarene bears
reference to the outward lowliness of the Messiah; accordingly,
the *netzer* in Isaiah 11:1 is analogous to the expressions used in
Isaiah 53:2, and to other descriptions of the humble appearance
of the Messiah."[35] Plumptre expresses the thought even more
appropriately. He says of the author of this Gospel: "He had
heard men speak with scorn of 'the Nazarene', and yet the very
syllables of that word had also fallen on his ears in one of the
most glorious of the prophecies admitted to be Messianic—'There
shall come forth a rod out of the stem of Jesse, and a *Netzer*
(Branch) shall grow out of his roots' (Isa. 11:1)."[36] It is of interest to note that "Nazarene" is the title regularly given to
Jesus and His disciples in the Jewish Talmud, where it is clearly
a term of contempt. Box thinks that *Nazoraios*, the Greek word
in Matt. 2:23—which he connects with the Hebrew *netzer*, by
way of Aramaic—may have been chosen by the early Christians

[32]*Op. cit.*, p. 25.

[33]*Ibid.* (italics omitted).

[34]H. A. W. Meyer, *Critical and Exegetical Hand-book to the Gospel of
Matthew* (New York: Funk and Wagnalls, 1884), p. 70.

[35]John Peter Lange, "Matthew," *Commentary on the Holy Scriptures,*
ed. J. P. Lange (Grand Rapids: Zondervan Publishing House, n.d.), p. 64.

[36]E. H. Plumptre, "Matthew," *Commentary on the Whole Bible,* ed.
C. J. Ellicott (Grand Rapids: Zondervan Publishing House, n.d.), p. 9.

as an "honorific title" in opposition to the contemptuous *Nazarenos.*[37]

It is very noticeable that all the Infancy Narratives of Matthew are told from the standpoint of Joseph. The announcement of Jesus' birth is to him, rather than to Mary (as in Luke). It was Joseph who was commanded to take the child Jesus and His mother into Egypt, and then to bring them back to the Promised Land. This is in striking contrast to the stories in the first two chapters of Luke, which are all written from the point of view of Mary.

## D. The Ministry of John the Baptist, 3:1-12

### 1. *His Appearance* (3:1-6)

The Greek suggests that **in those days** (1) John the Baptist "came along" or "arrived." Luke tells about the announcement of John's birth, and the circumstances surrounding his birth, as well as a bit about his childhood. But in Matthew's Gospel the forerunner of Jesus puts in his appearance suddenly at this point. All four Gospels present the ministry of John the Baptist as the preparation of the nation for Jesus' ministry.

John came **preaching.** The Greek word *kerysso* means literally "to be a herald, to proclaim."[38] It comes from *kerux,* a "herald" who stepped out in front of an army to make an announcement for the general, or before a crowd to deliver a proclamation for the ruler. He did not speak for himself, but for his superior. He did not give out his own message, but that which his commander had ordered him to proclaim. John was God's herald, announcing the important news that the Messiah was coming. Just so is every preacher of the gospel appointed to proclaim God's message of salvation. That is primarily what preaching is. This is why *kerysso* is the most frequently used verb in the New Testament for preaching, with *evangelizo*— "evangelize," "announce good news"—as a close second. These two significant verbs underscore the essential nature of New Testament preaching.

The parish where John preached was **the wilderness of Judaea.** This was a rocky, rugged area lying between the moun-

---

[37]G. H. Box, "Nazarene," *Dictionary of Christ and the Gospels,* ed. James Hastings (New York: Charles Scribner's Sons, 1908), II, 236.

[38]Abbott-Smith, *op. cit.,* p. 246.

tain plateau (2,500-3,300 feet above sea level) and the Dead Sea
(1,300 feet below sea level). It was a forbidding waste of crags
and canyons, inhabited mostly by wild beasts. W. L. Reed notes
that the word **wilderness** is rather an indefinite term. He says:
"An accurate translation is difficult, because the so-called wilderness regions included arid and semiarid territory, as well as sandy
desert, rocky plateaus, pasture lands, and desolate mountain ter-
rain."[39] W. F. Boyd and W. L. Reed express the opinion that
"desert" may be a better translation, since **wilderness** seems to
suggest a thick forest. They continue: "However, modern English
translations continue to employ both terms, doubtless due to the
fact that even 'desert' is not a perfect description; the regions
referred to are sometimes mountainous in nature, plains where
pastures exist after the rains, and settled regions such as that
part of the Wilderness of Judah near the Dead Sea where the
Qumran monastery and the Dead Sea Scrolls have been found."[40]

It should be noted that many scholars think John the Baptist
was probably an Essene and might even have had some association with the Qumran community. F. F. Bruce speaks favorably
of the idea. He notes John's residence in the wilderness of Judea,
his asceticism, and his baptismal teaching and practice—"Josephus's account of John's baptismal teaching accords more closely
with the Qumran doctrine than does the New Testament account."[41] He concludes: "John may have had some contact with
the Qumran community; he may even have belonged to it for a
time."[42]

The keynote of John the Baptist's preaching was **Repent** (2).
There is much superficial thinking on the subject of repentance.
It is commonly defined as "being sorry." But the Greek verb
means "to change one's mind." Repentance is primarily mental
and moral, rather than basically emotional. It involves a "change
of mind" with regard to sin and salvation. It means a renunciation of sin and commitment to Christ. Chamberlain says: "Repentance is the reorientation of a personality with reference to

---

[39]"Wilderness," *Interpreter's Dictionary of the Bible*, ed. George A. Buttrick, *et al.* (New York: Abingdon Press, 1962), IV, 844.

[40]"Wilderness, Desert," *Dictionary of the Bible*, ed. James Hastings (rev.
ed.; New York: Charles Scribner's Sons, 1963), p. 1037.

[41]F. F. Bruce, *Second Thoughts on the Dead Sea Scrolls* (Grand Rapids:
Wm. B. Eerdmans Publishing Co., 1956), p. 129.

[42]*Ibid.*, p. 130.

God and his purpose."[43] With regard to the exact meaning here, Robinson writes: "The Aramaic word which John used for 'repent' might be literally rendered 'be converted,' 'turn round and go back'; there is no safety in the course which men are now pursuing."[44]

In preaching repentance John was echoing the cries of the prophets of the Old Testament. In a very true sense, he was the last of this succession. He belonged to the old regime, but stood on the threshold of the new. He was doubtless steeped in the older Scriptures. When he cried, **Repent ye,** he may well have been thinking of the words of Isa. 1:16-17—"Wash you, make you clean; put away the evil of your doings; cease to do evil; learn to do well." Or Isa. 55:7—"Let the wicked forsake his way, and the unrighteous man his thoughts, and let him return unto the Lord, and he will have mercy upon him." Or, again, Jer. 7:3-7—"Amend your ways and your doings . . . for if ye throughly amend your ways and your doings, then will I cause you to dwell in this place, in the land that I gave your fathers for ever and ever."

Thayer says that the noun *metanoia* means: "especially the change of mind of those who have begun to abhor their errors and misdeeds, and have determined to enter upon a better course of life, so that it embraces both a recognition of sin and sorrow for it and hearty amendment, the tokens and effects of which are good deeds."[45]

Why should John's hearers repent? Because **the kingdom of heaven is at hand.** His preaching was not only ethical, but eschatological. Barnes suggests that the clause could best be translated: "the reign of God draws near."[46] There was a strong note of urgency in John's call to repentance. It was almost as if he said: "It's now or never!" The happenings of the next few years—culminating in the destruction of Jerusalem in A.D. 70— were to justify his look of eye and tone of voice. **Those days** proved to be "the last days," or "the days of the Messiah," cover-

43W. L. Chamberlain, *The Meaning of Repentance* (Grand Rapids: Wm. B. Eerdmans Publishing Co., 1943), p. 22.

44Theodore H. Robinson, *The Gospel of Matthew* ("Moffatt's New Testament Commentary"; New York: Harper and Brothers, 1927 [Preface]), p. 14.

45Joseph H. Thayer, *Greek-English Lexicon of the New Testament* (New York: American Book Company, 1889), p. 406.

46Albert Barnes, *Notes on the New Testament: Matthew and Mark* (Grand Rapids: Baker Book House, 1949), p. 22.

ing the time between His first and second comings (cf. Acts 2:17). But most of the Jews missed the point and suffered the consequences.

Matthew alone uses the phrase **the kingdom of heaven**—literally, "the kingdom of the heavens." It occurs some thirty-two times in this Gospel. Mark and Luke use "kingdom of God." The reason for Matthew's change of terminology is this: "In the Judaistic period previous to the Christian era, when a transcendent conception of God began to prevail, the use of heaven as a synonym for God came in."[47] Matthew did not wish to offend his Jewish readers and so conformed to this custom.

Almost all scholars are agreed that in the New Testament **kingdom** means "reign" rather than "realm." Arndt and Gingrich define the Greek word *basileia* as meaning: "kingship, royal power, royal rule, kingdom."[48] They further particularize it thus: "especially *the royal reign* or *kingdom* of God, a chiefly eschatological concept, beginning to appear in the prophets, elaborated in apocalyptic passages . . . , and taught by Jesus."[49] They insist (properly) that "kingdom of God" and "kingdom of heaven" mean essentially the same thing—they must, for they are used in exactly parallel passages in Luke and Matthew—but add: "The latter term may also emphasize the heavenly origin and nature of the kingdom."[50]

Morison pursues this last thought a little further. He writes: "Its origin is in heaven; its end is in heaven; its King is heavenly, all over, its subjects are heavenly in character and destiny; its laws are heavenly; its institutions are heavenly; its own culmination is in heaven, and is indeed heaven; its institutions on earth are earnests of the glory of heaven."[51]

In recent years there has been a good deal written on the subject of the kingdom of God. Some would identify it with the Church, as Augustine did fifteen hundred years ago. Others, like Harnack, make it purely subjective. Albert Schweitzer conceived of it completely in eschatological terms; that is, as future. On the other hand, C. H. Dodd made it wholly present, a "realized eschatology."

---

[47]A. B. Bruce, "The Synoptic Gospels," *Expositor's Greek Testament* (Grand Rapids: Wm. B. Eerdmans Publishing Co., n.d.), I, 80.

[48]*Op. cit.,* p. 134.

[49]*Ibid.*

[50]*Ibid.*

[51]*Op. cit.,* p. 29.

George Ladd has written several helpful books on the subject. In one of them he says: "The *primary* meaning of both the Hebrew word *malkuth* in the Old Testament and of the Greek word *basileia* in the New Testament is the rank, authority and sovereignty exercised by a king."[52]

The New Testament teaches that the Kingdom is both present and future, not just one or the other. In his exceedingly valuable survey of the history of interpretation of the kingdom of God during the last one hundred years, Bishop Lundstrom says: "To Jesus the present and the coming Kingdom of God stood side by side."[53]

To underscore his call to repentance, John quoted from Isa. 40:3. He identified himself as **The voice of one crying in the wilderness**—the wilderness of man's sin and spiritual need. Halford Luccock puts it very aptly when he says of Isaiah's word **wilderness**: "It is an up-to-the-minute description of much of our world."[54] John's description of himself as a **voice** is in line with his role as a herald (cf. "preaching," v. 1). He was not speaking for himself, but for Another.

As the forerunner of the Messiah, the task of John the Baptist was to warn men: **Prepare ye the way of the Lord.** They were to build a royal road on which their King might come. A few heard and heeded. But the leaders of the nation rejected the divine call and condemned their Messiah to death. **Make his paths straight** indicates what real repentance is. It is straightening out one's life.

The result was the ushering in of the gospel age, in which people are called upon to repent individually and receive Christ as Saviour. John's call was both national and individual. Today it is primarily the latter.

The appearance of John the Baptist befitted his mission and message. He was a rugged pioneer preacher. So his dress and food were rough and simple. His only clothing was **camel's hair** (4), a coarse sackcloth worn by ascetics and mourners. The **leathern girdle** (or "belt") held the loose garment together. This

[52]George E. Ladd, *The Gospel of the Kingdom* (Grand Rapids: Wm. B. Eerdmans Publishing Co., 1959), p. 19.

[53]Gosta Lundstrom, *The Kingdom of God in the Teaching of Jesus,* trans. Joan Bulman (Richmond, Va.: John Knox Press, 1963), p. 238.

[54]Halford E. Luccock, "The Gospel According to Mark" (Exposition), *The Interpreter's Bible,* ed. George A. Buttrick, *et al.,* VII (New York: Abingdon-Cokesbury Press, 1951), 649.

item is mentioned in the Old Testament description of Elijah (II Kings 1:8). Jesus identified John the Baptist as the New Testament Elijah (Matt. 17:10-13). The two men were very much alike in appearance, temperament, and mission.

John's **meat**—the word means "food," not just flesh—consisted of **locusts and wild honey.** Some have tried to identify the former with the pods of a tree, and the latter with the sweet sap that flows from certain trees. But probably the terms should be taken literally. Locusts were considered "clean" under Jewish law (Lev. 11:22) and are eaten by Arabs today. In fact, dried locusts can be bought in supermarkets in the United States. By **honey** is probably meant the "wild honey" (Mark 1:6) of bees, which would be found freely in the wilderness.

John the Baptist was a special messenger for a special time. J. C. Jones describes him as a "coarse man levelling mountains and filling up valleys, sternness in his looks, vehemence in his voice."[55] Josephus, the Jewish historian of the first century, says that John "was a good man, and commanded the Jews to exercise virtue, both as to righteousness towards one another, and piety towards God."[56]

John created a tremendous stir. We read that "there was going out to him" (imperfect tense) **Jerusalem, and all Judaea, and all the region round about Jordan** (5). The people from Jerusalem (about twenty-five hundred feet elevation) had to descend some four thousand feet to the Jordan River, which is thirteen hundred feet below sea level where it empties into the Dead Sea. John may have been baptizing about five miles up the river from its mouth. The eagerness of the people in coming to hear the prophet is shown by their willingness to face the long, rugged climb back up the Jericho Road.

John baptized only those who were **confessing their sins** (6). The Greek says "confessing out." This preacher required the candidates to acknowledge that they were sinners, and to expose themselves as such before he would baptize them.

### 2. *His Preaching* (3:7-10)

There were two main parties or sects in Judaism in Jesus' day. The first were the **Pharisees** (7). The name seems to be derived from the Hebrew *parash*, "one who is separated." The

---

[55]*The Biblical Illustrator: St. Mark,* ed. Joseph S. Exell (Grand Rapids: Baker Book House [reprint]), p. 8.

[56]*Antiquities* XVIII. 5. 2.

noted British scholar, Matthew Black, favors "the meaning of *perushim* as those who in their meticulous observance of the law and in particular of its Levitical observances, 'separated themselves' from uncleanness, and especially from the unclean, the 'people of the land' (*'am ha' ares*)."[57]

The beginnings of Pharisaism go back to the Babylonian captivity, when the Jews no longer had a temple in which to worship. So they became increasingly "the people of the Book." The law of Moses became the center of religious life. The study and teaching of the Law became the main task of the religious leaders (cf. Neh. 8:1-8). During the Maccabean period the Hasidim, or "pious ones," sought to maintain the purity of the Jewish religion against the encroachments of pagan Hellenism. Out of this "Puritan" laymen's movement arose the Pharisees. Josephus says that in the time of Herod the Great they numbered more than six thousand.[58]

The **Sadducees** were the second main sect of Jews. They were the priestly, aristocratic party. Whereas the Pharisees taught in the synagogues everywhere, the Sadducees held control of the Temple at Jerusalem (cf. Acts 4:1; 5:17).

It is commonly thought that the name was derived from Zadok. He was appointed high priest by Solomon (I Kings 2:35) in the place of Abiathar, who joined in the rebellion by Adonijah (I Kings 1:7). Thus Zadok became the ancestor of the succession of priests in Jerusalem. In Ezekiel's vision of the new temple it is "the sons of Zadok" who can "come near to the Lord to minister unto him" (Ezek. 40:46).

Rejecting theories of an earlier origin, Sundberg says: "It is more probable that the Sadducees arose as a party subsequent to the Maccabean Rebellion."[59] The first mention of them is in the days of John Hyrcanus (135-104 B.C.). Josephus writes: "Now there was one Jonathan, a very great friend of Hyrcanus's, but of the sect of the Sadducees, whose notions are quite contrary to those of the Pharisees."[60] The contrast which Josephus draws between the beliefs of these two sects[61] agrees well with what is stated in the New Testament.[62]

[57]Matthew Black, "Pharisees," IDB, III, 776.
[58]*Antiquities* XVII. 2. 4.
[59]A. C. Sundberg, "Sadducees," IDB, IV, 160.
[60]*Antiquities* XIII. 10. 6.
[61]See *Antiquities* XVIII. 1. 3-4.
[62]See the comments on Acts 23:8.

It is of interest to note that whereas the **Pharisees** are mentioned 100 times in the New Testament,[63] the name **Sadducees** occurs only 14 times.[64] Josephus affirms that the Pharisees were much more popular with the people.[65] After the final destruction of the Temple at Jerusalem in A.D. 70, the Sadducees disappeared from history. The Judaism that survived was that of the Pharisees.

John the Baptist had stern words of warning for the Pharisees and Sadducees that came to his baptism. He called them a **generation of vipers.** This seems like harsh language. But actually it was a character analysis. Morison expresses very well the implications, in these words:

> He looked through and through them, in a way impossible to ordinary men, and read what was in the heart of their hearts. He saw the grovelling element that cleaved to the dust. He saw the morally insidious element. There was poison too which they would not scruple, on occasion to eject and inject . . . He saw that there was in them an element of real antipathy to genuine humanity.[66]

The picture of vipers fleeing from **the wrath to come** (cf. I Thess. 1:10) finds vivid illustration in this description: "like a desert fire when the brown grass and thorns on the more fertile portions will blaze for miles, and the unclean reptiles creep out of their holes before its heat."[67]

These proud religionists are commanded: **Bring forth therefore fruits meet for repentance** (8)—"Then prove your repentance by the fruit it bears" (NEB). Real repentance always manifests itself in changed living.

John could sense the reaction of his hearers: **We have Abraham to our father** (9). We do not need to repent. We are Abraham's children, and so the elect people of God. It is the Gentiles and sinners who need repentance.

John's answer made short work of this false alibi. He declared that God could make children of Abraham out of the

[63]Thirty times in Matthew, twelve in Mark, twenty-eight in Luke, twenty in John, nine in Acts, and once in Philippians (3:5).

[64]Seven times in Matthew, once each in Mark and Luke, five times in Acts.

[65]*Ant.,* XVIII. 1. 4.

[66]*Op. cit.,* p. 34.

[67]George Adam Smith, *Historical Geography of the Holy Land* (20th ed.; London: Hodder & Stoughton, n.d.), p. 317.

stones that lay on the bank.[68] That is, physical descent, in which they gloried, meant nothing in God's sight. It was all on the material level, like stones. What God demands is moral character. Jesus repudiated the materialistic reasoning of the Jewish leaders on this point (John 8:33-39). Paul declares that those who have faith are "the children of Abraham" and will be blessed with "faithful Abraham" (Gal. 3:7, 9; see also v. 29; Rom. 4:11).

The statement that **the axe is laid unto the root of the trees (10)** might easily be taken as meaning that the axe is already striking the trees at their roots. But the Greek says: "The axe lies [*keitai*] at the root of the trees."[69] The idea is that of judgment ready to descend. At any moment the woodsman may pick up the axe and wield it. Every tree which is not producing fruit is being cut down and cast into the fire. Jesus uttered the same words later (7:19). The fire, says Johnson, is that "of Gehenna: 'Fire' in Jewish apocalypses often describes the final judgment."[70]

### 3. *Two Baptisms* (3:11-12)

John now refers more specifically to his role as the forerunner of the Messiah: **he that cometh after me is mightier than I, whose shoes I am not worthy to bear (11).** Luke (3:16) says, "the latchet of whose shoes I am not worthy to unloose." Characteristically, Mark makes it even more vivid: "the latchet of whose shoes I am not worthy to stoop down and unloose" (Mark 1:7). Tying and untying the "thongs" of the master's "sandals," and carrying the latter for him—these were the menial tasks of the humblest slave. Yet John did not feel worthy to do even these things for the Messiah. "Lightfoot (from Maimonides) shows that it was the token of a slave having become his master's property, to *loose* his shoe, to *tie* the same, or to *carry* the necessary articles for him to the bath."[71] Thus the words of all three accounts are appropriate.

---

[68]There may have been intended a play on the Hebrew words for "children" (*banim*) and "stones" (*ebhanim*).

[69]Abbott-Smith (p. 383) gives "at" as one meaning of *pros* with the accusative.

[70]Sherman Johnson, "Matthew" (Exegesis), IB, VII, 265.

[71]Henry Alford, *The Greek Testament*, rev. Everett Harrison (Chicago: Moody Press, 1958), I, 23.

Then comes the most significant statement in the preaching of John the Baptist. While he baptized **with,** or "in," **water,** the coming One would baptize **with the Holy Ghost, and with fire.** Other religions have baptized with water. The distinctive Christian baptism is that with the Holy Spirit. In the light of John's statement here it is difficult to justify the silence of most churches regarding the baptism with the Holy Spirit.

Matthew and Luke add to Mark's account at this point: **and with fire.** Many scholars have interpreted this, largely on the basis of verses 10 and 12, as referring to the fire of final judgment of sinners. But it also means the fire of the Holy Spirit, consuming the carnal nature. Alford says of the prediction here: "This was literally fulfilled at the day of Pentecost."[72] In a similar vein Micklem asserts: "The addition 'and fire' points to cleansing as the essence of Messiah's baptism."[73] He calls attention to the description of Christ's coming in Mal. 3:2—"He is like a refiner's fire."

Brown also disagrees with the reference to judgment. He says: "To take this as a distinct baptism from that of the Spirit—a baptism of the impenitent with hell-fire—is exceedingly unnatural."[74] He further observes: "Clearly . . . it is but the *fiery* character of the Spirit's operations upon the soul—searching, consuming, refining, sublimating—as nearly all good interpreters understand the words."[75]

G. Campbell Morgan echoes this thought. He paraphrases the Baptist's words thus: "He shall whelm you in the fire-whelming of the Holy Ghost, that burns your sin out of you, and remakes you."[76]

Especially striking are the comments of the late Bishop Ryle of the Church of England. He writes:

> We need to be told that forgiveness of sin is not the only thing necessary to salvation. There is another thing yet; and that is the baptizing of our hearts by the Holy Ghost. . . . Let us never rest till

[72]*Ibid.*

[73]Philip A. Micklem, *St. Matthew* ("Westminster Commentaries"; London: Methuen & Co., 1917), pp. 15-16.

[74]David Brown, "Matthew-John," *A Commentary . . . on the Old and New Testaments,* by Robert Jamieson, A. R. Fausset, and David Brown (Grand Rapids: Wm. B. Eerdmans Publishing Co., 1948 [reprint]), V, 12.

[75]*Ibid.*

[76]G. Campbell Morgan, *The Gospel According to Matthew* (New York: Fleming H. Revell Co., 1929), p. 23.

we know something by experience of the baptism of the Spirit. The
baptism of water is a great privilege. But let us see to it that we
have also the baptism of the Holy Ghost.[77]

There are three things that fire does: (1) It warms; (2) It
lights; (3) It cleanses. So the Holy Spirit brings to the human
heart that receives Him warmth, illumination, and cleansing from
all sin.

Airhart observes that this great message of John about
Jesus is related to the Christian doctrine of the baptism with the
Holy Spirit (1) by Jesus in His command to the disciples (Acts
1:4-5), (2) by Peter when interpreting the meaning of the
Gentile Pentecost (Acts 11:15-16). Also he notes that the promise to **gather his wheat into his garner** (12) suggests the positive
values of the baptism with the Holy Spirit. He writes: "Only the
chaff is burned, and this only in order that the wheat—the
genuine values in personality—may be garnered and set to use.
There is potential in our personalities which only God can
discern. There are possibilities of grace, dormant talents, buried
treasure, within believers' lives, but largely useless because as
yet encased in the chaff of an unsanctified nature. The baptism
with the Holy Spirit will provide the basis to bring to realization
the personality possibilities known to the Spirit, but otherwise
forever lost."[78]

The Messiah has in His hand a **fan** (12)—better, a "win-
nowing fork" (only here and Luke 3:17). The writer has watched
a man on the top of the hill Samaria throw threshed wheat into
the air with such a fork. The breeze blew away the chaff, and
the good grain collected on the ground.

John declared that Christ **will throughly purge his floor.**
The Greek compound verb, meaning "cleanse thoroughly," is
found only here in the New Testament. The **floor** is a threshing
floor, such as would be found near each village. It was usually
located on a high spot of ground, to take advantage of the breezes
that blow in from the Mediterranean. "It turns up at the edges
and is paved with stone or with tramped-down mud grown stone-
hard through centuries of use."[79] The newly harvested wheat or

---

[77]J. C. Ryle, *Expository Thoughts on the Gospels: Matthew-Mark*
(Grand Rapids: Zondervan Publishing House, n.d.), pp. 19-20.

[78]A. E. Airhart, "The Baptism with the Holy Spirit," *Preacher's Maga-
zine,* XXXVIII (May, 1963), 14.

[79]Madeleine S. Miller and J. Lane Miller, *Encyclopedia of Bible Life*
(New York: Harper & Brothers, 1944), p. 19.

barley is piled on it to the depth of about a foot and a half. Then a pair of oxen pull a threshing board over it, ridden by a woman or by children. The board, about four feet long by two and a half feet wide, has jagged pieces of stone or metal fastened to the bottom. These teeth tear the grain, while the oxen's feet also help to trample it out. One can still see these threshing floors in Palestine, sometimes with two pairs of oxen working on one floor.

After the grain has been threshed and winnowed, the wheat is gathered into the **garner**—"storehouse" or "granary"—and the chaff is burned up with **unquenchable fire**. The Greek word for **unquenchable** is *asbestos*.

### E. THE BAPTISM OF JESUS, 3:13-17

Jesus came **from Galilee** (13), specifically from His hometown of Nazareth, to the Jordan River where John was baptizing. When He presented himself as a Candidate, **John forbad him** (14). The Greek word, which occurs only here, means "to hinder, prevent." Since it is in the imperfect tense the best translation is "tried to prevent" (Moffatt). John felt that it was he who needed to be baptized by Jesus, not the reverse.

Jesus answered: **Suffer it to be so now** (15)—"Allow me now" (Berkeley). The reason He gave for it was: **thus it becometh us to fulfil all righteousness**—"so we ought to fulfil every religious duty" (Weymouth). John's protest and Jesus' reply are found only in Matthew.

Why was Jesus baptized? This question has haunted many minds. Why should He "who did no sin" (I Pet. 2:22) offer himself for baptism? John made every candidate confess his sins (v. 6). But Jesus had no sins to confess. Why, then, did He submit to baptism?

G. Campbell Morgan gives the following answer: "As Jesus left that in His life which was preparatory, and entered upon the actual work of the ministry, He devoted himself to the ultimate issue of His work, that namely, of an identification with men even to death." More specifically he says: "His being baptized was an act by which He consented to take His place among sinners."[80]

Identification with humanity—that is the key that unlocks this mystery. That is the real meaning of the Incarnation. It was

[80]*The Crises of the Christ* (New York: Fleming H. Revell Co., 1903), p. 120.

52

more than coming in a physical body. It was an entrance into
the human race. Often in Old Testament times God invaded
human history in a miraculous way. But now He invaded humanity itself. The Incarnation is the greatest of all miracles.
Christ's baptism was a prelude to the Cross. He fulfilled "every
religious duty" in order that He might be a perfect Sacrifice. How
the Sinless One could identify himself with sinful humanity is a
paradox that must always remain a mystery. But it was all related to His redemptive death at Calvary. Dietrich puts it this
way: "It is only later that the profound meaning of this act may
be grasped—that by this act Jesus identified himself with his
people, took on himself their guilt, and received with and for
them the baptism of repentance."[81]

Sadler says that the Baptism was, next to Jesus' death, "the
greatest instance of His submission to the will of His Father."
How? "For in it He consciously submitted to be reckoned
amongst sinners as if He were one Himself, and to receive the
outward sign of the cleansing away of that evil and defiling thing
in which He had no part."[82]

When Jesus had been baptized (aorist passive participle),
He **went up straightway out of the water** (16). The Greek says
*apo*—"from" the water. However Mark (1:10) says *ek*, "out of."
But neither one is conclusive proof for or against immersion.
The mode is not indicated, and we cannot go beyond what is
written.

The central factors in the baptismal scene were a vision and
a voice. The vision was that of **the Spirit of God descending like
a dove, and lighting upon him** (16). The voice declared: **This
is my beloved Son, in whom I am well pleased** (17). Erdman
comments: "The former was a symbolic indication of the divine
power by which his ministry was to be accomplished, the latter
was an assurance that he was the Messiah, the very Christ of
God."[83]

The expression **he saw** (v. 16; Mark 1:10) might seem to
suggest that the vision of the dove was seen only by Jesus. But

[81]Suzanne de Dietrich, "The Gospel According to Matthew," trans.
Donald G. Miller, *The Laymen's Bible Commentary*, XVI (Richmond, Va.:
John Knox Press, 1961), 23.

[82]M. F. Sadler, *The Gospel According to St. Matthew* (3d ed.; New York:
James Pott & Co., 1887), p. 35.

[83]Charles R. Erdman, *The Gospel of Matthew* (Philadelphia: Westminster Press, 1920), p. 37.

Luke says that "the Holy Ghost descended in a bodily shape like a dove upon him" (Luke 3:22). Also John's Gospel (1:32-34) indicates that the descent of the Spirit as a dove was the prearranged sign to John that this was really the Messiah. However, it is not stated anywhere that the vision was seen by the surrounding crowd. The dove was a fitting symbol of the gentleness of the Spirit.

The voice from heaven expressed the Father's approval of the Son's obedience. One meaning of **beloved** is "only." Thus did the Father in double fashion and with dual force declare the unique role of Jesus as His only Son and obedient Servant. Already Christ was functioning as the Servant of Jehovah described in Isaiah. The obedience to His Father's will which He first manifested publicly at His baptism found its culmination at the Cross. Calvary was the climax of His ministry as the Suffering Servant.

Matthew makes the message from heaven a public proclamation, **This is my beloved Son,** while Mark (1:11) and Luke (3:22) have the more direct and personal "Thou art my beloved Son." But Luke and John clearly indicate that the dovelike form was seen by at least John the Baptist (see above). So there is ample testimony to the fact that this was not a merely subjective experience on the part of Jesus alone.

With regard to the last clause, **in whom I am well pleased,** Meyer writes: "The *aorist* denotes: *in whom I have had good pleasure,* who has become the object of my good pleasure."[84] Lange explains it thus: "The verb is put in the aorist to denote the eternal act of loving contemplation with which the Father regards the Son."[85]

One of the significant features of the Baptism is that here we have for the first time in the Bible a clear and complete indication of the Trinity. As Jesus came up from the water, the Holy Spirit came down upon Him, and at the same time a voice from heaven declared: **This is my beloved Son, in whom I am well pleased.** Thus we enter upon the New Testament with an explicit revelation that God exists as Father, Son, and Holy Spirit.

F. THE TEMPTATION OF JESUS, 4:1-11

The Baptism was a glorious public event. But immediately after it came an excruciating private experience. "Great bless-

[84]*Op. cit.,* p. 87.
[85]*Op. cit.,* p. 77.

ings are usually followed by great temptations."[86] And it is still true: "It takes great temptation as well as great grace to make a great preacher."[87]

Why was Jesus tempted? The Epistle to the Hebrews goes further in answering that question than any other part of Scripture. We read of Christ: "Wherefore in all things it behoved him to be made like unto his brethren, that he might be a merciful and faithful high priest in things pertaining to God, to make reconciliation for the sins of the people. For in that he himself hath suffered being tempted, he is able to succour them that are tempted" (Heb. 2:17-18).

The last sentence declares a very revealing truth: He "suffered being tempted." This was no play-acting. It was warfare, hard and harsh. Jesus' temptations were just as real to Him as ours are to us—and just as agonizing. Some would say that, since Christ was the Son of God, He knew He could not fail, could not yield. But that would make His temptations an empty farce and would deny the clear statement of Hebrews. If He was "in all points tempted like as we are," He must have experienced the torment and torture *in His own consciousness* that we feel when severely tempted. It is true that, as the Son of God, He was omniscient. But there are many indications in the Gospels that Jesus limited this knowledge in His actual consciousness. That was a part of the Incarnation, of His becoming like us. This price He had to pay in order to be both our High Priest and our Sacrifice for sin.

Jesus was **led up** (1) from the Jordan Valley, over a thousand feet below sea level, to the craggy heights of the lonely wilderness of Judea. All three Synoptics say that He was led by **(of) the Spirit** into the wilderness. It was by divine appointment that He went. When things go wrong or we are severely tempted, it is easy to think that we may be out of the will of the Lord. But when Jesus was being tempted He was in the very center of God's will for him.

It was **into the wilderness** that He was led. The contrast between this and the setting of Adam and Eve's temptation is striking. They were in a beautiful paradise, the Garden of Eden. He was in the desolate wilds. They had everything to eat that

[86]G. A. McLaughlin, *Commentary on the Gospel According to Saint Matthew* (Chicago: Christian Witness Co., 1909), p. 40.
[87]*Ibid.*

one could wish. He was hungry. They had mutual companion-ship. He was alone. Yet they failed, while He won.

One of the most graphic descriptions of the Temptation is in Milton's *Paradise Regained*. Milton portrays Satan coming to Christ in the form of an old man. It would seem more likely that the specific temptations delineated here came as mental sugges-tions, as they usually do to us today. Broadus, however, thinks differently. He says: "During the forty days (Luke 4:2), and at other times, our Lord was doubtless tempted by suggestion to his mind, as we are; but in the three signal and final temptations here described, it seems to be distinctly declared that Satan appeared in bodily form and with actually spoken words, and this fitted the scene for distinct and impressive description."[88] But does it seem likely that Satan would take Jesus bodily to the pinnacle of the Temple? The conclusive argument against this view is that there is no mountain on earth from which one could see all the kingdoms of the world (8).

The divine purpose for which Christ was led into the wilder-ness was that He might be **tempted**. The Greek word is *peirazo*. In the earliest Greek literature (Homer) it is used in the sense "make proof of." Its main meaning is "test, try, prove."[89] Arndt and Gingrich say it means: *"try, make trial of, put to the test, to discover what kind of a person someone is."*[90] The Father was allowing His Son to be tested before He began His public work, as metal must be tested before it can be used dependably in a crucial place. But from the standpoint of Satan, Jesus was being **tempted**, seduced to sin, with the hope that He would fall. This is further indicated by the word "tempter" (*peirazon*) in verse 3.

Christ was tempted by **the devil**. Mark never uses this term, but instead has "Satan" (Mark 1:13). The latter, which means "adversary," comes directly from the Hebrew into Greek and English. The Greek word *diabolos* signifies "slanderer" or "false accuser." It became *diable* in French and **devil** in English. The two terms are used in the New Testament as equivalent.

To deny a personal devil is to lull ourselves to sleep in a false sense of security. It has been increasingly realized in recent

---

[88]John A. Broadus, *Commentary on the Gospel of Matthew* ("An Ameri-can Commentary on the New Testament"; Philadelphia: American Baptist Publication Society, 1886), p. 62.

[89]Abbott-Smith, *op. cit.,* p. 351.

[90]*Op. cit.,* p. 646.

years that one cannot explain the insidious influence of evil in this world without postulating a personal agent behind it.

Jesus **fasted forty days and forty nights** (2), as did Moses on Mount Sinai (Exod. 34:28) and Elijah in the wilderness (I Kings 19:8). Forty is generally thought of as indicating a period of probation. That is what it was for Jesus. And He did not fail the test.

At the end of the forty days, **he was afterward an hungred** (i.e., "hungry"). Apparently Jesus was so absorbed in spiritual conflict and contemplation that He did not feel hungry until the close of this period. Then there came surging in upon Him an intense craving for food.

Mark gives just a brief summary statement of the Temptation, without detailing the three specific attacks of Satan. Matthew and Luke give these three, but in different order (see comments on Luke 4:1-13). M'Neile suggests that Luke adopts a "geographical sequence," with the change from the wilderness to the city coming last, while "Matthew arranges a psychological climax: the first temptation is to doubt the truth of the revelation just received, the second to test it, and the third to snatch prematurely at the Messiahship which it involves."[91]

Doubt is one of the devil's favorite weapons. The first thing he said to Jesus was, **If thou be the Son of God** (3).[92] It was in similar fashion that he approached Eve: "Yea, hath God said . . . ?" (Gen. 3:1) Then the devil appealed to Jesus' physical appetite: **command that these stones be made bread.** As Maclaren says, "Satan had tried the same bait before on the first Adam. It had answered so well then, that he thinks himself wise in bringing it out once more."[93] Intrinsically there was nothing wrong in Jesus performing a miracle to provide himself with needed food. But to obey Satan is sin. Furthermore, Christ had come to share our humanity with us. He refused to use any power not at our disposal. He would not do anything that would be a denial of His incarnation. G. Campbell Morgan explains it thus: "The enemy asked Him to do a right thing in a wrong way, to satisfy a lawful appetite in an illegal fashion, to make use of the privileges of Sonship for violating its responsibilities."[94]

---

[91]*Op. cit.,* p. 37.

[92]Or, "Since you are the Son of God."

[93]Alexander Maclaren, *Expositions of Holy Scripture,* "St. Matthew" (Grand Rapids: Wm. B. Eerdmans Publishing Co., 1944 [reprint]), p. 78.

[94]*Crises of the Christ,* p. 168.

The first thing that Jesus said in reply was, **It is written** (4). This is in the perfect tense in Greek, which indicates completed action and also the resultant state as still continuing. The full meaning is: "It has been written, and still stands written." This emphasizes the eternal unchangeableness of God's Word.

Jesus met and conquered the devil with exactly the same weapon that is at our disposal: "the sword of the Spirit, which is the word of God" (Eph. 6:17). All three times He quoted from the Book of Deuteronomy. The first quotation was, **Man shall not live by bread alone, but by every word that proceedeth out of the mouth of God** (Deut. 8:3). Jesus lived by the Word of God, not by the whims of His own appetite. In this He set an example for all His followers.

In the second temptation the devil took Jesus into **the holy city** (5). In the New Testament this designation for Jerusalem is found only in Matthew and Revelation. It occurs four times in the Old Testament. The devil set Christ on a **pinnacle of the temple,** the highest place in the holy city. Morgan well remarks: "The choosing of the place is first evidence of the subtlety of the foe."[95]

In just such a setting, hallowed by sacred associations, probably with a waiting crowd below, Satan made an entirely different approach. This time he appealed to Jesus' complete trust in God. Before, the temptation was on the physical level. This time it was on a high spiritual plane: **If thou be the Son of God** (or, "Since you are the Son of God"), **cast thyself down** (6). So sacred was the setting that the devil became emboldened to quote scripture himself. He tried to quote Ps. 91:11-12. But he left out a significant phrase: "in all thy ways." Christ's ways were God's ways. If He stepped out of the divine will He could no longer claim the divine care. That is true of us today.

The Jews of that day expected that their Messiah would suddenly make a spectacular appearance in the Temple. Here was Jesus' opportunity to win the nation's acclaim as its Messiah. But He resisted this temptation to sensationalism. He would follow instead the simple path of humble obedience to His Father.

Jesus swung His Sword again—the Word of God. This time it was: **Thou shalt not tempt the Lord thy God** (7). Foolhardy conduct evidences, not faith, but presumption.

[95]*Ibid.,* p. 175.

The setting of the third temptation was still different: **an exceeding high mountain** (8). Here the devil made his highest bid. After giving Christ a vision of **all the kingdoms of the world, and the glory of them,** he made this overwhelming proposition: **All these things will I give thee, if thou wilt fall down and worship me** (9). What a temptation this was—to gain the whole world without going to the Cross! The essence of the temptation was to try to reach God-approved goals but to use Satan's strategy. Jesus rejected even this plausible appeal.

He told Satan to begone. Once more He quoted the Word: **Thou shalt worship the Lord thy God, and him only shalt thou serve** (10) (Deut. 6:13). Here is man's first and highest duty.

Satan tempted Jesus on three levels: (1) the physical—food; (2) the intellectual—do something sensational; (3) the spiritual—**worship me.** The devil still tempts men in these three ways.

In obedience to Christ's command, the devil left Him. Then **angels came and ministered unto him** (11). They probably provided Him with food (cf. I Kings 19:5-7) and also ministered to Him spiritually, rejoicing with Him in the victory He had won.

## G. THE BEGINNINGS IN GALILEE, 4:12-25

### 1. *The First Preaching* (4:12-17)

The arrest and imprisonment of John the Baptist furnish the chronological point for the beginning of Jesus' great Galilean ministry, as indicated in the first two Gospels (cf. Mark 1:14). When Jesus heard that **John was cast into prison**—or "arrested" —**he departed into Galilee** (12). That is, He returned to His home territory from the wilderness of Judea, far to the south. With John in prison, it was time for Jesus to begin His public ministry. And He was prepared for it—by His baptism and temptation.

But He did not stay in His hometown, Nazareth. Instead He **came and dwelt in Capernaum** (13), some twenty miles away on the north shore of the Lake of Galilee. The choice of this as His headquarters was wise. Nazareth was a small, obscure village in the hills. Its people were narrow-minded. They would not have received His ministry, as we know from the way they treated Him when He visited His old home (Luke 4:16-30). In its provincial atmosphere He would have been hindered and cramped.

On the other hand, **Capernaum** was a busy, bustling town, full of commercial activities. Here the crowds would be more open and receptive. Many would be coming and going, thus spreading the gospel. For the city was located on the main highway from Damascus in the north to Egypt in the south. It was a strategic location.

Again (14) occurs the formula for introducing a quotation from the Old Testament—**that it might be fulfilled which was spoken (14)** (cf. 1:22; 2:15, 23). This quotation is from Isa. 9:1-2. Matthew quotes fifteen times from this prince of Old Testament prophets. Because of its many Messianic passages, the book has sometimes been called "The Gospel According to Isaiah."

**Zabulon** and **Nephthalim** (15)—better, Zebulun and Naphtali —were the two tribal territories that largely comprised Galilee. Zebulun took in the western part, toward the Mediterranean, while Naphtali lay toward the east, near the Lake of Galilee. **The way of the sea** means the important highway from Egypt to Damascus, over which caravans of traders had passed for many centuries.

This area was called **Galilee of the Gentiles** because it had a larger Gentile population than Judea. The reason for this goes back to the days of Isaiah. When the Assyrians began invading Palestine they naturally took the outlying territories first. II Kings 15:29 says: "In the days of Pekah king of Israel came Tiglath-pileser king of Assyria, and took Ijon, and . . . Gilead, and Galilee, all the land of Naphtali, and carried them captive to Assyria." In place of the native inhabitants he put people from the countries of the East (II Kings 17:24). Thus the population of Samaria, and to a less extent of Galilee, became a mixture of Jews and Gentiles. It is also true that many Canaanites had remained in the area later known as Galilee, and thus it had been more largely Gentile through the period of the judges and kings (cf. Judg. 1:30-33; 4:2).

But Isaiah had predicted that in this region there would come **great light** (16). Matthew pinpoints the early Galilean ministry of Jesus as the fulfillment of this prophecy.

When Jesus began to **preach** (17)—same word, "herald, proclaim," as used of John the Baptist (3:1)—He took the same text as His forerunner: **Repent: for the kingdom of heaven is at hand.** The last phrase, **is at hand**, is literally, "has drawn near." As someone has said, "Jesus is God brought near." In Him the Jews were confronted with the kingdom of God. But they refused to accept it.

### 2. *The First Disciples* (4:18-22)

As Jesus was **walking by the sea of Galilee** (18), He saw two brothers fishing. One was **Simon.** This was a very common name among the Jews of Jesus' day, perhaps partly because of the Simon who was a great hero in the Maccabean revolt of the second century B.C. Nine different Simons are mentioned in the New Testament. Jesus gave to this one the surname **Peter,** which is the Greek word for "stone" (*petros*).

**Andrew** is known mainly as the **brother** of Peter, as he is here identified. Yet it was he who first brought his brother into contact with Christ (John 1:40-42). Andrew was the one who reported that a boy had a lunch, with which five thousand were fed (John 6:8-9). Just as Barnabas was overshadowed by Paul, so Andrew seems hidden in the shadow of Peter. But he played his own part faithfully and efficiently.

The two brothers were **casting a net into the sea.** This was done in the shallow water near the shore. A special type of casting net was used for this purpose. It had weights attached, so that it would sink to the bottom and enclose a school of fish. The same kind of net is still used around the warm springs on the shore of the Lake of Galilee south of the site of Capernaum.

Jesus spoke to these two fishermen with a command and a promise: **Follow me, and I will make you fishers of men** (19). He had a higher calling and a greater task for them. The most important business in the world is that of winning souls. Peter and Andrew were privileged to be the first two whom Jesus invited to join Him in this work.

This verse suggests the theme: "The Highest Calling." It may be outlined thus: (1) The divine call—**Follow me;** (2) The divine concern—**I will make you;** (3) The divine comission—**fishers of men.**

There was no hesitancy on the part of those who heard the call. They **straightway,** or "immediately," **left their nets, and followed him** (20). These fishermen recognized that it was the voice of the Master who spoke, and they obeyed.

A little farther on, Jesus saw a fishing boat near the shore. In it were **Zebedee** and his two sons, **James** and **John** (21). They were **mending their nets,** in preparation for another night of catching fish. Jesus **called them** also to follow Him. As had the other two, **immediately**—same Greek word as "straightway" (v. 20)—they **left** and **followed him** (22). The repetition of these two words underscores the fact that if one is going to follow Jesus in full-time service he must leave his previous occupation.

It is a striking fact that Christ called four fishermen as His first disciples. He still calls men from all walks of life to preach His gospel. He needs rugged men of courage, who have learned to face hardship with patience and perseverance.

These four men are always named first in the lists of the twelve apostles (Matt. 10:2-4; Mark 3:16-20; Luke 6:14-16; Acts 1:13). Three of them (Peter, James, and John) seem to have been especially close to Jesus. We see them with Him at the raising of Jairus' daughter, on the Mount of Transfiguration, and in Gethsemane. Two of them, Peter and John, are closely associated in the early chapters of Acts (e.g., 3:1; 8:14). Peter was the main spokesman in the apostolic circle, both in the Gospels and in Acts. It was he who preached the sermon on the Day of Pentecost (Acts 2). James was evidently an acknowledged leader of the group, for he became the first apostle martyr (Acts 12:2).

### 3. The First Crowds (4:23-25).

This paragraph comprises a very brief summary statement of a tour of **Galilee** (23) which Jesus made soon after enlisting His first four assistants. His ministry had three definite functions: **teaching ... preaching ... healing.**

The teaching took place at first in the **synagogues.** These were the local places of worship in the towns and villages. They also served as schools, where the Jewish boys could memorize the Scriptures. The local courts were connected with the synagogues. So they formed the center of community life. George A. Buttrick says: "The synagogue was at once school, local council, and church."[96]

Neither the Old Testament nor the Apocrypha tells us anything about the origin of the synagogue. But the reason for its appearance is rather obvious. When the Temple at Jerusalem was destroyed in 586 B.C. the Jews were left without a place of wor-

---

[96]"Matthew" (Exposition), IB, VII, 277.

ship. In the Captivity they would naturally gather together for prayer. The Greek word *synagoge* means "a gathering together." As with the word "church," it was used first for the congregation and then for the building in which it met.

Jesus was preaching the **gospel of the kingdom.** This was the good news that the kingdom of God was being offered to men in the person of Christ, the Messiah. In addition, He was healing **all manner of sickness and all manner of disease among the people.** There was no limit to His power. No case was too hard for Him. He was the Great Physician of bodies as well as souls.

His **fame** spread far and wide (24). **All Syria** would take in Palestine, as well as the territory north of it included in the present countries of Syria and Lebanon. As a result of this publicity, sick people were being brought to Him from everywhere. They are described as those who were **taken with divers** (diverse) **diseases and torments.** The word **torments,** which can be translated "tortures," emphasizes the pain and suffering brought on by illness. Among the ones who came were **those which were possessed with devils**—six words in English, one in Greek, *daimonizomenous,* "demonized ones." **Those which were lunatick** is likewise one word *seleniazomenous.* Literally it means "moonstruck." The term was used for epileptics, who were supposed to have been influenced by the moon. **Those that had the palsy** is simply *paralytikous,* "paralytics." Of all these difficult cases it is said, **he healed them.** The verb is *therapeuo,* from which come such words as "therapy" and "therapeutics."

The popularity of Jesus is underscored by the fact that He drew **great multitudes** (25)—literally "many crowds"—from all the surrounding territories. **Galilee** was the northern part of Palestine proper. **Decapolis** literally means "ten cities." This was the name given to a region lying mostly east of the Jordan Valley and embracing ten cities that were Hellenistic in culture and interest. These stretched from Damascus in the north to Philadelphia (modern Amman) in the south. This area was largely Gentile in character. Stendahl says that "in Decapolis the Jews must have been in the minority."[97] **Jerusalem** was the capital of **Judaea,** in the southern part of Palestine. The fact that people would travel a hundred miles north from Jerusalem to

---

[97]K. Stendahl, "Matthew," *Peake's Commentary on the Bible,* ed. Matthew Black and H. H. Rowley (London: Thomas Nelson and Sons, 1962), p. 774.

Galilee shows the tremendous drawing power of Jesus. **Beyond Jordan**—called in modern times Transjordan—was officially known then as Perea (literally, "across"). This region on the east side of the Jordan River was governed by Herod Antipas, ruler of Galilee.

Having given this general description of Jesus' early Galilean ministry, Matthew has now set the stage for the Sermon on the Mount. This is the first of five great discourses in this Gospel (see Introduction).

Section **II** *First Discourse:*
*Sermon on the Mount*

Matthew 5:1—7:29

Franzmann, in his *Follow Me: Discipleship According to Saint Matthew*, says of the Sermon on the Mount: "It builds upon the narrative of the beginnings (1:1—4:16), the genealogy and the seven fulfillments."[1] The latter phrase refers to the seven fulfillments of prophecy which occur in the first four chapters of Matthew. They are: (1) Emmanuel, 1:23; (2) birth in Bethlehem, 2:6; (3) called out of Egypt, 2:15; (4) Rachel weeping, 2:18; (5) called a Nazarene, 2:23; (6) a voice in the wilderness, 3:3; (7) a great light, 4:14-16.

Each of the five great discourses of Matthew, Franzmann feels, is preceded by a narrative which is related to it. This one, the first, is introduced by 4:17-25. He writes: "The Sermon on the Mount in this framework is to be understood and appreciated as the record of how the call of Jesus, issued by Him with Messianic authority, summoning men into the eschatological reality of the kingdom of heaven, is made to determine the whole existence of the disciple."[2] That is, "Jesus is, in the Sermon on the Mount, Messianically molding the will of His disciple."[3]

This idea seems to furnish the proper key to understanding the nature and purpose of this great discourse. The Master had just called His first four disciples. Now He is showing them what true discipleship means. He is describing the kind of life His disciples are to live.

There have been many ways suggested for interpreting and applying the Sermon on the Mount. McArthur devotes an entire chapter to describing twelve of these interpretations,[4] which he calls "Versions and Evasions of the Sermon on the Mount."[5] He

[1]Martin H. Franzmann, *Follow Me: Discipleship According to Saint Matthew* (St. Louis: Concordia Publishing House, 1961), p. 34.
[2]*Ibid.*
[3]*Ibid.*
[4]Harvey McArthur, *Understanding the Sermon on the Mount* (New York: Harper & Brothers, 1960), c. 4.
[5]*Ibid.*, p. 106.

begins by commenting that if "the proverbial visitor from Mars" were to visit "a characteristic Christian community," having read the Sermon on the Mount on the way, he would be perplexed by the contrast. "The gulf between the pattern of the Sermon and the pattern of conventional Christian life is so great that the visitor would suspect he had read the wrong Sermon or visited the wrong community."[6] McArthur's analysis and evaluation of these views is excellent.[7]

## A. THE SETTING OF THE SERMON, 5:1-2

One might deduce from the first verse of the fifth chapter that Jesus left **the multitudes** (1) and delivered this "sermon" to the disciples alone. But it appears that the crowd gathered around the outside of the inner circle and listened to the discourse (cf. 7:28).

The reference to a **mountain** is probably significant. Just as Moses received the old Law on Mount Sinai, so Jesus, the new Leader, enunciated the law of the Kingdom on a mountainside.

**Set** is literally "having sat down." Whereas preachers today follow the Greek and Roman custom of standing to speak, the Jewish rabbis always sat while they taught. **Disciples** literally means "learners." The word is found only in the Gospels and Acts (Matthew, seventy-four times; Mark, forty-five; Luke, thirty-eight; John, eighty-one; Acts, thirty). It is the earliest designation for the followers of Jesus.

## B. THE NATURE OF THE DISCIPLES, 5:3-16

### 1. *Their Blessedness* (5:3-12)

*a. The Poor in Spirit* (5:3). Each beatitude begins with **blessed,** which reminded the hearers of Ps. 1:1. Lenski comments: " 'Blessed!' intoned again and again, sounds like bells of heaven, ringing down into this unblessed world from the cathedral spires of the kingdom inviting all men to enter."[8]

The Greek word *makarios* means "happy." But it is obvious that ". . . the blessings contemplated in the Beatitudes can by no

---

[6]*Ibid.*, p. 105.

[7]*Ibid.*, c. 5.

[8]R. C. H. Lenski, *The Interpretation of St. Matthew's Gospel* (Columbus, O.: Wartburg Press, 1943), p. 183.

means be expressed in English by the word or concept 'happiness.' "[9] They refer rather to the blessedness that comes only to those who enjoy salvation in Jesus Christ. Hunter suggests: " 'Blessed' means 'Ah, the happiness of,' and beatitude is the happiness of the man who, in communion with God, lives the life that is life indeed."[10] Arndt and Gingrich write: "The translation *O, the happiness of* or *hail to those,* favored by some may be exactly right for the Aramaic original, but it scarcely exhausts the content which *makarios* had in the mouths of Greek-speaking Christians."[11] John Wesley has been followed by a number of more recent translators in adopting "Happy." But "Blessed" is perhaps a more adequate rendering.

**The poor in spirit** (3) are those who recognize their spiritual poverty. Luke (6:20) says: "Blessed be ye poor." But after the Babylonian captivity "the poor" was often a phrase used for the pious ones, in contrast to the wealthy, wicked, worldly oppressors of the poor. So the statements in Matthew and Luke mean the same thing. Perhaps the best translation of 5:3a is that of Goodspeed: "Blessed are those who feel their spiritual need."

Why are these poor blessed? Because **theirs is the kingdom of heaven.** The Beatitudes are in the form of synthetic parallelism, a type of Hebrew poetry in which the second line completes the meaning of the first. Thus here the second line defines more specifically the connotation of "blessed."

The first beatitude strikes right at the heart of man's need. Fitch declares: "Poverty of spirit is essentially the dethronement of pride."[12] After asserting that "pride is the very essence of sin," he goes on to say: "Pride is the sin of an exaggerated individualism, the sin of the usurper claiming a throne that is not his own, the sin that fills the universe with only an ego, the sin of dethroning God from His rightful sovereignty."[13]

b. *The Mourners* (5:4). When one realizes that he is bankrupt of all spiritual assets that would make him acceptable to

---

[9]John Wick Bowman and Roland W. Tapp, *The Gospel from the Mount* (Philadelphia: Westminster Press, 1957), p. 29.

[10]Archibald M. Hunter, *A Pattern for Life* (Philadelphia: Westminster Press, n.d. [British edition, 1953]), p. 30.

[11]*Op cit.,* p. 487.

[12]William Fitch, *The Beatitudes of Jesus* (Grand Rapids: Wm. B. Eerdmans Publishing Co., 1961), p. 24.

[13]*Ibid.*

God, he will **mourn** (4) over the fact. Lloyd-Jones writes, "To 'mourn' is something that follows of necessity from being 'poor in spirit,' " and adds: "As I confront God and His holiness, and contemplate the life that I am meant to live, I see myself, my utter helplessness and hopelessness."[14]

This mourning leads to repentance and conversion. But it does not stop there. It continues throughout the life of the conscientious Christian. The greatest saints realize most keenly how far they fall short of perfect Christlikeness, and they mourn over it. Only the shallow Christian can feel complacent.

The promise for the mourners is that **they shall be comforted** (cf. Isa. 57:18). This comes first in the comfort of forgiveness, and then in the comfort of communion. A compassionate Christ is especially close to those who mourn.

c. *The Meek* (5:5). The meaning of true meekness has often been sadly misunderstood. Too many times it has been conceived of in terms of a self-effacing, negative, almost false humility. But actually it is something far different, even as it relates one to his fellowman. Archbishop Trench writes of it: "Rather it is an inwrought grace of the soul; and the exercises of it are first and chiefly towards God."[15] He adds: "It is that temper of spirit in which we accept his dealings with us as good, and therefore without disputing or resisting."[16] In line with this Fitch says: "Meekness is yieldedness to God, submissiveness to His will, preparedness to accept whatever He may give, and readiness to take the lowest place."[17] Put in simplest terms, meekness is submission to the will of God. And this is not primarily negative, but positive. It is an active fulfilling of His will in our daily lives. Jesus Christ is the supreme Example of such meekness (cf. 11:29). This fulfilling of God's will includes a right estimate of self, an estimate that leads one "not to think of himself more highly than he ought to think" (Rom. 12:3).

Of the meek it is said that **they shall inherit the earth** (5). The world believes that the way to win is to assert oneself. But

[14]Martin Lloyd-Jones, *Studies in the Sermon on the Mount,* I (Grand Rapids: Wm. B. Eerdmans Publishing Co., 1959) 58.
[15]Richard C. Trench, *Synonyms of the New Testament* (Grand Rapids: Wm. B. Eerdmans Publishing Co., 1947 [reprint]), p. 152.
[16]*Ibid.*
[17]*Op. cit.,* p. 49.

Jesus said that those who accept His will shall someday reign with Him.

*d. The Hungry in Heart* (5:6). One of the early signs of life in a normal baby is hunger. So the one who has truly been born again will **hunger and thirst after righteousness (6)**—which in the Scriptures often means "salvation" (cf. Isa. 51:6). To such the promise is given: **they shall be filled.** The Greek word is *chortazo,* from *chortos,* which is usually translated "grass" in our English New Testament. The picture is that of cattle having eaten until they are full. The verb is also rendered "satisfied," and that fits very well here. Fitch observes: "Fulness is God's answer to the emptiness of man's heart."[18]

*e. The Merciful* (5:7). Those who have received mercy from God should show mercy to their fellowmen. The most vivid illustration of how unreasonable it is to refuse to forgive others is presented in the parable of the unmerciful servant (18:23-35). The parable of the Good Samaritan (Luke 10:30-37) gives an excellent example of mercy to one in need. Mercy has been defined as "kindness in action."

Bowman and Tapp suggest that the Beatitudes apparently represent "an original Aramaic poem in two stanzas of four verses each."[19] The first four beatitudes describe: "first, an awakening to one's state of inadequacy . . . ; secondly, the determination to 'turn' to God in repentance . . . ; thirdly, the adoption of a constant attitude of trust in God alone . . . ; and finally, the earnest longing to acquire the total 'righteousness' which constitutes 'salvation' for man."[20] Fitch holds that the first stanza describes the birth of the Christian, and the second his life as a Christian.[21]

*f. The Pure in Heart* (5:8). Of this condition Whedon says: "Here is a trait of character which God's Spirit can alone produce. This is sanctification."[22] McLaughlin writes: "A pure heart is a heart with nothing therein contrary to the love of God."[23]

---

[18]*Ibid.,* p. 66.
[19]*Op. cit.,* p. 27.
[20]*Ibid.,* pp. 35-36.
[21]*Op. cit.,* p. 72.
[22]D. D. Whedon, *Commentary on the Gospels: Matthew-Mark* (New York: Hunt & Eaton, 1860), p. 73.
[23]*Op. cit.,* p. 50.

Jesus declared that only the pure in heart **shall see God** (8). This means in life here, as well as hereafter. Sin is like dust in the eyes. It beclouds the vision and distorts the view. We can enter into full communion with the Lord only when our hearts are cleansed from all sin (cf. I John 1:7).

Heart purity is the end and summation of the previous beatitudes. The possibility of such inner rectitude is clearly implied; but it is also apparent both from Scripture and universal experience that no one is natively pure (Jer. 17:9); hearts can be pure only by being purified. Nor will human culture purge the depths of corruption; there must be a work of divine grace.

The heart must be purified from its pride (Prov. 16:5); if not, instead of being "poor in spirit" one will be haughty and self-sufficient; instead of being repentant (a true *mourner*) he will be self-complacent; instead of being "meek" a man will be stubborn and heady. The heart also must be purified from double-mindedness (Jas. 4:8), from selfishness and contention (Jas. 3:14), and from unbelief (Heb. 3:12).

*g. The Peacemakers* (5:9). James says in his Epistle that "the wisdom that is from above is first pure, then peaceable" (Jas. 3:17). That is the order here. Only the pure in heart, who have been cleansed from the carnal nature (the cause of all inward strife), can have "the peace of God" in its fullness in their souls. A divided heart is an unpeaceful heart. Only the peace of Christ controlling us can make us peacemakers.

Everyone dislikes a warmonger. But the challenge to a Christian is: Am I a peacemaker—in the community, in the church, in the home? The last is the hardest test of all.

**The children of God** (9) is in the Greek "sons of God." When the definite article is omitted in Greek it emphasizes kind or character. When people make peace they will be called "God's sons" because they act like God. In Eastern thinking "son of" means "having the nature of."

*h. The Persecuted* (5:10-12). Some scholars rate the Beatitudes as nine in number. Others count eight, considering verse 11 as a further extension of verse 10. We shall follow the latter method.

One must not fail to note that it is those who are **persecuted for righteousness' sake** (10) that are blessed. Some self-made martyrs complain of being persecuted for righteousness' sake, when it is really for their own foolishness' sake. When they are criticized for acting or talking unwisely, they quote this beatitude. But that is "handling the word of God deceitfully" (II Cor. 4:2).

When persecuted, the Christian is to **rejoice, and be exceeding glad** (12). Jesus cites the example of **the prophets** who were persecuted in Old Testament times. But actually He himself is the supreme Example of what is described in verse 11. Someone has said that the Beatitudes are an autobiography of Christ.

The virtues which Jesus extols in the Sermon on the Mount are almost exactly the opposite of those admired by the Greeks and Romans of His day. He said: Blessed are the poor in spirit, the pure in heart, the peacemakers, the persecuted; the mourners, the meek, the merciful; and those who hunger and thirst after righteousness. These still run counter to the spirit of the age. Bowman and Tapp express it thus: "It seems, then, that our Lord is sketching a saved personality forced to live in an unsaved world, righteousness surrounded by vice, with the consequent tensions thus created."[24]

One of the best summaries of the eight Beatitudes is that given by Fitch. He says:

> They divide naturally into four separate parts. The first three show us a man turning from his sin to God, and the fourth shows us God turning to the sinner and clothing him with the righteousness of Christ. The next three . . . show us the new-born child of God working the works of righteousness amongst men; and the final Beatitude shows how men react. . . . There are, first, three graces of a contrite soul, followed by God's answer in mercy, in righteousness, and in grace. Then follow three graces of a commissioned soul, followed by the world's answer in persecution and reproach.[25]

### 2. *Their Influence* (5:13-16)

Jesus used two symbols to describe the influence that Christians have on a non-Christian society. The first was salt, the second light.

*a. Like Salt* (5:13). **Salt** has two uses—for flavoring and preserving. (1) Such foods as oatmeal and gravy are very unpalatable without salt. In the Middle Ages in Europe when people raised most of their own food, they still had to travel to the annual markets to get salt. It was considered an absolutely essential ingredient. Just so, life without Christ and Christianity is

[24]*Op. cit.*, p. 42.
[25]*Op. cit.*, pp. 124-25.

unbearably insipid. As Christ has toned up life for the believer, so he in turn is to do for others.

(2) Salt preserves. Before the advent of iceboxes and modern refrigerators, salt was one of the main means of preserving food. When fish were shipped on the backs of donkeys one hundred miles from Capernaum to Jerusalem, they had to be heavily salted. So the follower of Christ is to act as a preservative in the world. One cannot help wondering what would happen to modern society with all its moral rottenness if it were not for the presence of the Christian Church.

b. *Like Light* (5:14-16). Jesus once declared, "I am the light of the world" (John 8:12). Here He says to His disciples: **Ye are the light of the world** (14). Just as the moon reflects the light of the sun onto the darkened side of the earth, so the Church is to reflect the rays of the "Sun of righteousness" (Mal. 4:2) on a world darkened by sin.

Christians are like **a city that is set on an hill**—a common sight in Palestine. Whether they like it or not, they are on display before the world all the time. One can no more escape his influence than he can run away from his own shadow.

**Candle** (15) should be "lamp"; **bushel** should be "peck measure," or "meal tub"; **candlestick** should be "lampstand." They did not use candles in Jesus' day, but little clay lamps about the size of the palm of a man's hand. Many of these from the time of Christ have been dug up in Palestine. In the windowless homes of that day the lamp would be placed on a stand, or more probably in a niche in the mud wall, and it would give light **unto all that are in the house.** This would be literally true in the one-room homes of the poorer people in Palestine. Olive oil was the fuel used in these lamps.

The **light** of the disciples was to be their **good works** (16). If these shone consistently with their profession, it would **glorify** God. To praise the Lord with one's life is even more important than praising Him with the lips.

C. THE RIGHTEOUSNESS OF THE DISCIPLES, 5:17-48

1. *Its Nature* (5:17-20)

Doubtless some of Jesus' hearers felt that He was revolutionary in His teaching. They may have thought that He intended to **destroy the law, or the prophets** (17). This He denied emphatically—**I am not come to destroy, but to fulfill.** In this very meaningful declaration He indicated His relationship to the Old Testament. He was to fulfill its commands and promises, its precepts and prophecies, its symbols and types. This He did in His life and ministry, His death and resurrection. To fulfill is to "fill full"—the same Greek word is used for both. Jesus filled up to the full the meaning of the Old Testament. When read in the light of His person and work, it sparkles with new meaning. Christ is the Key, the only Key, that unlocks the Scriptures.

What will happen to the Law? Solemnly the Master declared: **Verily I say unto you, Till heaven and earth pass, one jot or one tittle shall in no wise pass from the law, till all be fulfilled (18).** **Jot** represents the smallest letter of the Hebrew alphabet, the *yodh,* which looks much like an apostrophe. It would also correspond to the smallest Greek letter, *iota.* The **tittle** was the "horn" on some Hebrew letters which distinguished them from others. Often these distinctions are so minute that one has to look closely to be sure which letter is intended. The modern counterpart of this is very well expressed in Goodspeed's translation: "not one dotting of an *i* or crossing of a *t* will be dropped from the Law until it is all observed."

Consistent with this view, Jesus warned that whoever **shall break (19)** ("do away with, set aside") the least of the commandments and teach others to do so **shall be called least in the kingdom of heaven.** On the surface the last part of this statement seems surprising. How could one who broke the Law be in the Kingdom? The solution lies in translating the phrase: "in relation to the kingdom of heaven"; that is, in relation to the Kingdom he would be least, left outside. **Great** is the one who shall **do and teach** the commandments. The doing must precede the teaching.

Verse 20 is usually considered to be the key verse of the Sermon on the Mount. The righteousness of Christ's disciples must **exceed the righteousness of the scribes and Pharisees.** Jesus was calling for an inward, moral, spiritual righteousness, in place of the outward, ceremonial, legalistic righteousness of the Pharisees. "The trouble with the Pharisees," says Martin Lloyd-Jones, "was that they were interested in details rather than principles, that they were interested in actions rather than in motives, and that they were interested in doing rather than in being."[26]

[26]*Op. cit.,* I, 207.

It is proper for the Christian to thank God that he is not under Law but under grace. But if he thinks that the demands on him are less because of this, he has not read the Sermon on the Mount understandingly. Jesus stated emphatically that He requires a higher righteousness than that of the scribes and Pharisees. In the rest of the chapter He gives six concrete examples of exactly what He means. Basically He means a righteousness of inner attitude rather than merely of outward action. But this raises the requirement. One has to guard not only his actions, but also his attitudes; not only his words, but his thoughts as well. To keep the law of Christ is more demanding than keeping the law of Moses.

### 2. *Its Application* (5:21-48)

Each one of these six examples of higher righteousness is introduced by the phrase, **Ye have heard that it was said** (21, 27, 33, 38, 43),[27] except that in verse 31 it is modified to "It hath been said." **By them of old time** (21) (or "to them of old time"—the Greek could mean either) refers back to some command in the law of Moses.

In all six instances Jesus adds: **but I say unto you** (22, 28, 32, 34, 39, 44). The Greek is even more emphatic than the English. It says *ego de lego hymin*—"But *I* say unto you." In Greek, as in Latin, the pronoun is included in the verb form. It is expressed separately only when the speaker or writer wants to give strong emphasis to it. *Lego* means "I say." The *ego* **(I)** is not only added here, but also placed first in the clause—the emphatic position in a Greek sentence. So the clause should be read: "But *I* say unto you." In speaking thus Jesus was either the world's worst egotist, or He was what He claimed to be—the eternal Son of God, who spoke with divine authority. Nineteen centuries of Christian history have validated His claim. Blair rightly observes: "Matthew's portrait of Jesus centers in his representation of Jesus' authority."[28] And Taylor has well said: "Jesus will always remain a challenge to be met rather than a

---

[27]For some unknown reason the KJV translators changed this to "it hath been said" in verses 31, 33, 38, and 43. The Greek is exactly the same in all cases—*errethe*, "it was said."

[28]Edward P. Blair, *Jesus in the Gospel of Matthew* (New York: Abingdon Press, 1960), p. 46.

problem to be solved."[29] It is He who has the right to challenge us, not we to challenge Him.

*a. Anger* (5:21-26). **Thou shalt not kill** is the sixth commandment of the Decalogue (Exod. 20:13; Deut. 5:17). Jesus did not annul it. Rather, He gave it a higher interpretation: If you are angry with your brother, you have murder in your heart.

Whoever kills another will be **in danger of the judgment** (21). The reference is evidently to the local court, connected with the synagogue. But Jesus declared that whoever was **angry with his brother**[30] would be **in danger of**—a legal term, meaning "liable to"—**the judgment** (22). That is, he would be subject to court action. Whoever said to his brother, **Raca**—"a word of contempt, said to be from a root meaning to 'spit' "[31]—would be liable to action by the **council** (*synedrion*), the Great Sanhedrin at Jerusalem. Arndt and Gingrich define **Raca** as "a term of abuse, *fool, empty-head.*"[32] Whoever said, **Thou fool** (Greek, *moron*), would be liable to **hell fire** (literally, "Gehenna of fire").

Gehenna was the valley of Hinnom, just south of Jerusalem. The refuse and rubbish of the city were taken out through the Dung Gate (Neh. 3:14; 12:31) and cast onto what would now be called the city dump. As early as the first century B.C. the Jews had used Gehenna in a metaphorical sense to indicate the place of fiery torment. The lurid flames licking constantly at the edge of this dump formed the fitting symbol which Jesus here used for the fires of hell.

The application of the above warning is made in two spheres —that of worship (23-24) and that of legal suit (25-26). If a Jew brought a gift to the Temple to be offered on the altar—the altar of burnt offering before the sanctuary—and remembered that his **brother** (23) had anything against him, he was to go and be reconciled to his brother before offering his gift. The Greek word for **be reconciled** (24) (*diallasso*) is found only here in the New Testament. Paul uses *katalasso*, and the double compound *apokatallasso*, for the unilateral reconciliation that man must have with

---

[29]Vincent Taylor, *The Person of Christ in New Testament Teaching* (London: Macmillan & Co., 1958), p. 166.

[30]"Without a cause" is not in the two oldest Greek MSS and should be omitted.

[31]A. Carr, *The Gospel According to St. Matthew* ("Cambridge Greek Testament"; Cambridge: University Press, 1886), p. 120.

[32]*Op. cit.*, p. 741.

God. That is, man must cease his enmity against the Lord, and be reconciled through Christ. But *diallasso* denotes "mutual concession after mutual hostility."[33]

The significance of this is clear. When one is reconciled to God, he has to meet the divine conditions, because the wrong is all on one side. But when one is reconciled to his brother, both have to make concessions, because there are two sides to every human quarrel. The point Jesus is making, however, is that one's worship in the house of God is not acceptable as long as there is any bad feeling between the would-be worshiper and a "brother." One's relationship to God cannot be right when his relationship to his fellowman is wrong.

The second application (25-26) is a bit different. Your adversary is dragging you to **the judge** (25). Jesus said that it would be wiser to settle out of court. Otherwise you will not get out of prison until you have paid the last **farthing** (26)—"the last penny" (Goodspeed). The *kodrantes* was the smallest Roman copper coin, worth about a quarter of a cent. The point is that Christians should try to settle their differences as quickly and quietly as possible and settle them between themselves. Christians normally do not need a judge or court to decide what is right and fair between them (cf. I Cor. 6:1-8).

*b. Adultery* (5:27-30). Jesus quoted the seventh commandment (Exod. 20:14; Deut. 5:18), and then proceeded to give it a higher interpretation. He indicated that in God's sight wrong intention is sinful as well as the wrong deed. And God is equally cognizant of both.

Verses 29 and 30 show how serious a thing is lust. Jesus said: **if thy right eye offend thee, pluck it out, and cast it from thee** (29). The Greek word for **offend** is *skandalizo* ("scandalize"). It comes from the noun *skandalon* ("scandal"), which was first the bait-stick of a trap or snare, and then was used for the snare or trap itself. So the meaning here is, If looking is a trap or snare to you, by all means avoid looking. The verb is regularly translated "offend" in the King James Version and "cause to stumble" (a more adequate translation) in the American Standard Version. The translators of the Revised Standard Version struggled long over this word—delaying their vote on it until the very last—and finally settled for a variety of renderings, to fit

---

[33]J. B. Lightfoot, *Notes on the Epistles of St. Paul* (Grand Rapids: Zondervan Publishing House, 1957 [reprint]), p. 288.

the context. *The New English Bible* does likewise. Lenski insists on the literal meaning of the verb, and so translates it "entrap." Beck has "causes you to sin,"[34] which is a correct interpretive translation. It appears that the proper meaning is "set a trap for" rather than "put a stumbling-block in the way of."[35]

Christ declared that it was better for one to lose his **right eye** or **right hand** than to be cast into **hell** (Gehenna). We cannot believe that He was advocating the physical mutilation of the body—though in the past some have mistakenly taken His words literally. He was speaking metaphorically: If a close friend or favorite association of any kind is becoming a snare to you, cut it off! Better to be deprived of *anything* in this life than to be lost forever.

*c. Divorce* (5:31-32). Since the subject of divorce is discussed at greater length in a later chapter (19:3-12), extended consideration will be postponed until then. Suffice to say here that while the Law permitted divorce (Deut. 24:13), Jesus asserted that it often amounted to nothing less than legalized **adultery** (32).

*d. Oaths* (5:33-37). The Mosaic law said, **Thou shalt not forswear thyself** (33) (Lev. 19:12; Num. 30:2; Deut. 23:21), that is, "swear falsely"—the verb is found only here in the New Testament. But Jesus said, **Swear not at all** (34). He specifically forbade swearing by **heaven, earth, Jerusalem,** or one's **head** (34-36). The Jews held that swearing by God's name bound the oath-taker, but swearing by heaven was not binding. So the above items were substituted as a form of evasion of telling the truth. Bengel quotes the rabbinical saying: "As heaven and earth shall pass away, so shall the oath pass away which calls them to witness."[36] Jesus held that God is always present when men talk; so they should speak truthfully.

The command of Christ was: **But let your communication be, Yea, yea; Nay, nay** (37)—or, as Beck puts it: "Just say, 'Yes,

---

[34]William F. Beck, *The New Testament in the Language of Today* (St. Louis: Concordia Publishing House, 1963), p. 8.

[35]James Hope Moulton and George Milligan, *The Vocabulary of the Greek New Testament* (Grand Rapids: Wm. B. Eerdmans Publishing Co., 1949), p. 576.

[36]John Albert Bengel, *Gnomon of the New Testament*, 5 vols. (Edinburgh: T. & T. Clark, 1860), I, 180.

yes; no, no.' " The very practice of oaths is a sad reflection on human character. Jesus demands truthfulness all the time, whether a man is under oath or not. There is no double standard for the Christian.

    e. *Retaliation* (5:38-42). The basic principle of justice reflected in the law of Moses was: **An eye for an eye, and a tooth for a tooth (38)** (see Exod. 21:24; Lev. 24:20; Deut. 19:21). The purpose of this commandment was not to encourage men to strike back, but to forbid their exacting a penalty greater than the crime.

    Jesus introduced a higher law, that of non-retaliation. His command was: "Never strike back!" This principle He applied in five specific ways: turn the other cheek (39), let him take your coat (40),[37] go the second mile (41), give to the one who asks, and lend to the would-be borrower (42).

    Many people have assumed that these sayings of Jesus are to be taken with complete literalness. But a little thought will show how mistaken this position is. For instance, if a man begs for some money to get something to eat—suppose you give him what he asks and he uses it to get drunk. Have you done a good deed? Have you acted in keeping with intelligent love? Or may it be that what you intended as a blessing has become a curse? What Jesus was commanding was a generous, compassionate spirit toward the needy.

    What one must always remember is that "the letter killeth, but the spirit giveth life" (II Cor. 3:6). The new law of Jesus is primarily a new spirit. The Master was mainly concerned about attitudes. It should be recognized that "the Sermon on the Mount deals throughout with principles and not with rules."[38]

    f. *Love of Enemies* (5:43-48). In this sixth and last application of the higher righteousness demanded of the Christian, Jesus made one change of procedure. In the previous instances He had quoted only an Old Testament passage and then given it a loftier interpretation. This time to the scriptural command, **Thou shalt love thy neighbour (43)** (Lev. 19:18), He inserted an

---

    [37]The Greek for "coat" means the under garment, whereas "cloke" signifies the outer garment. The modern equivalents would be "shirt" and "coat."
    [38]Harvie Branscomb, *The Teachings of Jesus* (New York: Abingdon-Cokesbury Press, 1931), p. 186.

addition by the Jewish rabbis **and hate thine enemy.** This latter injunction is found nowhere in the sacred Scriptures. Henry has put the point well: "God said, *Thou shalt love thy neighbour;* and by *neighbour* they understood those only of their own country, nation, and religion . . . ; from this command . . . they were willing to infer what God never designed: *Thou shalt hate thine enemy.*"[39]

Jesus counteracted this false teaching with the strong command: **Love your enemies** (44). It is natural to love one's friends; it is supernatural to love one's enemies. But those who do so demonstrate that they are **the children of your Father which is in heaven** (45). The Greek says: "sons of your Father who is in heaven." Again note that the absence of the article denotes kind or quality—you show that in character you are God's sons. For He gives **sun** and **rain** to both **evil** and **good** people (45). If you exhibit kindness only to your friends, you are no better than the **publicans** (46-47). These were the tax collectors for the Roman government and were despised by most of their fellow Jews as being about as far down the ladder of evil as one could go.

Then comes the climax of this chapter: **Be ye therefore perfect, even as your Father which is in heaven is perfect** (48). This seems like a counsel of despair. But the proper interpretation is that in the *human* sphere we are to be perfect, as God is perfect in the *divine* sphere. This is the aim and goal of the Christian life.

The immediate context suggests that **perfect** must be interpreted as perfection in love. This can be experienced in life, here and now (I John 2:5; 4:12, 17-18). Filson writes: "*Perfect* emphasizes the measuring of all life by the perfect holy love of God himself, and makes v. 48 a fitting conclusion and summary of all that vss. 17-47 have said."[40]

The transcendent perfection of God's love is seen in (1) its *universality,* for all men are included; (2) its *compassion,* for it extends to the evil and unworthy, including those who do not love Him in return; (3) its *practicality,* for it actively seeks their welfare by sending rain and sunshine—and above all by sending His Son. Only as our love is thus perfect is it supernatural and

[39]Matthew Henry, *Commentary on the Whole Bible* (New York: Fleming H. Revell Co., n.d.), V, 66.
[40]*Op. cit.,* p. 91.

truly Christian. Such love is not only our present duty but our present privilege through the power of the Spirit. Without it, "what do ye more than others?"

God graciously imparts, to all who seek it, a perfect love for Him and for His will. Thereafter the Christian seeks for an ever more perfect manifestation of that love in his life and conduct. Because we are finite this perfect manifestation will never be completely attained in this world, but every consecrated follower of Christ must constantly strive toward it (cf. Phil. 3: 12-14).

The immediate context of vv. 17-47 is important, but that is not all. Perfection here must be explained in terms of the longer context—the entire fifth chapter. John Wesley's comment on this verse is: "referring to all that holiness which is described in the foregoing verses, which our Lord in the beginning of the chapter recommends as happiness, and in the close of it as perfection."[41]

These last six paragraphs of the chapter suggest six "Characteristics of Christian Perfection." They are: (1) peaceableness (21-26); (2) purity (27-30); (3) harmony (31-32); (4) honesty (33-37); (5) kindness (38-42); (6) love (43-48).

## D. THE RELIGION OF THE DISCIPLES, 6:1-34

### 1. *Three Religious Practices* (6:1-18)

(*Introduction*, v. 1). In the King James Version this verse seems to be a part of the discussion of almsgiving that follows (2-4). But the very oldest Greek manuscripts have "righteousness" instead of **alms**. That would make the first verse a broader introduction to the three following discussions of almsgiving (2-4), prayer (5-15), and fasting (16-18). However it should be noted that Kraeling includes the first verse with the paragraph on almsgiving, though he accepts the reading of the oldest manuscripts. He says: "Charitable giving was so important in this period that the Hebrew word for 'righteousness' acquired the meaning of 'almsgiving.' "[42] That is perhaps the reason that giving alms is discussed first here. Today prayer would probably receive first place, and almsgiving last.

---

[41]John Wesley, *Explanatory Notes upon the New Testament* (London: Epworth Press, 1941 [reprint]), p. 35.

[42]Emil G. Kraeling, *The Clarified New Testament* (New York: McGraw-Hill Book Co., 1962), I, 133.

John Wesley, who was a careful student of the Greek text and amazingly aware of the importance of textual criticism,[43] translated the first part of this verse as follows: "Take heed that ye practice not your righteousness before men, to be seen of them." More recent translations have: "Be careful not to perform your good works publicly to be noticed by the people" (Berkeley); "Beware of doing your good actions in the sight of men, to attract their gaze" (Weymouth); "Be careful not to make a show of your religion before men" (NEB). The simplest rendering is: "Don't parade your piety."

Jesus did not say that one is not to let anyone see his good deeds. He had already admonished His disciples: "Let your light so shine before men, that they may see your good works, and glorify your Father which is in heaven" (5:16). It is the motive that He is dealing with here. The significant phrase is: **to be seen of them.** We are to seek God's glory, not our own.

*a. Almsgiving* (6:2-4). Jesus warned His disciples against trumpeting their giving, **as the hypocrites** (2) did in public places. **They have their reward** is better translated: "They have received their reward." The papyri have proved that the verb *apecho,* which Matthew employs, was used regularly in receipts of that period. The full force of Jesus' statement is that when people crave and capture the praise of men, they virtually give a receipt, "Paid in full." There will be no further reward awaiting them in heaven.[44]

Some people have refused to make any public pledges, because of the admonition, **let not thy left hand know what thy right hand doeth** (3). But the Bible also says, "To him that knoweth to do good, and doeth it not, to him it is sin" (Jas. 4:17).

[43]In his translation of the New Testament, published in 1755, he made 12,000 changes from KJV. In over 6,500 of these John Wesley's *New Testament* agrees with the Revised Standard Version (1946) against the King James Version (1611). About 430 of these indicate that he was using a better Greek text than the so-called Textus Receptus, on which the King James Version was based.

[44]Adolf Deissman, *Bible Studies,* trans. A. Grieve (Edinburgh: T. & T. Clark, 1901), p. 229, writes: "The words *they have their reward* in the Sermon on the Mount, when considered in the light of the above [papyri], acquire the more pungent ironical meaning *they can sign the receipt of their reward:* their right to receive their reward is realized, precisely as if they had already given a receipt for it."

If one's pledging in public will encourage someone else to give, and the cause of the Kingdom is thus furthered, a consecrated Christian should be willing to do it.

   *b. Prayer* (6:5-15). Ostentatious praying, Jesus also indicated, is to be avoided. The **hypocrites . . . love to pray standing** in prominent places, **that they may be seen of men** (5). They too "have received their reward." The Master urged the importance of **secret** prayer (6). One of the most sacred spots in London is the little room where John Wesley prayed. It has one window, and is just off the bedroom in his home on City Road. The spirit of prayer still seems to linger there.

   Christ warned against the use of **vain repetitions** (7) in praying. Some people unconsciously repeat names for Deity over **and** over in public prayer, until it becomes annoying. It is unnecessary repetition. Our Heavenly Father knows that we are speaking to Him, and He knows what we need before we **ask him** (8). So we do not need to keep repeating our petitions.

   The Lord's Prayer is a perfect model of the simplicity and sincerity for which Jesus was pleading. It is also a beautiful example of poetic parallelism. Printed in the following form it has only ten lines. But how significant they are!

> *Our Father who art in heaven,*
> *Let Thy name be sanctified,*
> *Let Thy kingdom come,*
> *Let Thy will be done,*
>    *as in heaven, also upon earth.*
> *Our daily bread give to us today;*
> *And forgive us our debts,*
>    *as also we forgive those indebted to us;*
> *And do not lead us into temptation,*
>    *but deliver us from the evil one.*

   The address—**Our Father** (9), suggesting close fellowship, **which art in heaven**, requiring reverence—is followed by six petitions. The first three are for Kingdom interests. The second three are for personal needs. The order is most significant. The needs of the Kingdom must always have priority over everything else.

   Actually, the prayer begins, as all prayers should, with worship: **Hallowed be thy name.** The Greek says, "Let thy name be sanctified." This is a challenging petition: Let Thy holy name be sanctified by my life today, as I, bearing the name of Christ, live in a Christlike manner.

The second petition is, **Thy kingdom come (10).** This must take precedence over personal interests. George Ladd says: "This prayer is a petition for God to reign, to manifest His kingly sovereignty and power, to put to flight every enemy of righteousness and of His divine rule, that God alone may be King over all the world."[45] But this petition is also related to world evangelism. For it is particularly in the salvation of souls that God's kingdom comes.

The third petition, **Thy will be done in earth, as it is in heaven,** was echoed by Jesus in the Garden of Gethsemane (Luke 22:42). There is no greater prayer that one can offer. We should make it personal: Thy will be done first in my heart, as in heaven. Then: Thy will be done everywhere on earth.

The fourth petition is the first to express a personal need: **Give us this day our daily bread (11).** Physical sustenance should not come first; but it does have its place in due time. God is interested in our personal needs, and He wants us to bring them to Him in prayer. If we put His kingdom first, He has promised to supply our material necessities (v. 33). The exact meaning of *daily* (found only in the Lord's Prayer) is uncertain. The Greek word *epiousion* has been translated "necessary for existence," "for today," "for tomorrow," "for the future." **Daily** is best.

A more pressing need is that for forgiveness: **Forgive us our debts, as we forgive our debtors (12).** The one who bears an unforgiving spirit toward another should pause before he offers this prayer. Suppose God should take him at his word; what hope would there be for him? Luke's version of the Lord's Prayer has "sins" instead of debts.[46] Every human being is in debt, for "all have sinned" (Rom. 3:23). (See exposition of Luke 11:4.)

The last petition is, **And lead us not into temptation, but deliver us from evil (13)**—or "the evil one." **Temptation** may be "testing"; the Greek word can be translated either way. Morison paraphrases the petition thus: "And bring us not into trial,

---

[45]*Op. cit.,* p. 21.

[46]Matthew Black, *An Aramaic Approach to the Gospels and Acts* (2d ed.; Oxford: Clarendon Press, 1954), p. 102, points out that the same Aramaic word means "debt" and "sin." He says: "Sin was conceived of in terms of a debt." That is, something is owed to God.

severe trial, trial which, in virtue of its severity, is fitted to press hard upon the moral state."[47]

In the oldest Greek manuscripts the Lord's Prayer ends with this petition. The doxology that follows—**For thine is the kingdom, and the power, and the glory for ever. Amen**—was added very early, probably to give it more of a finished close when recited in public. The addition was finally incorporated by scribes into the text. It is best still to include it when reciting the Lord's Prayer in public.

In the two verses following the prayer (14-15) Jesus pointed out the great seriousness of the matter of forgiving others. The one who refuses to forgive shuts heaven's door in his own face. No unforgiving spirit can ever enter there. Regardless of what has been done to us, we must forgive—fully and forever.

*c. Fasting* (6:16-18). Again the **hypocrites** (16) are described, this time as being **of a sad countenance,** disfiguring their faces **that they may appear unto men to fast.** And again we are told that "they have received the reward."

Jesus' instructions, put in modern terms, are as follows: When fasting, comb your hair and wash your face. Don't look dismal to remind people that you are fasting. Rather, fast for the sake of the spiritual good of others and yourself. Note that Jesus says God has a reward for this kind of fasting.

On the spiritual value of fasting, Pink has this to say: "When the heart and mind are deeply exercised upon a serious subject, especially one of a solemn or sorrowful kind, there is a disinclination for the partaking of food, and abstinence therefrom is a natural expression of our unworthiness, of our sense of the comparative worthlessness of earthly things, and of our desire to fix our attention on things above."[48]

### 2. *Singleness of Purpose* (6:19-24)

*a. A Single Treasure* (6:19-21). Jesus warned of the folly of laying up treasure on earth. It can all be destroyed or lost. Expensive garments bulked large in the treasures of Oriental men and women. Moths would be a real threat to such wealth; also **rust** literally means "eating." So it may refer to worms eating

---

[47]*Op. cit.,* p. 92.

[48]Arthur W. Pink, *An Exposition of the Sermon on the Mount* (Grand Rapids: Baker Book House, 1951), p. 173.

clothing. At that time also it was common for thieves to "dig through" (**break through,** 19) the mud walls of the Palestinean home to **steal.** But in heaven all our treasures are safe (20).

Jesus here sets forth a very significant principle: **where your treasure is, there will your heart be also** (21). If you encourage a man to give to the Lord's work, you are helping to tie him to heaven. Even soliciting a sinner to contribute to a special project of the church may lead to his salvation. Thus we do people a definite service when we give them a chance to make their offerings to the Lord. Where their money goes, there also their hearts will go.

*b. A Single Eye* (6:22-23). Jesus declared that the lamp of the body is the eye. If the eye is **single,** the body is **full of light** (22). But if the eye is **evil** (strong word, *poneros*), the body is **full of darkness** (23). The point the Master was making is that only singleness of purpose, or purity of intention, can keep the inner being lighted with God's presence. The contrast between **light** and **darkness** is a favorite theme in the Bible, especially in John. It also plays a prominent part in the Dead Sea Scrolls, particularly in the scroll entitled "The War of the Sons of Light Against the Sons of Darkness."[49]

*c. A Single Master* (6:24). Filson observes: "Vs. 24 (cf. Lk. 16:13) states clearly the intent of the two previous paragraphs: God claims complete loyalty; the disciple cannot divide his loyalty between God and possessions."[50] **Mammon** (24) is the Aramaic word for money or wealth.

The three main emphases in the sixth chapter up to this point are simplicity, sincerity, and singleness. These are basic virtues in the life of discipleship, as Jesus described it. No amount of sophisticated ability or intellectualism will compensate for the lack of these.

3. *Simplicity of Trust* (6:25-34)

The sin which Jesus condemns in this section is that of worry. **Take no thought** (25) should be translated, "Do not be anxious." One is not to worry about food or clothing. **Life** is **more than meat** (food). It is a spiritual as well as material existence.

[49]See Matthew Black, *The Scrolls and Christian Origins* (New York: Charles Scribner's Sons, 1961), pp. 154-56.
[50]*Op. cit.,* p. 100.

The Master then gave the example of **the fowls of the air** (26). They neither **sow** seed nor **reap** harvests, yet the Heavenly Father feeds them. How much more will He care for His own children?

The meaning of **stature** (27) is not certain. It may be translated "measure of his life" (ASV) or "span of life" (RSV), but also "height" (NEB). The Greek word (*helikia*) occurs eight times in the New Testament. In John 9:21, 23 it very clearly means "age"—"he is of age; ask him." But in Luke 19:3 it just as clearly means "stature." Zacchaeus was lacking in height, not age. The question is: What does it mean here and in the parallel passage (Luke 12:25)? It would seem more natural to speak of adding a **cubit** (eighteen inches) to one's height than to his age. Abbott-Smith says: "But the prevailing usage in the Septuagint and papyri favours the former meaning [age] in these doubtful passages."[51] The context here also favors "length of life." Whatever the meaning of the word, Jesus' statement is forceful. Worrying cannot add to a man's height, age, or span of life.

Not only does God feed the birds, but He also clothes **the lilies of the field** (28). Though they do not **toil** or **spin,** yet they are arrayed in greater glory than that of Solomon (29). If God gives such care to the transient flowers—here today, gone tomorrow (for fuel in the baking **oven)**—how much more will He clothe His own children (30)? It is unanswerable logic. So the disciple is not to be anxious about what to eat, drink, or wear (31); his Heavenly Father knows what he needs (32).

Then comes the great passage on stewardship: **But seek ye first the kingdom of God, and his righteousness; and all these things shall be added unto you** (33). One is reminded of the order of petitions in the Lord's Prayer. First we should seek God's kingdom and righteousness for *ourselves.* Actually the kingdom of God is righteousness. Pink observes: "Now by 'the righteousness of God' we are to understand two things: an imputed righteousness and an imparted righteousness, one which is placed to our account or credit and one which is communicated to our souls."[52]

In the second place, we should seek God's kingdom and righteousness for *others.* That is, our main concern as disciples of the Lord should be the salvation of souls and the building of His

[51]*Op. cit.,* p. 199.
[52]*Op. cit.,* p. 253.

Church. If we put these first, He promises to supply material needs.

The chapter ends with a closing admonition not to worry about the future (34). Each day has sufficient **evil**; that is, troubles and cares of its own.

## E. THE LIFE OF THE DISCIPLES, 7:1-29

### 1. *Warnings and Exhortations* (7:1-23)

a. *Censoriousness* (7:1-5). A censorious spirit is a denial of true religion. This was one of the worst faults of the Pharisees. So Jesus warned His followers: **Judge not, that ye be not judged** (1). Using the term in the popular sense we might paraphrase it thus: "Don't be critical, or you will be criticized." A still better free rendering would be: "Don't condemn others, or you will be condemned yourself." As Buttrick says, "Critical censure is a boomerang."[53] The trouble with judging others is that we set ourselves above those we judge. Bowman and Tapp translate this verse: "Do not practice 'sitting in judgment' lest you come in for judgment!"[54] Oswald Chambers warns his readers: "Beware of anything that puts you in the superior person's place."[55]

It should be noted that a goodly number of commentators interpret the second clause of the first verse as referring to the final judgment day. If we judge others we shall be judged by God (or Christ).

In verse 2, Jesus states, in double form, one of the basic principles of life. It can be most briefly put this way: "You get what you give." Give a smile and you get a smile; give a growl and you get a growl.

Then Jesus illustrated the inconsistency of a critical spirit (3-5). A man sees a **mote** (3)—"speck" or "splinter"—in his brother's eye and wants to pull it out. But actually he has a **beam** or "log" in his own eye. The Master suggested that it might be well for the critic to cast the log out of his own eye first, so that he could see more clearly to pull the splinter out of his brother's eye.

[53]George A. Buttrick, "Matthew" (Exposition), IB, VII, 325.
[54]*Op. cit.,* p. 143.
[55]*Studies in the Sermon on the Mount* (Cincinnati: God's Revivalist Press, 1915), p. 84.

Obviously Jesus was speaking in hyperbole. But He was using the sound pedagogical principle that one remembers best what seems most ridiculous. No one could ever forget the picture He painted here.

One who shows a harsh, censorious spirit in criticizing some trifling fault in a fellow Christian actually has a sawlog in his own eye. Lack of love always distorts the vision. What Jesus is saying is: You can't help the other fellow until you get rid of that critical attitude you have.

*b. Sacredness* (7:6). Most commentators interpret this verse as a warning against sharing rich spiritual truths with unworthy listeners. Jones, however, objects that this does not fit in with the context, nor does it represent the mind of Christ. So he offers this alternative interpretation: "That we are not to take the holy thing of personality that is being perfected, and give it to the dogs of desire, nor take the pearl of our spiritual life and cast it before the swine of our lower appetites, lest they trample that holy thing in the mire, and turn and rend the most precious thing we have, namely, our spiritual life."[56]

*c. Asking* (7:7-12). In the English (not in the Greek) verse 7 has an acrostic: *Ask, Seek, Knock.* The first suggests sincere praying, the second earnest praying, the third desperate praying. It is perhaps suggested—and experience seems to bear it out—that sometimes one simply needs to **ask** (7) in order to get the answer. If it does not come, one should engage in persevering prayer; he should **seek.** If the answer is still delayed, one may need to **knock** in desperate, even agonizing, prayer. But the promise is that all these kinds of prayer will be rewarded (8).

Alexander Maclaren has a sermon based on this passage called "Our Knocking." He analyzes the truth with these probing questions: (1) To whom are such exhortations rightly addressed? (2) In what region of life are these promises true? (3) On what conditions do these promises depend?

Jesus used the analogy of a human parent. Not one of His hearers would give his son a **stone** for **bread,** or a **serpent** for a **fish** (9-10). The conclusion, then, is that if they, **being evil**—"bad as you are in comparison with the Father"[57]—give **good gifts** to

[56]E. Stanley Jones, *The Christ of the Mount* (New York: Abingdon Press, 1931), p. 250.

[57]A. Marcus Ward, *The Gospel According to St. Matthew* ("Epworth Preacher's Commentaries"; London: Epworth Press, 1961), p. 50.

their children, **how much more** will the Heavenly Father give **good things**—Luke has "the Holy Spirit" (Luke 11:13)—**to them that ask him?** (11) The logic is inescapable.

The so-called golden rule (12) summarizes **the law and the prophets;** that is, the Old Testament. Christianity is not anything less, but it is something more.

The golden rule had been stated in negative form before Christ appeared. Confucius said: "Do not unto others what you would not have them do unto you." The Jewish rabbis had a similar saying. But it is generally recognized that Jesus was the first to give it in positive form. This is something far different. To refrain from hurting is one thing; to lend a helping hand is another. This positive attitude is illustrated by the parable of the Good Samaritan (Luke 10:30-35).

d. *Two Ways* (7:13-14). The idea of two ways is a familiar one in the Old Testament (cf. Psalms 1; Jer. 1:8). But Jesus called attention to the entrances. **Strait** (13) means **narrow;** the same word as in v. 14. The literal translation is "compressed." The Greek for **broad** means "spacious." "Broadway Christianity" will not get one to heaven. It is a solemnizing thought that Jesus declared **few** would **find** the way that leads to **life.**

e. *False Prophets* (7:15-20). Jesus had to warn His disciples against those who would come in sheep's clothing. They would join the flock of believers, as if one with them, but **inwardly** (15) they would be **ravening** [ravenous] **wolves.** The Church of Jesus Christ has been afflicted with such false prophets throughout all its history. They have sometimes done much to destroy the flock. How can they be recognized? **Ye shall know them by their fruits** (16).

Christ used the analogy of fruit-bearing vines and trees. Each bears its own fruit. If the tree is bad, the fruit will be bad. The converse is also true. A tree that does not bear good fruit is **hewn down, and cast into the fire.** It is a solemn warning that those who are not bearing good fruit do not belong to Christ (19).

f. *False Profession* (7:21-23). Whereas the previous warning was particularly concerned with religious leaders, this one deals with the mass of members inside the Church. The real test of discipleship is obedience. Even preaching and performing miracles in Christ's name is no proof that a person is accepted with

89

God. **Devils** should be translated "demons." *Diabolos* ("devil") is always singular in the Greek. The word here is plural, *daimonia,* "demons." The penalty for disobedience is separation from God.

### 2. *Conclusion of the Sermon* (7:24-29)

*a. Closing Illustration* (7:24-27). The one who hears and does is like a man who built his house on the solid rock. When the storms beat on it in all their fury, it still stood firmly. **Floods** is literally "rivers." The climate of Palestine is like that of southern California in many ways. The riverbeds are dry most of the year. But when the winter and spring rains come, the floods follow. Jesus pictured the careless hearer as like a man who foolishly built his house on sand, and so lost it. The Palestine homes are built largely of stone or sun-dried brick. When the storm loosens the mortar, the walls are apt to collapse.

*b. Reaction of the Crowd* (7:28-29). When Jesus finished, the people were **astonished at his doctrine**—better, "teaching." He taught **as one having authority** (29). The common people sensed this divine authority which the **scribes** lacked, and bowed to it. The scribes were in the habit of quoting earlier rabbis for support of their teachings.

Section **III** *Narrative Resumed:*
*A Ministry of Miracles*

Matthew 8:1—9:34

One of the main characteristics of this Gospel is systematic arrangement (see Introduction). After three chapters of teaching we now find two chapters of mighty miracles. Jesus' *words* are followed by His *works*. Just as Moses after giving the Israelites the Law at Mount Sinai proceeded to perform miracles on behalf of the people, so the new Moses, after giving on the mountain the basic laws of the Kingdom, wrought miracles to prove the power of the Kingdom. Of Him, even more truly than of the first Moses, it could be said that He was "mighty in words and in deeds" (Acts 7:22).

"Miracle" may be defined very briefly and simply as "an interference with Nature by supernatural power."[1] Modern man has questioned the credibility of miracles. But C. S. Lewis puts the whole matter in its proper focus when he writes: "The central miracle asserted by Christians is the Incarnation. . . . Every other miracle prepares for this, or exhibits this, or results from this."[2]

There are ten "miracles of the Messiah" that are recorded in chapters eight and nine. Matthew's love for systematic arrangement is further shown in the grouping of incidents in these two chapters. He has first three miracles—the healing of a leper (8:1-4), a paralytic (8:5-13), and Peter's mother-in-law (8:14-17). These are followed by a brief section of teaching material (8:18-22). Then come three more miracles—the stilling of the storm (8:23-27), the deliverance of the two demoniacs (8:28-34), and the healing of another paralytic (9:1-8). Following that is the call of Matthew (9:9), the feast at his house (9:10-13), and a discussion of fasting (9:14-17). The third group of miracles includes the healing of the woman with a hemorrhage and the raising of Jairus' daughter, treated together (9:18-26), the healing of the two blind men (9:27-31), and the healing of the dumb demoniac

[1]C. S. Lewis, *Miracles* (New York: Macmillan Co., 1947), p. 15.
[2]*Ibid.*, p. 131.

(9:32-34). These are followed by a summary statement that Jesus went throughout Galilee, teaching, preaching, and healing; there is also a notice of the need of workers.

Of the ten miracles in these two chapters, nine are healings and the other is a nature miracle. Jesus showed His divine authority over disease, death, demons, and the storm.

A. THREE HEALING MIRACLES, 8:1-17

1. *Cleansing of a Leper* (8:1-4)

This incident is recorded also in Mark 1:40-45 and Luke 5:12-16. As usual, Mark's account is the most vivid of the three. Mark places this episode at the close of a preaching tour in Galilee. Luke has it following the call of the first four disciples. But Matthew puts it after the Sermon on the Mount. This fits in with his pattern of systematic arrangement, grouping together in one place teachings of Jesus and in another His miracles.

An interesting example of the difference in wording of the three Synoptic Gospels, yet with the same meaning conveyed, is found here. Matthew says that there came a leper **and worshipped him** (2). Mark has: "beseeching him, and kneeling down to him." Luke says: "fell on his face, and besought him." The three writers used considerable freedom in relating the same facts, as would be expected.

When Jesus **touched** the leper (3), He contracted ceremonial defilement according to the Law. But actually His power **cleansed** the disease. So we, rather than being contaminated by contact with sinners, should, by the power of the Holy Spirit, have a redemptive influence on them. Since leprosy in its spread and devastation in the body is a striking type of sin in the soul, it is altogether appropriate that its healing should be spoken of as "cleansing" (cf. Lev. 14:2).

Verses 2 and 3 suggest the topic "Love's Willingness," with these three points: (1) The Man's Fear—**if thou wilt;** (2) The Man's Faith—**thou canst make me clean;** (3) The Master's Fulfillment—**I will; be thou clean.**

Christ commanded the healed man to show himself to the priest, in order that he might be officially pronounced clean (cf. Lev. 14:1-52). **For a testimony unto them** (4) means to the priests. For Jesus had already given the order to **tell no man.** Mark relates that the healed man disobeyed this command, with the result that the Master was hampered in His teaching ministry by great crowds that came to be healed (Mark 1:45; cf. Luke 5:15). As usual, Matthew's narrative is the shortest of the three.

2. *Healing of the Centurion's Servant* (8:5-13)

This episode is not recorded by Mark, but is by Luke (7:1-10). It happened in **Capernaum,** which Jesus had chosen as His headquarters. A **centurion** (5)—officer in charge of a hundred Roman soldiers—came to Christ with an urgent request. One of his servants, "who was dear unto him" (Luke 7:2), was lying at home a helpless paralytic, **grievously tormented** (6). Luke says he was "sick, and ready to die."

Jesus immediately responded, **I will come and heal him** (7). But the centurion objected that he was not worthy for the Master to come into his home (8). All Jesus needed to do was to **speak the word only,** and his servant would be healed. He reasoned that, since he gave orders and they were obeyed, the Master's commands would likewise carry full authority for their execution (9). When Jesus heard this amazing declaration of faith in His divine power, **he marveled** (10), and said to His weak-faithed followers: **Verily I say unto you, I have not found so great faith, no, not in Israel.**

Only one other time is Christ said to have marveled, and that was at the unbelief of His own townspeople (Mark 6:6). The Master must have had mixed emotions as He heard the centurion's words—a thrill of joy at the faith of a Gentile, and a pang of sorrow at the unbelief of His fellow Jews. One cannot help wondering what His reactions often are to the attitudes of the members of His Church today. Are we gladdening His heart with our strong faith in Him?

Matthew alone records at this point[3] Christ's warning that many Gentiles would come **from the east and west** (11) to sit down with the patriarchs in the kingdom of Heaven, while **the children of the kingdom** (12) (the Jews) would be cast **into outer darkness** (11-12). This is one of several places where Jesus sounded a strong warning against being lost in eternity's night. Coming at the end of this exhibition of faith, the teaching is clear. Those who come into the **kingdom of heaven** do so by faith. Those who lack that faith are **cast out.**

The Master bade the centurion go home in faith. **And his servant was healed in the selfsame hour** (13).

[3]Luke has it in another connection (Luke 13:28-29).

William Barclay develops this story under three headings: (1) A Good Man's Plea (5-6); (2) Passport of Faith (7:12); (3) The Power Which Annihilates Distance (13).

On the surface it seems that Matthew and Luke have a serious contradiction in their accounts (see on Luke 7:1-10). Luke says that the centurion did not himself come to Jesus, but sent some "elders of the Jews" to make the request. These pleaded with Christ by saying that the centurion loved their nation and had built them a synagogue (Luke 7:5). While Jesus was on the way to the man's home, the latter "sent friends" to tell Him that He need not come, but just speak the word of healing.

The whole problem is resolved when we recognize Matthew's habit of "telescoping" events into a brief, general description, without giving all the details. Numerous examples of this phenomenon can be found in his Gospel. In this case the centurion **came** to Jesus in the person of his friends.

It is interesting to note that all the centurions mentioned in the New Testament appear in a good light. In addition to this one, all three Synoptics tell about the centurion at the Cross, who gave favorable testimony about Jesus at His death. The remaining centurions are all mentioned in Acts. One thinks of Cornelius in the tenth chapter and Julius in chapter 27. They show up better than the governors over them or the soldiers under them.

### 3. Healing of Peter's Mother-in-law (8:14-17)

This miracle is recorded in all three Synoptics (cf. Mark 1:29-34; Luke 4:38-41). Mark and Luke indicate that it took place when Jesus and His disciples returned from a synagogue service on the Sabbath day. But Matthew has grouped it in a series of healing incidents without chronological sequence.

Perhaps Peter was embarrassed that his mother-in-law was not able to wait on the guests in his home. But Jesus **touched her hand, and the fever left her** (15). The fact that she was immediately and completely healed is shown by the statement that **she arose, and ministered unto them.** What a thrill: "the touch of the Master's hand on mine"!

All three Synoptic Gospels also relate the many miracles of healing that took place at sunset, when the Sabbath had ended. A prominent feature of this occasion was the casting out of demons, or **spirits** (16). Typically, Matthew quotes an Old Testament passage as having been **fulfilled . . . Himself took our infirmities, and bare our sicknesses** (17).

In our English Bibles, Isa. 53:4 reads: "Surely he hath borne our griefs, and carried our sorrows." Morison says that these words as found in Matthew, **Himself took our infirmities, and bare our sicknesses,** are "a more literal translation of the original Hebrew than is given in our Old Testament version."[4] Furthermore, "the Hebrew word rendered *griefs* really means *sicknesses*, and is so rendered in almost all the other passages in which it occurs."[5] Filson notes that **took** and **bare** "have here the unusual meaning: took away, removed."[6]

## B. The Cost of Discipleship, 8:18-22

Jesus was a strenuous Worker. Yet He realized that He and His disciples must at times get away from the **great multitudes** (18) that thronged Him constantly. So He ordered a departure to **the other side**—the eastern shore of the Lake of Galilee, where they could hope to have a period of quiet rest and retirement.

An eager **scribe (19)**—teacher of the Law—came to **Jesus** with an offer that sounded like complete consecration: **Master, I will follow thee whithersoever thou goest.** But Christ tested this would-be disciple by reminding him that while **the foxes have holes, and the birds . . . have nests . . . the Son of man hath not where to lay his head (20).** In other words, He said: "Count the cost."

This is the first place in Matthew where the title **Son of man** occurs. It is used some eighty-three times in the Gospels—always on Jesus' lips and applied to himself. Outside the Gospels it occurs in the New Testament—with the definite article, "the Son of man"—only in Acts 7:56.

There has been a great deal of discussion about the meaning of this expression. Vincent Taylor writes: "It has been maintained that *bar nasha* cannot mean anything more than 'a man' or 'man' in general; but it is now widely recognized that it can bear the sense of 'the Man,' and so could be used as a name for the Messiah."[7] Manson finds a close correlation between Son of God, Servant of the Lord (in Isaiah), and Son of Man. He says: ". . . functions first attributed to the Davidic prince in the prophets and in the Psalms reappear in a form transfigured or infiltrated with suffering in the person of the Servant and finally are

[4]*Op. cit.,* p. 121.
[5]*Ibid.,* p. 122.
[6]*Op. cit.,* p. 112.
[7]*The Names of Jesus,* p. 25.

invested with every circumstance of apocalyptic glory and splendour in the figure of the supernatural Son of Man."[8] This last usage is found in Dan. 7:13.

Another of Jesus' disciples said to Him: **Lord, suffer me first to go and bury my father** (21). The Master's reply seems harsh: **Follow me; and let the dead bury their dead** (22). But we must not assume that the man's father was already dead and Jesus was trying to prevent his going to the funeral. It was the requirement in Palestine that the body must be buried the day a person died. Probably this man's father would live for years yet. But as the oldest son (implied here) it was his responsibility to see that when his father did die he had a proper burial. Jesus informed him that there was more important business to be taken care of. The spiritually **dead** could bury their physical **dead**.

This passage is paralleled only in Luke 9:57-62. There a third individual is described as offering to follow Christ. But first he wants to say farewell to those at home. This would mean days of feasting and paying social respects to all his relatives. Jesus warned him of the danger of "looking back."

Bonhoeffer has well expressed the main thrust of this section. He says: "Jesus summons men to follow him not as a teacher or a pattern of the good life, but as the Christ, the Son of God. . . . When we are called to follow Christ, we are summoned to an exclusive attachment to his person."[9]

## C. THREE MORE MIRACLES, 8:23—9:8

### 1. *Stilling the Storm* (8:23-27)

After the delay caused by the conversation with the two men (cf. v. 18), Jesus **entered into a ship** with His disciples (23). This was probably Peter's small fishing boat. As they crossed the lake, a **tempest** (*seismos*, "earthquake") arose (24). While the boat was being **covered with the waves,** Jesus kept on sleeping (imperfect tense). He was so weary that the storm did not waken Him (see also Mark 4:35-41; Luke 8:22-25).

Thoroughly frightened, the disciples roused Him with the cry: **Lord, save us: we perish** (25). He first reproved them for being **fearful** (26) (literally, "cowardly"), and then **rebuked** the

---

[8]William Manson, *Jesus the Messiah* (Philadelphia: Westminster Press, 1946), p. 141.

[9]Dietrich Bonhoeffer, *The Cost of Discipleship* (rev. ed.; New York: Macmillan Co., 1959), pp. 48-49.

winds and the waves. The result was **a great calm.** It is not surprising that **the men marvelled** (27). In their years of fishing on the lake they had been in many severe storms, but never in one that was suddenly quieted by a person's command. Their reaction is still pertinent today: **What manner of man is this!** As mere man He would be absolutely unexplainable.

### 2. *Gadarene Demoniacs* (8:28-34)

When Jesus and His disciples reached the east side of the Lake of Galilee—it was about seven miles across—they found themselves in the country of the *Gergesenes.* This may represent the village of Khersa, the ruins of which are near the one hill close to the eastern shore. But some Greek manuscripts have "Gerasenes" (the best reading in Mark and Luke). Gerasa was about thirty miles southeast of the lake. "Gadarenes" is what the oldest Greek manuscripts have in Matthew. Gadara was the nearest large city, about six miles away.

The fact that Matthew mentions **two** (28) demoniacs, whereas Mark and Luke have only one, may be due to his bookkeeping mind. As a tax collector he would have to keep careful statistics. The other two Evangelists may have mentioned only the more prominent of the two.

While Mark's description of the demoniac is more full and vivid, Matthew is the one who says he was **exceeding fierce, so that no man might pass by that way.** These two men were endangering the lives of the citizens of that countryside.

The demons, as on other occasions, recognized Christ as the Son of God and feared the **torment** that was inevitably to be theirs (29). At their request, Jesus permitted the demons to enter a herd of hogs nearby—Mark says there were about two thousand. The result was that the whole herd perished in the lake (30-32). The keepers fled to the city to report all that had happened (33). **The whole city**—so it seemed—**came out to meet Jesus** (34). The people, filled with fear (Luke 8:37), begged Him to leave their **coasts** ("borders," or "district"). They were afraid of Jesus' power.

As usual, Matthew's account is much shorter than that in Mark (5:1-20) or even Luke (8:26-39). He leaves out many of the details found in the other two, in line with his policy of telescoping narrative material.

Two questions have sometimes been asked about this incident. The first is: Why would Jesus permit these hogs to be destroyed? It has been suggested that He wanted to confirm the faith of the two healed demoniacs by this visible evidence that the demons had actually left them. Some think Jesus did it to show the crowd what awful power and destructive tendencies demons have. Trench writes of the account where only one demoniac is mentioned: "If this granting of the evil spirits' request helped in any way the cure of this sufferer, caused them to relax their hold on him more easily, mitigated the paroxysm of their going forth, this would have been motive enough for allowing them to perish. It may have been necessary for the permanent healing of the man that he should have this outward evidence and testimony that the hellish powers which held him in bondage had quitted their hold."[10]

A second question asked is this: What right did Jesus have to destroy other people's property? This is more difficult to answer. If we were sure that the owners were Jews, this would offer a simple solution. The Jews were supposed to avoid unclean meats, including pigs. But the Decapolis was predominantly Gentile in population. In any case, the character of Christ guarantees that He would do nothing unjust. The actions of God may not always be judged by the standards of men. If we knew more, we would understand better.

### 3. *Healing of the Paralytic* (9:1-8)

Leaving the Decapolis, as requested, Jesus **passed over** the lake westward (see map) to **his own city** (1). This was Capernaum, which He had chosen as the headquarters for His Galilean ministry. It was located on the northwestern shore of the Lake of Galilee.

There was brought to Him a **man sick of the palsy**—all one word in the Greek, *paralyticon*. When Jesus saw **their faith**—probably that of both the afflicted man and his friends—He said to the paralytic, **Thy sins be forgiven thee** (2). But the Greek says: "Your sins are forgiven." It was already an accomplished fact. The Jews believed that sickness was the consequence of sin in one's own life (John 9:2). There is a possibility that this man's paralysis may have been caused, in part, by a severe guilt complex, and that he needed to have this taken care of first of all.

Some scribes sitting there said to themselves, **This man blasphemeth** (3). Jesus, **knowing their thoughts**, asked: **Wherefore**

[10]*Notes on the Miracles*, pp. 133-34.

**think ye evil in your hearts?** (4) Christ's absolution of the man's sins put Him "on the spot" with these Pharisees. "Either He was the Son of God, or, as the scribes rightly said from their point of view, a blasphemer."[11] He had already sufficiently demonstrated His deity, but still they did not believe in Him. Now His performance of the miracle vindicated His claim to have the divine right to forgive sins.

**Which is easier, asked Jesus, to say, Thy sins be forgiven thee; or to say, Arise, and walk?** (5) Their answer would have been the first. For no one could check the results of this assertion. But Jesus healed the man's body—an observable fact—in proof that He had forgiven his sins.

The healing of this paralytic at Capernaum is "the first story which brings Jesus' divine power of healing into direct relation with his divine power and authority to forgive sins."[12]

As in the case of the previous incident, Matthew's account is much shorter and less vivid than that of Mark (2:1-12) or Luke (5:17-26). He says nothing about four men (Mark) taking the paralytic up on the roof and breaking a hole through it (Mark and Luke). A careful comparison of these three accounts will give a fair sampling of the typical differences of the three Gospels in handling narrative material.

### D. MERCY, NOT SACRIFICE, 9:9-17

#### 1. Call of Matthew (9:9)

As Jesus walked out of Capernaum, He saw a man named **Matthew**—"Levi" in Mark 2:14 and Luke 5:27—sitting **at the receipt of custom.** This may suggest a customs house near the city piers, where the fish were checked and tax collected on them. Another possible translation is **the place of toll** (ASV). This could be a tollhouse on the great highway between Damascus and Egypt, where caravans would be compelled to pay toll on their goods. Probably the best rendering is "tax office" (RSV). The Romans required the Jews to pay taxes on every fruit tree,

---

[11]J. R. Dummelow (ed.), *A Commentary on the Holy Bible* (London: Macmillan and Co., 1909), p. 656.

[12]Henry Offermann, "The Gospel According to Matthew," *New Testament Commentary,* ed. H. C. Alleman (rev. ed.; Philadelphia: Muhlenberg Press, 1944), p. 183.

well, piece of land, and on all the animals they owned. This taxation seemed oppressive, and being imposed by foreigners was especially offensive.

To the tax collector Jesus said just two words: **Follow me.** Without any hesitation, Matthew immediately **arose, and followed him.** This was a big step for Matthew to take. Bonhoeffer comments: "The disciple is dragged out of his relative security into a life of absolute insecurity (that is, in truth, into the absolute security and safety of the fellowship of Jesus)."[13]

### 2. *Eating with Publicans and Sinners* (9:10-13)

As Jesus **sat at meat** (literally, "reclined at table") **in the house**—Luke 5:29 identifies it as Levi's (Matthew's)—**many publicans and sinners** reclined at the table **with him and his disciples** (10). A more correct translation for **publicans** is "tax collectors" or "taxgatherers." The *publicani* were the wealthy men, usually Romans, who were responsible for the taxes of whole regions. The so-called **publicans** of the Gospels were the local tax collectors—Jews who were hated by their fellow Jews. They were considered "doubly base and despicable" because "they had sold their services to the foreign oppressor as against their own people, and they were engaged in literal robbery."[14]

The **sinners** were those who were considered such by the Pharisees because of their carelessness in observing all the many ceremonial requirements of the written and oral law. A strict Jew would not eat with publicans and sinners.

So the Pharisees complained to the **disciples** (11). Apparently they feared to attack Jesus directly. But the Master had an answer for them: **They that be whole need not a physician, but they that are sick** (12). This expresses a perfectly obvious fact and explains why the Pharisees spurned Jesus. They thought they were **whole.** The Master then quoted Hos. 6:6—**I will have mercy, and not sacrifice** (13). One of the keynotes of the Minor Prophets is the demand for righteousness rather than ritualism. That is what this Old Testament declaration means. It is true today. No amount of animal sacrifices—nor ritualism or outward righteousness—will compensate for the lack of love and mercy in one's life. Jesus did not come to call those who considered themselves **righteous,** but those who had need—these **despised sinners.**

---

[13]*Op. cit.,* p. 49.

[14]B. J. Bamberger, "Tax Collector," IDB, IV, 522.

### 3. *Question of Fasting* (9:14-17)

Mark (2:18) makes this incident more vivid by giving the actual setting: "John's disciples and the Pharisees were fasting" (ASV). That is, it was an actual fast day, and these two groups of strict Jews were observing the occasion carefully. They were shocked to see Jesus' disciples eating on a fast day. So they asked about it. The word **oft** (14) is not in the oldest Greek manuscripts. Leaving it out, Matthew's question is the same essentially as Mark's: "Why are we and the Pharisees fasting, but Your disciples are not fasting?"

Jesus replied by using the figure of a wedding. **The children of the bridechamber** (15) means the friends of the bridegroom. They cannot **mourn**—fasting is in a sense a sign of mourning— while the bridegroom is with them. But Jesus indicated the time would come when He would be taken away, and then His disciples would fast.

To illustrate the contrast between the Old and the New, Jesus gave two brief parabolic statements. The first was that of sewing a new patch on an old garment (16). When the garment was washed, the new, unshrunk patch would shrink and pull at the edges of the previously shrunk garment. This would cause a fresh tearing of the robe.

The second illustration was that of putting new wine into old wineskins (17). They did not have glass **bottles** in those days. Instead they used the skins of goats. The carcass would be removed, and then the skin sewed together, except for the neck. One can still see goatskins in Palestine being filled with water at a spring.

If new wine is put into "fresh" wineskins, those skins will stretch as the wine ferments and expands. But if new wine is put into old, brittle, already stretched wineskins, there will be disaster. The dry, stretched wineskins will have no capacity for stretching further with the fermentation of the new wine. Instead they will give way in some place, and both wine and wineskin will **perish.**

The application is clear. The new truths of Christianity must not be poured into the old forms of Judaism. The early chapters of Acts give some hint of the difficulties involved in replacing the old wineskins with the new. Entrenched institutions are apt to be brittle and unable to hold fresh truths.

The three incidents in this section (9:9-17) are found in all three Synoptics (see Mark 2:13-22; Luke 5:27-39).

E. THIRD GROUP OF MIRACLES, 9: 18-34

1. *A Double Miracle* (9: 18-26)

In all three Synoptic Gospels[15] the healing of the woman with a hemorrhage is put into the context of the raising of Jairus' daughter. So we are treating them together.

Jesus was approached by a ruler,[16] Jairus—the name is given in Mark 5: 22—with the request that He come and lay His hand on his daughter's head. Matthew reports Jairus as saying, **My daughter is even now dead** (18), while Mark has, "My little daughter lieth at the point of death" (Mark 5: 23)—literally, "at her last gasp." Mark and Luke tell of someone reporting on the way to the house that the daughter had died. But was she dead when Jesus started out with Jairus? Again for an explanation we fall back on Matthew's habit of telescoping a narrative. Mark and Luke give the correct details that fill in Matthew's meager account.

While Jesus was accompanying Jairus to his home, a timid woman who had suffered from a hemorrhage for twelve years came up behind Him and **touched the hem of his garment** (20) —or "tassel of His robe" (cf. Num. 15: 38). She believed that if she touched His garment, she would **be whole** (21). The verb here is *sozo*. It is used frequently in the Gospels, and sometimes in Acts, for physical healing. But in the Epistles it is used regularly for spiritual salvation. The Greek words for Saviour and salvation are from the same root as *sozo*. They emphasize the fact that salvation means spiritual health or wholeness.

It was not the touching of Jesus' robe that healed the woman; it was her faith (22). But her faith was expressed in action.

When Christ arrived at the home of the synagogue ruler, He found **the minstrels and the people making a noise** (23), or "tumult." These **minstrels,** or "flute players," would be the hired, professional mourners. The more noise they made at the funeral, the better they were paid. Since the body must be buried the same day, no time was to be lost.

What a contrast was the calm, dignified conduct of Christ! He bade the hired mourners, **Give place** (24). He assured every-

---

[15]See Mark 5: 21-43; Luke 8: 40-56.
[16]"Ruler" is identified in Mark and Luke (8: 41) as being a synagogue ruler, one who was in charge of the services in the synagogue.

one that the maid was not dead, but only asleep. Angered and frustrated, the professional mourners mocked Him.

Putting the unbelievers out of the room, Jesus took with Him only Peter, James, and John, plus the parents (cf. Mark and Luke). The Creator took the lifeless girl by the hand, and she got up (25).

The story of the raising of a girl from the dead naturally caused great excitement. It spread the fame of Jesus all over the land of Palestine (26).

### 2. Healing of Two Blind Men (9:27-31)

This incident, and the next one, are recorded only in Matthew. Here again we find two—this time **two blind men** (27). They cried out: **Thou son of David, have mercy on us.** Filson observes: "They accept him as the expected Messianic leader who will do wonderful deeds of mercy mentioned in Isaiah 35:5."[17]

When they asserted their faith in Him (28), Jesus replied: **According to your faith be it unto you** (29). This is a tremendously challenging statement for all Christians today. We can have what we believe for.

When the Great Physician touched their eyes, they were able to see. Then Jesus **straitly charged** them to tell no one about it (30). The verb is a very strong one in Greek. It indicates deep feeling on the part of the one who speaks or acts. Here it means "to admonish sternly."[18] The reason for Jesus' speaking so energetically was that He did not want further publicity to hinder His teaching ministry by causing multitudes to come for healing. But the admonition was in vain. The two men **spread abroad his fame in all that country** (31).

### 3. Healing of Dumb Demoniac (9:32-34)

The Gospels picture demon possession as causing insanity, and here dumbness. When delivered from the demon, the man spoke. Again the **multitudes marvelled** (33) at the power of God.

But the Pharisees had another explanation for it: Jesus was casting out "demons" through the prince of the demons (34). This was moral perversion on the part of these religious leaders, confusing the demonic and the divine. Elsewhere we find Jesus dealing sternly with this attitude on their part.

[17]*Op. cit.*, p. 123.
[18]Abbott-Smith, *op. cit.*, p. 148.

Section **IV** *Second Discourse:*

*Instructions to the Twelve*

Matthew 9:35—10:42

A. THE NEED FOR LABORERS, 9:35-38

The summary statement about Jesus' Galilean ministry in verse 35 is very similar to that in 4:23. In both places attention is called to His **teaching, preaching,** and **healing.** The Greek word for **sickness** means "disease"; that for **disease** denotes "infirmity."[1] So the correct translation is "every disease and every infirmity" (RSV).

**He was moved with compassion** (36) is all one word in the Greek, *esplangchnisthe.* The verb occurs five times in Matthew, four in Mark, and three in Luke. It comes from *splangchnon,* which means "the inward parts." It is used once literally in the New Testament (Acts 1:18), and ten times metaphorically, meaning "the heart, affections."[2] Here the thought is that Jesus' heart was stirred with compassion—which literally means "suffering with." Since the verb is in the aorist passive, it is better to translate it: "He was *gripped* with compassion." That was Christ's immediate reaction to human need.

This time His heart was stirred because He saw the crowds **scattered abroad, as sheep having no shepherd.** The religious leaders in Judaism were not fulfilling their responsible role as shepherds of the people. The sheep were "worn out" and "prostrate."

So He said to His disciples: **The harvest truly is plenteous, but the labourers are few** (37). The Master's compassionate eyes saw the multitudes as a great harvest field, ready to be reaped. He bade His disciples: **Pray ye therefore the Lord of the harvest, that he will send forth labourers into his harvest** (38). The prayer is a pertinent one today. For while the laborers have increased, they have not caught up with the colossal increase of the harvest. Nineteen centuries later there are countless millions who have never heard the good news that Christ died to save

[1]Thayer, *op. cit.,* p. 387.
[2]Abbott-Smith, *op. cit.,* p. 414.

them from sin. **Send forth** is a strong verb in the Greek. Jesus was urgent in this task of evangelism.

In this example and in these words of Jesus we see: (1) Our Lord teaching us how to look at men; (2) How that sight should touch us; (3) How Christ would have us act (Maclaren).

## B. The Mission of the Twelve, 10:1-42

### 1. *Appointment* (10:1-4)

Jesus chose **twelve disciples** (1) to go on a missionary tour of the twelve tribes of Israel. The boundaries of these tribes were no longer intact, but there were representatives of all twelve tribes in the remnant that stayed in the land as well as those that returned from the Captivity. The mission of the twelve was strictly to "the lost sheep of the house of Israel" (6).

To His messengers Jesus gave "authority"—the Greek word is *exousia*—**against unclean spirits.** An important part of their ministry, like His, was to be the casting out of demons, as well as the healing of the sick.

The expression **unclean spirits** occurs twice in Matthew, ten times in Mark, five times in Luke (plus "spirit of an unclean demon," 4:33), twice in Acts, and once in Revelation (16:13). It seems to be a particularly appropriate designation for "demons." The latter term, *daimonia,* is found eleven times in Matthew, thirteen times in Mark, twenty-two times in Luke, and six times in John—out of a total of sixty times in the New Testament. Luke also calls them "evil spirits" (Luke 7:21; 8:2; Acts 19:12-13, 15-16).

The twelve disciples are called **apostles** (2). The word comes from the Greek *apostolos,* which means "one sent on a mission." Walls notes that "the force of *apostolos* is probably 'one commissioned'—it is implied, by Christ."[3]

Lists of the **twelve apostles** will be found in all the Synoptic Gospels (cf. Mark 3:16-19; Luke 6:14-16) and in Acts 1:13. All the lists begin with Peter and end with Judas Iscariot (except the last, with Judas dead). The four fishermen are always named first, though in differing order. Matthew and Luke give them as pairs of brothers. Mark and Acts have Peter, James, and John first, as constituting the inner circle privileged to be alone with Jesus at the raising of Jairus' daughter, on the Mount of Trans-

[3]A. F. Walls, "Apostle," *New Bible Dictionary,* ed. J. D. Douglas (Grand Rapids: Wm. B. Eerdmans Publishing Co., 1962), p. 48.

figuration, and in Gethsemane. Furthermore, the second group of four names always begins with Philip, and the third group with James the son of Alphaeus. The slight differences may be seen by comparing the lists.[4]

**Simon** "is a [common] Greek name substituted for the Hebrew Symeon"[5] (cf. Acts 15:14). **Peter** is the Greek *petros* ("stone"). He is designated as being **first**. Tasker says: "There is little doubt that *The first* (*protos*) means 'first and foremost.' "[6] **Andrew** and **Philip** are Greek names. **Bartholomew, Thomas** ("twin"), and **Matthew** (3) are all Aramaic names. **Lebbaeus, whose surname was** should perhaps be omitted because not found in the two oldest Greek manuscripts (cf. Revised Versions). Mark has simply **Thaddaeus**. In place of this name Luke uses "Judas the brother [or son] of James" (Luke 6:16; Acts 1:13). Tasker observes: "It may be that Judas was his original name, but later owing to the stigma attaching to the name Judas Iscariot, Thaddaeus (meaning perhaps 'warm-hearted') was substituted for it."[7]

**Canaanite** (4) should be "Cananaean." Sherman Johnson says: "The word may be an Aramaic equivalent of the 'Zealot' of Luke 6:15."[8] The latter term may simply designate him as a Jew who was zealous for the Law (like Saul), or as previously

| [4]MATTHEW | MARK | LUKE | ACTS |
|---|---|---|---|
| *Peter* | *Peter* | *Peter* | *Peter* |
| Andrew | James | Andrew | John |
| James | John | James | James |
| John | Andrew | John | Andrew |
| *Philip* | *Philip* | *Philip* | *Philip* |
| Bartholomew | Bartholomew | Bartholomew | Thomas |
| Thomas | Matthew | Matthew | Bartholomew |
| Matthew | Thomas | Thomas | Matthew |
| *James* | *James* | *James* | *James* |
| (of Alphaeus) | (of Alphaeus) | (of Alphaeus) | (of Alphaeus) |
| Thaddaeus | Thaddaeus | Simon | Simon |
| | | (the Zealot) | (the Zealot) |
| Simon | Simon | Judas | Judas |
| (the Cananaean) | (the Cananaean) | (of James) | (of James) |
| Judas Iscariot | Judas Iscariot | Judas Iscariot | |

[5]W C. Allen, *A Critical and Exegetical Commentary on the Gospel According to St. Matthew* ("International Critical Commentary"; New York: Charles Scribner's Sons, 1907), p. 35.

[6]*Op. cit.*, p. 106.

[7]*Ibid.*, p. 107.

[8]IB, VII, 364

a member of the revolutionary group later known as "the Zealots."[9] **Iscariot** is usually explained as "man (Heb. *ish*) of Kerioth"—a village of Judah. If this is correct, Judas was apparently the only one of the Twelve who was not from Galilee.

### 2. *Instructions* (10:5-15)[10]

The first instruction the Master gave His twelve apostles (only in Matthew) was that they were not to evangelize the **Gentiles** or **Samaritans** (5). After Pentecost that would be done, as recorded in the Book of Acts. But before His crucifixion Jesus was concerned with offering the Kingdom to Israel. Paul indicated that the gospel of Christ was "the power of God unto salvation to every one that believeth; to the Jew first, and also to the Greek" (Rom. 1:16). **The lost sheep of the house of Israel** (6) must first be given the opportunity to accept their Messiah.

The message they were to **preach** ("proclaim") was: **The kingdom of heaven is at hand** (7). This was the message of Jesus and John the Baptist.

Along with their preaching they were to carry on a ministry of healing the sick and casting out demons (8). The command to **raise the dead** (found only in Matthew) has presented a problem. Adam Clarke rejects it as improbable.[11] Stier says: "We hold it as a spurious importation from a later time . . . their weak faith could not then be entrusted with this greatest of powers."[12] But the words are found in most of the earliest Greek manuscripts. A. B. Bruce says, "It is . . . too well attested to be omitted," and adds: "It must either have found a place in the autograph, or it must have crept in as a gloss at a very early period."[13] The problem is that the Gospels record only three times when Jesus raised the dead. It is difficult to think of the Twelve as doing it. But apparently the Master delegated His authority to His apostles, and this was included as a potentiality.

---

[9]Cf. Josephus *War* IV. 3. 9. See also W. R. Farmer, *Maccabees, Zealots, and Josephus* (New York: Columbia University Press, 1956), p. 124, n. 86, where the author indicates that the more general meaning of "Zealot" is "extreme nationalist."

[10]See also Mark 6:8-11; Luke 9:2-5.

[11]*The New Testament of Our Lord and Saviour Jesus Christ* (New York: Abingdon-Cokesbury Press, n.d.), I, 118.

[12]Rudolf Stier, *The Words of the Lord Jesus* (New York: N. Tibbals, 1864), I, 170.

[13]EGT, I, 160.

There is no record in the Gospels of their actually raising the dead, though Peter later raised Dorcas (Acts 9:36-43).

Next came specific instructions in answer to the unasked question, What shall we carry with us? The order was: **Provide**— the Greek word means "procure for oneself," or "acquire"— **neither gold, nor silver, nor brass in your purses** (9). These were the three kinds of money, **gold** taking the place of our present paper money. **Purses** is literally "belts"—money belts—the safest place to carry cash.

Also forbidden was **scrip** (10). The Greek *pera* was used for a traveler's leather bag or pouch. But on the basis of an inscription of this period in Syria, Deissmann asserts: "It clearly means the beggar's collecting-bag."[14] So Christ's twofold admonition means: "There is to be no earning, and also no begging of money."[15]

They were not to have two **coats.** The Greek word refers to the undergarment. So "shirts" (Moffatt) would be a better translation. **Shoes** is literally "bound under," and so means "sandals." They were to wear sandals, but not to carry an extra pair (cf. Mark 6:9).

**Staves** is singular in the oldest manuscripts—"neither a staff." Evidently some later scribe changed it to the plural because it seemed to conflict with Mark's form—"save a staff only." But Matthew says they were not to **provide,** or "procure," a staff; that is, an extra one. They were simply to take what they had and hurry off on their mission.

The reason for these stringent instructions is obvious. The disciples were on an urgent trip of short duration. The climate was warm, and the customs of the day guaranteed them free food and lodging wherever they went. So they were not to load themselves down with luggage.

They were to choose carefully their quarters in each city and remain in the same home while there (11). When they entered a house they were to **salute it** (12). The regular salutation was "Shalom," the Hebrew word meaning "Peace!"

When rejected, they were to wipe off their feet the very dust of the place (14), as a sign that God had in turn rejected that home or city because it had rejected His message. Jesus declared

[14]Adolf Deissmann, *Light from the Ancient East,* trans. L. R. M. Strachan (New York: George H. Doran Co., 1927), p. 109.
[15]*Ibid.*

that it would be **more tolerable for . . . Sodom and Gomorrha in the day of judgment, than for that city** (15). A great deal has been said in recent years about the "gentle teachings of the lowly Galilean." But on a number of occasions Jesus spoke with stern voice about the realities of a coming judgment. The destruction of Sodom is mentioned several times in the New Testament as a warning illustration (cf. 11:23-24; Luke 10:12; 17:29; Rom. 9:29; II Pet. 2:6; Jude 7). In fact Jerusalem is once called "Sodom" (Rev. 11:8).

### 3. *Warnings* (10:16-23)

Jesus warned His disciples that persecutions would overtake them. This prediction looks not only to the immediate tour they were taking, but also beyond it to the many years of ministry ahead. They were going out as **sheep** in the midst of **wolves** (16). The Book of Acts gives vivid documentation for this statement. The missionaries were to be **wise as serpents,** yet **harmless as doves.** The first adjective means "prudent," the second "pure" or "sincere." A successful Christian needs to be both.

The Master forewarned His apostles that they would be delivered up to **councils** (sanhedrins) and scourged in **synagogues** (17). They would also (18) be brought before **governors** (as Felix and Festus, Acts 24 and 25) and **kings** (as Agrippa, Acts 26). These were Gentile rulers. But it was the Jews who brought about the arrest of Paul. So the persecution was still Jewish in origin.

When delivered up, they were not to be anxious about their defense (19), for the Holy Spirit would give them the words to say (20).

Christ also declared that the coming of His kingdom would result in the division of families, so that children would even cause their parents to be put to death (21). This has happened many times in the past and is still happening today, especially in Communist countries. With the warning that they will be hated by all men for Jesus' sake comes the promise: **but he that endureth to the end shall be saved** (22). There is a sense in which one is saved when converted, another in which he is being saved day by day as he believes and obeys, and still another in which he will finally and forever be saved in heaven. It is with the second and third meanings that Jesus speaks in this verse.

If persecuted in one city, the missionaries were to move on to another (23). Jesus informed them that they would not

have covered **the cities of Israel, till the Son of man be come.**
Much ink has been used in trying to explain the meaning of this
statement. Perhaps as good an interpretation as can be given
is that of Tasker: "This very difficult verse, found only in
Matthew, is best understood with reference to the coming of the
Son of man in triumph immediately after His resurrection, when
He appeared to the apostles and commissioned them to make
disciples of all nations (xxviii. 18-20) ."[16]

### 4. *Discipleship* (10: 24-25)

The apostles could not hope to escape persecution, for **the
disciple is not above his master** (24)—literally, "teacher." **(Disciple** means "learner.") Neither is the **servant** (Greek, "slave")
above his **lord** (master). If they called the "house-master" (one
word in Greek) **Beelzebub,**[17] how much more **them of his household (25)**?

The origin and meaning of **Beelzebub** (or Beelzebul) are still
veiled in obscurity. The recent Ugaritic discoveries have suggested "prince of Baal." Other suggestions are "Lord of Dung"
or "Lord of the Abode [i.e. shrine]."[18] Davies says *"Beelzebub,*
originally 'lord of flies,' but by this time meant Satan, as lord of
the house of demons."[19]

### 5. *Assurance* (10: 26-33)

In spite of these predictions of persecution, Jesus told His
disciples not to be afraid. **For there is nothing covered, that shall
not be revealed** (26)—Greek, "uncovered." The day will come
when both persecutors and persecuted will be seen in their true
light. The Judgment Day will set the record straight. Therefore
the disciples were to preach boldly and openly the message of
Christ (27).

They were not to fear those who killed the body, but only
**him which is able to destroy both soul and body in hell (28)**—

[16]*Op. cit.,* p. 108.

[17]The form Beelzebub comes from the Latin. The Greek manuscripts
have Beelzeboul or Beezeboul.

[18]T. H. Gaster, "Beelzebul," IDB, I, 374.

[19]J. Newton Davies, "Matthew," *Abingdon Bible Commentary,* ed. F. C.
Eiselen, *et al.* (New York: Abingdon-Cokesbury Press, 1929), p. 972.

Gehenna. Most commentators are agreed that the reference here is to God rather than to Satan.[20]

As encouragement to the disciples' faith, Jesus cited the **sparrows** (29). Two of them were sold for a **farthing**. Here is a different Greek word from that translated "farthing" in 5:26 (see comment there). This one was worth about one cent. Though commercially worth only half a penny apiece, not one sparrow fell to the ground without the notice of the Creator. Only infinity can explain such a concept of God. Finite minds are frustrated. What is demanded is a "leap of faith" to believe in a God who is actually infinite in knowledge and power.

To make it a bit more personal, Jesus said: **But the very hairs of your head are all numbered** (30). Furthermore, you are of **more value than many sparrows** (31). So trust is the logical thing, not fear.

If the disciples were faithful to **confess** (32) Christ by preaching His truth fearlessly (cf. v. 27) and acknowledging Him loyally as their Lord, at whatever cost, He promised He would acknowledge them before His Father. But whoever would **deny Him** (33) would be denied before the Father. The context indicates that silence—a failure to speak out for Christ—could be one way of denying Him.

### 6. *Price of Discipleship* (10:34-39)

Jesus' statement, **I came not to send peace, but a sword** (34), is startling—one might say, literally, "shocking." It is obvious He is talking about the inevitable results of the demands of discipleship. Tasker rightly observes: "Consequences are often expressed in the Bible as though they were intentions."[21] It will always be true that some members of a family will accept Christ, while others reject Him. This brings inescapable conflict. For God demands our first love and loyalty (37). This cuts across the grain of selfish, worldly thinking. The one who would follow Christ must take up **his cross** (38) of full submission to the will of God.

One of the most significant sayings of Jesus is in verse 39.[22]

[20]Notable exceptions to this view are A. B. Bruce (EGT) and Carr (CGT). The latter thinks it can mean either God or Satan. Allen (ICC) says it is God. Sherman Johnson (IB) says, "probably God."
[21]*Op. cit.*, p. 108.
[22]It is recorded also in Mark 8:35; Luke 9:34; 17:33; John 12:25.

Of the first part, Filson says: "Self-seeking is self-defeating."[23]
Of the second part Davies writes: "Self-denial and self-sacrifice
are the only ways to self-discovery."[24] In the context of persecution described in the preceding verses the special application of
this truth would be: "He who under the pressure of persecution
desires to preserve his life will lose the true life of the soul;
while he who joyfully dies will live."[25]

### 7. *Privilege of Discipleship* (10:40-42)

The relationship of the disciple to his Lord is likened in a
sense to that of Christ to His Father—**him that sent me (40)**.
One is reminded of the language of Jesus in His high-priestly
prayer (John 17:21-23).

Lukyn Williams defines **prophet (41)** as "one upon whom the
mantle of the old prophets might in any sense be said to have
fallen," and **righteous man** as "one who is punctilious in performing all the details of the revealed will of God."[26] The prophet
and the righteous man are terms used here for the disciples. To
give even a cup of cold water **in the name of a disciple (42)** brings
a reward. The disciples are thus honored as emissaries of Christ.

As indicated by the headings, these last two paragraphs of
this chapter give us a two-point sermon outline: (1) The Price
of Discipleship; (2) The Privilege of Discipleship.

[23]*Op. cit.*, p. 134.

[24]*Op. cit.*, p. 972.

[25]P. P. Levertoff and H. L. Goudge, "The Gospel According to St. Mat-
thew," *A New Commentary on Holy Scripture*, ed. Charles Gore, H. L.
Goudge, and Alfred Guillaume (New York: Macmillan Co., 1928), p. 153
(NT).

[26]*Op. cit.*, I, 417.

Section **V** *Narrative Resumed:*
*Rejection of the Messiah*

Matthew 11:1—12:50

A. JESUS AND JOHN THE BAPTIST, 11:1-19

1. *Jesus' Answer to John* (11:1-6)

The first verse of this chapter is composed of a transitional statement between the second discourse and the resumption of the narrative. For the second time (cf. 7:28) there occurs the terminal expression, **And it came to pass, when Jesus had made an end (1)** (exactly the same in the Greek as 7:28). Then it is stated that Jesus started out—apparently alone—on a mission of teaching and preaching. In the next chapter we find the disciples once more with Him (cf. 12:1).

Only Matthew and Luke (7:18-35) tell of John's sending two of his disciples to Jesus. The prophet was languishing in prison, evidently tempted to be discouraged and disillusioned. He had introduced Jesus to the Jewish nation as its Messiah. He had meekly declared: "He must increase, but I must decrease" (John 3:30). He had assumed that Jesus would fulfill the expected role of the Messiah, destroying the foreign oppressor (Rome) and freeing His people from bondage. But this was exactly what Jesus was not doing.

The question John asked through his disciples was literally: "Are You the Coming One, or are we waiting for another?" In other words, Are You really the Messiah?

Instead of giving a categorical answer, Jesus bade the disciples go back to John and report what they had seen and heard. His healing of the **blind** and the **lame (5)** was a fulfilling of the Messianic role as described in Isa. 35:5-6. But the climax was the preaching of the gospel to the **poor** (cf. Isa. 61:1). The Greek says: "the poor are being evangelized" (*evangelizontai*). That was His main credential.

A little hint as to John's problem is suggested in verse 6—**And blessed is he, whosoever shall not be offended in me.** The verb is *skandalizo*, which we have already noted (see on 5:29). Apparently John stumbled over the fact that Jesus seemed to be making no effort to set up His Messianic kingdom. The Baptist had proclaimed: "The kingdom of heaven is at hand" (3:2). Was he mistaken? He had warned that the axe was ready to cut down the unfruitful tree (3:10). Judgment was ready to strike. He had preached that the Coming One would "throughly purge his floor," gathering His wheat into the storehouse, but burning up the chaff "with unquenchable fire" (3:12). John knew that the nation of Israel was ripe for judgment, and he expected the Messiah to judge His people. What he could not realize was that the first coming of Christ was in grace and mercy. Judgment must await His second coming.

Numbers of scholars have suggested that it was the disciples of John, not the Baptist himself, who doubted. But Lenski objects. He says: "This view casts reflection on the integrity of John as though he were asking a question when in reality it was being asked by his disciples."[1] Also Jesus told the disciples to go back and report to John. It is certainly not surprising that the prophet, locked up in prison, would be struggling with serious questions.

### 2. *Jesus' Commendation of John* (11:7-15)

After having comforted John, perhaps at the same time reproving him gently for his lack of faith (6), Jesus proceeded to give him the highest possible commendation before the crowd. He asked them what they had gone out into the wilderness to see, making the long journey to John's baptism. Was it **a reed shaken with the wind** (7), some cowardly, vacillating person? They all knew that John had been cast into prison for his fearless preaching to the king. Was it a man **clothed in soft raiment** (8) — "dressed in silks and satins" (NEB)? Everybody knew that John wore the very roughest of raiment—camel's hair sackcloth and a leather belt (3:4). Was it **a prophet?** The answer this time was: **Yea, I say unto you, and more than a prophet** (9). This was God's messenger, the forerunner of the Messiah, who was predicted in Mal. 3:1.

Then Jesus paid John the supreme compliment. He said that among all men that had been born there had not been a greater one (11). Perhaps this means that he was the greatest of the prophets.[2] Yet **he that is least in the kingdom of heaven is greater than he.** The famous fourth-century preacher Chrysostom interpreted **he that is least** as referring to Christ. A number of Church Fathers followed him in this, as did Erasmus and

---

[1]*Op. cit.*, p. 427.
[2]EGT, I, 172.

Luther. The idea was that Jesus, who was baptized by John and less in age and fame than the prophet, might be considered "least."[3] In recent times Cullmann has supported this view, based on his studies of the Dead Sea Scrolls. He presents it thus: "The smaller (i.e., Jesus, as the disciple) is greater than he (i.e., John the Baptist) in the kingdom of heaven."[4] But A. B. Bruce offers a convincing refutation. In regard to Chrysostom's view, he says: "In the abstract it is a possible interpretation, and it expresses a true idea, but not one Jesus was likely to utter then."[5] Evidently Christ meant that the "least" Christian is "greater" in privilege than John, who really belonged more to the Old Testament order.

The twelfth verse is difficult to explain. What is meant by the statement, **the kingdom of heaven suffereth violence, and the violent take it by force?** Thayer, in his treatment of the verb *biazo* **(suffereth violence)** writes: *"The kingdom of heaven is taken by violence, carried by storm,* i.e. a share in the heavenly kingdom is sought for with the most ardent zeal and the intensest exertion."[6] This seems to be a sound interpretation in the light of the introductory words—**from the days of John the Baptist until now.**[7] In other words, only those who are desperately in earnest can enter the Kingdom. Since the verb form *biazetai* may be either passive or middle (used in an active sense), Lenski prefers: "the kingdom of the heavens presses forward forcefully, and forceful people snatch it."[8] His conclusion is: "The trend of the entire discourse deals, not with violence against the kingdom, but with the indifference and the dissatisfaction that hinder men from entering it with zest."[9]

The substance of verses 12 and 13 is given in Luke 16:16, but in reverse order. The thought here seems to be: The entire Old Testament—**all the prophets and [even] the law—prophesied until John** (13). That is, the older Scriptures predicted the com-

---

[3]The adjective is in the comparative degree, *mikroteros*. But in the Koine Greek the comparative was often used for the superlative. This is the common NT usage.

[4]Oscar Cullmann, "Significance of Qumran Texts," *Journal of Biblical Literature,* LXXIV (1955), 219.

[5]EGT, I, 172.

[6]*Op. cit.,* p. 101.

[7]The alternative view, that the Kingdom suffers violence from its enemies, does not fit so well here.

[8]*Op. cit.,* p. 437.

[9]*Ibid.*

ing of Christ. But John filled a special role. He was the fulfilment of Mal. 4:5—the Elijah of the New Testament, the forerunner of the Messiah. **If ye will receive it** (14) probably means "if you can understand it." Jesus later definitely identified John the Baptist as the fulfillment of Malachi's prophecy (17:10-13).

**He that hath ears to hear, let him hear** (15) is a proverbial expression found for the first time here in Matthew, but twice later (13:9, 43) and several times elsewhere (Mark 4:9, 23; 7:16; Luke 8:8; 14:35; Rev. 2:7; 3:6; 13:9). It is both an invitation and a warning to listen carefully to the words of Christ.

### 3. *Jesus Contrasted with John* (11:16-19)

The analysis that Jesus gave of His **generation** is both humorous and pathetic. He said it was like children sitting in the **markets**—the Agora, main meeting place of people in any city of that day—and refusing to cooperate with their playmates in playing either wedding or funeral. Because John was an ascetic, they said: "He has a demon" (18). They refused to lament with him. Jesus was a sociable person, feasting with His friends. The verdict on Him: **Behold a man gluttonous, and a winebibber, a friend of publicans and sinners** (19). The Pharisees refused to recognize Jesus' friendship with the needy as His greatest glory and to rejoice with Him over the salvation of sinners.

The last part of verse 19 has caused considerable discussion. Perhaps **wisdom** should be personified (cf. Proverbs 8) and so capitalized. In Proverbs it seems to be almost identified with God. The two oldest Greek manuscripts (fourth century) say that wisdom is **justified** ("approved") by her "works," instead of **children.** But both ideas are much the same. Micklem seems to point the way to a possible synthesis of the two when he says: "The works of wisdom, which vindicate her character, are the results of her creative energy . . . as seen in the 'new creatures' (2 Cor. v. 17) which are the fruit of her work."[10] That is, wisdom is justified by its products. Thus Jesus defends himself against the criticism of the Pharisees.

### B. JESUS AND THE CITIES, 11:20-24

The Master began to **upbraid**—"reproach" or "rebuke"— **the cities** in which He had performed most of His **mighty works** ("powers"), because they had not **repented** (20). Cox says:

[10]*Op. cit.*, p. 113.

"It is noteworthy that repentance is regarded as the appropriate human reaction to the miracles of Jesus."[11]

Especially singled out for condemnation were **Chorazin** and **Bethsaida** (21). Both of these cities have long since disappeared, in fulfillment of the judgment here pronounced. In fact the exact location of **Chorazin** is uncertain. **Bethsaida** was on the east bank of the Jordan River near where it flows into the Lake of Galilee. Jesus declared that **Tyre and Sidon** (cities of Phoenicia) would have repented long before in sackcloth and ashes (signs of deep mourning) if they had witnessed the **mighty works** ("powers") done in the Jewish cities. Hence it will be **more tolerable for Tyre and Sidon in the day of judgment** than for these others (22). Jesus thus underscored the extreme seriousness of the sin of impenitence. Those who have the most light, but reject it, will be punished most severely.

The first part of verse 23 should be translated: "And you, Capernaum, will you be exalted to heaven? You shall be brought down to Hades" (RSV). The latter is the place of death. The proud, arrogant **Capernaum** was to be laid low. Today it is all in ruins. **Sodom** (24), wickedest city of the ancient world, will fare better **in the day of judgment** than Capernaum.

This paragraph stands as a stern warning to all who have witnessed Christ's presence and power manifested in their day. Those who refuse to repent will be doubly condemned for their rejection of the light they have received.

## C. Jesus and the Simple, 11:25-30

Though rejected by the proud cities, Christ was accepted by the simple, "the common people," who "heard him gladly" (Mark 12:37). **Answered and said** (25) is a typically fulsome Hebraic expression which simply means "said." **Thank** is the verb which is translated "confess" in 3:6, where the people are confessing their sins as John baptized them. Arndt and Gingrich note: "From the meaning *confess* there arose . . . the more general sense *praise*, of praise directed toward God."[12] Jesus addresses His Father as **Lord of heaven and earth.** In His sovereign wisdom the Father has hidden **these things**—the things concerning

---

[11]G. E. P. Cox, "The Gospel According to St. Matthew," *The Twentieth Century Bible Commentary,* ed. G. H. Davies, *et al.* (New York: Harper & Brothers, 1955), p. 393.

[12]*Op. cit.,* p. 276.

the Kingdom—from the **wise** and **prudent.** The former is *sophos,* which suggests the sophisticated, those who have "human intelligence and education above the average."[13] The second, *synetos,* means "intelligent, sagacious, wise."[14] These two expressions describe the Pharisees and scribes, who prided themselves on their superior learning. They had refused the light of the truth, and so were suffering from judicial blindness. Meanwhile the Father had revealed the way to **babes.** Carr comments: "The secrets of the kingdom are not revealed to those who are wise in their own conceit, but to those who have the meekness of infants and the child-like eagerness for knowledge."[15]

**All things** (27) have been given by the Father to the Son, so that the latter may fulfill His mission of redemption (cf. 28:18; John 3:35; 13:3; 17:2; I Cor. 15:25). This verse is almost exactly the same as Luke 10:22.

Jesus declared that no one knows the Son except the Father. Obviously He is not speaking in a relative sense—as knowing Christ for salvation—but in an absolute sense. No human being can fully understand the divine-human Christ. The union of two natures in one Person is beyond our comprehension. But we can believe it.

**Will reveal** is not a simple future, but a double expression in the Greek—"wills (or wishes) to reveal." Jesus is God revealed (John 1:18). We cannot know God apart from Christ.

Verses 28-30 are among the most beautiful in the Bible. Every Christian should memorize them, and thus possess them for comfort in the hour of sorrow or suffering.

Jesus did not say to sinful humanity, "Go away from Me," but, **Come unto me** (28). Who are invited? **All ye that labour and are heavy laden.** The first reference was to the Jews, under the yoke of the Law. As interpreted and applied by the rabbis, the Law—written and oral—became a burden too heavy to bear (23:4; Acts 15:10). The second clear reference is to the crushing weight of man's sin and guilt on the individual heart. But the invitation also comes to the Christian who may be weighed down and weary. To such Jesus says: **Come unto me . . . and I will give you rest**—literally, "I will rest you"; that is, with My presence.

[13]*Ibid.,* p. 767.
[14]*Ibid.,* p. 796.
[15]*Op. cit.,* p. 174.

To take Christ's **yoke** is to submit fully to His authority. With the rabbis, taking up one's yoke meant "going to school to." So the Master Teacher said in effect: Come to school to Me, **and learn of me** (29). Jesus declared: **I am meek and lowly in heart.** In true meekness there is rest of soul. Christ further declared: **For my yoke is easy, and my burden is light.** That is the testimony of those who have accepted this gracious invitation. Bonhoeffer wrote: "Grace is costly because it compels a man to submit to the yoke of Christ and follow him; it is grace because Jesus says: 'My yoke is easy, and burden is light.' "[16] The secret is in being filled with the Spirit of Christ (the Holy Spirit), so that one can say: "I delight to do thy will, O my God; yea, thy law is within my heart" (Ps. 40:8). When our hearts are filled with God's love, we delight to do His will. Someone has well said, "Love makes all burdens light."

The three imperatives here suggest three points under "The Rest That Jesus Gives." They are (1) **Come;** (2) **Take;** (3) **Learn.**

## D. Jesus and the Pharisees, 12:1-45

### 1. *Controversy over Sabbath Observance* (12:1-14)

*a. Harvesting Grain* (12:1-8). There were three things that particularly distinguished the Jews from the Gentiles in Jesus' day. The first was Sabbath observance. The Pharisees were especially rigid about this. The Talmud, which is the great depository of Pharisaic Judaism, has twenty-four chapters on the subject. The second distinguishing feature of Jewish life was circumcision. The third was the ban on eating "unclean" meat.

It happened that one Sabbath day Jesus went through **the corn** (1)—an adjective meaning "the sown" (plural). Used as a substantive it means "standing grain, grainfields." His disciples were **an hungred;** or, as we would say now, "hungry." They began to **pluck the ears of corn**—more correctly, "pick the heads of wheat." Even today wheat is called **corn** in the British Isles. But the picture of the disciples plucking **ears of corn** is misleading to the American reader.

The **Pharisees** (2) followed Jesus, not to receive help from Him, but to spy on Him with the hope of getting Him in trouble. So when they saw the apostles picking heads of wheat they immediately accused them of harvesting grain on the Sabbath. They complained to Jesus that His disciples were doing that **which is**

[16]*Op. cit.,* p. 37.

**not lawful to do upon the sabbath day.** The fourth commandment forbade the doing of "any work" on the Sabbath (Exod.
20:10). But the question is: What constitutes "work"? The
rabbis spelled this out with meticulous care in hundreds of minute
regulations. One is reminded of the little boy—whose mother
had just put him to bed with strict orders to keep quiet and not
beg for a single thing. However he did have one question to ask:
"Can I think?" Sometimes the smothering, stifling weight of
legalistic legislation must have tempted some Jews to inquire:
"Can we breathe?"

To the complaint of the Pharisees, Jesus had a rejoinder.
He cited the case of **David** (3), who with a band of hungry men
ate the **shewbread** (4)[17] which only the priests were permitted to
eat. In other words, human need is a higher law than religious
rules and regulations. Or, to put it more exactly, love is the
highest law in the universe and supersedes all other regulations.
And love demands that human need must be met, even if some
legal technicalities have to be laid aside in the process. This the
Pharisees could not see. Typical legalists that they were, they
lacked that love and common sense that together make life
function happily and smoothly. But love is the gift of God's grace
—yea, of himself, for "God is love." Legalism is a human denial
of divine love.

The Master also reminded His critics that the priests work
every Sabbath day in the Temple. Thus they **profane the sabbath,** yet are **blameless** (5). Common sense shows that in actual
practice some laws cancel out others. This is inevitable in an imperfect world like ours.

Then Jesus scored His main point. There was now present
something[18] **greater than the temple** (6). The True Temple,
meeting place of God and man, was Christ himself. The Jerusalem temple was God's house; Jesus was God's Son (cf. Heb. 3:
3-6). This is something infinitely **greater.**

---

[17]Literally, "loaves of the setting forth." The Hebrew name for it was
"bread of the presence." Twelve fresh loaves were placed on the golden
table in the holy place each Sabbath to symbolize God's presence in the
midst of His people, the twelve tribes of Israel.

[18]The best Greek text has the neuter of the adjective rather than the
masculine ("one greater," KJV). "The neuter gives the sense of indefinite
greatness" (Carr, *op. cit.,* p. 178).

Once more (cf. 9:13) Christ quoted Hos. 6:6—**I will have mercy, and not sacrifice** (7). It is obvious that this concept of true religion as consisting of a right attitude rather than ritual acts was central to Jesus' thinking. Whenever Christianity finds its main focus in liturgy rather than life it has retrogressed from the New Testament to the Old. And even then it has failed to catch the prophetic interpretation of the Mosaic law.

Jesus declared that if the Pharisees had **known** the meaning of Hos. 6:6—the Greek construction implies that they had not— they would not have condemned the **guiltless** (plural in the Greek). Condemnation is the work of the Holy Spirit (John 16:8), not of human beings. When we go around condemning people we are usurping divine authority (cf. 7:1).

The decisive point was that **the Son of man** (the Messiah) was **Lord even of the sabbath day** (8). Submission to Christ as supreme Lord will settle all basic controversies.[19]

b. *Healing a Man with a Withered Hand* (12:9-14). This miracle (cf. Mark 3:1-6; Luke 6:6-11) constitutes another item in Jesus' conflict with the Pharisees over the matter of Sabbath observance. There was in their **synagogue** (9)—probably at Capernaum (cf. Mark 2:1; 3:1)—a man who had his hand **withered** (literally, "all dried up"). The Pharisees asked Jesus a question: **Is it lawful to heal on the sabbath days?** (10) Their purpose was to secure, not information for themselves, but evidence against Him, **that they might accuse him.**

On the surface there seems to be a conflict with Mark 3:4 and Luke 6:9. Matthew says the Pharisees asked Jesus the question. In both Mark and Luke, Jesus is reported as asking the question of the Pharisees. But the Master's question may very logically have been asked in rhetorical form. In the presence of the crippled man the Pharisees asked Jesus, "Is it lawful to heal on the sabbath days?" In answer, Jesus asked them, "Is it lawful to do good on the sabbath days, or to do evil? to save life, or to kill?" Mark says immediately following this that "they held their peace." By answering the Pharisees' question with another one Jesus put theirs in its proper perspective and thus silenced His opponents.

To clinch His point, Christ asked them if they would not pull a sheep out of a pit on the Sabbath (11). Is not a man better than a

---

[19]For further comments on this incident see Mark 2:23-28; also Luke 6:1-5.

sheep? **Wherefore it is lawful to do well on the sabbath days** (12). Whatever is for the best good of humanity is always pleasing to God.

Then the Creator commanded His afflicted creature: **Stretch forth thine hand** (13). Morison thinks that only the hand was withered, not the arm, and that the purpose of stretching out his hand was that all might see its cure.[20] But does not stretching out the hand imply and involve a motion of the arm? So it seems that M'Neile is justified in saying: "The command called forth the faith which was operative towards the cure."[21] In other words, the man demonstrated his belief by his obedience. In actual life situations the two can never be divorced. In any case, the man's hand was **restored whole, like as the other.** The cure was complete.

Instead of being compelled by this miracle to believe in Jesus as their Messiah, the Pharisees "took counsel"[22] against Him, **how they might destroy him** (14). This action suggests the measure of their stubborn, willful rejection of Christ. There is nothing more unreasonable and unreasoning than religious fanaticism.

### 2. *Comfort from the Crowds* (12:15-21)

In contrast with the carping criticism of the religious leaders was the encouraging enthusiasm of the common people. When Jesus **withdrew** from the synagogue to escape the plot to assassinate Him, **great multitudes followed him** (15). Compassionately —and perhaps grateful for at least their faith in His healing power—**he healed them all.**

At the same time, he **charged,** or "warned," the people not to **make him known** (16). The reason for this warning is indicated in Mark 1:45. Jesus was seeking to avoid publicity in His healing ministry, lest it become a hindrance to His more important teaching ministry. Then, too, He wished to keep popular excitement from getting out of hand, with the consequent danger of a revolutionary uprising against Rome.

Once more Matthew employs his favorite formula for introducing Old Testament material, **That it might be fulfilled which**

---

[20]*Op. cit.,* pp. 220-21.

[21]*Op. cit.,* p. 171.

[22]Arndt and Gingrich (p. 785) explain this as a Latinism meaning "form a plan, decide, consult, plot."

**was spoken** (17). This time the rather lengthy quotation is from Isa. 42:1-4. It is not taken from the Septuagint, but is a somewhat free rendering of the Hebrew. This feature has been noted before in Matthew. Carr says about it here: "The divergence from the Septuagint points to an independent version, and the divergence from St. Matthew's vocabulary points to some translator other than the Evangelist."[23]

The word **servant** (18) is *pais,* which may mean either "servant" or "son," although the Hebrew word in Isaiah means only the former. Morison has this helpful comment: "The two-sidedness of the Greek word made it peculiarly applicable to the Messiah, in whom the two relationships were combined."[24] **I will put my spirit upon him** was fulfilled at the Baptism, when the Holy Spirit descended on Jesus. Judgment is the usual meaning of the Greek word *krisis* (cf. "crisis"). But here it carries the rare connotation of "justice."

The Servant of the Lord will not **strive** (19)—a Greek word, found only here in the New Testament, meaning "quarrel, wrangle." **Cry** is *kraugazo,* suggesting a loud outcry, calling attention to oneself. No one will **hear his voice in the streets,** making a bid for popularity. This verse, which forms the heart of the quotation, especially shows the reason why Matthew culled these words from Isaiah. He wanted to show the modesty of the Messiah, who sought to avoid publicity (16).

Verse 20 employs two metaphors in relation to the ministry of Christ. The first is that of a **bruised reed,** the second that of **smoking flax.** The latter indicates a flickering wick, almost burned out for lack of oil. Morison gives a clear and simple meaning of this interesting passage: "The bruised reed and the feebly-burning wick may be referred to the failing lives which Jesus restores and the sparks of faith which He revives."[25] Alford says that these metaphors represent "a proverbial expression for 'He will not crush the contrite heart, nor extinguish the slightest spark of repentant feeling in the sinner.'"[26] **Till he send forth judgment unto victory** means "until he makes his justice triumph, until he brings it to victory."

[23]*Op. cit.,* p. 179.
[24]*Op. cit.,* p. 202.
[25]*Op. cit.,* p. 179.
[26]*Op. cit.,* I, 127.

For verses 18-21, Charles Simeon suggests the topic: "The Compassion of Christ Towards the Weak." (1) His commission is given in 18. (2) His manner of carrying it out is indicated in 19-20: (*a*) Silently; (*b*) Tenderly; (*c*) Successfully. (3) Our duty toward Him is shown in 21.

### 3. *Contempt of the Critics* (12: 22-45)

This section shows the Pharisees in their crassest and cruelest opposition to Christ. Their carnal hearts are unmasked, and the picture revealed is a sordid commentary on the fruits of legalistic religion.

*a. The Blind, Dumb Demoniac* (12:22-30). Luke, who also records this healing miracle (Luke 11:14), mentions only the man's dumbness, not his blindness. Both he and Matthew indicate that he was "demonized." It may well be that this very difficult condition was brought to Jesus as a sort of test case. But He met the challenge with full success; the man was completely healed.

The reaction of the people was understandably one of amazement. They said, **Is not this the son of David?** (23) But the form of the Greek clearly indicates that a negative answer is expected: "This is not the son of David, is it?"[27] The question expresses surprised incredulity, perhaps mixed with hope—"Can this possibly be the son of David?"

The reaction of the Pharisees was something different. They said that Jesus cast out demons by Beelzebub[28] the prince of demons (24). Christ knew what they were thinking and proceeded to ask them some questions. After noting that every **kingdom, city,** or **house** divided against itself could not stand (25), He declared that if Satan was casting out Satan, he was divided against himself; how then could his kingdom stand (26)? The logic was simple and clear.

But Jesus pressed His point a little further. If He by Beelzebub cast out demons, **by whom do your children cast them out?** (27) Exorcism was practiced by at least some Jews in that day (cf. Acts 19:13).

[27]Hereon hangs a strange tale. The first edition of the King James Version (1611) correctly omitted "not." So also did four subsequent editions. Then it began to be introduced in some editions and finally took possession in 1769. See Morison, *op. cit.*, pp. 204-5.

[28]For the proper form of this word see the notes on 10:25.

Then the Master set the record straight. If **by the Spirit of God,** not "by Beelzebub" (24), He was casting out demons, **then the kingdom of God is come unto you** (28). This is exactly what had happened. In His person the Kingdom had "suddenly arrived" (aorist tense). But they were rejecting it.

Jesus drew a further picture. No one can enter a strong man's house and **spoil**—"steal, carry off, drag away"[29]—his **goods**—"his property"[30]—unless he first binds the strong man. Again the logic is unanswerable. Satan is a conquered foe or Jesus could not be seizing his property.

The first part of verse 30—**He that is not with me is against me**—seems, at first sight, to be in conflict with Luke 9:50—"He that is not against us is for us." But in Matthew, Jesus is talking about inward loyalty; in Luke, He is discussing outward opposition. The purposes of the two sayings were entirely different. In Luke, He is reproving a spirit of sectarianism; in Matthew, He is warning against the danger of divided loyalty. There is a difference also in who is against whom (cf. Matt. 12:30 and Luke 9:50 in RSV, NEB, *et al.*). In Matthew, Jesus declares that a man cannot be neutral in regard to Christ; if one is not for Him, he is against Him. In Luke, Jesus is speaking of His followers. A man does not always have to agree with every other Christian, or every group of Christians, in order to be for Christ. Nor should I demand that every other Christian agree with me. He may be doing Christ's work in his own way; if he is sincerely doing this, he is really for me because I too am seeking to get God's work done.

b. *The Unpardonable Sin* (12:31-32). Jesus asserted that **all manner of sin and blasphemy shall be forgiven unto men** (31), except the blasphemy against the Spirit. That will never be forgiven. In verse 32 He puts it even more strongly: whoever speaks **against the Son of man** will be forgiven, but not he who speaks **against the Holy Ghost.** The context suggests that the "unpardonable sin" is willfully attributing to Satan the work of the Holy Spirit. This was the opinion held by John Wesley and Adam Clarke. Wesley says: "It is neither more nor less than the ascribing those miracles to the power of the devil which Christ wrought by the power of the Holy Ghost."[31] But Morison, him-

[29]Arndt and Gingrich, *op. cit.,* p. 108.
[30]*Ibid.,* p. 761.
[31]*Op. cit.,* p. 64.

self a Wesleyan commentator of high scholarship, expresses the view most commonly held today with regard to the unpardonable sin. He expresses it this way: "Every sin and blasphemy shall be forgiven unto men except that which matures itself into unpardonableness by maturing itself into blasphemy against the Spirit."[32] Again he writes: "The blasphemy against the Spirit is the scornful rejection of the Spirit as the only Revealer of the holy propitiousness of God."[33] It is impenitence, "persevered in to the end of probation."[34]

c. *Good and Evil Hearts* (12: 33-37). Just as there are two kinds of trees, good and bad, so there are two kinds of hearts. And just as the tree is known by its fruit, so the true nature of the human heart is shown by what flows out of it (35). This is shown especially by what we say (36-37), for **out of the abundance of the heart the mouth speaketh** (34). The connection with the preceding paragraphs is shown by the first part of verse 34. The **evil** heart of the Pharisees was revealed by the blasphemous words they had just spoken.

Verses 36 and 37 utter a solemn truth. Blasphemous words are not the only words for which men are accountable to God. For every **idle word** that people speak they must render an account in the judgment day. The important question obviously is: What is meant by **idle?** The Greek word means "idle, lazy, useless." For this passage Arndt and Gingrich suggest "*a careless word* which, because of its worthlessness, had better been left unspoken."[35] Jesus is warning against carelessness in speech, since one's conversation reveals the condition of his heart. So by our words we are either **justified** or **condemned.**

d. *Seeking a Sign* (12: 38-42). The scribes and Pharisees tried to put Jesus "on the spot" by requesting that He show them a **sign** (38). This is the word commonly used in John's Gospel for the miracles that Jesus performed. The Master had just given them an amazing sign in His healing of the blind, dumb demoniac. But they craved something more sensational and spectacular. Luke 11:16 indicates that they were asking for "a sign from heaven" that would prove Him to be the Messiah. This Jesus refused to grant.

[32]*Op. cit.*, p. 211 (italics removed).
[33]*Ibid.*, p. 212.
[34]*Ibid.*
[35]*Op. cit.*, p. 104

Christ asserted that it was **an evil and adulterous generation** that was seeking a sign (39). The word **adulterous** is used in a spiritual sense here, as in Isaiah and Hosea, meaning untrue to Jehovah, estranged from God.

The only sign that Jesus would give they could find in their own sacred Scriptures. This is a salutary warning to those today who seek after sensational "signs." The Bible is the basis of our belief. "So then faith cometh by hearing, and hearing by the word of God" (Rom. 10:17). This is the only safe foundation for our faith.

As Jonah was three days in the stomach of the "great fish" (cf. Jonah 1:17)—"there are no whales in the Mediterranean"[36]— so **the Son of man** would be three days **in the heart of the earth** (40). Because of the difficulty of finding **three days and three nights** between Friday afternoon and Sunday morning, numbers of people have championed the idea of a Wednesday crucifixion. But this would require a resurrection on Saturday afternoon. Thursday would fit most easily, but for some reason this day is not often suggested by commentators. The important thing to note is that the Jews reckoned parts of days as whole days. So we find Friday, Saturday, and Sunday all right. Later Jesus declared definitely that He would be "raised again the third day" (16:21). The third day, beginning Friday, would be Sunday. When we place this with the strong tradition of the Early Church that the Crucifixion took place on Friday, it seems most reasonable to accept that day as correct. The Jews were much more flexible in their thinking about time than we are in our split-second age. The most accurate "clock" they had was a sundial.

Then Jesus warned His hearers that **the men of Nineveh** (41) and the queen of the south (42) (the queen of Sheba, cf. II Chron. 9:1-9) would both **rise up in the judgment with this generation** and condemn it for its unbelief. With far less light, they obeyed God's call and followed the gleam they saw.

e. *Swept but Empty* (12:43-45). The meaning of this paragraph in its context is well stated by Neil. He writes: "Israel has gone some way towards ridding herself of the major blots on her former record, through her verbal profession of allegiance to the Law, but seven worse devils have entered and possessed her

---

[36]Carr, *op. cit.*, p. 183.

religious life—bigotry, intolerance, prejudice and the rest of the sins of Judaism."[37]

**Dry,** or "waterless," **places** (43) means areas uninhabited by men, because there is no water available. Meyer says that deserts "were reputed to be the dwelling-place of the demons."[38]

Jesus was warning against the danger of having only a partial conversion—a reformation without regeneration. It is not enough to get rid of the bad habits of sin. That will only leave the life **empty, swept, and garnished** (44). The last term is the verb *kosmeo;* its basic meaning is "put in order."

If one has only a moral reformation without a spiritual transformation, the result may well be that **the last state of that man is worse than the first** (45). Christ must fill the cleansed life to keep it safe.

### E. JESUS AND HIS FAMILY, 12:46-50

This interesting little incident is related in all three Synoptic Gospels (cf. Mark 3:31-35; Luke 8:19-21). Jesus' **mother** and His **brethren** (see comments on 13:55) wanted to **speak with him** (46).

When informed of this (47), Jesus pointed to His disciples and said, **Behold my mother and my brethren!** (49) Then He stated a new, spiritual relationship: **For whosoever shall do the will of my Father which is in heaven, the same is my brother, and sister, and mother** (50). This is the new family of God. We enter it through the new birth. As long as we do the will of God we belong to it. Disobedience—if it is willful and persistent—shuts us out of it.

---

[37]William Neil, *Harper's Bible Commentary* (New York: Harper & Row, 1962), p. 342.

[38]*Op. cit.,* p. 247.

Section **VI** *Third Discourse:*

*Parables of the Kingdom*

Matthew 13: 1-52

The thirteenth chapter consists in the main of seven parables of the Kingdom. As has been noted previously, Matthew is marked by systematic arrangement of the material according to subject. And the main topic in this Gospel is the kingdom of Heaven. Following the longest and introductory parable, the sower, there are three other pairs—the tares and the dragnet, the mustard seed and the leaven, the hidden treasure and the pearl of great price. Each of these, except the sower, is introduced by the phrase: "The kingdom of heaven is like."

## A. The Setting, 13: 1-2

**The same day** Jesus left **the house** (see 12: 46)—probably Peter's home in Capernaum—went out of the city, and **sat by the sea side** (1). Capernaum was on the shore of the Lake of Galilee (see map). When **great multitudes** (2) gathered around Him, He was forced to get into a **ship**—better a "boat," probably Peter's fishing craft—and there He **sat.** This was the regular posture of Jewish rabbis while teaching (cf. 5:1). The vast crowd stood on the sloping **shore,** which formed a sort of natural amphitheater.

## B. The Seven Parables, 13: 3-50

### 1. *The Sower* (13: 3-23)

Sitting in the boat, Jesus told the people many things in **parables** (3). This word comes from the Greek *parabole,* which means something "thrown beside." The term is used only in the Synoptic Gospels (Matthew, seventeen times; Mark, thirteen times; Luke, eighteen times) and twice in Hebrews (9:9; 11:19), where it is translated "figure." Arndt and Gingrich state exactly what it means: "A parable is a short discourse that makes a comparison; it expresses a [single] complete thought."[1] The following is an interesting definition: "At its simplest the parable

[1]*Op. cit.,* p. 617.

is a metaphor or simile drawn from nature or common life, arresting the hearer by its vividness or strangeness, and leaving the mind in sufficient doubt about its precise application to tease it into active thought."[2]

Since Orientals are naturally given to the use of picturesque language, it is not surprising that a number of parables are to be found in the Old Testament, as well as in later Jewish writings. But Jesus made the most effective use of this method of teaching. To be valid and vigorous, a parable must be true to life. Consequently, "Jesus is Master of parable because He is Master of Life."[3] Only He who knew life perfectly could interpret it completely. A parable has been defined as "an earthly story with a heavenly meaning."

Such early Christian writers as Origen gave extreme allegorical interpretations of the parables of Jesus, although Tertullian and Chrysostom opposed this. The latter says in his Greek commentary on Matthew: "And, as I am always saying, the parables must not be explained throughout word for word, since many absurdities will follow."[4]

Most scholars have accepted the view that a parable was intended to teach only one point, and that allegorizing of various details must be studiously avoided. M'Neile, however, wisely warns that we must guard against "the refusal to admit that more than a single point can be illustrated in a parable."[5] He says: "When more than one truth is illustrated the picture approaches an allegory, and it is not always certain which details are intended to illustrate something, and which are merely part of the scenic framework."[6]

It so happens that the very first parable in this chapter proves the inadequacy of the "only one point" theory. For Jesus himself proceeded to give an allegorical interpretation of the various items in the parable of the sower. He also did this with the parable of the tares, as well as briefly with the parable of the

[2]C. H. Dodd, *The Parables of the Kingdom* (London: Nisbet & Co., 1936), p. 16.

[3]George A. Buttrick, *The Parables of Jesus* (New York: Harper & Brothers, 1928), p. xiii.

[4]Chrysostom, "Homilies on the Gospel of Saint Matthew," *A Select Library of the Nicene and Post-Nicene Fathers of the Christian Church,* ed. Philip Schaff (New York: Christian Literature Co., 1888), X, 292.

[5]*Op. cit.,* p. 186.

[6]*Ibid.*

dragnet. So three out of the seven parables here are treated allegorically by the Master.

*a. The Statement of the Parable* (13:3-9).[7] The picture Jesus painted in this parable was a very familiar one to His hearers. Even today one can see in Palestine a man striding across the field, taking seed from a bag slung over his shoulder, and scattering it broadcast with wide sweeps of his hand.

This story is sometimes called the parable of the soils, since its main point is a comparison of the four different kinds of soil—**the way side** (4), **stony places** (5), **among thorns** (7), and **good ground** (8). The seed which fell **by the way side** was devoured by birds. That which fell on **stony places**—shallow soil on top of rock—sprang up quickly but soon **withered away** because it had no root. The seed that fell **among thorns** (or "thistles") was **choked.** That which fell on **good ground** bore a rich harvest.

Jesus closed His story with the admonition: **Who hath ears to hear, let him hear** (9). Willingness to listen is the price of learning. This expression has occurred once earlier in Matthew (11:15), and is found again in the latter part of this chapter (43).

*b. The Reason for Speaking in Parables* (13:10-17). The disciples were curious as to why Jesus taught the multitudes in parables. When they asked Him, He replied that, while it was their privilege to **know the mysteries of the kingdom of heaven** (11), this was not granted to the crowds.

The term **mysteries** is from the Greek *mysteria.* In the Gospels it occurs only here and in the parallel passages in Mark (4:11) and Luke (8:10). It is found most frequently in Paul's Epistles (twenty times) and in Revelation (four times). In the time of Christ it had the technical meaning of secrets that were known only by the initiated, as in the mystery religions. The particular mystery of the Kingdom, as Paul defines it, is the salvation of the Gentiles as well as the Jews (Eph. 3:3-9).

In verse 12, Jesus set forth the significant principle that the one who has will receive abundantly more, while the one who has not will lose even what little he possesses. It is true in economics. The man with money to invest gets more money. He who has little is in danger of losing what he has when emergencies arise. The principle applies also to knowledge; the pupil must have a certain basic information before the teacher can lead him on to advanced understanding. Jesus here applies this principle

[7]See also Mark 4:1-9; Luke 8:4-8.

131

to the spiritual life. The disciples were the ones who already had some spiritual understanding and thus would receive more through the Master's teaching. Christ was speaking to the crowds in parables, not so they would lose the little they already had, but in order that those who had some grasp of spiritual life might add to it. **Because** of the people's difference of perception and understanding Jesus had to speak to them in parables (13). Carr expresses it this way: "The parable is suited (1) to the uninstructed, as being attractive in form and as revealing spiritual truth exactly in proportion to the capacity of the hearer; and (2) to the divinely wise as wrapping up a secret which he can penetrate by his spiritual insight."[8]

While Matthew's **because** (Greek *hoti*) presents no problem, the use of *hina* ("that," literally, "in order that") in Mark 4:12 and Luke 8:10 does create one of the greatest difficulties in the exegesis of the Gospels. Why should Jesus speak in parables "in order that" His hearers might not understand Him?

M'Neile suggests three possible answers. The first is the traditional one—"to prevent His teaching from being intelligible to any but those who sympathized with Him." The second would make *hina* ("in order that") "virtually equivalent to *hoste* [so that]: in accordance with a well-known Hebraic idiom, the *result* is ironically described as a *purpose.*" The third is expressed thus: "Mk.'s verse is possibly, like Mt., v. 14 f., an editorial comment: 'in order that Isaiah's words might be fulfilled' . . . , the grammar of the sentence being dominated by *hina*, as in Mt. xviii. 16."[9]

The second of these explanations finds strong support in a recent authoritative grammar of the Greek New Testament, which states that the causal use of *hina* ("because") has "good precedent" and makes "excellent sense" in Mark 4:12.[10]

Once more (14-15) Matthew quotes from his favorite Old Testament writer, the prophet Isaiah (6:9-10). Incidentally, this is the only place outside of II Peter (1:20-21) where an Old Testament passage is referred to as **prophecy** (14). This quotation, contrary to several earlier ones in the book, is taken verbatim from the Septuagint. The Hebrew of Isa. 6:9-10, as translated in our English versions, is imperative rather than fu-

---

[8]*Op. cit.*, pp. 186-87.

[9]*Op. cit.*, pp. 191-92.

[10]James Hope Moulton, *A Grammar of New Testament Greek:* Vol. III, "Syntax," by Nigel Turner (Edinburgh: T. & T. Clark, 1963), p. 102.

ture indicative. The former emphasized its application to Isaiah's ministry, the latter its prophetic application to later times.

**Heart** (15), in ancient Hebrew thought, referred to the seat of intelligence rather than the seat of the affections. That is the case in this quotation, as with many other Old Testament passages. In this verse Jesus gives a second hindrance to spiritual knowledge. In verses 11 and 12, He said spiritual understanding and growth are limited by ignorance, for which a man is not responsible. Here He declares that there is also a willful ignorance of gospel truth—**their eyes they have closed.**

Jesus reminded the disciples that their spiritual **eyes** were **blessed,** for they could **see** the truth (16); also their **ears,** because they could **hear.** This is the privilege of God's children—of all who have heard the gospel and who keep their hearts open to gospel truth.

The statement in verse 17 is further illuminated by I Pet. 1:10-11. What a privilege to live since Christ came!

*c. The Explanation of the Parable* (13:18-23). Jesus described four types of hearers of the gospel. There are first those **by the way side** (19). Their *stolid hearts*—made so by indifference or by the pressures of life—do not actually receive the truth, and the **wicked one** quickly snatches away the seed that lies on top of the ground. Luccock says: "Whatever is kept on the surface of life will be snatched away."[11]

The second are those in **stony places** (20), or rocky ground. Their *shallow hearts*—the shallowness partly inherited, partly acquired—respond with emotional enthusiasm, but they fail to put down their roots in deep repentance. So they live "thin lives." When **tribulation or persecution** (21) strikes them, they wilt and die. They are **offended** (*skandalizetai*)—caused to stumble, or trapped.

The third are those **among the thorns** (22). They receive the message, and are saved. But **the care of this world, and the deceitfulness of riches, choke the word.** These two things threaten the spiritual life of every Christian and cause the spiritual death of many. These are the *strangled hearts,* whose lives become overcrowded with *things,* until God-consciousness is choked out.

[11] IB, VII, 697.

The fourth are those described as **good ground** (23). These not only hear the Word but understand it. They bring forth fruit, but in varying degrees. The challenge to every Christian is to bear "more fruit" and "much fruit" (John 15:2, 5).

We might think of these four soils as suggesting "A Quartet of Human Hearts": (1) The Stolid Heart; (2) The Shallow Heart; (3) The Strangled Heart; (4) The Steady Heart.

Of course soil is entirely passive, but the human spirit is not. To infer some sort of fatalism or determinism from this story would be to fly in the face of the Scriptures as a whole, which everywhere assume individual responsibility. By the aid of the ever-willing Spirit we can break up the "fallow ground" of our hearts (Jer. 4:3). The removal of the stoniness of latent self-will and spiritual hardness is a promised privilege inherent in the new covenant (Ezek. 36:25-27) and is exactly what occurs in sound repentance, and more radically, in entire sanctification. As **for the care of this world, and the deceitfulness of riches,** the watchful, cleansed, Spirit-filled believer can refuse to allow temporal concerns to monopolize his attention and choke out his spirituality.

### 2. The Tares (13:24-30, 36-43)

This parable is found only in Matthew. It is probably placed right after the parable of the sower because both have to do with sowing grain. But there the similarity ends. The lessons taught by the two are entirely different.

*a. The Parable Stated* (13:24-30). Jesus compared the kingdom of Heaven to a man who **sowed good seed in his field** (24). But while everybody was sleeping, an **enemy** sowed **tares** ("darnel," a bearded weed resembling wheat) **among the wheat** (25). The damage was not discovered until the wheat began to head out (26), when the difference between it and the darnel could be discerned. The **servants** duly reported the matter to the **householder** (27). The owner recognized it as the work of an enemy.

When the servants asked if they should weed out the tares (28), the owner forbade them, lest they should pull up the wheat at the same time (29). He instructed them to let both grow together until the time of harvest. Then the darnel would be gathered into bundles for burning, while the wheat would be stored in the **barn** (30), or "storehouse." Jeremias explains how this was done: "By the gathering out of the darnel we are not to understand that it was rooted up immediately before the reaping of the grain, but that, as the reaper cut the grain with his sickle, he let the darnel fall, so that it was not gathered into the sheaves."[12] Later the darnel was picked up and bound for burning as fuel.

What was the occasion for this story being told? "The parable sounds like Jesus' reply to a critic—probably a Pharisee ... who had objected: 'If the Kingdom of God is really here, why has there not been a separating of sinners from saints in Israel?' "[13] In the original language the name Pharisee meant "separatist."

*b. The Parable Explained* (13:36-43). After Jesus had related the parables of the mustard seed and the leaven, He went into **the house** (see 13:1)—probably Peter's in Capernaum. In the privacy of the home the disciples asked for an explanation of the parable of the tares (36).

As in the case of the parable of the sower, Christ gave a detailed interpretation. The sower is **the Son of man** (37). **The field is the world; the good seed are the children of the kingdom** —here the Invisible Church, all who are true children of God— **but the tares are the children of the wicked one** (38). **The enemy is the devil; the harvest is the end of the world** ("age"); **and the reapers are the angels** (39). At the end of this age, said Jesus, He would send His angels to gather out of His **kingdom** (41)—the word appears here to have a wider connotation than usual, and different from the meaning in verse 38; here the word refers to the Visible Church, or more probably to the whole world of good men and evil men. **All things that offend** (*skandala*) means "everything that ensnares or tempts men to destruction."[14] **Iniquity** is, in the Greek, "lawlessness." These will be cast into **a furnace of fire,** where there will be **wailing and gnashing of teeth** (42)—a phrase found five times in Matthew (8:12; 13:42; 22:13; 24:51; 25:30) and once in Luke (13:28). It underscores the horror of hell. In contrast to this **the righteous** will **shine forth as the sun** (43). This is an echo of Dan. 12:3—"And they that be wise shall shine as the brightness of the firmament; and they that turn many to righteousness as the stars for ever and ever."

[12]Joachim Jeremias, *The Parables of Jesus*, trans. S. H. Hooke (New York: Charles Scribner's Sons, 1955), p. 156.

[13]A. M. Hunter, *Interpreting the Parables of Jesus* (Naperville, Ill.: SCM Book Club, 1960), p. 46.

[14]Carr, *op. cit.*, p. 192.

### 3. *The Mustard Seed* (13:31-32)

This parable is found in all three Synoptic Gospels (cf. Mark 4:30-32; Luke 13:18-19). The picture is that of a tiny seed being sown in the ground and growing to a tree-size plant, large enough for birds to perch on its branches. Actually, the mustard seed is not **the least of all seeds** (32), but this was a proverbial expression for something exceedingly small.

This brief parable suggests to us the topic "Little Is Much if God Is in It," and the three points: (1) Lost in the Soil; (2) Least of the Seeds; (3) Largest of the Herbs.

### 4. *The Leaven* (13:33)

This parable is found also in Luke (13:20-21), but not in Mark. Jesus portrayed a woman taking **leaven** (yeast) and hiding it in **three measures** (about a bushel) of **meal,** or "flour." The yeast affected the whole batch of bread dough, so that it all rose.

Since this parable is very closely related to the previous one, they may well be interpreted together. Two main interpretations are popular today.

The first is the traditional one, held from the early days of the Church. This view affirms that Jesus is here describing the twofold growth of the Church. In the parable of the mustard seed it is the outward growth; in the parable of the leaven it is the inward, spiritual growth—or its influence in leavening society.

During the past one hundred years a completely different view has been promoted by some Bible students. It is based primarily on the premise that **leaven** is always a symbol of evil. According to this interpretation the great growth of the **mustard** plant typifies the outward expansion of an apostate Church that would gain world domination. The **birds of the air** are the wicked men in high office in the various branches of the Church. **Leaven** symbolizes heretical teaching in the Church, by which it has become corrupted. Thus these two parables give a preview of the evil course of the outward Church in this age. The traditional interpretation seems much more consistent with the whole tenor of Jesus' teaching about the Kingdom.

### *Interlude: Summary* (13:34-35)

To the crowds Christ spoke only in parables (34). This made for both variety and vividness in His preaching. He used illustrations from fishing, farming, merchandising, and even cooking. Everyone could find something familiar here.

Again Matthew finds a fulfillment of Old Testament prophecy. He states that what follows **was spoken by the prophet** (35), but then quotes from Ps. 78:2. There is no such statement recorded in the Book of Isaiah.[15] As in other places, he translates the Hebrew rather than quoting from the Septuagint, as other writers of the New Testament commonly do. **Foundation** means "beginning." The Greek word is thus used by secular writers.

### 5. *The Hidden Treasure* (13:44)

In ancient times when in many places there were no banks, it was the custom to hide treasures in the ground. Jesus told of a man who unexpectedly discovered such a "find" and sold all he had to buy the field and get the treasure.

### 6. *The Pearl of Great Price* (13:45-46)

Similarly, a man who discovered a very valuable pearl sold all he had to purchase it. Both of these parables, found only in Matthew, clearly teach the same lesson.

Some have interpreted these two parables to mean Christ's giving His all to purchase the Church. But most scholars interpret them as meaning that one should be willing to give up all he has to gain salvation. The kingdom of God, the life of God in the soul, is the hidden treasure and precious pearl. It has been suggested that the hidden treasure typifies those who suddenly and unexpectedly find Christ, while the pearl of great price symbolizes those who search long before they find.

### 7. *The Dragnet* (13:47-50)

This and the parable of the tares are found only in Matthew and teach the same lesson. Both describe the final judgment day, with its separation of the good and the evil. In the present parable **the kingdom of heaven is like** is probably best understood if we read it to mean "God's work in the world is like . . ." This time the picture is that of a large dragnet which drew up from the lake a haul of fish **of every kind** (47). When the seine had been pulled to shore, the fish were separated. The **good** were put in **vessels** (48). But the fishermen cast away the **bad.** The word *sapra* usually means "rotten." But here it must mean "unusable, unfit

---

[15]Strangely, "Isaiah the prophet" is the reading of Codex Sinaiticus (4th cent.) and some good minuscules. It is not impossible that the Psalmist has quoted an oral saying of Isaiah. More probably the scribe of Sinaiticus made a mistake.

for use." Similarly, said Jesus, at the close of this age **the angels will sever the wicked from among the just** (49). The former will be cast into **the furnace of fire** (50), where there will be **wailing and gnashing of teeth** (cf. v. 42).

The lesson of the parables seems to be twofold. It is first a warning to each individual to be sure that he is among the **good** wheat or fish in the Kingdom, not the **bad**. In the second place, it is a warning to human leaders not to usurp the divine prerogative of separating the righteous from the wicked. Only at the judgment day can that task be properly performed.

## C. THE SEQUEL, 13:51-52

Having concluded His recital of the seven parables of the Kingdom, the Master asked His disciples if they had understood everything He said. They answered, **Yea, Lord** (51). Then He likened the **scribe** who is **instructed**—or "made a disciple"—in the truths of the Kingdom to a **householder** who brings out of his treasures things both **new** and **old** (52). This could mean the new truths of Christianity added to the teachings of the Old Testament.

# Section **VII** *Narrative Resumed: Journeys of Jesus*

Matthew 13:53—17:27

A. JESUS AND JOHN REJECTED, 13:53—14:12

1. *Rejection at Nazareth* (13:53-58)

Verse 53 contains the regular formula for closing each of the five discourses of Jesus. This is the third time that it has occurred (cf. 7:28; 11:1).

After giving the seven parables of the Kingdom, Jesus **departed thence** (53)—probably from Capernaum—and returned to **his own country** (54); that is, Nazareth (see map). There He **taught**—"was teaching" (imperfect tense)—**in their synagogue.** This was probably the very synagogue in which He had worshiped from the ages of twelve to thirty.

The attitude of His fellow townsmen was that which is usually accorded a hometown boy: **Whence hath this man this wisdom, and these mighty works?** Is it not strange that we so easily reject recognized wisdom and even mighty works when they appear in unexpected places? The people still thought of Him as **the carpenter's son** (55)—Mark has "the carpenter" (Mark 6:3). They knew His **mother** and His **brethren,** four of whom are named here. They are all very common Jewish names, found frequently in the New Testament. Jesus also had **sisters** (56), **all** of whom were still living in Nazareth—how many we are not told. The people were **offended in him** (57)—stumbled over the fact that they knew Him so well as a boy. This reaction indicates that Jesus lived a very normal life till the age of thirty and during those years had performed no supernatural feats.

The mention of Jesus' **brethren** and **sisters** immediately raises the question of the perpetual virginity of Mary, His mother —a Roman Catholic dogma with no support whatever in Scripture. In the fourth century Helvidius (*ca.* 380) claimed that these were children of Joseph and Mary. This is the most natural view, especially since the "brothers" are named here. The view is probably supported by a majority of Protestants.

Epiphanius (*ca.* 382) held that they were half brothers, children of Joseph by a former marriage. The fact that Joseph is never mentioned after the beginning of Jesus' public ministry has been taken as implying that he was an older man and now dead. This is the official view of the Greek Orthodox church and is favored by a considerable number of Protestants and Anglicans.

Jerome (*ca.* 383) went a step further. He took "brothers" as meaning "cousins." This interpretation was finally adopted by the Roman Catholic church. But it is a part of the elevation and adoration of "The Blessed Virgin," buttressed now with the official dogmas of her Immaculate Conception and Bodily Assumption.

Jesus answered the attitude of His former neighbors by quoting an old proverb (57). The sad thing is that He was prevented from doing **many mighty works there because of their unbelief** (58). Disbelief always deprives people of blessing.

This incident is recorded also in Mark 6:1-6. Whether this is the same trip to Nazareth as that described more extensively in Luke is a debatable point. Some good scholars favor two visits; others equally good find evidence for only one visit. See the comments on Luke 4:16-32.

### 2. *Death of John the Baptist* (14:1-12)[1]

**Herod the tetrarch** (1), who had built Tiberias on the west side of the Lake of Galilee as his capital city, was ruler of Galilee and Perea. Son of Herod the Great and a Samaritan woman, he was named Antipas, so that he is correctly called Herod Antipas. He ruled from 4 B.C. to A.D. 39. The word **tetrarch** literally means "ruler of a fourth part," but was used in a general sense for the ruler of a small region.

When Herod heard of **the fame of Jesus** as a Miracle Worker, he said to his **servants,**[2] **This is John the Baptist** (2). His conscience was still haunting him because he had killed the righteous prophet. He thought that only John could perform the miracles he heard attributed to Jesus. Herod had arrested, bound, and imprisoned John **for Herodias' sake** (3), because the prophet had told him, **It is not lawful for thee to have her** (4).

Herod Antipas had married the daughter of Aretas, king of the Nabatean Arabs. But on a visit to Rome he stayed at the home of his half brother, Philip. He became infatuated with his

[1]See also Mark 6:14-29; Luke 3:19-20; 9:7-9.

[2]The Greek is not the common *douloi,* which properly means "slaves," but *paides,* which is translated "children" in 2:16. Here it refers to Herod's "court attendants" (M'Neile, *op. cit.,* p. 208).

brother's wife and brought her back with him to Galilee. Hearing what had taken place, his first wife fled home to her father, who sent an army and severely defeated Herod Antipas. According to Josephus, many Jews considered this to be a divine judgment on the tetrarch for having killed John.[3]

After John had been imprisoned, Antipas **would have put him to death,** but **feared the multitude** (5). On the surface, this seems to clash with Mark's statement (as it reads in the best Greek text): "And Herodias had a grudge against him, and wanted to kill him. But she could not, for Herod feared John, knowing that he was a righteous and holy man, and kept him safe" (Mark 6:19-20, RSV). But it is necessary to remember again Matthew's habit of telescoping narratives, omitting details and giving only a general statement. It doubtless appeared to the public that Antipas wanted to have John executed. Carr makes this further helpful comment: "St. Mark's narrative gives a picture of the inner court intrigues, and bears evidence of keen questioning of some eye-witness as to facts."[4]

Herodias bided her time. She watched for the proper occasion to carry out her murderous designs on the prophet. Finally it came—**Herod's birthday** (6). With all the cunning and malice that a clever woman could muster, she laid her plot. So desperate was she to accomplish this dastardly deed that she was willing to disgrace her **daughter** (Salome) by having her go in and put on a sensual dance before a group of drunken men.

The ruse worked. Herod, drunk and passionate, **promised with an oath** to give the girl **whatsoever she would ask** (7). She, **being before instructed of her mother** (8), asked for the head of John the Baptist **in a charger**—rather, "on a platter." But this seems to conflict with Mark's statement that the girl went out and asked her mother what to request (Mark 6:24). The solution of the problem lies in simply correcting the translation in Matthew. **Being before instructed** should be rendered "being put forward" (ASV) or "prompted" (RSV). In keeping with his usual habit of generalization, Matthew merely states that Salome acted at the instigation of her mother. Mark typically fills in with the added detail that she went out and checked with her mother.

The **king** (9)—courtesy title for this tetrarch—**was sorry.** This agrees with Mark's picture of Antipas as perhaps liking John

[3]*Ant.* XVIII. 5. 1.
[4]*Op. cit.,* p. 197.

secretly and fearing him. But because of the guests, Herod kept his oath and ordered the execution. John the Baptist's head was given to the girl, and by her to her mother (11). His body was buried by sorrowing disciples (12). Human hate had won the battle.

This dramatic story lends itself easily to outlining. We could think of: (1) Dancing daughter; (2) Drunken despot; (3) Dastardly deed.

## B. FURTHER MIRACLES, 14:13-36

### 1. *Five Thousand Fed* (14:13-21)

The feeding of the five thousand has the distinction of being the only miracle of Jesus which is recorded in all four Gospels. It is found in Mark 6:30-44; Luke 9:10-17; John 6:1-14.

When Jesus, probably in the vicinity of Capernaum, heard of the assassination of John the Baptist, He crossed by boat to the eastern shore of the Lake of Galilee. Here it was quiet, **a desert place** (13); that is, an uninhabited area. Both He and His disciples needed a rest and a change.

But when the crowds heard where He had gone they followed **on foot,** or "by land," going around the north end of the lake. The speed of sailing in those days is measured by the fact that the people walked perhaps eight miles while the disciples were rowing or sailing some six miles.

When Jesus came out of the boat He found a big crowd waiting for Him. Instead of being annoyed at their presence, He was **moved** ("gripped") **with compassion toward them** and **healed their sick** (14).

As the day drew to a close, the disciples came to Jesus with a reminder that the **time** for supper was already **past** (15). Better send the crowd away, so that the people could go to the nearest villages and buy **victuals.**

Jesus' rejoinder was: **Give ye them to eat** (16). The disciples protested. There were only **five loaves, and two fishes** on hand (17). These loaves were the size and shape of a small pancake or a flat biscuit. The sum total of provisions available was just one boy's lunch (John 6:9).

But the disciples had made their computation without taking the Master into account. He asked that the single lunch be brought to Him (18). After commanding the crowd to **sit down**

142

(19) (the Greek is "recline") **on the grass**—Mark says the grass was "green," which shows that it was in the spring—Jesus took the five loaves and two fish, **blessed** and **brake,** and **gave** the broken loaves and fish to the disciples, who in turn served the crowd.

A significant point is that the disciples carried out the command of Christ. They actually fed the multitude—when they went into partnership with Jesus in doing it. The lesson for every Christian is that, no matter how impossible his assignment may seem, with divine help it can be done. "With God nothing shall be impossible" (Luke 1:37).

All the people ate and **were filled** (20). The verb *chortazo* **(were filled)** comes from the noun *chortos*, "grass." It was used first of animals grazing. The picture is that of cattle eating until they are full, and then lying contentedly on the grass. Arndt and Gingrich say that in the passive (as here) it means "eat one's fill, be satisfied."[5] This is the emphasis here. All these thousands of people ate their fill until they were "satisfied." That is the best translation.

From the **fragments that remained**—in the serving baskets of the disciples and probably in a pile on the clean grass in front of Jesus—they took up **twelve baskets full.** That is, each of the twelve disciples was able to fill his lunch basket with food for the next day.

The crowd that was fed was composed of **five thousand men** (21). Only Matthew, the statistician, adds: **beside women and children.** If the crowd was composed of pilgrims ready to go to the Passover, there would be only a few women and children (John 6:4-5). This distinction reflects the fact that in public— as often still among Orientals—the women and the children never ate with the men. Beyond debate that *was* a man's world.

### 2. *Jesus Walks on the Water* (14:22-27)[6]

The Master immediately **constrained** His disciples to leave (22). The verb is a strong one, meaning "compel, force." Arndt and Gingrich suggest the translation here: "He made the disciples embark."[7] Why? John gives the answer: "When Jesus

[5]*Op. cit.,* p. 892.
[6]Recorded also in Mark 6:45-56 and John 6:15-21, but not in Luke.
[7]*Op. cit.,* p. 51.

therefore perceived that they would come and take him by force, to make him a king, he departed again into a mountain himself alone" (John 6:15). He did not want His disciples staying around in such a revolutionary atmosphere, nor did He wish by His presence to stir such a movement. He was not there to set up a political kingdom in opposition to Roman rule but to establish His spiritual kingdom in the hearts of men. Jesus sensed the fact that these volatile Galileans were ready to launch another revolt against Rome. So He instructed His disciples to leave, dismissed the crowd, and went off to pray alone.

**When the evening was come** (23) is exactly the same in the Greek as "when it was evening" (15). But in between, the feeding of the five thousand had taken place. This activity must have taken at least an hour or two. How then can we harmonize these two expressions of time? The answer lies in the distinction between the "first evening" (beginning about 3:00 p.m.) and the "second evening" (after sunset). The word for **evening** is literally "late." The whole phrase (23) means "when it had become late." Arndt and Gingrich suggest: "The context often makes it easier to decide just what time is meant, whether before or after sundown."[8]

As darkness came on, Jesus was alone on the mountain. Meanwhile the boat was **in the midst of the sea** (24)—about halfway across the lake. Nestle's Greek text says it "held away from the land many stadia" (cf. RSV). This is in striking agreement with John's statement that the disciples had rowed about twenty-five or thirty furlongs (John 6:19)—three or four miles. At its northern end, where they were, the Lake of Galilee is about seven miles wide.

The boat was being **tossed with waves.** Carr comments: "The expression is forcible, 'tortured by the waves,' writhing in throes of agony, as it were."[9] The Lake of Galilee is notorious for its sudden, severe storms. The writer will never forget being in a storm on the same lake in 1953. It seemed that the fishing boat would certainly go to the bottom every time it plunged down into the deep trough between gigantic waves. But creaking, groaning, shuddering all over, each time it came up through the next waves, while torrents of water poured over its bow. The

[8]*Ibid.*, p. 606.

[9]*Op. cit.*, p. 200.

powerful motor in this modern fishing boat kept it moving ahead. But the disciples could only struggle vainly with their oars as they faced a strong headwind from the north.

When things were at their worst, **in the fourth watch of the night** (3: 00-6: 00 a.m.), Jesus drew near, **walking on the sea** (25). The disciples were **troubled** (26)—better, "terrified"—thinking Him to be a **spirit,** or "ghost" (Greek, *phantasma*). Terror-stricken by the storm and horror-struck by this phantom, they **cried out.** The verb means "cry out, scream, shriek."[10]

Immediately Jesus reassured them with the words: **Be of good cheer; it is I; be not afraid** (27). Literally the Greek says: "Have courage; it is I; stop being afraid." That is still Christ's message to His own in the midst of the storms of life.

### 3. *Peter Walks on the Water* (14: 28-33)

This is a unique incident, found only in Matthew. Peter was so challenged by seeing Jesus walking on the water that he said: **Lord, if it be thou**—or, "since it is You"—**bid me come unto thee on the water** (28). This is very much in keeping with Peter's impulsive nature. As M'Neile says to those who doubt its historicity: "A strong point in favour of the story is its faithful reflexion of the apostle's character."[11]

Confidently Peter responded to his Master's **Come** (29), and began walking on the water. The oldest Greek text has: "Peter walked on the water and came to Jesus." Apparently, then, he had practically reached Christ before his own faith failed. But when he **saw the wind** (30)—more precisely, its effects—he became afraid. **Beginning to sink**—the strong compound means "to sink into the deep sea"[12]—he cried, **Lord, save me.**

**Immediately Jesus stretched forth his hand, and caught him** (31)—literally, "took hold of him." This shows that Peter was within arm's reach. Gently the Master chided His ambitious disciple for his **little faith.** It had looked like great faith when he stepped out of the boat onto the water. But it seems to have been mixed with some presumption.

As soon as Christ entered the boat with Peter, **the wind ceased** (32). The Greek root suggests: "became weary, or tired."

[10]Arndt and Gingrich, *op. cit.,* p. 448.
[11]*Op. cit.,* p. 220.
[12]Carr, *op. cit.,* p. 201.

The disciples in the boat worshiped Jesus as God's Son (33). To them His presence and power proved His deity.

### 4. *Healing in Gennesaret* (14:34-36)

When they had **gone over** the lake from the east side to the west, they came to land at **Gennesaret** (34). This was a small plain, stretching about three miles along the western shore of the Lake of Galilee near its northern end, and reaching about a mile and a half inland. Josephus describes it glowingly as an exceedingly fertile area.[13]

Here was a heavily populated region. Soon the crowds gathered again to be healed. The sick begged to be allowed to touch **the hem of his garment** (36). This fringe on a Jewish robe is described in Num. 15:38-39. Carr explains it thus: "At each corner of the robe there was a tassel; each tassel had a conspicuous blue thread symbolical of the heavenly origin of the Commandments."[14]

**Were made perfectly whole** is all one word in the Greek. It is a strong compound, suggesting a complete cure.

### C. Ceremonial vs. Moral Defilement, 15:1-20

Of this section Carr writes: "These twenty verses sum up the great controversy of the New Testament, that between the religion of the letter and external observances and the religion of the heart, between what St. Paul calls 'the righteousness which is of the law and the righteousness which is of God by (or grounded upon) faith,' Phil. iii. 9."[15]

### 1. *Ceremonial Uncleanness* (15:1-9)

Once more Jesus came into conflict with the Pharisees. This time they were supported by scribes, or doctors of the Law, from **Jerusalem** (1), some one hundred miles away (see map). It is just possible that this was an official deputation from the Sanhedrin, sent to question Jesus (cf. John 1:19).

These scribes wanted to know why His disciples transgressed **the tradition of the elders** (2). The significance of this expression is explained by M'Neile: "The 'elders' were the great teachers of the past and present . . . ; the 'tradition' was the oral law, handed

---

[13]*War* III. 10. 8.
[14]*Op. cit.*, p. 202.
[15]*Ibid.*

down by them, not yet complete, and codified later in the Mishna."[16]

The specific transgression the Pharisees cited was: **they wash not their hands when they eat bread.**[17] This does not mean that the disciples ate with dirty hands but that they did not perform the elaborate ceremonial washing prescribed in the tradition of the elders. This custom is explained for his Roman readers by Mark (7:2-4). Matthew assumes that his Jewish readers will understand it.

Jesus countercharged the Pharisees by asking the question: **Why do ye also transgress the commandment of God by your tradition?** (3) Then He specified what He meant. He contrasted what **God commanded** (4) with what **ye say** (5). The fifth commandment says, **Honour thy father and mother** (Exod. 20:12). There is also the warning that whoever **curseth**—the Greek word literally means "speaks evil of"—his father or mother was to be put to death (Exod. 21:17).

The Pharisees had circumvented this divine commandment by their human tradition. They said that a son who was obligated to care for his parents—a supremely important point with Orientals—could declare that the money needed to support them was a **gift** (5); that is, dedicated to God. Thus they freed him from fulfilling his lawful obligation (6). In so doing they had "made void" the **commandment of God** by their **tradition.**

The unethical and irreligious implications of this rabbinical custom are described by Carr: "The scribes held that these words, even when pronounced in spite and anger against parents who needed succour, excused the son from his natural duty, indeed bound him not to perform it; and on the other hand, did not oblige him really to devote the sum to the service of God or of the Temple."[18] With this judgment M'Neile agrees. He says: "Its actual dedication is not really contemplated; it was dedicated (i.e. unavailable) only as regards the parent, or other person, who hoped to receive it."[19]

No wonder Jesus called the scribes **hypocrites** (7). To describe them He quoted (8-9) Isa. 29:13 (largely from the Septuagint, rather than the Hebrew text).

[16]*Op. cit.,* p. 222.
[17]The Law had no requirement on this point.
[18]*Op. cit.,* p. 203.
[19]*Op. cit.,* p. 223.

## 2. *Moral Uncleanness* (15:10-20)

To the **multitude** (10) Jesus explained that it was not what goes into one's mouth that **defileth** him, but what comes out (11). The verb is from *koinos*, "common," and so literally means "make common." But since the adjective took on the meaning "ceremonially unclean" (cf. Acts 10:14), the verb came to mean "defile" (in a ceremonial sense). Christ declared: "It is not what you eat that defiles you, but what you say." Montefiore, a Jewish writer, has well expressed the logic of what Jesus meant. "Things cannot be religiously either clean or unclean; only persons. And persons cannot be defiled by things, they can only be defiled by themselves, by acting irreligiously."[20]

This was a shocking denial of Pharisaic Judaism, with its main emphasis on ceremonial cleanness. It is not surprising that the disciples reported to their Master (12) that the Pharisees were **offended** ("scandalized"). He answered by implying that these critics were not of God's planting and would therefore be **rooted up** (13). He called them **blind leaders of the blind** (14).

Then **Peter** (15) asked for an explanation of **this parable**— evidently referring to verse 11. **Parable** (*parabole*) is here used in the limited sense of a short parabolic statement; that is, one that makes a comparison.

The Master expressed His surprise—and doubtless disappointment—that not even the disciples could **yet** understand Him (16). He tried to make the point of verse 11 a bit clearer by elaborating on it. Food has only a physical, not a spiritual, effect (17). But what comes out of **the heart** defiles a person (18). Though He mentions *mouth* again for the fourth time (cf. 11, 17), verses 19 and 20 make it clear that He is not just dealing with one's *words*, but also with his *deeds*.

**Evil thoughts** (19) seems to be a general, introductory expression, which is spelled out in six plurals describing external actions. But these all flow out of wrong attitudes in the heart. The sins are listed in much the same order as in the Ten Commandments. In the Scriptures the heart condition is all-important. This is the inner man as God sees him—his frame of mind, his imagination, affections, basic motives, and goals. When this inner self is evil, it is the fountainhead of all evil in life and conduct. No man can wholly avoid the defilement of sinful acts unless this

---

[20]Montefiore, *The Synoptic Gospels,* I, 169.

fountainhead of his character has been made pure. It was for this very purpose that Christ came among men.

D. MORE MIRACLES, 15:21-39

### 1. *Syrophoenician Woman's Daughter Healed* (15:21-28)

After this bout with the Pharisees, Jesus went northward to the **coasts**—"region" or "district"—**of Tyre and Sidon** (21). These two cities were in Phoenicia (modern Lebanon), which was Gentile territory (see map). Jesus wanted to be alone with His disciples to instruct them.

There came to Him **a woman of Canaan** (22). In Josh. 5:12, "the land of Canaan" (Hebrew) appears in the Greek Septuagint as "the country of the Phoenicians." This woman was a foreigner and a heathen. Yet she came to Christ. Mark, who is the only other writer to record this incident (Mark 7:24-30), calls her "a Greek, a Syrophenician by nation." So the two descriptions agree essentially.

She came out of the same **coasts**. This is an entirely different word in the Greek from the one translated "coasts" in verse 21. Here it is literally "boundaries" or "borders." In verse 21 it is "parts."

This woman addressed Jesus as **Lord, . . . son of David;** that is, Messiah. She may have been among those from "about Tyre and Sidon," who had come down to the Lake of Galilee to see Jesus (Mark 3:8). Now she pleaded for **mercy.** Her daughter was **grievously vexed with a devil;** or, as the Greek says, "badly demonized."

At first Jesus **answered her not a word** (23). Finally the disciples came and "kept asking him, saying, 'Send her away, because she is crying out behind us'" (literal translation). They were disgusted with a woman following them, "yelling" for help. They probably wanted the Master to grant her request, and so get rid of her.

In reply Christ informed the supplicant that He was sent only to **the lost sheep of the house of Israel** (24). First by silence, and then by direct statement, He rejected her plea. Carr rightly gives the purpose: "Jesus, by this refusal, tries the woman's faith, that He may purify and deepen it."[21]

---

[21]*Op. cit.,* p. 205.

Not to be put off, the woman came and **worshipped him**—
"knelt before Him"—pleading **Lord, help me** (25). The verb
means to come to the aid of someone who calls for help.

On the surface Jesus' reply seems to be nothing less than
insulting. He said that it was not **meet** (literally, "good") to take
the **children's** (Jews') bread and throw it to the **dogs** (26). The
Jews commonly called the Gentiles "dogs"; that is, "unclean."
This seems out of character on the lips of Christ. However the
Greek word means "little dogs." As Morison says, "Our Saviour
. . . refers not to the wild, fierce, filthy dogs, belonging to nobody,
that prowl about oriental cities, but to little pet dogs, in which
children are interested, and with which they play."[22] Also
Weatherhead thinks that Jesus may have used a tone of voice or
look of His eye that told the woman He was saying this primarily
as a reproof to the disciples for their narrow, nationalistic attitude.[23]

The woman's answer is remarkable in every way. Instead of
resenting Christ's classification of her as a "dog," she accepted it.
But she made the most of it. She would not claim to be one of the
children. All she asked was some of the **crumbs** that fall from
the table (27). She had faith that these **crumbs** would meet her
need. In other words, the Master's power was so great that it
would not take much of it to cast the demon out of her daughter.
No wonder Jesus answered, **O woman, great is thy faith** (28).
Her request was granted in full and at once.

The incident is well summed up by G. Campbell Morgan:
"Against prejudice she came, against silence she persevered,
against exclusion she proceeded, against rebuff she won."[24]

### 2. *Multitudes Healed* (15:29-31)

After His brief retirement with His disciples—with its usual
interruptions—Jesus returned to **the sea of Galilee** (29). Mark
(7:31) tells us that He went to the Decapolis, east of the lake.
There He **went up into a mountain,** and **sat down** to teach.

Great multitudes came to Him, bringing their **lame, blind,
dumb, maimed, and many others** (30). This gives some idea of

[22]*Op. cit.,* p. 267.

[23]Leslie Weatherhead, *It Happened in Palestine* (New York: Abingdon
Press, 1936), pp. 198-202.

[24]*Op. cit.,* p. 202.

the very high incidence of disease and affliction in those days of no hospitals and very poor physicians. Even today it is claimed that something like half the Arab children in cities have diseased eyes because of lack of sanitation.

Jesus healed all that came. This aroused great wonder and amazement among the people and caused them to glorify God (31).

### 3. *Four Thousand Fed* (15:32-39)

While the feeding of the five thousand is recorded in all four Gospels, this incident is found only in Matthew and Mark (8:1-9). A crowd had been with the Master for **three days,** and all food was gone. He was not willing to send the people away **fasting** (hungry), lest they **faint** on the way home (32). The disciples protested that there was no **bread in the wilderness** with which to feed them (33). All they had was **seven** loaves, **and a few little fishes** (34)—just a few biscuits and sardines.

The first thing Jesus did was to order the crowd to **sit down on the ground** (35). This is a different verb from that used in connection with the feeding of the five thousand (14:19). There it meant literally "lie back"; here it is "fall back." There is little essential difference. Both words really mean "recline." Whereas He "blessed" the bread in the feeding of the five thousand, here He **gave thanks** (36). The verb is *eucharisteo.* It is equivalent to our modern expression, "return thanks" at the table. Then Jesus broke the loaves, and again the disciples served the crowd.

This time they took up **seven baskets full** of the broken pieces that were left over (37). The word for **baskets** is different from that used in connection with the feeding of the five thousand (14:20). There it was the lunch baskets of the twelve disciples. Here a larger basket is meant. This is suggested by the fact that the same word is used for the basket in which Paul was let down over the wall of Damascus (Acts 9:25). It was probably a fisherman's basket, made with woven rope, and holding at least a bushel. So the **seven baskets** here may well have held more than the "twelve baskets" of the earlier occasion.

This time there were **four thousand men** (38). Again Matthew (and not Mark) adds: **beside women and children.**

Having dismissed the crowd, Jesus **took ship**—literally, "embarked in the boat"—and came into the **coasts** ("borders") of **Magdala** (39). This was the town from which Mary Magdalene

151

came. It was located in the fertile plain of Gennesaret (cf. 14:34). The oldest Greek manuscripts have "Magadan." Since the location of the latter is unknown, it is very easy to understand why some scribe should have changed it to the more familiar home city of the Magdalene.

E. BLIND PHARISEES AND SEEING DISCIPLES, 16:1—17:27

1. *The Demand for a Sign* (16:1-4)

The **Pharisees**—teachers in the synagogues—and **Sadducees** —priests in the Temple—came to Jesus, **tempting** ("trying," or "testing") Him (1). Ordinarily these two groups were antagonistic to each other, theologically and politically. The **Sadducees** favored cooperation with the Roman rulers, while the **Pharisees** resented them. But the two parties functioned together in the Sanhedrin at Jerusalem, and now a common hostility united them in opposition to Jesus.

These Jewish leaders **desired** (Greek, "asked") Him to show them **a sign from heaven.** They were not satisfied with the signs He was showing constantly in His healing ministry. These they did not accept as evidence that He was the Messiah. Rather, they demanded that He furnish a spectacular sign from the sky, something from out of the other world, as proof that He was what He claimed to be. His use of "Son of man" amounted to such a claim (see comments on 8:20).

In verses 2 and 3[25] we find a comparison between the signs of the weather and the **signs of the times.** This phrase, so frequently used in prophetic literature today, is found only here in the New Testament.[26] It refers to indications in world affairs of what is about to happen.

The words of Jesus quoted in verse 4 are the same as those found in 12:39. **Wicked** is the same Greek word as is there translated "evil." So the two passages are identical, except that **prophet** (4) is not in the Greek text.

Mark reports Jesus as saying: "There shall no sign be given unto this generation" (Mark 8:12). This might seem to conflict with Matthew's mention of the sign of Jonah. But obviously what Mark means is that no sign of the kind the Jewish leaders

[25]The entire quotation in these two verses (after "them") is omitted in the two oldest Greek manuscripts and bracketed in Nestle and Westcott and Hort, but retained in RSV. We cannot be sure about its genuineness.

[26]And its authenticity is in doubt here (see previous note).

demanded would be given them. (See also comments on 12: 38-42.)

## 2. *The Leaven of Pharisees and Sadducees* (16: 5-12)

Again Jesus left the western shore—where He experienced both the greatest popularity and the greatest opposition—and crossed to **the other side** of the lake (5). Somebody had forgotten to provide **bread** for the group. Two facts made it difficult to purchase food on the east side of the Lake of Galilee. In the first place it was rather sparsely inhabited. In the second place it was largely Gentile territory and it might not be easy to find "clean" food acceptable to the Jews.

Jesus warned His disciples to beware of **the leaven of the Pharisees and of the Sadducees** (6). Immediately they thought He referred to the fact that they had forgotten to bring bread (7). The Master attributed this conclusion to **little faith** (8); that is, a sad lack of spiritual perception. Apart from the grace of God men are incurably materialistic. To counteract the disciples' worry about not having bread on hand, Christ reminded them of how He had fed five thousand with five loaves and four thousand with seven loaves (9-10). It was not about physical **bread** that He was talking (11). Then the disciples understood that He was referring to the **doctrine** ("teaching") of the Pharisees and Sadducees (12). Typically, this explanation is added by Matthew (cf. 17: 13). It is not found in Mark (8: 13-21), the only other place where this incident is recorded.

Scholars have often argued that the feeding of the five thousand and the feeding of the four thousand are garbled variations of the same story. But the clear evidence is against this negative view. As already noted, the feeding of the five thousand is recorded in all four Gospels. The feeding of the four thousand is also described in Matthew and Mark. In the paragraph now under consideration Matthew and Mark refer back to both feedings. That makes six references to the feeding of the five thousand (Matt. 14: 20; 16: 9; Mark 6: 43; 8: 19; Luke 9: 17; John 6: 13). In all of these the Greek word for "basket" is *kophinos*. There are four references to the feeding of the four thousand (Matt. 15: 37; 16: 10; Mark 8: 8, 20). In all of these the word is *spyris*. It is difficult to see how anyone can account for these careful, consistent accounts except on the basis of accurate reporting of two distinct miracles. That is clearly the dual picture that is presented in the Gospels.

### 3. The Great Confession (16:13-20)

For a fourth time Jesus withdrew from the crowds in order to instruct His disciples (cf. 14:13; 15:21, 29). Northward (see map) He went, to the **coasts** ("parts") of **Caesarea Philippi** (13). This city was built by Philip, son of Herod the Great, and named **Caesarea** for the reigning emperor, Tiberius Caesar. It was designated further as **Philippi** to distinguish it from the Caesarea on the coast of the Mediterranean, built by Herod and in Jesus' day the seat of Roman government in Judea. The ancient Greek name of Caesarea Philippi had been Paneas, and this survives in its modern name Banias. It was located on a rocky terrace under the shadow of towering Mount Hermon (el. 9,166 ft.), which is snow-capped the year around. Nearby are cliffs that still bear marks of the ancient worship of the gods Baal and Pan (Greek word for "All"). This was a fitting place to confess the deity and messiahship of Jesus.

It was a critical moment in His career. M'Neile notes: "The public ministry in Galilee was at an end, the journey towards the Cross was soon to begin; and He wished to draw the disciples into closer sympathy with Himself than ever before."[27] It was necessary that the Twelve should have a firm belief in His messiahship as they faced a future which would severely test that faith.

As they reached the environs of Caesarea Philippi, Christ asked His disciples: "Who do men say that the Son of man is?" (RSV) They gave various replies: **John the Baptist, Elias** (Elijah), **Jeremias** (Jeremiah), **or one of the prophets** (14). Then He asked them the all-important question (15). Literally it is: "But you, who do you say me to be?" **Simon Peter** answered for the group: **Thou art the Christ, the Son of the living God** (16).

Verses 13-16 suggest the following outline: (1) The common question—**Whom do men say that I . . . am?** (2) The crucial question—**But whom say ye that I am?** (3) The confident confession—**Thou art the Christ.**

Mark (8:27-30) and Luke (9:18-21) both record this confession of Peter. But both of them limit it to "the Christ"; that is, the Messiah. Only Matthew adds: **the Son of the living God.** Carr rightly points out the implication: "This confession not only sees in Jesus the promised Messiah, but in the Messiah recognizes

[27]*Op. cit.*, p. 238.

the divine nature."[28] The Jewish leaders might have accepted a human Messiah. But it was precisely this claim to deity which caused them to reject Jesus and condemn Him to death on the charge of blasphemy (26: 64-65).

The rest of this section (17-20) is found only in Matthew. Jesus declared: **Blessed art thou, Simon Bar-jona; for flesh and blood hath not revealed it unto thee, but my Father which is in heaven (17).** Flesh and blood was a rabbinical expression for humanity in contrast with Deity. Only a divine revelation from the Holy Spirit can make us really *know* that Jesus is the Son of God. Such a revelation gives an inner certainty that cannot be shaken.

Christ went on to say: **Thou art Peter, and upon this rock I will build my church; and the gates of hell shall not prevail against it (18).** Peter is the Greek *petros*, which means "stone." Rock is *petra*, "a mass of . . . rock as distinct from *petros*, a detached stone or boulder."[29] Many scholars object that there is only one word in Aramaic for both of these, *Kepha*, and that since Jesus spoke in Aramaic no distinction between the Greek words applies here. But in this Gentile, Greek-speaking area it is altogether possible that Jesus spoke in Greek and changed words intentionally.

M'Neile thinks that Jesus spoke in Aramaic, using *Kepha*. He notes that this word is feminine, and so correctly represented by *petra*, "rock." He feels that *petros*, "stone," was not intended to be different in meaning, but was more suitable for a man's name because it was masculine. He adds, however, "It does not follow from the word-play that 'this rock' must be Peter," and concludes: "The reference is probably to the truth which the apostle had proclaimed; the fact of the Lord's Messiahship was to be the immovable bed-rock on which His 'ecclesia' would stand secure."[30] We believe this interpretation is preferable to that of Cullmann, who makes Peter the rock on which the Church is built. Cullmann, of course, means Peter as apostle and not as bishop.[31]

Jesus declared: **I will build my church.** The Greek word *ekklesia* occurs in the Gospels only here and in 18:17 (twice).

[28]*Op. cit.,* p. 210.
[29]Abbott-Smith, *op. cit.,* p. 359.
[30]*Op. cit.,* p. 241.
[31]Oscar Cullmann, *Peter: Disciple-Apostle-Martyr,* trans. Floyd V. Filson (Philadelphia: Westminster Press, 1953), p. 215.

But it is found some twenty-four times in Acts and over sixty times in Paul's Epistles. Its basic meaning is "assembly." In the Septuagint the word is used for the "congregation" of Israel. Its common meaning in Jesus' day was for the lawful assembly of free, voting citizens in a Greek city. In the New Testament it is employed in this secular sense three times (Acts 19:32, 39, 41). The literal meaning of *ekklesia* is "called out." So these free citizens were called out of the total mass. Likewise the Church of Jesus Christ is composed of called-out ones, who have the special privilege of functioning as the congregation of God.

The **gates of hell** (Hades) probably here means the "powers of death"; that is, all forces opposed to Christ and His kingdom. The Greek *Hades* was the place of departed spirits, and is equivalent to the Hebrew word *Sheol.* Morison says: "Our Saviour means that His true church . . . will never succumb to death and destruction."[32]

What did Jesus mean when He said to Peter, **I will give unto thee the keys of the kingdom of heaven** (19)? The Book of Acts seems to suggest the answer. Peter first used the keys when his preaching at Pentecost unlocked the door of the kingdom of Heaven to Jews and proselytes, and three thousand entered in one day. Later he used the keys to unlock the door to the Gentiles in the house of Cornelius. In a very real sense, "Every preacher uses the keys of the kingdom when he proclaims the terms of salvation in Christ."[33]

Even more striking is Jesus' statement that whatever Peter bound on earth would be bound in heaven, and whatever he loosed on earth would be loosed in heaven. What is meant by **bind** and **loose?** M'Neile explains: " 'Bind' and 'loose' appear to represent the Aramaic . . . technical terms for the verdict of a teacher of the Law who, on the strength of his expert knowledge of the oral tradition, declared some action or thing 'bound' i.e. forbidden, or 'loosed' i.e. permitted."[34] In other words, Peter would give decisions, based on the teachings of Jesus, which would be **bound in heaven;** that is, honored by God.

The Master **charged**—strong term, "strictly charged"—His disciples not to tell anyone that He was the Messiah (20). The

[32]*Op. cit.,* p. 284. John Wesley writes: "This phrase properly signifies the power and policy of Satan and his instruments" (*op. cit.,* p. 81).

[33]A. T. Robertson, *Word Pictures in the New Testament* (New York: Richard R. Smith, 1930), I, 135.

[34]*Op. cit.,* p. 243.

time was not ripe for this. With the political concept of a Messianic kingdom which the people held, there was danger of revolution.

### 4. *First Prediction of the Passion* (16:21-23)

**From that time forth began Jesus to shew unto his disciples** (21) suggests that Peter's confession at Caesarea Philippi constituted a turning point in Christ's ministry. From now on Jesus revealed to His disciples more and more the real purpose of His mission on earth. He was to die on the Cross and thus provide salvation. But this disclosure could not come until after they had confessed Him as Messiah.

Four things are included in the prediction: (1) going to **Jerusalem;** (2) suffering many things from the **elders and chief priests and scribes** (the Sanhedrin); (3) being **killed;** (4) being **raised again the third day.**

**Peter took him** (22) seems to suggest that the apostle excitedly grabbed hold of Jesus, as if to protect Him from such a fate. **Be it far from thee** is in the Greek *hileos soi.* It may be translated, "May (God) pity thee!" or simply, "Pity thyself!" Peter had a big heart of warm affection for his Lord.

But this time he had spoken the wrong word. Jesus **turned** —not away from him but toward him—and said, **Get thee behind me, Satan** (23). The word **Satan** means "adversary." In urging Jesus to avoid the Cross, Peter was acting the part of an adversary to the divine will for Christ's mission. He was tempting Jesus to turn aside, as had Satan in the wilderness temptation at the beginning of His public ministry.

Matthew adds (to Mark 8:33): **thou art an offence unto me.** The word is *skandalon,* "scandal." Without meaning to, Peter was setting a snare for Jesus. **Savourest** is simply "think," or "have in mind." Peter's thinking was contrary to God's.

In this conversation Peter is a perfect example of the double-mindedness which characterizes to a greater or lesser degree all believers who have not yet been sanctified wholly. It was not a conscious or intentional vacillation in devotion to Jesus which plagued Peter, but another frame of mind which coexisted subconsciously and which was incompatible with the true spirituality of the Kingdom. The fact of Christ's personal identity he saw: "Thou art the Christ." But the spiritual nature of His messiahship he did not see. This same ambivalence was evident not only here in Peter but in all, in various ways, until their eyes were opened and their souls spiritualized (adjusted to God's ways) in the baptism with the Holy Spirit on the Day of Pentecost.

### 5. *The Price of Discipleship* (16: 24-28)

One of the most significant sayings of Jesus (cf. 10: 38; Mark 8: 34; Luke 9: 23; 14: 27) is found in verse 24. Not only must Christ face the Cross, but so also must His disciples.

There is a whole sermon wrapped up in this verse. The Master said, **If any man will come after me**—rabbinical language for "be my disciple"—he must first **deny himself.** "Self-denial" is the word written over the gateway to the kingdom of God. Everyone has to humble himself, renounce his sins, and deny himself to **enter.** Secondly, he must **take up his cross.** This means death to self, being crucified with Christ (Rom. 6: 6; Gal. 2: 20), a full surrender of one's will to God's will. Bonhoeffer wrote: "Discipleship means adherence to the person of Jesus, and therefore submission to the law of Christ which is the law of the cross."[35] **Let him deny** and **take up** are both in the aorist tense, suggesting the crises of conversion and full consecration. **Follow** is in the present tense of continuous action, emphasizing the lifelong assignment of every Christian in following Christ.

All this suggests that the only way to life is through: (1) Denial of self (regeneration); (2) Death of self (entire sanctification); (3) Determination of self **(follow me).**

There is also a repetition of the thought in verse 25 (cf. 10: 39; Mark 8: 35; Luke 9: 24; 17: 33; John 12: 25). The only way to **save** one's life is to **lose** it.

Then Jesus asked what profit there was for the man who gained the whole world but lost his **soul.** The word is *psyche,* which is translated "life" in verse 25. Perhaps that would be the better rendering here. On the significance of the Greek word, Carr says: "*Psyche* had a wide range of meaning to the Greek; it was 'life' in all its extent, from the mere vegetative existence to the highest intellectual life."[36] He continues: "Christianity has deepened the conception by adding to the connotation of *psyche* the spiritual life of the soul in union with Christ."[37] F. C. Grant makes this observation: "It is the soul which thinks and feels

[35]Dietrich Bonhoeffer, *The Cost of Discipleship* (2nd ed., New York: Macmillan Co., 1959), p. 77.

[36]*Op. cit.,* p. 214.

[37]*Ibid.*

and is in general the living principle within the body."[38] He thinks that either "soul" or "life" fits this passage.

On 26, John Wesley has a strongly evangelistic sermon on "The Important Question." His main points are: (1) What is implied in *gaining* the whole world? (2) What is implied in *losing* one's soul? (3) What is a man profited if he gains the whole world and loses his soul?

The reason why one needs to give careful attention to losing his life for Christ's sake that he may find it is that **the Son of man** is one day coming as Judge to reward every man according to his works (27).

The prediction that **some standing here** would not die **till they see the Son of man coming in his kingdom** (28) has been variously interpreted. It has been applied to: (1) the Transfiguration, which follows. However, all scholars today seem agreed that this is not a correct interpretation. The verse has been applied to the fall of Jerusalem in A.D. 70. The main argument for this second interpretation is that it fits the emphasis on judgment in verse 27. But this seems to be a later Judgment Day, following the Second Coming. Taking everything into consideration it is best to interpret this verse as (3) referring to the Day of Pentecost, and the rapid spread of the gospel described in the Book of Acts.

M'Neile would broaden this a bit. He writes: "Christians can recognize that they received, or rather began to receive, their fulfilment at Pentecost, and that every subsequent catastrophe, or crisis, or demonstration of divine power, has been a gateway to a new era, a step in the age-long process of their complete fulfilment, the culmination of which is beyond our sight."[39] In a similar vein Morison says: "Our Saviour refers, we doubt not, though in an indefinite way, to the establishment and extension of His kingdom, and the manifestation of Himself as the victorious King that took place when Jerusalem and Judaism, both thoroughly corrupted to the core, were overturned."[40]

### 6. *The Transfiguration* (17:1-8)

This incident forms one of the great crises in the life of Christ. Along with the Baptism and the Temptation, it was a moment of

[38]F. C. Grant, *Introduction to New Testament Thought* (New York: Abingdon-Cokesbury Press, 1950), p. 162.

[39]*Op. cit.*, p. 248.

[40]*Op. cit.*, p. 293.

high spiritual significance. It is recorded in all three Synoptic Gospels (cf. Mark 9: 2-8; Luke 9: 28-36).

It happened **after six days** (1). Luke (9: 28) says, "about an eight days after." There is no contradiction here. Luke counts the days of the preceding and following incidents, Matthew and Mark only the six days between.

**After** what? Luke says, "after these sayings." That takes us back to the two important items in the previous chapters: (1) Peter's confession of Jesus' messiahship and deity, and (2) Christ's prediction of His passion.

It will be remembered that while Peter rose magnificently in response to the challenge of the Master's question, "But you, who do you say me to be?" his reaction to the Passion prediction was a miserable failure. He protested that Christ must not die. He failed, as did all the other disciples, to comprehend the meaning and necessity of a suffering Messiah.

It is noticeable that all three Synoptic Gospels begin this account by emphasizing the week between the Confession and the Transfiguration. G. Campbell Morgan feels that "during the period there had been a sense of estrangement between the disciples and the Master."[41] He goes on to say: "Those six days must have been among the saddest in the life of the Master; six days of silence, six days in which His loneliness was the supreme fact in His progress."[42] Even in anticipation, He must walk the Calvary road alone.

What was the purpose of the Transfiguration? The answer is clear now. It was to be a twofold confirmation: (1) of Jesus' deity, as the three disciples caught a glimpse of His eternal glory; (2) of the importance and necessity of the Passion. The latter point comes out in Luke, where it is stated that the topic of conversation with the two heavenly visitors was Christ's coming "decease" at Jerusalem (Luke 9: 31). The Greek word is *exodos*, which means "a going out" ("exodus"). So it included His crucifixion, resurrection, and ascension, which were to climax His earthly ministry.

For the viewing of this unique disclosure of His deity and coming death Jesus chose the same three disciples who had witnessed the raising of Jairus' daughter (Mark 5: 37). Later He

[41]*The Crises of the Christ,* p. 216.
[42]*Ibid.,* p. 217.

would take these of the inner circle—**Peter, James, and John** (1)
—with Him into the Garden of Gethsemane. Now He took them
up **a high mountain.** Though the traditional site of the Transfiguration is on Mount Tabor, in the Plain of Esdraelon, probably a
better choice would be one of the spurs of lofty Mount Hermon,
which stands like a lonely, white-haired sentinel at the head of
the Jordan Valley. This is near Caesarea Philippi, where Jesus
was in the previous incident.

Here Jesus was **transfigured** (2). The word is *metamorphoo,*
from which comes *metamorphosis.* Besides the parallel passage in
Mark (9:2), the word is found only in Rom. 12:2 ("trans
formed") and in II Cor. 3:18 ("changed"). The transformation of
Christ's appearance is described thus: **his face did shine as the
sun, and his raiment was white as the light.** Luke does not use
the word "transfigured," but he describes what took place in
almost exactly the same language. He alone notes that it was
while Jesus was praying that His appearance was altered. There
is a suggestion that our spiritual transfiguration will take place in
times of prayer.

All three Synoptics mention the surprise visit of **Moses and
Elias** (Elijah), who talked with Jesus (3). Moses represented the
Law, Elijah the Prophets. There are many places in the New
Testament where the Old Testament is referred to as "the law
and the prophets."[43] The implication here is that the entire Old
Testament pointed forward to Christ, and specifically that both
the Pentateuch and the prophets predicted the atoning death of
the Saviour. This was shown by type and symbol in the Law
(e.g., the sacrifices), but by statement in the prophets (e.g., Isaiah
53).

Peter was so pleased with the situation that he wanted to
prolong it. He suggested that the disciples might build **three
tabernacles** (4)—booths made from boughs of trees—one each
for Jesus, Moses, and Elijah. One can sympathize with the
apostle's feelings. It was a unique fellowship. But Peter showed
that the prediction of the Passion had not yet registered correctly on his mind. He wanted a glorified Messiah, not a suffering
one.

While Peter was still speaking, **a bright cloud overshadowed them** (5). The cloud here on the Mount of Transfiguration

[43]E.g., Matt. 5:17; 7:12; 11:13; 22:40; Acts 24:14; Rom. 3:21. Cf. "Moses
and the prophets"—Luke 16:29, 31; 24:27; Acts 26:22.

would alert the disciples to listen for the voice of God. It would bring to mind "the pillar of fire by night" (Exod. 13:22) that led the Israelites in the wilderness, as well as the Shekinah glory that dwelt on the Tabernacle (Num. 9:15, 22) and the Temple (I Kings 8:10). It was in a cloud that God appeared at Sinai (Exod. 19:9).

From the cloud a voice came clearly and distinctly, confirming the deity of Jesus—**This is my beloved [only] Son, in whom I am well pleased**[44]—and silencing Peter: **hear ye him.** The trouble with Peter was that he was quick to talk and slow to listen. Unfortunately, his tribe has not disappeared.

Overwhelmed by the vision and awed by the voice, the three disciples fell on their faces (6). This may suggest that they fell down as did Saul on the road to Damascus (Acts 9:4) or more probably that they prostrated themselves in worship. In either case, they were **sore afraid.**

But the Master **touched them** with tender comfort, bidding them to rise and not be afraid (7). When they opened their eyes, **they saw no man, save Jesus only** (8). The value of a vision is measured by its abiding results. No spiritual experience is of worth unless it leaves one with an increased consciousness of Christ's presence. When the heavenly visitors, the cloud, and the voice were gone, the disciples had **Jesus only.** He is the supreme need of every human life at all times.

### 7. *The Question About Elijah* (17:9-13)

Luke notes that it was "the next day" when they came down from the mountain (Luke 9:37). This implies that the Transfiguration took place at night, which fits the picture very well. Matthew's statement that Christ's **face did shine as the sun** (2) would be more meaningful if this happened in darkness.

On the way down the hill Jesus **charged** (9), or "commanded,"[45] the three disciples not to tell **the vision**—the Greek word means simply "that which is seen" (cf. Mark 9:9)—until after His resurrection (9). It would only be misunderstood and might lead to a popular Messianic uprising, a thing which Christ constantly sought to avoid.

The presence of Elijah on the mountain had pinpointed a question in the minds of the disciples (10). The **scribes,** teachers

[44]See notes on 3:17.

[45]"*Entello* points rather to the contents of the command" (Abbott-Smith, *op. cit.*, p. 156). This incident is found only in Matthew and Mark (9:9-13).

of the Law, said that Elijah's coming would precede that of the Messiah. They based this on Mal. 4:5. If Jesus was really the Messiah, as confessed by Peter at Caesarea Philippi and confirmed by the Father's voice on the mount, how was it that Elijah had not yet appeared?

By way of answer Jesus first endorsed the statement of the scribes. Elijah would come ahead of the Messiah, **and restore**[46] **all things** (11); that is, announce a new era in which all things would finally be restored in Christ (Col. 1:16; Eph. 1:9-11). But Jesus went beyond this to assert that "Elijah" had come already, and they (the people to whom John the Baptist had come) had done to him as they pleased, because they did not recognize him (12). Then He added: **Likewise shall also the Son of man suffer of them.** John the Baptist had been arrested and executed. The same fate would soon overtake the **Son of man,** the Messiah.

Matthew has the habit of adding explanations at points that might seem obscure in Mark. We have already met this in 16:12. Here it is stated that the disciples now understood Jesus to be speaking of **John the Baptist** (13).

### 8. *The Healing of the Epileptic Boy* (17:14-21)[47]

Peter had wanted to stay on the Mount of Transfiguration. But there was desperate need in the valley below. The same compassion that led Christ to leave heaven and come down into a world of sin and suffering now compelled Him to leave the glorious fellowship of the mountaintop and go down the hill to meet the need of a boy and his father. The greatest glory of Christ is this love that shone through His life.

As Jesus and the three disciples approached **the multitude** that always seemed to be waiting for Him, an earnest suppliant came, **kneeling down to him** (14). Immediately he presented his urgent request. He had a son who was **lunatick** (15). This comes from the Latin *luna*, "moon." It reflects the Greek word here which literally means "moonstruck." In the Revised Versions it is correctly translated "epileptic." The people of that day thought that epilepsy was sometimes caused by moonlight (cf. Ps. 121:6—"The sun shall not smite thee by day, nor the moon by night"). The seizures described here are typical of that affliction.

[46]The same Greek verb is used in the Septuagint of Mal. 4:6 (LXX, 3:23), where it is "turned" in English. See the significant prediction in Luke 1:16-17.

[47]Recorded also in Mark 9:14-29; Luke 9:37-43.

The distressed father informed Jesus that he had brought his boy to the disciples but **they could not cure him** (16). The verb is *therapeuo*, "heal." The Master had given them power to cast out demons (10:8). But for some reason they were unable to deal with this case.

The keen disappointment that Christ felt over this failure of His own commissioned apostles is reflected in the words of verse 17. They are filled with pathos. The disciples had learned so little from Him!

It must have been with added sternness in His voice that Jesus **rebuked the devil** (demon), which at once **departed out of him** (18). The **child** (*pais*) was **cured** (*therapeuo*) from that very hour. Christ was abundantly able to take care of this hard case.

It is not surprising that the disciples wanted to know why they had failed (19). Jesus informed them that it was because of their **unbelief** (20).[48] If they had **faith as a grain of mustard seed** (see on 13:31-32), they could command **this mountain** to be removed, and it would shift. Christ was probably not talking about a literal hill.[49] By **this mountain** He meant "this great difficulty," this hard case that was too much for them. Sherman Johnson observes: "Faith does not move physical mountains by magic, but its own proper triumphs are more marvelous than large-scale engineering."[50] In a similar vein George Buttrick writes: "Faith *has* removed mountains—mighty empires, pagan cults, entrenched wickedness."[51]

Verse 20 is climaxed with the astounding statement: **nothing shall be impossible to you.** How can this be? The answer is: "By faith." Mark, whose description of this healing is, as usual, much more vivid than that in Matthew or Luke, reports Jesus saying to the boy's father: "All things are possible to him that believeth" (Mark 9:23). That is because God is all-powerful, and faith brings the divine omnipotence to bear on human problems.

Verse 21 is not in the Revised Versions because it is lacking in the two oldest Greek manuscripts (Vaticanus and Sinaiticus), as

---

[48]The best Greek text says: "little faith" (cf. 6:30; 8:26; 14:31; 16:8).

[49]Lukyn Williams, however, says: "It seems rather that Jesus meant his words to be received literally" (*Pulpit Commentary,* "Matthew,") II, 178.

[50]IB, VII, 463.

[51]*Ibid.,* p. 464.

well as some ancient versions. In Mark the first part of the verse is genuine, but the words "and fasting" were added later. Then the entire verse was transcribed by some copyist to this parallel place in Matthew.

### 9. *Second Prediction of the Passion* (17: 22-23)

The first announcement of His coming death was made by Jesus right after Peter's confession at Caesarea Philippi. This second one was made after the next great crisis in His life, the Transfiguration. After both the confession and the confirmation of His deity and messiahship, Jesus made it clear to the disciples that His mission on earth was not to sit on a throne but to die on a cross.

The first prediction (16: 21) specified that Jesus would suffer many things from the Jewish Sanhedrin at Jerusalem. The second one adds the betrayal—**betrayed into the hands of men** (22). The words **into the hands of men** could include Pilate, as well as the Jewish leaders. Both predictions mention Jesus' death and resurrection **the third day** (23). Matthew adds here that the disciples were **exceeding sorry.**

### 10. *The Temple Tax* (17: 24-27)

This incident is found only in Matthew. When Jesus and His disciples returned home to Capernaum—after a considerable absence—Peter was approached with the question: **Doth not your master pay tribute?** (24) The Greek for tribute is *didrachma.* The drachma was a Greek coin with approximately the same value as the Roman denarius. The double drachma (here) was apparently worth about thirty or thirty-five cents. It was the half-shekel for the upkeep of the Temple, to be paid each year just before the Passover by every adult male Jew. The basis for this tax was the "half a shekel" prescribed as a poll tax in Exod. 30: 13. In the time of Christ the Jews all over the world were required to pay it. The Roman government approved this. Josephus quotes a letter from Caesar to Flaccus, which says: "Let those Jews, . . . who have been used, according to their ancient custom, to send their sacred money to Jerusalem, do the same freely."[52] After the destruction of Jerusalem (A.D. 70), when there was no more Temple to support, the emperor collected this tax. Josephus says: "He also laid a tribute upon the Jews wheresoever they were, and enjoined every one of them to bring two drachmae

[52]*Ant.* XVI. 6. 3.

every year into the Capitol, as they used to pay the same to the temple at Jerusalem."[53]

When Peter came into the house, Jesus **prevented** him— " 'Anticipated him' by answering his thoughts."[54] Jesus asked: **of whom do the kings of the earth take custom or tribute? of their own children, or of strangers? (25) Custom** refers to taxes on goods, **tribute** to taxes on persons (the Latin *census*). **Strangers** means those outside the king's family.

When Peter answered, **Of strangers,** Jesus said, **Then are the children free** (26). The point He was making was: "Shall he whom thou hast rightly named the Son of God pay tribute to the Temple of his Father?"[55]

But Jesus was in the habit of paying the Temple tax. That is shown by Peter's answer, **Yes,** above (25). So the Master said: **Lest we should offend them, go thou to the sea**—the Lake of Galilee, in front of Capernaum—**and cast an hook** (27). This shows that "hook and line" fishing was practiced then, as it still is on the shores of the Lake of Galilee. The first fish that Peter caught would have in its mouth **a piece of money** (Greek, *stater*). The stater was equal to a shekel in value. So this would pay the Temple tax for both Peter and his Lord.

---

[53]*War* VII. 6. 6.
[54]Carr, *op. cit.*, p. 219.
[55]*Ibid.*

Section **VIII** *Fourth Discourse:*
*The Christian Community*
Matthew 18:1-35

## A. THE CHRISTIAN AND CHILDREN, 18:1-14

### 1. *The Greatest in the Kingdom* (18:1-4)

The importance of this brief section on humility is shown by the fact that it is found in all three Synoptic Gospels (cf. Mark 9:33-37; Luke 9:46-48). It is also echoed in several other places in these books (see Matt. 20:26-27; 23:11; Mark 10:15, 43-44; Luke 18:17; 22:26). A strong case could be made for the proposition that Jesus emphasized humility more than any other Christian virtue. The careful student of the Gospels becomes increasingly impressed with this fact.

Mark gives the setting of this section. The disciples had been disputing along the way to Capernaum as to who was the greatest (Mark 9:33). In Matthew the disciples come to Jesus with the question: **Who is the greatest in the kingdom of heaven?** They asked this **at the same time** (1)—literally, "in that hour." This suggests that the immediately preceding events had roused them to excitement about the possibility of the Kingdom being soon set up on earth. They were like worldly politicians already jockeying for position.

In answer to their question, Jesus **called a little child unto him** (2). Here we get a glimpse of the Master's tenderness. Children were not afraid of Him, but felt drawn to Him.

Solemnly Jesus asserted (**Verily I say unto you**) that they could not enter the kingdom of Heaven unless they were **converted** (3). Literally this word means "turned." Abbott-Smith suggests for this passage the metaphorical meaning, "change."[1] Thayer gives "*to turn one's self* sc. from one's course of conduct, i.e. *to change one's mind.*"[2] Arndt and Gingrich say that here it means "*turn, change* inwardly, *be converted.*"[3] In the Greek **shall not enter** is a double negative for increased emphasis. It

[1]*Op. cit.*, p. 420.
[2]*Op. cit.*, p. 591.
[3]*Op. cit.*, p. 779.

connotes "shall *never* (or, by no means) enter." The disciples were talking about who would be greatest in the Kingdom. Jesus said: "Unless you are converted and become like a little child, you will not even get inside." The disciples needed to "change" their attitude, to "turn" from their proud, ambitious thoughts. Lukyn Williams observes: "The conversion here spoken of is confined to a change in the present state of mind—to a new direction given to the thoughts and wishes."[4] Shank translates this clause: "Unless you are completely changed in attitude and become as little children."[5]

In verse 4 the Master answered the disciples' question directly: **Whosoever therefore shall humble himself as this little child, the same is greatest in the kingdom of heaven.** In other words, the main characteristic of Christian greatness is humility. Not ability, but humility. Not achievement, but humility. Not impressive performance, but humility. No wonder we read in the Old Testament: "For my thoughts are not your thoughts, neither are your ways my ways, saith the Lord" (Isa. 55: 8). Christ's way runs directly counter to the way of the world.

The humility of a child consists mainly of a mood of trust and dependence. That is the attitude which God desires His children to take toward Him. The prevalent modern mood of self-sufficient, worldly-wise sophistication is inimical to genuine spirituality.

## 2. *A Solemn Warning* (18: 5-6)

While Jesus held the little child in His arms (cf. Mark 9:36), He used it for a further object lesson. Said He to His disciples: **Whoso shall receive one such little child in my name receiveth me** (5). This reveals the Master's deep concern for children. Then follows a startling truth. The one who rejects a child rejects Christ.

In verse 6 Jesus deepened His warning. He spoke of whoever shall **offend**—"cause to stumble" or "ensnare"—**one of these little ones which believe in me.** The last clause is found in the Synoptic Gospels only here and in the parallel passage in Mark (9:42). But it is common in John's Gospel. It is not "believe me," but "believe in me." This indicates personal trust in and commitment to Christ. It certainly implies His deity.

[4]*Op. cit.*, II, 208.

[5]Robert Shank, *Jesus—His Story* (Springfield, Mo.: Westcott Publishers, 1962), p. 119.

There is considerable difference of opinion among commentators as to whether **little ones** still refers to children, or whether Jesus here passes over to the idea of new converts. Perhaps we should allow *both* interpretations and applications—children, and those who have a childlike spirit.

Christ declared that if anyone should cause one of these to stumble, **it were better for him**—literally, "it is profitable"—that a **"millstone** of a donkey"—that is, a large one pulled round and round by a donkey—would be hanged around his neck, and he would be **drowned in the depth of the sea.** Williams gives this comment: "The punishment seems to have been reserved for the greatest criminals; and the size of the stone would prevent any chance of the body rising again to the surface and being buried by friends—a consideration which, in the minds of heathens, greatly increased the horror of this kind of death."[6] It is hard to conceive how Jesus could have given a more solemn warning concerning the heinousness of causing a new or weak Christian to stumble and be ensnared by sin because of one's influence. The need for a consistent, godly life here startles us like the flashing lights at a railroad crossing. We do well to heed the warning.

### 3. *The Seriousness of Sin* (18:7-10)

**Woe unto the world** (7)—or, "Alas for the world" (see 11:21)—because of **offences** (*skandalon*). This is one of the most difficult words in the New Testament to translate (see on 5:29). But it is a very strong term, much stronger than the English word "scandal," which comes from it. Lenski says that the noun *skandalon* and the verb *skandalizo* "go beyond the idea of stumbling (from which one may rise) and always denote spiritual destruction."[7]

Jesus indicated that snares, to entrap the unwary, will always exist. But **woe to that man** who is responsible for setting the trap.

It is difficult to see how Christ could have more vividly portrayed the seriousness of sin than He does in verses 8 and 9. If your **hand** or **foot offend** you ("causes you to sin," RSV), cut it off! Better to **enter into life** (eternal life, beginning here and reaching full flower in heaven) **halt** ("maimed" is better, referring to the loss of a hand) **or maimed** ("lame"), than having

[6]*Op. cit.*, II, 209.
[7]*Op. cit.*, p. 686.

**169**

both hands and both feet to be cast into **everlasting fire** (8). This phrase occurs here for the first time. It paints a horrible picture of eternal punishment.

If your **eye** causes you to sin, **pluck it out.** Jesus was not advocating a literal maiming of the physical, though that would be better than to be lost forever in **hell fire** (9). The Greek says "Gehenna of fire," which means "fiery Gehenna." Whatever hell will be like, it is worth any price to avoid going there.

These two verses (8-9) are closely paralleled in 5:29-30, except that the **foot** is not mentioned. It was noted there that the words should be taken figuratively, as suggesting close associates or associations (persons or things) that might lure one into sin. Williams writes: "Metaphorically, the expression signifies all that is as dear and as necessary as these important members."[8] Any hindering friendships or activities must be cut off, drastically and immediately.

Actually the foot, hand, and eye represent the *self* in its various avenues of expression. Whenever the foot goes astray, it is because of a straying heart. A holy self will have holy feet, hands, and eyes. Jesus therefore is urging that self be denied, that it be thoroughly sanctified by being purged from its sinful selfishness. It is when we become willing for life to be thus "pruned" that we approach true Christlikeness. To surrender what seem to be one's natural rights, whether represented by the foot, hand, or eye, seems surely to result in a maimed personality. But better save a maimed self than to lose a "whole" self. If in the heart there were no sin, the foot, hand, and eye would not so *easily* become the instruments of sinning.

Three thoughts are suggested here: (1) The hand is the symbol of *what we do;* (2) The foot is the symbol of *where we go;* (3) The eye is the symbol of *what we see.* All these must be kept under careful control.

Again Jesus comes back to **one of these little ones** (10; cf. 6). He asserts that in heaven **their angels do always behold the face of my Father.** Carr says, "In these words our Lord sanctions the Jewish belief in guardian angels," but also notes, "The reserve with which the doctrine is dwelt upon in the N.T. is in con-

[8]*Op. cit.,* II, 209.

trast with the general extravagance of Oriental belief on the subject."[9]

### 4. *The Parable of the Lost Sheep* (18:12-14)[10]

This story, which might also be called the parable of the seeking shepherd, is found in Luke 15:3-7. The picture was a very familiar one to Jesus' hearers.

The Oriental shepherd loves his **sheep (12)**—every one. Only a heart of love could lead a man to risk his life on the lonely, beast-infested **mountains** at night, to seek a single sheep which had gone astray. But love knows no limits.

When the shepherd finds his lost sheep, he rejoices more over it than over the ninety-nine **which went not astray (13)**. The application Jesus made of the parable is that it is not the will of **your Father** that **one of these little ones** (cf. 6, 10) **should perish (14)**. "The youngest, the weakest, the sickliest of His flock is as dear to Him as the strongest."[11]

The parable is a striking picture of Jesus' own mission on earth. He came seeking the lost sheep wherever He went.

## B. The Christian and His Brother, 18:15-35

### 1. *Discipline in the Church* (18:15-20)

Up to this point in the chapter Jesus had been warning against the danger of causing someone to stumble, of sinning against another. Now, in the second part, He deals with the other side of the picture. What are you to do if your **brother** (fellow church member) should **trespass**—the Greek says "sin" (*hamartese*)—against you? The answer is: **go and tell him his fault between thee and him alone (15). Tell . . . his fault** is one word in the Greek, *elenxon*. It means "convict" (as in John 16:8) or "rebuke." The latter meaning is in line with Lev. 19:17— "Thou shalt not hate thy brother in thine heart: thou shalt in any wise rebuke thy neighbour, and not suffer sin upon him." Too often church people go and tell everybody else about the trouble, rather than obeying what Jesus said here.

---

[9]*Op. cit.*, p. 222.

[10]While no truer statement is made in the Bible, verse 11 is not in the oldest Greek manuscripts of Matthew and so is omitted at this point in the Revised Versions. It is genuine in Luke 19:10, from which it was evidently copied here.

[11]Ryle, *op. cit.*, p. 223.

If the transgressor will listen, **thou hast gained thy brother**—"i.e. won over to a better mind—to Christ."[12] Meanwhile the unfortunate matter has not been publicized, resulting in people taking sides and thus starting a quarrel that might end in a church split. The time to deal with the situation is when it is small, before it gets too big to handle.

If the brother refuses to listen, then take along two or three witnesses, so that they can **establish** exactly what is said (16). This is often very necessary for protection against slander by one's opponent. If he refuses to listen to the committee, then tell it to the **church** (17). If he will not listen to the church, let him be excommunicated. That seems to be the meaning of the latter part of verse 17.

The word **church** is found elsewhere in the Gospels only in 16:18—"I will build my church." There it means the Church of Jesus Christ throughout the world. "Here it means the local congregation, which represents the whole Church, acting, of course, through its officers."[13]

Earlier (16:19) Jesus had told Peter that whatever he bound on earth would be bound in heaven, and whatever he loosed on earth would be loosed in heaven. Now He gives the same authority to all twelve apostles (18). This shows that Peter did not have a permanent place of unique preeminence. For the meaning of **bind** and **loose** see the notes on 16:19. The context here clearly indicates that Jesus is dealing with discipline in the church. The disciplines imposed by the church, in the spirit of love and in the ways Jesus directed, have God's sanction upon them.

Verse 19 must be related to this. The united prayer of two sincere believers will **bind** or **loose** affairs in the Kingdom. What a responsibility this puts on Christians to pray in the will of God! The Greek word translated **agree** is *symphoneo*. Its literal meaning is "agree in sound" (*phone*), "be in harmony." It came to be used, as here, in the sense "agree together." The use of the term in this passage suggests "a symphony of prayer." That makes a joyous harmony in the ears of God.

A church service—however small the group, or humble the place—is not just a meeting of people, but a meeting of people

---

[12]Carr, *op. cit.*, p. 223.

[13]W. K. Lowther Clarke, *Concise Bible Commentary* (New York: Macmillan Co., 1953), p. 738.

with God (20). Even if only **two or three** gather together **in my name,** the Divine Presence is promised.

## 2. *Unlimited Forgiveness* (18:21-22)

Peter had evidently been thinking of what Jesus said about a brother who had sinned "against thee" (15). He wanted to know how often he had to forgive his brother. He thought he was very generous when he suggested: **till seven times?** (21) "The Rabbinical rule was that no one should ask forgiveness of his neighbour more than thrice."[14]

The Master's answer must have been disturbing: **not . . . Until seven times: but, Until seventy times seven** (22). Some would translate this "seventy-seven times" (Goodspeed). But the traditional rendering seems better. Jesus was fond of hyperbole, as we know from other passages.

It should be obvious that Jesus did not intend for Peter to take His answer in any exact mathematical sense. He did not mean, "Forgive 490 times and then quit." He clearly meant unlimited forgiveness. Buttrick has caught the spirit of it when he says of **seventy times seven:** "We can 'do it in our heads.' But this is celestial arithmetic: we must 'do it in our hearts.' "[15]

## 3. *The Parable of the Unmerciful Servant* (18:23-35)

Since Matthew is presenting Jesus as King, a number of the parables he records refer to a king (cf. 22:2) or to the kingdom of Heaven (c. 13). This striking parable is found only in Matthew's Gospel.

**Therefore is the kingdom of heaven likened unto** (23)— this is virtually the same introductory formula which is found several times in chapter 13. Here it was **a certain king** who made an accounting with his servants. He found one who owed him **ten thousand talents** (24). Since a talent was worth about a thousand dollars, this would be "ten million dollars" (Goodspeed). The sum seems unbelievable. But it must be recognized that these **servants** were high court officials of an Oriental monarch. The documents that archaeology has discovered from the Assyrian and Babylonian periods indicate that these men handled immense sums of money. But we should recognize that Jesus may have again been using hyperbole. What He was seeking to emphasize was the utter hopelessness of our ever

[14]Carr, *op. cit.,* p. 224.
[15]IB, VII, 475.

paying the immeasurable debt of sin that we owe, until forgiven by God. To symbolize this it would be impossible to exaggerate the figures.

When the man could not pay, the order was given that he, his **wife,** and his **children** should all be sold into slavery (25). This was the custom in those days for treatment of debtors. But the man pleaded for mercy (26), and his master forgave him all the debt (27).

The forgiven servant **went out** from the master's presence and found a fellow servant who owed him a **hundred pence** (28). The **pence** was a Roman coin called the *denarius.* It is mentioned sixteen times in the New Testament, more often than any other coin. Always (in KJV) it is translated "penny" or "pence." It was worth about twenty cents. So the **hundred pence** would be about "twenty dollars" (Goodspeed)—a trifling sum compared with what this court official owed the king. Yet this servant grabbed his fellow servant by the throat and demanded payment at once. When the lower servant pleaded for time to pay, the higher servant refused. Instead he cast him into prison.

Naturally the fellow servants were incensed by this unfair attitude. They reported the matter to the king. The first servant was quickly summoned again into the royal presence and given the punishment he deserved. Jesus warned that His Heavenly Father would do the same **unto you, if ye from your hearts forgive not every one his brother their trespasses** (35).

This parable carries a vivid warning to every Christian. Each believer has been forgiven an incalculable debt of sin that he could never possibly pay. And yet some professing Christians will hold a grudge against a fellow church member for years, over a trifling word or act, which may have been said or done in innocence and ignorance. The instruction is **from your hearts forgive;** that is, with all your heart. That means "forgive and forget"! A person cannot harbor a grudge in his heart and at the same time be a true Christian.

Section **IX** *Narrative Resumed:*
*Discipleship and Controversy*

Matthew 19:1—23:39

## A. DISCIPLESHIP, 19:1—20:34

### 1. *Departure from Galilee* (19:1-2)

For the fourth time (cf. 7:28; 11:1; 13:53) we find the terminal expression: **And it came to pass, that when Jesus had finished these sayings** (1). This marks the end of the fourth discourse.

The "Great Galilean Ministry," which had lasted for perhaps a year and a half, was now ended. For the last time Jesus said farewell to His home territory, and began the fateful journey to Jerusalem. **He departed from Galilee** has in it the ring of finality. It marked the end of an epoch. Luke underscores the significance by his statement at this point: "And it came to pass, when the time was come that he should be received up, he stedfastly set his face to go to Jerusalem" (Luke 9:51).

Christ **came into the coasts** ("borders") **of Judaea beyond Jordan** (1). This is a strange geographical expression. Properly speaking, **Judaea** lay between the Jordan Valley and the Mediterranean Sea. The land **beyond Jordan** was at that time known as Perea, and was ruled by Herod Antipas, tetrarch of Galilee. But, as Plummer notes, " 'Judaea' here seems to be used in the wider sense of Palestine, the land of the Jews."[1]

In this area of Perea **great multitudes** again **followed Jesus, and he healed them** (2). In his parallel passage, Mark (10:1) says that "he taught them." The narrative indicates that He did both.

On this last journey to Jerusalem the Master and His disciples crossed the Jordan south of the Lake of Galilee (see map) and went down the east side of the river through Perea. This was the route generally taken by Galilean pilgrims when going to the annual feasts at Jerusalem. The shorter route through Samaria was less desirable because this territory was considered "unclean."

[1]*Op. cit.*, p. 251, n. 1.

Concerning Perea, Andrews writes: "The population was not purely Jewish, but rather a mixed one; not so largely heathen as in the Decapolis, and not likely to be so easily stirred up against the Lord as the inhabitants of Judaea, or even of Galilee."[2] He also calls attention to the Rabbinical saying that Judaea was the wheat, Galilee the chaff, and Perea the tares.[3]

### 2. Marriage (19:3-12)

*a. Divorce* (19:3-9). The question of divorce played an important part in the first century, as it does today. Jesus discussed it in the Sermon on the Mount (5:31-32). Now it appears again. Discussion of this subject had special significance and danger in the days of Jesus' ministry because of Herod Antipas' recent divorce of his wife.

This time the discussion was precipitated by the **Pharisees** (3), the strict keepers and teachers of the Law. They came to Jesus, **tempting him,** or "testing Him" (see notes on 4:1; 16:1).[4] The question they asked was: **Is it lawful for a man to put away his wife for every cause?**

The last phrase, **for every cause,** is particularly significant. It is not found in the parallel passage in Mark (10:2-12), for Gentile readers would not be aware, as would Matthew's readers, of the Jewish connotation. It highlights the controversy in the first century B.C. between the schools of Hillel and Shammai.

The conflict rose over the interpretation of Deut. 24:1— "When a man hath taken a wife, and married her, and it come to pass that she find no favour in his eyes, because he hath found some uncleanness in her: then let him write her a bill of divorcement . . ." Shammai held that "uncleanness" meant fornication: "A man shall not divorce his wife unless he has found in her a matter of shame."[5] His colleague, Hillel (*ca.* 60 B.C.—A.D. 20), who was much more liberal, emphasized the previous clause, "she find no favour in his eyes." He would allow a man to divorce his wife if she did anything that he disliked, even if she burned his food in cooking it.

In reply (4) to the question of the Pharisees, Jesus, as usual, referred them to the Word of God—a hint to us in theological

---

[2]Samuel J. Andrews, *The Life of Our Lord* (Grand Rapids: Zondervan Publishing House, 1954 [reprint]), p. 388.

[3]*Ibid.*, p. 388, n. 3.

[4]Cf. "trying him" (ASV), "tested him" (RSV, NEB).

[5]Quoted in M'Neile, *op. cit.*, p. 272.

controversies. He reminded them that at the beginning God made human beings **male and female** (Gen. 1:27). Then (5) He quoted Gen. 2:24, which gives the divine directive for human marriage. This passage is cited twice by Paul (I Cor. 6:16; Eph. 5:31). Jesus emphasized the last clause by repeating it (6). It is precisely because the marriage union thus makes two persons one that it is to be indissoluble—**let not man put asunder.** Stier says: *"One flesh,* i. e., one person, forming together one man, within the limits of this life in the flesh, for this world."[6]

Not satisfied yet, the Pharisees asked: Why then did Moses command the giving of a divorce certificate (7)? Jesus replied: **because of the hardness of your hearts ... but from the beginning it was not so** (8). God's original plan was "keep thee only unto her, so long as ye both shall live." By saying that Moses **suffered** ("allowed") them to give a certificate of divorce, Christ corrected the word **command** (7) used by the Pharisees. Moses only "permitted" divorce. The requirement that the husband had to furnish a **writing of divorcement** was intended to act as a curb on divorce, not to encourage it. A Moslem today has only to say to his wife three times, "I divorce you," and the divorce is recognized as legal. Moses would make the matter more difficult by requiring the man to employ the services of a scribe in drawing up a written document.

Christ put himself clearly on the side of the stricter interpretation of Deut. 24:1. He allowed only one cause for divorce—**except it be for fornication**[7] (9). This added clause occurs only in Matthew (here and in 5:32). Although some scholars take the position that these words were not uttered by Jesus, this view rejects the inspiration of Matthew. Adultery is a denial of the marriage vow. Jesus' position here is sound. Mark and Luke emphasize, more strongly even than Matthew, the divine abhorrence of divorce. In God's plan marriage is to be a permanent union.

*b. Celibacy* (19:10-12). The disciples seemed shocked by their Master's sternness and strictness. If marriage is going to be as binding as that, **it is not good to marry** (10). Ignoring their low, selfish point of view, Jesus defended the state of celibacy followed by himself and John the Baptist. **All men cannot re-**

[6]Stier, *op. cit.,* I, 352.

[7]The New Testament makes no technical distinction between fornication and adultery.

**ceive this saying** (11) "probably means that it is not given to every one to see that it is not good to marry, 'this saying' referring to the remark of the *disciples.*"[8]  In view of what Christ had just said about the divine institution of marriage, it should be obvious that celibacy is not God's usual plan. A married minister and father can enter more fully and helpfully into the domestic problems of his parishioners than can an unmarried man. It should go without saying that discipleship might demand celibacy. As A. B. Bruce says, "Jesus lifts the whole subject up out of the low region of mere personal taste, pleasure, or convenience, into the high region of the Kingdom of God and its claims."[9]

Jesus went on (12) to mention three classes of **eunuchs** (a Greek word). The first are those born with a physical defect that makes them eunuchs for life. The second are the ones who are **made eunuchs** by men. The word "eunuch" is from *eune,* "bed," and *echo,* "have." It was first used for a "keeper of the bedchamber in an Oriental harem . . . a jealous office, which could be entrusted only to such as were incapable of abusing their trust; hence one who has been emasculated."[10]

The third group is composed of those who have **made themselves eunuchs for the kingdom of heaven's sake**. This is ethical, not physical. Paul recognized the wisdom of this for some (I Cor. 7:32-35). But he also warned against the rise of false teachers, "forbidding to marry" (I Tim. 4:3). There is no scriptural support for enforced celibacy. It is only those who are **able to receive it,** "to whom it is given" (11), that are to **receive it.** The Greek word for **receive** means "make room." It is used here "metaphorically, of having or making room in mind or heart."[11]

### 3. *Blessing Little Children* (19:13-15)

This brief but beautiful incident is described in all three Synoptics (cf. Mark 10:13-16; Luke 18:15-17). Loving parents brought to Christ little children, **that he should put his hands on them, and pray** (13). Carr says: "It appears that it was customary for Jewish infants to be taken to the synagogue to be blessed by the Rabbi."[12] Marriage is sacred, and so are children.

---

[8]Plummer, *op. cit.,* p. 261.

[9]EGT, I, 247.

[10]*Ibid.*

[11]Abbott-Smith, *op. cit.,* p. 486.

[12]*Op. cit.,* p. 228.

The disciples resented this imposition on their Master's time and strength. They **rebuked** those who brought the infants. They considered children unimportant, as do some church workers today. But Jesus' attitude was far different. He said, **Suffer**— "permit," "allow"—**little children, and forbid them not**—"do not be hindering them"—**to come unto me** (14). His love welcomed them warmly. Then He added: **for of such is the kingdom of heaven.** The Greek can equally well mean "to such belongs the kingdom of heaven," or "the kingdom of heaven is composed of such." Actually, both ideas are true. "Love, simplicity of faith, innocence, and above all, humility, are the ideal characteristics of little children, and of the subjects of the kingdom."[13]

### 4. *Riches* (19:16-26)

*a. The Rich Young Ruler* (19:16-22). This story is told in all three Synoptic Gospels (cf. Mark 10:17-31; Luke 18:18-30). Matthew says that the man was "young" (20) and that he "had great possessions" (22). Luke indicates that he was a "ruler" and "very rich" (Luke 18:18, 23).

The man said to Jesus: **Master**[14] ("Teacher"), **what good thing shall I do, that I may have eternal life?** (16) This was a noble question, and revealed a hunger for a deeper relationship with God. **Eternal life** means "full and permanent fellowship" with God.[15] For the Jews it usually meant "life of the age to come."[16] The phrase, very common in John, is found here for the first time in the Synoptics.

In reply the Teacher asked, **Why callest thou me good?** (17) The best Greek text has, "Why do you ask me concerning the good?" **Good** is not a thing, but **God**. Then Jesus pointed the young man to the Scriptures: **keep the commandments.**

But the questioner was persistent. He asked, **Which?** (18) Literally *poia* means "Of what kind?" though here it may be equivalent to *tis*, "Which?" Jesus bypassed the first four of the Ten Commandments and cited the sixth, seventh, eighth, ninth, and fifth. He omitted the tenth, in place of which Mark has, "Defraud not" (Mark 10:19). Matthew alone adds: **Thou shalt love thy neighbour as thyself** (19; see Lev. 19:18), which is a

[13]*Ibid.*

[14]"Good" is omitted in the oldest Greek text.

[15]Filson, *op. cit.*, p. 209.

[16]Gustaf Dalman, *The Words of Jesus*, trans. D. M. Kay (Edinburgh: T. & T. Clark, 1909), p. 159.

summary of the last six commandments, describing one's duties to man. Jesus made no mention of the first four, which indicate duties to God, perhaps because He intended in a moment to probe the seeker at this point. The young man had broken the first commandment, because mammon had become his main god.

The assertion of the ruler that he had kept **all these things** (20) is found in all three Synoptics. Matthew alone adds: **what lack I yet?** It seems clear that he was not satisfied with his religion. He felt a lack inside.

Jesus met him on his own ground: **If thou wilt be perfect** (21). The word *teleios* has already occurred twice in 5:48 (and nowhere else in the Gospels; sixteen times in the Epistles). It comes from *telos,* "end." Thayer notes that its proper meaning is "brought to its end, finished; wanting nothing necessary to completion, perfect."[17] For the two passages in Matthew he suggests, "one who has reached the proper height of virtue and integrity."[18] Abbott-Smith thinks that here it expresses "the simple idea of complete goodness."[19] Arndt and Gingrich give for this passage: *"perfect, fully developed* in a moral sense."[20] The translation "complete" best answers the question, "What lack I yet?"

In the young man's case, perfection required that he sell all his possessions and distribute the proceeds to the poor. This was because money was the first goal of his life, not God. Discipleship demands that we surrender everything to Christ. For most people this does not mean giving up all material possessions. But in order to be sanctified wholly (I Thess. 5:23), every person must surrender that which he holds most dear, in order that God may actually have first place in his life. Bonhoeffer writes: "Is there some part of your life which you are refusing to surrender at his behest, some sinful passion, maybe, or some animosity, some hope, perhaps your ambition or your reason? If so, you must not be surprised that you have not received the Holy Spirit, that prayer is difficult, or that your request for faith remains unanswered."[21]

Refusing to surrender, the young man went away **sorrowful** (22; literally, "sorrowing"). He was plagued with an inner con-

17*Op. cit.,* p. 618.
18*Ibid.*
19*Op. cit.,* p. 442.
20*Op. cit.,* p. 817.
21*Op. cit.,* p. 57.

flict of desires. He wanted to follow Jesus, but he also wanted to enjoy his wealth. The latter desire was stronger, and won out.

Discipleship demands perfect obedience. Some people think that "Believe on the Lord Jesus Christ" (Acts 16:31) means simply mental assent. But, as D. L. Moody insisted, it is also moral consent. It means commitment to Christ. Bonhoeffer expressed it exactly when he wrote: "The man who disobeys cannot believe, for only he who obeys can believe."[22]

In the *Biblical Illustrator*, D. Macmillan outlines the story of the rich young ruler thus: (1) A hopeful meeting, 16; (2) An important conversation, 17-21; (3) A sorrowful parting (22); (4) Important lessons, 23-26.

*b. The Danger of Riches* (19:23-26). After the rich young ruler had left, the Master turned to His disciples and solemnly declared, **Verily I say unto you . . . a rich man shall hardly enter into the kingdom of heaven** (23). The adverb **hardly** means "with difficulty." And the difficulty is precisely that most rich men make gold their god.

Once more Jesus resorted to hyperbole—a statement exaggerated for effect. Attempts to reduce the word **camel** (24) to a rope—as George Lamsa does, on the basis of a supposed Aramaic original—or to enlarge the **eye of a needle** to a small gate in the wall of Jerusalem are both mistaken. We should take the passage just as it reads. The Jewish Talmud uses the figure of an elephant going through a needle's eye to express the idea of an impossibility. That is the same thing that Jesus does here.

The disciples were **exceedingly amazed** and asked, **Who then can be saved?** (25) This question reflects the common Jewish belief that material prosperity was the evidence of God's blessing. Although this belief is reflected often in the Old Testament, the Book of Job refutes the idea.

By way of reply, Jesus first **beheld them** (26)—literally, "having looked upon them." Carr observes: "These heart-searching looks of Christ doubtless gave an effect to His words which it is impossible to recall, but which would never be effaced from the memory of those who felt their meaning."[23] Then the Master declared that while **this**—the salvation of the rich—was impossible with men, there is no limit to what God can do when men permit Him to have His way.

[22]*Ibid.*
[23]*Op. cit.*, p. 232.

### 5. *Rewards of Discipleship* (19:27—20:16)

There are two incidents in this section. They are tied closely together by the fact that both end with essentially the same saying (19:30; 20:16).

*a. Peter's Concern* (19:27-30). The refusal of the rich young ruler to give up his wealth prompted Peter to say: **Behold, we have forsaken all, and followed thee** (27). But his testimony was vitiated by his self-interested plea: **What shall we have therefore?** The apostle was still hopelessly materialistic and selfish in his outlook on life.

Jesus assured **them** (28)—Peter was the spokesman for the whole group of disciples—that all who followed Him would be rewarded abundantly in the **regeneration.** The word *palingenesia* means "new birth, renewal, restoration, regeneration."[24] It occurs only here and in Titus 3:5—"the washing of regeneration," referring to individual spiritual experience. But here it means "the new world," as it is translated in the Syriac Version and found in the Apocalypse of Baruch (44:12).[25] It is further identified as the time **when the Son of man shall sit in the throne of his glory.** This combination is reflected strikingly in Rev. 21:5—"And he that sat upon the throne said, Behold, I make all things new." Bengel comments: "There will be a new creation, over which the second Adam will preside, when the whole microcosm of human nature, by means of the resurrection, and also the macrocosm of the universe, will be born again."[26]

The reward of the disciples is thus expressed: **ye also shall sit upon twelve thrones, judging the twelve tribes of Israel.** As might be expected, this apocalyptic statement, clothed in Jewish language, has found varied interpretations. The best we can do is to interpret scripture by scripture. Paul says: "Do ye not know that the saints shall judge the world?" (I Cor. 6:2) This seems to reflect Dan. 7:22—"Until the Ancient of days came, and judgment was given to the saints of the most High."

But many refer the language here to "reigning," rather than "judging" in a judicial sense. Williams says: "The verb 'judge' sometimes signifies 'govern or direct,' and perhaps may be here used to denote that the saints shall, in the new Messianic king-

[24]Abbott-Smith, *op. cit.,* p. 335.
[25]Dalman, *op. cit.,* p. 177.
[26]*Op. cit.,* I, 365.

dom, be Christ's vicegerents and exercise his authority."[27] With regard to **the twelve tribes of Israel,** Williams writes: "More probably **Israel** means the spiritual Israel, or the whole body of the Church; and the number twelve . . . imports the complete number of those who are being judged."[28]

Jesus also promised that everyone who left relatives and property to follow Him would **receive an hundredfold (29).** Mark adds "in this time." But the ultimate reward is **everlasting life.** This is better translated "eternal life"—something primarily qualitative as well as quantitative. It is not just life that lasts forever **(everlasting),** but the life of eternity (God himself) in the soul of man.

Verse 30 is a rebuke to Peter's self-complacency. Though he was the **first** of the disciples, if he showed the wrong spirit he would be **last.** And Christians who in the eyes of the world are **last** will be **first.**

b. *Parable of the Laborers in the Vineyard* (20:1-16). This is another one of Matthew's parables of the Kingdom, beginning with the formula: **the kingdom of heaven is like unto (1)** (cf. c. 13). It is found only in this Gospel.

**Householder** means literally "house-master" (*oikos,* "house," compounded with *despotes,* "master"). This man went out **early in the morning,** perhaps at sunrise, to hire workers for his vineyard. "In all big cities people wanting work would be gathered *proi* about 6 a.m."[29] When the grapes became ripe they must be picked promptly, or the harvest would be lost.

He found men and agreed with them to pay **a penny** per day **(2).** The Greek indicates a Roman *denarius,* a silver coin worth about twenty cents (some say fifteen or seventeen). But it represented much more in buying power than that amount would today; it was a fair and customary day's wage.

Again he went out about **the third hour** (9:00 a.m.) and found men standing idle in the **marketplace (3)**—the *Agora,* central meeting place in every city for children playing (11:16), people purchasing (*agorazo*="buy"), magistrates judging (Acts 16:19), and philosophers disputing (Acts 17:17). The house-

[27]*Op. cit.,* II, 252.

[28]*Ibid.*

[29]Eric F. Bishop, *Jesus of Palestine* (London: Lutterworth Press, 1955), p. 203.

holder hired these with simply the promise: **whatsoever is right I will give you** (4).

At about the **sixth** (noon) and **ninth hour** (3:00 p.m.) he hired others on the same terms (5). About the **eleventh hour** (5:00 p.m.) he discovered still others **standing idle** in the Agora (6). When he asked them why they were not at work, they replied: **Because no man hath hired us** (7). So he sent them into the vineyard with the promise that they would receive **whatsoever is right**. **At even** (8)—the custom then was to pay laborers at the end of each day (cf. Lev. 19:13)—**the lord of the vineyard** (same man as "householder" above) ordered his **steward** (the one "entrusted" with his master's business) to call the workers and give them their pay, **beginning from the last unto the first.** So the "manager" (Berkeley) lined up the laborers and proceeded to pay them.

To the **eleventh hour** men he gave each a denarius, a full day's wage (9). When it came the turn of those who had worked all day, they naturally expected more. But each one received a denarius (10). This caused immediate discontent. They **murmured** (11)—the sound of the Greek word suggsts the buzzing of bees—against the **goodman of the house**. This phrase is all one word in the Greek, *oikodespotes,* translated "householder" in verse one.

On the surface, the complaint of these men (12) was not unnatural. But it betrayed a spirit of selfishness. The men who worked only one hour needed as much to feed their families as those who worked all day. The owner reminded one of those who complained that the agreement had been for a fair day's wage of one denarius (13). It was the master's privilege to give more, if he wished. **Is thine eye evil, because I am good?** (15) The worker was stingy; the householder was generous and kind.

The principle which this parable was intended to illustrate is expressed in verse 16—**So the last shall be first, and the first last**[30] (cf. 19:30). It is obvious that the story was told in rebuke for the kind of spirit reflected in Peter's question, "What shall we have therefore?" (19:27) Peter considered himself first. But some who came last might prove to be first.

Carr makes a good suggestion about the mentioning of different hours. He says: "Possibly the element of time is introduced

[30]The rest of the verse (KJV) is not found in the two oldest Greek manuscripts, though genuine elsewhere (22:14).

to illustrate in a parabolic form the *apparent* degrees of service, and to signify that no man can estimate the comparative merit of work for God."[31]

As always, Trench has done an excellent job in explaining the purpose of this story. Basically, "the parable is directed against a wrong temper and spirit of mind."[32] Its meaning is this: " 'Not of works, lest any should boast;' this was the truth which they were in danger of missing, and which He would now by the parable enforce; and if nothing of works, but all of grace for all, then no glorying of one over another, no claim as of right upon the part of any."[33]

J. C. Gray in *The Biblical Illustrator* develops this passage under the story title "The Vineyard Labourers." He uses a strikingly simple outline: (1) Idling, 1-3; (2) Calling, 2, 4; (3) Working, 7; (4) Paying, 8-16.

### 6. *Third Prediction of the Passion* (20:17-19)

It is noticeable that Christ's announcements of His coming death at Jerusalem are given only to **the twelve disciples apart** (17). He wanted no publicity in the matter. But the importance of these predictions is shown by the fact that each of the three is recorded in all the Synoptic Gospels (for this one see Mark 10:32-34; Luke 18:31-34). This third prediction is more detailed and specific than the other two (cf. 16:21; 17:22-23). Jesus will be **betrayed** to the **chief priests** and **scribes**, and **they** (the Sanhedrin) **shall condemn him to death** (18). Then the Jews will **deliver him to the Gentiles**, who will **mock . . . scourge . . . and crucify** Him (19). This is the first mention of the Crucifixion, as well as the first definite statement that He would be executed by Gentiles, not Jews. The Resurrection is featured in all three predictions.

### 7. *Personal Ambition of James and John* (20:20-28)

In Mark 10:35-45, the only other place where this incident is recorded, it says that James and John made the request. Here it is their mother, **with her sons** (20). Obviously the three together presented the petition. Matthew here departs from his usual practice and becomes more specific than Mark. **Worshipping him** means bowing down before Him.

[31]*Op. cit.*, p. 234.
[32]*Op. cit.*, p. 138.
[33]*Ibid.*, pp. 138-39.

The request was that two sons might sit, **the one on thy right hand, and the other on the left, in thy kingdom (21).** After the second prediction of the Passion, the disciples had asked: "Who is the greatest in the kingdom of heaven?" (18:1) Jesus had answered by setting a child in the midst and saying: "Whosoever therefore shall humble himself as this little child, the same is greatest in the kingdom of heaven" (18:4). The present incident shows how abysmal was their lack of understanding of this truth as well as of Jesus' teaching about the coming Passion. They had failed utterly to catch the spirit of their Master. They were still looking for the setting up of an earthly kingdom. And they had already decided who was to be "the greatest" in it, though perhaps not who was to sit on the **right hand**—the place of highest honor—and who on the **left.**

Jesus' answer was to the point: **Ye know not what ye ask (22).** Some people are always seeking the privileges of a position, without recognizing the responsibilities involved. Those who would be closest to Christ must suffer the most. For He is the Suffering Saviour. Did they want to hang on a cross, one on each side of Him? There was no vying for these positions! Yet when He asked, **Are ye able . . . ?** they blithely and ignorantly responded, **We are able. To drink of the cup** was a familiar figure to the Jews (cf. Ps. 75:8). Williams says: "Here the cup signifies the internal, mental, and spiritual sufferings which Christ endured (ch. xxvi. 39, 42)."[34]

The Master warned His two disciples that they would **drink indeed of my cup**[35] **(23).** James was the first of the apostles to be martyred (Acts 12:2). Concerning the last days of John there are many legends, but nothing certain is known except that he suffered on the Isle of Patmos (Rev. 1:9).

Jesus added that to assign seats on His right hand and left **is not mine to give, but (it shall be given to them)**—the words in parentheses are in italics, indicating that they are not in the original—**for whom it is prepared of my Father.** This seems like a disclaimer of authority on the part of Christ. It is more probable that **but** (*alla*) means "except" (*ei me*) in this passage, as al-

[34]*Op. cit.,* II, 281.

[35]The reference to baptism in verses 22 and 23 is not found in the oldest manuscripts, though genuine in Mark 10:38-39, where treatment will be found.

lowed by Blass-Debrunner[36] and J. H. Moulton.[37] The passage would thus mean, "It is not Mine to give except to those for whom God has planned it." It is not favoritism but fitness that will govern one's place in the Messianic kingdom.

When the other ten apostles heard what James and John had done, they were **moved with indignation** against them (24). The verb means "be aroused, indignant, angry."[38] They resented the two sons of Zebedee trying to "steal a march" on them. But unfortunately there is no evidence that their motives were any purer than those of the two brothers.

Jesus called the Twelve together and warned them that the policies of His kingdom were very different from those of earthly rulers. He reminded them that **the princes of the Gentiles exercise dominion over them** (25)—literally, "lord it over them"— **and the great ones exercise authority** (found only here and in the parallel passage in Mark 10:42). The verb **exercise authority** may perhaps mean "tyrannize over someone."[39]

But it is not to be so among Christ's followers (26). In ascending scale Jesus first said that the one who would be **great** must be **minister.** This is *diakonos,* from which comes "deacon." But its original meaning was simply "servant." In the second place, whoever would be **chief** must be **servant** (27)—literally, "slave." This illustrates the old saying, "The way up is down." He who becomes servant of all will find himself honored and promoted.

Verse 28 is a great theological passage. Jesus declared that **the Son of man came not to be ministered unto** (*diakonethenai*), **but to minister** (*diakonesai*)—"not to be served, but to serve"— **and to give his life a ransom for many.** The word for life is *psyche.* Ransom is *lytron* (only here and Mark 10:45), from *lyo,* "loose." It meant *"price of release, ransom* (especially also the ransom money for the manumission of slaves . . .)."[40] This usage is illustrated fully in the papyri, as Adolf Deissmann has shown. He cites three papyrus documents dated A.D. 86, 100, and 107 (or 91) which use the word this way. His comment is: "But when anybody heard the Greek word *lytron,* 'ransom', in the first

[36]*Op. cit.,* p. 233.
[37]*Op. cit.,* I, 241.
[38]Arndt and Gingrich, *op. cit.,* p. 4.
[39]*Ibid.,* p. 422.
[40]*Ibid.,* p. 483.

century it was natural for him to think of the purchase-money for manumitting slaves."[41]

**For (many)** is *anti*. The common meaning of this preposition in the papyri of that period was "instead of."[42] This connotation shows up rather clearly in the only two other passages in Matthew where this word occurs. In 2:22 we read that Archelaus reigned "in the room of" (*anti*) his father, Herod. He had taken his place. In 5:38 we hear of an eye "for" (*anti*) an eye, and a tooth "for" (*anti*) a tooth. Obviously it means an eye taken "in place of" an eye, and a tooth "in place of" a tooth. In some mysterious way, known only to God, Christ gave His life a ransom "instead of many," to free them from the slavery of sin and to save them from eternal death.

The use of **many** here does not deny the fact that Christ died for all. Paul writes in I Tim. 2:6 that Christ Jesus "gave himself a ransom [*antilytron*] for [*hyper*] all." Christ died for "all," but many are saved as the result of His death.

Under the title "True Greatness" one can think of: (1) The price of greatness—**Are ye able to drink of the cup . . . and to be baptized with the baptism?** (2) The practice of greatness—**Whosoever will be great among you, let him be your minister** (servant); (3) The paragon of greatness—**The Son of man came not to be ministered unto, but to minister.**

### 8. *Two Blind Men Healed* (20:29-34)

This incident is recorded in all three Synoptics (cf. Mark 10:46-52; Luke 18:35-43). But whereas Matthew mentions **two blind men** (30),[43] Mark and Luke have only one. Mark alone identifies him as Bartimaeus. Evidently he was the more prominent of the two, and probably a well-known Christian when Mark wrote his Gospel.

It happened as they **departed from Jericho** (29), on their way to Jerusalem. But Luke says the blind man called for help as Jesus "was come nigh unto Jericho" (Luke 18:35). The difference in the accounts has caused considerable comment (see notes on Luke 18:35-43). The simplest solution is perhaps to take Luke's statement as merely indicating that the healing miracle took place near Jericho.

[41]LAE, p. 327.
[42]Moulton and Milligan, VGT, p. 56.
[43]For previous "doubles" in Matthew, see 8:28 and 9:27.

The cry of the blind men—**Have mercy on us, O Lord, thou son of David** (30)—is the same as that of the Syrophoenician woman (15:22). When the crowd tried to silence them, telling them to hold their peace, the blind men earnestly repeated their plea (31). This caused Jesus to stop and ask them, **What will ye that I shall do unto you?** (32) The answer was quick and clear: **Lord, that our eyes may be opened** (33). "Gripped with compassion" (literally), Jesus **touched their eyes** (34). This act was perhaps more to strengthen their faith than to produce healing. **Immediately their eyes received sight** (literally, "they looked up," or "they saw again"). Making good use of their new eyesight, **they followed him.** Thus the crowd increased as the Master made His way to Jerusalem to offer himself as an atoning Sacrifice for all men's sins. He who healed the bodies came especially to heal men's souls.

## B. Controversy, 21:1—23:39

### 1. *The Triumphal Entry* (21:1-11)

This event marked the beginning of Passion Week.[44] Its importance is shown by the fact that it is recorded in all four Gospels (cf. Mark 11:1-10; Luke 19:29-38; John 12:12-19). Hitherto John has had very little material in common with the Synoptics, except for the feeding of the five thousand. But all four Gospels record the events of Passion Week with far greater detail than any other period in the life of Christ.

The Triumphal Entry happened on Sunday. After the healing of the blind men at Jericho (20:29-34), Jesus and His disciples, in company with Galilean pilgrims on their way to the Passover, had walked up the Jericho road toward Jerusalem. This was on Friday. From sunset Friday to sunset Saturday (the Jewish Sabbath) Jesus and His disciples rested, perhaps in the home of Martha and Mary at Bethany.

Sunday they went into Jerusalem. On the way they evidently stopped at Bethphage (pronounced beth-fa-jee). This village is not mentioned in the Old Testament, and only in con-

---

[44]*Webster's Unabridged Dictionary* (2d ed., p. 1788) defines "Passion Week" as follows: "Originally the week before Easter; Holy Week; now, commonly, the week between Passion Sunday and Palm Sunday." We are using the expression in its original sense.

For an outline of the events of the week see chart in connection with the treatment of Mark 11:11.

nection with the Triumphal Entry in the New. The Talmud speaks of it as being near Jerusalem. Dalman says, on the basis of rabbinical literature: "It must have been a district situated outside Jerusalem (a suburb, but not a separate unit), beginning at the border of the sanctuary, i.e. before the eastern wall of Jerusalem."[45] This would suggest a territory including the Kidron Valley and the western slope of the Mount of Olives.

Jesus sent **two disciples**—were they Peter and John? (cf. Mark 14:13 with Luke 22:8)—with instructions to **Go into the village over against you,** where they would find an ass tied and a **colt** with it (2). These they were to bring to the Master. If anyone protested, they were to say: **The Lord hath need of them** (3). It is interesting to note that only here and in the parallel passage in Mark 11:3 is Jesus called the Lord in the first two Gospels. Luke, however, employs this usage sixteen times.

As usual, Matthew quotes a prophecy as having been fulfilled in this event in Christ's life. The quotation is from Zech. 9:9 (cf. also Isa. 62:11). There it is predicted that the Messiah-King would come, meekly riding on a donkey (5). This act of Jesus showed that He was officially presenting himself to the Jewish nation as its Messiah. Josephus records the popular belief that the Messiah would appear on the Mount of Olives.[46]

The disciples carried out their commission (6). Apparently the triumphal procession began near the top of the Mount of Olives. The disciples placed their clothes on the donkey, in lieu of a saddle, for the Master to sit on.[47]

**A very great multitude**—"most of the crowd" (Weymouth, Williams, Goodspeed, RSV)—**spread their garments in the way** (8). This shows the almost tumultuous enthusiasm of these Galilean pilgrims, who had seen the many miracles which Jesus had performed. Now they acclaim Him as their Messiah (9).

---

[45]Gustaf Dalman, *Sacred Sites and Ways* (London: S.P.C.K., 1935), pp. 252-53.

[46]*War* II. 13. 5; *Ant.* II. 8. 6.

[47]Critics have sometimes made fun of Matthew's supposed picture of Jesus riding two animals at once. But this implies a degree of stupidity for the writer of this Gospel which is denied by the nobility of its contents. The Greek text of verse 7 is somewhat uncertain. In Zech. 9:9 the "ass" and the "colt" are the same animal (Hebrew poetic parallelism). The other Gospels mention only one animal, called a "colt" (Mark 11:2; Luke 19:30) or a "young ass" (John 12:14).

The language used here—**the son of David**—is clearly Messianic.[48]
**Hosanna** means "Save now," or "Save, we pray." Here it is
probably equivalent to "God save the King!" Hosanna is the
opening word of Ps. 118:25, "a verse which was sung in solemn
procession round the altar at the feast of Tabernacles and on
other occasions."[49]

When Jesus entered Jerusalem, **all the city was moved** (10).
Everybody asked, **Who is this?** The answer of the crowd was:
**This is Jesus the prophet of Nazareth of Galilee** (11).

For a Palm Sunday sermon "The Triumphal Entry" could
be treated thus: (1) The preparation, 1-5; (2) The procession,
6-8; (3) The praise, 9.

### 2. *The Cleansing of the Temple* (21:12-13)

This incident is given by Matthew immediately following the
Triumphal Entry, as if it occurred the same day. Mark (11:15-19)
spells out the details by noting that the cleansing took place on
Monday. This is another example of Matthew's habit of "telescop-
ing" two narratives together. In this case Luke follows Matthew
(Luke 19:45-48).

John records a cleansing of the Temple (John 2:13-17) near
the beginning of Christ's ministry. All three Synoptics (cf. Mark
11:15-19; Luke 19:45-48) describe a similar event at the beginning of Passion Week. Most scholars assume that there were
not two cleansings. But Alfred Plummer says: "There is nothing
incredible in two cleansings."[50] And Salmon writes: "We are
at liberty to accept St. John's account, that our Lord made His
protest against Temple profanation on an earlier visit to the
sacred House, and to believe that after an absence of a year or
more, coming back with a number of Galilean disciples, He
enforced His requirements more vigorously."[51]

The cleansing of the Temple is described vividly. **Jesus cast
out all them that sold and bought in the temple** (12)—*hieron*,

---

[48]Carr (*op. cit.*, p. 242) says: " 'He that cometh' was a recognized
Messianic title." But M'Neile (*op. cit.*, p. 151) and Vincent Taylor (*Names
of Jesus*, p. 79) deny this. The latter thinks it originated with John the
Baptist.

[49]Carr, *op. cit.*, p. 241.

[50]*Op. cit.*, p. 287.

[51]George Salmon, *The Human Element in the Gospels* (New York: E. P.
Dutton & Co., 1907), pp. 433-34.

"Temple Area," covering about twenty-five acres. In the Court of the Gentiles there was a market where sheep and oxen were sold for sacrifices (cf. John 2:14). Since the Law specified that these must be "without blemish" (Exod. 12:5), it was safer to buy them in the Temple market, which was run by relatives of the high priest. Everything bought here would be approved. Then, too, it would be inconvenient for the pilgrims from Galilee to bring a sheep on the long journey. Those who were too poor to offer a sheep were permitted to substitute doves (Lev. 12:8). There would be a brisk sale of these every day.

**Money changers** also reaped their harvest. Every adult male Jew had to pay an annual Temple tax of half a shekel (cf. 17:24). This must be paid with the Phoenician coin. Since the money the Jews handled ordinarily was Greek or Roman, this meant that most of the people had to get their money changed. The priests were permitted to charge something like 15 percent for making the exchange. Edersheim thinks this alone would amount to between $40,000 and $45,000 each year,[52] a tremendous income in those days.

Jesus reminded the offenders that it was written in the Scriptures (13), **My house shall be called the house of prayer** (quoted from Isa. 56:7), **but ye have made it a den of thieves** (quoted from Jer. 7:11). The Greek says "a cave of robbers." The phrase would be a familiar one to Jews of the first century.

Christ's condemnation of the operators of the Temple market as "robbers" finds ample support in the rabbinical writings. They speak of "the Bazaars of the sons of Annas"—the former high priest who was succeeded by five of his sons, and whose son-in-law, Caiaphas, was high priest at this time. Edersheim calls attention to the statement that "the Sanhedrin, forty years before the destruction of Jerusalem [i.e., A.D. 30, the year of the Crucifixion], transferred its meeting-place from 'the Hall of Hewn Stones' (on the south side of the Court of the Priests . . .) to 'the Bazaars,' and then afterwards to the City."[53] A little later, "popular indignation, three years before the destruction of Jerusalem, swept away the Bazaars of the family of Annas."[54] The seriousness of the situation is reflected in this statement: "The Talmud also records the curse which a distinguished Rabbi of Jerusalem

[52]*Op. cit.*, I, 368.
[53]*Ibid.*, p. 371.
[54]*Ibid.*, p. 372.

(Abba Shaul) pronounced upon the High-Priestly families (including that of Annas), who were 'themselves High-Priests, their sons treasurers, their sons-in-law assistant-treasurers, while their servants beat the people with sticks."[55]

The cleansing of the Temple was the second Messianic act of Jesus in Passion Week. It formed a fitting sequel to His welcome as "the son of David" in the Triumphal Entry and fulfilled the prophecy in Mal. 3:1-3.

A careful reading of the four accounts of the cleansing of the Temple will not support the idea that Jesus used physical violence on people or robbed them of their property. He simply made the men and their belongings leave the sacred area.

### 3. The Children's Praise (21:14-17)

This section is found only in Matthew. When Jesus had cast the wicked transgressors out of the Temple, **the blind and the lame came to him** there, **and he healed them** (14). This was something quite different from the wrangling of buyers and sellers. It reveals God's deep concern for the suffering of men.

The change, however, was not pleasing to the **chief priests** (15). This term probably included the high priest, former high priests, male members of their families, and perhaps the heads of the twenty-four priestly courses. When these (Sadducees) and the **scribes** (Pharisees) heard the children crying out, **Hosanna to the son of David**, they **were sore displeased**. This is exactly the same word as the one translated "were moved with indignation" in 20:24. In reply to their petulant complaint, **Hearest thou what these say?** (16) Jesus quoted a part of Ps. 8:2 from the Septuagint (8:3). When religious leaders refuse to praise Him, little children make up for the lack.

This is the first place in the Synoptic Gospels where the Sadducees are mentioned as being in open opposition to Jesus. Up to this point it had been mainly the Pharisees with whom He came in conflict. But when Jesus cleansed the Temple, He struck at both the prestige and the pocketbooks of the priests. For this they never forgave Him. It was they who led the final attack on Him (cf. 27:1, 12; Mark 14:55; 15:10). E. F. Scott says, "He had openly defied them, and they had now to reconsider what measures they should take to effect his speedy death."[56]

[55]*Ibid.*

[56]E. F. Scott, *The Crisis in the Life of Jesus: The Cleansing of the Temple and Its Significance* (New York: Charles Scribner's Sons, 1952), p. 101.

The critical, jealous attitude of the Pharisees and Sadducees, right in the house of God, doubtless saddened the Master. **He left them** (17) and went out to **Bethany** (two miles away, see map) for the night. There—probably in the home of Martha, Mary, and Lazarus—He found love and understanding. It was a haven for His troubled soul in these crucial days.

### 4. *The Cursing of the Fig Tree* (21:18-22)

This incident is recorded in Matthew and Mark (11:12-14, 20-25). As the split reference indicates, Mark separates this story into two parts: the cursing of the fig tree on Monday morning, and the withering of the fig tree observed on Tuesday morning. Again, Matthew here telescopes two incidents into one narrative, with no chronological break.

It happened **in the morning** (18), as Jesus was returning to Jerusalem from Bethany. Feeling hungry—we do not know how He happened to miss breakfast that morning—He spotted a fig tree **in the way** (19). This is literally, "upon the path." When He reached the tree, He found nothing but **leaves.** Usually the figs hide under the leaves. But here there was no fruit. So Jesus cursed the tree as a sign of God's displeasure with hypocrisy.

Matthew says, **presently the fig tree withered away.** But the Greek is stronger than this. **Presently** is *parachrema,* which means "on the spot, forthwith, instantly."[57] The disciples noted the change in the tree's appearance, and exclaimed: **How soon is the fig tree withered away!** (20) **Soon** is *parachrema* again (translated "immediately" both times in ASV).

How is this to be harmonized with Mark's clear indication that it was some twenty-four hours later when the disciples observed the withering of the tree? We have already noted Matthew's custom of telescoping incidents together. But his use of "immediately" does undeniably pose a problem. The best solution may be to treat **withered away** (19-20) as an ingressive aorist, "began to wither away." Even a day after Jesus pronounced the tree's doom the disciples would be surprised to see it withered, and might well use "immediately" in describing the quick change.

Some have found fault with Jesus for destroying the tree. It should be noted that this was not private property; it was "upon the path." Furthermore, Trench makes this sane observa-

---

[57]Abbott-Smith, *op. cit.,* p. 344.

tion: "Man is the prince of creation, and all things are to serve him, and they rightly fulfil their subordinate uses when they do serve him,—in their life or in their death,—yielding unto him fruit, or warning him in a figure what shall be the curse and penalty of unfruitfulness."[58] He adds: "Christ did not attribute moral responsibilities to the tree, when He smote it because of its unfruitfulness, but He did attribute to it a fitness for representing moral qualities."[59] Certainly the loss of one tree, belonging to no one in particular, was well worthwhile in order to teach the disciples a lesson.

What was that lesson? Actually there were two. The first was a vivid warning against hypocrisy—having the leaves of a false profession, but no fruit of God's grace. One specific application of this was to the nation of Israel, professing to be God's children, but denying it by ungodly conduct (cf. John 8:33-47).

The second lesson is spelled out in verses 21 and 22. Jesus solemnly declared (**Verily I say unto you**), **If ye have faith, and doubt not,** you can not only do what I have done, but greater things.[60] Then He gave one of the outstanding prayer promises of the Bible: **And all things, whatsoever ye shall ask in prayer, believing, ye shall receive** (22). This may seem like a senseless *carte blanche.* But there is an all-important condition—**believing.** One cannot really believe for anything contrary to the will of God. Morison has caught the spirit of the passage when he writes: "What you really wish, *if your wish has merged itself in the wish of Christ and of your Father,* you always will get when you present your wishes at the throne of grace."[61]

### 5. *Controversies with Jewish Leaders* (21:23—22:46)

*a. By What Authority?* (21:23-27) This incident is recorded in all three Synoptics (cf. Mark 11:27-33; Luke 20:1-8). When Jesus came into the Temple on Tuesday morning, He was immediately challenged by **the chief priests and the elders of the people** (23). The latter term seems to be a general designation for members of the Great Sanhedrin at Jerusalem. These asked Him: **By what authority doest thou these things? and who gave**

---

[58]R. C. Trench, *Notes on the Miracles of Our Lord* (Philadelphia: Wm. Syckelmoore, 1878), p. 346.

[59]*Ibid.*

[60]For the meaning of removing mountains, see notes on 17:20.

[61]*Op. cit.*, p. 384.

**thee this authority?** By **these things** is meant His cleansing of
the Temple on the previous day, and the miracles He was performing. Taken off guard by the cleansing of the Temple, the
Jewish leaders had not collected their wits at that time. But
overnight they had evidently decided to challenge His right to
do what He did. So they asked: "Who gave You the authority to
upset the established regime in the Temple?"

Very wisely Christ answered by saying that He would ask
them one question. If they answered His question, He would answer theirs (24).

His question hit them like the burst of a shell: **The baptism
of John, whence was it? from heaven, or of men?** (25) Their
reasoning shows no ethical concern whatever. It was not a
matter of what was right, but of what was expedient. Not, What
is true? but, What will this do to us? They were caught on the
horns of a dilemma from which there seemed to be no escape.
They *would* not say it was **from heaven;** and they *could* not, for
fear of the people, say it was **of men.** So they deliberately lied
by saying, **We cannot tell** (27). Justifiably Jesus declined to
answer their question. The answer to both questions is exactly
the same: the source was heaven.

*b. Parable of the Two Sons* (21:28-32). This parable is
found only in Matthew. Jesus started with a good attention-
getter, **But what think ye?** (28) A story about two boys is always
interesting. This one has definite affinities with the parable of the
prodigal son (Luke 15:11-32). Both begin with the same words
(in English): **A certain man had two sons.** But here the word
is literally "children."

To the first the father said: **Son, go work to day in my vineyard.** He refused, but later **repented** (29) and went. This is not
the more common verb *metanoeo* (thirty-four times in NT), but
the less common *metamelomai* (five times). Both are always
translated "repent" (in KJV), and seem to be used rather inter-
changeably. But *metamelomai* could be rendered "regret."

The second child at first agreed to go. But actually he did
not obey his father's command. When Jesus asked which one did
his father's will, the obvious answer was, **The first** (31). Then
Jesus made the application: **The publicans and the harlots go
into the kingdom of God before you** (31). He chided the Jewish
leaders with refusing to believe John the Baptist, and failing to
repent (*metamelomai*) afterward. They claimed to be obeying

196

God, but were not. They were like the boy who said, **I go,** but
**went not.**

In the Greek text of Nestle and of Westcott and Hort the
order of the two sons is reversed (RSV, however, retains the
same order as KJV). Trench thinks the order was changed by
some scribe who thought that the application was to Jews (first)
and Gentiles (second). He says: "But the parable does not
primarily apply to the Jew and Gentile, but must be referred
rather to the two bodies within the bosom of the Jewish people"[62]
—the Pharisees on the one hand, and the **publicans** and **harlots**
on the other.

     *c. Parable of the Wicked Husbandmen* (21:33-46). Of
Trench's list of thirty parables, only three are found in all three
Synoptic Gospels. The two previous ones are the parable of the
sower (13:3-9) and the parable of the mustard seed (13:31-32).
This is the third (cf. Mark 12:1-12; Luke 20:9-19).

     Jesus told about a **householder** (*oikodespotes*) who planted
a **vineyard,** an exceedingly common thing in Palestine. He
**hedged it**—probably with a stone wall—**and digged a winepress
in it** (33). This would be a depression lined with stone or mortar
where the juice would be tramped out of the grapes. Such wine-
presses can be seen today in the Holy Land. To keep watch
over the vineyard, so that no one would steal the ripe grapes, he
built a tower—a raised wooden platform which the rabbis specified should be fifteen feet high and six feet square. Then he
rented the vineyard out to **husbandmen,** or "vine-dressers," and
went abroad.

     **When the time of the fruit drew near** (34)—September of
the fifth year after planting (Lev. 19:23-25)—the owner sent
some servants to collect his share of the crop. The tenants **beat**
one servant, **killed** another, and **stoned** a third (35).

     Finally, in desperation, the owner sent his son, thinking
they would **reverence,** or "respect," him (37). But they killed
him, foolishly thinking they could inherit his estate (38-39). Instead they were destroyed and the vineyard rented to more
worthy tenants (41).

     In verses 40 and 41 Jesus let His enemies pass judgment on
their own conduct and pass sentence for their sin. He then
clinched the truth of the parable by quoting Ps. 118:22-23. **The**

---

[62]*Notes on the Parables,* p. 155.

**stone which the builders rejected** (42)—the verb means *"reject (after scrutiny), declare useless"*[63]—had become **the head of the corner.** This stone refers to either the cornerstone of the building or the keystone of an arch.

Jesus left no room for doubt as to what He meant by the parable. He said that the kingdom of God would be taken away from the Jewish leaders and given to another nation (43, only in Matthew). Whoever fell on **this stone** (Christ) would be **broken** (cf. Isa. 8:14-15), but whoever it fell upon would be ground to **powder** (44). The first figure here seems to refer to someone stumbling over Christ and being "crushed" (literal meaning of rare word), like a water jar of pottery shattered when falling on a rock. The second figure is clearly that of judgment.

The **chief priests and Pharisees** could not fail to see that this parable was spoken against them (45). They were the wicked husbandmen representing the preceding leaders of the nation who had killed the prophets (**servants**). Now they themselves were about to kill the Son. The Kingdom would be given to the Gentiles. Enraged, they wanted to kill Jesus, but they feared the people, who believed Him to be a **prophet** (46).

*d. Parable of the Marriage Feast* (22:1-14). This story has some similarities to the parable of the great supper, which is found only in Luke (14:16-24). These parables are connected mainly by the refusal of the invited guests to come and the orders to the servants to go out into the highways and bring in anybody they could find.

The differences so far outweigh the likenesses that they must be considered as separate stories. In Matthew it is a **king** making a **marriage** feast for his son. In Luke it is a "man" who makes a "great supper." Here it is said that the invited guests **would not come** (3). There they make varied excuses. Here we have **other servants** sent out, urging the guests to come to the elaborate wedding feast, where **oxen** and **fatlings** are **ready** (4). The guests **made light of it** (5). They **went their ways, one to his farm, another to his merchandise.** This has some resemblance to the first two excuses in Luke. But the killing of the servants by the invited guests (6) and the king's destruction of their city (7) are ideas alien to Luke's parable.

The Greek for highways in verses 9 and 10 is interestingly different. In 10 it is the simple *hodous,* "way" or "road." But in

---

[63]Arndt and Gingrich, *op. cit.,* p. 90.

9 it is *diexodous ton hodon. Diexodous* is found only here in the New Testament. Arndt and Gingrich think that phrase probably means "the place where a street cuts *through* the city boundary and goes *out* into the open country."[64]

The meaning of the parable is quite obvious. The Jews were first invited to enjoy the good things of the Kingdom. When they rejected the opportunity, the Gentiles would be brought in.

When the king surveyed his guests, he discovered one who was not wearing **a wedding garment (11)**. Questioned, the man remained **speechless (12)**. The king ordered him to be bound and cast **into outer darkness**—in great contrast to the brightness and happiness of the wedding feast. There, we are told, will be **weeping and gnashing of teeth (13)**. The same expression occurred in 8:12. It is a terrible picture of torment. Again (cf. 20:16) appears the statement: **For many are called, but few are chosen (14)**.

This story teaches two important lessons. The outstanding one is that not all who are called will be saved. **Many are called**—salvation is universal in its provision—**but few are chosen.** That is not because God (the king) rejects men, but because they reject His call. There is no place here for the idea of "effectual calling." One may reject God's call to salvation and be lost.

The other lesson is found in the incident of the man without the wedding garment. Rather obviously, each guest was furnished with one by the king. But one man refused to wear his. He is a type of those who prefer their own righteousness to the righteousness provided by Christ. Such will be cast into outer darkness.

It is clear that the final and determinative qualification for the wedding feast was not the invitation, or even the acceptance, but the wedding garment. For the full import we must associate the parable with Rev. 19:7-9, where the raiment is "fine linen, clean and white: for the fine linen is the righteousness of the saints"; only now the saints are not *guests* merely but comprise the *bride* herself. If it is legitimate to see in the wedding garment of Matthew a foreshadowing of the identification in Revelation, then it must be affirmed that personal righteousness and holiness is the *sine qua non* for participation in the marriage supper of the Lamb.

[64]*Op. cit.*, p. 193.

This is much more than an automatic imputation of righteousness to all who respond to the invitation. It is rather an imparted righteousness which, while provided by the blood of Jesus, must nevertheless be obtained by each guest, voluntarily and individually. If the invitation and the provision of the garment depend on the initiative of the King, the procurement and wearing of the garment depend on the initiative of the guest. While it would be straining the parable to make it directly teach two works of grace, it is not straining to recognize in it the basic requirement of holiness, the means to which include both justification and sanctification.

In his sermon "On the Wedding Garment," John Wesley says that the wedding garment signifies "holiness, without which no man shall see the Lord." He makes these two points: (1) Without the righteousness of Christ we could have no *claim* to glory; (2) Without holiness we could have no *fitness* for it.

*e. Question of the Herodians* (22:15-22). In this chapter three groups of Jewish leaders question Jesus. In each instance He answers them, and then He asks a question which effectually silences His hecklers. All four of these items are recorded in each of the Synoptic Gospels (cf. Mark 12:13-37; Luke 20:20-44). These controversies apparently took place on Tuesday or Wednesday of Passion Week.

The **Pharisees** were the instigators of the first question. They counseled as to how they might **entangle him in his talk** (15)—literally, "in a word," or "in a saying." The verb is used in the Septuagint, but nowhere in classical Greek. It is a hunting term, meaning "set a snare." Arndt and Gingrich translate the clause, "in order that they might entrap him with something that he said."[65] They had a malicious motive.

Josephus describes "three philosophical sects among the Jews": the Pharisees, the Sadducees, and the Essenes[66] (now usually identified with the Qumran community that produced the Dead Sea Scrolls). The Essenes are not named in the New Testament. Strangely, Josephus does not mention the **Herodians**, who are named three times in the Gospels (cf. Mark 3:6; 12:13). Nothing certain is known about them. Their name suggests that

[65]*Op. cit.*, p. 607.

[66]*Ant.* XVIII. 1. 2-5; *War* 8. 2-14. Josephus also writes: "But of the fourth sect of Jewish philosophy Judas the Galilean was the author" (*Ant.* XVIII. 1. 6). This seems like a reference to the Zealots.

they were followers of Herod Antipas, and that is as good a guess as any.[67]

It was a clever ruse which the **Pharisees (15)** employed. They sent to Jesus some of **their disciples with the Herodians (16)**. Ordinarily these two groups were at swords' points, because the Pharisees opposed Roman rule. But now they united in common enmity against Christ.

The flattering approach which these men made was utterly unethical. They tried to throw Jesus off His guard by suggesting that He always told the truth and did not care what anybody thought about Him. They thus hoped to get Him to incriminate himself by an uncautious statement.

Then they set their trap: Should they pay taxes to the emperor, or not? **(17)** The word for **tribute** is *kensos* (Latin, *census*). This was the poll tax, which was particularly offensive to the Jews because it reminded them that they were in subjection to a foreign power.

The inquirers thought they had the Master firmly fixed on the horns of a dilemma, so that He could not possibly escape. If He said, "Yes," the Pharisees would expose Him to the people as a disloyal Jew. If He said, "No," the Herodians would report Him to the Roman government as guilty of sedition. One of the worst offenses that a person could commit, in the eyes of the Romans, was to oppose taxation.

**Jesus perceived** (saw through) **their wickedness, and asked, Why tempt ye me, ye hypocrites? (18)** Carr well observes on verse 16: "Nothing could exceed the insidious hypocrisy of this attack on Jesus."[68]

Christ countered with a request: **Shew me the tribute money (19)**—"the coin of census," which was used in paying the poll tax. In response they brought Him a **penny**. This was a silver denarius, worth about twenty cents.

Jesus asked, **Whose is this image and superscription? (20)** The ready answer was, **Caesar's (21)**. The denarius of that particular time carried on one side the head of the Emperor Tiberius, with the following **inscription** in Latin: "Tiberius Caesar, the son of the deified Augustus, (himself Augustus)."

Then the Master uttered a profound but simple command: **Render therefore unto Caesar the things which are Caesar's;**

[67]So S. Sandmel, "Herodians," IDB, II, 595.
[68]*Op. cit.*, p. 253.

**and unto God the things that are God's.** The verb **render** is literally "give back." If the denarius carried on it Caesar's name and picture, it must be his property. So give back to him what belongs to him. Paul reiterates this principle (Rom. 13:6).

But one should also give back what belongs to God—and what do we have that He has not given us? "The Jewish doctors laid down the principle that 'He is king whose coin passes current.' "[69] The one who refuses or fails to pay his tithe is denying that Jesus Christ is Lord of his life. He is rejecting the kingship of Christ.

But rendering to God what is due is more than paying one's tithe—and even giving additional offerings. Erasmus made this excellent comment: "Give back to God that which has the image and superscription of God—the soul."[70]

Those who had come to question Jesus left Him in utter amazement. He had completely foiled their attempt to trap Him.

f. *Question of the Sadducees* (22:23-33). On the same day there came to Jesus **the Sadducees, which say that there is no resurrection** (23). This description of the Sadducees is corroborated not only in Acts 23:8, but also by Josephus. He writes: "But the doctrine of the Sadducees is this: That souls die with the bodies; nor do they regard the observation of anything besides what the law enjoins them; for they think it an instance of virtue to dispute with those teachers of philosophy whom they frequent: but this doctrine is received but by a few, yet by those still of the greatest dignity."

The Sadducees began their conversation with Jesus by quoting Moses (Deut. 25:5) for the so-called levirate law (from Latin *levir*, "brother-in-law"). Practiced by other Oriental nations, the law was simply this: If a husband died childless, his brother was to marry his widow and **raise up seed unto his brother** (24). Thus any sons born would carry the deceased brother's name.

Then the Sadducees posed a very improbable, hypothetical situation. Seven brothers in succession married the same woman, but all died without having a child (25-26). Finally, **the woman died also** (27). Now, asked the Sadducees, **in the resurrection whose wife shall she be of the seven?** (28) This is typical of the

[69]*Ibid.*

[70]Quoted by A. M. Hunter, *Gospel According to Mark* (London: SCM Press, 1948), p. 117.

kind of question with which little minds like to plague sensible people. Probably this was a stock argument that the Sadducees had often used in disputing with the Pharisees. In the quotation from Josephus above it is noted that these people were fond of carrying on philosophical disputations with their opponents.

Jesus called their hand immediately. He said: **Ye do err, not knowing the scriptures, nor the power of God** (29). The only way that the church, or individuals, can be saved from error today is by knowing both of these. True orthodoxy can be preserved only by a careful, constant study of the Word of God, coupled with an experience of the power and presence of the Holy Spirit.

The Master went on to say that there is no marriage in the next life, but all are **as the angels of God in heaven** (30)[71]; that is, immortal and not reproductive. Then Jesus challenged them with their own Scriptures. It will be noted that Josephus said the Sadducees disregarded "the observation of anything besides what the law enjoins." That is, they accepted only the Pentateuch (Torah), rejecting the Pharisees' use of the rest of the Old Testament. Specifically, they denied the resurrection because they said it was not taught in the Torah. So Jesus met them on their own ground. He quoted Exod. 3:6—the words of the Lord to Moses at the burning bush—and made the application: **God is not the God of the dead, but of the living** (32). If at the time of Moses, God was the God of Abraham, Isaac, and Jacob, and these men had long since died, the clear implication was that they were living in a state of immortality though no longer living on the earth. The relation of this passage to the resurrection is thus expressed by Bengel: "God . . . is not the God of that which is not: He is the living God; they therefore who possess God must themselves also be living, and as to any portion of them in which life has been suspended, must revive forever."[72]

The effect of Christ's words on the crowd is vividly described (33). The people were **astonished at his doctrine** (Greek, "teaching"). The verb literally means "to strike out," and so in the passive "to be struck with astonishment."[73] Furthermore, it is in the imperfect tense. Carr explains the force of this. He says:

[71]Luke (20:35-38) gives this a bit more fully, in line with Paul's teaching in Phil. 3:11 and Rom. 14:8.

[72]*Op. cit.,* I, 398.

[73]Thayer, *op. cit.,* p. 199.

"The imperfect well expresses the thrill of amazement passing through the crowd from one to another."[74]

g. *Question of the Pharisees* (22:34-40). When the Pharisees heard that Jesus had effectually silenced—the Greek says "muzzled," "gagged"—their opponents, the Sadducees, they were doubtless delighted. But they decided they would try their hand again (cf. 15).

One of their number, **a lawyer**—that is, a teacher of the Mosaic law—asked Christ a question, **tempting him** (35). Once more we have the problem as to how we should translate *peirazon*, whether "trying" (ASV), "to test" (RSV, cf. NEB), or "tempting" (KJV). The fundamental meaning of the verb is "try, make trial of, put to the test."[75] If a malicious motive is suggested by the context, the word may be translated "tempt." One might assume that such was the case here, were it not for Mark's parallel account. He says of this questioning "scribe" (teacher of the Law), "he had answered them well," and pictures a mutual appreciation between Jesus and the lawyer. So probably "testing" would be the best translation here.

The scribe asked: **Master** (Greek, "Teacher"), **which is the great commandment in the law?** (36) **Which** is literally "what kind." Plummer suggests that this lawyer wanted "a canon of classification." He says: "The Rabbis divided the 613 precepts of the Law (248 commands and 365 prohibitions) into 'weighty' and 'light,' but the sorting of them caused much debate."[76]

In answer Jesus quoted Deut. 6:5—**Thou shalt love the Lord thy God with all thy heart, and with all thy soul, and with all thy mind** (37). Mark and Luke add, "with all thy strength." Actually, the Hebrew of the Old Testament passage reads "heart," "soul," and "might." The Septuagint has "heart," "soul," and "power" (*dynamis*), with some manuscripts giving "mind" (*dianoia*). It appears that Jesus combined all four of these. Carr explains the three terms in Matthew thus: "*Kardia* includes the emotions, will, purpose; *psyche*, the spiritual faculties; *dianoia* the intellect, the thinking faculty."[77] But it is impossible to distinguish these words accurately and fully. For instance, for *psyche* Arndt and Gingrich give, with supporting scriptures, the

[74]*Op. cit.*, p. 255.

[75]Arndt and Gingrich, *op. cit.*, p. 646.

[76]*Gospel According to Mark*, p. 283.

[77]*Op. cit.*, pp. 255-56.

following meanings (among others): *"life, life-principle"; "earthly life"; "the soul* as seat and center of the inner life of man in its many and varied aspects"; *"the soul* as seat and center of life that transcends the earthly."[78] They observe: "It is often impossible to draw hard and fast lines between the meanings of this many-sided word."[79] The same could be said for *kardia* (heart).

But the clear meaning is that one is to love the Lord with all his being. The Greek word for **love,** *agapao,* means far more than affection or emotion (expressed by *phileo*). Cremer says of *agapao:* "It does not in itself exclude affection, but it is always the moral affection of conscious deliberate will which is contained in it, not the natural impulse of immediate feeling."[80]

After identifying Deut. 6:5 as the **first and great commandment** (38), Jesus went on to give the **second,** which is: **Thou shalt love thy neighbour as thyself** (39). This is quoted from Lev. 19:18. The verb again is *agapao.* Abbott-Smith says of it: *"Agapao* is fitly used in the New Testament of Christian love to God and man, the spiritual affection which follows the direction of the will, and which, therefore, unlike that feeling which is instinctive and unreasoned, can be commanded as a duty."[81]

Jesus added (only in Matthew): **On these two commandments hang all the law and the prophets** (40)—that is, the entire Old Testament. These are the two key commandments, which unlock the meaning of all the rest.

Since the gist of the entire Old Testament is in these commandments, it is obvious that holiness as a standard for God's people is not unique to the gospel dispensation. That which is special to the new covenant is the *means* by which men are to meet the standard, and the *measure,* or degree of perfection, with which they may meet it. Power for inner fulfillment now becomes the heritage of every child of God. It is a power which so alters the affections and fills the self with the Holy Spirit that loving God with all the being is a natural and spontaneous attitude (Rom. 5:5). When God promises that in the new covenant He will put His "laws into their mind, and write them in their hearts" (Heb. 8:10; Jer. 31:33), He means these two laws above all, for they include all.

78*Op. cit.,* pp. 901-2.
79*Ibid.,* p. 901.
80Hermann Cremer, *Biblico-Theological Lexicon of New Testament Greek,* trans. William Urwick (Edinburgh: T. & T. Clark, 1878), p. 11.
81*Op. cit.,* p. 3.

*h. Question of Jesus* (22:41-46). The Pharisees had been questioning Christ, and He had answered them effectively. Now He asks them a question which they cannot answer.

Taking advantage of the fact that He had a considerable group of Pharisees before Him (41), Jesus asked first: **What think ye of Christ,** the Messiah? **whose son is he?** They answered, **The son of David** (42). This was the popular conception of that time,[82] based on such scriptures as Ps. 89:20-37; Isa. 9:2-7; 11:1-9; Jer. 23:5-6; 33:14-18; Ezek. 34:23-24; 37:24.

**How then,** asked Jesus, **doth David in spirit call him Lord?** (43) **In spirit** means "inspired by the Spirit" (RSV); that is, the Holy Spirit. Thus did Jesus, at one and the same time, assert the Davidic authorship of Psalms 110 and its divine inspiration. Then He quoted the first verse of this Messianic psalm.[83] **The Lord said unto my Lord** (44) is in the Hebrew "Jehovah [or Yahweh] said to my Adonai." In the Old Testament (KJV) usually Lord is the translation of *Yahweh* and Lord of *Adonai.* In the Greek *kyrios* is used for both.

The Jews could not, or would not, answer the pointed question: **If David then call him Lord, how is he his son?** (45) The Christian answer is that David's Lord became David's son in the Incarnation.

Verse 46 indicates that Jesus had effectually silenced all His opponents. No one after that momentous day dared to ask Him any more questions.

6. *Denunciations of the Pharisees* (23:1-36)

*a. Position and Pride* (23:1-12). Jesus addressed himself **to the multitudes, and to his disciples** (1). The Pharisees had revealed the wickedness of their hearts in their efforts to trap Him. Now He who "knew what was in man" (John 2:25) portrayed the inner sins of these religious leaders.

The position **the scribes and the Pharisees** (2) had was that of sitting in Moses' **seat** (*kathedra*). Therefore they spoke *ex cathedra*—with official authority—and so their words were to be obeyed (3). But their **works** were not to be imitated, for they said one thing and did another. Obviously the injunction to do what the scribes said is to be taken in a modified sense, since

---

[82]See notes on 9:27; 15:22; 20:30.

[83]It is quoted five other times in the New Testament (Acts 2:34; Heb. 1:13; 5:6; 7:17, 21).

elsewhere the Master condemns them for annulling the Word of God by teaching the tradition of the elders (15:1-6). Morison suggests the true meaning here, as follows: "Whatsoever things the scribes and Pharisees inculcate upon you, when they translate to you the words of the Book of God, and whatsoever things they prove, in their teachings, to be agreeable to the mind of God, as made known in His Book, all these things do."[84]

The heartlessness of these teachers of the Law is denounced by Jesus: **they bind heavy burdens and grievous to be borne, and lay them on men's shoulders; but they themselves will not move them with one of their fingers** (4). Carr has caught the figure in these words: "The picture is of the merciless camel- or ass-driver, who makes up . . . burdens, not only heavy but unwieldy and so difficult to carry, and then placing them on the animal's shoulders, stands by indifferent, raising no finger to lighten or even adjust the burden."[85] This is in startling contrast to the gracious invitation of the Master in 11:28-30. Legalistic religion is always a heavy burden to be borne. There is no joy in it.

Ostentatious pride was one of the besetting sins of the Pharisees. Jesus accused them of doing their good works **to be seen of men** (5). Of course, not all Pharisees were like that, but too many were. In keeping with this outward display of piety they wore large **phylacteries.** This is a Greek word found only here in the New Testament. It was taken over into English by way of the Geneva Bible. In classical Greek it meant an "outpost" or "fortification." Plutarch uses it for an "amulet"; that is, a protecting charm. The word comes from the verb meaning "guard." But here it refers to small leather prayer cases worn on the forehead and left arm at the daily morning prayers. The one for the head had four little compartments, in each of which was a tiny scroll bearing a portion of scripture. The four passages were: Exod. 13:1-10, 11-16; Deut. 6:4-9; 11:13-21. The phylactery worn on the arm had only one compartment, with the scriptures on one roll. The commands to bind the words of scripture "for a sign upon your hand" and "as frontlets between your eyes" were taken literally, when they were probably meant to be figurative.

Jesus also said that the Pharisees **enlarge the borders of their garments.** The Law enjoined pious Israelites to make fringes on their garments, with "a ribband of blue" (Num. 15:38). The

[84]*Op. cit.,* p. 424.
[85]*Op. cit.,* p. 4.

Jews therefore fastened tassels of blue to the corners of their robes. But Christ declared that the scribes did this for public display, not for reasons of personal piety.

Their selfish pride also asserted itself in the way they sought the **uppermost rooms at feasts** (6). These were literally "first couches"—those on which they reclined around the table while eating (except in the poorer homes). **Chief seats** is also a rare compound. M'Neile says: "The chief seats were on the platform facing the congregation, with their backs to the chest in which the rolls of Scripture were kept."[86]

Jesus went on to say that the scribes loved **greetings in the markets** (Agora) and to be called **Rabbi** (7).[87] This was "the usual form of address with which the learned were greeted."[88] It means "my master" (the final *i* representing "my" in Hebrew). Dalman says that "by general consent 'Rabbi' is reckoned to be higher than 'Rab,' and 'Rabban' higher than 'Rabbi.' "[89]

But the disciples were not to be **called Rabbi** (8). This command should be taken "in the spirit, and not in the letter" (Rom. 2:29), "for the letter killeth, but the spirit giveth life" (II Cor. 3:6). Jesus is not giving precise regulations about the use of such technical titles as "Doctor" and "Reverend." Rather He is speaking against the spirit of pride that makes men crave honor from others. The proper attitude is to recognize that only one is **Master**—the best Greek has "teacher"[90]—**even Christ; and all ye are brethren.** It is always proper to call a fellow Christian man "brother" (cf. Acts 9:17).

Jesus also warned against calling anyone on earth **your father,** because **one is your Father, which is in heaven** (9). Schurer says: "The Rabbis required from their pupils the most absolute reverence, surpassing even the honour felt for parents."[91] He quotes a considerable number of very strong statements from the Jewish rabbis to support this assertion. That attitude was exactly what Christ was condemning.

[86]M'Neile, *op. cit.,* p. 331.

[87]The second "Rabbi" in this verse is not in the oldest manuscripts.

[88]Dalman, *Words of Jesus,* p. 331.

[89]*Ibid.,* p. 332.

[90]The earliest use of the English word "doctor" was not for a physician, but for a teacher (*Oxford English Dictionary,* III, 570).

[91]Emil Schurer, *A History of the Jewish People in the Time of Jesus Christ,* Eng. trans. (Edinburgh: T. & T. Clark, 1885), II. i. 317.

Neither, said Jesus, are you to be called **masters,** because **one is your Master, even Christ** (10). The word for **master** is *kathegetes.* The term is found only here in the New Testament. It comes from a verb meaning "go before, guide." So its proper meaning is "guide." But it came to be used for "teacher" and in modern Greek signifies "professor." **One is your Master** emphasizes Jesus' unique authority as the Son of God.

Then Jesus laid down the general principle (already enunciated in 20:26): **he that is greatest among you shall be your servant** (11). The last word is *diakonos,* the origin of which is unknown. But it was used in classical Greek for such persons as waiters on table. That is the idea it conveys here. This paragraph concludes with the warning that whoever exalts himself will be **abased** ("humbled"), but whoever will **humble** (same Greek word) himself will be exalted (12).

b. *Woes upon Hypocrites* (23:13-36). In this section there are seven[92] woes pronounced upon the scribes and Pharisees for their hypocrisy. Each one begins with the formula, **Woe unto you, scribes and Pharisees, hypocrites** (13, 15, 23, 25, 27, 29), except verse 16, which has **Woe unto you, ye blind guides.** Counting verse 13 as 14, M'Neile gives the following summary: "Three woes (vv. 14-22) deal with the teaching of the Scribes, three (vv. 23-28) with the life of the Pharisees, and the last (vv. 29-32) is directed against the nation as a whole."[93]

**Woe unto you** may be translated "Alas for you!" Thayer says that *ouai* is "an interjection of grief or of denunciation."[94] It would seem best to treat the term here as expressing both ideas. The compassion of Christ made Him grieve over the selfishness of the scribes and Pharisees. His holiness compelled Him to denounce their sins and pronounce their sentence.

**Hypocrites** is an exact transliteration of the Greek *hypocrites* (singular). The term is used in classical Greek for an actor, or player on the stage. In those days when there were no electronic means of amplification it was difficult for actors on the stage to be heard by an audience of 25,000 or more in an amphitheater. So they wore masks with small megaphones hidden in them. Thus

---

[92]The King James Version has eight. Though verse 14 is omitted in the Revised Versions on the evidence of the early manuscripts, the content is genuine in Mark 12:40 and Luke 20:47. See notes there.

[93]*Op. cit.,* p. 332.

[94]*Op. cit.,* p. 461.

a hypocrite is literally one who wears a mask, or who shows a false face to the public.

(1) *Perversity* (23:13). This is a terrible charge that Jesus brings against the Jewish leaders. He accuses them of shutting up the kingdom of Heaven against men by rejecting Him in whom the Kingdom was embodied, neither entering themselves nor letting others do so. This is the most severe denunciation of all, and so Luke places it at the end of his list as the climax (Luke 11:52). On the order here M'Neile comments: "In Mt. its position produces a sharp contrast between the deterrent effect of the Scribes' teaching and their efforts at proselytizing (v. 15), and also between 'the Kingdom of Heaven' and 'Gehenna.' "[95] John the Baptist had opened the door of repentance into the Kingdom. The scribes had slammed it shut. For comment on verse 14 see treatment of Mark 13:40 and Luke 20:47.

(2) *Proselytizing* (23:15). The typical zeal of the Jews is vividly portrayed by Jesus when He said that they compassed sea and land to **make one proselyte.** This is illustrated by what took place in Rome, where Jews lived as early as the second century b.c. Pope writes: "From the first the Jews in Rome exhibited such an aggressive spirit of proselytism that they were charged with seeking to infect the Romans with their cult, and the government expelled the chief propagandists from the city in 139 B.C."[96] Pope also says that the latter part of this verse, **ye make him twofold more the child of hell,** ". . . has reference to the Pharisaic obsession with ritual purity, which they impressed with double force on the proselyte."[97]

(3) *Swearing* (23:16-22). The ridiculous casuistry of much rabbinical reasoning is vividly illustrated here. These **blind guides** taught that to swear by the Temple meant nothing, but to **swear** by the gold of the Temple made the oath binding. There seems to be no explanation available as to why this kind of religious thinking developed among the Pharisees. Jesus riddled such nonsense with simple logic. The only thing that makes the gold sacred is the fact that it is attached to the Temple (17). The same goes for the gift on the altar (18-19). Christ clearly warned against taking careless oaths (20-22).

[95]*Op. cit.*, p. 333.
[96]M. H. Pope, "Proselyte," IDB, III, 925.
[97]*Ibid.*, p. 930.

(4) *Tithing* (23:23-24). The Pharisees were very scrupulous about paying a tithe of their **mint and anise** (or "dill") **and cummin** (23) (small herbs). The Israelites were commanded in the Law to tithe their crops—"all the increase of thy seed"—and specifically grain, wine, and oil (Deut. 14:22-23). "The rabbis, in building a fence about the law, included vegetables, fruits, and nuts in the command."[98]

In their scrupulous attention to the minute details of tithing, the scribes and Pharisees had **omitted** ("neglected") **the weightier matters of the law.** This seems to reflect the rabbinical distinction between "heavy" and "light" commandments.[99] The Jewish Talmud makes this statement: "Observance of the lesser precepts is rewarded on earth; observance of the greater precepts is rewarded in heaven."[100] The **weightier** things of the Law are **judgment** ("justice"), **mercy, and faith** (or "faithfulness"). Jesus said that they ought to have done **these** (the latter) and not to have "neglected" (same verb as **omitted** above) **the other** —the payment of various tithes.

**Strain at a gnat** (24) suggests the mental picture of a man straining to catch a gnat out of the air. This is completely foreign to what the Greek says. The correct translation is "strain out," as Tyndale had in the first printed English New Testament (1525). Since the King James Version is the only English translation known that has **strain at,** it is commonly thought that this must represent a typographical error. Goodspeed, for instance, says: "This is an admitted misprint in the King James Version, which for some reason has never been corrected."[101]

The true picture is that of a rigid Pharisee carefully straining his drinking water through a cloth strainer, to make sure that he does not accidentally swallow a gnat, the smallest unclean animal. While engaged in this meticulous task, lo and behold, he swallows a whole camel—one of the largest of the unclean animals. As in the reference to a camel going through the eye of a needle (19:24), Jesus was purposely using a figure of speech to shock His hearers into getting the point. Rigid legalists today often

[98]IB, VII, 535.
[99]*Ibid.*, p. 536.
[100]Carr, *op. cit.*, p. 261.
[101]Edgar J. Goodspeed, *Problems of New Testament Translation* (Chicago: University of Chicago Press, 1945), p. 38.

furnish examples of the pharisaic attitude that Jesus was talking about.

From this chapter Richard Glover points out the dangers of hypocrisy. (1) Hypocrisy is a hard taskmaster, 4; (2) Hypocrisy lives only for the praise of man, 5-7; (3) The mischief of hypocrisy 13-22; (4) Hypocrisy concerns itself with the small things of religion, 23-24.

(5) *Cleansing* (23:25-26). Jesus said that the Pharisees cleansed the outside of the **cup** and **platter** ("dish"),[102] but inside they were full of **extortion**—"plundering, robbery"—and **excess** ("incontinence," or "self-indulgence") (25). He commanded the **blind Pharisee** (26) to cleanse first the inside of the cup and dish. The meaning is as follows: "The outside of the cup and platter is the external behaviour and conduct of the Pharisee, the inside of the cup is his heart and real life."[103] These two concerns sum up graphically the basic difference between the Judaism of that time and Christianity.

(6) *Whited sepulchres* (23:27-28). The explanation of what Jesus was saying is thus given by M'Neile: "To walk over a grave caused pollution, which must be avoided by anyone who wished to enter the temple (cf. Num. xix. 16); hence the custom . . . of chalking graves with white marks on the 15th Adar [March-April] before the Passover."[104] Jesus was pleading for something better than whitewashed Christianity, nice-appearing on the surface but full of sinful attitudes.

The chief indictment is the lack of inward sincerity. Their righteousness was entirely on the surface; therefore it was a sham. It was further condemned for its exaggerated piety in comparative trifles as a facade for the neglect of the primary principles, judgment, mercy, and faith. If we are to escape the same scathing condemnation, our ethics must be thoroughly sound and our hearts must be genuinely holy. We must be beautiful *within*, first and always, in God's sight, even if we do not always achieve perfect beauty of conduct without. Such holiness requires a sanctifying Saviour and an indwelling Holy Spirit.

(7) *Worshiping the past* (23:29-36). There are three stages in the life of every religious organization. First it is a movement,

---

[102]The word occurs (in NT) only in these two verses.
[103]Carr, *op. cit.*, p. 261.
[104]*Op. cit.*, p. 337.

vibrant and vigorous, active and aggressive. Then it becomes an institution with "more harness than horse." Finally its vitality disappears and it becomes a museum, where the bones of the ancient leaders are put on display. Judaism had reached this third stage. Ironically, but sadly, Jesus bade the scribes: **Fill ye up then the measure of your fathers** (32); that is, complete the persecutions they began. They were admitting that they were the **children** (descendants) of those who **killed the prophets** (31). The words of verse 33 sound strange on the lips of Christ. But those He addressed were already plotting to kill the sinless Saviour of mankind. The Book of Acts (e.g., 7:58; 8:1-3; 9:1-2) relates the fulfillment of the predictions of verse 34.

**Abel** (35) was the first man to be murdered. The case of Zacharias[105] is recorded in the book that comes at the close of the Old Testament in the Hebrew Bible (Chronicles). So the expression here is somewhat like the current phrase "from Genesis to Revelation."

Verse 35 suggests national participation in the guilt of previous generations. This generation had committed the climactic sin of rejecting Jesus Christ. In a sense the accumulated guilt of previous generations in persecuting the prophets was therefore to fall on this one.

The words of verse 36 were fulfilled with horrible literalness in A.D. 70, when Jerusalem was taken by the Romans and its Temple destroyed.

### 7. *Lament over Jerusalem* (23:37-39)

The pathos of these words defies description. Jesus had offered himself to the Jews as their King and Messiah. The leaders had rejected Him and soon would condemn Him to die. **And ye would not** (37) are the words written as the epitaph of the centuries. Christ declared that the Jews would not see Him until they welcomed Him at His second coming with the acclamation which the Galilean pilgrims had given Him in the Triumphal Entry (39; cf. 21:9).

---

[105]In II Chron. 24:20-22 his father's name is given as Jehoiada, not Barachias. This difference has not yet been solved. But "son" sometimes means "grandson"; also men in Bible times occasionally had two names.

## A. THE END OF THE AGE, 24:1-51

The Olivet Discourse, so called because given on the Mount of Olives, is the only long discourse recorded in all three Synoptic Gospels (cf. Mark 13:1-37; Luke 21:5-36). It is significant that it should deal with the Second Coming and the end of the age. In place of this John's Gospel has the last discourse of Jesus in the Upper Room. The subject of that is the Holy Spirit, who makes the presence of Christ real to us today.

There has been a great deal of discussion and disagreement about the interpretation of this twenty-fourth chapter. Some would refer it all to the destruction of Jerusalem in A.D. 70. Others think it relates entirely to the end of the age. Probably both views are wrong. There seems to be considerable overlapping of material, and some predictions can apparently be applied to both periods. Chrysostom and some other Fathers of the Early Church held that everything down through verse 22 related to the fall of Jerusalem.[1] This is more satisfactory than to apply the entire chapter either to the fall of Jerusalem or to the end of the age. However so sharp a division is probably too exact.

### 1. *Questions of the Disciples* (24:1-3)

For the last time, as far as the record shows, Jesus **departed from the temple** (1). He had been rejected there by the leaders of the Jewish nation. Now their house was to be left to them desolate, and soon destroyed.

The disciples were eager to show Him **the buildings of the temple.** Josephus indicates that the sanctuary itself was 150 feet long and 150 feet high.[2] Herod the Great rebuilt the Temple of 516 B.C., beginning in the eighteenth year of his reign (20/19 B.C.). He wished to make it as great and glorious as was Solomon's magnificent edifice. Work was still in progress on this project during Jesus' ministry (John 2:20), and it is thought that it may not have been entirely finished when it was destroyed in A.D. 70.[3]

[1]Carr, *op. cit.*, p. 265.
[2]*Ant.* XV. 11. 3.
[3]W. F. Stinespring, "Temple, Jerusalem," IDB, IV, 550.

To the shocked surprise of the disciples, their Master informed them: **There shall not be left here one stone upon another, that shall not be thrown down** (2). The literal fulfillment of this prediction in A.D. 70 is corroborated by Josephus, who was an eyewitness. The Temple area was just inside the east wall of Jerusalem, and he says that all except the west wall of the city "was so thoroughly laid even with the ground by those that dug it up to the foundation, that there was left nothing to make those that came thither believe it had ever been inhabited."[4]

While Jesus was seated on the slopes of the Mount of Olives, which overlooks the Temple area, the disciples asked Him a threefold question: **when shall these things be? and what shall be the sign of thy coming, and of the end of the world?** (3) This is much more specific than are the parallel passages in Mark and Luke. But it is difficult to separate the answers to these questions. They definitely do not appear to be answered in order.

The last word of the disciples' question, **world,** is literally "age" (*aion*). **Coming** is *parousia,* "presence" (literally "being beside"). It is translated "presence" in II Cor. 10:10 and Phil. 2:12, where the literal meaning applies. It is also used of "the coming of Stephanas" (I Cor. 16:17), the coming of Titus (II Cor. 7:6-7), and the coming of Paul (Phil. 1:26). Throughout the rest of the New Testament it is employed for the second coming of Christ (eighteen times). Four of the instances are in this chapter (3, 27, 37, 39). It is not found in the other three Gospels, in Acts, or in Revelation. Deissmann writes of it: "From the Ptolemaic period down into the 2nd century A.D. we are able to trace the word in the East as a technical expression for the arrival or the visit of the king or the emperor."[5] Arndt and Gingrich say that it is used "of Christ, and nearly always of his Messianic Advent in glory to judge the world at the end of this age."[6]

### 2. *Signs of the End* (24:4-14)

Jesus seems to answer the disciples' last question first. In this section there are given no less than ten signs of the end of the age. The first is the appearance of false messiahs (5): **many will come saying, I am Christ** (i.e., "the Messiah").

The second sign is the report of **wars and rumours of wars** (6). These have plagued just about every generation. But they

---

[4]*War* VII. 1. 1.
[5]LAE, p. 368.
[6]*Op. cit.,* p. 635.

will increase toward the close of the age. Jesus said, **the end is not yet;** that is, the end is approaching, but not here.

The third sign is **famines,** the fourth **pestilences**—these two often go together—and the fifth **earthquakes** (7). **All these,** said Jesus, **are the beginning of sorrows** (8). The last word literally means "birth-pangs" (cf. I Thess. 5:3, where it is translated "travail," coming "upon a woman with child"). The troubles enumerated here will be characteristic of the period preceding the Messianic age in its final manifestation in the millennium.

The sixth sign is persecution. The followers of Christ will be delivered up **to be afflicted** (9)—literally, "unto tribulation." The noun *thlipsis* comes from the verb *thlibo*, "press." Aristotle uses it in the literal sense of "pressure." In the Septuagint and the New Testament it is used metaphorically for "tribulation." This is from the Latin *tribulum*, a "flail" used for beating grain or beans out of husks or pods. The Greek verb was used to describe pressing wine out of grapes. These two ideas convey the sense of what "tribulation" or "affliction" is.[7] The term vividly describes the pressure of constant persecution.

The seventh sign, closely connected, is that many, being **offended** (*skandalizo*), will **betray one another,** and **hate one another** (10). The eighth sign is the appearance of **false prophets,** who will **deceive many** (11). One cannot forbear mentioning the multiplicity of false cults in recent years. The ninth sign (only in Matthew) is lack of love: **because iniquity** (literally "lawlessness") **shall abound, the love of many shall wax cold** (12). The last verb is found only here in the New Testament. It is a solemn warning, and a very pertinent one in these lawless times.

It is interesting to note the noun *agape* **(love)** occurs only here in Matthew, not at all in Mark, and once in Luke (11:42), though the verb *agapao* is found numerous times in all three. The heavy use of *agape* is in the Epistles.

To the persecuted a promise is given: **But he that shall endure unto the end, the same shall be saved** (13). Mark (13:13b) has exactly the same words. Luke (21:19) says: "In your patience possess ye your souls." But the noun "patience" is from the same root as **endure** here. Furthermore, "possess" means "gain" or "acquire." So the form of the saying in Luke has the same meaning as that in Mark and Matthew.

---

[7]The noun is translated (KJV) "tribulation" twenty-one times and "affliction" seventeen times out of a total forty-five occurrences in the NT.

The tenth sign (only in Matthew) is the evangelization of the world (14). This **gospel of the kingdom**—same as "the gospel of Jesus Christ" (Mark 1:1)—**shall be preached** ("heralded, proclaimed") **in all the world** (*oikoumene*, "inhabited earth") **for a witness unto all nations; and then shall the end come.** The word *oikoumene* was used first for the Greek world (as by Demosthenes), later for the Roman Empire, and finally for the whole world. Since probably all **nations,** in the general sense of that term, have heard the gospel in a measure—and radio is speeding that process very rapidly these days—it would seem that no one should deny the possibility of this sign having already been fulfilled. The end of the age could come at any time.

### 3. *The Abomination of Desolation* (24:15-22)

This expression means "the abomination that maketh desolate" (cf. Dan. 11:31; 12:11). Arndt and Gingrich define it as "the detestable thing causing the desolation of the holy place.."[8]

It is identified as **spoken of by Daniel the prophet** (15). Found three times in Daniel (9:27; 11:31; 12:11), it also occurs in I Macc. 1:54—where it apparently is used for the altar of Zeus erected on the sacred altar in the Temple in 168 B.C. Daniel seems to refer to the same thing. Here it has a dual reference: to A.D. 70 and to the end of the age.

The phrase is found elsewhere in the New Testament only in the parallel passage in Mark (13:14). For this cryptic, apocalyptic expression Luke (21:20) has substituted a plain statement for his Gentile readers—"when ye shall see Jerusalem compassed with armies." The **abomination** might then be the Roman eagles on the standards of the besieging soldiers. The margin of Dan. 9:27 reads, "Upon the battlements shall be the idols of the desolator." The Zealots' massacre of their fellow Jews during the siege may also be another application, as they desecrated the Temple. Since all three Gospels go on to urge flight to the mountains, it would seem that they all refer to the same event. But that does not rule out an application also to the setting up of an image of the Antichrist in Jerusalem at the end of this age (Rev. 13:14).

Eusebius tells how the order for those in **Judaea to flee into the mountains** (16) was literally carried out. He writes: "The whole body, however, of the church at Jerusalem, having been

---

[8]*Op. cit.*, p. 137.

commanded by a divine revelation, given to men of approved piety there before the war, removed from the city, and dwelt at a certain town beyond the Jordan, called Pella."[9] A. B. Bruce thinks this flight must have taken place before the siege began.[10] But it may be that conditions were relaxed temporarily when Vespasian was called to Rome as emperor in A.D. 69 and his son Titus succeeded him as commander of the Roman army around Jerusalem.

So urgent was the flight to be that a man who was on a flat **housetop** was not to descend into the house for anything, but to flee down the outside stairway (17). The one in the field was not to turn back for his coat (18). Sudden flight would be especially hard for those who were expecting or who had small babies (19). In **winter** it would be very cold at night, and the Jordan River—which they must ford—would be swollen by winter rain (20). For his Jewish readers Matthew adds what would be meaningless in Mark: **neither on the sabbath day.** Strict Jews would not travel more than half a mile on the Sabbath, and thus they might be caught by the enemy.

Jesus predicted that at that time there would be **great tribulation, such as was not since the beginning of the world to this time, no, nor ever shall be** (21). Mark has almost the same words. **Tribulation** is *thlipsis* (see comment on v. 9). Swete suggests: "*Thlipsis* is here used almost in its literal sense for the daily tightening of the meshes of the siege."[11] It has been objected often that the words of this verse are too strong to be applied to A.D. 70. But Josephus writes: "It appears to me that the misfortunes of all men, from the beginning of the world, if they be compared to those of the Jews, are not so considerable as they were."[12] Carr summarizes the situation thus:

> No words can describe the unequalled horrors of this siege. It was the Passover season, and Jews from all parts were crowded within the walls. Three factions, at desperate feud with each other, were posted on the heights of Sion and the Temple Mount . . . The Temple-courts swam with the blood of civil discord, which was literally mingled with the blood of the sacrifices.[13]

[9]Eusebius *Ecclesiastical History,* trans. C. F. Cruse (Grand Rapids: Baker Book House, 1955), III, 5.
[10]EGT, I, 292.
[11]H. B. Swete, *The Gospel According to St. Mark* (London: Macmillan and Co., 1898), p. 289.
[12]*War,* Preface, 4.
[13]*Op. cit.,* p. 269.

Josephus claimed that over a million Jews perished in this catastrophe, and that nearly 100,000 were sold as slaves.[14] It seems that the best way to interpret verse 21 is to allow the double application—to the fall of Jerusalem in A.D. 70 and also to "The Great Tribulation" at the end of this age.

The shortening of **those days** (22) applies to the final siege of Jerusalem, which surprisingly lasted for less than five months (April to September, A.D. 70). This was **for the elect's sake**—lest all the Christian Jews of Judea be wiped out in a war of Jewish extermination. Or the phrase **for the elect's sake** could mean for the sake of the prayers of the Christians in Pella, prayers for the Jews they had left behind.

Morison gives half a dozen factors in the shortening of the siege. Vespasian's attention was turned more and more toward Rome, where he was soon to become emperor. Revolts on the northern border of the empire required attention. Titus, who was left in charge when Vespasian went to Rome, was naturally generous. Josephus was a favorite of his, as was Agrippa's sister Bernice (cf. Acts 25:23). Titus was eager to get to Rome to share in the inaugural ceremonies of his father. Also divine judgment came on the disobedient Jews through the appearance of mutually murderous factions in the city. This brought the siege to a close more quickly.

4. *The Coming of the Son of Man* (24:23-28)

Again the prediction is made that there would be **false Christs** (messiahs) and **false prophets** (24), who would seek by **great signs and wonders** (cf. Deut. 13:1-3) to **deceive the very elect.** Carr suggests that the latter part of the verse should be translated: "with the view of deceiving if possible (*ei dynaton*), i.e. by every possible means, even the elect."[15] But Christ forewarned His disciples (25) that they were not to follow any false leaders who trumped up a following **in the desert** or hid away in **secret chambers** (26). The work of God is honest, and can be done where all may see it.

The Parousia of the Son of Man will come suddenly without warning, like lightning (27). But the language here also implies that it will be visible, as lightning is, from one horizon to the other. The figure clearly implies a worldwide awareness of the second coming of Christ.

[14]*War* VI. 9. 3.
[15]*Op. cit.*, p. 270.

**For wheresoever the carcase is, there will the eagles be gathered together** (28) is a statement that has puzzled interpreters from the early days of the Church. Because of the complexity of the situation we can only summarize several views, without giving documentation. Chrysostom held that the eagles were "angels, martyrs, and saints." Jerome agreed, but explained **carcase** as referring to the death of Christ. Calvin spoke of believers flocking together "to the Author of life, by whom alone they are truly fed." Erasmus, Zwingli, and Beza held much the same view. Trapp represents the Puritans when he seemingly endorses the following rather crude view: "The sacrificial body of Christ hath a most fragrant smell, inviting the saints (like birds of prey) to fly from far with marvellous swiftness to this dead but all-quickening carcase."[16]

On the other hand, Adam Clarke followed Whitby in interpreting the **carcase** as referring to the Jews and the **eagles** as the Roman armies, with the eagle as ensign. John Wesley says that the Jewish nation "is already before God a dead carcass, which the Roman eagles will devour."[17]

It is difficult to fit this verse into its immediate context. But the general emphasis of the chapter is on divine judgment, and it seems best to interpret this particular passage—perhaps a current proverb[18]—in terms of that larger contextual setting. Lange says: "The figure gives a profound and strong expression of the necessity, inevitableness, and universality of judgment."[19] He then gives the following comprehensive and convincing interpretation, based on sound exegesis:

> In the destruction of Jerusalem, the judgment will begin by the appearance of the great carrion eagles (there is included a manifest allusion to the Roman eagles). From that time it will go on through the whole new period. . . . At last the judgment will extend to the whole morally corrupt and spiritually dead world.[20]

### 5. The Sign of the Son of Man (24:29-31)

Matthew alone has the disciples asking, "What shall be the sign of thy coming?" (3), and so he is the only one who furnishes

---

[16]John Trapp, *Commentary on the New Testament* (Grand Rapids: Zondervan Publishing House, 1958 [reprint]), p. 249.

[17]*Explanatory Notes*, p. 115.

[18]So M'Neile, *op. cit.*, p. 351.

[19]*Op. cit.*, p. 426.

[20]*Ibid.*, p. 427.

a direct answer here. Verse 29 is reminiscent of Joel 2:31; 3:15. The language is definitely apocalyptic and very vivid. But in this age of atomic power there could take place a greater natural, physical fulfillment than anyone has yet envisioned.

What is intended by **the sign of the Son of man** (30)? No categorical answer can be given. It may mean some visible sign before the Second Coming. Or it could refer to "the Son of Man is Himself the sign,—the sign that the consummation of the age has arrived; in which case there may be a direct reference to Daniel vii, 13: 'Behold there was coming with the clouds of heaven one like unto a son of man.'"[21] The reference to the fact that the **tribes** will **mourn** is based on Zech. 12:12. The last part of the verse reflects Dan. 7:13. The combination of these two scriptures is found again in Rev. 1:7. The sound of a trumpet recalls Isa. 27:13. The Son of Man will gather together His chosen people **from the four winds** (all directions), and **from one end of heaven to the other** (31)—"from horizon to horizon."

### 6. *The Parable of the Fig Tree* (24:32-35)

This is found in all three Synoptics (cf. Mark 13:28-31; Luke 21:29-33). The fig tree is generally thought of as representing Israel. Her revival will be a harbinger of summer. Luke adds "and all the trees," which may reflect his interest in the Gentiles as well as the Jews. But these fine, allegorical points should not be pressed. **It is near** (33) is perhaps better rendered "He is near."

The solemn **Verily I say unto you** statement of verse 34— **This generation shall not pass, till all these things be fulfilled**—is another difficult passage. What is meant by **all these things?** Does this relate only to the destruction of Jerusalem in A.D. 70, or does it include the Second Coming? If the latter, what does this verse mean?

**Generation** is *genea*. It first meant "family, descent, race." It sometimes refers to a "nation." Its primary sense in the Gospels is thus stated by Arndt and Gingrich: "basically, the sum total of those born at the same time, expanded to include all those living at a given time; generation, contemporaries."[22]

If we take the word in this strict meaning, the reference can only be to the events of A.D. 70 in Judea. The early Fathers of

---

[21]Plummer, *op. cit.*, p. 335.
[22]*Op. cit.*, p. 153.

the Church preferred to broaden the concept. Chrysostom and Origin said it represented that generation of believers. Jerome suggested that it meant the Jewish race or the race of men. But most modern commentators feel that the word should be taken in its more limited natural sense. The only way that this can be related to the Second Coming is to say that the generation that sees the beginning of the definite fulfillment of the signs will see the end of the age. Though a bit nebulous, this interpretation should not be dismissed too lightly.

**Heaven** (35) does not mean the abode of God but the blue sky above the earth. The combination **heaven and earth** probably represents all material creation. Everything material will **pass away,** but never the Word of God. The Greek has a double negative (*ou me*) which adds force—"not by any means," or *"never."*

7. *Suddenness of the Second Coming* (24:36-51)

a. *"In Such an Hour as Ye Think Not"* (24:36-44). Jesus asserted that no one knows the hour of His coming, **not the angels,** "neither the Son,"[23] **but my Father only** (36). Those who set dates for the Second Coming are definitely ignoring Scripture.

The time preceding the coming of Christ is likened to **the days of Noe** (Noah, 37). People were living normal, secularized lives, ignoring God (38). But suddenly the **flood** (Greek, *kataklysmos,* "cataclysm") swept them all away (39). So, said Jesus, **shall also the coming of the Son of man be** (phrase found for the third and last time in this chapter).

Ultimately the human race is divided into two groups— those who watch for Christ's coming and those who do not. The principle of separation is illustrated here graphically. Of two **in the field,** one will be **taken,** the other **left** (40). The same will be true of two women **grinding at the mill** (41)—a little hand-mill turned by two women, as can still be seen in Palestine. Then Jesus made the application: **Watch therefore: for ye know not what hour your Lord doth come** (42). This is the keynote of the Olivet Discourse (cf. 25:13). **Watch** is literally, "Stay wide awake!" For no one knows when Christ may come.

Verse 43 contains a brief parabolic statement. If the **goodman of the house** (*oikodespotes,* see 20:1, 11) had known when the thief was coming, he would have been watching for him. Be-

---

[23]This addition in Mark (13:32) is also found here in Matthew in the oldest Greek manuscripts.

cause we do not know when Jesus may come, we must always be ready (44). To be ready at every moment for the return of Christ is the first responsibility of every Christian.

*b. The Faithful and Unfaithful Servant* (24:45-51). The closing admonition of this chapter is cast in the form of a brief parable about **a faithful and wise servant** (45) (slave) and an **evil servant** (48). The first keeps busy, faithfully performing his assigned tasks. So he is ready when his master returns.

But if the slave should decide that his master will be delayed for some time and should begin to carouse and to mistreat his fellow servants, his master will return at an unexpected hour. The result will be severe punishment—**cut him asunder** (51) (literally, "cut in two") and consign him to the place of hypocrites, where there is **weeping and gnashing of teeth** (cf. 8:12; 13:42, 50; 22:13; 25:30; Luke 13:28). Eternal judgment is the fate of the unfaithful.

Maclaren titles this section (42-51) "Watching for the King." He notes: (1) The command of watchfulness enforced by our ignorance of the time of His coming, 42-44; (2) The picture and reward of watchfulness, 45-47; (3) The picture and doom of the unwatchful servant, 48-51.

## B. THREE PARABLES ON PREPAREDNESS, 25:1-46

Chapter 25 is usually treated as a part of the Olivet Discourse (cf. 25:13 with 24:42). Only Matthew gives this material. The chapter very clearly consists of three parts. The first two are parables of the Kingdom. The third describes a judgment scene, which involves the parabolic language of sheep and goats.

### 1. Parable of the Ten Virgins (25:1-13)

No more striking story could be told to illustrate the need for being constantly ready for the coming of Christ. Jesus used a familiar figure, and one that comes close to people's hearts—that of a wedding.

He described **ten virgins** (1) who took their **lamps** (Greek, *lampas*) and went out to meet the bridegroom. Five were **wise** (2)—"prudent, i.e. mindful of one's interests"[24]—but the other five were **foolish** (Greek, *morai*).[25] The prudent ones **took oil in**

[24]Thayer, *op. cit.*, p. 658.
[25]The best Greek text reverses "wise" and "foolish" (cf. RV).

**their vessels with their lamps** (4), but the foolish failed to do so (3).

While the bridegroom **tarried**—literally, "spent time"—all the virgins **slumbered** and **slept** (5). The first verb is aorist and means "to nod." So it suggests "began to nod and doze." The second verb is in the (continuous) present tense and indicates that they kept on sleeping.

The picture here is of a typical Jewish wedding in Palestine. The bridegroom, accompanied by his friends, goes to the bride's house and takes her in a joyful procession to his own home. On Christmas afternoon of 1949 the writer met a large bridal procession on the road from Jerusalem to Amman. The men were riding on horseback, or walking, while the bride and her attendants were perched on camels, with large blankets draped over their heads to protect them from being seen.

Trench thinks the virgins "joined the procession at some convenient point, and entered with the rest of the bridal company into the hall of feasting."[26] On the other hand, Edersheim says the parable implies that the bridegroom had come from a distance, and was on his way to the bride's house. "Accordingly, the bridal procession is to meet Him on His Arrival, and escort Him to the bridal place."[27] Morison simply comments that **to meet the bridegroom** means: "To welcome him on occasion of his coming for his bride."[28]

There were **ten virgins**, since this was the number required for the ceremony. No bride is mentioned, for in the spiritual lesson of the parable the virgins take the place of the bride.

At midnight there came a cry: **Behold the bridegroom!** (6) [29] All the virgins rose quickly and **trimmed their lamps** (7). The Greek verb is *kosmeo*, from which comes "cósmetics." It means "to order, arrange, prepare," or "to adorn, furnish."[30] They probably clipped the charred ends of the wicks. There were no glass chimneys to clean.

In desperation the **foolish** turned to the wise, with the request for oil; **for our lamps are gone out** (8). But the Greek

---

[26]*Notes on the Parables*, p. 193.

[27]*Op. cit.*, II, 455.

[28]*Op. cit.*, p. 494.

[29]The added "cometh" is not in the oldest manuscripts.

[30]Abbott-Smith, *op. cit.*, pp. 254-55.

very clearly says: "Our lamps are going out"—literally, "are being quenched." This is a much stronger truth and a more comprehensive warning. There are many Christians who have not lost all their spiritual life, but whose lights are burning dimly. They need to realize that they are in danger of being left in outer darkness, as the foolish virgins were.

The wise refused the request (9). At first thought this might seem selfish. But from the standpoint of the spiritual truth being taught it was inevitable. Trench rightly interprets the intention of this verse: "It tells us that every man must live by his own faith."[31] The grace of God is not transferable from one human being to another. Each one must secure his own supply.

But while the foolish virgins went to buy more oil, the bridegroom arrived. Those that were **ready** (same word as in 24:44) went in with him to the **marriage**—the "marriage feast," which normally lasted from one to three weeks—and **the door was shut** (10). This suggests the solemn warning that someday the period of probation will be ended for each individual. Then the door of his eternal destiny will forever be **shut.** There is no second chance in the next life.

Finally the foolish virgins arrived, but they found the door closed against them. Inside were light and joy and gladness; outside was dismal darkness. The virgins cried out in desperation: **Lord, Lord, open to us** (11). But it was too late. The bridegroom did not recognize their voices (12), and at that hour of the night he dared not open the door to strangers who might be "party-crashers."

What is the lesson of this parable? It is summed up in verse 13: **Watch therefore, for ye know neither the day nor the hour wherein the Son of man cometh.** It teaches us that we must be prepared every moment for the imminent return of our Lord, ready to meet Him when He comes. To do this we must keep our Christian experience up-to-date. Since oil is a recognized type of the Holy Spirit, both in the Old Testament and the New, it is suggested that we must be filled with the Spirit if we would be properly prepared. Every man needs all of the grace of God available to him if he is to do the whole will of God and to be ready for our Lord's return.

[31]*Notes on the Parables,* p. 203.

## 2. *Parable of the Talents* (25:14-30)

This parable is somewhat similar to the parable of the pounds (Luke 19:11-28). In both, money is entrusted to servants, the reports of three are given, the first two are commended, and the third is condemned. But the differences outweigh the likenesses, so that the two are to be considered as separate parables given on different occasions. In Matthew the master gives one servant five talents, another two, and a third one, whereas in Luke he gives a pound to each of ten servants. The amounts gained are different, and so are the rewards given. Yet the two parables teach much the same lesson, that of the importance of being faithful in service.

Jesus here pictures himself as **a man travelling into a far country** (14)—anticipating His ascension to heaven. This man entrusted his money to three servants, giving to one five talents, to another two, and to another one—**to every man according to his several ability** (15). The talent was worth about a thousand dollars. The fact that today the term is used for one's personal ability gives added point to the parable.[32] All our God-given talents must be used for His glory and the good of humanity.

The man who had received five talents doubled them (16), as did also the one who had received two (17). But the one-talent man dug a hole in the ground, **and hid his lord's money** (18). It is too often true in church circles that a person who feels he has only one talent buries it instead of using it in the work of the Kingdom.

When the lord (master) returned, **he reckoneth with them** (19). The Greek literally says, "he takes up an account together with them"; that is, he "settled accounts" with them. The same expression is used in 18:23, where it is translated "take account." Probably Matthew's background of keeping books in his tax office is reflected in his use of this business phrase (*synairo logon*), which is found only in this Gospel.

The first two men reported that they had doubled the talents given them (20, 22). In reply the master said exactly the same words of commendation to both servants. The reward he promised was based on faithfulness, not ability. It is extremely signifi-

---

[32]Cf. Carr (*op. cit.*, p. 277): "It is from this parable that the word 'talents' has passed into modern languages in the sense of 'abilities,' or 'mental gifts,' though it seems properly to mean 'opportunities' or 'spheres of duty.'"

cant that both servants were commended for being **good and faithful** (21, 23), not for being capable and clever. These are two honest, solid virtues everyone can have—the poor as well as the rich, the uneducated as well as the brilliant intellectual. These are the only two things God requires of everyone—that he be **good** in character and **faithful** in service.

The one-talent man came with his whining complaint and his stupid alibi (24-25). If he knew his master was so demanding, it was all the more reason why he should have traded with his talent and gained something. **Gathering where thou hast not strawed** (24) means "gathering from a place where you have not threshed";[33] that is, gathering into your storehouse from another man's threshing floor. What the servant implied was: "exacting interest where you have not invested money."

The French have a good proverb for this man's actions: *"Qui s'excuse s'accuse"* ("He who excuses himself accuses himself"). The master condemned the selfish, do-nothing servant as **wicked** and **slothful** (26). The last word means "idle, lazy, indolent."[34] The man should have taken his master's money to the **exchangers** (27) ("bankers," only here in NT). Then his owner— **servant** in this parable is "slave"—would have received back his talent with **usury.** The Greek word literally means "birth" or "offspring," but was used metaphorically for "interest" (only here and Luke 19:23).

The Master then commanded his servants to take this man's talent and give it to the one who had ten talents (28). How often have ten-talent men had to do the work in the church that one-talent men should have cared for!

A universal life-principle is stated in verse 29. The man who uses his many talents always gains more. The one who uses not, loses. And the final tragedy for **the unprofitable servant** is **outer darkness,** where there is **weeping and gnashing of teeth** (30).

Whereas the parable of the ten virgins emphasizes the importance of keeping one's spiritual life up-to-date, fresh and full, the parable of the talents shows the necessity for being faithful and vigorous in the service of the Kingdom. It takes both to be ready for the return of our Lord.

Under the title "The Condemnation of the Buried Talent," we may observe: (1) God gives men differing gifts, 14-15; (2) The

[33]Meyer, *op. cit.,* pp. 441-42.
[34]Arndt and Gingrich, *op. cit.,* p. 565.

227

reward of work well done is still more work to do, 20-23; (3) The man who is punished is the man who will not try, 24-28; (4) To him that hath shall be given, and from him that hath not shall be taken away that which he has (WILLIAM BARCLAY).

### 3. *The Sheep and the Goats* (25:31-46)

Verse 31 describes the second coming of Christ in power, when He shall **sit upon the throne of his glory.** He will then act as the Judge. Before Him will be gathered **all nations** (neuter) and He will separate **them** (masculine, referring to people) as a shepherd **divides his sheep from the goats** (32). It is not nations, as such, that are saved or lost, but individuals. The language of verses 32 and 33 is reminiscent of Ezek. 34:17.

Carr calls attention to the formal structure of verses 34-46. He writes: "These verses are constructed according to the rules of Hebrew poetry: they fall into two divisions, the *first* extends from v. 34-40, the second from v. 41-46."[35] It will be noted that 34 is parallel to 41, 35 and 36 are parallel to 42 and 43, 37-39 to 44, and 40 answers to 45. Also in verses 35 and 36 there is a climactic effect in recognized duties; "the last three are voluntary acts of self-forgetting love."[36]

There has been considerable discussion as to what is meant by **my brethren** (40). Some have held that this expression refers to the Jews and that it is the Gentile nations that are being judged on the basis of their treatment of God's chosen people. It seems better to hold that, in the Incarnation and in His compassionate love for all men, Christ is referring to suffering humanity as **my brethren.** In their emphasis on separatism, the evangelical churches have too often failed to recognize the social implications and applications of the gospel of Jesus Christ. Works of mercy are not the only basis upon which eternal rewards and punishments are based. But can any man read these words of Jesus and believe that a Christian dares be unconcerned and inactive when his fellowman is in need?

The last verse of this chapter has strong theological overtones. The thing to note especially is that **everlasting** (46) and **eternal** are translations of the same Greek word—*aionion,* "pertaining to the ages." **Punishment** is just as **everlasting** as is **life.**

[35]*Op. cit.,* p. 279.
[36]*Ibid.,* p. 280.

One who believes in eternal bliss must also believe in eternal gloom. That seems to be the clear teaching of this passage.

Tasker has done a good job of connecting the three items of this chapter. He notes that it is sins of omission and not sins of commission that bring condemnation and eternal punishment. That is the main thrust of this chapter. "The door is shut against the foolish virgins for their negligence; the unenterprising servant is cast out as good-for-nothing for doing nothing; and those *on the left hand* are severely punished for failing to notice the many opportunities for showing kindness which had been given them."[37]

[37]Tasker, *op. cit.*, p. 239.

Section **XI** *The Passion*

Matthew 26:1—27:66

A. PREPARATION FOR DEATH, 26:1—27:31

1. *Preliminaries* (26:1-5)

*a. The Prospect* (26:1-2). For the last time we find the formula, **And it came to pass, when Jesus had finished all these sayings** (1), which occurs at the close of each of the five great discourses of Jesus in Matthew (cf. 7:28; 11:1; 13:53; 19:1). **And it came to pass** is *kai egeneto,* a Septuagint expression found commonly in Luke, but used by Matthew only with this formula.

Three times Jesus had predicted His passion (16:21; 17:22-23; 20:17-19). Now He tells them that His betrayal is only **two days** away (2). Since Jesus ate **the passover** with His disciples on Thursday night, this would be Tuesday. It would appear that the Master may have spent Wednesday in seclusion, privately instructing His disciples. **Is betrayed** should be "is being betrayed" (prophetic present).[1]

*b. The Plot* (26:3-5). **The chief priests, and the scribes,**[2] **and the elders of the people** (3) comprised the Great Sanhedrin at Jerusalem, which was the supreme judicial body of the Jewish nation. This group gathered at the **palace** (Greek, "court") of the high priest, **Caiaphas,** who was in office A.D. 18-36.

These **consulted** ("took counsel") how they might take Jesus **by subtilty**—the word originally meant a "bait" or "snare," and so "craft" or "deceit"—**and kill him** (4). They wished to avoid doing it **on the feast day,** so there would be no **uproar** ("tumult," mob action) **among the people** (5). Fanatical feelings always ran high during the Passover season, which commemorated the release of the Israelites from Egyptian bondage. It was a time when it would take only a spark to ignite the fire of revolution against Roman rule. This the Jewish leaders knew very well. They

[1]See F. Blass and A. Debrunner, *A Greek Grammar of the New Testament and Other Early Christian Literature,* trans. Robert W. Funk (Chicago: University of Chicago Press, 1961), p. 168—"In prophecies it is very frequent in the New Testament."

[2]Omitted in the earliest manuscripts.

would have preferred to wait until the million or more Passover pilgrims had left Jerusalem. But when Judas offered to betray his Master, they evidently decided to go ahead right away.

## 2. *The Anointing at Bethany* (26:6-13)

John (12:2-8) places this anointing—not to be confused with the one in Luke 7:36-50 (see comments there)—"six days before the passover" (John 12:1). That would be on Friday or Saturday night preceding Passion Week. But Mark (14:3-9) and Matthew record it here just ahead of the Betrayal. It seems best to follow the Johannine chronology, where the time connection is more precise. Andrews suggests the most satisfactory solution to the problem: "A close examination of Matthew and Mark shows that their account of the supper is brought in parenthetically."[3] The reason for this is that apparently they wanted to show that it was the anointing which precipitated Judas' action in going to the chief priests (14). Plummer agrees with this when he writes: "Evidently we are to suppose that the proposal was a consequence ... of that incident."[4]

The anointing took place **in Bethany** (two miles out of Jerusalem, see map), **in the house of Simon the leper** (6). Simon was a very common name, and this man may have been cured of his leprosy by Jesus.

There came **a woman**—John identifies her as Mary (the sister of Martha)—with an **alabaster box** (7). The Greek simply says *alabastron*. Arndt and Gingrich define this word as meaning: "*alabaster,* then an *alabaster flask* for ointment, a vessel with a rather long neck which was broken off when the contents were used."[5] The ointment was **very precious** (literally, "of heavy value"). It may well have represented her whole life's savings. This she **poured** on Jesus' head. She did not apply it drop by drop, as expensive perfume would ordinarily be used. Rather she broke the narrow neck of the flask (Mark 14:3), and with an abandonment of love and devotion poured out the contents on the Master's **head**. John (12:3) says on His feet. It was the custom to anoint both the head and the feet (cf. Luke 7:38, 46); so Mary naturally did both. **As he sat at meat** should be translated "as He reclined at the table."

[3]*Op. cit.,* pp. 426-27.
[4]*Op. cit.,* p. 354.
[5]*Op. cit.,* p. 33.

The disciples **had indignation** (8)—same word as in 20:24 and 21:15 (see notes there)—because of this waste. John (12:4) tells us that it was Judas Iscariot who especially found fault. He seems to have been infuriated at seeing all this "waste." Matthew implies that all the disciples (Mark says "some") were materialistically minded. They caught nothing of the fragrance of Mary's devotion, symbolized by the perfume.

But Jesus defended her action. He said (10): "She has done a beautiful thing to me" (RSV).[6] The **poor** they would always have—history certifies this—but Jesus would soon be gone (11). Then the Master explained the significance of her action; **she did it for my burial** (12). Though He was to die on a cross rather than sit on a throne, He was still the King. Mary, because she listened more carefully (cf. Luke 10:39), may possibly have understood His mission more fully than anyone else.

For her love and loyalty Mary would have a **memorial** known **in the whole world** (13). Millions of copies of the Gospels in a thousand languages have told the story wherever the gospel has gone. Because she gave her all, Mary's name is immortal.

William Barclay calls Mary's anointing of Jesus "Love's Extravagance." In the story we see that (1) There are times when the commonsense view of things fails, 6-9; (2) There are certain things which must be done when the opportunity arises, or they can never be done at all, 10-12; (3) The fragrance of a lovely deed lasts forever, 13.

### 3. *The Treachery of Judas* (26:14-16)[7]

The greedy mind of Judas Iscariot had reacted violently to the "waste" of nearly a year's wages (cf. Mark 14:5; Matt. 20:2). Also Judas had expected Jesus to set up His kingdom at Jerusalem. But all the Master seemed to talk about was His crucifixion, not His coronation. It appears evident that Judas was actuated by a double motive, that of greed and disappointed political ambitions. Some believe that He wanted Jesus to come out openly as King and thought that the betrayal would force the issue.

Judas went to the **chief priests** (14)—now the main enemies of Jesus—and asked how much they would give him for betray-

---

[6]The Greek word *kalos* means "good, beautiful." Carr (*op. cit.,* p. 286) comments: "The Lord passes a higher commendation on this than on any other act recorded in the New Testament."

[7]Recorded also in Mark 14:10-11; Luke 22:3-6.

ing the Master to them (15). **They covenanted with him.** The Greek says, "they weighed out to him." This use of *histemi* for "set in a balance"[8] or "place in a scale," and so "weigh" is found only here in the New Testament, though it occurs in classical Greek and the Septuagint. The amount they weighed was **thirty pieces of silver.** These were silver shekels. The total amount would be equal to 120 denarii, or about 25 dollars. This was the price of a slave (Exod. 21:32), which gives added force to Jesus' words in 20:28 and to Paul's statement in Phil. 2:7-8.

### 4. *The Last Passover* (26:17-29)

*a. The Preparation* (26:17-19). One of the last things that Jesus did with His disciples before His death was to eat the Passover meal with them. This was particularly appropriate, since in a few hours He was to give himself as the paschal Lamb to atone for all men's sins.

**The first day of the feast of unleavened bread** (17) was the day the Passover lamb was slain (see Mark 14:12; Luke 22:7). According to the Mosaic law this was called the Passover and was followed by seven days of the Feast of Unleavened Bread (Lev. 23:5-6). But at this time the whole period was known by this name. Josephus says: "We keep a feast for eight days, which is called the feast of unleavened bread."[9]

The three Synoptic Gospels agree in portraying Jesus as eating the Passover with His disciples the night before His crucifixion. But John's Gospel seems to conflict with this. He says that the Jews would not enter Pilate's Praetorium the morning of the Crucifixion "lest they should be defiled; but that they might eat the passover" (John 18:28).

The problem of harmonizing the Synoptic and Johannine accounts at this point is the most difficult one in New Testament chronology. Most scholars today feel that they are irreconcilable, and choose the Johannine chronology as correct and the Synoptic one as in error. Some seek a moderate position by saying that it was not really the Passover meal which Jesus ate with His disciples—the Synoptics seem definitely to say it was—or else that He intentionally ate it early, knowing that He would be dead at the regular time.[10]

8Abbott-Smith, *op. cit.,* p. 219.
9*Ant.* II. 15. 1.
10Cf. Plummer, *op. cit.,* p. 357.

Edersheim insists that the Last Supper of the Synoptic Gospels was actually the Passover.[11] So does Jeremias, who calls attention to the fact that the supper was held in Jerusalem, during the night, with the Twelve, with bread and wine, and with a hymn.[12] He seems to have proved this point rather conclusively. There seems to be no way of sidestepping the fact that Jesus did eat the Passover with His disciples before His death.

What is the solution to the problem? Andrews holds that John used the term "passover" in its broader sense. He writes: ". . . the phrase 'to eat the passover' naturally came to embrace the whole feast."[13] Again he says: "Passover, with John, is a term denoting the whole festival; and why, if the paschal supper was past, might he not employ it to designate the remaining feasts?"[14]

Stauffer has another explanation. He accounts for the surprising fact that no lamb is mentioned by saying that an apostate was not permitted to eat the Passover lamb. So, without the lamb, "Jesus held his Passover twenty-four hours before the official Passover meal of the members of the temple community."[15]

Two other solutions have been offered by recent writers. One is this: "In that particular year the Jews in Palestine observed Passover on Saturday; those in the Dispersion observed it on Friday."[16] Mark followed the Dispersion calendar. So both the Synoptics and John are right. ("Friday" means Thursday evening, as the Jewish day began at sunset.)

Freedman claims the Dead Sea Scrolls show that many pious Jews held to the older solar calendar of Israel (364 days) and rejected the new lunar calendar. He thinks Jesus ate the Passover with His disciples Tuesday evening, whereas the priests and

[11]*Op. cit.*, II. 480-82.

[12]Joachim Jeremias, *The Eucharistic Words of Jesus,* trans. Arnold Ehrhardt (New York: Macmillan Co., 1955), pp. 14-37.

[13]*Op. cit.*, p. 456.

[14]*Ibid.*, p. 471.

[15]Ethelbert Stauffer, *Jesus and His Story,* trans. Richard and Clara Winston (New York: Alfred A. Knopf, 1959), p. 113.

[16]Massey H. Shepherd, Jr., "Are Both the Synoptics and John Correct About the Date of Jesus' Death?" *Journal of Biblical Literature,* LXXX (1961), 125.

others ate it on Friday, after the Crucifixion.[17] He thinks that
Jesus was held prisoner from Tuesday night until Friday.

With these many proposed solutions from which to choose, it
is obvious that one does not have to settle for an unresolvable
contradiction between John and the Synoptics. While no solution
has won universal acceptance, that of Andrews perhaps has the
least difficulties and the most evidence for it.

Matthew's habit of omitting details shows up again in this
narrative. He does not say who was sent to prepare the Passover.
Mark says it was "two disciples" and Luke designates them as
"Peter and John." Matthew says they were to meet **such a man**
(18), whereas Mark and Luke say "a man bearing a pitcher of
water."

The disciples were to carry the message: **I will keep the
passover at thy house with my disciples.** Following directions,
**they made ready the passover** (19).

*b. The Last Supper* (26:20-25). Jesus **sat down** (rather,
"reclined") with the twelve apostles (20). While they were
eating, He announced that one of them would betray Him (21).
The shocked and saddened disciples asked, one by one, **Lord,
is it I?** (22) The Greek indicates that a negative answer was
expected—"Lord, it isn't I, is it!" The Master informed them it
was the one **that dippeth his hand with me in the dish** (23). This
fact made Judas' crime all the more heinous. For to eat with a
person meant that you were his friend and guaranteed you
would not harm him. Even the betrayer joined in asking the
question, though he addressed Jesus as Master (Greek, "Rabbi"),
not Lord. Christ answered, **Thou hast said** (25), which seems to
be a direct affirmative answer. In spite of this warning from
Jesus, and even after this opportunity to reconsider his decision,
Judas went through with his plans for the actual betrayal.

*c. The Lord's Supper* (26:26-29). In connection with the
Last Supper, Jesus instituted the Lord's Supper. He **blessed** and
**brake** bread, and said to His disciples: **Take, eat; this is my body**
(26). It should be clear that the meaning is, "this *represents* my
body."

Then the Master took the **cup** (27). Carr thinks this was the
third cup of the Passover meal, called the "cup of blessing."[18] He

---

[17]David Noel Freedman, "When Did Christ Die?" *Perspective,* III (1962),
257.

[18]*Op. cit.,* p. 289.

instructed them: **Drink ye all of it.** It is unfortunate that these words, repeated thousands of times every Sunday around the world, were translated so incorrectly. The Greek very clearly says: "All of you drink of it" (cf. RSV). Jesus then went on to identify the contents of the cup as representing **my blood of the new**[19] **testament** ("covenant") **which is shed** (Greek, "poured out") **for many for the remission of sins.**

Christ declared that He would not again drink of the fruit of the vine, **until that day when I drink it new with you in my Father's kingdom** (29). There is a sense in which Christ shares with believers in the Communion service. Paul asserts: "For as often as ye eat this bread, and drink this cup, ye do shew the Lord's death till he come" (I Cor. 11:26).

### 5. *On the Mount of Olives* (26:30-56)

*a. Prediction of Peter's Denials* (26:30-35). At the close of the supper they sang a **hymn** (30). Edersheim says: "Probably we are to understand this of the second portion of the *Hallel* [Psalms 115—118], sung some time after the third cup, or else of Psalm cxxxvi, which, in the present Ritual, stands near the end of the service."[20]

To His disciples the Master made another sad announcement (cf. v. 21): **All ye shall be offended because of me this night** (31). Lenski has: "All you shall be trapped in connection with me."[21] The verb is *skandalizo*. Certain it is that all the disciples fell into the trap of Satan that night, when they forsook their Master. Christ quoted Zech. 13:7, changing the imperative (both Hebrew and Septuagint) to a future tense. He added that when He had **risen again** (32), He would **go before** them into Galilee. The latter verb literally means "lead the way." It carries on the figure of the **shepherd** (31).

Peter always had a word to say. As usual, it was a self-confident one. Even if everyone else should "fall away" (RSV, NEB), he **never** would (33). Unfortunately he did not know his own weakness. Christ was compelled to warn him that on that very night before the cock should crow he would thrice deny his Master (34). Typically, Peter replied that he would die before he would deny his Lord (35). It might have been more

[19]The oldest manuscripts omit "new."

[20]*Op. cit.,* II, 533.

[21]*Op. cit.,* p. 1033.

the part of wisdom for him to have asked humbly for strength to meet the test. **All the disciples** joined him in asserting their determined loyalty.

b. *Prayer in Gethsemane* (26:36-46). The name Gethsemane (only here and Mark 14:32) means "oil-press." The Mount of Olives was naturally an appropriate place for pressing out the olive oil which was used in that day as fuel for lamps, food, and healing ointment.

Jesus left eight of His eleven disciples at the garden gate. Taking only the inner circle of three—**Peter and the two sons of Zebedee** (37)—He walked inside the olive grove and bared His heart to these nearest associates. He said: **My soul is exceeding sorrowful, even unto death** (38). It was the weight of a world's sins on His shoulders that was crushing Him. He begged them: **Tarry ye here, and watch with me.** But they failed.

**Jesus went a little farther** (39), not only physically, but spiritually. Had He not gone a **little farther,** we could not be saved. And unless we go a **little farther**—in compassionate, consecrated service—many others will not be saved.

The Master **fell on his face.** This reveals something of His agony of soul. He prayed that if possible the **cup** might pass from Him. What was this cup? Certainly it was more than physical death. Jesus was no coward. It would seem that the bitterest dregs of this cup of sorrow were separation from His Father's face, when He who knew no sin should be made "sin" (or a Sin Offering) for us (II Cor. 5:21). His final prayer was: **nevertheless not as I will, but as thou wilt.** That is always the prayer of a consecrated soul.

When Jesus returned to the three disciples who were supposed to be watching (38), He found them fast **asleep** (40). Since Peter had boasted so loudly, the Master chided him a bit. Could he not stay awake even one hour? Then Christ uttered another solemn warning: **Watch and pray, that ye enter not into temptation** (41). That is an admonition that every Christian needs to heed every hour of every day. "Eternal vigilance is the price of liberty." That is true militarily, and it is true spiritually. Jesus recognized that **the spirit indeed is willing, but the flesh is weak.** This does not mean the carnal nature, but the physical body. The disciples were so tired and so saddened with sorrow that they fell asleep.

The second time Jesus prayed essentially the same prayer, with perhaps slightly more emphasis on **thy will be done** (42). Once more He found the disciples sleeping, **for their eyes were heavy** (43). They had come through a hard week. Their intentions were good, but their performance left something to be desired.

A third time the Master prayed, saying the same words (44). When He returned this time He said: **Sleep on now, and take your rest** (45). This apparent exhortation in the King James Version seems inconsistent with verse 46: **Rise, let us be going: behold, he is at hand that doth betray me.** The solution of the problem is simple. The Greek of the above quotation from verse 45 can with equal accuracy be translated as a command or a question—the form for both is exactly the same. But here the command does not fit at all, whereas the question fits perfectly. The correct translation is: "Are you still sleeping and taking your rest?" At such a time as this, when the Son of Man "is being betrayed"—the action was already taking place—are you sleeping as sentries at their post?

c. *Betrayal and Arrest* (26:47-56). Even as the Master was seeking to rouse His disciples, Judas, **one of the twelve**—what a pathetic note, found in all three Synoptics!—put in his appearance. With him was a great **multitude** (47). Stauffer thinks this was "a small army of a thousand soldiers."[22] But this seems unlikely in view of their mission to arrest one Man—or even a dozen men. It was a motley mob with **swords and staves.** They certainly had false ideas about the Prince of Peace. These men were sent by **the chief priests and elders of the people;** that is, the Sanhedrin.

Judas had given a **sign** (48). He would identify Christ by kissing Him. This was a particularly atrocious act, since the kiss was a symbol of friendship and honor. The hard "brass" of Judas' character is revealed here. He stepped up to Jesus and greeted Him affectionately with a kiss and the words: **Hail, master** (49) (Greek, "Rabbi"). With gentle compassion the Master said: **Friend** (literally, "companion" or "comrade"), **wherefore art thou come?** (50) But there was no time for further talk. The mob quickly surrounded Jesus and seized Him.

One of Jesus' disciples—John (18:10) tells us it was Peter—drew his sword and tried to defend his Master. He swung his

---

[22]*Op. cit.,* p. 120.

sword, probably intending to cut off the head of the man who dared to lay hands on Christ. The man perhaps tried to dodge the blow and so lost an ear instead of his head. John also tells us that the name of the high priest's servant was Malchus. He had this information probably because he was acquainted with the household of the high priest (cf. John 18:15).

Jesus ordered His zealous disciple to put his sword away, uttering the significant truth: **all they that take the sword shall perish with the sword** (52). He also intimated that He could call for **more than twelve legions of angels** (53). He did not lack for defense. But He must submit, in order that God's will, revealed in **the scriptures** (our OT), might be fulfilled (54).

Then Christ chided the mob (55) for coming out as if against a **thief** (Greek, "robber"), with **swords and staves** ("clubs"). He reminded them that they had had ample opportunity to take Him while He taught daily in the Temple. But what was happening was in fulfillment of the **scriptures of the prophets** (56). Appended is the sad note: **Then all the disciples forsook him, and fled.** Where was their boasted loyalty of a few hours before (cf. 35)?

### 6. *The Jewish Trial* (26:57—27:2)

*a. Before the Sanhedrin* (26:57-68). The mob that had seized Jesus took Him to Caiaphas, the high priest, where **the scribes and the elders** (the Sanhedrin) had assembled (57). Peter, though having been rebuffed for his efforts to protect his Master, **followed him afar off** (58). He at least should get credit for following. His love for the Lord made him go along, though afraid. He entered the **priest's palace** (Greek, "courtyard") and sat down with the servants, **to see the end** (58). He probably realized by now something of the seriousness of the situation.

**All the council**—composed of chief priests, elders, and scribes—sought **false witness against Jesus, to put him to death** (59). So determined were these leaders to slay Him that they were willing to stoop to any falsehood to bring this about. But even this effort failed, for the false witnesses could not agree in their fabricated stories (60).

Finally two did get together in a common accusation. They charged Christ with having said: **I am able to destroy the temple of God, and to build it in three days** (61). Of course Jesus never said any such thing. It was probably a false interpretation of His saying recorded in John 2:19.

The high priest challenged Christ to answer the accusations leveled against Him (62). But the Master remained silent. Finally the high priest put Jesus under oath to tell the facts of His origin (63). Under their duress, Christ replied: **Thou hast said** (64). The same expression occurs in verse 25. Carr writes: "This is a formula of assent both in Hebrew and Greek, and is still used in Palestine in that sense."[23] Jesus then added a highly apocalyptic statement about the Son of Man sitting on the right hand of **power**—a typical Jewish substitute for "god"—and **coming in the clouds of heaven.** This is the sort of thing the Messiah was expected to do.

The effect of Jesus' words was electric. Caiaphas **rent his clothes** (65). This the high priest was forbidden by law to do under ordinary circumstances (Lev. 10:6; 21:10), "but the custom which required it on hearing a blasphemy may have grown up by the 1st century."[24]

There was no need for further witnesses: **behold, now ye have heard his blasphemy.** It would not have been blasphemy to claim to be a human messiah, which many expected. But the high priest had put Jesus under oath to tell whether He was "the Son of God" (63). He had answered in the affirmative. This, put with the rest of verse 64, shows why the Sanhedrin might have held Him guilty of blaspheming.

When questioned, the court said: **He is guilty of death** (66). The actions that followed are a sad commentary on the ethical level in the Judaism of that day. For the religious leaders of the nation to stoop to such disgraceful acts as spitting in His face, buffeting Him, and slapping Him (67) shows the failure of Judaism.

Verse 68 becomes clear in the light of Luke 22:64, where it is stated that they blindfolded Jesus and then asked Him to identify the ones who slapped Him.

*b. Peter's Denials* (26:69-75). While the trial before Caiaphas was going on, Peter was sitting **without in the palace** (69)— Greek, "outside in the courtyard." A **damsel** accosted him with the accusation: **Thou also wast with Jesus of Galilee.** Peter denied, asserting: **I know not what thou sayest** (70). Then, to escape further detection by the bright light of the fire (cf. Mark 14:54), he slipped out into the **porch,** or "vestibule" (71). But

[23]*Op. cit.,* p. 290.
[24]M'Neile, *op. cit.,* pp. 402-3.

here another maid spotted him and said to those standing around: **This fellow was also with Jesus of Nazareth.** Again he denied, this time **with an oath, I do not know the man** (72). Here Peter was guilty of perjury.

After a while the bystanders closed in on him with the assertion: **Surely thou also art one of them; for thy speech bewrayeth** ("betrayeth") **thee** (73). A better translation would be: "Your accent gives you away." The Galileans spoke with a different accent from the Judeans. It was easy for people in Jerusalem to recognize a Galilean when they heard him speak.

When Peter found himself really in a corner, he began **to curse and to swear, saying, I know not the man** (74). This would easily be interpreted as meaning that he used profane language. But what it really means is that he called down upon himself the curses of God if he were not telling the truth, and swore an oath that he was. Thus he was guilty of double perjury (cf. 72).

Just then **the cock crew.** Peter recalled Christ's prediction of what he had just done (75). **And he went out, and wept bitterly.** These were tears of genuine repentance, as the sequel shows.

When Peter affirmed vigorously that he would never deny his Lord, he was sincere. But he did not know the depths of depravity in his own heart. This experience of denying Christ revealed it to him. He was thus prepared to wait, with the others, for the filling of the Holy Spirit at Pentecost that cleansed his heart and made him fully loyal to his Lord.

c. *Morning Session of Sanhedrin* (27:1-2). The meeting of the Sanhedrin at night was illegal. So the court met at daylight to pass official sentence on Jesus. The Jews were not allowed by the Roman government to execute anyone—except in the case of a foreigner who invaded the sacred precincts of the Temple; that is, went beyond the Court of the Gentiles. All the Sanhedrin could do was to bind Jesus and deliver Him over to Pilate for the final trial. **Pontius Pilate** was **governor** (2) (*hegemon*), or "procurator," of Judea, A.D. 26-36.

7. *The Remorse of Judas* (27:3-10)

Though all three Synoptic Gospels tell of Judas Iscariot's compact with the chief priests to betray Jesus and all record the actual betrayal, only Matthew relates the remorse and suicide of the betrayer. It is a solemnizing thought that a man whom Christ

chose as His apostle and sent out to preach should end his career
thus.

When Judas saw that Jesus was **condemned** by the Sanhedrin—and this verdict was irrevocable[25]—he **repented himself**
(3). The verb is not *metanoeo,* "change one's mind," but *metamelomai,* "regret." He regretted the consequences of his act of
betrayal, but he had no genuine repentance for his sin. Back to
**the chief priests and elders** (Sanhedrin) he brought the thirty
pieces of silver. The money was burning in his purse.

To his religious leaders he made his confession: **I have sinned
in that I have betrayed the innocent blood** (4). But he received
no comfort or help from them. Their only reply was: **What is
that to us? see thou to that.** When the spiritual leaders could talk
that way to their people, things were in a sorry way with Judaism.

Judas could not stand the sight of his ill-gotten gain any
longer. Literally, "having hurled the silver pieces into the Sanctuary"—the inmost court of the Temple where only the priests
could enter—he went and hanged himself (5).

The **chief priests** picked up the **silver pieces,** but were perplexed as to what to do with them. They could not use them in
the Temple, because they were **the price of blood** (6). They held
a conference and decided to buy with them **the potter's field** (7).
The Greek says "the field of the potter," which may suggest that
it was a well-known place near Jerusalem. The **strangers** they
wanted to **bury** there would be Jews from abroad who died at the
annual festivals or came in their old age to die in the Holy Land.[26]

In keeping with his usual custom, Matthew cites a prophecy
from the Old Testament (9-10). The quotation is attributed to
**Jeremy,** or Jeremiah. (In reading the Scriptures aloud prominent Old Testament names mentioned in the New Testament
should always be given the familiar form they have in the older
Scriptures.) But the passage seems to be quoted from Zech.
11:12-13. Bengel thought that Jeremy was a gloss, added by a
copyist.[27] John Wesley, who depended heavily on Bengel's *Gnomon* for his own *Explanatory Notes on the New Testament,*
writes: "The word Jeremy, which was added to the text in later
copies, and thence received into many translations, is evidently a

---

[25]Stauffer, *op. cit.,* p. 128.

[26]The problem of harmonizing verses 5-8 with Acts 1:18-19 will be
handled in connection with the latter passage.

[27]*Op. cit.,* I, 471.

mistake; for he who spoke what St. Matthew here cites, or rather paraphrases, was not Jeremy, but Zechariah."[28] Adam Clarke likewise says: "It is very likely that the original reading was *dia tou prophetou* ['through the prophet'], and the name of no prophet mentioned."[29]

The textual problem is that "Jeremiah" is the reading in practically all the Greek manuscripts, including the oldest now extant. The Wesleyan commentator Morison thinks that it is a typographical error which somehow got into "the original edition of the Gospel, the first published edition," as "strain *at* a gnat" instead of "strain *out* a gnat" got into the first edition of the King James Version and remained uncorrected (cf. 23:24).[30]

### 8. The Roman Trial (27:11-31)

a. *Jesus Before Pilate* (27:11-14). Having been condemned by the Jews in a model of mistrial, Christ now stood before the **governor** (11). All three Synoptic Gospels have Pilate asking, **Art Thou the King of the Jews?** and all three give His answer: **Thou sayest.** M'Neile says that this seems to imply: "Thou art verbally correct, but the truth is beyond thy comprehension."[31]

Accused by the Jewish leaders, Jesus answered **nothing** (12). "The silence, which met the accusations and Pilate's next question, is of the same kind as in xxvi. 62 f.; legally it might be taken as a confession of guilt, but actually it produced an uncomfortable effect upon the judge: Caiaphas was led by it to extort a confession, Pilate to a series of attempts to extricate the Prisoner and himself."[32] At the perfect poise of Christ, Pilate **marvelled greatly** (14).

b. *Jesus or Barabbas?* (27:15-23) During the annual **feast** (15) of the Passover the governor was in the habit of releasing to the people a prisoner of their choice. Attention has been called many times to the fact that this custom is not mentioned outside the Gospels. Carr makes a good suggestion as to how it gained an entrance among the Jews. After noting that the release of prisoners took place at certain festivals in Rome, he says: "It is not, therefore, improbable that Herod the Great, who certainly fa-

[28]*Op. cit.*, pp. 130-31.
[29]*Op. cit.*, I, 270.
[30]*Op. cit.*, pp. 573-74.
[31]*Op. cit.*, p. 409.
[32]*Ibid.*, pp. 409-10.

miliarized the Jews with other usages of Greece and Rome, introduced this custom, and that the Roman governor, finding the
custom established and gratifying to the Jews, in accordance with
the Roman practice . . . retained the observance of it."[33] It is significant that Pilate says: "Ye have a custom" (John 18:39).

There was a **notable prisoner** there, called **Barabbas** (16).
This is an Aramaic name, meaning "son [*bar*] of a father [*abba*]."
Mark (15:7) and Luke (23:19) state that Barabbas had committed murder in an insurrection. Pilate now asked the Jewish
leaders (17) whether they wished him to release **Barabbas** or
**Jesus** the Messiah **(Christ).** It is obvious that the governor
hoped they would prefer the harmless Prophet in their midst
rather than the dangerous murderer. He knew that their hatred
of Jesus was because of **envy** (18). This should have impelled
him to release Christ. Added to this was a message from his
wife (recorded only in Matthew), urging him, "Be careful how
you get involved with this innocent man." Lenski makes this
comment: "In her dream Jesus appeared wholly guiltless, and the
dream probably suggested that Pilate was on the verge of condemning this just man."[34] This is why she had **suffered many
things** (19).

During the time that Pilate was busied with this message
from his wife, the **chief priests and elders** made the most of the
opportunity to harangue the crowd into asking that Barabbas be
released and Jesus destroyed (20). So when Pilate took up
where he had left off, asking whom he should release, the people
answered, **Barabbas** (21). Then Pilate asked a question which
has taken on cosmic proportions in its evangelistic thrust: **What
shall I do then with Jesus which is called Christ?** (22) One is
reminded of the words of the song: "What will you do with
Jesus? Neutral you cannot be." No man can be neutral toward
Jesus Christ.

This passage suggests three points. Pilate was: (1) Confronted by Christ, 11; (2) Concerned with Christ, 17; (3) Condemned by Christ, 23. The main text would be 22.

In reply to the governor's question, the people cried out:
**Let him be crucified.** In his powerful novel, *Behold the Man,*
Kagawa has perhaps caught well what was happening here. He

[33]*Op. cit.,* p. 303.
[34]*Op. cit.,* p. 1090.

portrays the crafty old ex-high priest Annas (cf. John 18:13) acting now in desperation. "Surreptitiously, he was sending his servants into the crowd with sacks of coins which they distributed, whispering to each bystander as they did so."[35] What they were telling the people, of course, was to ask for the release of Barabbas and the crucifixion of Jesus.

c. *Jesus Scourged* (27:24-26). Pilate finally quailed before the crowd. He could see that the mob was getting out of hand, that a **tumult** (uproar) was being made. There was nothing that a Roman governor feared more. If word got back to Rome that he had let a riot take place, his public career would be finished. Better to let one prisoner suffer a miscarriage of justice than for him to risk his own future. So Pilate took water and washed his hands before the crowd, saying: **I am innocent of the blood of this just person: see ye to it** (24). Insanely the people answered: **His blood be on us, and on our children** (25). The horrible holocaust of A.D. 70 forms a tragic footnote to this epitaph of a nation.

Pilate **released** Barabbas, **scourged** Jesus, and **delivered him to be crucified** (26). The Roman scourge was a cruel instrument —a short whip of leather thongs, with sharp pieces of metal or bone fastened to the ends. The prisoner was forced to bend over and the lash was brought down with terrible force on his bare back. The taut skin would quickly be cut to shreds. It was not uncommon for men to die under the whip. It appears to have been the Roman practice to scourge victims just before crucifying them. Josephus notes at least two such instances.[36]

d. *Jesus Mocked* (27:27-31). The soldiers of the governor took Jesus into the **common hall**—one word, *praitorion,* from the Latin *praetorium.* It was used first for the headquarters in a Roman military camp, and then for the official residence of the governor of a province. The location of the Praetorium in Jerusalem is a debatable question. Some scholars think it was Herod's palace in the southwestern part of the city, near the present Jaffa Gate. Others prefer the Tower of Antonia, the Roman barracks at the northwest corner of the Temple area. The evidence of Josephus seems to favor the former: he mentions the

[35]Toyohiko Kagawa, *Behold the Man* (New York: Harper and Brothers, 1941), p. 302.

[36]*War* II. 14. 9; V. 11. 1.

governor setting up his tribunal "at the palace."[37] Schurer says: "On special occasions, especially during the chief Jewish feasts, when, on account of the crowds of people that streamed into Jerusalem, particularly careful oversight was necessary, the procurator, went up to Jerusalem [from Caesarea, the Roman seat of government in Palestine] and resided there in what had been the palace of Herod."[38] This view is favored by M'Neile,[39] by George Adam Smith,[40] by Sherman Johnson,[41] and by perhaps a majority of scholars today.

The soldiers gathered together the whole **band,** or "cohort." This ordinarily consisted of a tenth of a legion, about six hundred men. But they may not have all been on duty at one time. These soldiers stripped Jesus and put on him a **scarlet robe (28)**—the outer cloak of a Roman soldier. Here it was a quick and mocking substitute for a royal robe of purple. Next they wove a **crown of thorns** and placed it on His head, and placed a **reed** (mock scepter) in His right hand. Bowing down before Him they jeered at Him as **King of the Jews (29).** Spitting contemptuously on Him, they took the reed and **smote him on the head (30).** Never was one treated with more cruel disdain and more undeserving of it. After the soldiers had mocked Him until they were tired of their cruel game, they took off the scarlet robe and led Jesus out to be crucified (31).

## B. DEATH AND BURIAL, 27:32-66

### 1. *The Crucifixion* (27:32-50)

*a. The Morning Hours* (27:32-44). As the soldiers left the Praetorium, they impressed into service to carry Jesus' cross a man from **Cyrene (32)**—north Africa. Jesus started out carrying His cross. But weakened by all He had gone through, He was unable to carry it far. So the soldiers picked out a passerby and placed it on his shoulders.

**Golgotha (33)** is a transliteration of the Aramaic word for **skull.** It is found in Matthew, Mark, and John, but not Luke. All

[37]*War* II. 14. 8.

[38]*Ibid.,* I. i. 48.

[39]*Op. cit.,* p. 414.

[40]George Adam Smith, *Jerusalem* (New York: A. C. Armstrong and Son, 1908), II, 574.

[41]IB, VII, 599-600.

four Gospels have the Greek word *kranion*, which has reached into English by way of the Latin form, *cranium*. In Matthew, Mark, and John this is translated **skull** in the King James Version. But it is translated "Calvary" in Luke (23:33). This is the only place in the entire Bible (KJV) where this word occurs. It comes from the Latin Vulgate, where *calvaria* is the regular translation of the Greek *kranion* (found only here and the three parallel passages in the other Gospels—Mark 15:22; Luke 23:33; John 19:17). Yet the term "Calvary" has become very deeply imbedded in our theological thinking and holds a prominent place in our homiletics and hymnology.

The location of Golgotha is a matter of great dispute and uncertainty. There is general agreement today, however, that it does not mean a "place of skulls"—that is, of execution—but rather a skull-shaped knoll. The two main proposed sites are the Church of the Holy Sepulcher inside Old Jerusalem, and "Gordon's Calvary," outside the north wall of the city, near the Damascus Gate. While archaeologists tend to favor the former, the latter gives one much better "the feel" of the Crucifixion— and the Garden Tomb nearby gives "the feel" of the Resurrection.

Arrived at the place of execution, the soldiers offered Jesus **vinegar to drink mingled with gall** (34). Tradition has it that the women of Jerusalem were accustomed to furnish this pain-killing narcotic out of pity for prisoners who were being crucified. But when Jesus had tasted it, **he would not drink.** He did not want His senses deadened nor His consciousness impaired while He suffered for our sins.

Finally **they crucified him** (35). His garments were divided among the four soldiers. The **casting lots** is explained by John (19:23-24) as being specifically for the seamless undergarment (*chiton*). Matthew again has his favorite formula: **that it might be fulfilled.** This time the quotation is from Ps. 22:18, the great Messianic psalm on the Crucifixion.

Verse 36 is sometimes interpreted as another evidence of the callous cruelty of the soldiers. But M'Neile is probably nearer the truth when he writes: "It does not mean that they gloated over the Sufferer; they sat and guarded Him, as was customary, to prevent the possibility of escape."[42]

Over Jesus' head was a tablet bearing the **accusation** ("charge") against Him (37). The exact wording differs a little

[42]*Op. cit.,* p. 418.

in the four Gospels. Mark has the shortest form, "The King of the Jews," which is incorporated in the other three. Putting them all together we have: "This is Jesus of Nazareth, the King of the Jews."

With Jesus there were crucified two **thieves** (Greek, "robbers"), one on either side (38). It is altogether possible that they were fellow insurrectionists with Barabbas. If so, it is probable that Barabbas was the one slated to die on the middle cross. But Jesus took his place—a parable of His taking every sinner's place on the Cross.

Even the passersby mocked Jesus in a heartless manner. They recalled the charge that He had claimed power to destroy and rebuild the Temple. If He were the **Son of God** (40), why not assert His divine power and come down from the Cross? The **chief priests, scribes, and elders** (comprising the Sanhedrin) jeered at Him. Unintentionally they uttered a profound truth: **He saved others; himself he cannot save** (42). That was exactly it. Had He saved His own life, we would still be dead in sin. The cruelty of these men is seen in their insinuation that God the Father did not want Jesus (43). The fact, of course, was that the Father had to turn His back, as it were, on His Son and leave Him to die alone. That was part of the price of our redemption. Even the "robbers" on either side **cast the same in his teeth** (44) —just two words in the Greek, "reproached him."[43]

b. *The Afternoon Hours* (27:45-50). All three Synoptic Gospels mention the change that took place at the **sixth hour** (noon), when there was darkness until the **ninth hour** (45) (3:00 p.m.). This was over all the **land.** The Greek word is *ge,* which may be translated "earth" or **land.** If the latter, it may refer to the whole of Palestine, or only to Judea. Probably the last interpretation is best. Since the moon is always full at the Passover season, which comes in the middle of the lunar month between new moons, this could not have been an eclipse of the sun. It was either a supernatural darkness or due to very heavy, black clouds. In either case the timing was miraculous.

About the **ninth hour**—the time of offering the evening sacrifice—Jesus cried out with a loud voice: **Eli, Eli, lama sabachthani?**—Hebrew-Aramaic words that mean, **My God, my God,**

---

[43]For the difference in Luke's account see the comments on Luke 23:29-43.

**why hast thou forsaken me?** (46) In what way was Jesus forsaken? M'Neile says: "The cry was an expression of His agony of soul and body, but in that agony is involved the mystery of the Atonement."[44]

Some bystanders thought Jesus was calling for the prophet Elijah. One of them soaked a sponge in vinegar and offered it to Him, to quench His unbearable thirst (48). But the rest sought to restrain him. Better wait and see if Elijah would come to save Him (49). Once more Jesus cried out with a loud voice, and then **yielded up the ghost** (50)—better, "dismissed His spirit." Jesus had declared that He had power to lay down His life and to take it again (John 10:18).

### 2. *Accompanying Events* (27:51-54)

When Jesus died, **the veil of the temple** was rent in two from top to bottom (51). This was the inner veil, which separated the holy of holies from the holy place. The spiritual meaning of this is stated clearly in Heb. 9:1-14; 10:19-22. Through the rent veil of Christ's flesh the way was now opened into the very presence of God. It may also have been a hint that soon the old sanctuary would be destroyed (A.D. 70). In Christianity one can worship God anytime, anywhere. There may be a connection also between this event and the conversion of many priests (Acts 6:7).

The rending of the veil is recorded in all three Synoptics (cf. Mark 15:38; Luke 23:45), but the earthquake and the resurrection of some saints is recorded only here (51b-53). Whether there was any connection between the earthquake and the rending of the veil we do not know; nothing is stated here. They would seem to be two separate, supernatural consequences of that earth-shaking death. Neither are we told what happened to the saints who rose. Any suggestions here would be pure speculation.

When the **centurion** (officer in charge of a hundred men) saw the things that had happened, he was filled with awe and said, **Truly this was the Son of God** (54). There is no definite article here in the Greek. It is accurately translated "a son of God" (RSV) or perhaps "God's Son" (Berkeley). But there is something to be said for the translation "the Son of God" in this place. E. C. Colwell has made out a strong case for it in his study of the use and nonuse of the definite article in the Greek New

[44]*Op. cit.*, 421.

Testament.[45] Moule apparently agrees with him.[46] Omission of
the definite article is no evidence against the deity of Jesus taught
clearly throughout the New Testament. The omission here would
only suggest that a heathen Roman soldier was unlikely to have
had the background to understand and assert the deity of Jesus.
Luke reports the centurion as saying, "Certainly this was a
righteous man."

### 3. *Accompanying Women* (27: 55-56)

In sharp contrast to the scurrilous attitudes and actions of
the Jewish leaders around the Cross (41-43) is the reaction of the
centurion (54) and of these women. With loving devotion they
had followed the Master from Galilee, **ministering** (*diakonousai*)
**unto him** (55). Carr calls this: "The beginning of the ministry of
women—the female diaconate—in the Christian Church."[47] The
men had all fled in fear (26:56). It was the women who stayed in
sight of the Cross. What a comfort it must have been to Christ!

**Mary Magdalene** (56) is mentioned here for the first time in
this Gospel. Her name indicates that she came from Magdala, on
the western shore of the Sea of Galilee. Jesus had cast seven
demons out of her (Luke 8:2) and she was filled with gratitude
to Him. Her deep devotion caused her to be the first at the
empty tomb on Easter morning and the first to see Jesus after
His resurrection (John 20:1-18). About the other **Mary** we know
very little. **The mother of Zebedee's children** was probably
named Salome (cf. Mark 15:40).

### 4. *The Burial* (27:57-61)

**When the even was come** (57)—late afternoon, before sunset, when the sacred Sabbath would begin—Joseph of Arimathaea took action to bury the body of Jesus. Among the Jews it
was considered a horrible thing for the body of a friend or fellow
Jew to remain unburied. The apocryphal Book of Tobit emphasizes this strongly.

Joseph is here called **Jesus' disciple.** This seems to be the
first time that he had come out openly for Christ. It took courage

[45]"A Definite Rule for the Use of the Article in the Greek New Testament," *Journal of Biblical Literature,* LII (1933), 20.

[46]C. F. D. Moule, *An Idiom Book of New Testament Greek* (Cambridge:
University Press, 1953), p. 116.

[47]*Op. cit.,* p. 312.

to go in to Pilate and ask for the body of Jesus. But Joseph did it, and his request was granted.

There was no time for any extended treatment of the body. He simply **wrapped it in a clean linen cloth, and laid it in his own new tomb, which he had hewn out in the rock** (59-60). He rolled a great stone against the door and left. The two Marys were watching carefully where the Lord was laid (61).

### 5. *The Posting of the Guard* (27:62-66)

While all four Gospels record the burial of Jesus, only Matthew tells about the setting of the guard. It was on the **next day** (62), Saturday. The **chief priests** (Sadducees) and the **Pharisees** (representing the Sanhedrin) came to Pilate. They had heard of Jesus' prediction that He would rise the third day. They were taking no chances. They requested that a guard be posted in front of the tomb lest the disciples come and steal the body away and then claim He had risen. The last clause of verse 64 is thus explained by M'Neile: " 'The last error' would be the belief in the resurrection of Jesus, 'the first' the belief in His Messiahship."[48]

Pilate replied: **Ye have a watch: go your way, make it as sure as ye can** (65). **Watch** is *koustodian* ("custodian"). Perhaps the verb **have** should be treated as an imperative instead of an indicative (same form in Greek in the second person plural). Lenski translates it this way—"Have a guard!"[49] Probably Pilate was angry and spoke curtly. These men had pushed him into a corner, and he was doubtless disgusted with their asking for further favors. But he evidently gave them a small group of soldiers for an official guard at the tomb (66).

48*Op. cit.,* p. 428.
49*Op. cit.,* p. 1145.

Section **XII** *The Resurrection*

Matthew 28: 1-20

Matthew gives two post-resurrection appearances of Jesus. The first was to the women on the day He rose. The second was to the eleven apostles on a mountain in Galilee. Mark has no appearances in the first eight verses of chapter 16, but lists several in the last twelve verses.[1] Luke gives three, besides a reference to a fourth (to Simon Peter). He describes the appearances to the two disciples on the road to Emmaus, the meeting in the Upper Room at Jerusalem the first Sunday night, and the final time at the Ascension. John has the earliest appearance—to Mary Magdalene—the visits with the disciples on the first two Sunday nights in Jerusalem, and the appearance at the Lake of Galilee (four in all).

## A. THE DAY OF THE RESURRECTION, 28: 1-15

### 1. *The Women at the Sepulchre* (28: 1-10)

**In the end of the sabbath** (1) means "after the sabbath."[2] **As it began to dawn toward the first day of the week** shows that it was early Sunday morning. **Mary Magdalene and the other Mary** came to see the **sepulchre.** It would seem likely that this is the same visit as that described in John 20:1, where Mary Magdalene alone is mentioned. The two women went to tell the disciples (Peter and John in the Fourth Gospel) and perhaps the other Mary did not return to the tomb until later, after Mary Magdalene had first seen the risen Lord.

Matthew alone tells of the **earthquake** when an angel came and **rolled back the stone from the door** (2). He alone describes the angel's appearance (3) and the fright of the **keepers,** or "guards" (4).

The words of the angel (5-7) are rather similar in Matthew and Mark (16: 6-7). In both, the women are commanded to tell the disciples that Jesus will meet them in Galilee (7). Both tell of the mixed feelings of the women as they left the empty sepulcher (8).

---

[1]For discussion of their relation to the Gospel, see notes at that place in the commentary on Mark.

[2]Blass-Debrunner, *op. cit.,* p. 91 (164, 4).

252

Only Matthew relates the appearance of Jesus to these women as they were hastening to report to the disciples (9). He greeted them with the words, **All hail.** The single Greek word is *chairete*. Literally it means "rejoice, be glad." Lenski says: "The verb *chairein* is used to express all manner of greetings and always conveys a wish of happiness and well-being."[3] For this passage Arndt and Gingrich suggest "Good morning."[4] The two women fell at His feet and **worshipped him** as their risen, living Lord.

Just as the angels had bade the women not to fear (5), so now Jesus says to them: **Be not afraid** (10). Literally this is, "Stop being afraid!" Then He repeated the instructions of the angel that they were to tell the disciples to go north to Galilee, where Jesus would meet them. But it appears that they stayed in Jerusalem for a week, before leaving for Galilee (cf. John 20:28).

Under the title "The Message of the Empty Tomb," one could consider: (1) The mystery of the empty tomb—**He is not here;** (2) The miracle of the empty tomb—**He is risen;** (3) The meaning of the empty tomb—(*a*) An accepted sacrifice, Rom. 4:25; (*b*) An abiding presence, John 20:16; (*c*) An appointed judgment, Acts 17:31.

### 2. *The Bribing of the Guard* (28:11-15)

Since Matthew is the only one who tells of the posting of the guard (27:62-66), it is natural that he alone should mention the guards in verse 4 as well as give this incident.

After the women left the tomb, some of the **watch** ("guard") went into the city to tell the **chief priests** about the angel, the earthquake, and the fact that Jesus' body was gone (11). The chief priests summoned the **elders** (12) for a quick meeting of the Sanhedrin to decide what to do. The decision was to give **large money** ("many pieces of silver") to the soldiers, instructing them to say that Christ's disciples stole His body at night, while the soldiers slept (13). Since for a sentry to sleep at his post was a crime punishable by death, the chief priests promised that, if the governor heard, they would **persuade him,** and **secure you** (14). Carr cites examples to show that both of these verbs had a technical usage at that time, meaning "persuade (by bribes)"

[3]*Op. cit.,* p. 1157.
[4]*Op. cit.,* p. 882.

and **secure** with "judicial bribery." It is a sad commentary on the morals of the day.

The purpose of Matthew's inserting this paragraph was obviously to counteract the false story about Jesus' body being stolen. The story was **commonly reported among the Jews until this day** (15)—that is, the time of the writing of this Gospel.

### B. THE GREAT COMMISSION, 28:16-20

Obedient to Christ's command, **the eleven disciples** went northward to Galilee, to **a mountain** where Jesus had agreed to meet them (16). Nowhere are we told what mountain this was. When they saw Jesus, **they worshipped him: but some doubted** (17). This seems to imply a larger group than the eleven, and may be the same meeting where the risen Christ was seen by "above five hundred brethren at once" (I Cor. 15:6).

The Great Commission is given in verses 18-20. Blair calls this "the key passage of this Gospel," and adds: "Here many of the emphases of the book are caught up."[5] He mentions the absoluteness of Jesus' authority, "its derivative character," the command to evangelize the whole world, the nature of discipleship, and the assurance of Jesus' presence.[6]

**Power** (18) is *exousia*, "authority." **Teach** (19) is "make disciples"—a different word entirely from **teaching** (20). **Alway** (20) is literally "all the days." No matter what days—good or bad, happy or sorrowful—may meet us, Jesus has promised to be with us "all the days"—**even unto the end of the** "age" (*aion*). Blair rightly observes: "The statement on Jesus' lips at the very end of the Gospel—'All authority in heaven and on earth has been given to me'—simply catches up the thrust of the entire story."[7]

---

[5]Edward P. Blair, *Jesus in the Gospel of Matthew* (New York: Abingdon Press, 1960), p. 45.

[6]*Ibid.*, pp. 45-46.

[7]*Ibid.*, p. 46.

# BIBLIOGRAPHY

## I. COMMENTARIES

ALFORD, HENRY. *The Greek Testament.* Revised by EVERETT HARRISON. Chicago: Moody Press, 1958.

ALLEN, W. C. *A Critical and Exegetical Commentary on the Gospel According to St. Matthew.* "International Critical Commentary." New York: Charles Scribner's Sons, 1907.

ATKINSON, BASIL F. C. "Gospel According to Matthew." *New Bible Commentary,* edited by F. DAVIDSON. Second Edition. Grand Rapids: Wm. B. Eerdmans Publishing Co., 1954.

BARCLAY, WILLIAM. *The Gospel of Matthew,* Vol. I. Second Edition. "The Daily Study Bible." Philadelphia: Westminster Press, 1958.

BARNES, ALBERT. *Notes on the New Testament: Matthew and Mark.* Grand Rapids: Baker Book House, 1949.

BENGEL, JOHN ALBERT. *Gnomon of the New Testament.* 5 vols. Edinburgh: T. & T. Clark, 1860.

BROADUS, JOHN A. *Commentary on the Gospel of Matthew.* "An American Commentary on the New Testament." Philadelphia: American Baptist Publication Society, 1886.

BROWN, DAVID. "Matthew—John," *A Commentary . . . on the Old and New Testaments,* Vol. V, by R. JAMIESON, A. R. FAUSSET, and DAVID BROWN. Grand Rapids: Wm. B. Eerdmans Publishing Co., 1948 (reprint).

BRUCE, A. B. "The Synoptic Gospels." *Expositor's Greek Testament.* Grand Rapids: Wm. B. Eerdmans Publishing Co., n.d.

BUTTRICK, GEORGE A. "Matthew" (Exposition). *Interpreter's Bible.* Edited by GEORGE A. BUTTRICK, et al., Vol. VII. New York: Abingdon-Cokesbury Press, 1951.

CARR, A. *The Gospel According to St. Matthew.* "Cambridge Greek Testament." Cambridge: University Press, 1886.

CHRYSOSTOM. "Homilies on the Gospel of St. Matthew." *A Select Library of the Nicene and Post-Nicene Fathers of the Christian Church.* Edited by PHILIP SCHAFF. New York: Christian Literature Co., 1888.

CLARKE, ADAM. *The New Testament of Our Lord and Saviour Jesus Christ,* Vol. I. New York: Abingdon-Cokesbury Press, n.d.

CLARKE, W. K. LOWTHER. *Concise Bible Commentary.* New York: Macmillan Co., 1953.

Cox, G. E. P. "The Gospel According to St. Matthew." *The Twentieth Century Bible Commentary.* Edited by G. H. DAVIES, et al. New York: Harper & Brothers, 1955.

DAVIES, J. NEWTON. "Matthew." *Abingdon Bible Commentary.* Edited by F. C. EISELEN, et al. New York: Abingdon-Cokesbury Press, 1929.

DE DIETRICH, SUZANNE. "The Gospel According to St. Matthew." Translated by DONALD G. MILLER, *The Layman's Bible Commentary,* Vol. XVI. Richmond: John Knox Press, 1961.

DUMMELOW, J. R. (ed.). *A Commentary on the Holy Bible.* London: Macmillan and Company, 1909.

255

ERDMAN, CHARLES R. *The Gospel of Matthew*. Philadelphia: Westminster Press, 1920.

FILSON, FLOYD V. *A Commentary on the Gospel According to St. Matthew*. "Harper's New Testament Commentaries." New York: Harper & Brothers, 1960.

GIBSON, JOHN M. *The Gospel of St. Matthew*. "The Expositor's Bible." New York: A. C. Armstrong & Son, n.d.

GRANT, FREDRICK C. "Matthew." *Nelson's Bible Commentary*, Vol. VI. New York: Thomas Nelson & Sons, 1962.

GREEN, F. W. *The Gospel According to St. Matthew*. "The Clarendon Bible." Oxford: Clarendon Press, 1936.

HENRY, MATTHEW. *Commentary on the Whole Bible*. New York: Fleming H. Revell Company, n.d.

JOHNSON, SHERMAN. "Matthew" (Exegesis). *Interpreter's Bible*. Edited by GEORGE BUTTRICK, et al., Vol. VII. New York: Abingdon-Cokesbury Press, 1951.

KENT, HOMER A., JR. "Matthew." *Wycliffe Bible Commentary*. Edited by CHARLES F. PFEIFFER and EVERETT F. HARRISON. Chicago: Moody Press, 1962.

KRAELING, EMIL G. *The Clarified New Testament*. New York: McGraw-Hill Book Company, 1962.

LANGE, JOHN PETER. "Matthew." *Commentary on the Holy Scriptures*. Edited by J. P. LANGE. Grand Rapids: Zondervan Publishing House, n.d.

LENSKI, R. C. H. *The Interpretation of St. Matthew's Gospel*. Columbus, Ohio: Wartburg Press, 1943.

LEVERTOFF, P. P., and GOUDGE, H. L. "The Gospel According to St. Matthew." *A Commentary on the Holy Scriptures*. Edited by CHARLES GORE, H. L. GOUDGE, and ALFRED GUILLAUME. New York: Macmillan Co., 1928.

MACLAREN, ALEXANDER. *Exposition of Holy Scripture*. "St. Matthew." Grand Rapids: Wm. B. Eerdmans Publishing Co., 1944 (reprint).

MCLAUGHLIN, G. A. *Commentary on the Gospel According to St. Matthew*. Chicago: Christian Witness Co., 1909.

MEYER, H. A. W. *Critical and Exegetical Hand-Book to the Gospel of Matthew*. New York: Funk & Wagnalls, 1884.

MICKLEM, PHILIP A. *St. Matthew*. "Westminster Commentaries." London: Methuen & Co., 1917.

M'NEILE, ALAN H. *The Gospel According to St. Matthew*. London: Macmillan & Co., 1915.

MONTEFIORE, C. G. *The Synoptic Gospels*. 2 vols. London: Macmillan & Co., 1909.

MORGAN, G. CAMPBELL. *The Gospel According to Matthew*. New York: Fleming H. Revell Co., 1929.

MORISON, JAMES. *A Practical Commentary on the Gospel According to St. Matthew*. London: Hodder & Stoughton, 1899.

NEIL, WILLIAM. *Harper's Bible Commentary*. New York: Harper & Row, 1962.

OFFERMANN, HENRY. "The Gospel According to Matthew." *New Testament Commentary*. Edited by H. C. ALLEMAN. Revised Edition. Philadelphia: Muhlenberg Press, 1944.

PLUMMER, ALFRED. *An Exegetical Commentary on the Gospel According to St. Matthew*. London: Elliot Stock, 1909.

PLUMPTRE, E. H. "Matthew." *Commentary on the Whole Bible.* Edited by C. J. ELLICOTT. Grand Rapids: Zondervan Publishing House, n.d.

ROBINSON, THEODORE H. *The Gospel of Matthew.* "Moffatt's New Testament Commentary." New York: Harper and Brothers, 1927.

RYLE, J. C. *Expository Thoughts on the Gospels: Matthew—Mark.* Grand Rapids: Zondervan Publishing House, n.d.

SADLER, M. F. *The Gospel According to St. Matthew.* Third Edition. New York: James Pott & Co., 1887.

STENDAHL, K. "Matthew." *Peake's Commentary on the Bible.* Edited by MATTHEW BLACK and H. H. ROWLEY. London: Thomas Nelson & Sons, 1962.

TASKER, R. V. G. *The Gospel According to St. Matthew.* "Tyndale New Testament Commentaries." Grand Rapids: Wm. B. Eerdmans Publishing Co., 1961.

TRAPP, JOHN. *Commentary on the New Testament.* Grand Rapids: Zondervan Publishing House, 1958 (reprint).

WARD, A. MARCUS. *The Gospel According to St. Matthew.* "Epworth Preacher's Commentaries." London: Epworth Press, 1961.

WESLEY, JOHN. *Explanatory Notes upon the New Testament.* London: Epworth Press, 1941 (reprint).

WHEDON, D. D. *Commentary on the Gospels: Matthew—Mark.* New York: Hunt & Eaton, 1860.

WILLIAMS, A. LUKYN. "St. Matthew" (Exposition). *Pulpit Commentary.* Edited by JOSEPH S. EXELL. Grand Rapids: Wm. B. Eerdmans Publishing Co., 1950 (reprint).

## II. OTHER BOOKS

ABBOTT-SMITH, G. *A Manual Greek Lexicon of the New Testament.* Second Edition. Edinburgh: T. & T. Clark, 1923.

ANDREWS, SAMUEL J. *The Life of Our Lord.* Grand Rapids: Zondervan Publishing House, 1954 (reprint).

ARNDT, W. F., and GINGRICH, F. W. *A Greek-English Lexicon of the New Testament and Other Early Christian Literature.* Chicago: University of Chicago Press, 1957.

BLAIR, EDWARD P. *Jesus in the Gospel of Matthew.* New York: Abingdon Press, 1960.

BONHOEFFER, DIETRICH. *The Cost of Discipleship.* Revised Edition. New York: Macmillan Co., 1959.

BOWMAN, JOHN WICK, and TAPP, ROLAND W. *The Gospel from the Mount.* Philadelphia: Westminster Press, 1957.

BRANSCOMB, HARVIE. *The Teachings of Jesus.* New York: Abingdon-Cokesbury Press, 1931.

BUTTRICK, GEORGE A. *The Parables of Jesus.* New York: Harper & Brothers, 1928.

CHAMBERS, OSWALD. *Studies in the Sermon on the Mount.* Cincinnati: God's Revivalist Press, 1915.

DEISSMANN, ADOLF. *Bible Studies.* Translated by A. GRIEVE. Edinburgh: T. & T. Clark, 1901.

————. *Light from the Ancient East.* Translated by L. R. M. STRACHAN. New York: George H. Doran Co., 1927.

DODD, C. H. *The Parables of the Kingdom.* London: Nisbet & Co., 1936.

EDERSHEIM, ALFRED. *The Life and Times of Jesus the Messiah.* Eighth Edition. New York: Longmans, Green and Co., 1903.

FARMER, W. R. *Maccabees, Zealots, and Josephus.* New York: Columbia University Press, 1956.

FITCH, WILLIAM. *The Beatitudes of Jesus.* Grand Rapids: Wm. B. Eerdmans Publishing Co., 1961.

FRANZMANN, MARTIN H. *Follow Me: Discipleship According to St. Matthew.* St. Louis: Concordia Publishing House, 1961.

HAYES, D. A. *The Synoptic Gospels and The Book of Acts.* New York: Methodist Book Concern, 1919.

HUNTER, A. M. *Gospel According to Mark.* London: S.C.M. Press, 1948.

————. *Interpreting the Parables of Jesus.* Naperville, Ill.: S.C.M. Book Club, 1960.

————. *A Pattern for Life.* Philadelphia: Westminster Press, n.d. (British Edition, 1953).

JEREMIAS, JOACHIM. *The Eucharistic Words of Jesus.* Translated by ARNOLD ERHARDT. New York: Macmillan Co., 1955.

————. *The Parables of Jesus.* Translated by S. H. HOOKE. New York: Charles Scribner's Sons, 1955.

JONES, E. STANLEY. *The Christ of the Mount.* New York: Abingdon Press, 1931.

JOSEPHUS, FLAVIUS. *Works.* Translated by WILLIAM WHISTON. Philadelphia: Henry T. Coates & Co., n.d.

LADD, GEORGE E. *The Gospel of the Kingdom.* Grand Rapids: Wm. B. Eerdmans Publishing Co., 1959.

LIGHTFOOT, J. B. *Notes on the Epistles of St. Paul.* Grand Rapids: Zondervan Publishing House, 1957 (reprint).

LLOYD-JONES, MARTIN. *Studies in the Sermon on the Mount.* 2 vols. Grand Rapids: Wm. B. Eerdmans Publishing Co., 1959.

LUNDSTROM, GOSTA. *The Kingdom of God in the Teaching of Jesus.* Translated by JOAN BULMAN. Richmond: John Knox Press, 1963.

MANSON, WILLIAM. *Jesus the Messiah.* Philadelphia: Westminster Press, 1946.

MCARTHUR, HARVEY. *Understanding the Sermon on the Mount.* New York: Harper & Brothers, 1960.

MORGAN, G. CAMPBELL. *The Crises of the Christ.* New York: Fleming H. Revell Co., 1903.

PINK, ARTHUR W. *An Exposition of the Sermon on the Mount.* Grand Rapids: Baker Book House, 1951.

ROBERTSON, A. T. *Word Pictures in the New Testament,* Vol. I. New York: Richard R. Smith, 1930.

SCHURER, EMIL. *A History of the Jewish People in the Time of Jesus Christ,* Vol. II. English Translation. Edinburgh: T. & T. Clark, 1885.

SCOTT, E. F. *The Crisis in the Life of Jesus: The Cleansing of the Temple and Its Significance.* New York: Charles Scribner's Sons, 1952.

SMITH, GEORGE ADAM. *Historical Geography of the Holy Land.* Twentieth Edition. London: Hodder & Stroughton, n.d.

——. *Jerusalem.* New York: A. C. Armstrong & Son, 1908.

STAUFFER, ETHELBERT. *Jesus and His Story.* Translated by RICHARD and CLARA WINSTON. New York: Alfred A. Knopf, 1959.

STREETER, B. H. *The Four Gospels.* Revised Edition. London: Macmillan & Co., 1930.

TAYLOR, VINCENT. *The Names of Jesus.* London: Macmillan & Co., 1953.

——. *The Person of Christ in New Testament Teaching.* London: Macmillan & Co., 1958.

TRENCH, RICHARD C. *Notes on the Miracles of Our Lord.* Philadelphia: Wm. Syckelmoore, 1878.

——. *Synonyms of the New Testament.* Grand Rapids: Wm. B. Eerdmans Publishing Co., 1947 (reprint).

——. *Notes on the Parables of Our Lord.* Philadelphia: Wm. Syckelmoore, 1878.

WIKENHAUSER, ALFRED. *New Testament Introduction.* Translation by JOSEPH CUNNINGHAM. New York: Herder & Herder, 1958.

ZAHN, THEODOR. *Introduction to the New Testament.* Translated by JOHN M. TROUT, et al. 3 vols. Grand Rapids: Kregel Publications, 1953 [reprint].

*The Gospel According to*

# MARK

A. Elwood Sanner

# Introduction

## A. ORIGIN

Although Mark's Gospel itself is anonymous (the titles of the fourfold Gospels having been added later), it is virtually a certainty that the author was John Mark, a native of Jerusalem, a cousin of Barnabas, and a close associate of Peter and perhaps of Paul as well. From the beginning of the second century, Mark's name, and no other, has always been associated with the Gospel. This is a remarkable fact. In a time when the Church sought to assign apostolic authorship to its literature, it is highly unlikely that a secondary name would be linked with a Gospel unless there was good reason for doing so. Papias, Justin Martyr, the *Anti-Marcionite Prologue to Mark*, Irenaeus, and the Muratorian Canon all attribute the Gospel to Mark as an interpreter of Peter. In the words of Vincent Taylor, "There can be no doubt that the author of the Gospel was Mark, the attendant of Peter."[1]

Some question has been raised whether this Mark is to be identified with the Mark of the New Testament,[2] but the objections are not weighty, and the consensus is that the identification should be made. "We may take it as virtually certain that the Mark who wrote the Gospel and who is referred to in I Pet. 5:13 and the Mark of Acts and the Pauline letters are one and the same person."[3]

The implication of all this should be clear. If the earliest Gospel came from the pen of a man who had close contact with the earliest leaders of the young Christian Church, we may be confident that he has given us an accurate, historically reliable account of the life and ministry of Jesus. More than this, one may be sure that Mark reflects the theological beliefs and convictions of the first generation of Christians, which included eyewitnesses of the mighty works of Jesus. This is of immeasurable importance. Man's only hope is in "Jesus of Nazareth, a man approved of God . . . by miracles and wonders and signs, which God did by him . . . whom God hath raised up, having loosed the pains of

---

[1]*The Gospel According to St. Mark* (London: Macmillan and Co. Ltd., 1959), p. 26.

[2]Acts 12:12, 25; 13:13; 15:37-39; Col. 4:10; II Tim. 4:11; Philem. 24; I Pet. 5:13. *John* was his Jewish name, *Mark* his Greek name.

[3]C. E. B. Cranfield, "Mark, Gospel of," *The Interpreter's Dictionary of the Bible* (New York: Abingdon Press, 1962) III, 268.

death . . ." (Acts 2:22, 24). A dependable, trustworthy account of such good news is priceless.

## B. Date and Place

The time of writing is often fixed at A.D. 65-70. This is on the assumption that Mark wrote after the death of Peter (which probably occurred during the Neronian persecution of A.D. 64-65) but before the reduction of Jerusalem in A.D. 70. Many, however, believe the Gospel was written earlier, perhaps in the fifties. This dating is based upon the belief that Luke and Acts were written before the death of Paul (c. A.D. 64), and hence that Mark (one of Luke's sources) was written earlier.

A stronger case can be made for Rome as the place of writing than for any other ancient city, although Alexandria and Antioch have also been mentioned. Because Mark explains Jewish customs (e.g., 7:3-4) and translates Aramaic terms (5:41, *et passim*), it is clear that he was writing for non-Jewish readers. The testimony of tradition (the *Anti-Marcionite Prologue,* Irenaeus, Clement of Alexandria) points to Rome, as does also the presence of a number of words borrowed from Latin (e.g., *centurion, denarius,* etc.). The overtones of persecution and suffering also support this view. Peter (I Pet. 5:13) specifically states that Mark, "my son," was with him in "Babylon," thought to be a reference to Rome. If the Rufus of Mark 15:21 is to be identified with the Rufus mentioned in Rom. 16:13, the case for Rome is further strengthened.

## C. Sources

According to Papias, bishop of Hierapolis (c. A.D. 140), Mark was the interpreter of Peter and wrote an accurate account of all the things he remembered from the preaching and teaching of Simon.[4] This tradition, confirmed by other second-century writers, has been played down by those who question the historical reliability of the Gospel. Considerable internal evidence, however, links the Gospel with Peter: Mark begins at the point where Peter became a disciple and features the Galilean ministry as it centered in Capernaum, Peter's home; vivid details suggest an eyewitness account; events favorable to Peter are omitted, whereas less favorable events, such as the denial, are told with

---

[4]Papias, whose statement was preserved by Eusebius in his *Ecclesiastical History* (III. 39), was actually quoting from someone he calls "the Elder," probably the elder John of Ephesus. *Ibid.,* p. 267.

considerable fullness. The prevailing opinion is that Peter was one of Mark's principal sources: "In the main he [Mark] records what he heard Peter tell, supplementing this with other materials which he knew to be reliable."[5]

Another factor to be considered, often associated with negative results, is known as form criticism. This discipline attempts to discover the oral sources behind the Gospels. If Mark was the first Gospel to be written, as it is widely believed, there was a period of twenty-five years or more when the gospel message circulated chiefly in oral form.[6] Form critics have studied what are thought to be units of tradition in the Gospels and have classified them under a wide variety of categories or "forms" (e.g., Pronouncement-Stories, Miracle-Stories, etc.). The more radical critics have taught or implied that these units were the creation of the Church and devoid of historical basis.

The subjectivism of the radical advocates of form criticism, as evidenced by the absence of agreement, has discredited the movement in its negative form. Some scholars, by contrast, have used form criticism to demonstrate the accuracy and dependability of the Gospel records. It is undoubtedly true that the various units of the gospel story were preached and taught widely by means of certain forms advantageous to memorization and catechetical usage. But "those forms crystalized when there was every possibility of checking their accuracy."[7] John Mark could not have written and circulated successfully an account of the life and teaching of Jesus which was contrary to the facts still widely known during the generation after the Crucifixion. There is a sense in which the Gospel of Mark is the fruit of the combined witness of the first generation of believers.

This viewpoint has been summarized movingly: "As through a glass darkly, we can see the Evangelist at work and in the background many others to whom he is debtor . . . Behind him lay the teaching activity of a living Church. In it he had shared and upon it he was dependent . . . His Gospel is far more than a private undertaking; it is a product of the life of the Church inspired by the Spirit of God."[8]

[5]C. L. Mitton, *The Good News: Bible Guides No. 13,* eds. William Barclay and F. F. Bruce (London: Lutterworth Press, 1961), p. 24.

[6]Numerous efforts have also been made to establish the existence of written sources back of Mark but with little success, although it is usually conceded that such documents probably did exist.

[7]Samuel A. Cartledge, "The Gospel of Mark," *Interpretation,* IX, No. 2 (April, 1955), 189.

[8]Taylor, *op. cit.,* pp. 103-4.

Mark's sources, then, were principally the preaching and teaching ministry of Peter, together with elements of oral tradition, his own personal recollections, and possibly certain written documents.

## D. The Miracles

It is perhaps fair to say that the Church has come through a period during which the miraculous element in the Bible was widely discredited. The atmosphere of our day is friendlier to the idea of miracles. Science has a humbler view of the limits of natural law. "No longer is there any reason for denying, on the basis of science or philosophy, that God can use forces or laws that man has not yet discovered."[9]

It has also become clearer in biblical and theological studies that the earliest Christian tradition is shot through with a belief in the miracles of the Gospels. One is certainly free, on the basis of his own philosophy and presuppositions, to reject the miracles, but he must at the same time admit that such a position is inconsistent with historic Christianity. We are grateful for the contemporary resurgence of historic evangelical Christianity with its firm confidence that Jesus of Nazareth was indeed "a man approved of God . . . by miracles and wonders and signs" (Acts 2:22).

However worthy the motives of men like Bultmann may be, it is possible they have misread the modern mind, for a profound hunger resides there. In any case, the preaching of the Cross has always been foolishness to them that perish, and it is still true that, in the wisdom of God, He has chosen to save men "through the folly of what we preach" (I Cor. 1:21, RSV). And, happily, "many of the finest scientists, philosophers, and biblical scholars are humble believers in a supernatural approach to historic Christianity."[10]

## E. Purpose

One of the sure conclusions of biblical studies is that the Gospels were written with a religious and theological purpose. Although Mark did not state his purpose as overtly as John did, it would not be essentially different. "These are written, that ye might believe that Jesus is the Christ, the Son of God; and that believing ye might have life through his name" (John 20:31).

[9]Cartledge, op. cit., p. 191.
[10]Ibid., p. 192.

This is not to say that the Evangelists had no interest in the facts of history. There is good reason to believe that their work is historically reliable. It is to say, however, that they wrote with a religious purpose in mind and not with the thought of conforming to the canons of modern historical research.

Through the testimony of Peter and other eyewitnesses (including possibly his own reminiscences), John Mark caught a vision of the Man of Nazareth, who was also the Messiah, the heavenly Son of Man, and the Son of God. In Him the kingdom of God had come near. This strong Son of God engaged Satan and his minions—demons, disease, and death—in mortal conflict and emerged as Victor. Mark wanted all mankind to see the Suffering Servant and follow Him all the way to Golgotha, through the empty tomb, and into glory that is to come. He wanted to hearten and galvanize believers as they girded themselves to face ostracism, ridicule, and brutal martyrdom under hostile Roman emperors.

And thus it was that John Mark, once a failure and a disappointment to the Apostle Paul (Acts 13:13; 15:36-39), set a reed pen to papyrus and recorded for all time his story. He told it breathlessly, using the historical present and the imperfect tense, as if the events were taking place before his eyes. Punctuating the account with the word *euthus* ("immediately," "at once") and connecting his clauses with *kai* ("also," "and"), he wrote the Gospel of action with vividness, color, and detail such as an eyewitness would recall. Though apparently simple and artless, the result was in fact a profound religious document, soundly based on fact, and verily the Word of God.

> Strong Son of God, eternal, living Saviour—
> He knows the way; He'll take us safely through.[11]

[11]Kathryn Blackburn Peck, from "No Other Name."

# Outline

I. The Beginning of the Gospel, 1:1-13
   A. The "Keynote," 1:1
   B. John the Baptizer, 1:2-8
   C. The Baptism of Jesus, 1:9-11
   D. The Temptation, 1:12-13

II. The Early Galilean Ministry, 1:14—3:6
   A. First Steps in Galilee, 1:14-20
   B. A Sabbath in Capernaum, 1:21-34
   C. The First Preaching Tour, 1:35-45
   D. Conflicts with the Pharisees, 2:1—3:6

III. The Later Galilean Ministry, 3:7—6:13
   A. Withdrawal to the Seaside, 3:7-12
   B. The Appointment of the Twelve, 3:13-19
   C. Friends and Foes, 3:20-35
   D. A Ministry in Parables, 4:1-34
   E. A Ministry of Mighty Works, 4:35—5:43
   F. A Prophet Without Honor, 6:1-6
   G. The Mission of the Twelve, 6:7-13

IV. A Ministry Beyond Galilee, 6:14—8:26
   A. The Ghosts of Herod's Fears, 6:14-29
   B. Miracles and Teaching Around the Sea, 6:30-56
   C. Conflict over the Tradition of the Elders, 7:1-23
   D. Two Healings Among Gentiles, 7:24-37
   E. Gifts of Food and Sight, 8:1-26

V. The Road Toward Jerusalem, 8:27—10:52
   A. The Great Confession and Transfiguration, 8:27—9:29
   B. En Route Through Galilee, 9:30-50
   C. The Ministry in Perea, 10:1-52

VI. The Jerusalem Ministry, 11:1—13:37
   A. Events Preceding the Ministry, 11:1-26
   B. Teaching and Debate in Jerusalem, 11:27—12:44
   C. The Discourse on the Mount of Olives, 13:1-37

VII. The Passion Narrative, 14:1—15:47
   A. Events Leading to the Arrest, 14:1-52
   B. The Trials, Crucifixion, and Burial, 14:53—15:47

VIII. The Resurrection, 16:1-20
   A. The Empty Tomb, 16:1-8
   B. The Epilogue, 16:9-20

# Section I · The Beginning of the Gospel

Mark 1:1-13

## A. THE "KEYNOTE," 1:1

These opening words, **the beginning of the gospel** (1), are reminiscent of Gen. 1:1, "In the beginning God," and John 1:1, "In the beginning was the Word." Is this first verse to be regarded as a title to the book as a whole or as simply an introduction to John's ministry, described in 2-8? The view that this is a title for Mark's entire Gospel is widely held and is reasonable, though other interpretations are also possible.[1] Mark may have had in mind the ministry of John the Baptist as the point where the proclamation of **the gospel** actually began. This would be in line with Acts 10:36 ff.

A refreshing explanation is offered by Sherman E. Johnson,[2] who speaks of this verse as a "keynote" of the Gospel of Mark. The thought of 1:1 does permeate the book and sets forth the essence of it.

The word **gospel** (*euangelion*) and its corresponding verb (*euangelidzo*) are rich in biblical and historical associations. In the Greek Old Testament (the Septugint), the terms are related to the announcement of good news, especially of victory (see I Kings 1:42; I Sam. 31:9). The terms also had a pagan usage in connection with the announcement of the birth of a royal heir and of his advancement to succeeding levels of attainment. The **gospel** is the publication of good news, the inbreaking of the long-expected Kingdom.

Do the words **the gospel of** mean *about* Jesus Christ or *by* and *through* Him? They mean both. Jesus came in order that there might be a **gospel**. The story of His incarnation, crucifixion, resurrection, and ascension are the facts of the gospel. However, Jesus also came preaching (telling about) **the gospel.**

---

[1]C. E. B. Cranfield, *The Gospel According to Saint Mark* ("The Cambridge Greek Testament Commentary"; New York and London: Cambridge University Press, 1959), pp. 34-35, cites ten possible views on the relation of 1:1 to the book as a whole.

[2]*A Commentary on the Gospel According to St. Mark* ("Harper's New Testament Commentaries"; New York: Harper and Brothers Publishers, 1960), p. 31.

Whether this verse be thought of as a title to the book or only as a pointer to the ministry of John the Baptist, it serves well as a "keynote" for the whole of Mark's Gospel. In the phrase **Jesus Christ, the Son of God,** Mark has given us the heart of his story: Jesus is the Greek equivalent of *Joshua* ("the Lord is salvation"); Christ is the New Testament term for *Messiah;* and the **Son of God**[3] is the loftiest title possible. Our Lord's deity was the rock upon which the first Christians built their faith.

## B. JOHN THE BAPTIZER, 1: 2-8

**As it is written** (2) should have special emphasis as a precise fulfillment of scripture: *Just* as it is written. **In the prophets** should read, "in Isaiah the prophet," as the better MSS have it. Both Mal. 3:1 and Isa. 40:3 are quoted in vv. 2-3, but Mark evidently referred to Isaiah as representative of the two appropriate references.[4] The gospel had already begun in the "long thoughts of God" found in the prophets. God had promised to send a forerunner ahead of the Anointed One to prepare the way for His coming. **My messenger ... the voice of one crying** (2-3) refers to the "Elijah" whom the Jews expected before the coming of Messiah (9:11 ff.). On the basis of Mal. 3:1 ff., the forerunner was one who threatened judgment to come and therefore stressed the need for purification. Straight paths, personal rectitude, were needful for those who would receive the coming One. We may therefore connect vv. 2 and 4 thus: **As it is written ... John did baptize.**

Why did the Baptizer appear **in the wilderness?** (4) The answer is found in Israel's long association with the waste places of the Near East. It was in the wilderness where God gave the Law and led His chosen people with a mighty hand and outstretched arm. It was thought by the Jews that Messiah would also appear in the wilderness to bring Israel's final salvation. The Qumran community, made famous by the Dead Sea Scrolls, was located in a desolate area. John evidently preached in Perea, for it was Herod Antipas who later arrested him.

**John did baptize,** of course, but more than this he was an earnest preacher. He was the voice of one crying aloud in the

---

[3]While it is true that this phrase does not appear in some of the better MSS, it is generally accepted as genuine because it is characteristic of Mark's theology and because the omission is more likely an error than the inclusion. Six singular genitives, several of which were probably abbreviated, follow in succession.

[4]For a more accurate rendering, see any recent translation.

wilderness. To **preach,** in the sense of the Greek term, meant to announce with a loud voice. In the Baptizer, Israel heard the self-authenticating voice of prophecy, so long silent in the land. John proclaimed repentance—not a sentimental penitence or sorrow, but a radical turning to God. Without this, the **remission or forgiveness of sins** was impossible. Converts to Judaism (proselytes) were required, among other things, to be baptized. But here was a rugged prophet who required repentance, baptism, and confession of sins even of the children of Abraham.

Despite the fact that his hearers had to come on foot some twenty miles and descend four thousand feet, **there went out unto** (5) John great throngs of people from all over Judea, including, of course, Jerusalem. John was the leader of a truly great religious movement, a fact confirmed by Josephus.[5] The Baptizer's influence eventually came to the attention of Herod Antipas, with tragic results; that influence was still a factor in the religious outlook of the people shortly before the Crucifixion (11:27-33). As the repentant converts were being baptized they were **confessing their sins.** Some take the verb baptized as middle voice (same form in the Greek as passive). Grant writes: "Baptized by him means 'in his presence,' or 'at his direction;' Jewish baptism, and probably the earliest Christian as well, was self-administered: 'baptized themselves in his presence.' "[6] But this is not the most natural way to take the language here, nor in Acts 8:38; 16:33.

John's appearance was as rugged as the region where he ministered, for he was **clothed with camel's hair** (6) and wore a belt of animal skin. His daily fare included **locusts,** despised by all but the poorest (even though approved in Lev. 11:22), and **wild honey,** from the crevices of the rocks. John was a prophet, in line with the great prophets of the Old Testament, as his garb indicated (II Kings 1:8; Zech. 13:4). Jesus later spoke with affection of him and ranked him with the noblest of his era (Matt. 11:11). All of this notwithstanding, John knew his ministry to be only a preparatory one: **There cometh one . . . after me** (7). John was a genuinely humble man. As important as his message and ministry were, he knew himself to be no more than the fore-

[5]*Ant.* XVIII, 5. 2.

[6]F. C. Grant, "The Gospel According to St. Mark" (Exegesis), *The Interpreter's Bible,* ed. George A. Buttrick, *et al.,* VII (New York: Abingdon-Cokesbury Press, 1951), 650.

runner of One mightier than he. It was the duty of slaves to carry their masters' sandals and to tie or loosen the **latchet** or thong, but the Baptizer felt unworthy to perform even the service of a slave for Him who would **baptize . . . with the Holy Ghost** (8).

In speaking of the baptism of the Holy Spirit, Mark certainly must have had the Pentecost in mind. In numerous places the Old Testament speaks of the coming of the Holy Spirit (see Joel 2:28 f.; Ezek. 36:25-27; *et al.*). Also, the bestowal of the Spirit was related to the coming of Messiah.[7] A radical turning to God with confession of sins—symbolized by the washing of baptism— is significant, but only preparatory to the coming of Him whose medium of baptism is the fiery Holy Spirit.

## C. THE BAPTISM OF JESUS, 1:9-11

In those days, sometime during the great religious revival under John, perhaps near the close, Jesus came from Galilee to begin His ministry. Nazareth was to the north and west; Perea, where John was baptizing, was to the south and east of Jordan. (See map.) Jesus' crucial hour of decision had come. The village He left, **Nazareth** (9), had been His home since childhood (Matt. 2:23), but was an obscure place. It is not mentioned in the Old Testament, Josephus, or the Talmud. This was in line with the Messianic veiledness of our Lord. But the word of John's powerful ministry had reached even Nazareth, far beyond Judea and Perea.

Christians have often read with perplexity that Jesus sought baptism at the hands of John. Apart from the fact that He wanted to identify himself with John's religious movement, the question arises, Why? He had no sense of personal need, as His testimony in John 8:46a makes clear; He did not, as others, confess sin. Moreover, as Matthew records, Jesus had to override the objections of John himself (Matt. 3:14 f.). Cranfield answers the question well: "Jesus' submission to John's baptism of repentance was his mature self-dedication of his mission of self-identification with sinners which in due course would take him to the Cross."[8] He here, literally, numbered himself "with the transgressors" (Isa. 53:12).

---

[7]Cranfield, (*op. cit.*, p. 50) says: "There is evidence that a general bestowal of the Spirit was expected as a feature of the last days."

[8]*Ibid.*, p. 52.

Somewhat later (10:38), Jesus referred to His sufferings and death as a baptism. We may believe this symbolism was present even here. One other consideration may be mentioned. The fact that our Lord submitted to baptism is sufficient warrant for the practice of Christian baptism.

As Jesus came **up out of the water** (10), He **straightway,** or immediately, **saw the heavens** "torn open." The Greek word here (*schizomenous*) is a vivid, apocalyptic expression and will be recognized at once for its modern connotations. It is a present participle indicating the action was in progress. Man's anguished prayer, "Oh that thou wouldest rend the heavens" (Isa. 64:1), was fully answered in the experience of Jesus. Coming down from the opened heavens upon (or, possibly, *into*) Jesus, was **the Spirit** in the "tenderness, purity, gentleness"[9] of **a dove.** The brooding of the Spirit, like a bird, in Gen. 1:2, may be suggested.

We shall have ample occasion to observe Mark's emphasis upon the true deity of Jesus Christ. But we may well note here that the **voice from heaven** (11), expressing the approval of the Father, must have been a source of unutterable assurance to our Lord. Like us, He walked by faith rather than by sight (Heb. 4:15). **My beloved Son** may be rendered, "My Son, the beloved." The words mean that He was the *only* Son of the Father, F. C. Grant notes that the divine voice usually speaks in the words of Scripture—in this case, Ps. 2:7, combined with Isa. 42:1. More than a Messianic title, these words of divine approval were a confirmation for Jesus of His own consciousness that He was the Son of God. "There can be no question that for Mark . . . Jesus' divine sonship was unique, and wholly supernatural."[10] Luke adds a moving note to the whole story in recording that Jesus was praying (Luke 3:21) during this experience.

Though Mark's description of this scene is brief, we cannot doubt that for Jesus it was pivotal. The baptism was for Him "the moment of decision . . . identification . . . approval . . . equipment."[11]

Stressing verse 9, G. Campbell Morgan notes that Jesus came (1) To baptism, (2) To anointing, (3) To temptation, and ex-

[9]Ralph Earle, *The Gospel According to Mark* ("The Evangelical Commentary on the Bible," ed. George A. Turner, *et al.*; Grand Rapids: Zondervan Publishing House, 1957), p. 31.

[10]IB, VII, 654.

[11]William Barclay, *The Gospel of Mark* ("The Daily Study Bible"; Philadelphia: The Westminster Press, 1954), pp. 9-11.

plains these, respectively, as coming (1) To man in his sin, (2) To God for the Spirit's anointing, (3) To Satan for conflict.

## D. THE TEMPTATION OF JESUS, 1:12-13

Mark records only the barest details of the Temptation. See the parallels in Matt. 4:1-11 and Luke 4:1-13 for a fuller description. These probably represent expanded accounts of Mark's terse story. Because Jesus was alone at the time of the temptations we may assume the information in all three accounts came from our Lord himself.

Mark's favorite adverb, **immediately** (12), indicates the close connection between the Baptism and the Temptation. The mountaintops of vision are often followed quickly by the valleys of temptation. "A person begins a life of discipleship with a lift, an exhilaration. Then comes the wilderness of doubt and wonder."[12]

It was not by chance or fancy that Jesus encountered Satan in the **wilderness** (13). **The spirit driveth him** (12) there. The verb (*ekballo*) is a strong one, meaning to "cast out," and is used later in the accounts of Jesus casting out demons. A strong inner persuasion of the Spirit compelled Jesus to take the offensive in this encounter with Satan. The route of the Suffering Servant lay before Him. The location of the wilderness is unknown, but it was a desolate place such as is elsewhere associated with demons (e.g., Luke 8:29; 11:24). The place of test and trial is a lonely one.

To be **tempted of Satan** (13) meant, first of all, that Jesus was put to the test, as the verb *peirazo* implies. The context, however, suggests more. It was "not just 'being tempted,' but being tempted to turn aside from his appointed path."[13] The temptation was strenuous and long, some **forty days** (cf. Moses' experience in Exod. 34:28 and Elijah's in I Kings 19:8). **Satan,** the agent, means "adversary." Matthew and Luke use the term "devil," which means "slanderer." The great mission of Jesus was to oppose and defeat the kingdom of Satan; therefore it was desirable for Him at the outset to engage the enemy in a decisive encounter. Jesus repudiated the way of a revolutionary Messiah and chose the path of sacrificial love. Only Gethsemane and Golgotha could reveal how costly this choice was.

---

[12]Halford E. Luccock, *The Gospel According to St. Mark* (Exposition), IB, VII, 654.

[13]Cranfield, *op. cit.*, p. 58.

In that lonely place of trial, Jesus had a strange contrast in companions. The **wild beasts** were with Him, as were **the angels** who **ministered unto him**. Mark alone notes the animals, possibly as a picture of desolation and the absence of human help, but perhaps also as a hint of companionship. Fasting and hunger are implied in the ministration of the angels. The verb is in the imperfect tense and may indicate a continuation of action, although the strengthening may have come after the ordeal. The angels brought assurance of God's presence as well as physical strength, an experience to be repeated later under the shadow of the Cross (Luke 22:43).

## A. First Steps in Galilee, 1:14-20

### 1. *The Preaching of Jesus* (1:14-15)

The progress of the Kingdom cannot be blocked. The muzzling of John by Herod Antipas was the signal for Jesus to begin His preaching. **Put in prison** (14) literally means "handed over to another." It was evidently a technical term in the police jargon of the day. But more than this is implied, for the same language is used of Jesus and His betrayal; He too was "handed over" and "delivered up" to His enemies.

**Jesus came . . . preaching** (14) the "good news of God."[1] Would that we could sense the bright promise of these words! Not gloom and doom but good news—and that from God himself. Hope, salvation, life abundant—all are implicit. At long last, "God's clock was striking the hour";[2] **the time** was **fulfilled.** Here the word for **time** is not *chronos* (a space of time), but *kairos* ("opportune or seasonable time").[3]

> *There is a tide in the affairs of men*
> *Which, taken at the flood, leads on to fortune;*
> *Omitted, all the voyage of their lives*
> *Is bound in shallows and in miseries.*
> *We must take the current when it serves,*
> *Or lose our ventures.*[4]

So it was with Israel. The crucial hour of her destiny had come and she would miss it. A generation later Jerusalem lay in devastation, while the Gentiles heard and received the gospel (cf. Eph. 1:10).

---

[1]The phrase *of the kingdom* is not found in the two oldest MSS, but not all scholars favor omitting it here.

[2]Earle, *op. cit.,* p. 33.

[3]Abbott-Smith, *A Manual Greek Lexicon of the New Testament* (3rd ed.; Edinburgh: T. & T. Clark, 1937), p. 226.

[4]*Julius Caesar*, Act IV, Sc. 3.

**The kingdom of God** (15) may properly be thought of as the unifying theme of the entire Bible.[5] It was not unfamiliar to those who heard Jesus. The word **kingdom** (*basileia*) may be used in an abstract or concrete sense, as either *reign* or *realm.* The sovereignty or authority of God is a present fact in our moral world, but it is contested by the rebellion of man. Nevertheless "God is on the throne," and He does *reign,* making even the wrath of man to praise Him. One day, however, the Kingdom will become a *realm* over which God will rule without contradictions. These two themes interpenetrate the idea of **the kingdom of God** throughout Scripture: present reality, future expectation and hope. When **Jesus came into Galilee . . . preaching,** the Kingdom was truly **at hand.** "The kingdom of God has come close to men in the person of Jesus, and in his person it actually confronts them."[6] In 14:42 the same Greek word is used of the betrayer being at hand.

The first word of Jesus, as with John, was **repent,** turn to God with a radical *change of mind.* John saw only the threat of judgment, however, and said little more. Jesus saw also the promise of redemption and included the positive note: **believe (in) the gospel.** This is a literal rendering of the Greek and is said to be the only clear instance of the phrase in the New Testament. "Repentance toward God, and faith toward our Lord Jesus Christ" (Acts 20:21) remain the two key words of the gospel.

### 2. *The Call of Four Fishermen* (1:16-20)

This story is a natural sequence to the proclamation of the gospel in the previous section. Men sensed an authority in the word of Jesus and responded to His call as to One who had a right to make such demands.

It was a casual yet critical moment when Jesus **walked by the sea** (16). Luke, who had sailed a real sea (the Mediterranean) speaks of the "lake" of Gennesaret (5:1). The dimensions of the **sea of Galilee** are approximately eight by thirteen miles, not a large body of water, but a busy center of fishing activity in Galilee. Simon (New Testament equivalent for Simeon) and Andrew were plying their trade, **casting a net into the sea.** This was a weighted, circular net with a drawrope to enclose the fish, as in a purse.

[5]John Bright, *The Kingdom of God* (New York: Abingdon-Cokesbury, 1953).
[6]Cranfield, *op. cit.,* p. 68.

When Jesus said, **Come ye after me** (17), He was calling busy and brave men. Accustomed to the dangers of the unpredictable sea and acquainted with the fisherman's requirement of patience, they would have the qualities needed as **fishers of men.** They had more to learn, as the words **I will make you to become** imply. The real purpose of discipleship is seen in the reason Jesus gave for calling these men. "Christ calls men, not so much for what they are, as for what He is able to make them become."[7]

The call and response seem quite abrupt—**straightway** (18), in the language of Mark's "nervous style"—but it is possible they may already have known Jesus through the ministry of John the Baptist.

A short distance further, Jesus met another pair of fisherman brothers, **James . . . and John his brother** (19). The colorful details of this scene convince many scholars that we are close to the testimony of an eyewitness, Peter. The first pair of brothers is described as actively fishing, the second pair as quietly mending their nets, "putting them in order" (Goodspeed). The term **mending** is an interesting one, used also for the "rebuilding of a ruin or setting of a broken bone."[8]

Jesus promptly called the sons of **Zebedee.** To be a disciple was by invitation only. This biblical term is fraught with theological significance. Jesus later reminded His disciples, "Ye have not chosen me, but I have chosen you" (John 15:16).

Simon and Andrew **forsook their nets** (18), their means of livelihood, while James and John **left their father Zebedee** (20), as well as his good business (indicated by the presence of **hired servants).** It was a costly choice, but not more so than with any follower of the Lord. "Each left all that he had; that is always the minimum requirement for the Christian" (Luke 14:33).[9]

### B. A Sabbath in Capernaum, 1:21-34

#### 1. *A Demoniac in the Synagogue* (1:21-28)

Several characteristic aspects of Mark's style may be noted in this section (Earle): the historical present, constant use of

[7]C. E. Graham Swift, "The Gospel According to Mark"; *The New Bible Commentary,* ed. F. Davidson (Grand Rapids: Wm. B. Eerdmans Publishing Co., 1953), p. 810.

[8]Earle, *op. cit.,* p. 35.

[9]R. A. Cole, *The Gospel According to St. Mark* ("The Tyndale New Testament Commentaries"; Grand Rapids: Wm. B. Eerdmans Publishing Co., 1961), p. 60.

*kai* ("and," "also") and *euthus* ("immediately," "straightway").
All of this makes for vividness of expression and possibly reflects
Peter's style of preaching as Mark recalled it.

Although Nazareth was the village where Jesus grew up,
Capernaum became His headquarters in Galilee.   An important city on the northwest shore of the lake (see map), some
two miles from the Jordan, **Capernaum** (21) was near the border of Antipas' territory, hence the presence of a receipt of custom
or toll-booth (2:14). Here Jesus, **on the sabbath day . . . entered
into the synagogue** to worship and to teach.

Jesus made it a practice to worship regularly in the Temple
at Jerusalem, and in the synagogue, wherever He was.  The synagogue, built to point toward Jerusalem, was a place of worship
on the Sabbath, and, during the week, a school for the children
and a courtroom for minor offenders.  Here Jesus **taught.** Mark
recorded the doings of Jesus more than His sayings, but this does
not mean that the Evangelist felt our Lord's teaching ministry
was secondary. Sixteen of the seventeen times where the verb
*taught* appears in Mark, it has reference to Jesus.

The hearers **were astonished** (22) not merely at Jesus' **doctrine,** *what* He taught, but more especially because of the *way*
He taught. His word carried **authority** and was not merely an
echo of other religious leaders and their ideas, as was true of
**the scribes.**

Among those present, one who hitherto was neither helped
nor disturbed, was **a man with an unclean spirit** (23). Mark
uses this expression ten times, Matthew twice, Luke six times.
Demon possession is an idea offensive to some modern minds,
even while we talk of the *demonic* forces of our day!  Perhaps
nothing could please Satan more than for the Church to regard
him and his underlings as mythological.  Consider the unclean
spirits which control men: malice, vanity, greed, sensuality, loneliness, despair, brutality. A literal translation of this verse is "a
man *in* an unclean spirit."

Recognizing Jesus as **the Holy One of God** (24), the demoniac
cried out in consternation, **What have we to do with thee?** The
unclean demon had nothing in common with Jesus. His ego impaired, the man was but an instrument of his tormentor. **I know
thee who thou art** is a statement of fact found several times in
the Gospels. "Demons often sensed the power of the exorcist."[10]

[10]Grant, IB, VII, 662.

The answer to the question, **Art thou come to destroy us?** was, "Certainly!" "For this purpose the Son of God was manifested" (I John 3:8). What is here termed a question may also be regarded as a statement. Both fear and defiance were expressed by the demons.

**Jesus rebuked him** (25). This verb is used in the Septuagint to represent the divine word of rebuke, a counterpart of the divine creative word. **Hold thy peace** is often translated, "Be muzzled!" or, "Silence!" Cf. Matt. 22:12, where the wedding guest, without the proper garment, was speechless; also Matt. 22:34, where Jesus silenced the Sadducees. Jesus would not accept testimony from an unworthy source, nor did He wish at this stage to stress His messiahship.

The unclean spirit **came out of him** (26), but not before he had torn the man. The demons in their vengefulness seemed always to obey with as much destruction as possible, crying out, convulsing their victims, often leaving them as if dead. Nevertheless the kingdom of Satan gave way to the kingdom of God.

We have in v. 27, as in v. 22, an indication of the impression Jesus created. Men were **astonished** at His teaching and **amazed** at His works. The works authenticated the words. "Amazement (v. 22) deepened into awe."[11] "What is this? A new teaching!" (RSV) Quite naturally, **his fame spread abroad** (28), though it was not altogether a blessing.

### 2. *The Healing of Peter's Mother-in-law* (1:29-31)

These verses contain another reminiscence of Peter; the story is told from his point of view and is specifically located in his home.

The healing evidently took place on the Sabbath, for Jesus and His disciples came at once, **forthwith** (*euthus*), from the **synagogue** service to **the house of Simon and Andrew** (29). Whether this means it was Andrew's home as well as Peter's is not clear. His name may have been included because of his relationship with Peter. In any case, this home became a kind of headquarters for the ministry of Jesus in Galilee.[12] With **James**

[11]Henry Barclay Swete, *The Gospel According to St. Mark* (Grand Rapids: Wm. B. Eerdmans Publishing Co., 1956 [reprint]), p. 21.

[12]John 1:44 states that Bethsaida was the home of Peter and Andrew, but there was evidently some connection between the two cities, possibly through the fishing industry; see NBC *in loco*.

**and John** present, it is evident that all four of the disciples were now accompanying Jesus wherever He went.

Peter was somewhat taken aback to find that his **wife's mother lay sick of a fever** (30). And with Sabbath guests present! Peter was thus a married man at the time of his calling. In the light of I Cor. 9:5, his wife may have traveled with him on later missionary trips. Luke speaks of "a great fever" (4:38), possibly malaria, due to the swampy marshes around the lake.

In his need, the host turned to his Guest for aid. **Anon** ("immediately") **they tell him of her.** With characteristic compassion and tenderness, Jesus **came and took her by the hand** (31) (cf. v. 41). The physician Luke recalls that "he stood over her" (4:39). **The fever left her,** and the memorable event left an indelible impression on Peter's mind. Without any of the typical adverse aftereffects, Peter's mother-in-law arose and **ministered unto** the distinguished visitors. "So gratitude finds expression in service."[13]

### 3. *A Healing Service at Sundown* (1:32-34)

It was impossible that a Man of such authority and deeds could be concealed. The crowds would have come to Jesus sooner that day, but they were restrained by the Jewish law forbidding burden-bearing on the Sabbath (Jer. 17:21-22). Now **at even, when the sun did set** and the Sabbath was over,[14] **they brought unto him all that were diseased, and . . . possessed** (32). (The Greek word here translated **devils** should be rendered "demons"; the word for "devil," *diabolos,* is used in the singular only.) After the casting out of the demons from the man in the synagogue and the healing in Peter's home, those with both afflictions naturally were brought.

The great crowds, so much in evidence later, had begun to appear. **All the city** crowded about **the door** (33). Wherever Jesus went He was sensitive to human need. In the synagogue, in the home, and now in the streets He responded to the plea for health, healing many. The **all** of v. 32 and the **many** of v. 34 are not in contrast. The words are transposed in Matt. 8:16.

---

[13]A. M. Hunter, *The Gospel According to Saint Mark* ("A Torch Bible Commentary," ed. David L. Edwards, *et al.;* New York: Collier Books, 1962 [reprint]), p. 35.

[14]"The law was that the Sabbath was ended and the day had finished when three stars came out in the sky" (Barclay, *op. cit.,* p. 31).

Once more those possessed **knew him,** but He **suffered not the devils to speak** (34). The Messianic secret was not to be tossed about prematurely, especially by unworthy witnesses. Johnson writes: "Jesus' nature must not be disclosed until he is ready to reveal it."[15]

## C. The First Preaching Tour, 1:35-45

### 1. *Jesus Alone at Prayer* (1:35-39)

Very early the following morning, "while it was still dark" (35, Phillips), Jesus **departed into a solitary place** to be alone with the Father. The temporal phrase of v. 35 is an unusual one, meaning, "at an early hour, while it was still night."[16] A. T. Robertson thinks Mark has reference to the early part of the last watch of the night, from 3:00 to 6:00 a.m.[17] Despite the exhausting demands of preaching and healing on the previous day, Jesus early sought the reinvigoration of His spirit in prayer.

> *Lord, what a change within us one short hour*
> *Spent in Thy presence will avail to make!*
> *What heavy burdens from our bosoms take!*
> *What parched grounds refresh as with a shower!*[18]

Mark makes special note of Jesus praying at the beginning, middle, and close of His ministry (here; 6:46; and 14:32). He prayed at many other times, of course, as Luke especially records. Is it not a haunting question: If Jesus needed to pray, how much more do we?

With a suggestion of dismay, **Simon and they that were with him** (36) "tracked him down" (Barclay). Peter could not understand why, in the face of mounting popularity, Jesus would adopt such a course of action. It must have been puzzling indeed when the Master replied, **Let us go into the next towns, that I may preach there also** (38). The crowds came and were amazed at the miracles, but few remained to believe the gospel. With almost

---

[15]Sherman Johnson, *A Commentary on the Gospel According to St. Mark* ("Harper's New Testament Commentaries"; New York: Harper and Brothers, 1960), p. 50.

[16]Vincent Taylor, *The Gospel According to St. Mark* (London: Macmillan & Co., Ltd., 1959), p. 182.

[17]*Word Pictures in the New Testament* (Nashville: Broadman Press, 1930), I, 263.

[18]Robert C. Trench, "Prayer," *The World's Great Religious Poetry*, ed. Caroline M. Hill (New York: The Macmillan Co., 1943), p. 416.

a fierce determination, Jesus pursued the purpose for which He **came . . . forth** from God (cf. John 8:42; 13:3). To **preach** the gospel was more significant to Him than to heal the sick. Therefore He left the environs of Capernaum to embark on a preaching tour of the towns . . . **throughout all Galilee** (39). "Literally, 'village-cities' . . . Towns as to size, villages as without walls."[19] This would seem to suggest a journey lasting several weeks or months. However long this first preaching tour may have been, wherever Jesus went He **preached** the good news and **cast out demons.** The kingdom of Satan was under attack by the mighty Son of God.

### 2. The Curing of a Leper (1:40-45)

As the fame of Jesus spread abroad, the word of hope reached some dismal abode where a **leper** dwelt. In the desperation of his misery, "he comes (literally) to him [Jesus] begging him and kneeling down saying to him, 'If you are willing you are able.'" The leper had more faith in the power of Jesus than in His goodwill.

Lepers were required to avoid human contact, remain outside of dwellings, and cry, "Unclean," as a warning to others (cf. Leviticus 13). This leper must have been a pitiful sight: "His clothes rent, his hair loose, his upper lip covered, and his hoarse cry, 'Unclean.'"[20] In the Bible leprosy included skin disorders other than a true leprosy; it also included fungus found on clothing or on the walls of a house (Lev. 13:47; 14:34). This man was "full of leprosy" (Luke 5:12).

**Moved with compassion** (41) (Earle translates, "Gripped with compassion"[21]), Jesus **put forth his hand** and, risking ceremonial pollution, **touched** the untouchable.[22] Jesus often touched those whom He healed (e.g., 7:33) and was touched by those who sought healing (cf. 3:10). The Master was both able and willing

---

[19]Hunter, *op. cit.,* p. 36.

[20]*Ibid.,* p. 36.

[21]Earle, *op. cit.,* p. 40.

[22]There is an interesting textual problem here. A few MSS have "moved with anger" (*orgistheis*) instead of **moved with compassion.** Some commentators see a connection between this and v. 43, where Jesus **straitly charged** the man. If Jesus was angry, it was not with the poor leper, whom He touched with love and tenderness, but with the causes of leprosy, including the kingdom of Satan. The alternate reading does not commend itself generally, although Cranfield accepts it (*op. cit.,* p. 92).

to cure the leper and **saith unto him, I will; be thou clean.** The inexpressible compassion of Him who is "touched with the feeling of our infirmities" (Heb. 4:15) could scarcely be described in more moving language.

The cleansing of the leper was instantaneous and complete: **immediately the leprosy departed** (42). Jesus' word, **be thou clean,** was similar to the expression used by the priests and may be a hint of His priesthood.

When Jesus **straitly charged him, and . . . sent him away** (43), He felt strongly about it. *Embrimesamenos,* **straitly charged,** "originally means to snort or groan, and is used in the Greek Bible to express indignation, disapproval and other strong emotions; cf. 14:5; John 11:33, 38."[23] The man was **charged,** first of all, to **say nothing to any man** (44) about his wonderful deliverance, and then to **shew** himself **to the priest . . . for a testimony.**

The ex-leper's disobedience to the first charge, however excellent his motives, only served to impede the Lord's work in the cities; He **could no more openly enter into the city** (45), but was **without in desert places.** No doubt the healed man made the journey to Jerusalem to **offer for** his **cleansing those things which Moses commanded** (Lev. 14:1-7). This would be an expression of gratitude to God as well as a fulfillment of legal requirements. In so doing he would bear a **testimony** unto the priests who inspected him and to the people who witnessed the mighty work, said by the rabbis to be "as difficult as raising the dead."[24]

Under the topic "The Master and His Men," one might consider: (1) The Master's message, 14-15; (2) The Master's men, 16-20; (3) The Master's ministry, 21-45.

D. CONFLICTS WITH THE PHARISEES, 2:1—3:6

1. *Healing and Forgiveness* (2:1-12)

This chapter opens a section describing the development of opposition to Jesus. At first the antagonism lay unspoken in the thoughts of the scribes (2:6), but soon found expression in attacks upon the disciples (2:16), and then in plots against the Lord himself (3:6).

23Johnson, *op. cit.,* p. 53.
24*Ibid.,* p. 51.

As Matthew indicates (9:1), **Capernaum** (1) (see map) had now become our Lord's "own city" and was to be a base of operation throughout the Galilean ministry. Upon Jesus' return, word was **noised** through the community that He was in **the house,** quite probably Peter's. "He could not be hid" (7:24). The exact meaning of Mark's time indication, **after some days,** remains a mystery. It suggests that a few days after Jesus came to Capernaum news of His presence got around.

So **many were gathered together** (2) that the house could not contain them, nor was there room **about the door.** It was a humble home, without a porch or vestibule. The crowded conditions notwithstanding, Jesus **preached,** or proclaimed, **the word,** "the message" (NEB), **unto them.**

To this crowded house, four men brought a paralytic in faith that Jesus would heal him. Climbing the outside stairway to the flat top of the one-story dwelling, the men **uncovered the roof** (4), breaking through the baked clay (or tile, Luke 5:19), as well as the branches, twigs, and saplings below the surface, and **let down the bed** (a pallet to be spread out at night and rolled up by day). Their cooperation and toil had found a way.

Seeing **their faith**—made visible by their works—Jesus announced, with affection for the troubled man, **Son, thy sins be forgiven thee** (5). It is a moot question whether this man's affliction had a spiritual cause. Some contend that it did;[25] others hold that Jesus warred against both disease and sin.[26]

At once **the scribes** (6), professional instructors in the Law, questioned Jesus' statement. They reasoned, **This man** (implying contempt) speaks **blasphemies** (7) (an act punishable by death, according to Lev. 24:15); only God **can forgive sins.** It is striking that the critics were **sitting,** perhaps in places of honor near Jesus, while the rest stood inside and out. Unwittingly **the scribes** made a profound confession. **The Son of man** (10) was more than a man. He was the expected Messiah, and as the strong Son of God could make such a statement without blasphemy.

**Immediately** (*euthus*) Jesus **perceived** (8) the reasoning going on in the hearts of His opponents and was disturbed at their thoughts. Which is easier, Jesus asked them, **To say . . . Thy sins be forgiven,** or, **Arise . . . and walk?** The answer was simply,

25NBC, p. 811.
26Cranfield, *op. cit.,* p. 98.

Neither, for both are impossible to man, but both are possible to God. Both were evidences of God's power.

Jesus then proceeded "to prove the validity of His words of forgiveness by the power of His words of healing."[27] Thus all present would know that **the Son of man**[28] had **power on earth to forgive sins** (10). **The sick of the palsy** was commanded to rise, take up his bed, and go home without assistance.

Again Mark records the amazement produced by the mighty works of Jesus: **We never saw it on this fashion** (12).

Under the theme "The Faith That Works," we may note: (1) The setting, 1; (2) The scene, 2-4; (3) The sequel, 5-11.

### 2. The Calling of Levi (2:13-14)

As the doors of the synagogues began to close on the ministry of Jesus, the hillsides and seashore beckoned. Thus **he went forth again by the sea side** (13) (the Sea of Galilee, see map) and **taught** the multitudes as they were coming and going (indicated by the imperfect tense of **resorted**). **As he passed by**, walking along and teaching in a typical rabbinical fashion, **he saw Levi** (14), better known as Matthew,[29] **sitting at the receipt of custom**, a place where taxes of some type were collected.

Several of the great roads of the ancient world crossed Galilee, one of them coming through Capernaum, a city near the frontier of Herod Antipas' territory. Levi was one of Herod's despised agents for the collection of revenue either from these crossing the border into Galilee or possibly from those engaged in the fishing industry. For the orthodox Jew, a publican was as defiling ceremonially as a leper. Many publicans were not only

---

[27]IB, VII, 672.

[28]This is the first instance in Mark of this self-designation of Jesus. It occurs only once more in this Gospel (2:28) before Peter's great confession (8:27-30), but often thereafter. It no doubt refers both to the heavenly "Son of man" in Dan. 7:13-28 and to the fact that Jesus was the Representative Man, the Second Adam. In the Gospels it is found only on the lips of Jesus and is used elsewhere in the New Testament only in Acts 7:56 and Rev. 1:13. See the special note on this subject in Earle (*op. cit.*, p. 44), and the additional references he gives there.

[29]Some question exists as to the relationship between Levi and Matthew. The name *Levi* is used three times: here and in Luke 5:27, 29. Matt. 9:9 has *Matthew* instead. While some textual problems remain in reconciling the lists of the Twelve, it is probably best to assume that Levi, like Peter, had more than one name. Barclay flatly calls him *Matthew* (*op. cit.*, pp. 45-49).

avaricious in levying taxes, but also corrupt in personal morals. They were hated by everyone. Nevertheless Jesus **said unto him, Follow me.** The man, who must have had a desire in his heart for a new way of life, **arose and followed.**

It is noteworthy that Levi renounced more than any of the four who had so recently left all to follow Jesus. They could return to their nets and boats, but Levi had made an irrevocable decision. No man gives up more to follow Christ, however, than he receives in return. The contribution of Levi (or Matthew) through the first Gospel has made his name imperishable.

### 3. *Levi's Farewell Dinner* (2:15-17)

When **Jesus sat** (or "reclined," as the custom was) **at meat** (15) in Levi's house, it was a "kind of reception given by Levi to his old business acquaintances, to enable them to meet his new-found Master"[30] (cf. Luke 5:29). Thus his motive was a missionary one. The guests, who were many and who had followed Jesus, were a disreputable lot. The **publicans** were the hated tax collectors, and the **sinners** were Jews who ignored the Mosaic law, in both its moral and ritual sense.[31] The more orthodox Jews, such as the **scribes** and the **Pharisees** (16), would not associate with these people, especially when food was involved, lest they suffer ceremonial defilement. They complained to the **disciples,** perhaps hoping to undermine their loyalty, that Jesus was careless about the requirements of the Law when He ate and drank with such persons.

Jesus was eager to help sinners but He was never "soft" on sin. The implication of the scribes, who were also Pharisees, was baseless. When a man began to follow Jesus, he had to forsake sin. Jesus consorted with **publicans and sinners** (a phrase employed three times in this paragraph) because they sensed their need.

---

[30]Cole, *op. cit.,* p. 69.

[31]The KJV, following Wycliffe and the Latin Vulgate, uses the term *publicans* to translate the New Testament word *telonai.* The *telonai* were successors to the *publicani,* who had made big business out of tax collections under the Roman Republic. The *telonai* had no responsibility for the major taxes, but harassed the populace with numerous petty taxes on the use of roads, bridges, harbors, on commerce, salt, and other items. See *Harper's Bible Dictionary,* ed. Madeleine S. Miller and J. Lane Miller (sixth ed.; New York: Harper & Brothers, Publishers, 1959), p. 592.

When **Jesus heard** (17) the criticism, He replied with a statement strong in irony. He had not come to heal them **that are whole,** nor **to call the righteous.** These poor, blind Pharisees, whose very name was a symbol of tenacious loyalty to Judaism, were satisfied with their own condition, confident that they were not among the **sick** nor the unrighteous. However, the despised publicans and the rejected sinners, acutely aware of their need, welcomed the Physician who was not afraid of their defilement. Indeed, it was to **call** such that Jesus came from the Father.

### 4. *The Debate over Fasting* (2:18-22)

The **disciples of John** (18) the Baptist, who formed a separate group for some time, and the **Pharisees** "were keeping a fast" (18, Goodspeed). The disciples of John, whose master may have already suffered martyrdom, perhaps felt that festivities were not in order. Their complaint probably also reflects their Jewish orthodoxy. The Pharisees, who now suspected that Jesus repudiated the Law, reached a new level of open opposition to Him: **Why do . . . thy disciples fast not?**

Jesus had not required His disciples to fast, but He had taught them (Matt. 6:16) that the practice of fasting should spring from spiritual motives and should not be an occasion for display. "Jesus sanctions fasting without enjoining it."[32]

Replying in parabolic language, Jesus asked His critics if they would expect wedding guests, **children of the bridechamber**[33] to fast **while the bridegroom is with them** (19). Hardly. At such a time **they cannot fast.**

The biblical metaphor of the bridegroom and his bride is rich in meaning. In the light of Isa. 54:5, Jesus may have referred to His consciousness as the Son of God.[34] Further, respecting the relationship between John the Baptist and Jesus, it was John himself who said, "He that hath the bride is the bridegroom: but the friend . . . which standeth" near him "rejoiceth greatly" (John 3:29). It was appropriate for John's disciples to fast, as they mourned their master, but not so for the disciples of Jesus, as long as **the bridegroom** was **with them.**

---

[32]NBC, p. 812.

[33]The term here is *numphios* and refers to "the bridegroom's friends who have charge of the nuptial arrangements" (Abbott-Smith, *op. cit.*, p. 306).

[34]Cranfield, *op. cit.*, p. 110.

Here and in v. 20 is a clear hint, the first in Mark, of the passion and death of Jesus. Like John, **the bridegroom** would be **taken away** violently. Then it would be proper for His disciples to fast. Perhaps as Mark penned these words he knew all too well what **those days** were like, when fasting was inevitable. H. Orton Wiley used to say to his students, "No man really prays until he is crushed to his knees."

Two parables follow, in vv. 21-22, "to teach that in the Gospel message and fellowship there is a spirit of joy and power that must find its own appropriate form."[35] It is sometimes thought that these verses have been misplaced, but in fact Jesus pursues the answer to His critics on a deeper level.

New spiritual life calls for new forms of expression. If one should sew a **piece of new cloth** (21), untreated and unshrunken, on **an old garment,** in the process of time the new piece would shrink and tear **away from the old,** making the hole worse. Likewise with **new wine** (22). Old wineskins (not **bottles**) cannot contain new wine. The vigor of the new destroys the rigidity of the old, marring the wineskins and spilling the wine.

In the gospel something new and dynamic has come. As the critics berated Jesus for not fasting, they failed to see that the Christian movement could not be forced into the old, static forms of Judaism. **New wine must be put into new bottles** (22).

### 5. *The Lord of the Sabbath* (2: 23—3: 6)

*a. Threshing Grain on the Sabbath* (2: 23-28). In this section (2: 1—3: 6) we note the growth of opposition to Jesus. The Pharisees criticized our Lord on four counts: they denied Him the right to forgive sins, objected to His friendship with the outcast, complained when His disciples did not fast, and fussed with Him about the keeping of the Sabbath.

Mark describes, in the narrative before us, how Jesus and His disciples were making their way **through the corn fields**[36] **on the sabbath day** (23). It was perfectly legal for travelers to pluck grapes from a vineyard or heads of grain in a field of barley or wheat, so long as they did not use a vessel for the grapes or a sickle on the grain (Deut. 23: 24-25).

[35]*The Westminster Study Edition of the Holy Bible* (Philadelphia: The Westminster Press, 1948), *in loco.*

[36]More accurately, "grainfields," where the disciples **plucked** "the heads of wheat" (23, Goodspeed); all grains were customarily called corn in England, where KJV was translated.

Attacking Jesus through His disciples, **the Pharisees** said to him, **Behold, why do they . . . that which is not lawful?** (24) The simple procedure of plucking a few grains of wheat and of rubbing them between the hands had, because it was done **on the sabbath day,** become threshing! However insignificant the occasion, this was a serious charge, for violation of the Sabbath was punishable by stoning, providing the offender had been warned.

**The Son of man** (28), who is **Lord . . . of the sabbath,** defended the "unlawful" action of His followers with the argument that human need stands above ritual law. Jesus cited an example from their own Scriptures to show that even the immortal David, in a time of urgent flight, ate the shewbread, which was not lawful for him to eat, and gave also to the men with him (see I Sam. 21:1-7). This is not to say that necessity always dictates what is right, but to point out that under similar conditions David's act was not condemned; thus the Pharisees did not understand the implications of their own law. The "bread of the Presence" (26, RSV), normally to be eaten only by the priests as part of a significant ritual, was not so sacred that it could not serve human need.

Thus the great principle was enunciated that **the sabbath was made for man, and not man for the sabbath** (27). Let it be noted, however, that the Sabbath is for the benefit of the total man: physical, mental, and spiritual needs. "To ignore this law is only to prove its necessity."[37] D. Elton Trueblood warns that the neglect of institutions such as the Sabbath can only lead to the dissolution of biblical religion.[38] Judah, with the Sabbath, survived the Exile, whereas Israel, without it, did not.

Jesus concluded the controversy with what must have been, for His critics, a shocking assertion: **Therefore** (since the Sabbath is for man), **the Son of man is Lord also of the sabbath.** "The Sabbath has been given for man's benefit. Therefore the Representative Man may decide how it can be used."[39]

*b. Sabbath for Man* (3:1-6) "As his custom was" (Luke 4:16), Jesus **entered . . . the synagogue . . . on the sabbath** (1-2). What follows is the fifth in a series of conflicts with the scribes

[37]Earle, *op. cit.,* p. 49.

[38]*Foundations for Reconstruction* (New York: Harper & Brothers, 1946), c. 4.

[39]NBC, p. 812.

and Pharisees (see on 2:23-28). **There was a man (1)** in the synagogue who had **a withered hand,** probably "hand-paralysis followed by contracture."[40] Therein lies a parable. How many there are in God's house with all the right ideas, but with no ability to translate them into fruitful service! Luke records (6:6) that it was the right hand which was withered. There is an old tradition that the man was a bricklayer and needed the hand as a means of livelihood.

With "squinting eyes . . . intent on everything Jesus did,"[41] the Pharisees **watched him (2).** Here is a devastating picture of the legalist, modern as well as ancient, who looks on only to find fault, completely insensitive to human suffering! The Pharisees permitted healing on the Sabbath only if it was a matter of life and death, obviously not the case here.

Jesus **saith unto the man . . . Stand forth (3),** literally, "Arise into the midst." Johnson translates, "Stand up in front."[42] Knowing the malice of their thoughts, Jesus lifted the matter of Sabbath observance to a higher and positive level. **Is it lawful to do good . . . or to do evil? (4)** That is, which is more truly consistent with the law, to restore life to this man's afflicted hand, even on the Sabbath, or to kill his hopes and future by observing a senseless human tradition? **But they held their peace.** "They could not deny His arguments, and they refused to admit their validity."[43]

Our Lord **looked round about on them with anger . . . grieved for the hardness** (or blindness) **of their hearts (5).** This is the only place in the Gospels where anger is attributed to Jesus. What was the nature of this anger? Perhaps Heb. 1:9 gives us a clue: "Thou hast loved righteousness, and hated iniquity." But note also Mark's explanation for this angry look—Jesus **was grieved** ("to be moved to grief by sympathy")[44] over their tragic situation. No other kind of anger has a place in God's kingdom.

Turning from His critics, Jesus addressed the man with a command: **Stretch forth thine hand (5).** The man's will combined with Christ's power to bring the impossible to reality. **He stretched it out: and his hand was restored.**

[40]Hunter, *op. cit.,* p. 48.
[41]IB, VII, 680 (Exposition).
[42]*Op. cit.,* p. 70.
[43]Earle, *op. cit.,* p. 51.
[44]Abbott-Smith, *op. cit.,* p. 431.

In the blindness of their hearts, the Pharisees went forth at once to confer with the Herodians on how they might destroy Jesus. What strange bedfellows enmity makes! The Pharisees hated the Herodians as traitors to their nation, yet, as on a later occasion (12:13), they joined forces with them to destroy the Man who disturbed them.

Mark 3:7—6:13

A. WITHDRAWAL TO THE SEASIDE, 3:7-12

When opposition to Jesus mounted to the pitch described in
3:6, **Jesus withdrew himself with his disciples (7)** to the open
seashore, where He was surrounded by friends. This act of
withdrawal suggests the breach developing between Jesus and
the leaders of Judaism. "He came unto his own, and his own
received him not" (John 1:11). **A great multitude from Galilee,**
actually a tumultuous throng, **followed him,** while additional
crowds came from as far south as Judea and **Idumaea (8),** from
Transjordan on the east, and from the Roman province of Syria
**(Tyre and Sidon)** on the north (see map). These words give us a
remarkable picture of the geographical extent of Jesus' ministry
even at this early stage.

**When they had heard what great things he** (Jesus) **did,**
they **came unto him (8).** "Great happenings draw great multitudes, and where human need is truly met there is no lack of
seeking souls."[1]

As a precautionary measure, Jesus instructed His former
fishermen-disciples to keep **a small ship (9)** (Mark's colloquial
diminutive) in readiness so that He could escape the crush of the
eager crowd as **they pressed upon him for to touch him (10).**

There is something moving about the hopefulness of those
who had been plagued (scourged)[2] by their diseases, and who
knew that Jesus **had healed many.** Like the woman who later
said, "If I may touch but his clothes, I shall be whole" (5:28),
they also longed to **touch** Him. It was characteristic of Jesus to
respond to such longing, for He often put forth a hand to touch an
afflicted person (e.g., 1:31, 41, *et al.*).

However, when the **unclean spirits . . . saw him** and cried
out, **Thou art the Son of God (11),** Jesus "warned them repeatedly that they must not make him known" (12, Phillips). Jesus
steadfastly and vigorously rejected the unworthy testimony of
demoniacs and regularly charged those who had witnessed a

[1]NBC, p. 813.
[2]The word "plagues" (*mastigas*) literally means a whip or scourge.

miracle to keep silent about it. Apart from His wish not to inflame nationalistic hopes for a political Messiah, Jesus refused such testimony lest men follow Him from improper motives. His words and mighty works would lead them to see who He was, if they were capable of seeing (cf. Luke 7:19-23).

### B. The Appointment of the Twelve, 3:13-19

As the breach between Jesus and official Jewry widened (3:6), our Lord began the building of His own *ecclesia*, the new Israel. Going up **into a mountain** (the hill country of Galilee), **He calleth unto him whom he would** (13). The wording (literally, "whom He himself wanted") stresses the sovereign choice of Jesus: "Ye have not chosen me, but I have chosen you" (John 15:16). In the mystery of His own will, Jesus called the Twelve, including Judas Iscariot, **and they came unto him,** in the uncoerced response of their free agency.

Jesus **ordained** (better, "appointed") **twelve** (14) to **be with him** for formal and informal training. Such instruction would lead to a mission of preaching, healing, and deliverance. Through intimate fellowship with the Lord, the disciples would receive a commission **to preach** and an authority (*exousia,* **power** in the sense of delegated authority) **to heal sicknesses, and to cast out devils** (15). Was there ever a program of ministerial training so simple or so effective? "Their appointment involved communion . . . companionship . . . commission."[3]

The New Testament gives us four lists of the Twelve: in addition to Mark's list, Matt. 10:2-4; Luke 6:14-16; Acts 1:13. **Simon . . . surnamed Peter** (16) always heads the list, with Judas Iscariot always last (except in Acts, where his name is omitted). **James . . . and John . . . surnamed . . . The sons of thunder** (17) complete the inner circle.

Mark's use of "loving personal nicknames"[4] is unique. Peter, the name Jesus gave Simon, means "a stone" and was more of a promise than an evaluation. The sons of Zebedee had tempestuous personalities (cf. 9:38; Luke 9:54), but their surname may have been complimentary, implying that their Christian witness would be as mighty as thunder.

Andrew, the fourth member of the fisherman-group, was an effective disciple, but not a member of the "inner circle." Bar-

---

[3]NBC, p. 813.
[4]Cole, *op. cit.,* p. 80.

tholomew and Nathanael are regarded as the same person, inasmuch as John joins Philip and Nathanael, while the Synoptics link Philip and Bartholomew (meaning "son of *Talmai*"). Matthew is also called Levi and described as a publican only in the first Gospel. Thomas means "twin." **James the son of Alphaeus** (18) is sometimes identified as "James the less" (15:40) and may have been a brother of Levi, who was also a "son of Alphaeus" (2:14). **Simon the Canaanite** should read "the Cananean," a Jewish revolutionary group also called the Zealots (Luke 6:15; Acts 1:13).

Iscariot may mean that Judas was from Kerioth, a town in southern Judah, or it may be a nickname meaning "assassin." Grant feels the term "probably means 'sicarious' ('assassin'), a name ('sicarii') given the Zealots . . . in A.D. 70."[5] Jesus must have once seen in the man **which also betrayed him** (19) significant possibilities for good. It was by transgression that Judas fell, not by an inexorable divine determinism.

There were twelve disciples. These were all ordinary men with imperfect and different personalities. Yet, with the exception of Judas, because of their companionship with Jesus they were all destined to become effective Christian witnesses.

## C. FRIENDS AND FOES, 3:20-35

### 1. *The Unpardonable Sin* (3:20-30)

**And they went into an house** (19).[6] Going back to His home in Capernaum, after the brief respite in the hill country (3:13), Jesus once more plunged into the demanding ministry before Him. So great and insistent was **the multitude** (20) which came **together again** that Jesus and His disciples **could not so much as eat bread**; there was no time even for meals.

Fearing for the health and sanity of Jesus, certain friends, evidently from Nazareth, **went out to lay hold on** ("seize") **him** (21). It is probable that v. 21 anticipates v. 31, where **his brethren and his mother** are described as sharing the alarm over His safety. They were sure He was **beside himself.** The picture Mark gives us is one of incredible zeal and strenuous activity on the part of Jesus.

[5]IB, VII, 689.
[6]The list of apostles ends in the middle of verse 19. The latter part of the verse logically goes with what follows.

Another group now appears—a delegation of **scribes (Phari-sees) which came down from Jerusalem** (22). These men carried greater prestige and authority than the local scribes. Whenever a devout Jew came from Jerusalem, it was "down," and likewise "up" when he journeyed to the holy city. These official examiners had another and more serious charge: He **hath Beelzebub**[7] and is in league with the **prince of the devils.**

Replying **in parables** (23) (or parabolic sayings; the first use of the term in Mark), Jesus said three things. First, **How can Satan cast out Satan?** Satan is too wise to tolerate destructive division in his kingdom. Second, whoever casts out Satan must be stronger than he; hence, also, someone other than Satan. Jesus implies in verse 27 that He himself has come to enter into the strong man's house and spoil his goods. Stronger than Satan, He can bind him and spoil his house. This is why "the Son of God was manifested, that he might destroy the works of the devil" (I John 3:8).

Third, and finally, Jesus sounded a chilling warning to those who attributed the work of God to the power of Satan. **Verily I say unto you, . . . he that shall blaspheme against the Holy Ghost hath never forgiveness** (28-29). Prefaced with the solemn affirmation **Verily** (literally, "Amen"; the first of thirteen occurrences in Mark), the statement contains a sublime promise and the most serious warning possible. That all sins shall be forgiven is the wonder of the gospel. That one may be in danger of an eternal sin[8] is sobering.

What is the *unpardonable* sin? The answer lies in Mark's own explanation: **Because they said, He hath an unclean spirit** (30). The scribes had attributed the mighty works of Jesus to *Beelzebul,* the name for a corrupt pagan god which the Jews of that day applied to Satan. To ascribe the work of the Holy Spirit in the ministry of Jesus to the power of the devil was to exhibit a hopeless spiritual blindness. It was to become guilty of an eternal sin and to become liable to **eternal damnation** (29). Why?

---

[7]Most Gk. MSS have *Beelzebul.* "Beelzebul, or Baalzebul, was an intentional caricature of Baalzebub. Baalzebub means 'Fly-god.' The Jews said, Baalzebul, i.e., 'Filth-god,' and applied it to Satan" (Hunter, *op. cit.,* p. 51). An alternate explanation of the term is, "Lord of the house," or "dwelling," in which case v. 27 would be a play on words.

[8]The correct text is *hamartematos* ("sin") rather than *kriseos* ("damnation" or "judgment").

When one says, "Evil, be thou my good,"[9] he has turned his face toward the darkness and his back toward the light. "And for this cause God shall send them strong delusion, that they should believe a lie: that they all might be damned who believed not the truth" (II Thess. 2:11-12a).

Unscriptural preaching on this subject has done lamentable damage to tender souls. No one is likely to commit the unpardonable sin who is distressed over the possibility.[10] This is not to minimize but only to think clearly on the somber warning of Jesus. "If therefore the light that is in thee be darkness, how great is that darkness!" (Matt. 6:23b)

### 2. *"My Mother and My Brothers"* (3:31-35)

Among those who came "to lay hold" on Jesus (21), fearing that He was "beside himself," were **his brethren and his mother** (31). Unable to "come at him for the press" of the crowd (Luke 8:19), they stood **without** and **sent unto him, calling him.**

Mary, who appears only at this point in Mark, and her sons[11] were troubled over the intense zeal and activity of Jesus. Many things Mary had "kept" and "pondered . . . in her heart" (Luke 2:19). She did not fully understand her Son and "neither did his brethren believe in him" (John 7:5). Now, standing outside the house, or on the fringes of the crowd, they sent an anxious message that they were seeking for Him.

What follows is an application of Jesus' own requirement: "If any man come to me, and hate not his father, and mother . . . and brethren . . . he cannot be my disciple" (Luke 14:26). In Mark's vivid description of a characteristic gesture, Jesus looked round about on them sitting nearby and said, **Behold my mother and my brethren!** (34) Jesus meant no affront to those related to Him by blood; this is clear from the way He cared for His mother even in the agony of the Cross (John 19:26-27). Our Lord was simply driving home a point with a forceful dramatic

---

[9]*Paradise Lost*, Bk. IV, 1. 110.

[10]Cf. Cranfield's wholesome word on this, *op. cit.*, p. 142.

[11]What relationship did His brethren bear to Jesus? Several explanations have been offered: that they were children of Joseph by a previous marriage; that they were cousins; or that they were younger sons of Joseph and Mary. The reference to Jesus as Mary's firstborn Son (Luke 2:7) would seem to support the last position. See Taylor, *op. cit.*, pp. 247-49, for a detailed discussion.

gesture. **Whosoever shall do the will of God, the same is my brother, and my sister, and mother** (35).

"Obedience to God rather than physical relationship binds men close to Jesus."[12] Grant notes that this episode must have been most heartening to the Early Church, hurt by broken families, ostracism, and persecution.[13] Let it also be said that, if obedience to the will of God be so commanded, it is, by God's grace, a human possibility.

## D. A MINISTRY IN PARABLES, 4:1-34

### 1. *The Parable of the Sower* (4:1-9)

Turning from those who misrepresented and misunderstood Him, Jesus came **again** (see 3:7) to **the sea side** to instruct **the great multitude** (1). Among them were followers whose spiritual kinship with Him was stronger than His family ties.

Perhaps to escape the pressure of the crowd, ofttimes a personal threat, Jesus **entered into a ship** (boat). Here He had a "floating pulpit" (Hunter), and **sat in the sea** to teach **the whole multitude** sitting **by the sea** in what must have been a natural amphitheatre. That Jesus could sit down to teach is evidence of the power in His words. Vivid truth more than dramatic presentation gripped the attention of the people. The doctrine He taught was not in this instance a theological discourse, but the **many things by parables** (2) such as appear in this chapter.

It will be useful at this point to consider the meaning of the word *parable*. The New Testament word may be defined as "a placing beside . . . a comparing, comparison . . . illustration, analogy, figure."[14] It may refer not only to the stories which Jesus told, but also to the figures of speech and analogies He often used (e.g., 2:17, 19 ff.). "A parable is an earthly story with a heavenly meaning."[15]

The use of parables was common among the Hebrew people, but Jesus used them with penetrating purpose, especially as the listeners increased who might misunderstand or misuse His teaching. A story would quite naturally catch and hold the attention of friend and foe alike; but more, the parable probed the heart,

12Cranfield, *op. cit.*, p. 146.
13IB, VII, 694.
14Abbott-Smith, *op. cit.*, p. 338.
15Barclay, *op. cit.*, p. 81.

compelling deeper thought and application. The parables were "moral weapons to surprise and stir the conscience."[16]

Jesus began by calling for the careful attention of the hearers: **Hearken** (3). "Listen!" (RSV) The cryptic warning of v. 9, closing the parable, coupled with this request would seem to stress the need for thoughtful listening.

This parable of the sower stands at the head of a series of parables in all the Synoptics. It has to do with the reception of the teaching of Jesus, the divine **sower** who went out **to sow.**

The occasion for the parable is found in the attitude of official Jewry which misrepresented Jesus, and in the reaction of His own family, who failed to understand Him. Why does the preaching of the gospel not produce uniform results in all hearers? The reply of the parable is: "The operation of the divine word is not automatic . . . the nature of the divine response is dictated by the nature of the heart that receives it."[17]

The Father "maketh his sun to rise on the evil and on the good, and sendeth rain on the just and on the unjust" (Matt. 5:45); thus also He sows the seed on all kinds of soils: the **way side** (4), the **stony ground** (5), **among thorns** (7), and on **good ground** (8) (literally, "the good earth"). "The hard heart, the shallow heart, the over-crowded heart, and the good heart—all are in fact present, whenever the Word of God is preached."[18]

To mix metaphors, there is doubtless a responsibility for those who would "prepare . . . the way of the Lord" (1:3) also to help in the cultivation of the soil. Nevertheless, everyone who hears the Word has a plain duty: **He that hath ears to hear, let him hear** (9).

### 2. *An Explanation of the Parables* (4:10-20)

The multitudes had gone and Jesus was **alone,** except for those **that were about him with the twelve** (10). These were sympathetic followers who had been among the larger audience. They **asked of him the parable.**[19]

This very query illustrates the purpose and effectiveness of the parables: to set people to thinking in order that the message might sink down into their ears (cf. Luke 9:44).

---

[16]NBC, p. 814.

[17]Cole, *op. cit.,* p. 89.

[18]*Ibid.,* p. 90.

[19]Although the more recent versions put **parable** in the plural, Grant (IB, VII, 699) thinks the KJV reading "probable."

Before explaining the parable, Jesus reminded His disciples that they were blessed with spiritual insight, given to them by revelation, whereas those **without** (11), or outside their circle, were not. The **mystery** ("secret," RSV) **of the kingdom of God,** through faith and obedience, had been made plain to them. To those yet in moral blindness, Jesus purposely spoke **all these things . . . in parables.**

Here follows (12) a most perplexing verse. As the words stand, Mark seems to say that the purpose of the parables was to (*hina*, "in order to") obstruct understanding and to thwart conversion. So strong is the language that a moderate exegete like Vincent Taylor concludes that "Mark has given an unauthentic version of a genuine saying."[20]

No such conclusion is required by the evidence. The background of this verse is Isa. 6:9-10, where the commission of the prophet is given in ironical language. Barclay's exposition is helpful: "The explanation is that no man can translate or set down in print a tone of voice. When Isaiah spoke he spoke half in irony and half in despair and altogether in love."[21]

Isaiah, who said, "Here am I; send me" (Isa. 6:8), and Jesus, "whom the Father . . . sanctified, and sent into the world" (John 10:36), toiled at the task of helping men to see. The language of v. 12 is irony. Jesus had at first used a direct approach, but when men rejected His words, He turned to the more indirect approach of the parables with the hope that curiosity would lead to deeper reflection and, finally, acceptance. Nevertheless, in the end, He knew that hardened, shallow, crowded hearts would spurn the truth.

An understanding of this parable was crucial. Those who **know . . . not this parable** (13) would have difficulty with **all parables.** This is so not only because the parable of the sower is simple, but because it reflects their reaction to parabolic teaching in general. It is a key to the teaching value of all other parables.

The seed is **the word** (14); and if Jesus had confidence in the vitality of that seed, so should we. The harvest is sure. What about the soils where the seed is sown? The four classes of soil typify (1) The hardened life, 4, 15; (2) The shallow life, 5-6, 16-

---

[20]*Op. cit.,* p. 257. See Cranfield, *op. cit.,* pp. 158-61, for a careful study of the issues and his reasons for accepting the authenticity of these verses.

[21]*Op. cit.,* p. 90.

17; (3) The crowded life, 7, 18-19; and (4) The receptive life, 8, 20.[22]

The hardened heart has no opening for a seed to enter; hence **Satan cometh immediately, and taketh away the word** (15). Somehow that soil will have to be broken up if the seed is ever to lodge there.

The stony ground, where shallow soil covers rock, produces flashy results. But, with no root in themselves, these followers of Christ **endure but for a time** (17), only to "stumble *and* fall away" (*Amplified NT*) in the face of **affliction or persecution.** A theology which teaches a *positional* salvation has no encouragement here, nor does the doctrine known as "eternal security." But neither is there ground for that pessimism which sees no hope for the "easy-come, easy-go" Christian. If he can once touch God for the cleansing of inbred sin, his shallowness can be replaced by depth and his wobbling can give place to stability.

It is alarming that forces exist capable of choking the word so that it **becometh unfruitful** (19)! Daily **cares, the deceitfulness**[23] **of riches,** together with **lusts,** or longing, for **other things** not in the divine will, may combine to smother **the word.** (The word translated **choke** literally means "to squeeze together," thus "to strangle, throttle.")[24]

The picture thus far is pessimistic, but the climax is not. There is **good ground** (20), too, and perhaps more of it in a field than the less productive soil. **These are they which . . . hear the word, and receive it** (20) ("welcome it," Goodspeed). Faith is more than assent to truth, or consent to duty; it is also a commitment and an acceptance from the heart. These **bring forth fruit** in immense quantities.

### 3. *An Exhortation to Understanding* (4:21-25)

Once more Jesus takes the common features of daily life and makes them luminous with meaning. Note the **candle** (or lamp), the **bushel** (a container holding about eight quarts), the **bed** (a mat to be rolled up by day), the **candlestick** (a small shelf jutting from the wall). All of these were basic furnishings in a typical Palestinian home.

[22]Earle, *op. cit.,* p. 63.
[23]This term, *apate,* may also be rendered *delight* or *pleasure.*
[24]Robertson, *op. cit.,* p. 284.

> *Earth's crammed with heaven*
> *And every common bush afire with God,*
> *But only he who sees takes off his shoes . . .*[25]

Why is a **candle brought** (21) into the house? Is it **to be put under a bushel, or under a bed?** (Putting the lamp under a bed was not impossible, for the mat could be raised slightly to shade the light.) The answer is obvious. The lamp is brought into a home to dispel the darkness and so stands in an unobstructed position.

Why, then, has the Christ come into the world? To be sure, He spoke in mysterious parables and went about incognito, revealing "the mystery of the kingdom of God" (4:11) to only a few. Nevertheless **there is nothing hid** (22) "except to be made manifest," **neither . . . any thing kept secret** "except to come to light" (RSV).

The temporary hiding of His message in parabolic form, and the temporary veiling of His person ("And he straitly charged them that they should not make him known," 3:12) was really in order to reveal the truth. "The veil sharpens attention, stimulates curiosity, quickens effort, and so becomes positively subsidiary to the great purpose of revelation . . ."[26]

The hearer, then, quite clearly has an obligation. "If anyone has ears for hearing, let him hear" (23, S. E. Johnson). **Take heed what ye hear** (24) and "how ye hear" (Luke 8:18). If the man in the pulpit must have a care lest "the hungry sheep look up, and are not fed,"[27] it follows that the man in the pew has a responsibility to listen with earnest thoughtfulness. "The measure you give will be the measure you get" (24, RSV). "Response to the truth is the condition for receiving further truth."[28] Moreover, a refusal to respond to the truth will lead to moral atrophy and decay. In this sense, "the rich get richer and the poor get poorer." **And he that hath not, from him shall be taken even that which he hath** (25). "As for the man who has nothing, even his nothing will be taken away" (Phillips).

[25]Elizabeth Barrett Browning, from *Aurora Leigh.*

[26]Alexander Maclaren, *Expositions of Holy Scripture: St. Mark* (Grand Rapids, Michigan: Wm. B. Eerdmans Publishing Co., 1938 [reprint]), p. 150.

[27]John Milton, from *Lycidas.*

[28]NBC, p. 815.

## 4. *The Parable of the Seed Growing Secretly* (4:26-29)

This parable, found only in Mark, follows in line with the parable of the sower but has been subject to more varied interpretations. The central thrust of the parable is surely that "the growth of God's kingdom in the world is beyond man's understanding and control."[29] **The kingdom of God, [is] as if a man should cast seed into the ground . . . and the seed should spring and grow up, he knoweth not how** (27). As the sower goes about his daily routine, sleeping and rising night and day, the earth **bringeth forth fruit of herself** (28) (literally, "automatically," *automate*).

The servant of the Lord certainly has a duty to cultivate the soil, sow the seed, and water the plants, but it is "God that giveth the increase" (I Cor. 3:7). We may deduce other truths, such as man's limitations and the need for patience; but the parable teaches, first of all, "the certainty . . . the inevitability of the kingdom's coming, once the seed"[30] is **cast . . . into the ground** (26).

It may be that the parable is not intended to teach the gradualness of the Kingdom's coming, but that coming does occur in sure and orderly stages: **first the blade, then the ear, after that the full corn** (grain) **in the ear** (28). As Halford Luccock reminds us,[31] the first and the last stages of this process are exciting. But the in-between stage, the "adolescence" of Christian growth, is less glamorous. Whether in the life of the young Christian, a young church, or in society at large, **the blade** and **the full corn in the ear** are cause for rejoicing. The more painful experience of growing up requires patience and fidelity.

**When the fruit is brought forth** (29), i.e., "when the grain is ripe" (RSV), it is time **immediately** to put **in the sickle,** (cf. Joel 3:13) **because the harvest is come.** One's view of the parable as a whole will govern his interpretation of the harvest. Some regard the harvesttime as the end of the world. In that case the Christian worker would have no responsibility for putting in the sickle. It seems better, while not rejecting eschatological implications, to apply this parable to the growth of the Kingdom whenever and wherever it may take place. The men who **cast**

[29]*The Oxford Annotated Bible,* eds. Herbert G. May and Bruce M. Metzger (New York: Oxford University Press, 1962) p. 1218.
[30]IB, VII, 706.
[31]IB, VII, 705 (Exposition).

**seed into the ground** (26), and who watched the earth bring forth fruit of itself, will yet have an urgent task. "The harvest truly is plenteous, but the labourers are few" (Matt. 9:37).

## 5. *The Parable of the Mustard Seed* (4:30-32)

Jesus here continued His effort to help the disciples understand the true nature of **the kingdom of God** (30). (And how slow they were to learn! Cf. Acts 1:6.) He asked, **Whereunto shall we liken it?** graciously including the hearers in the project. Parenthetically, we may note the importance of pictorial thinking in spiritual matters. **With what comparison shall we compare it?** Translated literally it is, "In what parable might we put it?"[32] Abstract ideas need to be clothed in stories and pictures if they are to reach the mind and heart.

The point of the parable is that, although the Kingdom may have had the smallest possible beginning, it would one day grow to a stupendous size. **A grain of mustard seed** (31) was used proverbially to represent something very small (see Matt. 17:20). Despite its size, however, the mustard seed produced a plant or shrub greater than any other vegetable in the garden, about ten feet or more tall. The branches of the plant were of sufficient size to permit **the fowls** (birds) **of the air** (32) to make nests and **lodge under the shadow of it.** (Birds were fond of the mustard seed.)

The figure of a large tree, with birds lodging in its branches and animals resting in its shade, is reminiscent of the Old Testament teaching on the fate of great empires and the rise of God's kingdom. The great cedar of Assyria was cut down, and the strong, fair tree of Nebuchadnezzar also (Ezek. 21:3-13; Dan. 4:10-14), but the tree of the Lord flourished (Ezek. 17:22-24).

It must have been a source of enormous encouragement in Mark's day for the young, struggling Church to hear the assurance of Christ in this parable. It is still a probing question: "Who hath despised the day of small things?" (Zech. 4:10)

## 6. *On the Use of Parables* (4:33-34)

It is clear from the words **with many such parables** (33) that Mark has given only a selection from a larger group. "In keeping with his stress on action, Mark has less of Jesus' teaching than

[32]Marvin R. Vincent, *Word Studies of the New Testament* (Grand Rapids, Michigan: Wm. B. Eerdmans Publishing Co., 1946), I, 183-84.

the other Synoptic Gospels but proportionately more of His miracles."[33]

By means of such parables, or figures, Jesus spoke **the word,** the good news of the Kingdom, **unto them** (33). By whatever means, let the man of God "preach the word" (II Tim. 4:2) and so "follow [in] his steps" (I Pet. 2:21).

As the Master Teacher, Jesus **spake ... the word ... as they were able to hear it** (33). A good teacher adapts his materials and methods to the capacity of his learners. Even at the last, Jesus said to His disciples, "I have yet many things to say unto you, but ye cannot bear them now" (John 16:12). This speaks a word to both teacher and student. Let the teacher take a sincere interest in his pupils for their own sake, and let the student remember that "none may move to advanced lessons till he has mastered the elementary studies."[34]

It was the practice of Jesus not to address the multitudes **without a parable** (34), a figure of speech of some sort. "Had he spoken to the crowds in a direct way, he would have forced them to make a final decision at once ... a decision of unbelief and rejection."[35] (See on 4:10-20.) But when the disciples were with Him **alone, he expounded** (literally, "loosened," "set free") **all things** to them. Eager, interested learners stayed after class for a fuller explanation of the lecture!

In neglecting exposition of the Scriptures, preachers have hardly improved on the method of Jesus. It is still true that men's hearts will burn within them when someone opens to them the Scriptures (cf. Luke 24:32).

### E. A Ministry of Mighty Works, 4:35—5:43

#### 1. *Stilling the Tempest* (4:35-41)

The scene of the "ministry in parables," recorded in chapter 4, was "by the sea side" (1). Jesus had "sat in the sea" with a boat as His pulpit. **The same day** (35), one full of public teaching and private explanation, **he saith, ... Let us pass over unto the other side.** Jesus referred, of course, to the Sea of Galilee (see map), a freshwater lake in northern Palestine, heart-shaped,

---

[33]Ralph Earle (ed.), *Exploring the New Testament* (Kansas City, Missouri: Beacon Hill Press, 1955), p. 114.

[34]Cole, *op. cit.,* p. 95.

[35]Cranfield, *op. cit.,* p. 171.

about thirteen miles long and eight miles wide, 680 feet below
sea level. The sea was a place of inspiring beauty; it was a center
of commercial activity in Jesus' day. With mountains skirting
most of the lake, it was subject to violent storms, because of
the fierce downdrafts of cold air from the higher elevations to the
lower.[36]

It was at **even** when Jesus gave the invitation, **Let us pass
over.** There is here a suggestive word of tender compassion on the
lips of a pastor as he shares an hour of bereavement with his
flock.

Leaving **the multitude,** the disciples took Jesus with them
**even as he was** (36), perhaps without leaving the boat mentioned in verse 1. The time comes when one must turn away from
the crowded life and seek out a place of rest and recuperation.
Jesus sought to put several miles of water between Him and the
cities of the western shore as He and the disciples "took ship"
for the more desolate eastern side. That such solitude was rare
is evident from the words **there were also with him other little
ships** (boats). This detail, unnecessary to the story, is another
authentic reminiscence, very probably from Peter himself. The
storm apparently soon turned back the other boats.

For geographical reasons described above there soon **arose
a great storm of wind** (37), of hurricane proportions, with crash-
ing waves threatening to sink the boat.[37] Evincing both fatigue
and faith, Jesus had fallen **asleep on a pillow** (38) in the stern
of the boat. But this was "no soft luxurious pillow . . . [rather]
the low bench at the stern on which the steersman sometimes
sits, and the captain sometimes rests his head to sleep."[38] The
**pillow** was perhaps a leather cushion. Only here does the New
Testament speak of Jesus sleeping, although John 4:6 records
that Jesus "being wearied . . . sat thus on the well."

In stark terror, the disciples aroused Jesus and said, re-
proachfully, " 'Teacher, are we to drown, for all you care?' "(38,
Moffatt) The roughness of their reproach and the severity of
Jesus' rebuke are further examples of details in the memory of

[36]*Harper's Bible Dictionary,* eds. Madeleine S. and J. Lane Miller (New
York: Harper and Brothers, Publishers, 1952) pp. 213-14.

[37]Cf. Earle's literal translation, *op. cit.,* p. 67.

[38]A. B. Bruce, "The Synoptic Gospels," *The Expositor's Greek Testament,* ed. W. Robertson Nicoll (Grand Rapids, Michigan: Wm. B. Eerdmans,
n.d.), I, 370.

Peter, from whom Mark is believed to have secured much of the content of his Gospel.

Rudely awakened, Jesus addressed the storm in the language of an exorcist confronting one possessed. He spoke two words: one to the noisy wind, "Silence!"; the other to the raging waters, "Be muzzled!" As if weary from exertion, **the wind ceased** (39) and the water became very **calm.**

Under the title "With the Master on Board," one may note: (1) Crisis, 37-38; (2) Christ, 39; (3) Calm, 39.

The miracles of Jesus, especially the "nature miracles," are an offense to those who reject the supernatural. But has it not ever been so? (Cf. I Cor. 1:23.) When one grants the greatest of all miracles, the Incarnation, the miracles of the New Testament are quite in order. In any case, a rejection of this miracle simply discounts Mark's responsible account.[39]

Having rebuked the elements, Jesus turned to His distraught followers and chided them. **Why . . . so fearful?** (40) If He rebuked their lack of courage, would He commend our fears? Ours is an age of anxiety. Worry is not a mild opponent. But opposite **fear,** Jesus sets **faith.** Our Lord has help for us at this point. "What time I am afraid, I will trust in thee" (Ps. 56:3).

Speechless, the disciples now **feared exceedingly** (41). Literally, "They were frightened with a great fear." Life's greatest question was asked by the disciples, **What manner of man is this?** The correct answer to this question is the only solution to the problem of miracles. The singular of the verb *obey* indicates that each element was thought of separately. "Even the wind, even the sea, obeys Him."[40]

The text, **What manner of man is this?** may be used to open up an exposition of 4:39—5:43. The subject, "Christ's Power": (1) Over danger, 4:36-41; (2) Over demons, 5:1-19; (3) Over disease, 5:24-34; (4) Over death, 5:20-23, 35-43.

### 2. *The Demoniac of Gerasa* (5:1-20)

How uneventful the words, **they came over unto the other side of the sea** (1), yet how much wiser and stronger the disciples must have been for their recent experience (cf. 4:35-41)! "Now no chastening for the present seemeth to be joyous, but grievous: nevertheless afterward..." (Heb. 12:11). As Jesus and

[39]See Hunter, *op. cit.,* pp. 61-62, for a helpful discussion on miracles.
[40]EGT, I, 370.

His disciples came **into the country of the Gadarenes,**[41] from a storm-tossed sea, they immediately confronted a storm-tossed soul, **a man with an unclean spirit** (2).[42]

The description of the Gerasene demoniac (3-5) is a description of the wretchedness and brutality of sin. **His dwelling** [was] **among the tombs** (3), a real possibility, for tombs were often located in the shelter of caves. **No man** was able to **bind him** nor strong enough to **tame him.**[43] **Chains had been plucked asunder** . . . and **fetters broken in pieces** (4). The demoniac was simply unmanageable. (A series of negatives in the Greek stresses this fact.) His great strength brought only misery as **night and day** he raged through **the mountains, and in the tombs, crying,** and lacerating **himself with stones** (5).

Sin is "Public Enemy No. 1," for it means: (1) Suicide—dwelling in the place of death, 3; (2) Insanity, 4; (3) Self-destruction, 5.

Here we see another example of that mysterious recognition of Jesus by those possessed. Though some distance from the shore, when the demoniac **saw Jesus . . . he ran and worshipped him** (6), i.e., fell prostrate before Him. Even the disciples had not yet come to understand who Jesus truly was, yet the demoniac cried out, "What have You to do with me, Jesus, Son of the Most High God?" (7, *Amplified NT*) The expression **the most high God** reflects an Old Testament name for God used "mainly by non-Israelites to denote the God of Israel."[44] The words **I adjure thee by God** are the language of one who casts out demons. Do we have here an attempt at exorcism in reverse?[45] **Torment me not** probably reflects the fright of the demons that Jesus would cast them out (cf. Matt. 8:29). The tormentor was pleading for escape from torment; Jesus "was saying to him, 'You foul spirit, come out of this man'" (8, Goodspeed).

---

[41]Several variant readings of this location appear in the Synoptists, including *Gerasenes* (best attested reading in Mark) and *Gergesenes*. About a mile from the modern Kersa or Koursi is a slope some forty yards from the lake. The site was in the general region of Gadara.

[42]Sherman, *op. cit.,* p. 101, refers to "some well-attested stories of demon-possession." Something more than a psychosis is involved here. Dr. F. C. Sutherland, a distinguished Nazarene missionary from China, affirms that belief in demon possession is something "no one can take from us."

[43]The only other New Testament usage of the word for **tame** (*damasai*) is with respect to the tongue, "which no man can tame" (Jas. 3:7-8).

[44]Cranfield, *op. cit.,* p. 177.

[45]Sherman, *op. cit.,* p. 102.

Perhaps to assist this disordered soul to come to himself, Jesus **asked him, What is thy name?** (9) For an adversary to obtain the name of his opponent was, it was thought, the first step in seizing control over him. **He answered, . . . My name is Legion: for we are many.** The intermingling of we and I in the demoniac's conversation suggests the extent of his split personality due to the presence of demon forces. He was overwhelmed by "a conglomeration of evil forces,"[46] and the 4,000 to 6,000 in a Roman legion may have been an accurate description of his condition.

The desperate plea of the demons that Jesus **would not send them away out of the country** (10) evidently reflects their fear of eternal punishment (cf. Luke 8:31, "into the deep," or "the bottomless pit," *Amplified NT*). Recognizing the authority of Jesus and their own defeat, **all the devils** (demons)[47] **besought** (12) Jesus for permission to go among **a great herd of swine feeding** (11) nearby and to **enter into them.**

The story then "bristles with difficulties" (Cranfield), for **Jesus gave them leave** (13). The numerous **unclean spirits** left their victim and **entered into the swine. Running violently down a steep place,** some **two thousand** pigs were drowned **in the sea.**

Why did Jesus permit this loss of property? Some scholars, seeking to soften the offense, conclude that the last wild cries of the demoniac startled the animals and caused the disaster. Others write it off as a legendary Jewish tale.

The story remains an integral part of the Synoptic record and must carry a significant truth. Perhaps the best explanation is that the poor demented Gerasene needed some outward evidence of his deliverance. The flight and destruction of the swine were an "ocular demonstration to the demoniac that the demons had in fact departed from him."[48] The observation of Barclay is also in order.

> How could the fate of the pigs possibly be compared with the fate of a man's immortal soul? . . . There is a cheap sentimentalism which will languish in grief over the pain of an animal and will never turn a hair at the wretched state of millions of God's men and women. In God's scale of proportions, there is nothing so important as a human soul.[49]

[46]NBC, p. 816.
[47]Cf. any recent version.
[48]NBC, p. 816.
[49]*Op. cit.*, p. 119.

"The herdsmen fled and told it in the city and in the country" (14, RSV). Where else could the story be told? Quite naturally men, no doubt including the owners of the swine, **went out to see what . . . was done** (14). **They** came **to Jesus** (15), but saw the demoniac, the very one who **had the legion,** and "they were really frightened" (15, Phillips). Afraid of sanity! He who once raged among the tombs, wore "no clothes" (Luke 8:27), and was completely bereft of reason, now was **sitting** peacefully, **clothed, and in his right mind** (from a word meaning to "be of sound mind").[50]

The mighty works of Jesus brought amazement and awe to those who looked on. Recall that the disciples "feared exceedingly" when they witnessed the stilling of the storm on Galilee (4:41). Men have always felt a *mysterium tremendum* in the presence of God. Moses took off his shoes before the burning bush (Exod. 3:5); Isaiah cried, "Woe is me!" (Isa. 6:5), in the glory-filled Temple; and when John saw the glorified Christ, he "fell at his feet as dead" (Rev. 1:17). Mark wants us to sense, as well as read, that Jesus is the Christ, "the Son of God" (1:1).

When eyewitnesses described the deliverance of the demoniac and the destruction of the swine, the townspeople of Gerasa **began to pray** (17) ("beg," "implore") Jesus **to depart out of their** area. Perhaps they feared that a greater loss of some kind would occur. Unwilling to remain where He was unwanted, Jesus "gave them their request; but sent leanness into their soul" (Ps. 106:15).[51] It has been said that no other miracle Jesus ever wrought received such a negative response.

In sharp contrast was the eloquent plea of the man **that had been possessed with the devil** (18). **When he [Jesus] was come into the ship** (better, "As he was getting into the boat," RSV), the healed man **prayed** ("besought" or "implored") Jesus **that he might be with him.** Jesus put considerable responsibility on the Gerasene, so young in the faith, in that He **suffered him not** (19) to go along. **Go home . . . and tell . . . how great things the Lord hath done . . . and hath had compassion on thee.** Those who drove Jesus from their shores would thus have a messenger preaching in His stead.

[50]*A Greek-English Lexicon of the New Testament,* eds. William F. Arndt and F. Wilbur Gingrich (Chicago: The University of Chicago Press, 1957), p. 809.

[51]Cf. Cole, *op. cit.,* pp. 99-100.

Courageously but vigorously the ex-demoniac obeyed, apparently at once, **and began to publish** (20)[52] in Decapolis[53] the **great things Jesus had done.** Note that the Gerasene identified **the Lord** with Jesus (19-20; see Luke 8:39). His indisputable testimony evoked amazement. **All . . . did marvel.**

### 3. *The Raising of the Daughter of Jairus* (5:21-43)

In the section before us, two "stupendous miracles"[54] are described. They are unique in that one interrupts the progress of the other without frustrating it. The first represents those who seek for help, the second those who must receive help through the instrumentality of others. The one illustrates Christ's power over disease, the other His power over death.

*a. A Father's Plea* (5:21-24). Returning from the eastern side of the Galilean Sea, and the experience with the Gerasene demoniac, Jesus **passed over again by ship** (21) to the more populous western side. In sharp contrast to the unfriendly reception among the Gerasenes, a great many people **gathered unto him** as soon as He stepped ashore near Capernaum.

The first to break through the curious throng was one of the most distinguished members of the community, **one of the rulers of the synagogue, Jairus by name** (22). Something of a chairman of the congregation, he would have "to do especially with the conduct of public worship, in its various parts of prayer, reading of Scripture, and exhortation."[55] In his desperation, Jairus forgot his "prejudices . . . dignity . . . pride . . . friends"[56] and fell at the feet of Jesus. No man really prays until he is crushed to his knees.

**My little daughter** (the diminutive, peculiar to Mark, was an endearing term) **lieth at the point of death . . . come and lay thy hands on her** (23). Jairus had great faith in Jesus and must

---

[52]A word also translated "preach."

[53]A league of ten cities which had developed under the influence of Alexander the Great and so were Grecian in culture. The presence of the swine, repugnant to a loyal Jew, would indicate Gentile influence. Nine of the cities were east of the Jordan, one on the west. They were scattered from Damascus in the north to as far south as Philadelphia (Rabbath-Ammon). Gergesa and Gadara were about midway between these.

[54]IB, VII, 718.

[55]S. D. F. Salmond, *St. Mark*, "The Century Bible" (Edinburgh: T. C. and E. C. Jack, n.d.), p. 173.

[56]Barclay, *op. cit.*, pp. 126-27.

have known of His power to heal. It is attractive speculation
that he may have been among the "elders of the Jews" who
besought Jesus to heal the servant of a friendly centurion in
Capernaum (Luke 7:2-5).

Although pressed on all sides by those who **thronged him**
(24), Jesus **went with** the distraught father, bringing hope that
his daughter would **be healed** (literally, "saved").

*b. A Pathetic Interruption* (5:25-34). Among those who
**thronged** Jesus (24), as He set out for the home of Jairus, was
**a certain woman** (25) "who had had a flow of blood for twelve
years" (*Amplified NT*). Her ailment was as old as the child who
at that moment lay "at the point of death" (23). This unnamed
woman had sought relief from **many physicians** (26) but was
**nothing bettered.** Mark is blunt and uncomplimentary about the
physicians of the time. The woman **had suffered many things**
at their hands, **had spent all that she had,** and was **worse.** The
beloved physician, Luke, is somewhat friendlier to the members
of his profession and notes that the malady could not be cured
(Luke 8:43).

The plight of the woman was pathetic—"presumably a
chronic hemorrhage, debilitating, embarrassing . . . impoverish-
ing . . . discouraging."[57] It is not surprising that **when she had
heard of Jesus** (27), whose fame was now widespread, she
sought deliverance from Him. Hoping "to steal a miracle,"[58] she
came in the throng behind Jesus and **touched his garment.**

The practice of healing has usually been associated with a
touch. We have already noted how Jesus, "moved with compassion, put forth his hand and touched" a leper to heal him (1:41).
The multitudes often "pressed upon" the Master in order "to
touch him" (3:10). This is also in line with James's instructions concerning prayer for the sick (Jas. 5:14). **If I may but
touch his clothes** (28), the woman reflected in profound hope,
**I shall be whole.** The men of Israel were required to wear a
border on their garments: "the fringe of the borders a ribband
of blue" (Num. 15:38). It was perhaps this tassel she touched
(Luke 8:44).

**Straightway** (Mark's favorite adverb, *euthus*) **the fountain
of her blood** (cf. Lev. 12:7) **was dried up** (29), and she sensed

---

[57]IB, VII, 720.
[58]Hunter, *op. cit.,* p. 66.

that **she was healed of that** scourge (the literal rendering of **plague**). The word **healed** (*iatai*) is in the perfect tense and implies that the "consequences remain."[59]

For the moment, the unspeakable joy of the woman turned to alarm, for Jesus, **knowing**[60] that power (*dynamis*) had "gone forth from him" (30, RSV), **turned him about . . . and said, Who touched my clothes?** Why did Jesus raise the question? Probably to help the woman make that open confession so important to salvation (Rom. 10:10), but also to make it clear that the object of her faith was himself, not His clothes.

The disciples were obviously amused and a little exasperated at the question of Jesus. Why should He ask, **Who touched me?** (31) when a multitude was **thronging**[61] them from all sides? Their question was not very respectful, and a bit sarcastic. But it reflects the antiquity and reliability of Mark's source.

The healing of the woman reminds us that there is a "world of difference between thronging Jesus and touching Him in personal faith."[62]

Ignoring the comment of His disciples, Jesus **looked round about** (32) for the one **that had done this thing.** Again reporting a detail such as an eyewitness would recall, Mark gives us a vivid picture of Jesus searching the faces of the crowd, as in 3:5, except that here it is with kindness rather than anger.

Fully aware that she had rendered Jesus ceremonially unclean (Lev. 15:19) and **trembling** with uncertainty lest He be angry, the woman nevertheless came forward "and told Him the whole truth" (33, RSV). The kindly words of Jesus assuaged her fearful spirit. **Daughter, thy faith hath made thee whole** (34). No group has more to gain by serving Christ, or more to lose by rejecting Him, than the women of the world.

Jesus made it clear that it was the woman's faith in Him, not some magic in the touch of His clothes, that made her whole. His words were also an outward confirmation of what had transpired in her.

**Go in peace, and be whole.** As one who now was sound in body and free from her scourge, she could indeed **go in**

---

[59]Cranfield, *op. cit.,* p. 184.

[60]A word meaning exact knowledge, thorough and complete.

[61]In the New Testament, only here and in v. 24, "pressed together" (Earle).

[62]NBC, p. 817.

**peace.** The blessings of good health and the consequent feeling of well-being are gifts of God. In substance, Jesus said, " 'May your trouble never worry you any more.' "[63]

Mark has thus preserved for all time another of the mighty works of Him who is "the same yesterday, and to day, and for ever" (Heb. 13:8).

*c. Life from the Dead* (5:35-43) One can imagine the intense anxiety of Jairus during the interruption described in vv. 25-34. If he had such fears, they were confirmed when some callous soul appeared **while** Jesus **yet spake** (35) to the woman and reported that his **daughter** was **dead.** Their question, **Why troublest**[64] **thou the Master any further?** implies that they thought Jairus was annoying Him. They had no expectation of a resurrection.

Overhearing **the word that was spoken** (36), but ignoring the implication,[65] Jesus quickly saith unto Jairus, **"Be not afraid; continue to believe."** How often Jesus rebuked fear and encouraged faith!

At that point Jesus turned back the curious throng and **suffered no man to follow him** (37), except the inner circle of **Peter, and James, and John,** his brother. The privilege of these three to witness this and other remarkable events (the Transfiguration, 9:2; the agony of Gethsemane, 14:33) was balanced by later responsibility. Peter was the chief spokesman at Pentecost; James early faced martyrdom; and John exercised immeasurable influence as the apostle of love.

When at last Jesus and those with Him reached **the house of the ruler of the synagogue** (38), they beheld a **tumult,** a great din and confusion caused by the loud weeping and wailing.[66] It was customary to employ professional mourners, although undoubtedly close friends were present who wept with a sincere grief.

Possibly distressed by some who **wept and wailed** for gain, Jesus, having come into the home or its courtyard, **saith unto**

---

[63]Hunter, *op. cit.,* p. 66.

[64]A softened form of a term meaning "to skin, flay, rend." Abbott-Smith, *op. cit.,* p. 411.

[65]The better reading is *parakousas,* "to overhear" or "hear carelessly," hence "ignore," as in Matt. 18:17.

[66]"A descriptive word of the hired mourners crying al-a-lai!" (Vincent, *op. cit.,* p. 191).

**them, Why make ye this ado** (literally, "make a tumult," as in
v. 38), **and weep?** (39) "The child is not dead; she is asleep"
(39, NEB).

The death of the child must have been real, for the story is
the climax of a series of "mighty works." To the power of God
in Jesus, her death was no greater obstacle than a person asleep.
"The other world . . . is within reach of the Saviour's voice."[67]

Confident that **the damsel** was indeed not asleep but **dead,**
the mourners **laughed Jesus to scorn** (40). The term (*kategelon*)
implies derision. "They . . . jeered at Him" (*Amplified NT*). The
scornful contribute nothing to an atmosphere of faith, so Jesus
**put them all out.**[68] "Only the real mourners were to be comforted; only they needed it."[69]

Accompanied by the three disciples, Jesus rendered a touching pastoral service, such as a good minister of Jesus Christ must
often do. **He taketh the father and the mother . . . and entereth
in where the damsel was.** The presence of others with Jesus in
the room would have evidential value and also satisfy the sense
of Jewish propriety.

In a characteristic move (cf. 1:31), Jesus took the little girl
**by the hand** (41) and called her as perhaps her parents had
often called her from sleep. " 'Get up, my child' " (NEB). **Talitha
cumi** are perhaps the very words Jesus spoke, for Aramaic was
the language He used. The response of **the damsel** was immediate.
**Straightway** (42) she **arose, and walked.** Mark notes that she
was **of the age of twelve years** and thus old enough to walk.

Once more we learn of the emotional reaction of those who
witnessed the divine power of Jesus. **They were astonished with
a great astonishment,** i.e., "they were utterly amazed" (42, Goodspeed). "The great fact of the Christian life is that that which
looks completely impossible with men is possible with God."[70]

It was impossible, of course, to hide the fact that a great
miracle had occurred; nevertheless, Jesus **charged them straitly**
("strictly," RSV) **that no man should know it** (43). Our Lord
refused to inflame the false hopes of the Jews that He was the
political Messiah they looked for.

[67]NBC, p. 817.

[68]"Some degree of force is implied" (Vincent, *op. cit.,* p. 396).

[69]Hunter, *op. cit.,* p. 68.

[70]Barclay, *op. cit.,* p. 137.

The story closes with a note on the thoughtfulness and practicality of Jesus. He **commanded that something should be given** the child to eat. This would also prove the reality of the miracle. "The dead was now living and could take food."[71]

This chapter portrays "Christ the Conqueror": (1) Over demons, 1-20; (2) Over disease, 25-34; (3) Over death, 35-43.

## F. A Prophet Without Honor, 6:1-6

Leaving Capernaum, Jesus **went out from thence** (1) on the first leg of a teaching circuit in Galilee. About a day's journey away He **and his disciples** (who were now experiencing in-service training!) came **into his own country,** i.e., Nazareth, His hometown (see map).

On **the sabbath day** (2), Jesus **began to teach in the synagogue.** Here was a "large audience" (Moffatt) of old friends. The ministry of Jesus often evoked astonishment (5:42), but it was different in Nazareth. " 'Where did this man get all this?' " (RSV) There may have been dark hints that the **wisdom** and the **mighty works** of Jesus were **given unto him** from some source other than God (cf. 3:22).

" 'There is always a shadow under the lamp,' "[72] and so it was in Nazareth. "He came unto his own, and his own received him not" (John 1:11). They had known Him as the **carpenter** ("the joiner," Moffatt), **the son of Mary** (3).[73] His brothers and sisters they could name.[74] **And they were offended** (a transliteration would be "scandalized")[75] **at him.** "Astonished" at His wisdom and power, they nevertheless stumbled over His person.

Jesus replied with a proverb common to the day and region.

[71]IB, VII, 725.

[72]Hunter, *op. cit.,* p. 70.

[73]Cranfield, *op. cit.,* p. 195, takes this to be "an important piece of evidence in support of the historicity of the Virgin Birth." For a contrary view, see IB, VII, 727.

[74]The family was evidently devout, for the sons were named after Old Testament heroes: Jacob (James), Joseph, Judah, Simeon, and Joshua (Jesus) (Hunter, *op. cit.,* p. 71). James later became head of the Jerusalem church. The sisters are not mentioned elsewhere.

[75]"The kindred noun is *skandalon* . . . the stick in a trap on which the bait is placed, and which springs up and shuts the trap at the touch of an animal" (Vincent, *op. cit.,* p. 41).

" 'A prophet will always be held in honour except in his home town' " (4, NEB). It is evident elsewhere (Luke 13:33) as well as here that Jesus spoke of himself as a Prophet and was popularly so regarded (15). He was a Bearer of truth.

There follows in verse 5 what has been called one of the "boldest statements in the Gospels," one that creates a "deep impression of historical accuracy."[76] **He could there do no mighty work** (5). (Literally, "He was not able there to do . . .") What we call miracles, John called "signs," and the Synoptists called "mighty works" (*dynameis*). Except for **a few sick folk** on whom Jesus **laid his hands** to heal, no one witnessed any "signs" or "mighty works" in the hometown of Him who has always been known as Jesus of Nazareth.

Wherever the Master went, His ministry aroused amazement, but in Nazareth the reverse was true. The **unbelief** of His kinsmen and friends astonished Him. Jesus **marvelled because of their unbelief** (6). As He **went round about the villages** of Galilee, **teaching**, He must have carried a wound in His soul (cf. Matt. 17:17).

## G. The Mission of the Twelve, 6:7-13

This section seems properly to begin with verse 6b. The teaching ministry of Jesus in Galilee was extended through the work of **the twelve,** whom He now **called** and sent **forth** (*apostellein,* from whence comes our word "apostle") with **power** (*exousia,* "authority") **over unclean spirits** (7).

What an incomparable theological education these unlettered fishermen received! They "learned by doing" under the guidance of One who spoke as "never man spake" (John 7:46).

Going out **two and two,** "for purposes of witness and fellowship,"[77] they were to travel with frugality and urgency, depending upon God and the hospitality of those who received them. Notice the progression in restriction: carrying **a staff only** (8)[78] (possibly as a protection against vicious dogs), they were to

---

[76]Taylor, *op. cit.,* p. 301.

[77]NBC, p. 818.

[78]"Matthew's (10:10) and Luke's (9:3) prohibition against even this seems to mean that they were not to acquire a staff if they did not already have one" (Earle, *op. cit.,* p. 80).

take **no bread, no scrip** (8) (bag) [79] for carrying bread, nor any **money** (copper coin!) **in their purse** (belt) to buy bread. **Shod with sandals** (9), they were not to **put on two coats** (a tunic or shirt worn next to the skin). "Two shirts are a luxury unsuitable for travelling." [80]

Such requirements would apply literally only to the short period of this ministry in Galilee, but in principle they are applicable for all time. "The service of the Word of God is still a matter of extreme urgency, calling for absolute self-dedication." [81]

Jesus further commanded the disciples to **abide** (10) in **what place soever** they should **enter** until they were ready to **depart from that place** for another village. They were not to offend their hosts by seeking other more comfortable surroundings or perhaps lingering too long. In the second century it became necessary for the Church to develop rules governing traveling prophets. [82]

On the other hand, **whosoever** would **not receive . . . nor hear** (11) them was to receive a stern warning. When the disciples departed from **thence,** they were to **shake off the dust under** their **feet for a testimony against** that place. The responsibility for rejection was to rest upon the head of the rejecters. It was the practice of the Jews, upon leaving a pagan land, to shake off the dust of that land from their shoes, lest their own sacred land be defiled. The gesture required by Jesus would declare that village heathen, with the hope that repentance would follow (cf. Acts 13:51). [83]

The disciples, who had been (1) *Called* from their secular tasks, (2) *Chosen* to be apostles, and finally (3) *Commissioned* [84] to go out with "power over unclean spirits," 7, **went out, and preached that men should repent.** [85] They not only received authority but employed it successfully. As fine as preparation and planning may be, how much finer is performance!

[79]The word order as it appears in the earlier MSS.

[80]Taylor, *op. cit.,* p. 305.

[81]Cranfield, *op. cit.,* p. 200.

[82]Cf. *Didache* xi. 3—xii. 5. Johnson, *op. cit.,* p. 116.

[83]"The latter part of verse 11 is omitted by RV, RSV, NEB, following the principal uncial MSS. It was no doubt added here because of Matthew x. 15" (Cole, *op. cit.,* p. 109).

[84]Hunter, *op. cit.,* p. 72.

[85]See on 1:15.

> *Knowledge we ask not—knowledge Thou hast lent,*
> *But, Lord, the will—there lies our bitter need,*
> *Give us to build above the deep intent*
> *The deed, the deed.*[86]

In the power given them by Jesus, the disciples **cast out many devils (13)**, (demons) and anointing **with oil many . . . sick** (cf. Luke 10:34; Jas. 5:14), **healed them.** In the person of Jesus and in the preaching of His disciples, the kingdom of God indeed had come near (cf. 1:15).

Section **IV** *A Ministry Beyond Galilee*

Mark 6:14—8:26

The story of Herod and the martyrdom of John the Baptist (6:14-29) introduces a period in the ministry of Jesus when He began to withdraw from Galilee and prepare to turn toward Jerusalem and the Cross. This action may have been due to the rising hostility of Herod Antipas (Luke 13:31) as well as to the need for rest and solitude as He and the disciples entered the shadow of the Cross.

This section provides an interlude between the mission of the Twelve (7-13) and their return (30). Mark gives us no record of what Jesus was doing during the preaching tour of the disciples, although it is evident from verse 6*b* that He was similarly employed.

A. THE GHOSTS OF HEROD'S FEARS, 6:14-29

Herod Antipas, popularly called king, was tetrarch[1] of Galilee and Perea from 4 B.C. to A.D. 39. His reign thus spanned the life and public ministry of Jesus. From a family characterized by intrigue and violence, "he appears as a sensual, cunning, capricious, cruel, weak, unscrupulous, superstitious, despotic prince (Matt. 14:9; Luke 3:19; 13:31, 32)."[2]

"Quite naturally, especially after the mission of the Twelve, **Herod heard** (14) of the fame of Jesus. A rumor prevailed, in which Herod concurred,[3] **That John the Baptist was risen from the dead.** "It is on account of this," Herod reasoned, "that such mighty powers are at work in Him." Others said, "It is Elijah" (cf. Mal. 4:5; Matt. 16:14), while still others asserted, " 'It is a prophet, like one of the prophets of old' " (15, RSV).

It is a commentary on the prophetic power of Jesus' preaching that His contemporaries likened Him to such rugged men as Elijah and John the Baptist. Whatever public opinion may have been, Herod's own tormented soul concluded, **It is John, whom I beheaded: he is risen from the dead** (16).

At this point (17) Mark recalls some earlier history, the sad facts which now troubled Herod. Some time before, Herod had

---

[1]Literally, one who rules one-quarter of a domain.
[2]CB, p. 184.
[3]Some MSS read (14) "he said" and others "they said."

been in Rome, where he had fallen in love with Herodias, **his brother Philip's wife.**[4] Herodias, actually a niece of Antipas, left her husband, Philip, for the ruler of Galilee. Herod divorced his first wife, the daughter of an Arabian king, Aretas IV, causing an international incident. According to Josephus,[5] Aretas made war on Herod's armies with considerable success.

For this incestuous marriage, John the Baptist had rebuked the king. **It is not lawful for thee to have thy brother's wife** (18). Neither Jewish nor Christian standards would support such a marriage. John's words stung Herodias, so that thereafter she "nursed a grudge against him and would willingly have killed him" (19, NEB) but **could not.** Paradoxically, the restraining hand was Herod's, who **feared John** (20), knowing he was **a just man and . . . holy.**

John was a preacher of holiness, by his life and by his word. Filled with the Holy Spirit, "even from his mother's womb" (Luke 1:15), John the Baptist called men to repentance and to a life of righteousness. That the holiness of his character was ethical in quality, and not merely ceremonial or positional, is seen in the fact that it is linked with righteousness. **He was a just** (righteous) and **holy man** (20). In a state of divided mind, Herod kept John safe in prison (the meaning of **observed)** and yet often **heard him gladly.** As rulers of the Jewish people, the Herods were "dillettanti in religion"[6] and often sampled religious instruction (cf. Acts 26:1-3). Yet when Herod heard John "he was much perplexed"[7] (20, *Amplified NT*), as well he might have been. One recalls the perplexity and confusion of Festus and Agrippa, on another occasion, when Paul preached the gospel to them (Acts 26:24, 28).

Like another Jezebel, Herodias waited for an opportune time to lay a trap for the outspoken prophet. She found **a convenient day** (21) when **Herod on his birthday made** a feast for **his lords** ("great ones"), **high captains** (*chiliarch,* "captain of a thousand"), **and chief estates of Galilee** ("leading men"). The banquet was characteristic of a sensual oriental monarch. Drunk-

[4]Certain apparent difficulties in this account have led some critics to reject it as legendary. For a step-by-step analysis of each objection, see Cranfield, *op. cit.,* p. 208. Before a "cool appraisal" (Taylor) the difficulties are seen to be without substance.

[5]See his *Ant.* XVIII. 5. 1 ff. for another account of the whole affair.

[6]Cole, *op. cit.,* p. 110.

[7]A better attested reading than "he did many things."

enness and the voluptuous dancing by Salome, Herodias' own daughter,[8] influenced the king to make a rash vow. **Whatsoever thou shalt ask of me** (23), he **sware unto** the girl, **I will give it thee.** "Rash vows are condemned by the Lord in Matthew v. 34; rash vows brought Jephthah into agony (Judg. xi. 31 ff.) and nearly undid Saul (I Sam. xiv. 38 ff.)."[9]

The decisive influence of the home is illustrated by the action of Salome. She went straight **unto her mother** (24) with the question, **What shall I ask?** The lives of children and youth may be twisted and blighted or ennobled and refined by their parents. Such power is frightening! The mother who outraged the standards of even that poor day by exposing her princess-daughter in a sensuous dance now seized the opportunity her smoldering malice sought. Her reply: **The head of John the Baptist.** Feverish urgency is seen in the words which follow: the daughter returned **straightway with haste** (25) and demanded "at once" (the meaning of **by and by**) her grisly trophy. No opportunity would be given Herod to change his mind.

**And the king was exceeding sorry** (26). This is strong language and used elsewhere by Mark only once (14:34, where Jesus said, "My soul is exceeding sorrowful unto death"). The grief and regret of the king are in line with his attitude toward John and must have been genuine. The pressure of public opinion was more than he could bear. Because of the oaths he had made in the presence of those **which sat with him** "he did not want to break his word" (26, RSV).

Like a weak-willed Ahab, dominated by Jezebel, **the king sent an executioner** (27) (probably a guard)[10] at once and **beheaded** John **in the prison.** The scene took place at Machaerus, located on "a lonely ridge, surrounded by terrible ravines, overlooking the east side of the Dead Sea. It was one of the loneliest and grimmest and most unassailable fortresses in the world."[11]

[8]Later married to her paternal uncle, Philip, tetrarch of Trachonitis, and, following his death, to a second cousin, Aristobulus. Merrill F. Unger, *Unger's Bible Dictionary* (Chicago: Moody Press, 1957), p. 955.

[9]Cole, *op. cit.*, p. 112.

[10]"One of Mark's Latin words, *speculator*. A speculator was a guardsman, whose business it was to *watch* or *spy out* (*speculari*). It came gradually to denote one of the armed body-guard of the Roman emperor . . . Herod imitated the manners of the Roman court" (Vincent, *op. cit.*, pp. 194-95).

[11]Barclay, *op. cit.*, p. 150.

The bleak dungeons, with their instruments of imprisonment, are still there for the visitor to see. "Herod the Great had built a palace there,"[12] so it is not impossible that the banquet took place at Machaerus. With no friend but God to witness his execution, John the Baptist paid dearly for being a preacher of righteousness.

To complete the ghastly business, Herod caused John's head to be **brought** (28) on **a charger** (platter) and given **to the damsel. She in turn gave it to her mother.**[13] The **disciples** of John (cf. 2:18; Acts 19:3), hearing of it, **came** and **laid** his body **in a tomb** (29). Matthew adds (14:12) a tender note, that John's disciples "went and told Jesus." The labors of Jesus and John intertwined, and very shortly Jesus too confronted His passion and death.

In discussing "A King's Uneasy Conscience," we may note: (1) Cutting conscience, 16-18; (2) Crafty conniving, 19-25; (3) Cruel compliance, 26-28.

## B. Miracles and Teaching Around the Sea, 6:30-56

### 1. *The Feeding of the Five Thousand* (6:30-44)

Mark is now ready to describe the return of the Twelve after their preaching and healing tour of Galilee. No doubt with joy and exuberance **the apostles** (30), so called because of their mission (an apostle, "one sent"), "rejoined Jesus" (Goodspeed) **and told him all things, both what they had done, and . . . taught.** Deeds and words, a happy order! One recalls Chaucer's line

*That first he wroghte, and afterward he taughte.*

After listening to their reports, the Good Physician, knowing the physical and emotional weariness of the disciples, said, **Come ye yourselves apart into a desert** (lonely, deserted) **place, and rest a while** (31).

> The watchful care of health and strength is a primary religious duty. When we fail to take that care, we sin against God. We snatch away from his full use the instrument he ought to have . . . If we are too busy to allow strength to be renewed by withdrawal and rest, we are too busy to serve God with our best.[14]

[12]Taylor, *op. cit.,* p. 317.
[13]Herodias was ultimately the downfall of her husband. She prodded Herod to seek the title of "king," an act which led to his banishment. To her credit, Herodias shared her husband's disgrace. See Branscomb, *op. cit.,* p. 110.
[14]IB, VII, 738 (Exposition).

As upon numerous other occasions,[15] the little band took a boat and set out on the lake. They sought **a desert place . . . privately** (32). What their destination was is not stated, perhaps the northeast shore of the sea. More miles by foot than by boat, **the people** (33) who **saw them departing, and . . . knew** them, **ran afoot thither . . . and outwent them.** If there were only a slight breeze for their sails or a contrary wind, the boat would move slowly, a fortunate happenstance availing at least some little respite from the crowds.

When Jesus, coming out of the boat, **saw much people** (34) gathered **together unto him,** "he was gripped with compassion toward them" (Earle). **Compassion** is a term used only of Jesus or by Him of characters in His parables and "denotes a pity which expresses itself in . . . assistance."[16] The helplessness and confusion of **sheep not having a shepherd** is proverbial in all lands (cf. Num. 27:15-17; Ezek. 34:1-6). **And he began to teach them many things** ("at length," Moffatt). Matthew (14:13) and Luke (9:11) add that He healed the sick as well, "but a vigorous crowd of runners would not have many sick."[17] Presently He was to feed them all.

In sharp contrast to the attitude of Jesus, the disciples knowing that **the day was now far spent** (35) and that they were indeed in **a desert place** apart, approached Jesus with the suggestion that He dismiss the people. Surely somewhere in **the country round about** (36), or in **the villages,** they could **buy themselves bread.**

Jesus resisted the suggestion with the words, **Give ye them to eat** (37). "Such words come as a lasting rebuke to the helplessness of the Church, in face of a starving world . . ."[18] The reply of the disciples, so characteristic of Mark's bold style, again reflects his authentic early sources. **Shall we go and buy two hundred pennyworth of bread?** A penny (*denarius*) was a silver coin worth about twenty cents, but it represented a day's wages (Matt. 20:2). **Two hundred pennyworth** would be thirty-five or forty dollars, with a purchasing power then of many times that amount—probably an impossible sum.

---

[15]"Mark alone notes no less than eleven occasions on which Jesus retired from his work . . ." (Vincent, *op. cit.*, p. 175).

[16]Cranfield, *op. cit.*, p. 216.

[17]Robertson, *op. cit.*, p. 315.

[18]NBC, p. 819.

**How many loaves have ye?** (38) Jesus sent them to take stock of their resources. **And when they knew, they say, Five, and two fishes.** "The five *loaves* would be small round loaves, . . . slightly larger than our baker's buns."[19] John adds the fact that the loaves and fish were from the lunch of a boy in the crowd (6:9).

However meagre our resources may be, Jesus can make them adequate for the necessary demands, but He calls for the full dedication of what we possess. "What is that in thine hand?" (Exod. 4:2) The paltry provisions available were sufficient. Jesus directed them at once **to make all sit down** (39) (recline) company by company **upon the green grass.** What follows is the vivid description of an eyewitness. **And they sat down** (literally, "threw themselves down") **in ranks** (literally, "garden beds by garden beds") **by hundreds and by fifties** (40)—"with the regularity of arrangement of beds of herbs, looking like so many garden plots" (*Amplified NT*). Perhaps in fifty groups of one hundred each, the crowd, seated in orderly rows and dressed in colorful garments, resembled flower beds upon the "fresh grass" (Goodspeed).

Showing himself to be the Master and Host, Jesus took the **loaves** and **fishes** and, in a characteristic attitude (7:34; John 11:41), **looked up to heaven, and blessed, and brake the loaves** (41). "The recognized form of the blessing was . . . : 'Blessed art Thou, O Lord our God, King of the world, who bringest forth bread from the earth.' "[20] It is said that the object of the blessing was not the loaves and the fishes but God, who gave bread to the earth (Deut. 8:10).[21] Nevertheless, "the broken bread was held to be hallowed . . ."[22] The multiplication of the loaves and fishes evidently followed. The verb **brake** is in the aorist tense, signifying instantaneous, completed action, whereas the word **gave** is in the imperfect tense, indicating past continuous action: "kept on giving them to the disciples" (*Amplified NT*). The once reluctant disciples were now drawn into the miracle as they **set before** the people the broken loaves and divided fish. The language here is reminiscent of the sacrament of the Lord's Supper (cf. 14:22).

[19]IB, VII, 741.
[20]Swete, *op. cit.,* p. 134.
[21]Cranfield, *op. cit.,* p. 219.
[22]Cole, *op. cit.,* p. 144 n.

**And they** (some five thousand men) **did all eat, and,** quite literally, **were filled** (42). The Greek word (*echortasthesan*) was normally used of animals and meant "to feed, fatten . . . fill or satisfy with food."[23] With due regard for the divine gift of food, the disciples **took up twelve baskets full of fragments** (43). "Each waiter received his tip—a basket full of food for the next day."[24] The baskets were wicker containers in which a Jew carried his food. The **fragments** that remained were much more than the original supply and were a testimony to the divine generosity.

Mark illustrates the compassion of Jesus, hints at the Lord's Supper, and describes Jesus as the true Bread of Heaven. The incarnate Son of God had wrought another "mighty work."

This incident suggests: (1) The disciples' problem, 34-37; (2) The disciples' provisions, 38-40; The disciples' presentation, 41-44.

## 2. *Walking on the Water* (6:45-52)

**Straightway** (immediately), after the feeding of the five thousand (30-44), Jesus **constrained** (45), or directed, **his disciples** to take a boat for **the other side,** while He dismissed **the people.** The vigor of the constraint (it may mean compelled) was apparently necessary because of a Messianic excitement in the air. Jesus "perceived that they would . . . take him by force, to make him king" (John 6:15) and did not want the disciples to abet the movement.

A geographical problem exists because of their destination, Bethsaida. The disciples were starting from the northeastern shore. **The other side** would apparently not be **Bethsaida,** located just east of the mouth of the Jordan. Moreover, when they came to land it was at Gennesaret (53), a short distance down the western shore from Capernaum. However, because of the oval contour of the lake, Bethsaida could be described as on **the other side** from the eastern shore. The effect of the contrary wind (48) may have been to blow them off course and land them on the western side at Gennesaret.[25]

---

23Abbott-Smith, p. 482.

24Earle, *op. cit.*, p. 87.

25Cf. Johnson, *op. cit.*, p. 126. Others posit two Bethsaidas, one associated with Capernaum and the other east of where the Jordan River enters the Lake of Galilee.

Earlier (36) the disciples had vainly urged Jesus to send the crowds away. Now, having met their needs by teaching, healing, and feeding them, Jesus was ready more gently and kindly to send them away. He himself was impelled to depart **into a mountain to pray** (46). "The death of John and the attitude of the people made another crisis in his career, which required prayer and thought."[26] Did He face once more the temptation to win the people through popular acclaim rather than by the way of the Cross (Luke 4:5-8)? Thus, for a time, the disciples were separated from the Lord, they out on **the sea, and he alone on the land** (47).

From the mountains overlooking the Sea of Galilee (some 700 feet below sea level) Jesus could see the disciples **toiling in rowing** (48), against a **contrary** wind. The language is strong: "They were distressed in rowing" (RSV). Moffatt translates, "buffeted as they rowed." The word **toiling** (*basanizomenous*) literally means they were "being examined by torture," hence, "tormented" or "distressed." They were undoubtedly buffeted not only by the wind but also by the realization that the storm had come in the path of duty and that the One who had sent them was absent.

**About the fourth watch of the night** (3:00 a.m.), Jesus came to His beleaguered disciples, **walking upon the sea,** and, literally, "purposed to pass by them." As in the case of the Emmaus' disciples (Luke 24:28), "the purpose . . . was to try, and by trial strengthen faith (cf. Jo. vi. 6)."[27] Frightened by what seemed to be a ghost, as well as alarmed lest He would pass by them, the disciples cried out (49). It was no apparition. **They all saw him, and were troubled** (50), for they could not apprehend this Man who had quieted a tempest, fed hungry thousands, and now had come **walking upon the sea.** How slowly faith grows! The reason was their recurrent hardness of heart (cf. 8:17). The word "hardened" (*peporomene*) suggests the setting of concrete, so that they were unimpressionable. On the surface they were frequently amazed and wondered, but their amazement was short-lived and skin-deep. This tendency to revert to spiritual hardness is one of the deepest tendencies of the carnal heart. After Pentecost there was no such recurrence. One of the central

[26]CB, p. 194.
[27]Swete, *op. cit.,* p. 138.

promises pertaining to the new covenant was the declaration, "I will take away the stony heart out of your flesh" (Ezek. 36:26).

If this miracle seems mysterious to us, let us recall that those who witnessed it **were sore amazed . . . beyond measure, and wondered** (51). Nevertheless, Jesus came to them in their distress, saying, **Be of good cheer . . . be not afraid.** And when **he went up unto them into the** boat, **the wind ceased.** "It is the simple fact of life . . . that when Christ is there the storm becomes a calm . . . the unbearable becomes bearable, and men pass the breaking point and do not break."[28]

### 3. *Healings in the Region of Gennesaret* (6:53-56)

What follows is a summary statement of the activities of Jesus perhaps for some days in the region of Gennesaret, a lovely and fertile plain, densely populated, approximately three miles long and something over a mile wide, located just south of Capernaum. Having **passed over** (53) the sea, following the feeding of the five thousand and the night of tempest and toil, **they came into the land of Gennesaret, and drew** ("moored") **to the shore.** Although it must have been very early in the morning, Jesus was immediately recognized. His popularity had reached its greatest height at this period. Eager to aid their afflicted friends, the people "hurried all over the countryside" (55, Goodspeed) and brought **in beds**[29] **those that were sick.**

Evidently Jesus was moving about through the area, for the sick were brought to the place **where they heard he was,** whether **villages . . . cities . . . or country** (56). **They laid the sick** "in the market-places" (NEB), i.e., in some prominent place along Jesus' route, and **besought him that they might touch** "even the tassel of His robe"[30] (Barclay). **As many as touched him** (cf. 3:10; 5:28) **were made whole** (literally, "were saved").

The insistent demand of the crowds never went beyond their physical needs; nevertheless Jesus ministered to them, even though He must have longed to meet deeper needs. Mark records no teaching ministry at this time. Perhaps Jesus was still seeking a place of solitude apart from the multitudes.

[28]Barclay, *op. cit.,* p. 163.

[29]"The word for 'beds' . . . means mattresses or perhaps sleeping rugs, such as the paralytic carried off when Jesus said to him, 'Take up thy bed'" (H. D. A. Major, *et al., The Mission and Message of Jesus* [New York: E. P. Dutton and Co., Inc., 1938], p. 96).

[30]Cf. Num. 15:37-39

## C. CONFLICT OVER THE TRADITION OF THE ELDERS, 7:1-23

The material before us falls naturally into three parts: verses 1-8, the question of ceremonial defilement; verses 9-13, the countercharge of Jesus; verses 14-23, an explanation of defilement, its real nature and source. Jesus addresses three groups—the hostile critics (6), the people (14), the disciples (18). He who is "the end of the law" (Rom. 10:4), i.e., the fulfillment *(telos)* of the law, herein rebukes legalism for all time.

In another clash with official Judaism (cf. chapters 2 and 3), Jesus was confronted by a delegation of **Pharisees,** some from the local area; others, **the scribes** (also **Pharisees), from Jerusalem** (1). Reports concerning the Prophet of Galilee had begun to trouble the Holy City. The critics were not long in finding fault.[31] The Pharisees noted that **some of his disciples** (2) ate **bread with defiled, that is ... unwashen hands.** The question was not one of hygiene, but of religion and ceremony.

Mark goes on to explain to his Gentile readers that the **Jews** practiced all manner of ablutions to avoid ceremonial defilement,[32] thus **holding the tradition of the elders** (3). Unless they washed **their hands oft** ("in a particular way," Goodspeed),[33] they would not eat. There were **many other things** (tradition) which they observed faithfully, from washing themselves after jostling in **the market** (4),[34] to ceremonial ablutions for everything from **cups** and **pots** to **tables** (more accurately, "beds").[35] So burdensome had **the tradition of the elders** (5)[36] become, it was no wonder the common people, including the disciples, did not **walk** (live) **according to** them.

[31]The last three words of verse 2 are not found in the most ancient MSS. Vv. 3-4 are often taken to be a parenthesis, with verse 5 completing an otherwise incomplete sentence. Cf. Cranfield, *op. cit.,* p. 231.

[32]The expression *defiled* stems from a term *(koinos)* which means "'common' as opposed to 'private'" and came in New Testament times to mean "ritually unclean" (*Ibid.,* p. 232).

[33]Back of the word *oft (pykna)* lies a textual problem. Another word, *pygme,* has better support, but is difficult to translate (the RSV leaves it untranslated). It probably means "'with the fist', i.e., in the hollow of the other hand ... perhaps with a handful" of water (IB, VII, 748).

[34]Or, possibly, sprinkling what they had bought in the market.

[35]**Tables** is usually omitted because of manuscript evidence.

[36]"The oral tradition of legal interpretation handed down in the schools, eventually culminating in the written Mishnah and the two Talmuds, and the later massive commentaries upon them" (IB, VII, 749).

Jesus replied with a quotation from Isaiah (29:13, Septuagint) and likened His critics to **hypocrites (6)** (literally, "actors"), whose outward appearance is at variance with inner reality. Honoring God with **their lips**, their **heart** was far from Him. Their **worship (7)** was **in vain**, for they taught **the commandments of men** in place of **the commandment of God** (8).[37] Their oral tradition was not a hedge about the law to protect it, but a massive human subversion of the divine law. Such a serious charge was certain to arouse fury.

Pursuing His charge against the Pharisees, Jesus with great irony replied, **Full well** ("how splendidly," 9, Johnson) **ye reject the commandment of God** in order to **keep your own tradition.** He went on to cite what must have been a flagrant example of using **the commandments of men** to distort the word of God. Their practice has been called "Corban casuistry"[38] and was a device to evade the fifth commandment. Moses had said, **Honour thy father and thy mother (10)** (Exod. 20:12), and, **Let him die the death** who **curseth father or mother** (Exod. 21:17; Lev. 20:9). This was **the commandment of God.** Nevertheless, if a son in anger vowed to make a gift (perhaps to the Temple) of possessions really needed for the support of his parents, the vow was binding thereafter, no matter what distress it caused. The meaning of verse 11 is, This money with which I might have helped you has been dedicated to God. **Corban** thus became a "rigorous, heartless, inhumanly logical casuistry."[39] It not only provided a means whereby selfish children might escape the care of their parents (for the **gift** was not necessarily ever delivered), but it also became a barrier to some repentant son who regretted the vow and wished to break it. The Pharisees would **suffer him no more to do ought for his father or his mother (12).** A vow was a vow!

Through such a tradition as this, which they were careful to hand on to the next generation, the Pharisees made **the word of God of none effect (13)** ("render invalid," Barclay). **Many such like things** they did. What frightening power the infinite God has put in the hands of mortal men that they can "choke the word" (4:19) and render it ineffectual!

---

[37]Verse 8 should end with the word **men.** The balance of the verse is not found in the best MSS.

[38]Major, *op. cit.,* p. 99.

[39]IB, VII, 751.

Turning from His adversaries to **the people,** who always seemed to be at hand, Jesus rather sternly commanded, **Hearken unto me every one . . . and understand** (14). "Get it straight!" Jesus often pleaded for attentive, thoughtful listening. He regarded the following principle as of crucial importance. The source of defilement is not **from without a man** (15), as the Pharisees were teaching, but from within the heart of man, **the things which come out of him.** "The merely external cannot defile man's spiritual nature . . . [nor] purify it."[40] What would our Lord say to those in our time who "desire to make a fair shew in the flesh" (Gal. 6:12) by identifying Christian holiness simply with externals? "Cleanse first that which is within the cup . . . , that the outside may be clean also" (Matt. 23:26).[41]

When the crowd had dispersed and Jesus was alone with His **disciples** ("learners"), they **asked him concerning the parable** (17) (cf. 4:10). The word "parable" is a broad term and includes what may be called a "dark saying" (15).[42] Troubled and perplexed by their slowness to learn, Jesus queried, " 'So you do not understand, either?' " (18, Moffatt) Indeed they, as well as the Church later, **did not perceive** that even ceremonially unclean food **cannot defile** (18) a man, **because it entereth not into his heart** (19) but into the digestive tract "and so passes on" (RSV). It was after Pentecost that Peter heard the word, "What God hath cleansed, that call not thou common" (Acts 10:14; cf. Gal. 2:12). The phrase **purging all meats** (food) is not a part of Jesus' statement. It is Mark's comment that Jesus "thus . . . declared all foods clean" (19, NEB).

What, then, is it **which cometh out of the man, that defileth** (20) him? The corruption of his inmost being, proceeding **from within, out of the heart** (21), is what defiles and stains the man. The unholy catalog which follows (21-22) is stark evidence that "the heart is deceitful above all things, and desperately wicked: who can know it?" (Jer. 17:9) Only a radical salvation can purify the corrupt human heart. But this is exactly what Jesus came into the world to provide.

[40]Swete, *op. cit.,* p. 150.

[41]Many recent versions omit verse 16 because it does not appear in the best MSS. However, Taylor includes it in his Greek text. The expression is elsewhere used by Jesus (cf. Matt. 11:15).

[42]Taylor, *op. cit.,* p. 344.

**Evil thoughts** are generally taken to be the origin of the sinful acts and vices described. "Mark begins where all sin begins, in the realm of thought."[43]

The first six terms in the Greek are in the plural, the remaining six in the singular.[44] The former possibly refer to evil acts, the latter to moral defects or vices. **Adulteries** are the sins of the married, **fornications** "usually of the unmarried,"[45] while **murders** are often the fruit of both. **Thefts** (22): stealings of any sort; **covetousness:** an insatiable desire for "more and more";[46] **wickedness:** iniquity, "malice" (NEB); **deceit:** literally, a bait or snare, hence, "fraud"; **lasciviousness:** "unrestrained sex instinct" (Robertson), licentiousness, indecency; **evil eye:** envy, "jealous grudge" (Swete); **blasphemy:** railing or slander, whether against God or man;[47] **pride:** literally, "showing oneself above others," hence, arrogance; **foolishness:** lack of moral sense, an appropriate ending of the sordid list.

If this be the character of man's unregenerate heart, his plight is desperate. **All these evil things** (23), proceeding from a carnal heart, as a matter of fact do **defile the man.** Forgiveness, then, is not enough. Man requires "the washing of regeneration and renewing of the Holy Ghost" (Titus 3:5). Holiness of heart and life is the only adequate remedy.

Under "Ritualism Versus Reality" one might consider: (1) Carping critics, 1-2; (2) Ceremonial cleansing, 3-8; (3) Case of corban, 9-13; (4) Carnal contamination, 14-23.

## D. Two Healings Among the Gentiles, 7:24-37

### 1. *The Syro-Phoenician Woman* (7:24-30)

Perhaps because of rising religious and political opposition, or more probably because of a desire for rest and privacy, Jesus **went into the borders** (regions) **of Tyre and Sidon** (24).[48] These

[43]NBC, p. 820.
[44]The order of these terms in the KJV differs somewhat from that of the accepted Greek text.
[45]Robertson, *op. cit.,* p. 325.
[46]*Ibid.* "Sometimes . . . associated with terms describing sexual sins (cf. Eph. iv. 19 . . . )" (Taylor, *op. cit.,* p. 345).
[47]In the New Testament blasphemy may be evil-speaking generally or it may be railing against God. The word is here used in a different sense than in 3:29, where it is identified with the unpardonable sin. See 3:28-29 for a clear instance of both uses.
[48]Some ancient MSS omit the words "and Sidon."

independent cities, forty to sixty miles north of Capernaum (see map), had a long history going back to antiquity, when the Phoenicians led the world in navigation. Both Tyre and Sidon had natural harbors and were fortress-like in their position. Phoenicia, which nearly surrounded northern Galilee, was a part of Syria. Because of the close proximity, it was quite natural for a traveler in Galilee to cross over into the territory of Tyre. The prophet Elijah once made a similar journey into this area and brought miraculous assistance to another widow (I Kings 17:8-23). Jesus **entered into an house** of some unnamed friend (cf. 3:19) and sought seclusion in vain, for **he could not be hid.** A burdened mother, whose little daughter (a diminutive and an endearing term) was afflicted, came in great desperation and **fell at his feet** (25).

A **Greek** (26) by culture and religion, possibly by language also, and a **Syrophoenician** by race (hence, not to be confused with Carthaginian Phoenicia), the woman pleaded with Jesus to cast out the unclean spirit from her daughter. Matthew's account (15:21-28), as well as the imperfect tense here, indicates that her entreaty may have persisted for a time.

The response of Jesus calls for reflection. **It is not meet** (right, proper) **to take the children's bread, and . . . cast it unto the dogs** (27). The term "children" of course refers to Israel (Isa. 1:2), and "the dogs" represent the Gentiles. This appears to be a harsh rejoinder, but several factors soften the words. Jesus was in Gentile territory and felt the cost of carrying out His mission to the house of Israel. In the divine plan the Suffering Servant must go to "the tribes of Jacob" before He could be "a light to the Gentiles" (Isa. 49:6). The gospel was to be preached "to the Jew first" and then "to the Greek" (Rom. 1:16; cf. 15:8-9). Jesus could not turn aside from the path that led to Jerusalem and the Cross.

The apparent harshness is further softened by the fact that Jesus referred, not to the vicious scavenger dogs of the streets, but to the little house dogs (*kunarioi*), perhaps puppies, of the children. These might well play **under the table** (28), especially if they received **the children's crumbs** on the sly. "A delightful picture. Little dogs, little scraps of bread . . . little children."[49]

The woman's wit, faith, and persistence found a way through the hindrances. Agreeing that **the children** must **first be filled**

---

[49]Robertson, *op. cit.*, 326.

(27), and accepting the implication that the Gentiles were **dogs** of a sort, she asked, sought, and knocked (Luke 19:9-10) until her prayer was answered. **Jesus said unto her, For this saying go thy way; the devil** (demon) **is gone . . . When she** came **to her house, she found** (29-30) it so. The demon was gone out, but evidently not without a parting blow. The mother discovered **her daughter laid** ("thrown," 30, *Amplified NT*) **upon the bed.**

### 2. *The Deaf-mute of Decapolis* (7:31-37)

On His return **from the coasts of Tyre** (31), Jesus took a circuitous route by the way of **Sidon** through the territory of the **Decapolis**[50] (see map) to **the sea of Galilee.** He thus skirted the realm of the hostile Antipas while He avoided the more populous areas.

The people of Decapolis in the vicinity of the Sea of Galilee brought to Jesus a deaf-mute. It is entirely possible that this event took place in the country of the Gerasenes; if so, it would represent a marked change of attitude (cf. 5:17) on their part. The testimony of the ex-demoniac of Gerasa must have been fruitful (5:20). Far from pleading with Him to depart, the people besought Jesus **to put his hand upon** (32) the man who **was deaf** and who **had an impediment in his speech.**

In order to avoid publicity, as well as to communicate with the man more clearly, Jesus took him **aside from the multitude** (33). The Master restored his hearing and speech through a series of acts evidently designed to arouse and fortify faith. Putting His **fingers into** the man's **ears** (33) and touching his tongue with saliva from His own mouth, Jesus looked up to heaven with a sigh—a prayer without words (cf. Rom. 8:26; also John 11:33, 38). Jesus thus spoke in signs to the man who could not hear. His gestures declared that with power from above and by the word of His own mouth He would open the closed ears and release the bound tongue. The deaf-mute must have read the Lord's lips as He said **unto him, Ephphatha . . . Be opened** (34) ("open completely," Earle).

At once the afflicted man could hear, and also speak plainly (supporting the view that he was not entirely dumb but spoke with difficulty). The promise of Isa. 35:6 had been fulfilled: "Then shall the . . . tongue of the dumb sing."

Herein lies a parable: dumbness follows deafness. Until one has heard the word of God he has nothing significant to speak.

[50]See note on 5:20.

"If our ears are open to hear the word of the Lord, then our tongues will surely be loosed in praise, prayer, and testimony."[51] Perhaps Mark also wanted his readers to see that the disciples, who were spiritually deaf, dumb, and blind, were now beginning to hear and see as the Master took them aside for instruction. Soon they too would begin to speak (8:27 ff.).

As upon so many other occasions, Jesus **charged them** (36) to **tell no man.** It was in vain. The more he **charged them . . . the more . . . they published it.** It is not strange, of course, that such disobedience should follow, for they **were beyond measure**[52] **astonished** (37). Echoing Gen. 1:31, "Behold, it was very good," the people said of Jesus, **He hath done all things well.**

Centering his thought on verse 37, G. Campbell Morgan gathers round this text not only the healing of the deaf-mute, but also Christ's dealings with the Syrophoenician woman (7:24-30), the Pharisees (8:11-21), and the blind man of Bethsaida (8:22-26). He notes: (1) Christ's understanding of each case; (2) His quick sympathy; (3) His sustained loyalty to principle.

## E. GIFTS OF FOOD AND SIGHT, 8:1-26

### 1. *The Feeding of the 4,000* (8:1-10)

The question is often discussed whether this story is simply another account of the earlier feeding of the 5,000 (6:30-44). The significant differences in detail and purpose make this conclusion highly unlikely. Mark "deliberately recorded both the Feeding Miracles with a view to the development of a main theme of the first half of his Gospel, the opening of the blind eyes of the disciples."[53]

While Jesus and His disciples were still in the land of the Decapolis (7:31-37), a great crowd gathered again. It should be noted once more that this was the area in which the Gadarene (Gerasene) demoniac, after his deliverance, had been commissioned to tell what great things the Lord had done for him (5:19). We may have here "a glimpse of what the witness of one man can do for Christ."[54]

[51]NBC, p. 821.

[52]An unusual word, *hyperperissos,* "a term found only here in all Greek literature" (Earle, *op. cit.,* p. 98).

[53]Alan Richardson, *Interpretation,* IX (1955), 144; cf. Earle, *op. cit.,* pp. 98-99.

[54]Barclay, *op. cit.,* p. 188.

Moved with **compassion** because **the multitude** had **nothing to eat (2)**, Jesus was unwilling to **send them away fasting (3)** lest they **faint by the way.** They had been in His company for **three days,** and their food had finally given out. Some **(divers) of them** had come **from far** (cf. 3:8 for an example of the distances people traveled to hear Jesus).

The compassion of Jesus led Him to challenge the hesitancy of the disciples.[55] Their question seems to be singularly obtuse. **From whence can a man satisfy these . . . here in the wilderness? (4)** Did they not recall the miracle of the loaves and fishes and the feeding of the 5,000? In their defense it should be said that mature Christians sometimes have doubt even after a great experience with God. Moreover, considerable time must have elapsed since the earlier miracle of feeding. Perhaps their attitude was now not one of disrespect but of personal embarrassment because they could not help, or even of expectancy regarding what Jesus might do.[56]

This time, with **seven loaves (6)** and a **few small fishes (7)** at hand, Jesus again **commanded the people** to recline **on the ground,** while He **took** the bread and **gave thanks.**[57] Nothing is said in this account of the people reclining in groups, nor of any grass to sit upon. Once again the disciples took the broken bread from the hands of Jesus and set it **before the people.** Likewise with the **few small fishes,** Jesus **blessed** them and **commanded** the disciples to distribute them.

The people **did eat, and were filled (8).** The rendering, "They all ate to their hearts' content" (NEB), conveys the implication of the original language. The precious scraps **of the broken meat** were taken up in **seven baskets.** The word used here would probably mean that more food remained than on the previous occasion when "they took up twelve baskets of fragments" (6:43). The **basket** in the present case (*sphuris*) was larger than the wicker basket used before (*kophinos*). The smaller container, shaped somewhat like a waterpot, was used by the Jew to carry his food about and so avoid ritual contamination. The larger one was made of rope or reeds and was something like a hamper. It was in one of these that the Apostle Paul escaped over the wall at Damascus (Acts 9:25).

[55]*Ibid.,* p. 186.
[56]Cf. Cranfield, *op. cit.,* p. 205.
[57]*Eucharistesas,* from whence comes the word *Eucharist.*

The **four thousand** (9) whom Jesus sent away well filled represented the non-Jewish world (the Decapolis had a large Gentile population). The 5,000 whom Jesus fed on the previous occasion represented the Jewish world. The "bread which cometh down from heaven" was adequate to satisfy them both.

**Straightway** (10), following this episode, Jesus and **his disciples** took a boat for **the parts of Dalmanutha,** some unidentified place on the western shore of the Sea of Galilee. Alternate readings give Magadan or Magdala, from whence Mary Magdalene may have come.

### 2. *A Captious Demand for Proof* (8:11-13)

As upon other occasions (cf. 7:1), **the Pharisees** (11), joined this time with the Sadducees (Matt. 16:1), **came forth** to debate and **question with him.** They sought **a sign from heaven, tempting him,** that is, testing His claim to be from God. Ignoring the quiet, helpful signs already given, the critics called for something spectacular, perhaps a bolt of lightning or a voice out of heaven.

Jesus had already rejected the temptation to dazzle men into the Kingdom (Matt. 4:6-7). Under such conditions, faith as personal decision is impossible. God has His signs, but they are not such as unbelief requires. With great feeling, Jesus **sighed deeply**[58] **in his spirit** (12) and replied, **There shall no sign be given unto this generation.** The language of the original implies: "If I do such a thing, may God punish me!"[59]

The sequel suggests how unbelief cuts men off from Christ. **He left them** (13), and taking a boat, **departed to the other side** of the lake. Spiritual religion is hindered also in our time by those who "require a sign" (I Cor. 1:22). Jesus promised only one sign, the sign of the prophet Jonah (Luke 11:29), that is, Christ himself, crucified and risen. "A holy life and the manifestation of perfect love are far surer signs that one has been filled with the Spirit of God"[60] than any physical evidence.

### 3. *The Leaven of the Pharisees* (8:14-21)

To understand the teaching of Jesus in these verses, one should refer to the material just preceding (11-13) and should

[58]A strengthened form of *stenazo* (cf. 7:34), found only here in the New Testament.
[59]Cf. EGT, p. 394.
[60]Earle, *op. cit.,* p. 101.

read the parallel reference in Matt. 16:5-12. Two thoughts are apparently interwoven here. **The disciples had forgotten to take (14)** sufficient **bread** with them, having no **more than one loaf** with them **in the ship** (boat). Since this caused them some anxiety, Jesus upbraided them for their little faith and short memory. He reminded them that when He broke the **loaves among** the **five thousand (19),** they took up twelve **baskets full** of fragments, and seven **baskets full** when He fed the **four thousand (20).** They should have had no concern because of being short on provisions. Some months later Jesus asked them if they had lacked anything when He sent them out on a mission without resources. "And they said, Nothing" (Luke 22:35). At this point, however, they had not fully learned that God would supply all their need (Phil. 4:19).

Another thought, however, dominates this section, causing one to ask himself if Jesus is still saying, **How is it that ye do not understand? (21)** Because the disciples were reasoning about bread, Jesus used the occasion to warn them against something bread suggests, namely, **leaven,** the pervasive power of evil. **Beware** ("Be on your guard," 15, NEB) **of the leaven of the Pharisees, and of ... Herod.** In the making of bread a small lump of dough was left unused in order that fermentation might occur and so provide yeast for the next baking. In the Hebrew mind, this leaven came to symbolize the sinister and expanding influence of sin in the human heart.

**The leaven of the Pharisees** was hypocrisy, propagated by their teaching (Matt. 16:12; Luke 12:1). Critical, harsh, and blind, they demanded of Jesus a sign from heaven even while signs abounded. **The leaven of Herod** was the godless worldliness of a third-rate ruler who had silenced John and would have destroyed Jesus. "That fox" (Luke 13:32), Jesus once called him.

Anxious about their lack of bread and bewildered by the point Jesus was trying to make, the disciples seemed to have eyes without sight and ears without hearing (cf. Jer. 5:21; Ezek. 12:2). Nevertheless, they were willing to learn; so Jesus continued to deal patiently with them. By contrast, He left the Pharisees in their willful blindness and departed to another place.

The force of this paragraph should linger with us. Let all believers be on the lookout for the leaven of evil, whether hypocrisy or worldliness, and flee both of them as a plague.

### 4. *The Blind Man of Bethsaida* (8:22-26)

Moving slowly from the western side of the Sea of Galilee
(10, 13) toward **the towns of Caesarea Philippi** (27) to the north
(see map), Jesus and the disciples came quite naturally **to
Bethsaida**, Julias, a sizable town located a mile from the northeast
corner of the lake.[61] "It was originally a small town; but Philip
the tetrarch, having raised it to the rank of a city, called it Julias,
after Julia, the daughter of the emperor."[62]

Someone who had faith in Jesus and compassion for the
needy brought **a blind man** (22) to the Master and **besought him**
to do what He normally did—**touch** the sick. Characteristically,
Mark notes details such as an eyewitness would recall. Jesus
**took the blind man by the hand, and led him out of the town**
(23), seeking "privacy and quiet for treatment."[63] Putting spittle
upon the man's eyes (widely thought to have healing properties),
Jesus did indeed **touch him** and then **asked him if he saw** anything. Step by step, as in the case of the deaf-mute of Decapolis
(7:31-37), Jesus encouraged and strengthened the blind man's
faith.

The language of the man's reply, in the original, expresses
his excitement. "We might translate: I can actually see people,
for they look to me like trees—only they walk!"[64] The point is
simply that the man could see, but not distinctly. Cole, an Eng-
lishman, remarks that "any who have been betrayed into apolo-
gizing to a lamp post, bumped in a London fog, will appreciate . . .
at once" the "columnar similarity" between the "trunk" of a tree
and of a man![65]

A second time the Lord **put his hands** (25) upon the afflicted
eyes. "The man looked intently . . . and he was restored, and
saw everything distinctly—even what was at a distance" (*Amplified NT*).[66] The work was thorough and complete. The man
was neither nearsighted nor farsighted! Why Jesus performed
this miracle in two stages is not clear from the scripture, although
many explanations have been offered by Bible scholars. It may

[61]See discussion on 6:45, also article on "Bethsaida" in *Harper's Bible
Dictionary*, p. 70.

[62]*Unger's Bible Dictionary*, p. 142.

[63]IB, VII, 763.

[64]Cranfield, *op. cit.*, p. 265.

[65]*Op. cit.*, p. 133.

[66]This translation reflects the better Greek text, such as found in WH
and Nestle.

be that Mark introduced the story as a kind of parable concerning the disciples, who had only begun to understand Jesus. "Presently, after the second touch of His Spirit at Pentecost, they will see all things clearly."[67]

As in the case of the paralytic (2:11), Jesus **sent (26)** the man **away to his house,** apparently in the country, where his family would be the first to learn the joyous news. He was not permitted to **go into the town,** nor **tell** the glad word to **any in the town,** lest the publicity thwart the journey toward Caesarea Philippi. Jesus spurned the temptation to be known as a miracle-worker.

[67]NBC, p. 822.

Mark 8:27—10:52

A. The Great Confession and Transfiguration, 8:27—9:29

Commentators generally regard this as the midpoint of Mark's Gospel and the beginning of an important division. The Cross was but a scant six months away, and much remained to be done in the preparation of the disciples for that traumatic event. The ministry of Jesus heretofore had been principally with the multitudes, but hereafter it would be chiefly with His immediate followers.

1. *The Confession of Peter* (8:27-30)

It was imperative that Jesus should take His little band away from the crowds and out of the jurisdiction of unfriendly Antipas. Thus they **went out . . . into the towns of Caesarea Philippi** (27). Herod Philip, said to be the best son of Herod the Great, had rebuilt and refurbished this city in honor of his emperor, Tiberius. Situated at the foot of towering Mount Hermon and near one of the principal sources of the river Jordan, it was a beautiful city. The worship of the Greek god Pan flourished there, as did also the worship of the Roman emperor. The city was a center of pagan religion. It was a dramatic locale for the Great Confession.

Testing their spiritual insight, Jesus asked His disciples, **Whom do men say that I am?** It is noteworthy that they did not report any who thought Him to be Christ, the Messiah; **John the Baptist . . . Elias** (28) (Elijah), Jeremiah (Matt. 16:14), **one of the prophets**, but not the Christ. Oddly enough, this was fortunate. The popular concept of the Messiah was such that Jesus took great pains to prevent the masses from so acclaiming Him.

Then followed the searching question no man can avoid when he comes into contact with Christ, **But whom say ye that I am?** (29) In a flash of revelation Peter replied, **Thou art the Christ.** Jesus of Nazareth was indeed the Christ, the long-awaited Messiah; but His people were expecting a political leader, the glory of whose coming would parallel roughly the Christian's understanding of the Second Advent.[1] Such vain hopes could then

[1]See Barclay's discussion, "The Jewish Ideas of the Messiah," *op. cit.,* pp. 197-203.

341

only lead to a holocaust—and under pretended Messiahs tragedies occurred. However joyful Jesus may have been at this expression of Peter's (Matt. 16:17), it was understandable why **he charged them that they should tell no man of him** (30). Peter's own reach had exceeded his grasp, as the next verses make plain.

### 2. *The First Passion Prediction* (8:31-33)

Peter had just confessed that Jesus was the Christ, the long-awaited Messiah (29). Because the disciples shared the mistaken concept of a Messiah who would overpower the enemies of Judaism with apocalyptic vengeance, Jesus at once **began to teach them** (31) of His sufferings soon to come. This was the first prediction of His passion; others were to follow (9:31; 10:32-34). **The Son of man**[2] **must suffer many things.** As one who came to do the will of the Father, it was necessary (as the Synoptists all have it) for Him to suffer.

Although the prophets had spoken of a Suffering Servant (cf. Isa. 52:13—53:12), the idea that the invincible Christ would **be rejected**[3] by the Great Sanhedrin (made up of the three groups cited in verse 31) and **be killed** was incomprehensible to Peter and his fellows. The assurance that **after three days**[4] He would **rise again** went unheard. Probably with a patronizing air, **Peter took** (32) Jesus aside **and began to rebuke him.**

The reply of Jesus must have startled the group. Turning away from Peter and looking **on his disciples** (33), He **rebuked Peter** before them all. **Get thee behind me, Satan.**

Why was the rebuke so strong? It was because, with the popular view of the Messiah in mind, Jesus once more heard the voice of Satan calling Him away from the Cross (Matt. 4:3-10). "The tempter can make no more terrible attack than when he attacks in the voice of those who love us, and who think they seek only our good."[5] Peter did not have the divine mind but rather the human. "You are not on the side of God, but of man" (33, RSV).

---

[2]For a helpful discussion of the critical issues in the use of this phrase, see Cranfield, *op. cit.*, pp. 272-77. It was Jesus' favorite self-designation, one related to the Messianic expectation but not identified with the popular understanding of it.

[3]Literally, rejected after examination.

[4]Matthew and Luke clarify this phrase by saying, "the third day." Far from being a prediction "after the fact," Mark's untouched language may be evidence to the contrary.

[5]Barclay, *op. cit.*, p. 205.

We find here: (1) The confusion of the people, 27-28; (2) The confession of Peter, 29-30; (3) The consecration of Christ, 31; (4) The contradiction of the Cross, 32-35.

### 3. *The Cost of Spurning Discipleship* (8:34—9:1)

Calling **the people** (34), who never seemed to be far away, Jesus made it plain to them and **his disciples** that the servant is not above his lord (Matt. 10:24). If the Son of Man was to suffer rejection and death (31), whosoever would **come after** Him must first **deny himself** and **take up his cross** in order to **follow** Him. In decisive acts the would-be follower must say "no" to himself and shoulder his cross. This must lead to a continuous relationship of following the Leader. It was as if Jesus said, "If you want to be my disciples, you must begin to live as men on the way to the gallows."[6]

For those who may have felt that the cost of discipleship was too high, Jesus had a further word on the cost of *spurning* discipleship: "Whoever wants to preserve his own life will lose it" (35, Goodspeed). **Soul** and **life** are interchangeable here, because they are translations of the same word (*psyche*), but a double reference is intended. An apostate might **save his life** (35) by denying the Son of Man in this **sinful generation** (38), but he would **lose his . . . soul** (36). If, in the process he should **gain the whole world, what** would his **profit** be? The parable of the rich fool is a case in point (Luke 12:16-21). When one has paid the ultimate penalty and forfeited his **soul**, what will he **give in exchange for** (37) the return of **his soul**? However great his possessions may have been, he will have nothing with which to buy it back.

By contrast, those martyrs who **lose** their lives for Christ's **sake and the gospel's, the same shall save** (35) them. Ridicule is a weapon which has slain its thousands, but what will it be for those of whom **the Son of man** shall **be ashamed** when He comes in the Father's **glory** surrounded by **the holy angels**? (38) **Adulterous** here means spiritually disloyal.

This description of the *parousia* prompted Jesus to go on to say something puzzling (9:1). What could He have meant by the words that **some** standing there would not die before seeing **the kingdom of God come with power**? (1) He did *not* say the Second Coming would occur within the lifetime of those present.

---

[6]Hunter, *op. cit.*, p. 94.

Within six days (9:2) three of the disciples witnessed the Transfiguration. Within a year or so all of the disciples save one witnessed the power of the Resurrection and Pentecost, and within the lifetime of many present the gospel spread with astonishing vigor throughout the world of that day. In these ways they saw **the kingdom ... come with power.**

### 4. *The Transfiguration* (9:2-8)

About a week after Peter's confession, and the resultant teaching on the suffering Messiah (8:27—9:1), Jesus took the inner circle of His disciples **up into an high mountain** (2) (probably a spur of Mount Hermon) apart from the crowds, where **he was transfigured before them.**

What were the nature and the purpose of the Transfiguration? The term, from *metamorphoo,* means "to transform." It is used in the New Testament only here and in Matt. 17:2 (the parallel reference); Rom. 12:2; and II Cor. 3:18. This change of form, making His **raiment** (3) shine **exceeding white,** more dazzling "than any earthly bleaching could make them" (Goodspeed), must have been "an effulgence from within ... a manifestation of the Son of God in his true nature."[7] It was a restoration of the glory which He had with the Father before the world was (John 17:5; cf. Mark 14:62; Acts 7:55).

The purpose of the Transfiguration was first to strengthen Jesus for the ordeal of the Cross. The Son of Man found reassurance from heaven at crucial points in His ministry (e.g., 1:11; Luke 22:43). On this occasion **there appeared ... Elias** (Elijah) **with Moses: and they were talking with Jesus** (4) about His (literally) "exodus" (Luke 9:31). Both men, representing the law and the prophets, respectively, had experienced something of a transfiguration: Moses on Sinai (Exod. 34:35), and Elijah in the fiery chariot (II Kings 2:11).

The Transfiguration also served to convince the disciples that Peter's inspired confession (8:29) was true. The idea of a suffering Messiah was not at variance with the Old Testament. The disciples, who had not always listened well, were instructed to give greater heed to the teaching of Jesus. **This is my beloved Son: hear him** (7).

Luke records that Peter and the others were "heavy with sleep" (9:32), which may explain the apparent confusion. Star-

[7]IB, VII, 775.

tled beyond measure, Peter **wist not what to say** (6). Knowing that it was **good** for them to be on the mount of vision, and hoping to cling to that sacred hour, Peter proposed the building of **three tabernacles.** He may have been thinking of the booths such as were used in the Feast of Tabernacles, or he may have had something more permanent in mind, possibly the Tent of Meeting, where God met His people in the wilderness (Exod. 35:11).

The **cloud** (7) which then **overshadowed** or enveloped **them**[8] was a symbol of the Divine Presence, the Shekinah of the Old Testament (cf. Exod. 13:21; 14:19; Ps. 78:14). Clouds are also linked in the New Testament with God's presence (e.g., 13:26; I Thess. 4:17). God came near and announced that His Son was also a Prophet[9] (Deut. 18:15): **hear him.**

Matthew describes the Transfiguration as a "vision" (17:9). It was factual, a miraculous vision divinely brought about as a revelation to the disciples. Anticipating the Resurrection and the Parousia, the Transfiguration strengthened Jesus and the disciples for the crushing experiences ahead and announced to all that Jesus was unmistakably the Son of God.

Alexander Maclaren draws from verse 8: (1) The solitary Saviour, (2) The vanishing witnesses, (3) The waiting disciples.

### 5. *The Coming of Elijah* (9:9-13)

**As they came down** (9) from the Mount of Transfiguration, the disciples must have pondered deeply what they had seen. They may have wondered why Jesus **charged them** to **tell no man** until He was **risen from the dead.** It was not safe as yet to reveal the Messianic secret. Not until the Cross and the open tomb taught them what they needed to learn about the Messiah would it be expedient for them to describe their transcendent experience.

"They did not forget what he said" (10, Goodspeed), but they were greatly perplexed as to **what the rising from the dead should mean.** They were not prepared to accept the idea that **the Son of man . . . must suffer many things** (12); so they could not imagine a rising from the dead. This raised a further question. If Jesus was indeed the Christ, as they now believed, what

---

[8]Probably Jesus, Elijah, and Moses, for the voice spoke out of the cloud to the disciples.

[9]In Semitic thought, "the highest possible category of divine revelation" (IB, VII, 777).

about the assertion of **the scribes that Elias** (Elijah)[10] **must first come?** (11) The last two verses of the Old Testament canon (Mal. 4:5-6) were meaningful to the Jewish people.

Agreeing with the scribes, Jesus replied, Elijah **verily cometh first** "to restore all things" (12, RSV), a process under way but incomplete. But He probed further with a question: **How is it written of the Son of man, that he must suffer . . . and be set at naught** ("treated with contempt," NEB)?[11] In other words, the scribes were correct in noting that Elijah would be the forerunner of the Messiah but wrong in their blindness to the Messiah's sufferings.

Elijah had come already, in the person of John the Baptist (Matt. 17:13), and had suffered at the hands of another Jezebel. If men did this to the forerunner, what would they do to the Messiah? "As Elijah's coming was a heralding of the Lord's coming, so Elijah's rejection was a warning of the Lord's rejection: and all alike was in fulfillment of Scripture."[12]

### 6. *Powerless Disciples* (9:14-29)

The scene which follows is in sharp contrast to the account of the Transfiguration (2-8). Raphael has portrayed this fact movingly in a painting depicting Jesus in the glory of the mount while the disciples are in the gloom of the valley. When Jesus and the inner circle of followers **came to** (14) the rest of the **disciples, surrounded by a great multitude** and in a dispute with **the scribes,** they confronted the world in miniature: "Youth in the grip of evil, parental anguish, nine disciples to whom the necessary power had been given . . . so that they ought not to have failed . . . , and finally . . . a collection of critical and hostile religionists."[13]

Immediately **all the people** (15) were astonished at the appearance of Jesus and ran toward Him with excitement. What caused them to be **greatly amazed,**[14] "overcome with awe"

---

[10]The KJV uses a transliteration of the Greek term for *Elijah*, which in turn stems from the Greek version of the Old Testament, the Septuagint (LXX).

[11]This term reflects the ideas of Isa. 53:3, "He is despised and rejected . . ."

[12]Cole, *op. cit.*, p. 145.

[13]NBC, p. 824.

[14]"Used by Mark only in New Testament, here, and in xiv. 33 and xvi. 5 in connections which demand a very strong sense" (EGT, p. 26).

(NEB)? The Master had arrived unexpectedly and at a most opportune time, but this seems hardly to account for the crowd's astonishment. Jesus must have returned "from the holy mount, His face and person yet glistening" (15, *Amplified NT*).

When Jesus asked them, **What question ye with them?** (16) the answer came not from the scribes, but from **one of the multitude** (17), a troubled father whose son was an epileptic. Matthew describes him as "lunatick" (17:15), i.e., "moonstruck," "epilepsy being supposed to be influenced by the moon."[15]

The father had brought his son, hoping to see Jesus. Disappointed at not finding Him, the distraught parent had spoken to the **disciples that they should cast him out; and they could not** (18) (literally, "they were not strong enough"). "Note the tragic brevity of the final words."[16] The man's despair was understandable.

The reply of Jesus has been called "'a cry of homesickness . . . for his heavenly Father.'"[17] **O faithless generation, how long shall I be with you? . . . bring him unto me (19).** He rebuked not only those present, but also the whole world of unbelief standing in the way. Even as **the foul spirit**, recognizing Him, convulsed the lad again, Jesus engaged the father in a conversation intended to awaken faith (21-22). **If thou canst do any thing,** came the plaintive plea, "help us, having compassion on us" (22, Earle).

The real implication of Jesus' answer is somewhat obscured in the KJV. Phillips has a clearer rendering, "*'If you can do anything!'*" responded Jesus. "'Everything is possible to the man who believes.'"[18] The confidence of Jesus in the power of faith is startling. "With the same utter confidence in God with which he rebuked the raging tempest (4:39), and met the dangerous maniac from the tombs (5:8), and took the daughter of Jairus by the hand (5:41), here he advances upon the powerful spirit that holds the epileptic boy in its grasp (cf. 5:36)."[19] Perhaps reacting to the challenge of Jesus, **the father** (24) immediately **cried out** a confession of his paradoxical condition. **Lord, I be-**

---

[15]Abbott-Smith, *op. cit.*, p. 404.

[16]IB, VII, 780.

[17]Hunter, *op. cit.*, p. 99.

[18]*The Westminster Study Edition of the Holy Bible* reflects the original thus: "'As for your *If thou canst*, all things are possible . . .'" (*in loco*).

[19]IB, VII, 782.

**lieve; help thou mine unbelief.** Let him cast the first stone who has not shared that man's experience!

Under the theme "Unbelieving Belief," Alexander Maclaren discusses v. 24 as follows: (1) The birth of faith, 17-18; (2) The infancy of faith, 21-22; (3) The cry of faith, 23-24; (4) The education of faith, 25-29.

Seeing that **the people came running together** (25), Jesus moved at once to stop the spread of meddling curiosity. **Thou dumb and deaf** (a new detail) **spirit . . . come out of him, and enter no more into him.** These were surely heartening words telling a distraught parent that the promised deliverance would be permanent. The Master spoke to the demon as an agent separate from the boy. "This makes it difficult to believe that Jesus was merely indulging popular belief in a superstition."[20]

"Convulsing him terribly" (26, RSV), the unclean spirit **came out of him,** leaving the boy **as one dead.** Most of those present said, **He is dead.** Characteristically, the powers of darkness had one last fling as they left their victim. As in the case of Jairus' daughter (5:41), Jesus **took** the youth **by the hand, and lifted him up** (27). This token of the tender compassion of Jesus has a corollary in a detail Luke records: "And Jesus . . . healed the child, and delivered him again to his father" (9:42).

Somewhere in the multitude was a group of nine chagrined and defeated disciples. Later, **when** they had all **come into the house** (28), they asked Jesus **privately, Why could not we cast him out?** The reasons for their failure lay in their lack of faith (Matt. 17:20), which in turn was due to their prayerlessness and absence of self-discipline. **This kind can come forth by nothing but by prayer and fasting** (29).[21]

The disciples evidently thought that the power and authority given them earlier (6:7) was theirs to exercise at will. "They had to learn God's power is not given to men in that way. It has ever to be asked for afresh and received afresh."[22] Whatever gift one may have cannot be maintained in strength and power without continuous reliance upon the Giver. Problems of the kind

---

[20]Robertson, *op. cit.,* p. 343.

[21]The words "and fasting" are not found in the oldest and most reliable manuscripts. Some scholars, however, do not regard this evidence as conclusive (NBC, p. 824; Cole, *op. cit.,* p. 148).

[22]Cranfield, *op. cit.,* p. 305.

the disciples faced cannot be *driven out* except by a life of persistent, effectual prayer. Spasmodic requests in emergencies only will not suffice. The warning, however, is also a promise. "The effectual fervent prayer of a righteous man availeth much" (Jas. 5:16).

The first two incidents of this chapter suggest: (1) Worship on the mountain, 2-13; (2) Work in the valley, 14-29. Peter wanted to enjoy the pleasant situation on the mountaintop, but there was work to do below. We must worship in the place of prayer and then go to work in the place of need.

B. En Route Through Galilee, 9:30-50

1. *The Second Passion Prediction* (9:30-32)

Departing **thence** (30), evidently from the regions of Caesarea Philippi, Jesus and the disciples **passed** along **through Galilee**[23] with the purpose of avoiding recognition. Traveling incognito was difficult for anyone as well known as Jesus and had not always been possible (7:24). Secrecy was needful so that He could be alone with the disciples and instruct them further on the events impending in Jerusalem.

The labor of Jesus to change the thinking of His disciples is a lesson in the teaching-learning process. Repeatedly He warned them of His sufferings and death, **but they understood not** (32). With what persistent patience, then, must the pastor and teacher toil as they lead their listeners to a fuller understanding of the Christian life!

The words of verse 31 are but the substance of what Jesus continued to teach them along the way. **The son of man is delivered**[24] **into the hands of men.** These words may refer either to the divine plan (as in Rom. 8:32) or to the nefarious process by which Jesus would be handed over to the Sanhedrin by Judas, and from thence to Pilate and the soldiers. Perhaps both are implied (cf. Acts 2:23).

Although **they understood not that saying** (32), the disciples **were afraid to ask** for an explanation. Perhaps they did not wish to face the realities which would dash their political hopes to the ground.

[23]"Some take the *para* in the compound verb to mean, went along byways, to avoid publicity" (EGT, p. 404).

[24]Futuristic or prophetic present, "is being delivered."

## 2. *The Dispute over Greatness* (9:33-37)

When they **came to Capernaum (33)**, Jesus and the disciples were back at what had been their base of operations during the Galilean ministry. When they had gathered **in the house**, probably Peter's, **he asked them** what they were arguing about **by the way.** The question was embarrassing, for while Jesus had been talking of His coming death **they had disputed among themselves, who should be the greatest (34)**. Little wonder **they held their peace.**

What prompted the dispute? Such questions were of great moment in Palestine, a land where one's position in the synagogue or at meals was a source of frequent bickering. The argument may also have been touched off by recognition which the inner circle—Peter, James, and John—often received, as at the Transfiguration. In any case, the squabble was a shabby performance.

In a gesture of inspiring patience, Jesus **sat down (35)**, the characteristic position of a Jewish teacher, **and called the twelve.** He taught them: Let the one who wants to be **first** become the **last of all** and everyone's **servant.** There can be no doubt as to the meaning of this ethical ideal. It is "identical with the sayings about the chief commandments, the so-called Golden Rule, and the saying of Jesus preserved in Acts—'it is more blessed to give than to receive.' "[25]

In an "action-sermon"[26] Jesus then "took a child, set him in front of them, and put his arm round him" (36, NEB). **Whosoever shall receive one of such children in my name, receiveth me (37).** Apart from Jesus' underlying intent of these words, their effect upon the valuation of children should be noted. "If today men show a solicitude for little children that would have amazed the ancients, that solicitude takes its concern from one Man."[27]

The purpose of Jesus' action was to illustrate the principle found in verse 35. True greatness is seen in humble service. When one receives (literally, "welcomes") a child, out of regard for Christ (i.e., in His name), he does so without thought of reward and unwittingly "welcomes" Christ. In receiving Him, he receives the Father who sent Him, for a messenger from the

[25]Branscomb, *op. cit.*, p. 169.

[26]Hunter, *op. cit.*, p. 100.

[27]*Ibid.* See Johnson, *op. cit.*, p. 164, for an instance of common cruelty in the treatment of children among the Egyptians of that day.

king is the king himself. The object lesson was a dramatic rebuke to the disciples in their scramble for first place.

### 3. *The Unknown Exorcist* (9:38-41)

These verses have been called "a lesson in tolerance," and "a warning against sectarianism." John, who is seldom prominent in the Synoptics, spoke up at this point, **saying, Master, we saw one casting out devils** (demons) **in thy name . . . and we forbad him** (38) (literally, "we tried to stop him"). The Son of Thunder, who shortly would have called fire down upon an inhospitable Samaritan village ("even as Elias did," Luke 9:54), was rigorous in his party loyalties.

In a rebuke of intolerance and sectarianism, **Jesus said, Forbid him not . . . he that is not against us is on our part** (38-39). An interesting parallel is found in Num. 11:26-29. In a time of crisis, the Lord had poured His Spirit upon the leaders of Israel, and also upon two "unauthorized" men, Eldad and Medad. Joshua urged Moses to put a stop to their prophesying. Moses refused, saying, " 'Are you jealous for my sake? Would that all the Lord's people were prophets' " (Num. 11:29, RSV). One does not easily combine commitment to his own cause with charity for other movements, but the effort will have Christ's blessing. Edwin Markham said it well:

> He drew a circle that shut me out—
> Rebel, heretic, thing to flout.
> But love and I had the wit to win—
> We drew a circle that took him in.

The sum of the matter is pictured in verse 41. Christians are to welcome sincere cooperation even though it may come from unexpected sources. If one should offer a **cup of water (41)** to a believer on the ground that he is a follower of Christ, that man, Jesus affirms, **shall not lose his reward.**

### 4. *The Threat of Gehenna* (9:42-50)

These verses are a collection of certain sayings of Jesus, one often growing out of another. The relationship may not be chronological. Sometimes verse 41 is included with this paragraph.

**These little ones that believe in me (42)** refers to young and immature Christians, including perhaps the "weak brother" of Romans 14. **Whosoever shall offend,** "scandalize," or cause to fall into sin, **one of these** should have died first, so serious such an offense would be. The millstone was a "huge grinding stone of an ass-driven mill."[28] To be **cast into the sea** with this weight **hanged about** one's **neck** would mean certain death. Execution by drowning was a form of Roman capital punishment. To blight or maim the faith of another, so as to cause him to fall from grace, is a heinous crime.

We are warned that offenses, i.e., "occasions of stumbling" (Luke 17:1, ERV), are certain to come. Some may come from the outside, as in verse 42, but other provocations may come from oneself (43-48). Concerning these Jesus issued the most solemn of warnings.

Although one can speak of "the hand, which steals; the foot, which trespasses; the eye, which lusts or covets,"[29] we are not thereby to infer that these physical members are the real cause of sinning. It is the heart which controls the hand, the foot, and the eye. To dismember ourselves literally might prevent us from committing certain sins outwardly, but would not remove the inner corrupt desire. Jesus is speaking both hypothetically and metaphorically. On the hypothesis that the loss of physical members would save us from sinning, then better far to lose them, no matter how humanly indispensable they may seem to be, than to be cast into hell. Metaphorically, we are here reminded that in life things as legitimate and natural as the hand, foot, and eye may become an occasion of temptation; and if so, we can well afford to sacrifice them, no matter how painful the severance may be. The offending member could be a friendship, a membership, an ambition, anything near and dear to us which proves subversive to spiritual victory.

In verses 45 and 47, the divine judgment is described in the words **cast into hell.** But beginning with verse 43, it is clear that it is the offender who chooses (literally) "to go away" **into hell** through his own action.

The word for **hell,** that melancholy place with **the fire that never shall be quenched** (Gk., *asbestos*), may be transliterated *Gehenna,* the Valley of Hinnom. This valley, below Jerusalem, had become infamous during the time of the later kings of Judah because of the sacrifice of children to the pagan god Molech (Jer. 7:31; 19:5-6; 32:35). It was later officially desecrated

[28]IB, VII, 791.

[29]Major, *op. cit.,* p. 123.

(II Kings 23:10), and ultimately became the depository of offal and rubbish for Jerusalem. "There the corrupting worm crawled and fires were kept continually burning for the purpose of destroying the refuse."[30]

It should be remembered that the description of the future state of the impenitent in these verses comes from Jesus himself. However severe the language may be, it is biblical (Isa. 66:24) and is an integral part of our Lord's teaching.

The message is plain: No sacrifice is too great in order **to enter into the kingdom of God** (47) (synonymous with eternal **life,** verses 43 and 45) and avoid *Gehenna*,[31] **where their worm dieth not, and the fire is not quenched** (48).[32] **Worm** may refer to gnawing memory and **fire** to unsatisfied desire.

The remaining verses (49-50) contain three sayings, well summarized in the phrase, "salting inevitable and indispensable."[33] The words **every one shall be salted with fire** (49) are usually taken to mean that all disciples must go through the fires of purification, primarily by the Spirit, but also through discipline and persecution. Just as **every sacrifice** was required to be **salted with salt** (Lev. 2:13),[34] so every follower of Christ must be cleansed by fire to be acceptable to God.

**Salt** (50) is indeed **good.** What insipidity and corruption follow in its absence! When a believer has lost **his saltness,** he is useless (cf. Matt. 5:13). He "is like an exploded shell, a burned out crater, a spent force."[35] Christians must be careful to **have salt** in themselves, i.e., possess the Christian graces, in order to be at **peace one with another.** The disputing disciples (33) needed this admonition.

## C. The Ministry in Perea, 10:1-52

This section marks another crucial turning point in the ministry of Jesus. For the *last* time He left Galilee and turned with resolution toward Jerusalem. It was in reality the way to the

---

[30]*Ibid.*

[31]**Hell,** the translation of *Gehenna,* is not to be confused with *hades,* the realm of the dead, also translated "hell" (e.g. Rev. 1:18; 6:8; 20:13-14).

[32]"Note that the better MSS (followed by RV, RSV, NEB) omit verses 44 and 46 which are identical with verse 48" (Cole, *op. cit.,* p. 153).

[33]EGT, p. 407.

[34]V. 49b is omitted by the most ancient MSS but it gives an added clue to the meaning of the verse.

[35]Robertson, *op. cit.,* p. 347.

Cross. The journey led down the cleft of the Jordan valley **into the coasts** (region or district) **of Judaea** (1) and from thence to **the farther side** of the river Jordan, the land of Perea.

### 1. *Teaching on Divorce* (10:1-12)

The days of withdrawal and privacy were now over for Jesus and His disciples, as **the people** (1) thronged about **him again.** As was His custom, **he taught them.**[36]

Once more **the Pharisees came to him** (2) with a question, **tempting** or "testing" **him.** The attempt to ensnare Jesus in His own words would proceed apace to the end. They now hoped to embroil Him either with Antipas, a divorcee, or with the Sanhedrin, through a conflict with the Law. Their question was on the subject of divorce. **Is it lawful?** (2) Matthew phrases their inquiry differently: Is divorce lawful for any and every cause? (19:3) Jesus replied to their trick question with another query. **What did Moses command?** (3)

The dispute centered about Deut. 24:1-2, where Moses ordered that "a bill of divorcement" be given a woman at the time of separation, so she would be free to marry again. This command was no encouragement whatever to the loose practice of divorce. It was rather a merciful provision in a day when womanhood had no rights. The Pharisees softened the words by saying **Moses suffered** (4) or permitted the practice. In so doing, they yielded ground in the debate. It was an admission that the **bill of divorcement** was a concession because of **the hardness** (5) ("perversity," Goodspeed) of their **heart.** Jesus reminded them that it was not so at **the beginning** (6) when **God made them male and female** and called upon a man to forsake his previous family ties **and cleave to his wife** (7).[37]

God's full ideal for the human family was monogamy, which ruled out both polygamy and divorce. The sanctity of marriage derives from the divine command: **What . . . God hath joined . . . let not man put asunder** (9). The later concession of the Law (5), which Jesus by implication criticized and yet recognized, is "consonant with the idea of God's adaptation of his general pur-

---

[36]The Perean ministry of Jesus, described in detail by Luke, included some of His most memorable parabolic teaching; e.g., the parables of the Good Samaritan and the Prodigal Son.

[37]Earle notes that the word *cleave* literally means "stick to" and observes, "God give more glue to the modern marriage" (*op. cit.*, p. 123).

pose to immediate circumstances and needs."[38] The exceptions allowed in Matt. 19:9 (cf. 5:32) and I Cor. 7:15 are apparently in line with this principle.

It had become the practice among many in Judaism to take the Mosaic concession as an encouragement to license. The point was debated at the time by the schools of Rabbi Hillel and Rabbi Shammai. Shammai allowed divorce only for adultery. Hillel's views encouraged laxity. One of his devotees, e.g., permitted a man to put away his wife when he discovered a more attractive woman, on the ground that his spouse no longer found "favour in his eyes" (Deut. 24:1). The same reference was employed to allow divorce on even more trivial grounds: " 'If the wife cook her husband's food ill, by over-salting or over-roasting it, she is to be put away.' "[39] Jesus rebuked their callous disregard of God's intention (cf. Mal. 2:13-16).

One wishes that we, like the **disciples,** could turn aside privately and ask Jesus of **the same matter** (10). His reply **in the house** was that man is not to **put away his wife** (11), nor is a **woman** to **put away her husband** (12) (something unheard of in Judaism, but possible among the Romans, to whom Mark wrote). Matthew records the consternation of the disciples: "If such is the case . . . it is not expedient to marry" (19:10, RSV).

Devout interpreters divide as to the implication of Christ's words in verses 11 and 12. Some hold that in effect they became a new legislation. The following is an example of such a view: "Christ's view of divorce . . . was to forbid it absolutely. According to Him marriage was indissoluble save by death, and remarriage was therefore impermissible within the lifetime of both partners."[40] Others would say that "Jesus was not attempting to legislate on divorce but was setting forth principles which would raise the entire question . . . to the spiritual level of God's will."[41] To dissolve the marriage union brings one under judgment, but "it may nevertheless be proper for the state and also the church to make provisions for situations in which because of human sinfulness divorce may be the lesser evil."[42] Neither the hardness

[38]IB, VII, 796.

[39]*A Commentary on the Holy Bible,* ed. J. R. Dummelow (New York: The Macmillan Co., 1956 [reprint]), p. 688.

[40]A. R. G. Deasley, "The New Testament and Divorce," *Interchange,* I, No. 1, 16.

[41]Earle, *et al.,* ENT, p. 136.

[42]Cranfield, *op. cit.,* p. 321.

of man's heart nor the mercy of God, as reflected in Deut. 24:1-2, has changed.

### 2. *Children and the Kingdom* (10:13-16)

This discussion of children and their relation to the Kingdom appropriately follows the teaching of Jesus on divorce. Children are the first and saddest casualties in broken homes. Both womanhood and childhood owe much to the defense Jesus gave them.

When certain **young children** (13) were **brought** to Jesus, **that he should touch them,** as in healing, the **disciples** reproved **those** who were bringing **them.** Their action was doubtless taken with the thought of shielding Jesus from the crowds.

Noting what His disciples had done, Jesus was **much displeased,** "indignant *and* pained" (14, *Amplified NT*). Jesus was capable of moral indignation (cf. 3:5; 9:19): "Let the children come to me, do not hinder them" (14, RSV). The absence of a conjunction in the Greek before **forbid them not** suggests impatience.[43] **The kingdom of God** belongs to **such** as have the qualities of children. A child is receptive and trustful; he has the "capacity to *act* at once"[44] upon what he understands. No one can merit the Kingdom; he must receive it through grace. **Whoever shall not receive the kingdom . . . as a little child . . . shall not enter therein** "at all" (15, NASB). Why Jesus was vexed with His disciples should be clear.

As if to illustrate how strongly He felt, Jesus **took** (16) the children **up in his arms**[45] and, putting **his hands upon them, . . . blessed them.** "He blessed them fervently, in no perfunctory way, but with emphasis, as those who were capable of a more unreserved benediction than their elders."[46]

### 3. *The Rich Young Ruler and Discipleship* (10:17-31)

As Jesus was starting out on another leg of His journey, **there came one running** (17),[47] perhaps apprehensive lest he be

---

[43]*Ibid.*, p. 323.

[44]IB, VII, 800.

[45]"Folded them in His arms" (Earle, *op. cit.*, p. 125).

[46]Swete, *op. cit.*, p. 222. This incident reputedly encouraged infant baptism in segments of the early Christian Church.

[47]The combined record of the Synoptists, that he was young (Matt. 19:22), rich (Mark 10:22), and "a certain ruler" (Luke 18:18), gives us the traditional description, "the rich young ruler."

too late to meet the Master, **and kneeled to him** in respect and reverence. Mark's details ("running," "kneeled") are a testimony to the impression Jesus made upon men.

The young man's question, **Good Master, what shall I do ... ?** revealed an inner dissatisfaction. He whose judgments are according to truth replied, **Why callest thou me good?** (18) The assertion of Jesus that **there is none good but ... God** was not an admission of sinfulness, but a rejection of the idea, as in this man's view, that goodness is by achievement. There is nothing one can **do** to **inherit eternal life.** " 'Jesus did not rest in Himself, but referred Himself wholly to His Father . . .' "[48] (See esp. John 5: 19.)

**Thou knowest the commandments** (19) of this good God, Jesus said, and reviewed in substance the second table of the Decalogue. Perhaps Jesus omitted mention of the first commandments because in a moment He intended to probe the young man more deeply at the point of his devotion to God. The answer of the youthful ruler was touching. **Master** (omitting the word "good"), **all these have I observed** (literally, "guarded") **from my youth** (20). It is said that the ancient Jew was the most conscientious of men. Another Hebrew, who later made a similar profession (Phil. 3: 6), also found that "by the works of the law shall no flesh be justified" (Gal. 2: 16).

As if to peer into this young man's very soul, "Jesus looked straight at him" (21, NEB) and **loved him.** What promise and possibility, and yet what spiritual poverty, the Master must have seen! The young man's question, "What lack I yet?" (Matt. 19: 20), found an answer in the candid reply of Christ. **One thing thou lackest . . . sell whatsoever thou hast . . . and come . . . follow me.** This earnest seeker, who had lack of nothing which wealth could purchase, nevertheless was in great want (cf. Rev. 3: 17-18). The young ruler who had done no wrong to his neighbor (19) possessed a love of wealth and self which violated the first commandment.

In contrast to the way he came, the rich young ruler **went away grieved** (22). Refusing the rare invitation to **follow** Jesus to Jerusalem, he chose to cling to his own **great possessions** rather

---

[48]Cranfield, *op. cit.,* p. 327. "In an absolute sense goodness belongs to God the Father alone. By contrast, the goodness of Jesus was in some sense subject to growth and testing in the circumstances of the incarnation wherein He learned obedience by the things which He suffered" (Heb. 5: 8) (NBC, p. 826).

than to **have treasure in heaven.**[49] It is a parable on the joy of obedience and the tragedy of disobedience that he **went away** with a gloomy countenance, like the sky on a somber, cloudy day.[50]

Seeing the man of wealth refuse to do what He had already asked His disciples to do, **Jesus looked round about**[51] and said, " 'With what difficulty will those who have money enter into the Kingdom of God!' " (23, Barclay) The disciples were not prepared for that statement and **were astonished at his words** (24). Abraham the faithful, Job the righteous, and Solomon the wise were all men of wealth. Were not riches a sign of divine approval? **But Jesus answereth again,** with a tender reproach, " 'Children, how hard it is[52] to enter the kingdom of God!' " (24, NASB) If at best there be few who find the strait gate and narrow way (Matt. 7:14), with what difficulty will those who rest in the false security of wealth **enter into the kingdom of God!**

The language of verse 25 has called forth several ingenious explanations, but "the difficulty is only in the minds of the unimaginative occidentals."[53] The point, clothed in Oriental hyperbole, is simply that from a human viewpoint it is impossible **for a rich man** to be saved. The figure of the **camel** and the **eye of a needle,** like those of the beam and the splinter (Luke 6:41) and the gnat and the camel (Matt. 23:24), is a dramatic way of expressing "what, humanly speaking, is impossible or absurd."[54]

Still **astonished out of measure** (26), the disciples were assured by Jesus that **with God all things are possible.** To enter into the Kingdom and eternal life is beyond the achievement of man; but in the grace of God all men, rich and poor alike, may enter. The entrance fee is the same for everyone; the pearl of great price costs all that any man has (Matt. 13:45-46).

Doing some quick mental arithmetic, **Peter** (28), usually the spokesman for the group (8:29; 9:5; 11:21), **began to say ... Lo,**

[49]Did this man ever reconsider and return? "An interesting conjecture is that he did, and that his name was Barnabas" (NBC, p. 826).

[50]The literal meaning of the verb *stygnazo,* here translated "he was sad" (22); cf. Matt. 16:3.

[51]Another vivid Petrine reminiscence, as in verse 21.

[52]Later MSS add, "for them that trust in riches."

[53]Earle, *op. cit.,* p. 128.

[54]Taylor, *op. cit.,* p. 431.

**we have left all, and have followed thee.**[55] Matthew adds, "What shall we have therefore?" (19:27).

The answer of Jesus was that He will have no man in His debt. If a man should leave **house,** *or* family, **or lands, for my sake, and the gospel's** (29), that man shall receive "a hundred times over" (30, Phillips) *in this present age,* **houses** *and* family,[56] **and lands, with persecutions;**[57] and in the age that is coming **eternal life.** Contrast the *or* of verse 29 with the *and* of verse 30. "What is gained will far outweigh what is lost."[58] Lest the disciples conclude that their position gave them special favor, Jesus reminded them that **many . . . first shall be last** (31), and vice versa. Matthew appends at this point the parable of the laborers in the vineyard who received the same wage no matter how long their day had been (20:1-16).

### 4. *The Third Passion Prediction* (10:32-34)

Mark's story gathers power as one follows it consecutively. The events and teaching of Galilee and Perea were now in the past, as **they were in the way going up**[59] **to Jerusalem** (32). The climax of Jesus' ministry was approaching.

Reflecting upon the sober fact that He would be **delivered unto the chief priests** (33) and condemned **to death,** amidst mockery and abuse, **Jesus went before them.** What a scene to envision: "Jesus a great lonely figure striding ahead, and the disciples following, awe-stricken, at a distance"![60] The disciples **were amazed** at the courage with which Jesus moved toward an encounter with His foes, "and those who still followed were afraid" (32, Goodspeed).

It seems that two groups were en route with Jesus, the Twelve, and another party of pilgrims (possible including the

---

[55]"The aor. and perf. are here to be distinguished from each other, the aor., *we left,* as denoting simple past action, the perf., *we have followed,* as denoting action continuing into the present" (Ezra P. Gould, *A Critical and Exegetical Commentary on the Gospel According to St. Mark,* "The International Critical Commentary" [Edinburgh: T. & T. Clark, 1955 Impression], p. 195 n.).

[56]Cf. Rom. 16:13. "Salute Rufus . . . and his mother and mine."

[57]"Adds an element which was to temper the compensations of the present, and warns against dreams of unbroken peace" (Swete, *op. cit.,* p. 232).

[58]Cranfield, *op. cit.,* p. 333.

[59]Very literally true. The Jordan cleft is hundreds of feet below sea level; Jerusalem, some twenty-five hundred feet above sea level.

[60]Hunter, *op. cit.,* p. 110.

women of 15:40). This conclusion finds support in the statement that **he took again the twelve**, i.e., took them apart from the rest, and once again **began to tell them what things should happen unto him** (32) (cf. 8:31; 9:31). This time the prediction was in detail:[61] **the Son of man** (33) would **be delivered** to the members of the Sanhedrin, who would **condemn him to death** and hand Him over to the Romans. With mocking, spitting, and scourging, these **Gentiles** would **kill him** (34). Notwithstanding, three days later He would rise again. It is perplexing that the disciples not only "understand none of these things" (Luke 18:34), but continue their scheming for advantage, as the next verses make clear (35-45).

Considering "Christ on the Road to the Cross," Maclaren describes Him as: (1) The heroic Christ, (2) The self-sacrificing Christ, (3) The shrinking Christ, (4) The lonely Christ.

### 5. *The Ambition of James and John* (10:35-45)

As one reads these verses, he is struck by the unspirituality of the disciples—their short memory (9:33-35), and their unabashed selfishness. But one is equally impressed by the incredible patience and wisdom of their Master. Jesus had scarcely finished giving them in detail another prediction of His forthcoming passion, when **James and John** (35), evidently abetted by their mother (Matt. 20:20-21), approached Him with a request such as a child would make. **Do for us whatsoever we shall desire.** This was like asking for a signed check with the amount left blank! Patiently Jesus queried, **What would ye that I should do for you?** (36)

Believing that Jesus was about to establish the Messianic kingdom, the Sons of Thunder asked as largely as possible. **That we may sit . . . on thy right hand, and . . . on thy left . . . in thy glory** (37). "The grand vizier stood at his sovereign's right hand, the commander-in-chief at his left."[62] They sought the positions of greatest authority. What pain this must have caused the Lord!

> While He was thinking of a cross, they were thinking of crowns. His burden was matched by their blindness, His sacrifice by their selfishness. He wanted only to give, they to get. His motive was service; theirs was self-satisfaction.[63]

[61]See Cranfield, *op. cit.*, p. 334-35, for a rejection of the position that such detail must have been given "after the event."

[62]Major, *op. cit.*, p. 135.

[63]Earle, *op. cit.*, p. 130.

**Ye know not what ye ask** (38), was Jesus' sad rejoinder. Then came questions to probe the spirits of these ambitious young men and to lead them to a better understanding of the Kingdom. **Can ye drink of the cup** of inward suffering and agony **I drink of** (cf. Ps. 75:8; Isa. 51:22; John 18:11) and undergo **the baptism** of overwhelming sorrow (cf. Isa. 43:2; Luke 12:50)—or outward persecution and affliction—**I am baptized with?** In other words, "Can you bear to be plunged into the trials into which I am plunged, and which are about to overwhelm Me?" Like would-be martyrs from the Maccabean days, James and John **said unto him, We can** (39). Their brashness is astonishing, even appalling. And yet they spoke a measure of truth. In due time they did **indeed drink** from Christ's **cup** of agony and experienced something of His **baptism** of death, as Acts 12:2 and Rev. 1:9 confirm.[64]

With respect to the request for positions of authority, Jesus implied that "it is merit, not favour . . . not self-seeking, which secures promotion in the Kingdom of God."[65] **To sit on my right . . . and on my left . . . is not mine to give,** "but it is for those for whom it has been prepared" (40, RSV). Places of honor—*and corresponding responsibility*—are not distributed upon request. These come, in the very nature of the Kingdom, to those who are prepared for them by qualities of character and spirit (cf. Ps. 75:6).

If the two sons of Zebedee appeared in a poor light, the remaining ten disciples were no better, for when they **heard of it** "they burst into indignation at James and John" (41, Moffatt). The earlier dispute over "who should be the greatest" (9:34) flared again. With unflagging persistence, **Jesus called them to him** and sought to show them His "transvaluation of values."[66] **Ye know that they which are accounted to rule** (literally, "seem to rule") **over the Gentiles** "lord it over them" (42, ERV). The disciples would feel the sting of these words as they recalled the oppressive tactics of the provincial governors. **But so shall it not be among you** (43). **The great** among the followers of Jesus

---

[64]For the pros and cons on whether John experienced early martyrdom, as some think these verses imply, cf. the arguments of Grant (IB, VII, 814-15) and Cranfield, (*op. cit.,* p. 339).

[65]Major, *op. cit.,* p. 135.

[66]Cranfield, *op. cit.,* p. 341.

is the one eager to be a **minister** (servant) and **servant** (slave) **of all** (44).

> *The Kingdoms of the earth go by*
> *In purple and in gold;*
> *They rise, they flourish, and they die,*
> *And all their tale is told.*
>
> *One Kingdom only is Divine,*
> *One banner triumphs still,*
> *Its King a servant, and its sign*
> *A gibbet on a hill.*[67]

And why should this be so? "For the Son of Man himself has not come to be waited on, but to wait on other people" (45, Goodspeed). In this Christ has left us an example that we should follow in His steps (I Pet. 2:21).

The remaining portion of verse 45 is basic to the doctrine of the atonement. **The Son of man came . . . to give his life a ransom** (*lutron*, "the redemption money paid for the freeing of a slave"[68]) **for many.** The word **for** (*anti*), which literally means "instead of" or "in place of," points to the element of substitution essential to a biblical understanding of the atonement. This great passage "shows clearly how Jesus knew himself called to fuse in His own destiny the two roles of the Son of Man (Dan. 7) and the Servant of the Lord (Isa. 53)."[69]

Verses 32-45 may be outlined thus: (1) Self-giving sacrifice, 32-34; (2) Selfish seeking, 35-40; (3) Selfless service, 41-45.

### 6. *Blind Bartimaeus of Jericho* (10:46-52)

As noted previously (32), Jesus had left Perea, crossed the river Jordan a short distance above the Dead Sea, and had begun the ascent toward Jerusalem. Jericho was situated astride this route. As Jesus, along **with his disciples** (46) and a multitude **of people,** came **out of Jericho,**[70] He passed near **blind Bartimaeus**

---

[67]G. F. Bradby, quoted in Major, *op. cit.,* p. 135.

[68]Earle, *op. cit.,* p. 132.

[69]Hunter, *op. cit.,* p. 112.

[70]Divergent details appear in the Synoptic accounts. Matthew (20:30) speaks of two beggars, and Luke (18:35) locates the event at the approach to the city. "These differences do not affect anything vital, being such as one would expect to find in all evidence given by trustworthy witnesses" (NBC, p. 828). Luke means nothing more than that the healing took place in the vicinity of Jericho, and Mark may recall only the better known of the two men Matthew mentions. Cf. Earle, *op. cit.,* p. 132.

(which means **son of Timaeus**), who sat by the side of the road **begging**. Blindness and defective eyesight are common in the East.[71]

Learning **that it was Jesus** (47) the Nazarene who was passing by in the crowd, **he began to cry** aloud in language no one else had used as yet. **Jesus, thou son of David, have mercy.** "The Messianic secret had begun to leak out."[72] The **many** (48) who **charged him** to **hold his peace** may have regarded his cries as a nuisance (cf. 10:13), or they may have feared the band of pilgrims would be marked as revolutionary. Whatever the reason, Bartimaeus saw a ray of hope and "shouted all the more" (48, NEB) **Thou son of David, have mercy on me.** No word of rebuke or warning came from Jesus.

What follows is dramatic, especially in Mark's vivid language. **Jesus stood still** (49). No longer did the crowd hinder him. **Be of good comfort, rise; he calleth thee.** The heartening word, **Be of good comfort** (" 'It's all right now,' " Phillips), appears seven times in the New Testament, all on the lips of Jesus, except here, where it is related to Him. Paul later received the same encouragement from the glorified Christ (Acts 23:11).

The blind man needed no further prompting. Throwing aside his outer garment and leaping up,[73] he hurriedly **came to Jesus** (50). **What wilt thou that I should do unto thee?** (51) may seem like a superfluous question. But it undoubtedly served to strengthen the man's faith by requiring him to make his desire articulate. In asking questions, Jesus "encouraged others to express their wishes, hopes, aspirations, and gave them opportunity to express their faith, upon which he could then act and build."[74] Bartimaeus replied, " 'Rabboni,[75] I want to regain my sight!' " (51, NASB). Without any of the usual gestures of healing, **Jesus said unto him, . . . Thy faith hath made thee whole** (52) (literally, "has saved you").

At once **he received his sight** and, literally as well as spiritually, **followed Jesus in the way** toward Jerusalem and the Cross. "Bartimaeus . . . had done the best bit of begging in his life."[76]

---

[71]Vincent, *op. cit.*, p. 213.
[72]Hunter, *op. cit.*, p. 112.
[73]The only instance of this word (*anapedesas*) in the New Testament.
[74]IB, VII, 822.
[75]An affectionate term of reverence and respect (cf. John 20:16).
[76]Hunter, *op. cit.*, p. 133.

Mark 11:1—13:37

## A. Events Preceding the Ministry, 11:1-26

### 1. *The Entry into Jerusalem* (11:1-11)

Jesus and His disciples, along with other pilgrims, had now come **nigh to Jerusalem** (1), a goal toward which His ministry had long pointed. **Bethphage** ("the house of unripe figs") **and Bethany** ("house of dates") were two small towns on the slopes of **the mount of Olives,** the former probably a suburb of Jerusalem, the latter about two miles distant from the city (see map).

Stopping at Bethany, where He would retire for sanctuary during the Passion Week, Jesus sent **forth two of his disciples** to the village opposite them, probably Bethphage (cf. Matt. 21:1). Perhaps Peter was one of the two and so recalled the details recorded. They were to **find a colt tied, whereon never man sat; loose him, and bring him** (2) to Jesus. The Master, who was born of a virgin, and at the end ascended to the right hand of God, would thus ride on an unbroken ass. "In the ancient world . . . an animal intended for sacred use must be unbroken."[1]

If the owner, who may well have been a follower of Jesus, should question their action, they were to say that **the Lord** had **need of him** (3) and would return the animal promptly. This is the only instance in Mark where **the Lord** is used as a description of Jesus. It was sufficient identification for the owner of the colt and sufficient reason to devote his property to the Lord's service. Who will follow the example of that anonymous disciple? The disciples **found the colt tied by the door** "out in the open street" (4, RSV) and loosed him.

When **certain** (5) persons who **stood there** raised a question as to their action, they replied **as Jesus had commanded** and were permitted to bring **the colt to Jesus** (7). It has been suggested that these rather mysterious arrangements were either the result of previous planning, perhaps on one of the journeys to Jerusalem mentioned in John, or that they were an evidence of the supernatural knowledge of Jesus. Either was certainly possible.

[1]IB, VII, 825.

The important question is, Why did Jesus choose to ride into the Holy City? His purpose was to fulfill the prophecy of Zechariah (9:9):

> *Rejoice greatly, O daughter of Zion; shout, O daughter of Jerusalem: behold, thy King cometh unto thee: he is just, and having salvation; lowly, and riding upon an ass, and upon a colt the foal of an ass.*

It was "an open and deliberate assertion of Messiahship,"[2] but of a sort Judaism did not expect and, as a consequence, did not understand nor accept. "His purpose was not the overthrow of Rome but the breaking of the power of sin."[3] His messiahship was still veiled from the people by their blindness, a fact which caused Jesus to weep over the city (Luke 19:41-42).

After they had **cast their garments on** the unsaddled colt, Jesus **sat upon him** and started toward Jerusalem (some two miles west of Bethany) amidst the excitement and acclaim of those who "carpeted the road with their cloaks" (8, NEB) and with "leafy branches which they had cut from the fields" (RSV). **They that went before** (9) in the procession, possibly some who had come out from the city, and **they that followed,** perhaps the pilgrims from Galilee, **cried, saying, Hosanna** ("God save!" or "Save now!" cf. II Sam. 14:4; Ps. 20:9).

The shouts of **Hosanna, and Blessed is he that cometh in the name of the Lord,** echoed one of the Hallel Psalms (118:25-26), "which were sung antiphonally by pilgrims nearing Jerusalem and by the Levites receiving them at the holy gate."[4] Doubtless, however, many in the multitude hoped that this "prophet of Nazareth" (Matt. 21:11) would in some manner hasten the coming of the Messianic kingdom. "Blessed is the coming kingdom of our father David; Hosanna in the highest"[5] (10, NASB). It was these nationalistic zealots who would be distressed to learn that Jesus had come in peace and for righteousness, not as a warrior for political revolution. Nevertheless Jesus had determined to offer himself to the Chosen People at the very gates of the Holy City, whatever their reaction. "He came unto his own, and his own received him not" (John 1:11).

---

[2]NBC, p. 828.

[3]*Ibid.*

[4]*The Westminster Study Edition of the Holy Bible, in loco.*

[5]The second clause possibly means, " 'Save, thou who dwellest . . . on high!' " (IB, VII, 826.)

The so-called Triumphal Entry over, **Jesus entered into** (11) the city and **into the temple,** where He **looked round about upon all things,** feeling grief and anger for the corruption in evidence. But because it was late in the day, **he went out unto Bethany** again **with the twelve** and bided His time until the morrow.

It may be helpful at this point to include an outline of Mark's chronology for the Passion Week:

Sunday ("Palm"): Entry into Jerusalem and return to Bethany (11:1-11)

Monday: Cursing of the fig tree and cleansing of the Temple (11:12-19)

Tuesday: Parables, controversy stories, and other teachings (11:20—13:37)

Wednesday: Anointing at Bethany and the treachery of Judas (14:1-11)

Thursday: Passover preparation, Last Supper, Gethsemane, arrest, and ecclesiastical trial (14:12-72)

Friday: Trial before Pilate, condemnation, crucifixion, burial (15:1-47)

Saturday: Jesus in the grave

Sunday (Easter): Resurrection (16:1-20)[6]

### 2. The Fruitless Fig Tree (11:12-14)

**On the morrow** (12), i.e., Monday, the day after the Triumphal Entry, Jesus and the disciples returned to Jerusalem **from** the nearby village of **Bethany.** This was to be the pattern of the week: Jerusalem in the daytime, Bethany at night.

It was evidently early in the day, and Jesus **was hungry.** The humanity of Jesus was always in close juxtaposition with His divine nature. **Seeing a fig tree** at a distance, **having leaves,** "he went to see if he could find anything on it" (13, RSV).

The presence of leaves on the tree was an indication that normally fruit would be present, even though the usual season **for figs was not yet.**

> While the main crop of figs does not ripen in the vicinity of Jerusalem until August, smaller figs begin to appear . . . as soon as the leaf buds are put forth . . . Even these immature figs were eaten by the peasants . . . The lack of any fruit on the tree was proof of its barrenness.[7]

[6]Adapted from C. Milo Connick, *Jesus: The Man, the Mission, and the Message* (Englewood Cliffs, New Jersey: Prentice-Hall, Inc., 1963), p. 327.

[7]Earle, *et al.*, ENT, p. 139.

What followed was another "action-parable." The week would bring a bruising encounter with a barren, fruitless Judaism. When Jesus **said unto** (14) the fig tree, **No man eat fruit of thee hereafter for ever,** He was pronouncing in symbol the certain doom of the Holy City. **And his disciples heard it.**

### 3. *The Cleansing of the Temple* (11:15-19)

Upon His arrival in Jerusalem the day before, Jesus had "entered into . . . the temple: and . . . had looked round about upon all things" (11). What He saw must have stirred His moral indignation, but He waited until the following day to take action.

The place where **the moneychangers** (15) and those who **sold doves** plied their trade was called the Mountain of the House or the Court of the Gentiles. It was a spacious court surrounding the Temple proper and open to Gentiles as well as to Jews.[8]

Every adult male Jew was required to pay an annual tax of a half-shekel for the support of the Temple. Special money changers were present to exchange foreign coins "for the standard ancient Hebrew or Tyrian money which was required."[9] This exchange cost about 15 percent. The principal abuse, however, was in the sale of doves and sacrificial animals, controlled by the wealthy and hated Sadduccean priests. These practices were rebuked by Jewish rabbis, and the markets were destroyed by the public in A.D. 67.[10]

The wrath of Jesus was aroused chiefly because the offensive odors, din, and confusion of the place made it impossible for the Gentiles to worship God in the only area of the Temple open to them. Isaiah had described the day when Jew and Gentile would worship God together in "an house of prayer for all people" (see Isa. 56:6-7). Those who **sold and bought in the temple** had converted **the house of prayer** (17) into "a den of robbers" (Jer. 7:11). He who "loved righteousness, and hated iniquity" (Heb. 1:9) **overthrew the tables** and **the seats** of the greedy merchants and put a stop to the practice of those who made the Temple area simply a convenient shortcut (16).

When **the scribes and chief priests** (18) (Pharisees and Sadducees) saw a source of Temple revenue threatened, they

[8]See Connick, *op. cit.*, pp. 331-33, for a helpful description of the Temple.
[9]IB, VII, 830.
[10]Branscomb, *op. cit.*, pp. 204-5; Connick, *op. cit.*, p. 335.

plotted **how they might destroy him,** but **feared him,** "because the whole crowd was spellbound by his teaching" (NEB). Knowing their malice, Jesus again **went out of the city** (19), for sanctuary among His friends in Bethany. In the second Messianic act of the week, the Lord of the Temple had "suddenly come to his temple . . . like a refiner's fire, and like fullers' soap" (see Mal. 3:1-3).

### 4. *The Withered Fig Tree* (11:20-26)

Mark records that on the **morning** (20) following the cleansing of the Temple (15-19), **as they passed** along the return route to Jerusalem, the disciples **saw the fig tree dried up from the roots.** On the previous day Jesus had rebuked the tree for its pretense in having leaves but no fruit (see on 12-14). **Calling to remembrance** (21) this event, Peter, presumably with some excitement, directed the attention of Jesus to **the fig tree** now **withered away.** The destruction of the fig tree was so complete as to be startling.[11]

At the time when Jesus cursed the tree, He was concerned to show His displeasure with sham and hypocrisy. The results of that rebuke in the withering of the fig tree became the occasion for a lesson on another subject: the power of faith when linked with effectual prayer. **Have faith in God** (22), Jesus said, and more than this will be possible. Perhaps pointing to the Mount of Olives, on which they stood, and looking to the Dead Sea in the distance, Jesus said that a person of faith and prayer could say **unto this mountain,** " 'Get up and throw yourself into the sea' " (23, Phillips), and it would **come to pass.**

Mountains were commonly regarded among the Hebrews as symbols of great obstacles and difficulties. In rabbinical literature, a teacher who could explain an obscure passage was referred to as a "mountain-mover." Zechariah had said of a respected Jewish leader, "Who art thou, O great mountain? before Zerubbabel thou shalt become a plain" (Zech. 4:7). The day would come when the disciples would face mountainous problems. Jesus challenged them to pray "the prayer of faith" (Jas. 5:15). This prayer brings its difficulties to God for His solution and moves in a spirit of expectancy and charity. "Believe that you have received everything for which you pray and ask, and

---

[11]Matthew abridges the story and so telescopes the action (21:18-20).

it will be done for you" (24, Barclay).[12] Jesus set no limitations to the possibilities of prayer.

He who prays in expectancy with **faith in God** must also meet another condition. **When ye stand praying** (cf. I Kings 8:14, 22; Luke 18:11, 13), "if you have a grievance against anyone, forgive him" (25, NEB), otherwise the Father will be unable to **forgive you your trespasses.**[13] He who withholds forgiveness cannot receive it, for an unforgiving spirit is alien to a petition for forgiveness.[14]

## B. TEACHING AND DEBATE IN JERUSALEM, 11:27—12:44

### 1. *The Question of Authority* (11:27-33)

Jesus and the disciples had **come again**[15] **to Jerusalem** (27). **As he was walking** about **in the temple** (27), engaged in "teaching the people . . . and preaching the gospel" (Luke 20:1, RSV), an official delegation of the Sanhedrin[16] challenged the action of Jesus in ridding the Temple area of the money changers and merchants. Their opposition was prompt and vigorous. " 'What authority have you for what you're doing?' " (28, Phillips) Their question was rhetorical, for they recognized no authority in the Temple other than their own.

While Jesus taught and healed in Galilee, official Judaism was suspicious of Him (cf. 7:1), but in that northern province He was under the government of Herod Antipas and out of their jurisdiction. Now that the Prophet of Nazareth was on their doorstep, they set about to trap Him. If, in response to their question, Jesus had claimed divine authority, He would have been charged with blasphemy. If He claimed authority as the

---

[12]"All things whatever ye pray and ask for, believe that you received them" (Gould, *op. cit.,* p. 216). "The aor. is a rhetorical exaggeration of the immediateness of the answer: it antedates even the prayer in the mind of the petitioner" (*Ibid.*).

[13]" 'A falling beside or away' . . . First . . . 'a false step, blunder.' Then . . . 'misdeed, or trespass' " (Earle, *op. cit.,* p. 141).

[14]Verse 26 is clearly an accurate reflection of Jesus' teachings and is relevant to the thought of this passage but it "is omitted in several important MSS. and may be by 'attraction' from the very similar saying in Matthew vi. 15" (Cole, *op. cit.,* p. 182).

[15]Tuesday, according to Mark's chronology.

[16]**The chief priests** (Sadducees), **the scribes** (Pharisees), **and the elders** ("laymen of position and influence") (Johnson, *op. cit.,* p. 149) were the constituent elements of this high tribunal.

Son of David, He would have been charged with treason against Rome. If He had claimed no authority at all, He would have been branded an impostor.

In the style of rabbinical discussion, Jesus replied with a counterquestion. **The baptism of John, was it from heaven, or of men?** (30) And then, in the imperative mood, He made it clear who was on trial: **answer me.** The question was unanswerable, for the ministries of John and Jesus had been related (see on 1:2 ff.; 6:14 ff.). The authority of both was **from heaven** and *not* **of men.** The members of the Sanhedrin were impaled on the horns of a dilemma. **All men counted John** (32) as a bona fide **prophet.** To deny this would be to endanger their lives: "all the people will stone us" (Luke 20:6). Nor could they admit the divine inspiration of John, for they had not believed in him. Moreover, such an admission would be a tacit confession that the authority of Jesus was also **from heaven.** Their answer, after some reasoning among themselves, was to plead ignorance. **We cannot tell** (33). In doing so, "they virtually abdicated from their office as teachers of the nation, and had no further right to question the authority of Jesus."[17] The response of the Master closed the debate. **Neither do I tell you.** Jesus did not say, "I do not know," only that He would not tell. One of the tragic fruits of disobedience is to be shut off from the Source of truth and light.

Under "Jesus Asserts His Authority," we might note: (1) The demonstration of His authority, 15-18; (2) The defense of His authority, 27-33.

### 2. *The Rebellious Tenants* (12:1-12)

As Jesus resumed a public teaching ministry, **he began to speak unto them** (1) (the people in the Temple area, including His enemies) again **by parables,** or "figures." It had been the practice of Jesus to address the crowds in parables, in order to capture their attention and puzzle them into thinking. "Without a parable spake he not unto them" (see on 4:33-34). When He was alone with the disciples He addressed them more directly and plainly.

The parable He now used was allegorical in form and was an obvious adaptation of Isa. 5:1-7, a story familiar to His listeners. In a land where vineyards dotted the hillsides, the details of the

[17]NBC, p. 829.

parable were commonplace: a **man** who **planted a vineyard; an hedge,** or fence, probably made of stones cleared from the soil; a pit dug for the winepress;[18] **a tower** (some fifteen feet high and six feet square), which was both a lookout for the watchman and "a lodge for the keeper of the vineyard";[19] and the practice of letting the vineyard **out** on shares to **husbandmen** (literally, "workers in the ground")[20] while the absentee landlord **went into** another **country.**

The point of the parable must have been painfully clear from the start. The owner of the vineyard was God. The vineyard itself was Israel. The wicked husbandmen were the leaders and rulers of Israel, while the servants, who were beaten ("flayed" or "skinned"), **wounded . . . in the head** (4), and insulted, were the prophets whom God had **sent unto them** (see II Chron. 36: 15-16; Neh. 9:26; Jer. 25:3-7; Matt. 23:29-30). The only **son** (6), the **wellbeloved,** who was **killed, and cast . . . out of the vineyard** (8), was Jesus himself. The destruction of **the husbandmen** by **the lord** ("master," "owner") **of the vineyard** (9) pointed to A.D. 70 and the doom of Jerusalem. As severe a condemnation as this was, more crushing was the prediction that the vineyard would be given **unto others.** That Israel's choice heritage might become the possession of the Gentiles was a possibility unthinkable to the Jewish people (cf. Acts 22:21-22).

The parable tells us that God is generous, trustful, patient, and just. It tells us that Jesus thought of himself as the beloved **son,** not as one of the servants; that He clearly foresaw not only His certain death and rejection outside **the vineyard** but also His final vindication.[21] So prophetic are the details of this parable—the Cross, the Resurrection, the destruction of Jerusalem (A.D. 70), the mission to the Gentiles—that many reject it as unauthentic. It is unfortunate that in the minds of some critics any prediction of the future in the Gospels is *prima facie* evidence that it was contrived after the event. This is only on the *a priori* assumption that Jesus could not and did not know the future. Through the supernatural knowledge which He here

---

[18]**Winefat** (KJV) is old English for *winevat* and is a translation of *hupolenion,* literally, "under the winepress." It was "the under vat of the wine press, into which the juices trampled out . . . flowed" (EGT, p. 420).

[19]Gould, *op. cit.,* p. 220.

[20]Robertson, *op. cit.,* p. 364.

[21]Cf. Barclay, *op. cit.,* pp. 294-95.

exercised, Jesus was giving the leaders of Israel the clearest warning possible.

The parable describes a failure in stewardship. In the story familiar to Judaism (Isa. 5:1-7), the owner of the vineyard lavished care upon it and "looked that it should bring forth grapes, and it brought forth wild grapes" (Isa. 5:2). The vineyard of the Lord was "the house of Israel, and the men of Judah his pleasant plant," but when He looked for justice He found oppression and bloodshed, and when He sought "for righteousness . . . behold a cry" (Isa. 5:7). For such a disappointment, the Lord promised incredible devastation upon the vineyard: "I will lay it waste."

If Jerusalem, that lovely "vineyard in a very fruitful hill," was finally laid waste by the crushing juggernaut of the Roman army, how seriously should we, personally and collectively, regard our stewardship of the gospel entrusted to us by the Lord (cf. Rom. 11:13-24)?

Pursuing His point even further, Jesus asked them if they had **not read** (10) even **this scripture** (Ps. 118:22-23) about **the stone which the builders** of the Temple had once **rejected,** only later to find that it had **become the head of the corner** (joining two walls either as a cornerstone or as a crown at the crest). In the original, the Psalmist thinks of Israel as **the stone** set aside and rejected by the world powers "but finally restored to the place of honour designed for it by God among the nations."[22] This action **was** indeed **the Lord's doing,** and **marvellous** in **Israel's eyes** (11). This quotation, strongly Messianic in tone, Jesus obviously applied to himself, as did the Church later (Acts 4:11; Eph. 2:20; I Pet. 2:4-8).

The members of the Sanhedrin could not escape the implication, **for they knew that he had spoken the parable against them.** "They tried to arrest him" (12, RSV), but fearing the people, **they left him** for the moment **and went their way.**

C. H. Spurgeon found in these verses: (1) The amazing mission, 6; (2) The astounding crime, 8; (3) The appropriate punishment, 9.

### 3. *The Question of Tribute to Caesar* (12:13-17)

The chief priests, scribes, and elders (11:27), who had just retired after the previous skirmish (12), now sent representatives

[22]CB, p. 277.

from **the Pharisees** (13) and **the Herodians** to **catch**[23] Jesus **in his words** (literally, "in a word;" cf. 3:6).

They approached Jesus with fulsome praise. **We know that thou art true** and "truckle to no man, whoever he may be" (14, NEB). **Is it lawful** among us **to give tribute to Caesar?** The **tribute** was an aggravating poll tax paid annually to the emperor. As a popular Leader, Jesus would be expected to have strong views on the subject of taxation. His enemies posed a dilemma. If He should tell them not to pay the tax, He would be subject to arrest by the Roman governor Pilate. If He should tell them to pay the **tribute,** He would alienate the people. "He would either be discredited or imperiled."[24]

**Knowing their hypocrisy,** Jesus **said unto them,** " 'Why try this trick on me?' " (15, Phillips) **Bring me a penny.** Jesus asked for a *denarius,* a silver coin used in paying the poll tax, worth about twenty cents and bearing the image of the emperor. This coin was particularly offensive. Other local coins were struck with less annoying inscriptions, such as "leaven of the native trees."[25] When they had brought the coin, Jesus asked them, **Whose is this image?** (16) They must have squirmed as they replied, **Caesar's.** They professed hatred for Caesar but carried his effigy in their purses!

The response of Jesus astonished them. They had inquired, "Shall we *pay* this unjust assessment?" **Jesus ... said unto them, Render** (17) as a just obligation **to Caesar the things that are Caesar's.** "The tax is not much, and the coin is Caesar's anyway—give it back to him!" And then, to show there is no necessary conflict between one's civil and religious duties, Jesus concluded, **and to God the things that are God's.** (Perhaps Jesus also implied that, if the Jewish nation had followed the will of God, **Caesar** would not have been in the land.) "Duty to God and duty to State are not incompatible; we owe a debt to both, and it is clearly possible to be a good Christian and a loyal citizen."[26] (See Rom. 13:7; I Pet. 2:13-14.)

### 4. *Controversy over the Resurrection* (12:18-27)

The next group to challenge Jesus in this series of questions was **the Sadducees** (18), a smaller party than the Pharisees, but

---

[23]"To catch or take by hunting or fishing" (Abbott-Smith, p. 7).
[24]Taylor, *op. cit.,* p. 479.
[25]CB, p. 279.
[26]NBC, p. 830.

powerful through their control of the Temple. They were wealthy, worldly, harsh, arrogant. They clung to the older beliefs of
Judaism and rejected the newer developments of the Pharisees,
including the doctrine of the **resurrection**. The Sadducees faded
out with the fall of Jerusalem, whereas the Pharisees persisted.

These well-educated aristocrats approached the Prophet of
Galilee (the "backwoods" of Palestine) with a question typical
of intellectual skepticism and snobbery. It concerned the levirate
law of Israel (Deut. 25:5-10) designed to perpetuate the family
line of a man who had suffered the great calamity of dying childless, "that his name be not put out of Israel." **In the resurrection**
(23), they queried, **whose wife shall she be** who, in succession,
had been married to **seven** brothers, all of whom had died leaving
no seed? This puzzle may well have been the stock-in-trade of
the Sadducees in their debates with the Pharisees. It was a problem intended to reduce to an absurdity belief in the resurrection
from the dead. One can imagine that the questioners could
scarcely contain their mirth.

Jesus did not debate the issue with His opponents on their
own grounds but went instead to the heart of the issue: their
ignorance of **the scriptures** and **the power of God** (24), both of
which they should have known as priests in the Temple of God.
They were rationalistic conservatives (accepting, like the Samaritans, only the Torah as scripture). They were thus passed by in
the developing revelation of God. "Is not this where you wander
*and* go wrong . . . ?" (24, *Amplified NT*) These are correlative:
**the scriptures** and **the power of God**. Apart from a knowledge
of the gospel, available only in the Bible, one's search for the
living God is frustrating, if not futile. Apart from the power
of the Spirit of God, the Scriptures are devoid of spiritual
life, "for the letter killeth, but the spirit giveth life" (II Cor. 3:6).
The written Word rightly related to the living Word gives us our
only sure hope for the preservation of pure religion.

Those who know **the power of God** through **the scriptures** do
not find the promise of **the resurrection** incredible. The God of
the Bible is a God of miracles and has the ability "to create new
orders of existence"[27] quite different from the one we now know.
In the words of Luke, "those who are accounted worthy to attain
to that age and to the resurrection from the dead neither marry
nor are given in marriage, for they cannot die any more, be-

---

[27]Hunter, *op. cit.*, p. 123.

cause they are equal to angels . . ." (20:35-36, RSV). The Sadducees were wrong in rejecting the resurrection, but the Pharisees (like the Moslems later) were wrong in supposing that the resurrection body would perform marriage functions. **The angels (25)** (whose existence the Sadducees also denied) were created directly by God, not by procreation. The believers' "equality with the angels consists in their deliverance from mortality and its consequences."[28]

And then, **as touching the dead (26)**, whether or not **they rise,** Jesus turned the tables on His adversaries and quoted directly from their own Scriptures. **Have ye not read . . . how in the bush**[29] **God spake . . . saying, I am the God of Abraham, . . . of Isaac, and . . . of Jacob?** (Exod. 3:6) The living **God** is the **God** of **living** men. "God called these men his friends (says Jesus) and God does not leave his friends in the dust . . . When God loves once, he loves forever."[30]

The argument of Jesus for life after death is not based upon philosophical analyses of the nature of man but upon the character of God. If Abraham, Isaac, and Jacob were among the living in the day of Moses, "we may be confident that at the last God will raise up their bodies, so that they may share the final blessedness."[31] To the skeptics of any age—Sadducean or modern—Jesus would say, "You are quite wrong" (27, RSV).

### 5. *The First Commandment of All* (12:28-34)

While Jesus was **reasoning (28)**, or disputing, with His adversaries (13-27), **one of the scribes** of nobler mind **came** up and perceived that the Master **had answered them well.** The atmosphere of the ensuing discussion was warm and friendly, in sharp contrast with the previous debates. Apparently with sincere motive, the scribe **asked him, Which is the first commandment of all?** He may well have meant, "What is the *kind* of commandment that is entitled to rank first?"[32] Many attempts had been made to distinguish between the "weighty" or "heavy" com-

---

[28]Swete, *op. cit.,* p. 281.

[29]Some scholars hold that this phrase refers to a passage in the Sadducean canon bearing the title "The Bush." "The Jewish Scriptures were at this time divided into sections, the most notable of which had distinctive titles" (Major, *op. cit.,* p. 150).

[30]Hunter, *op. cit.,* p. 124.

[31]Cranfield, *op. cit.,* p. 376.

[32]CB, p. 285.

mandments and those "light" or "little." Some principle of classification or some way to sum up the complex system of laws was sought. It is said that a Gentile once came to the great Rabbi Hillel and agreed to become a proselyte if the whole law could be taught him while he stood on one foot.[33]

**Jesus answered** (29) the scribe by quoting the first part of the Shema (Deut. 6:4-5): **Hear, O Israel; The Lord our God is one Lord.**[34] It was a vigorous confession of monotheism. " 'The Lord your God is the only Lord' " (NEB). The God who is one and undivided calls for undivided love and loyalty. **Thou shalt love the Lord thy God** (literally, in each case) "out of the whole of" **thy heart . . . soul . . . mind, and . . . strength** (30). It is impossible to exactly define each of these faculties though it seems clear that some differentiation is intended. The commandment calls for a complete response of man's whole being. This is the perfect love of Christian perfection.

Although it was unsolicited, Jesus went on to add a **second** (31) commandment **like** unto the first, **Thou shalt love thy neighbour as thyself.** So far as is known, no one had ever previously linked these two statements (Deut. 6:4-5; Lev. 19:18) as the substance of all the Law. Jesus was not saying that these were the first and second commandments, respectively, in a long list of requirements, but rather that they combined to give a distillation of man's whole moral obligation. "On these two . . . hang all the law and the prophets" (Matt. 22:40).

As significant as the second commandment is, it is important to see its dependence upon the first. "The love of God is the only secure and permanent basis for a love of man . . . A love of man which is not based on the love of God is always liable to succumb to the temptations of self-gratification, self-interest, and sentimentality."[35]

The scribe was deeply moved by Jesus' answer. "Excellently . . . answered, Teacher!" (32, *Amplified NT*) To do this is much **more than all whole burnt offerings and sacrifices** (33). In turn, Jesus was touched by the scribe's response. Seeing **that he answered discreetly** (34) ("intelligently"),[36] Jesus said with poignancy, **Thou art not far from the kingdom.** Could this

---

[33]Cranfield, *op. cit.*, p. 377.

[34]Or, " 'Hear, O Israel: The Lord our God, the Lord is one' " (29, RSV).

[35]Major, *op. cit.*, p. 152.

[36]Literally, "as one who had a mind (of his own)" (EGT, I, 425).

scribe have been one of those in Jerusalem who was converted after Pentecost (cf. Acts 6:7)? It may have been so.

The enemies of Jesus were now muzzled. "After that no one dared ask him any question" (34, RSV).

The three preceding paragraphs could be treated together under the topic: "Christ Can Answer Your Questions." Here we have questions: (1) Concerning the present life—taxation, 13-17; (2) Concerning the future life—resurrection, 18-27; (3) Concerning the heart of religious life—the Great Commandment, 28-34.

### 6. The Messiah and David (12:35-37)

When Jesus' enemies no longer dared ask Him questions, He took the initiative again (cf. 11:30) and **answered** the implied denials of His messiahship with a question of His own. **How say the scribes,** the teachers of the Law, **that the Christ is the son of David?** (35) Such a query would have the attention of all His listeners in **the temple** area, for the Jewish people held and the Old Testament taught that the Messiah would be a Descendant of David's line (Isa. 9:6 f.; 11:1 f.; Jer. 23:5 f.).

Quoting Ps. 110:1, from the leading Messianic psalm and often alluded to in the New Testament (e.g., Acts 2:34; Heb. 1:13), Jesus noted that **David . . . himself** (37), inspired by the Holy Spirit, had called the Christ his **Lord. Whence is he then his son?** In other words, this is not the language of a father addressing his son, but the opposite.

Jesus, who was indeed "of the seed of David according to the flesh" (Rom. 1:3), was trying to correct the erroneous ideas of the scribes concerning the Messiah. **The son of David** to them meant another popular, political leader. David, by divine inspiration, plainly saw that the Messiah was more than this, as Jesus knew himself to be. The Father had said, "Thou art my beloved Son" (1:11). How much greater was the Messiah than any mere offspring of David! "The vast crowd heard this with great delight" (37, Phillips).

### 7. A Warning Against the Scribes (12:38-40)

To **the common people** (37), who listened to Him with delight, Jesus said, in the course of His teaching, **Beware of the scribes** (38). The office of scribe had a long history in Israel (cf. Jer. 8:8) and had included the "ready scribe" Ezra (Ezra 7:6). By the time of Jesus the numbers and influence of this group had multiplied until their responsibilities as interpreters and teachers of the Law, as well as jurists, made them a dominant influence in Judaism. Jesus had condemned their teaching as erroneous and now attacked their religious practices as insincere.

There were four things these men liked, all of which indicated their hunger for recognition and preference (see John 5:44; 12:43): to walk about in the **long** robes of the scholars, to receive **salutations** in public places (Matt. 23:7-8), to sit in the **chief** synagogue **seats** (while the congregation stood), and to have the places of honor **at feasts.** Their **long prayers** (40) were but "a cloak for greed" (I Thess. 2:5, RSV), as they devoured **widows' houses** through exorbitant fees or through the abuse of hospitality or generosity. Their judgment would be in direct proportion to their **pretence** of piety.

These severe criticisms were not unjust. Josephus speaks of the "great influence" certain Pharisees had with women, and the Talmud refers to some of them as a "plague."[37] But let not these warnings fall unheeded on twentieth-century ears.

### 8. *The Widow's Offering* (12:41-44)

Mark has concluded his account of the controversial discussions between Jesus and His opponents (11:27—12:40) and now introduces as welcome relief the inspiring story of the **widow** (42) and her sacrificial giving.

**The treasury** (41) "was probably a section or room in one of the porticoes of the Court of the Women"[38] in the Temple proper. In **the treasury** there were thirteen receptacles with trumpet-shaped mouths to receive the several types of offerings. It is said that contributors were required to state the amount of their donation and its purpose.[39] Thus as **Jesus sat over against the treasury** He could probably see and hear what **the people** were giving.

As He **beheld how . . . many that were rich cast in much . . .** a **certain poor widow** appeared and **threw in two mites,** together worth half a cent. They were the smallest copper coins in circulation and represented the smallest contribution lawful to make.

He who looks on each time the collection plate moves through a congregation **called . . . his disciples** (43) and said, **This poor**

[37]Hunter, *op. cit.,* p. 126.
[38]Connick, *op. cit.,* p. 350.
[39]*Ibid.*

**widow hath cast more in than all** the rich with their large gifts. Those with wealth had given easily from their **abundance** (44); the widow in love and out of **her want** (cf. Phil. 4:11) had given **all her living** ("livelihood") in complete dependence upon God. Could this **poor widow** have been one whose house the scribes had devoured (40)? Could the gifts of the rich have been from the proceeds of such greed?

From this story the poor may learn the value of their giving, however meagre, and the rich may discover a measure for their giving, however munificent.

> Give as you would if an angel
> Awaited your gift at the door.
> Give as you would if tomorrow
> Found you where giving is o'er.
>
> Give as you would to the Master
> If you met His loving look.
> Give as you would of your substance
> If His hand your offering took.[40]

## C. The Discourse on the Mount of Olives, 13:1-37

This chapter has been called "one of the most difficult . . . in the New Testament for a modern reader to understand."[41] This is true for several reasons. The language reflects Jewish ideas and history understood by the people of that day but strange to us. Further, at least two themes are interwoven: prophecies concerning the destruction of Jerusalem and warnings concerning the second coming of Christ. There are also predictions of persecution and warnings of perils to appear in the last days. As a result, it is sometimes charged that the chapter is a composite of authentic sayings of Jesus mingled with a Jewish-Christian apocalypse (an "unveiling") written on the eve of Jerusalem's destruction. It is heartening to read the comments of scholars like Barclay and Cranfield, who take the whole of the chapter as genuine.[42]

[40]*Christianity Today*, VI, No. 8, 364.

[41]Barclay, *op. cit.*, p. 317.

[42]*Ibid.*, pp. 317-37; Cranfield, *op. cit.*, pp. 387-91.

### 1. *The Impending Destruction* (13:1-2)

The occasion for the discourse was an exclamation of awe from **one of the disciples** (1) as the group was leaving **the temple** enclosure. "Look, Teacher, what wonderful stones and . . . buildings!" (RSV) Herod's Temple was acknowledged as one of the wonders of the world. Some of the **stones** were said to be forty feet long, by twelve feet high, by eighteen feet wide. Situated on an eminence looking eastward toward the Mount of Olives, the **buildings** of the Temple complex were impressive.[43] In the heart of every loyal Jew was a profound love for the house of God on Zion's hill:

> *How amiable are thy tabernacles, O Lord of hosts!*
> *My soul longeth, yea, even fainteth for the courts of the Lord* (Ps. 84:1-2).

And yet that massive Temple represented implacable opposition to the Prophet of Nazareth. "One greater than the temple" (Matt. 12:6) had come and had gone unrecognized and scorned. Judaism moved surely toward open revolt against Rome and consequent annihilation. When the destruction of Jerusalem was complete in A.D. 70, the prediction of Jesus was fulfilled with dreadful accuracy. There was **not . . . left one stone upon another** (2).

### 2. *Questions and Answers Concerning the End* (13:3-8)

On the natural route to Bethany from Jerusalem, Jesus and the disciples came to **the mount of Olives over against the temple** (3), i.e., opposite the Temple across the Kidron Valley about half a mile east. It was a **mount** associated with Messianic expectation (cf. Zech. 14:4). Rising some two hundred feet about the city, its summit provided the observer with a breathtaking view.

As Jesus **sat** there, the "inner circle" **(Peter, James, and John)**, plus dependable **Andrew** (3), **asked him privately** when **these things** (4) would be and what **sign** they could expect to assure them of fulfillment. The disciples quite naturally associated the destruction of the Temple with the whole series of events in the end time (Matt. 24:3). In general, Jesus said that much was yet to come before the end (5-23), that certain signs would

---

[43]See *Harper's Bible Dictionary* for an excellent description of the three temples successively built by Solomon, Zerubbabel, and Herod (pp. 730-36); cf. also the record of Josephus in his *Wars* V. 5. 1-8.

herald the Second Coming (24-27), and that watchfulness was imperative (28-37).[44]

The disciples, like so many others since that time, wanted one unmistakable sign, such as would make watchfulness unnecessary. Jesus gave them, not one, but many. "The purpose of his reply was not to impart esoteric information but to strengthen and sustain faith."[45] There is a curiosity about such matters that is purely intellectual, and so there is also a divine reserve in the unveiling of future events (cf. Acts 1:7). "The Bible knows no solely intellectual truth; all is moral as well."[46]

Jesus warned His disciples of "impostors . . . commotions . . . calamities."[47] **Many shall come in my name, saying, I am Christ (6).**[48] The Christian faith may be more than sound doctrine, but it is not less. Heresy subverts the faith.

False Messiahs (e.g., Bar Cochba, A.D. 132), **wars (7), earthquakes (8)** (Pompeii and Laodicea in A.D. 61-62), **famines** (Acts 11:28)—all would quite literally soon appear. But the disciples were **not** to be **troubled,** for **these are** but **the beginnings of sorrows.** The term translated **beginnings** (from *odin*) means "a birth-pang, travail pain . . . metaphorically of extreme suffering."[49] "These are merely the beginning of birth pangs" (8, NASB). **The end shall not be yet (7).** This is also "a continual picture of the present age of turmoil, in the midst of which the Christian church must live and witness."[50]

### 3. Preparation for Persecution (13:9-13)

Jesus could foresee that His followers would experience bitter opposition, often from heartbreaking sources. He sought to prepare them. Four times in this chapter the Lord said, **Take heed** (5, 9, 23, 33): " 'Take care' . . . 'Be on your guard' . . . 'Be alert' " (NEB). This admonition is relevant in all ages. The danger of spiritual defeat is always present. It is largely a forgotten truth that "the role of the Christian church during this age is unquestionably one of suffering . . . Worldly favor and

---

[44]See Cranfield, *op. cit.,* pp. 394-407.
[45]*Ibid.,* p. 394.
[46]Cole, *op. cit.,* p. 198.
[47]NBC, p. 832.
[48]The word *Christ* is supplied in KJV; note italics. " 'I am he!' " (RSV)
[49]Abbott-Smith, p. 490.
[50]Cole, *op. cit.,* p. 200.

prosperity . . . have always had an enervating and enfeebling effect upon it."[51]

The early generations of Christians faced intense persecution, first from the Jews and later from the Gentiles, as is indicated here and in Acts. The local **councils** (9), or sanhedrins, had authority to try and punish heresy by means of scourging. As the gospel spread, the disciples were **brought before rulers and kings,** on behalf of Christ, **for a testimony against them** (literally, "unto them").[52] It is noteworthy that in the Book of Acts most of the preaching was not before receptive audiences but in the courts and before unfriendly hearers. Paul is the classic example and counted his imprisonments as providential openings for the preaching of Christ (cf. Acts 26:2). In this and in countless other ways, **the gospel must first be published** (literally, "preached") **among all nations** (10) before the end (Matt. 24:14). The divine necessity **(must)** promises the universal publication of the gospel as a part of God's purpose for the end of the age.

Instructions, especially for the apostolic period, and warnings of familial treachery follow. When handed over to authorities, believers were not "to give a premeditated and perhaps softened answer."[53] Martyrs were later carefully prepared for their ordeal. This injunction is no encouragement to carelessness in the preparation of sermons!

Has our time forgotten the chilling words of Jesus, **Ye shall be hated of all . . . for my name's sake** (13)? Let a man of God disturb entrenched ignorance, prejudice, or evil—personal and social—and he will face the sinister, stolid face of hate. It is then that endurance becomes a virtue and duty. He who endures **unto the end,** "to the last degree,"[54] **shall be saved.**

### 4. *The Desolation of Desecration* (13:14-23)

It has already been noted that the two themes, the destruction of Jerusalem and the coming of the end, intertwine in chapter 13. Commentators generally agree that the section before us refers especially to the sacking of Jerusalem. However, it seems wise to consider the presence of a double reference in these

---

[51]NBC, p. 832.

[52]The term translated "testimony" (*martyrion*) is obviously related to our word "martyr."

[53]Earle, *et al.,* ENT, p. 146.

[54]IB, VII, 860.

words, Jesus seeing in the demise of the Holy City a picture of later judgments and, finally, the end of all things. Prophecy may be at once both the *forthtelling* of the mind of God and the *foretelling* of the purpose of God. "Here God's judgment on Jewry is almost insensibly dovetailed into God's judgment on all mankind at the end of time."[55]

**The abomination of desolation,** or "the desolating sacrilege" (14, RSV), is reminiscent of Daniel[56] (9:27; 11:31; 12:11). "The dreadful desecration" (Goodspeed) refers to some detestable profanation of the Temple which would drive God and His people away, leaving it desolate. The **abomination of desolation** was taken by the Jews to refer to the defilement of the holy place by Antiochus Epiphanes in 168 B.C. The hated Syrian ruler had set up an idol in the Temple and caused swine to be sacrificed on the great altar. In the present instance it has reference to the threat of desecration posed by the Roman armies (Luke 21:20). This was to be a signal for the Christians in Judea to **flee to** the safety of the **mountains** east of the Jordan. **Let him that readeth understand** is a note inserted by the Evangelist, urging his readers to give careful attention to what Jesus said.

So pressing was the danger, great haste was urged. Anyone **on the housetop** (15) was to go down by the outside stairway and **take** nothing **out of his house.** Those at work **in the field** (16) were not to **turn back again** to their houses for an outer **garment,** however needful in the night chill. Such desperate flight would be especially difficult for those with children. Because of the heavy rains which would flood the wadis and the Jordan River, they were to **pray** (18) that their **flight** would **not** be **in winter.** This warning of Jesus evidently saved the Judean Christian community. "Just prior to A.D. 70 the Christians of Jerusalem did in fact make their escape in this way and Eusebius, the church historian, tells us that they fled to Pella, in Perea, east of the Jordan."[57]

Contemporary records confirm the **affliction** or "tribulation" (19, ASV)[58] of **those days.** Josephus records[59] the horrors of the

---

[55]Cole, *op. cit.,* p. 203.

[56]Although the phrase "Daniel the prophet" does not have adequate MS support here, it is clearly authentic in the parallel passage, Matt. 24:15.

[57]NBC, p. 833.

[58]The Greek word and this translation combine "the ideas of pressing out grapes and threshing grain" (Earle, *op. cit.,* p. 158).

[59]*Wars of the Jews* Book V.

siege of Jerusalem in A.D. 70 as one of the grimmest events in all history. As the masses crowded into the city, the Romans literally pressed them to death by means of starvation. Nearly 100,000 were captured, and more than a million persons perished in agony. Perhaps in answer to the prayers of the believers (**for the elect's sake,** 20) in Pella (see above), **the Lord . . . shortened the days,** as He had in Old Testament times (II Sam. 24:16; Isa. 65:8). Impelled by matters of pressing personal concern, the Roman generals hastened back to Italy.

The "double reference" noted at the beginning of this section may be recalled. The prophetic telescoping of future events and the consequent foreshortening of time are evident here. Prefigured in the tribulation of those days are the judgments of the last times, and in the warnings of **false Christs** (22) is the admonition to watch for **false prophets** in the end time. "Thus in the crises of history the eschatological is foreshadowed. The divine judgments in history are, so to speak, rehearsals of the last judgment . . . The fulfillment of these verses is past, present, and future."[60]

We have been warned and should be alert. **Behold, I have foretold you all things** (23).

5. *The Parousia* (13:24-27)

These verses are generally regarded as descriptive of the Second Coming, the *parousia* ("presence," "coming," the principal New Testament term for the second advent of Jesus). The language contains imagery strange to us but familiar to the disciples. Jesus did not create these symbols but employed well-known prophetic and apocalyptic terminology (Isa. 13:10; 24:23; 34:4).[61]

To what extent these words are to be taken literally is an issue on which devout commentators divide. In the apocalyptic drama of our atomic-space age, these figures no longer seem incredible. The second advent of our Lord will certainly be a cataclysmic event.

In any case, **after that tribulation** (24) (a summary of the totality of suffering through which the Church will have gone), **the Son of man** (26) (Dan. 7:13-14) will come **with great power and glory,** bringing an end to the painful period of walking by faith rather than by sight. **Then shall they** see Him. Then shall

---

[60]Cranfield, *op. cit.,* p. 404.

[61]See also Barclay, *op. cit.,* pp. 333-35, for examples from noncanonical literature.

the Son of Man **gather together his elect** ("chosen ones") from
"the farthest bounds of earth to the farthest bounds of heaven"
(27, NEB). Whatever torment the Church may suffer in this
unstable world, we should maintain this confidence, that it is the
*Lord* who will "summon his chosen together from every quarter"
(27, Phillips).

### 6. *The Lesson of the Fig Tree* (13:28-31)

**The fig tree** (28), a common sight in Palestine, along with
"all the trees" (Luke 21:29), has a lesson for those who will learn.
In the spring of the year when the stirrings of life have made the
branches **tender** in preparation for the budding of leaves, everyone knows **that summer is near.** Likewise, when **these things
come to pass** (29), the disciples are to **know that it is nigh**[62] ...
**at the doors.** With the most solemn affirmation, Jesus went on to
say, **This generation shall not pass, till all these things be done**
(30). As a final assurance that this prediction would be fulfilled,
Jesus added, **My words shall not pass away** (31).

To what does the phrase **all these things** refer? The reference
seems to be first of all to the fall of Jerusalem, a tragic event
which did take place before the members of that **generation**
passed on. Nevertheless the imminency of the end is also implied.
The coming of Christ in the flesh was D day; His coming in glory
will be V day. "Ever since the incarnation men have been living
in the last days."[63] For further discussion of this point see the
notes on Matt. 24:32-35.

### 7. *The Virtue of Watchfulness* (13:32-37)

The intent of this concluding paragraph of the Olivet discourse is, like the chapter as a whole, practical and moral. The
purpose of the "Little Apocalypse," as the discourse is often
called, is "not speculative but practical, not to enable us to fore-
cast the future but to interpret the present, not to satisfy curiosity
but to deliver from perplexity."[64]

These things stand out: first, the Lord will certainly come
again[65] (36); second, **no man** (32), nor **the angels**, not even **the**

---

[62]Often translated, "he is near," i.e., the Christ. Luke takes this to mean
"the kingdom of God" (21:31).

[63]Cranfield, *op. cit.*, p. 408.

[64]NBC, p. 832.

[65]By **of that day** "the day of the Parousia is clearly intended. In the
O.T. 'that day' is an eschatological technical term" (Cranfield, *op. cit.*,
pp. 410-11).

Son,[66] can possibly know when; third, therefore we must **all** (37) be watchful, alert, prayerful, and prepared for His sudden return.

The very emphatic assertion of verse 32 that absolutely no one can know **that day and that hour** should have muzzled the date-setters. And yet some quibble over the statement, saying that the *year* of the Parousia may be known, if the **day** and **hour** are not! Their condemnation is just. **Ye know not when the time is** (33).

The simile of **the porter** (34) ("doorkeeper," 34-35) conveys the message of Jesus. The doorkeepers of the Temple were on guard through the night and were under obligation to be wakeful and alert. "Any guard found asleep on duty was beaten, or his garments were set on fire"[67] (cf. Rev. 16:15). It is moving to notice that **when the master of the house cometh** (35), early or late,[68] it is during the night, when wakefulness and alertness are difficult.

What Jesus said unto the disciples, He says **unto all, Watch** (37).

The contents of this chapter may be outlined thus: (1) Prediction of the Temple's destruction, 1-8; (2) Patience in persecution, 9-23; (3) Preparation for Christ's coming, 24-37.

---

[66]A self-imposed limitation until He should return to the Father; cf. Phil. 2:5-8; John 17:5.

[67]Vincent, *op. cit.*, p. 225.

[68]Mark gives the four watches of the night familiar to the Romans, three hours each from 6:00 p.m. to 6:00 a.m. For the Jewish practice, cf. Luke 12:38.

Mark 14:1—15:47

## A. EVENTS LEADING TO THE ARREST, 14:1-52

### 1. *Dark Intrigue* (14:1-2)

The smoldering wrath of **the chief priests and the scribes** over the words and actions of Jesus now burst into flame as they **sought how they might take him** "by stealth, and kill him" (1, RSV). How to do this without **an uproar** (2), which would bring the fury of the Roman legions upon their heads, was a question. Jerusalem and environs were jammed with possibly more than a million people,[1] including Galilean pilgrims, friendly to Jesus. With but **two days** remaining until **the passover** and the feast of **unleavened bread,**[2] cautious haste was imperative.

### 2. *The Alabaster Box* (14:3-9)

Each night during the Passion Week, Jesus went to nearby **Bethany** (3) or to the Mount of Olives, for sanctuary among friends. On this occasion He was **in the house of Simon the leper.** Nothing more is known of this man. Perhaps he had been healed of leprosy by Jesus.[3]

As Jesus reclined **at meat,** a woman came with **an alabaster** flask of **ointment** (perfume) "of pure nard, very costly *and* precious" (3, *Amplified NT*). Breaking the jar, **she poured it** in

---

[1]A census in A.D. 65 of lambs slain at the Passover was said to total more than a quarter of a million animals. The minimum number for each party of pilgrims was ten persons per lamb. Josephus says that there were three million at the Passover that year (*Wars*, II. 14. 3).

[2]These two were in reality separate events, but were often conjoined in thought. The Passover, celebrating Israel's deliverance out of Egypt, was observed on the evening of Nisan 14, the Feast of Unleavened Bread during the following seven days. ". . . The *unleavened bread* . . . was to remind them of the bread they had eaten in haste when they escaped from slavery" (Barclay, *op. cit.*, p. 350). See *Unger's Bible Dictionary*, pp. 352-56, for a helpful treatment of these festivals.

[3]The parallel accounts present problems. Luke 7:36-50 certainly refers to a different event. John locates the anointing in the home of Lazarus and seems to date it several days earlier. Perhaps there was some connection between Simon and the other friends of Jesus in Bethany. Mark has evidently "sacrificed the chronological order for homiletical reasons" (NBC, p. 834).

loving generosity **on his head.** In the homes of the wealthy, guests were often anointed with a drop or two of costly ointment.

Such a display of wholehearted devotion seemed an extravagant waste to **some** (4), including Judas (John 12:4-6), who grumbled indignantly. It was certainly an expensive gesture of love and faith. **It might have been sold for more than three hundred pence** (5) (denarii), or about as much as a man could earn in a year.[4]

Typical of complainers in every age, **they murmured against her.** It might be said that they "growled" or "glowered" as they "scolded" her. Their concern for **the poor** was specious. There are values of the spirit that transcend humanitarianism. Moreover, Jesus himself was a poor Man and, in quoting Deut. 15:11, underlined the command, "Open thine hand wide unto thy brother, to thy poor, and to thy needy."

Jesus came to the woman's defense. " 'Let her alone . . . She has done a beautiful thing to me' " (6, RSV). The word for **good** (KJV) in this case refers to form rather than essence and implies something lovely or fair. The cause of *goodness* in the world would be strengthened if all its advocates cultivated what is *beautiful* and *lovely* (Phil. 4:8) as well as what is *right.*

Consciously or not, the woman had acknowledged Jesus as the suffering Messiah. Like those who bathed and perfumed their beloved dead before laying them to rest, she at unbelievable cost had **come aforehand to anoint** (8) His body **to the burying.** "Her act said more plainly than words to Christ 'I know that you are the Messiah, and I know also that a cross awaits you.' "[5]

Confident of what lay beyond the grave, including the preaching of the gospel **throughout the whole world** (9), Jesus promised that this story of reckless, loving generosity would be told everywhere as a **memorial of her.** "There is that scattereth, and yet increaseth; and there is that withholdeth . . . but it tendeth to poverty" (Prov. 11:24).

Why this good work wrought on Jesus was beautiful: (1) It was altogether a glorifying of Jesus; (2) It was an act of pure love; (3) It was done with considerable sacrifice; (4) It was done with preparation (C. H. Spurgeon).

[4]A denarius, worth about twenty cents, was a day's wage.
[5]Hunter, *op. cit.,* p. 133.

### 3. *Judas and His First Step* (14: 10-11)

The fabric of Mark's story is thoughtfully woven. The priests had decided to destroy Jesus (1-2). **Judas Iscariot** (10) [6] had witnessed a lavish display of devotion and was angered (John 12: 6). Evil men joined forces. The betrayer **went unto the chief priests,** and **they were glad** (11).

Why would **one of the twelve** (cf. Ps. 41:9; John 13:18) do this great wrong? The most likely conjecture is that he was disillusioned with Jesus and His role as the suffering Messiah. At some point along the way he yielded to the dark thoughts in his soul and flung the door wide to Satan (John 13:2, 27). With avarice moving his will (Matt. 26:15), Judas (literally, "Judah," which means, ironically, "praise") set about to salvage what he could. He **sought** at once an opportunity to (literally) "hand over" Jesus "by craft" (1).

### 4. *Preparing for the Passover* (14: 12-16)

The time was swiftly approaching when "the Lamb of God" (John 1: 29) would be slain and so become "our passover" (I Cor. 5: 7), "our paschal lamb" (RSV). **The first day of unleavened bread** (12) [7] was on the fourteenth of the month Nisan (March-April), or Thursday of the Passion Week. The Passover lambs were slain in the Temple during that afternoon, and the Passover meal was eaten between sunset and midnight of the same day.[8]

The **disciples** wondered where Jesus would have them **go and prepare . . . the passover.** Residents of Jerusalem were required to open their homes to the Passover pilgrims for this purpose. Jesus sent **two of his disciples** (13) (cf. 11:1)—John and Peter, according to Luke 22: 8—into the city with instructions designed to prevent discovery of where their Passover would be eaten. They were to follow **a man bearing a pitcher of water.** In a land where "women bear water jars and men carry water-skins"[9] the sign would be clear enough.

**Wheresoever** that man should **go in,** they were to inquire of **the goodman**[10] ("householder") **of the house** about a guest room

---

[6]See on 3:19 for a discussion of his name.

[7]In the popular sense, as the following words ("when they killed the passover") show. The Feast of Unleavened Bread began on Nisan 15.

[8]See note on vv. 1-2 for a discussion of the Passover and the Feast of Unleavened Bread.

[9]Connick, *op. cit.,* p. 368.

[10]"Beautiful old English for the head of the family" (IB, VII, 873).

where **the Master** and His disciples could **eat the passover** (14). They could expect to find **a large upper room furnished** (15) "with carpets and cushions, prepared for the meal by being furnished with a table and with couches."[11]

To **make ready** the Passover was no small task. "The Passover was a formal meal and required bitter herbs such as lettuce, chicory, and endives, a sauce (charosheth), water, wine, and unleavened cakes, in addition to the lamb which must be brought from the Temple and roasted."[12] It was customarily consumed with a great deal of ceremony and ritual.[13] It is an attractive hypothesis that this home may have been that of John Mark, a place which later figured in the activity of the Jerusalem church (Acts 12:12; 1:13).

When the disciples had gone **forth . . . into the city** (16), they **found** it as Jesus **had said** and there prepared **the passover.**

### 5. *Prediction of Betrayal* (14:17-21)

The Passover meal had been prepared, **and in the evening**[14] Jesus **cometh with the twelve** (17) to commemorate Israel's escape from Egypt and the birth of her life as a nation. It was a sacred hour intended to strengthen the brotherhood and bind the Chosen People to God.

It is believed that the guests at the Passover meal reclined on couches, about on a level with the tables, each person on his left arm, his feet extending outward. **As they** (18) thus observed the paschal feast, Jesus spoke a frightening word, **One of you . . . shall betray me.** Dismayed and **sorrowful,** the Twelve began **one by one** to ask, " 'Surely it is not I' "[15] (19, Taylor). Underlining the horror of the crime, Jesus replied, **It is one of the twelve, that dippeth with me** in the "same"[16] **dish** (20) (Ps. 41:9; John 13:18). During the meal a common **dish** or bowl, containing the sauce, was passed from one to another. Into this bowl the

[11]Earle, *op. cit.,* p. 165.

[12]Earle, *et al.,* ENT, pp. 149-50. It has been noted (NBC, p. 835) that the account of the Last Supper makes no reference to a lamb and that one may not have been used by Him who was the Lamb of God.

[13]Cf. Connick, *op. cit.,* pp. 369-70, for a description in detail.

[14]See discussion on vv. 1-2 and vv. 12-16.

[15]In the language of the original a negative reply is expected.

[16]An alternate reading (see RSV, NEB, *Amplified NT*), stressing the perfidy of Judas' treachery.

bitter herbs or cakes of unleavened bread were dipped. **Treachery after such close fellowship was unthinkable.**

The patience, devotion, self-restraint, and suffering love of Jesus in this hour are ineffable. He submitted to the divine necessity of His sacrifice: **The Son of man indeed goeth, as it is written of him** (21) (Isa. 53:12, Septuagint). He did not isolate Judas nor humiliate him, but proffered His redeeming love in one last word of warning and appeal: **Woe to that man** through **whom** (perhaps suggesting that Judas was a link in some nefarious scheme) **the Son of man is betrayed!** Judas may still have been present when Jesus said, "It would have been better for that man if he had not been born" (RSV). Men bear the responsibility for their crimes even though God in His sovereign will uses them to advance His kingdom. "The fact that God turns the wrath of man to his praise does not excuse the wrath of man."[17]

Matthew (26:25) and John (13:26) both imply that Jesus pointed out Judas as the betrayer. Hunter suggests that John and Judas may have been on either side of Jesus; in the reclining position a word could have been given them not heard by the rest.[18] At some time during the meal, not indicated by Mark, Judas left the light and love of that fellowship and went out into the dark, never to return (John 13:27, 30).

### 6. *The Last Supper* (14:22-25)

As they were eating the Passover meal,[19] a lengthy occasion embodying considerable sacred ceremony, **Jesus took bread . . . blessed** (22) the Father who had given it, **brake it** (cf. 6:41; 8:6), and **gave to them.** Earlier in His ministry Jesus had taught that He was the Bread from Heaven, and that unless men ate His flesh and drank His blood, they would have no life in them

---

[17]Cranfield, *op. cit.,* p. 424.

[18]*Op. cit.,* p. 136.

[19]It seems reasonable to believe that this is what Mark is saying. However, John places the Passover a day later, so that Jesus was dying on the Cross at precisely the same time as the paschal lambs were being slain in the Temple (cf. John 18:28; 19:14, 31, 42). In that case, the Last Supper would have been either "a hurried anticipation of the Passover . . . or Passover *Kiddush* ('sanctification'), i.e., a social-religious meal, held by groups of pious Jews, in order to prepare for the Passover" (Hunter, *op. cit.,* pp. 134-35). In either case, the presence of the Passover would have been uppermost in the minds of the disciples, "so that, in one sense, the question is almost irrelevant" (Cole, *op. cit.,* p. 214).

(John 6:51, 53). Perhaps the disciples recalled this and began to see what Jesus meant. In any event, the injunction, **Take, eat: this is my body,** remained in their hearts.

Taking **the cup** (23), which was passed around during the paschal meal, having **given thanks** (*eucharistesas* = Eucharist), **he said unto them,** " 'This is my blood of the covenant' "[20] (24, RSV; cf. Exod. 24:8), **which is shed for many** (Isa. 53:11-12). As Paul had recorded (I Cor. 11:23-26), even before the writing of Mark, the sacrament of the Lord's Supper was thus instituted.

Although Jesus solemnly affirmed that He would never again **drink** of the cup with them, He looked beyond the Cross and the tomb to a time of fellowship with them when He would **drink it new in the kingdom of God** (25), after the resurrection and in the heavenlies. With Christ, the last word is always one of hope.

### 7. *The Scattering of the Sheep* (14:26-31)

The Passover meal concluded with the singing of a **hymn** (26), in this case probably the second part of the Hallel (Ps. 115: 118).[21] Probably on their way out to **the mount of Olives,** half a mile east of Jerusalem, Jesus made a startling announcement. **All ye shall be offended** (27), i.e., "stumble," or "fall away." When **the shepherd** is smitten, **the sheep** are **scattered** (Zech. 13:7).

Such words must have brought great perplexity and distress to the minds of the disciples. Only slowly did they come to understand that the Son of Man was also the Suffering Servant. This was not the last word, however. **After that I am risen, I will go before you into Galilee** (28), their home province in the north, now some distance away. "Jesus scarcely ever referred to His death without looking beyond it."[22] Though His death would scatter **the sheep,** His resurrection would bring the Shepherd back to reunite them.[23]

---

[20]Although the word *new* does not have adequate MS support, it is theologically accurate; the whole statement reflects Jer. 31:31 and Ezek. 37:26.

[21]Psalms of praise so called because they begin (Ps. 113:1) with "Hallelujah."

[22]NBC, p. 835.

[23]The word *proaxo,* "I will go before," continues the analogy of a shepherd leading his sheep.

Jesus was never unprepared. The colt was ready when He needed it for the entry into Jerusalem. The upper room was available and furnished when He sent His disciples to see the "goodman" of the house. Judas and the chief priests did not take Jesus by surprise. However bitter the disappointment may have been, the falling away of the disciples and the denial of Peter were not unexpected to Jesus.

Wounded at the announcement, Peter asserted with emphasis that *he* would not fall away whatever *the others* might do. With emphasis just as pointed, Jesus replied, **This day . . . this night, before the cock crow twice,**[24] "you yourself will disown me three times" (30, Goodspeed). With inordinate vehemence, protesting "too much, methinks,"[25] Peter bludgeoned down his fears and professed readiness to **die** with Jesus. It is sometimes forgotten that Peter was not alone in his protestations. **Likewise also said they all** (31).

Two conclusions may be drawn from this experience. First, apostasy is a real possibility (cf. I Cor. 10:12). The example of Peter, however, is better than that of Judas; though a man fail, he can repent and be a stronger disciple forever after. Second, divine foreknowing is consistent with human freedom and responsibility. The knowledge of Jesus concerning forthcoming events was not the *cause* of them.

### 8. *The Agony of Gethsemane* (14:32-42)

Jesus and the disciples now **came** to the mount of Olives, to a particular **place** (32) called **Gethsemane** ("oil press"). John (18:1) describes it as a "garden," possibly a private walled area among the olive trees still characteristic of that mount. It was probably a place they had often visited (Luke 22:39), known to Judas as well as to the rest.

The night of the Passover was to be "a night of watching kept to the Lord by all the people of Israel throughout all their generations" (Exod. 12:42, RSV). Knowing what events lay before Him during that dark night, Jesus felt His great need of prayer and fellowship. He wanted His friends nearby even as He prayed alone.

[24]"The time is defined with ascending accuracy" (Cranfield, *op. cit.*, p. 429). "The cock-crowing marks the third watch of the night" (Robertson, *op. cit.*, p. 383).

[25]Shakespeare, *Macbeth*, Act III, Scene II.

Leaving eight of the disciples at the entrance to the garden, Jesus took the privileged inner circle further into Gethsemane. He was thus ringed about with two circles of followers who were to serve as guards of a sort. Those who had once witnessed His glory would now share His agony.

The full import of the Cross, and what it meant to bear the sin of the world, began to come over Jesus. Mark describes it in the strongest possible language. "Horror and dismay came over him" (34, NEB). It was as if He were sick unto death. " 'My heart is nearly breaking . . . Stay here and keep watch for me' " (34, Phillips). The shadow of the Cross had long lain across His path, but now it loomed before Him a few scant hours away. The cost of rejecting the easy way became very clear. "Now in the garden Satan returns in force and in all his majesty as the prince of this world, to avenge his earlier defeat; and Jesus sees now in appalling immediacy the full cost of his steadfast obedience."[26]

"Going a little farther" (35, RSV), as our Lord always does, Jesus **fell on the ground, and prayed.** Earle notes that the imperfect tense here "seems to suggest the picture of Jesus staggering and stumbling until He fell on the ground, crying aloud in agony of soul."[27] The prayer life of Jesus is both an example and a rebuke to prayerless Christians.

The request of Jesus in this prayer is evidence both of His humanity and of His unalterable devotion to the will of the Father. As a man He recoiled from the Cross and the separation from God this would bring. In His identification with sinful men, Jesus became the Object of God's wrath against sin (cf. II Cor. 5:21; Mark 15:34). Now He pleaded with the One for whom **all things are possible** (36) to **take away this cup . . . nevertheless . . . what thou wilt.**

It is significant that Jesus saw the **cup** of suffering as proffered to Him by the **Father.** The hour of anguish or frightening responsibility is bearable when it is the God of holiness and love who beckons us to endure it. In the end one will be stronger if he accepts the cup than he will be if he refuses it. Submission to the will of God is the soul of a Spirit-filled life.

> *May Thy Spirit divine fill this being of mine.*
> *Not my will, but Thy will, be done, Lord, in me.*[28]

---

[26]Cranfield, *op. cit.*, p. 432.
[27]*Op. cit.*, p. 170.
[28]© 1951 by Lillenas Publishing Co.

The loneliness of Him who has "trodden the winepress alone" (Isa. 63:3) was never more poignant than when Jesus returned to **Peter** (37) and the others to find **them sleeping.** Only a few hours before He had urged, "Watch ye therefore . . . lest coming suddenly he find you sleeping" (13:35-36). His reproach singled out **Peter,** whom He now addressed as **Simon** rather than Cephas ("rock"). No reply is recorded. The hour *was* late and the disciples *had* partaken of a full meal, and so **the flesh** (38) would incline to sleep in spite of a **spirit truly . . . ready.** Nevertheless they were cautioned again to be watchful and prayerful, a needful and effective combination.

A second time Jesus **went away** (39) the distance of "a stone's cast" (Luke 22:41) **and prayed** as before. Returning again to the hoped-for fellowship of the disciples, He found them asleep as before. In sad embarrassment they **wist** not **what to answer him** (40) (cf. 9:6). When Jesus had prayed "the third time, saying the same words" (Matt. 26:40), He returned with His soul at rest to announce that His **hour** had now **come** (41). "'Still asleep? Still resting? The End is far away? The Hour has struck.'"[29]

Never taken by surprise and always prepared, Jesus called the disciples to get up and join Him[30] as He was delivered up **into the hands of sinners** (41). What pathos in the words, "'My betrayer is upon us'" (42, NEB)!

The incident in Gethsemane suggests this significant contrast: (1) The sorrowing Master, 32-36; (2) The sleeping disciples, 37-42.

### 9. *The Arrest* (14:43-50)

At the very moment that Jesus was arousing the sleepy disciples and urging them to face the betrayer with Him, **Judas** (43) appeared, along with a motley crowd armed with swords and cudgels. The betrayer, who was **one of the twelve,**[31] knew where the Master would be and must have suspected that the disciples would be asleep. The implication is that the **great multitude,**

[29]Taylor (*op. cit.*, p. 557) accepts the alternate reading, *apechei to telos.* However, most scholars believe *apechei* should stand alone and be translated, "It is enough!" or words to that effect.

[30]The words, **Let us go** (42), may represent a military expression and mean, "Forward!"

[31]An identification Mark never allows us to forget.

although authorized by the Sanhedrin,[32] was hurriedly assembled and was something of a mob or gang.

A man of worldly wisdom, Judas left nothing to chance. Those accompanying him were armed to forestall any resistance (cf. Luke 22:38). Lest in the darkness there be confusion as to who Jesus was, the traitor had made prior arrangements to identify Him with the typical salutation of a devoted follower. The **token** (44) or "sign" was to be a **kiss** and greeting. Going straight to Jesus, he hailed Him as **Master** (45) and "kissed him affectionately"[33] (45, Goodspeed). This was a device not only to identify Jesus but also to hold Him until His arrest. Without doubt apprehensive **(lead him away safely,** 44), Judas must have felt some relief when the mob **laid their hands on** (46) Jesus and seized Him.

The motives of Judas remain inscrutable. How one who lived so near to Jesus during His ministry could close his own soul to the Son of Man is perplexing and disturbing. It is a sobering thought to consider that one chosen by Jesus, and one who commanded sufficient confidence to be responsible for the funds of the group (John 12:6), could be guilty of such treachery. "If you feel sure that you are standing firm, beware! You may fall" (I Cor. 10:12, NEB).

In a last futile gesture of disappointment, bewilderment, and rage, "a certain one of those who stood by"[34] (47, NASB) **drew a sword,** and struck a slave of **the high priest,** cutting **off his ear.** It was fortunate for Peter, not to mention the victim, that the slave (one "Malchus," John 18:10) evidently ducked his head, leaving only the ear exposed.[35]

In a protest against the lawlessness of His seizure, Jesus confronted the crowd with a question which staggered them (cf. John 18:6): " 'Have you come out as against a robber, with swords and clubs to capture me?' " (48, RSV) He reminded them that day

---

[32]**The chief priests and the scribes and the elders** (43) were the constituent elements of that body.

[33]The compound verb (*katephilesen*), translated *kissed,* "denotes a certain profuseness in the act" (Gould, *op. cit.,* p. 274).

[34]John (18:10), who wrote after Peter's death, plainly states it was "Simon Peter."

[35]The parallels (Matt. 26:51-53; Luke 22:49-51; John 18:10-11) should be read for other details.

after day[36] He had taught them **in the temple** (49) grounds. Why had they not seized Him there, if their charge was just?

Because it is useless to reason with moral blindness, and because He had already lifted the "cup" of suffering (36) to His lips, Jesus submitted to their indignities with the words, "But let the scriptures be fulfilled!" (49, Goodspeed) This was but another way of saying, "Nevertheless not what I will, but what thou wilt" (36).

When the disciples saw that Jesus did not intend to resist and that heaven did not interfere, **they all** (50), to the last man, **forsook him, and fled.** He was not the Messiah they had looked for, in the hope that He would redeem Israel (Luke 24:21). Their failure was not so much one of courage as of faith. "But doubt removes courage; the disciples fled because their faith wavered."[37]

### 10. *The Anonymous Young Witness* (14:51-52)

Why did Mark include this brief and apparently trivial episode? Matthew and Luke, who incorporate almost all of Mark's Gospel, omit these verses. The most reasonable explanation is that this is a personal reminiscence. However, some have spiritualized it in terms of Amos 2:16 and Gen. 39:12, or relate it to 16:5.

When it is recalled that the earliest center of the Jerusalem church was the home of Mary, the mother of Mark (Acts 12:12), it is at least probable that the Last Supper took place in the upper room of that house. It is further possible that John Mark himself, somehow awakened by the dramatic events of the night, **followed** (51, literally, "followed with") Jesus and was a witness to all that transpired in the garden.[38] In any event, the **young man** was so close he barely escaped arrest. The men **laid hold on him,** but **he left the linen cloth** (52), which had been **cast about** him, **and fled.**[39]

This little story is surely Mark's "modest way of saying, 'I was there.' "[40]

---

[36]Possibly suggesting a more extensive teaching ministry than Mark's brief account indicates.

[37]Gould, *op. cit.,* p. 275.

[38]Cf. Barclay, *op. cit.,* pp. 365-66.

[39]The word translated **naked** (*gymnos*) may also be rendered "scantily clad."

[40]Hunter, *op. cit.,* p. 142.

B. THE TRIALS, CRUCIFIXION, AND BURIAL, 14:53—15:47

1. *The Ecclesiastical Trial* (14:53-65)

The Gospels record that Jesus was examined in four trials before He was finally put to death. The first was before Annas (John 18:12-14, 19-24), a former high priest, several of whose sons and sons-in-law followed him in office. The second is the one here recorded. It was conducted by **the high priest** (54), Caiaphas (Matt. 26:57; John 18:13). The third was in the presence of Pilate (noted in all the Gospels), and the fourth before Herod Antipas (Luke 23:6-12).[41]

Obviously expecting the arrest and detention of Jesus, the several elements of the Sanhedrin were **assembled** in the palace of Caiaphas, where his father-in-law, Annas, may also have been. It was the intent of **the council** (55) to secure the condemnation of Jesus under Jewish law before handing Him over to Pilate for execution under Roman law. Whether the Jewish authorities had the power to impose capital punishment is a moot question.

In the meantime Peter, accompanied by John,[42] had **followed** Jesus (albeit **afar off**) "right into the courtyard of the high priest" (54, RSV). The spring night was chilly, so Peter **sat with the servants** ("attendants," Goodspeed) in the firelight and **warmed himself**.[43] Love and fear mingled in Peter's heart. It is entirely possible that he was close enough to witness the trial, although the details may have come later from some member of the council (cf. John 7:50; 19:39; Acts 6:7).

Acting not as impartial judges but as vindictive prosecutors, the members of **the council sought for** (55) witnesses whose testimony would condemn Jesus. Their effort was in vain; for those who testified gave a garbled account of what Jesus had taught, and **their witness agreed not together,** i.e., "their statements did not tally" (56, NEB). Jewish law (Deut. 19:15) required that at least two witnesses must give consistent testimony before a charge could be sustained.

Certain **false** witnesses (57) recalled that Jesus had said something about destroying a **temple . . . made with hands** (58)

---

[41]See Major, *op. cit.,* p. 180, for supporting evidence.

[42]See John 18:15. This is probably why Peter was able to get so close.

[43]The word for *fire,* in this case *(phos),* "is never used of the *fire itself,* but of *the light* of the fire" (Vincent, *op. cit.,* p. 229). It was this light which drew the attention of the maid to Peter (66).

and of building **another made without hands.** This report was evidently a blend of two statements Jesus had made, one concerning the destruction of the Temple (13:2), the other concerning His own death and resurrection (John 2:19-22). Once more **their witness** (59) "did not tally."

Failing in the attempt to find damaging testimony, **the high priest stood up in the midst** (60) of the council, making up "by bluster the lack of evidence,"[44] and sought to browbeat Jesus into hasty and incriminating answers. The testimony of the witnesses required no answer and received none. Jesus **held his peace** (61). However when Caiaphas came to the nub of the matter—the implied claim of Jesus to be the Messiah—it was different. When required upon oath (Matt. 26:63) to answer the question, **Art thou the Christ?** Jesus said openly, **I am** (62). He was indeed the Messiah, **the Son of the Blessed.**[45]

As we have seen, throughout His ministry Jesus kept His messiahship veiled from the public lest its disclosure defeat His mission. The hour had now come for Him to make His claim in fullest terms before the highest authority of His nation. **Ye shall see the Son of man sitting on the right hand of power, and coming in the clouds of heaven** (cf. Ps. 110:1; Dan. 7:13).

If it is sometimes wrong to speak, it is also at times a crime to remain silent. Jesus chose to speak and thus to give His enemies all the evidence they sought. Rending "his mantle" (63, RSV), in a gesture of deep feeling,[46] **the high priest** said, **What need we any further witnesses?** By means of a leading question, improper because self-incriminating, Caiaphas accomplished what all the false witnesses had failed to do. **They all condemned him to be guilty of death** (64), i.e., liable to that punishment.

It has been repeatedly noted that the Sanhedrin broke most of its own laws of procedure in this preliminary trial and condemnation. As many as fourteen such violations have been totaled.[47] The council was not permitted to meet at night,[48] nor on a feast day. If a defendant was sentenced to death, the penalty

---

[44]Robertson, *op. cit.*, p. 387.

[45]The Messiah was not always regarded as the Son of God, but Jesus had already intimated that He was (see Matt. 11:27; Luke 10:22).

[46]"The law forbade the High Priest to rend his garment in private troubles (Lev. 10:6; 21:10), but when acting as a judge, he was required by custom to express in this way his horror of any blasphemy uttered in his presence" (Swete, *op. cit.*, p. 360).

[47]IB, VII, 887.

[48]See 15:1 for the attempt to "legalize" the action.

could not be carried out until a night had passed. Each member of the court was to be polled individually, but Jesus apparently was sentenced by group action. Relentless malice and implacable hatred crushed legal restraint in destroying Jesus.

Evidently it was members of the Sanhedrin who engaged in the inexcusable abuse and ridicule which followed. They then turned Jesus over to the officers or guards, who "received him with blows" (65, RSV). "He came unto his own, and his own received him not" (John 1:11).

### 2. *The Three Denials of Peter* (14:66-72)

Doubtless neither too much nor too little should be made of Peter's fall. Peter did show considerable courage in following Jesus right into the courtyard of the palace, where the trial was in progress (54). Moreover, only Peter could have told this story in the first place and preserved it for all time. His gratitude for the grace of God must have been boundless.

Nevertheless, "light thoughts on sin ultimately lead to light thoughts on redemption, and ultimately rob the cross of its glory."[49] The bitterness of Peter's tears (72) gives some indication of how seriously he regarded his own failure of courage and faith.

Out in the courtyard, around which the rooms of the palace were built, Peter had been warming himself at a fire (54). That this did not preclude some visual contact with Jesus is evident from Luke 22:61. **One of the maids of the high priest** (66), who perhaps had seen Peter with Jesus in the Temple area, noticed him in the firelight. Gazing "intently at him" (67, *Amplified NT*), she identified Peter, perhaps contemptuously, with the words, " 'You also were with the Nazarene, Jesus' " (67, RSV). He denied any knowledge of what she meant and **went out into the porch** (68), or vestibule, where he would be less conspicuous. **And the cock crew.**[50]

When the maid saw him again, she spread the word to bystanders: **This** man **is one of them** (69).[51] For the second time

---

[49]Cole, *op. cit.,* p. 231.

[50]Cranfield (*op. cit.,* p. 447) believes this reading, as well as the last clause in v. 70, should be retained "in spite of the impressive witnesses for omission."

[51]Even a cursory reading of the Gospels will reveal differences in the accounts of Peter's denials. These do not affect the historicity of the event. "Obviously, there is no collusion here" (Major, *op. cit.,* p. 183).

Peter denied any association with Jesus, fearful that a confession of the truth would lead to his arrest. The bystanders quite naturally took up the charge and insisted that Peter was a follower of Jesus. The broad, rough accent of his Galilean dialect was proof enough for the Judeans.

Now quite beside himself with terror and shame, Peter took an oath and swore that he did not know the **man of whom** (71) they spoke. It is commonly supposed that Peter lapsed back into the profanity probably quite characteristic of Galilean fishermen. This is obviously a distinct possibility, but it is not the meaning of the words here. The verb **to curse** (*anathematizo*) means to be bound with an oath and is used elsewhere in the New Testament only in Acts 23:12, 14, 21. The verb **to swear** (*omnyo*) means to swear or affirm by an oath and is used with reference to God in Acts 2:30. *The Amplified NT* gives the sense of the verse: "Then he commenced invoking a curse on himself [if he were not telling the truth] and to swear, I do not know the Man..." (71).

Immediately and for **the second time the cock crew** (72).[52] Peter, stabbed broad awake, remembered **the word** of **Jesus** (cf. also Luke 22:61) that he would **deny** Him **thrice** before **the** cock crew **twice.** "And he broke down[53] and wept" (72, RSV). The cowardice of Peter's heart was corrected later by the baptism of the Holy Spirit and by the purity of heart that this experience brings (Acts 15:8-9).

### 3. *Jesus Before Pilate* (15:1-5)

**Straightway in the morning** (1), i.e., as early as possible, the Sadducean **chief priests,** now leading the opposition, **held a consultation** with **the whole council** (Sanhedrin) to prepare their case against Jesus in the Roman court. The ecclesiastical "trial" during the night had fixed the crime of Jesus as blasphemy, but this would carry no weight with Pilate. The charge before the Roman procurator must be of a political nature and cast Jesus in the role of a threat to Caesar. With this accusation in mind and probably in writing, they **bound Jesus** and led Him to **Pilate.**

---

[52]This may refer to a note of time, "a bugle call which was called the *gallicinium* . . . Latin for the *cockcrow*" (Barclay, *op. cit.,* p. 371). If so, it would signal the change of the guard, probably at three o'clock in the morning.

[53]The exact meaning of this word, *epibalon,* is uncertain.

Pilate, who governed Judea and Samaria, A.D. 26-36, was disliked by the Jews and was finally recalled because of the harsh control he exercised over his subjects. If Pilate could only have known that it was he who was on trial! Whenever the Apostles' Creed is repeated, the judgment of history upon him is remembered. Our Lord "suffered under Pontius Pilate."

Noting the charge against Jesus, **Pilate asked him,** " 'You, are you the king of the Jews?' " (2, Earle) Because Palestine was a seething cauldron of political unrest, the Roman governors were watchful for signs of insurrection. The confession of Messiahship during the night (14:62) had been twisted into a political offense. The reply of Jesus, **Thou sayest it,** probably means, "Yes, I am, but not in the way you mean it."[54]

As "the high priests kept heaping accusations upon him" (3, Goodspeed), and Jesus remained silent, Pilate was puzzled **and asked him again . . . Answerest thou nothing?** (4) "But Jesus made no further answer—to Pilate's astonishment" (5, Phillips). It was quite clear that this uncommon Prisoner was innocent of the charge.

Sometimes silence spells tragedy. It was so in the days of Amos, when Israel turned to false gods:

> . . . I will send a famine on the land. It will not be a famine of
> bread or water, but of hearing the words of the Lord.[55]

It was so with Pilate.

### 4. Jesus Bar-Joseph and Jesus Barabbas (15:6-15)

It was evidently the custom of Pilate, a man described by the Jews as merciless and stubborn, to soften his rule a bit at the Passover season by releasing **one prisoner, whomsoever they desired** (6). No certain knowledge of this practice, apart from the Gospels, has come to light, but "the granting of amnesty at festival times is well known."[56]

Considerable sentiment had apparently developed in Jerusalem for the release of **one named Barabbas** (7) ("son of a father") because of his part **in the insurrection.**[57] Perhaps he

---

[54]John's account (18:33-37) relates a fuller conversation between Pilate and Jesus inside "the judgment hall." Cf. all the parallels for a more complete picture.

[55]Amos 8:11, Phillips.

[56]Connick (*op. cit.,* p. 389) cites Roman custom, also a rule from the Talmud which "may reflect Jewish practice in Jesus' time."

[57]Some well-known Jewish uprising against Rome.

was a member of the fanatical *Sicarii* ("assassins"), whose trade-
mark was the daggers they carried. Barabbas had shed blood.
A multitude of Barabbas' supporters "came up"[58] to Pilate's
palace and began to beg him to do as he habitually had done for
them (8). "To the chief priests this was a heaven-sent opportunity."[59] With their own crowd present, it would be easy to fan the
clamor for the release of the insurrectionist.

Pilate's thoughts were different. Assured in his own mind of
Jesus' innocence, he saw in the request of **the multitude** an opportunity to save Him, **for he knew that the chief priests (10)** were
motivated by **envy.** But his question, **Will ye that I release . . .
the King of the Jews? (9)** was received with roars of opposition.
**The chief priests moved**[60] **the people (11)** to choose **Barabbas**
instead.

In certain dependable manuscripts of Matthew, the name of
the insurrectionist is "Jesus Barabbas" (27:16 f.), and it is quite
likely that the same phrase once appeared in 15:7. The original
choice of the crowd may well have been between "Jesus Bar-
Joseph" and "Jesus Barabbas."[61] The prisoner they chose "was
just what the Jews accused Jesus of being, a man who had
raised a revolt against the Roman power."[62] How *lawless* the
human heart, but how *sublime* the divine atonement (cf. Heb.
2:9)!

The question is often raised how the Jerusalem crowds
could be so fickle as to acclaim Jesus on Sunday and yet cry
for His death on Friday. Such fickleness is not unknown (cf. Acts
14:11-19), but another explanation is sounder here. The answer
is simply that these were two different crowds. The pilgrims
who rejoiced as Jesus entered the Holy City perhaps were not
even aware of the events of Thursday night and early Friday
morning. As noted above, the multitude at Pilate's palace certainly contained the chief priests' own supporters and very probably also included a crowd already bent on the release of
Barabbas.

Torn by the conflict between his Roman sense of justice
and his unworthy desire to please the people,[63] **Pilate . . . said**

[58]A better attested reading than **crying aloud (8).**
[59]Barclay, *op. cit.,* p. 376.
[60]"*Shook up* like an earthquake" (Robertson, *op. cit.,* p. 393).
[61]Cf. Cranfield, *op. cit.,* p. 450, and Connick, *op. cit.,* p. 390.
[62]Gould, *op. cit.,* p. 285.
[63]See also Matt. 27:19.

**again unto them,** " 'Then what shall I do with the man you call the king of the Jews?' " (12, Goodspeed)  The question was in reality a taunt and was heavy with sarcasm. But in its essence it is a question which still haunts men. Eternal destiny hangs on the answer they make. The crowd's response was immediate and vigorous: **Crucify him** (13).

Undoubtedly prodded by his own conscience (cf. Matt. 27:24) and yet eager to test the strength of public pressure, **Pilate** replied, **Why, what evil hath he done?** (14)  The resounding shout gave him the answer to his crafty question. "Their voices rose to a roar, 'Crucify him!' " (14, Phillips)  Pilate made his decision as a political opportunist, morally weak and devoid of integrity. "Wishing to satisfy the crowd" (15, RSV), he set Barabbas free, and after scourging[64] Jesus, **delivered** him **to be crucified.** Just one more Galilean (cf. Luke 13:1)!

It is an interesting sidelight of early Christian history that Pilate was canonized by the Abyssinian church because of his belief in the innocence of Jesus. The Greek church gave his wife similar recognition. The judgment of history is different. Pilate could have released Jesus, and the Jews should have received Him. Both have tasted the judgment of Almighty God.

### 5. *The Mocking by the Soldiers* (15:16-20)

Pilate had given the command for Jesus "to be crucified" (15). It was the responsibility of the Roman soldiers to carry out his order. Perhaps while the Cross was being prepared, these tough, callous men, aliens on Judean soil, led Jesus away **into the hall** (16), i.e., the courtyard of the **Praetorium,** either Herod's royal palace (on the western edge of Jerusalem) or the Tower of Antonia (attached to the northwest corner of the Temple grounds).

What followed is shocking, but evidently it was a common occurrence.[65] It was a sort of sport or game with these military machines, whose prime loyalty was to Caesar and who had no regard for the Jews, especially for one who seemed to be a pretender to the imperial throne. As brutal as the mocking was, it may have caused Jesus less personal pain than some of the other indignities of the trials and Crucifixion.

---

[64]A brutal preparation for crucifixion. The whip of leather cords, carrying pieces of metal and bone, left the victim's back in shreds.

[65]Cf. Taylor, *op. cit.,* pp. 646-48.

Calling **together the whole band** ("battalion," RSV),[66] the soldiers attired Jesus with grotesque symbols of kingship and made Him an Object of their jest and abuse. Clothing Him with "a scarlet military cloak . . . a part of their own uniform"[67] (cf. Matt. 27:28), and pressing a wreath of **thorns . . . about his head** (17),[68] they saluted Him as the Emperor[69] **of the Jews** (18). In a series of continuous insults (evident from the imperfect tense), **they smote him on the head with a reed** (19) ("scepter"; cf. Matt. 27:29, also 36), spat **upon him,** and bowed **their knees** in mock homage (Isa. 50:6).

The buffoonery by the "goon-squad" over, they removed the **purple** cloak, reclothed Jesus with His own garments, and "took him out of the city to crucify him" (20, Goodspeed).

Ridicule and mockery have always been among the most effective weapons of Satan. Whether the scorn be crude or refined, from barbarians or from men of learning, it is certain to come. Jesus has warned the Church: "The servant is not above his lord" (John 15:20).

### 6. *The Crucifixion* (15:21-41)

*a. The Forenoon of Ignominy* (15:21-32). As the centurion and his four soldiers led Jesus through the streets of Jerusalem, en route to the place of execution outside the walls (Heb. 13:12), the Master's physical strength evidently broke under the weight of the heavy crossbeam.[70] The strain of the harrowing events, from Gethsemane to the scourging and mocking by the soldiers, was crushing.

**One Simon a Cyrenian** (21) (a north African), just entering the city, was "impressed"[71] into the service of Rome and carried **the cross** for Jesus. Such civil compulsion normally aggravated the relationship between Jew and Roman. In this instance, something memorable must have transpired. Why would Mark record that **Simon** was **the father of Alexander and Rufus** if the family

---

[66]A *cohort* numbered 600 men, a *maniple* 200.

[67]Major, *op. cit.,* p. 188.

[68]"In cruel imitation of the laurel wreath worn by the Emperor" (*ibid.*).

[69]The meaning of **King** (*basileus*) to them.

[70]Part of a condemned person's punishment was to carry the horizontal piece of the cross. It weighed "about eighty or ninety pounds" (Connick, *op. cit.,* p. 392).

[71]Cf. Matt. 5:41, where the same word is used.

was unknown to his readers? (See Acts 11:20; 13:1; Rom. 16:3.) What he saw at the Crucifixion evidently led Simon to become a Christian convert.

The place of execution was **Golgotha** (22) (Aramaic) or Calvary (Latin), assumed to be a skull-shaped knoll outside the first-century walls of Jerusalem. The exact location is not agreed upon by competent authorities. In such a place of crucifixion, permanent upright beams would be located where passersby would see and take note. As a humanitarian measure, it was customary for women of the city to prepare drugs for the condemned in order to deaden the searing pain of crucifixion. In this case they offered Jesus "drugged wine" (23, Goodspeed), **but he received it not.** He preferred to keep a clear mind to the end (cf. 14:25). It was the third hour—nine o'clock in the morning—**when they . . . crucified him** (24).

Crucifixion was a harsh form of capital punishment which the Romans had used for generations. It was reserved for those of lower social or legal position. Roman citizens were exempt. The soldiers first of all removed the clothing of the condemned and **parted his garments** among themselves. The victim's arms were affixed to the crossbeam. His body was lifted to the upright post and supported by means of a peg. The feet were then impaled or the ankles tied to the post, a few inches above the ground. "Exposure, loss of blood, maltreatment by sadistic spectators, torture by insects, and impaired circulation caused excruciating pain."[72] Death was slow in coming and welcomed as a friend.

So that all observers might know the nature of the crime, a placard of wood covered with white gypsum was prepared, bearing in black letters the charge. This inscription was suspended from the prisoner's neck or carried before him by the executioners. The placard was then fastened to the cross above his head.[73] **The superscription** (26) of the charge against Jesus read, **THE KING OF THE JEWS.** John (19:21 ff.) makes it clear that Pilate found some revenge in the wording of the charge, for the chief priests resented it.

Prisoners were executed in groups, and it would seem that an execution had been planned, possibly for Barabbas and two of his accomplices. The men who were crucified with Jesus, **the one on his right hand, and the other on his left** (27), were rob-

[72]Connick, *op. cit.*, p. 393.
[73]*Ibid.*, p. 395.

bers (a stronger term than **thieves**) and probably rebels. It was James and John who had sought these positions at our Lord's right hand and at His left. They had professed their ability to occupy them (10: 37), but, indeed, they did *not* know what they asked. Jesus was, instead, **numbered with the transgressors.**[74]

Once more Jesus was subjected to taunts and ridicule.[75] All the jeers and abuse had one point: If Jesus be the Messiah, the Saviour of the world, **the King of Israel** (32), let Him prove it by a demonstration of supernatural power. Twentieth-century rabbis have been heard to make the same accusation—"Jesus of Nazareth was not the Messiah because He was a failure!" They that passed by railed on him, **wagging their heads** (29).[76] The Sadducean **chief priests** and the Pharisees **(scribes)** also "made sport of him to one another" (31, Goodspeed), saying, **He saved others; himself he cannot save.** Even the robbers **crucified** (32) with Jesus **reviled him.**

. . . *behold, and see if there be any sorrow like unto my sorrow* . . .[77]

Unwittingly, and with incredible moral blindness, those who mocked spoke the bitter truth. Jesus himself had said, "Whosoever will save his life shall lose it . . ." (8: 34), and, "Except a corn of wheat fall into the ground and die, it abideth alone . . ." (John 12: 24). This was the struggle of the Temptation and a continuing test during His public ministry. At times Jesus had been deeply troubled over the cost of redemption and wondered if He should ask the Father to save Him from "this hour." But He never yielded. "For this cause came I unto this hour" (John 12: 27).

The enemies of Jesus had long sought a miraculous confirmation of His claims (8: 11; cf. I Cor. 1: 22), **that we may see and believe.** But no supernatural sign would "change a Pharisee, a narrow-minded, formal, and hypocritical legalist, into a spiritual man, in sympathy with Christ's principles and purposes."[78] The only way to salvation is the way of the Cross and the Empty Tomb.

---

[74]Verse 28 is missing in the most significant MSS.

[75]"The Evangelists record six mockings of Jesus by (1) the High Priests' servants, (2) Herod Antipas and his soldiers, (3) the soldiers of the Roman garrison, (4) the general public, (5) priests and scribes, (6) the two crucified brigands" (Major, *op. cit.,* p. 189).

[76]"An oriental gesture of scorn" (Johnson, *op. cit.,* p. 255). Cf. Isa. 37: 22; Jer. 18: 16.

[77]Lam. 1: 12. Cf. *The Messiah,* by G. F. Handel, No. 30.

[78]Gould, *op. cit.,* p. 293.

   *b. Darkness at Midday* (15:33-39). **When the sixth hour
(noon) was come** (33), Jesus had been on the Cross three hours
(25).[79] From then until three o'clock in the afternoon **(the ninth
hour), there was darkness over the whole land.** This was only
one of the portents associated with the death of the Son of God.
Even if the result of natural causes, such as the black clouds of
the sirocco, the **darkness** was a prophetic symbol of judgment.

> On that day, the Lord God declares,
> I will make the sun go down at noon
> And darken the earth in broad daylight.[80]

   **At the ninth hour** (34), the strange cry came from the Cross,
**My God, my God, why . . . ?** The words of Jesus give us a
"Hebrew-tinged Aramaic version of Ps. 22:1."[81] The cry may
have been uttered originally in Hebrew, for the first two words
(as in Matt. 27:46) would then be more easily mistaken as a call
for Elijah (35).

   The real question is the meaning of these words. If they are
taken in the context of the New Testament as a whole, they give
us an insight into the cost of the atonement. In the will of God,
Jesus was "in all things . . . made like unto his brethren" (Heb.
2:17), except in respect to the experience of sin (Heb. 4:15). The
anguished cry of forsakenness must be seen in the light of 14:36;
II Cor. 5:21; and Gal. 3:13. "The burden of the world's sin, his
complete self-identification with sinners, involved not a felt, but
a real, abandonment by his Father. It is in the cry of dereliction
that the full horror of man's sin stands revealed."[82]

   **Some of** the bystanders supposed that Jesus was calling for
help from heaven, as their previous taunts had implied He should
(30-32). "See, he is calling Elijah" (35, Gould). Someone, probably a soldier, soaked a sponge with sour wine (cf. Ruth 2:14;
Ps. 69:21) and gave it to Him on a reed, **saying, Let alone; let
us see whether Elias will come to take him down** (36).

   The phrase **Let alone** raises the question as to who was
speaking. Matthew (27:49) says that "the rest [plural] said,
Let be" (singular). In Mark's account **saying** is singular in the
Greek, indicating that one person was speaking. A natural ex-

---

[79]On the apparent conflict with John 19:14, see Earle, *op. cit.*, p. 183.
[80]Amos 8:9, Phillips.
[81]Cranfield, *op. cit.*, p. 458.
[82]*Ibid.*

planation would be that Mark writes as though one bystander spoke for the group. Another solution assumes that the last part of verse 36 was spoken, as the words themselves seem to indicate, by the one who offered Jesus the sour wine. Gould offers this explanatory paraphrase: "Let me give him this, and so prolong his life, and then we shall get an opportunity to see whether Elijah comes to help him or not" (p. 295).

In that **hour,** after some six hours on the Cross,[83] **Jesus cried with a loud voice** (37) and expired. As the other Evangelists indicate,[84] the moment of separation from the Father passed, and Jesus died in peace and triumph. His last cry, perhaps the single word of John 19:30 (*tetelestai,* "It is finished"), was "the shout of a victor."[85] **The veil of the temple** (38), separating the holy of holies from the holy place, **was rent in twain,** giving us "boldness to enter into the holiest by the blood of Jesus" (Heb. 10:19), perhaps also pointing to the impending destruction of the Temple.[86]

The cumulative effect of Jesus' conduct from the scourging to the Crucifixion was to wrench an amazing confession from the hard-bitten **centurion** (39) who had **stood** facing Jesus. Hearing the shout of victory from the Cross, the man who was inured to savage death said, **Truly this man was the Son of God.**[87]

We find here: (1) The Crucifixion, 24-28; (2) The cruel mockery, 29-32; (3) The cries of Christ, 33-38; (4) The confession of the centurion, 39.

c. *The Women of Galilee* (15:40-41). The women's side of the Crucifixion story is told in this brief footnote. It is in tender contrast with the foregoing verses, and is a commentary on the life of the Church. Although "looking on from a distance" (40, *Amplified NT*), the **women** from Galilee were there and the disciples were not. The women shared in the burial (47) and were the first at the empty tomb (16:1). (They could thus have been among Mark's informants.) They were among those who

[83]Thought to be about half the time victims usually require to die.

[84]Luke and John each give three other "words" from the Cross. Matthew and Mark report the same utterances. Those from Luke are 23:34, 43, 46. Those from John are 19:26-27, 28, 30.

[85]IB, VII, 907.

[86]Acts 6:7 may give us a clue as to the effect of such a portent.

[87]Whatever **the centurion** may have meant (see Luke 23:47), it is clear what Mark intended (cf. 1:1).

had supported Jesus with their service and substance while He was in Galilee (cf. Luke 8:3) and had joined His band of pilgrims on the last journey to Jerusalem.

These choice spirits whose names Mark made immortal were: **Mary** of Magdala, who owed Jesus a special debt (see Luke 8:2); **Mary**, the mother of "the younger" **James** ("the son of Alphaeus," Matt. 10:3) **and of Joses;** and **Salome,** the mother of James and John (Matt. 27:56). They looked on with grief and shock but with love. "It is only love which can give us a hold on Christ that not even the most bewildering experiences can break."[88]

### 7. *The Burial of Jesus* (15:42-47)

"Crucified, dead, and buried." These blunt facts Christians have confessed for centuries. The death of Jesus was no illusion, for He was truly man as well as truly God, the God-man.

Jesus expired on Friday afternoon, about 3:00 p.m., a few hours before the Sabbath, which began at sunset. Friday was the day of preparation. No burials were permitted on the Sabbath, and the Law required that the body of Jesus be taken down from the Cross and buried before nightfall (Deut. 21:23).

With this sense of urgency, one **Joseph of Arimathaea,**[89] "a respected member of the Council" (43, NEB), i.e., the Sanhedrin, plucked up his courage and asked **Pilate** for **the body of Jesus.**[90] **Joseph** was a man of wealth (Matt. 27:57), of noble character (Luke 23:50), and a secret disciple of Jesus (John 19:38). He and Nicodemus were evidently among those "chief rulers" who believed on Jesus but did not confess Him publicly (John 12:42). It took the tragedy of the Cross to bring them out into the open (cf. John 12:32). Nevertheless **Joseph** was looking for **the kingdom of God** and was a man of faith. His was "a life lived in expectation of God's action in the world."[91]

One cannot but wonder what thoughts flooded Pilate's mind as Joseph made his courageous request. Startled at the report of Jesus' early death, Pilate summoned **the centurion** (44), who

---

[88]Barclay, *op. cit.,* p. 384.

[89]Possibly to be identified with Rathamin, about twenty miles northwest of Jerusalem (cf. I Sam. 1:1).

[90]Not only did Joseph risk the ire of Pilate, but also the ostracism of his fellow councillors.

[91]IB, VII, 910 (Exposition).

was well qualified to confirm that Jesus was in fact dead (39).
Pilate then **gave the body to Joseph** (45).

Mark succinctly and movingly notes five aspects of Joseph's
ministry to Jesus: He purchased **fine linen** (46), removed the
body from the Cross and wrapped it in the linen shroud (see
John 19:40), **laid him in** his own new rock-hewn **sepulchre**
(which was in a garden on a nearby hillside), **and rolled a** heavy
**stone** against **the door** of the tomb (as a protection against
marauders).

*Finis* (end)? No, *telos* (destination, goal)! ". . . History
shows that God never notices stones. Earth's finalities are never
his."[92]

The devoted women of Galilee (40-41) **beheld where he was
laid** (47), and made their plans to assist in the embalming after
the Sabbath (16:1; Luke 23:56). Many of the details Mark has
given us must have come from them.

[92]*Ibid.*

Section **VIII** *The Resurrection*

Mark 16:1-20

A. THE EMPTY TOMB, 16:1-8

In a few, swift strokes, Mark paints a picture of the ultimate proof that the gospel is of God: **Jesus of Nazareth . . . is risen** (6) from the dead, and is "declared to be the Son of God with power" (Rom. 1:4). One becomes weary both of those who magnify the differences in the several accounts and of those who labor over-much to reconcile them. A. M. Hunter has a barbed quote from Lessing on this point: " 'Cold discrepancy hunters, do ye not see then that the evangelists do not count the angels? There were not only two angels, there were millions of them.' "[1]

**Very early in the morning** (2), on **the first day of the week,**[2] the faithful women of Galilee (14:40-41, 47) **came unto the sepulchre.** On the previous evening, **when the sabbath was past,** they had purchased additional **spices** (cf. Luke 23:56) for the anointing of His body. As they approached the tomb, they expressed anxiety as to who would remove **the stone from the door** (3). Looking up (as the original language indicates),[3] they were puzzled to see that the very large **stone was rolled away** (4).

Stooping down to enter **into the sepulchre** (5), a chamber perhaps six or seven feet square and in height, they were terrified to see an angel sitting **on the right side.** He knew in advance why they had come: to seek **Jesus** (6), the **crucified.**[4] **He is risen; he is not here: behold the place.** "The three statements . . . are cumulative: (a) the central fact; (b) the reason why He is not seen; (c) the evidence that He has been there . . ."[5] **Be not affrighted.**[6]

No human eye witnessed the Resurrection, but the angels did. "So the angel's word to the woman . . . is as it were the

---

[1]*Op. cit.,* p. 154.

[2]Soon to be known as the Lord's day (Rev. 1:10).

[3]Suggesting either a downcast attitude or that the tomb was on a hill-side above them.

[4]This may be in the form of a question: Seek ye?

[5]IB, VII, 913.

[6]The word may also be translated "greatly amazed" and is so translated elsewhere in Mark (KJV). See 9:15; cf. 14:33.

412

mirror in which men were allowed to see the reflection of this eschatological event."[7]

**The young man ... clothed in ... white** then instructed them to go and to **tell his disciples** (7), especially **Peter** (lest he banish himself in shame), that they should keep their appointment with Him in **Galilee** (14:28). Startled beyond words, the women **fled from the sepulchre; for they trembled and were amazed** (8). For the moment, so great was their fright, "they said nothing about it to anyone" (8, *Amplified NT*). It was a different matter later, when understanding brought a surge of joy (Matt. 28:8; Luke 24:9).

The empty tomb has never been successfully explained away. If the enemies of Jesus could have produced the body, they would have destroyed the young faith. They did not because they could not. To believe that the disciples stole and hid the body in order to preach a fraud is beyond belief.[8] On the other hand, a great many disciples (cf. I Cor. 15:3-9) had no doubt whatever that they had seen the Lord. There are at least three great witnesses to the reality of the Resurrection: the Church, the New Testament, and the Lord's day. None would have come into existence unless Jesus had risen. "But now is Christ risen from the dead, and become the firstfruits of them that slept" (I Cor. 15:20).

This paragraph suggests: (1) The women's anxiety, 1-3; (2) The women's amazement, 4-6; (3) The women's assignment, 7-8.

## B. THE EPILOGUE, 16:9-20

These concluding verses pose what has been called "one of the major textual problems of the New Testament."[9] The facts are as follows. The two oldest and most reliable manuscripts (Vaticanus and Sinaiticus) omit these verses altogether and close the Gospel of Mark at 16:8. The verses are also missing from several other ancient manuscripts and versions.

Several fathers of the Early Church confirm this omission, including the great church historian Eusebius and the translator

---

[7]Cranfield, *op. cit.*, pp. 465-66; q.v. for a protest against the contemporary dismissal of angels as "pious fancy."

[8]"Even a Jew like Klausner pronounces this incredible" (Hunter, *op. cit.*, p. 157).

[9]NBC, p. 839.

of the Vulgate, Jerome. In addition, the earliest extant commentary on Mark ends at 16:8. Still other evidence might be advanced, including the fact that Matthew and Luke, who otherwise include almost all of Mark, do not use these verses as they are recorded here.

Another fact, not evident in the King James Version, should be noted. One Latin and several Greek manuscripts include a "shorter ending" (in addition to verses 9-20, the so-called "longer ending"), between verses 8 and 9. These "endings" are believed to be early but non-Markan attempts to complete the Gospel. It is just as serious a mistake to add to the Bible as it is to take away from it (Rev. 22:18-19).[10]

Some scholars believe that Mark intended to close his message with verse 8, not on a note of fear but on one of amazement.

Most scholars, however, believe that the abrupt ending at 16:8 means that the very end of the ancient scroll was damaged and thus lost, or that Mark was prevented from completing his Gospel, perhaps by martyrdom. The implication of 14:28 is that Mark originally recorded at least one appearance of Jesus in Galilee. The warm reference to Peter in verse 7 (cf. I Cor. 15:5) may suggest an unrecorded reconciliation with Jesus.

The following provides a handy summary of verses 9-20.[11]

9-11  are an abridged version of John 20:11-18 (the *Rabboni* story).

12-13  summarize Luke 24:13-35 (the walk to Emmaus).

14-15  recall Luke 24:36-49 and Matt. 28:16-20.

17-18  most of the signs here described can be paralleled in the Acts.

19-20  Cf. Acts 1:9-11.

Exposition of the content will be found at the appropriate places in Matthew, Luke, John, and the Acts.

The message of verses 15 to 20 is that the task of the Church is one of preaching and healing, to be done in the power of the ever-present Christ.

---

[10]See Earle, *op. cit.*, p. 20, for a helpful summary of the problem.

[11]Hunter, *op. cit.*, p. 156.

# BIBLIOGRAPHY

## I. BOOKS

ABBOTT-SMITH, G. *A Manual Greek Lexicon of the New Testament*. Edinburgh: T. & T. Clark, 1937.

ARNDT, W. F., and GINGRICH, F. W. (eds.). *A Greek-English Lexicon of the New Testament*. Chicago: The University of Chicago Press, 1957.

BARCLAY, WILLIAM. *The Daily Study Bible: The Gospel of Mark*. Philadelphia: The Westminster Press, 1954.

BRANSCOMB, B. HARVIE. *The Gospel of Mark*. "The Moffatt New Testament Commentary." Edited by JAMES MOFFATT. New York: Harper and Brothers Publishers, n.d.

BRIGHT, JOHN. *The Kingdom of God*. New York: Abingdon-Cokesbury, 1953.

BRUCE, A. B. "The Synoptic Gospels." *The Expositor's Greek Testament*. Edited by W. ROBERTSON NICOLL, Vol. I. Grand Rapids: Wm. B. Eerdmans Publishing Co., n.d.

COLE, R. A. *The Gospel According to St. Mark*. "The Tyndale New Testament Commentaries." Edited by R. V. G. TASKER. Grand Rapids: Wm. B. Eerdmans Publishing Co., 1961.

CONNICK, C. MILO. *Jesus: The Man, the Mission, and the Message*. Englewood Cliffs: Prentice-Hall, Inc., 1963.

CRANFIELD, C. E. B. *The Gospel According to Saint Mark*. "The Cambridge Greek Testament Commentary." New York and London: Cambridge University Press, 1959.

DUMMELOW, J. R. (ed.). *A Commentary on the Whole Bible*. New York: Macmillan Co., 1956 (reprint).

EARLE, RALPH, et al. *Exploring the New Testament*. Kansas City: Beacon Hill Press, 1955.

EARLE, RALPH. *The Gospel According to Mark*. "The Evangelical Commentary on the Bible." Edited by GEORGE A. TURNER, et al. Grand Rapids: Zondervan Publishing House, 1957.

GOULD, EZRA P. *A Critical and Exegetical Commentary on the Gospel According to St. Mark*. "The International Critical Commentary." Edited by S. R. DRIVER, et al. Edinburgh: T. & T. Clark, 1955 impression.

GRANT, F. C. "The Gospel According to St. Mark" (Exegesis). *The Interpreter's Bible*. Edited by GEORGE A. BUTTRICK, et al., Vol. VII. New York: Abingdon-Cokesbury Press, 1951.

*Harper's Bible Dictionary*. Edited by MADELEINE S. MILLER and J. LANE MILLER. Sixth ed. New York: Harper and Brothers, Publishers, 1959.

HUNTER, A. M. *The Gospel According to Saint Mark*. "A Torch Bible Commentary." Edited by DAVID L. EDWARDS, et al. New York: Collier Books, 1962 (reprint).

JACOB, PHILIP E. *Changing Values in College*. New York: Harper and Brothers, Publishers, 1957.

JOHNSON, SHERMAN E. *A Commentary on the Gospel According to St. Mark*. "Harper's New Testament Commentaries." New York: Harper and Brothers, Publishers, 1960.

LUCCOCK, HALFORD E. "The Gospel According to St. Mark" (Exposition). *The Interpreter's Bible.* Edited by GEORGE A. BUTTRICK, et al., Vol. VII. New York: Abingdon-Cokesbury Press, 1951.

MACLAREN, ALEXANDER. *Expositions of Holy Scripture: St. Mark.* Grand Rapids: Wm. B. Eerdmans Publishing Co., 1938 (reprint).

MAJOR, H. D. A. "The Gospel According to St. Mark: Text and Commentary." *The Mission and Message of Jesus,* by H. D. A. MAJOR, T. W. MANSON, and C. J. WRIGHT. New York: E. P. Dutton and Co., 1938.

MITTON, C. L. *The Good News.* "Bible Guides." Edited by WILLIAM BARCLAY and F. F. BRUCE. No. 13. London: Lutterworth Press, 1961.

*Oxford Annotated Bible.* Edited by HERBERT G. MAY and BRUCE M. METZGER. New York: Oxford University Press, 1962.

ROBERTSON, A. T. *Word Pictures in the New Testament,* Vol. I. Nashville: Broadman Press, 1930.

SALMOND, S. D. F. *St. Mark.* "The Century Bible." Edited by W. F. ADENEY. Edinburgh: T. C. and E. C. Jack, n.d.

SWETE, HENRY BARCLAY. *The Gospel According to St. Mark.* Grand Rapids: Wm. B. Eerdmans Publishing Co., 1956 (reprint).

SWIFT, C. E. GRAHAM. "The Gospel According to Mark." *The New Bible Commentary.* Edited by F. DAVIDSON. Grand Rapids: Wm. B. Eerdmans Publishing Co., 1953.

TAYLOR, VINCENT. *The Gospel According to St. Mark.* London: Macmillan and Co., Ltd., 1959.

TRENCH, ROBERT C. "Prayer." *The World's Great Religious Poetry.* Edited by CAROLINE M. HILL. New York: The Macmillan Co., 1943.

TRUEBLOOD, D. E. *Foundations for Reconstruction.* New York: Harper and Brothers, Publishers, 1946.

UNGER, MERRILL F. *Unger's Bible Dictionary.* Chicago: Moody Press, 1957.

VINCENT, MARVIN R. *Word Studies of the New Testament,* Vol. I. Grand Rapids: Wm. B. Eerdmans Publishing Co., 1946.

*Westminster Study Edition of the Holy Bible.* Edited by F. W. DILLISTONE, et al. Philadelphia: The Westminster Press, 1948.

## II. ARTICLES

CARTLEDGE, SAMUEL A. "The Gospel of Mark." *Interpretation,* IX, No. 2 (April, 1955), 186-99.

CRANFIELD, C. E. B. "Mark, Gospel of." *The Interpreter's Dictionary of the Bible.* Edited by GEORGE A. BUTTRICK, et al., Vol. III. New York: Abingdon Press, 1962.

DEASLEY, A. R. G. "The New Testament and Divorce." *Interchange,* I, No. 1 (Winter, 1961-62), 12-17.

REES, PAUL. "As in Thy Sight. *Christianity Today,* VI, No. 8 (Jan. 19, 1962), 10-12.

RICHARDSON, ALAN. "The Feeding of the Five Thousand." *Interpretation,* IX, No. 2 (April, 1955), 144-49.

SCHINDLER, JOHN A. "Your Mind Can Keep You Well." *Reader's Digest,* LV, No. 332 (December, 1949), 51-55.

416

*The Gospel According to*

# ST. LUKE

Charles L. Childers

# Introduction

Luke's Gospel has been called "the most beautiful book in the world," and, along with Acts, "the most ambitious literary undertaking of the ancient church." If such expressions of praise seem extravagant, they at least help to prepare one for the study of a work which is, beyond all doubt, both a very significant portion of the Bible and one of the literary masterpieces of ancient times.

## A. AUTHORSHIP

Both ancient tradition and modern scholarship agree that the author of the third Gospel was Luke, "the beloved physician" and companion of the Apostle Paul. Statements to the effect that Luke was the author of both the third Gospel and the Acts can be found as early as the second half of the second century; from that time on, tradition is unanimous in its support of this contention. In fact, there is no evidence that this Gospel was ever ascribed to any other author than Luke.

We can accept the verdict of tradition more readily when we remember that there were many spurious "gospels" which were falsely assigned to various apostles and other eyewitnesses of Christ's ministry. Luke however was neither an eyewitness nor was he prominent enough in the New Testament for a book to be assigned to him unless he was indeed the author.

Though Luke nowhere asserts that he is the author of either the third Gospel or the Acts, the internal evidence from the New Testament solidly supports the position that he was the author of both books. In the first place, it is evident that both Luke and the Acts were written by the same person. Both are addressed to the same man, Theophilus; and the Acts, in its preface, speaks of a "former treatise." Also, a close examination of the literary style and vocabulary of the two books reveals a similarity too close to be accounted for on any other ground than that they are the work of the same author.

Another link in this chain of evidence is formed by the famous "we" sections in Acts.[1] These passages clearly indicate that the author was a companion of Paul. Since Luke is the only one of Paul's known companions (with the exception of Titus)

[1]These passages are: Acts 16:10-17; 20:5-15; 21:1-18; 27:1—28:31.

419

who is not otherwise identified in the Acts, it seems obvious that he was the author.[2]

Very little is known about Luke. His name is mentioned only three times in the New Testament. In his Colossian letter (4:14) Paul refers to him as "the beloved physician," and in his Epistle to Philemon (24) Paul calls him his "fellowlaborer." Then in Paul's last letter—his Second Epistle to Timothy (4:11)—Luke is said to be Paul's only companion at the time the Epistle was written.

The "we" sections in Acts indicate that Luke joined Paul's party at Troas on his second missionary journey (16:10) and was a companion of Paul at least as far as Philippi. When the Apostle moved on to Thessalonica the third personal pronoun indicates that Luke was no longer with him. The next "we" section (20:5) shows that Luke again joined Paul's party as he was returning from Greece on his third missionary journey. He joined the missionary party at Philippi and accompanied it to Jerusalem. The final "we" section (27:1) indicates that Luke accompanied Paul on his voyage to Rome. He was with Paul in Rome at the time of the writing of the Epistles to Philemon and the Colossians and later at the time of the Second Epistle to Timothy—just before Paul's death.

There are a few interesting references to Luke in the writings of the early Church Fathers, but these references add little which can be accepted as fact, for the accounts are often contradictory. However, Paul's reference to him as a physician is not only in harmony with tradition, but the use of medical language in both the Gospel and Acts corroborates this assertion.[3]

## B. Place and Date of Writing

The ancient sources are either vague or silent about the place of writing. The Gospel could have been written at Caesarea while Paul was in prison there. This certainly must have been the time when Luke collected much of his material. It is also possible that Luke wrote his Gospel in Rome while Paul was in prison there. Though it could have been written somewhere else

---

[2]Since there was no early tradition in favor of Titus' authorship of these books, and since what is known about the author fits Luke much more than it does Titus, the latter can be dismissed as a possible author.

[3]William Kirk Hobart, *The Medical Language of St. Luke* (Grand Rapids: Baker Book House, 1954 [reprint]. Though this work has been partially discredited, its major thesis—that Luke's Gospel contains distinct medical terminology—is probably valid.

—in Greece or Asia Minor, after Paul's release from his first imprisonment in Rome—Caesarea seems to be the most likely place, with Rome the place where Acts was either written or completed.

The date of writing was sometime between 58 and 69, for it is not likely that he could have written his Gospel before his stay in Palestine. Luke's handling of Jesus' prophecies of the destruction of Jerusalem makes it clear that the book must have been written before the fulfillment of these prophecies.[4] If, as has been suggested above, the Gospel was written in Caesarea, then 58 is the probable date.

## C. Purpose

Luke states his purpose for writing in the preface. He is writing primarily to give Theophilus more complete and more satisfactory knowledge concerning Jesus Christ. He had received rudimentary information, but Luke felt that he needed further instruction, and possibly Theophilus had asked Luke to furnish him a more adequate account. But Luke undoubtedly had a larger audience in mind than one prominent inquirer. He probably felt that the Church as a whole needed a more complete Gospel than was then in existence.

## D. Sources

New Testament scholars now generally believe that Mark and other written accounts of certain phases of Jesus' ministry were used by Luke in the composition of his Gospel. Usually two of these other sources are named: "Q" is the designation given to the supposed document which contains material used by both Luke and Matthew but not found in Mark; "L" designates the document from which Luke is supposed to have gotten the material which is peculiar to his Gospel.

That this explanation is an oversimplification of the case is also widely recognized, and other documents—an indeterminate number—are generally believed to have been used. It is certainly possible, even very probable, that Luke made use of such written sources. In his preface he mentions "many" who had undertaken

---

[4]Liberal scholars have insisted on a later date—as late as the nineties—but this position seems to depend upon their unwillingness to accept the truth of predictive prophecy. The contention is that Luke's prophecies—of the destruction of Jerusalem—are so much like the historical facts that they must have been written after the facts. The destruction of Jerusalem was in A.D. 70.

to give an account of the gospel. Though he clearly thinks these are inadequate for his purpose, he nevertheless might have made use of them. At least he would have read them to see what they could add to his other sources.

But an additional source that Luke certainly made use of was the preaching, and undoubtedly the private conversation, of his companion, the Apostle Paul. He had ample opportunity to take advantage of this. Also, while the Apostle was in prison in Caesarea, Luke had two years for detailed research in Jesus' native land. While there he could have talked to a great number of eyewitnesses of Jesus' ministry, including Mary, the mother of Jesus, from whom he might well have learned the facts which he used in his Nativity narrative. He might also have found written sources in Palestine.

## E. CHARACTERISTICS

### 1. The Most Literary

The structure, the vocabulary, and the style of Luke's record mark it as the most literary of the Gospels. Some of the parables which only Luke records are among the world's best-loved stories —"The Good Samaritan," "The Prodigal Son," *et al.*

### 2. A Gospel of Song

Closely allied to its literary significance is the fact that Luke gives us some of the great songs of Christendom. He is sometimes referred to as the first Christian hymnologist. Among these songs are: the "Benedictus," the "Magnificat," the "Nunc Dimittis," the "Ave Maria," and "Gloria in Excelsis"—all in the first two chapters.

### 3. The Gospel of Women

The place accorded women was low in Palestine, as it was throughout the ancient world, but Luke's Gospel is notable for the attention it gives to women. This fact is clearly demonstrated by the significance in this Gospel of Elizabeth; Mary, the mother of Jesus; the sisters, Mary and Martha; Mary Magdalene; and others.

### 4. The Gospel of Prayer

Luke has more to say about prayer than any other Evangelist. At the great moments in Jesus' life Luke shows Him at prayer. Only Luke gives us the parables of the "Friend at Midnight (11:5-

13), the "Unjust Judge" (18:1-8), and the "Pharisee and the Publican" (18:9-14).

## 5. *The Gospel for the Gentiles*

That Luke's Gospel was written specifically for Gentiles is shown by the facts (*a*) that it was addressed to a Gentile, Theophilus, (*b*) that Jewish terms are either avoided or they are explained or their Greek equivalents are given, (*c*) that he seldom quotes from the Old Testament, and (*d*) that he begins his dating from the reigning Roman emperor and the current Roman governor.

## 6. *The Gospel of the Universal Saviour*

Luke presents Jesus as the Saviour for all men. Such parables as "The Good Samaritan," "The Prodigal Son," and "The Pharisee and the Publican" reflect an interest in the downtrodden and the outcast.

# Outline

I. Preface (1:1-4)

II. The Nativity and Boyhood of Jesus (1:5—2:52)
   - A. Annunciation to Zechariah (1:5-25)
   - B. The Annunciation to Mary (1:26-38)
   - C. Mary's Visit to Elisabeth (1:39-56)
   - D. The Birth of John (1:57-80)
   - E. The Birth of Jesus (2:1-20)
   - F. The Infancy and Boyhood of Jesus (2:21-52)

III. The Preparation for Christ's Ministry (3:1—4:13)
   - A. The Preaching of John (3:1-20)
   - B. The Baptism of Jesus (3:21-22)
   - C. The Lineage of Jesus (3:23-28)
   - D. The Temptation of Jesus (4:1-13)

IV. The Galilean Ministry (4:14—9:50)
   - A. The First Period (4:14-44)
   - B. The Second Period (5:1—6:11)
   - C. The Third Period (6:12—8:56)
   - D. The Fourth Period (9:1-50)

V. The Journey to Jerusalem—The Perean Ministry (9:51—19:27)
   - A. First Stage (9:51—13:21)
   - B. Second Stage (13:22—17:10)
   - C. Third Stage (17:11—19:27)

VI. The Ministry at Jerusalem (19:28—21:38)
   - A. The Entry into Jerusalem and the Cleansing of the Temple (19:28-48)
   - B. Teaching Daily in the Temple (20:1—21:4)
   - C. Revelation of the Future (21:5-38)

VII. The Passion of Christ (22:1—23:56)
   - A. The Final Preparation (22:1-13)
   - B. The Last Supper (22:14-38)
   - C. Gethsemane (22:39-53)
   - D. The Jewish Trial (22:54-71)
   - E. The Roman Trial (23:1-25)
   - F. The Crucifixion and Burial (23:26-56)

VIII. The Risen Christ (24:1-53)
   - A. The Resurrection (24:1-12)
   - B. Appearances of the Risen Lord (24:13-49)
   - C. The Ascension (24:50-53)

Section **I** *Preface*

Luke 1:1-4

Luke's Gospel opens with a short preface which follows the form of introduction used by the Greek historians—Herodotus, Thucydides, Polybius, and others. It is the only instance in the four Gospels where the author steps forward and, using the pronoun "I," declares his purpose and plan of writing. Luke is also the only Gospel which is specifically addressed to a person or persons.

**Forasmuch as many have taken in hand** (1) indicates that there were many gospels or narratives of at least parts of the ministry of Jesus before Luke wrote his Gospel. They could have included collections of sayings, miracles, parables, etc. This is usually understood as a proof that Luke used written sources, and it can be so interpreted (see Introduction). Luke, however, does not say that he used them as sources. He strongly implies that they were either unsatisfactory or inadequate. Had he been perfectly satisfied with any of these, he would not have attempted to write a Gospel. Whether they were merely incomplete or were inaccurate is not stated. But the complete absence of adverse criticism and the implication that they, like his own, were from the testimony of eyewitnesses make it rather clear that his objection is to their incompleteness.

**Those things which are most surely believed among us** is better translated "the things which have been accomplished among us" (RSV). This refers to the facts of the Gospel—the historical life, deeds, and teachings of Jesus. They are established, provable, historical facts which must be accepted as such.

**Which from the beginning were eyewitnesses, and ministers** (2) suggests that the information which Luke is presenting in his Gospel came from those who from the beginning of Jesus' ministry were eyewitnesses. This would refer primarily to the apostles. But Luke is also informing us that he was not an eyewitness. This reveals both his humility and his honesty.

**Having had perfect understanding . . . from the very first** (3) is literally "having been acquainted from the first with all

425

things accurately." This is not an assertion that he was an eye-witness. It is a claim that his research has made him acquainted accurately with all the pertinent facts concerning the life of Jesus. It also seems to be an implication that he has gone back beyond the apostolic tradition—which begins with the beginning of Jesus' ministry. Luke has not only gone back to the birth of Jesus but to the annunciations of both Jesus and His forerunner, John.

**In order** is literally "one after another." Luke purposes to give an orderly presentation of the ministry of Jesus. As we look at the completed Gospel we see that this "order" included both logical and chronological arrangement.

The name **Theophilus** means either "God-lover" or "Friend of God." It could also be interpreted to mean "Beloved of God." Some commentators have suggested that it might refer to a class of persons—God-lovers—but the singular number of the name would forbid such usage. There is no reason to doubt that this was the name of an individual.

**Most excellent** is a title of respect used for persons in authority. Theophilus was probably a Roman official. This probability is strengthened by the fact that the author uses the same title three times in the Acts, and all three times it is spoken to a Roman official.[1]

**That thou mightest know the certainty . . . wherein thou hast been instructed** (4) suggests that Theophilus was either a convert to Christianity or an interested inquirer into the facts and teaching of the gospel. His knowledge is incomplete, and it is possible that there is some danger of his being misled by false information. He seems to have been previously instructed by Luke or someone close to him, and Luke feels an obligation to perfect this instruction.

We need not suppose that Luke's Gospel was written to Theophilus alone. The extent of his work, its literary perfection, and the great amount of time and effort which it required would surely imply that the author was beaming his Gospel to all those Gentiles who, like Theophilus, were interested, or might be made interested, in a true account of the ministry of Jesus of Nazareth. It has been noted in the Introduction that this Gospel was the "Gospel of the Gentiles."

---

[1]Acts 23:26; 24:3; 26:25. The KJV translates the latter two as "most noble," but the same Greek word is used in all three instances, and it is the same word as that used in Luke 1:3.

# Section II  *The Nativity and Boyhood of Jesus*

Luke 1: 5—2: 52

This Scripture portion contains the most complete account of the birth and childhood of Jesus to be found in the New Testament. Two of the Gospels (Mark and John) have no Nativity story. Matthew's Nativity account differs from Luke's in three particulars: (a) it is shorter than Luke's; (b) it is written from Joseph's viewpoint while Luke's is from that of Mary; and (c) the facts which Matthew chose to narrate are almost completely different from those chosen by Luke.

There is a change of style in the original Greek when going from the preface to the Nativity story. The former is an excellent example of classic Greek; the latter abounds in Hebraisms. Some have suggested that these indicate slavish copying of his sources. But the fact that the characteristic elements of Luke's style can be found in this section disproves the contention. It is quite possible that he is purposely giving us the authentic Jewish character of the stories. One thing seems certain: Luke followed his sources closely enough to preserve the Hebrew flavor of the account.

## A. ANNUNCIATION TO ZECHARIAH, 1: 5-25

### 1. *Zechariah Introduced* (1: 5-7)

**In the days of Herod, the King** (5) is one of many illustrations of Luke's carefulness in dating events. The device helps assure their accuracy, because this specific dating would enable his readers to validate his stories.

This Herod is usually surnamed "The Great." He was not a Jew by birth but an Idumean, the son of Antipater. He professed himself a proselyte of the Jewish religion, but his whole life makes it clear that he supported no religion except as it might further his own selfish interests and ambitions. Herod was a tool of the Romans. He was made King of the Jews by the Roman Senate at the suggestion of Antony after Herod had promised him a large sum of money.[1]

**The course of Abia,** or Abijah, was the eighth of the twenty-four courses—work shifts into which David divided the priests

[1]Josephus *Antiquities* XIV.

(I Chron. 24:10). Every male descendant of Aaron was a priest. These became so numerous that many of them would never have had opportunity to serve without some such organization as that carried out by David. Priests were permitted to marry only women of pure Jewish lineage, and it was considered especially meritorious to marry a woman who was a descendant of Aaron. Thus the marriage of Zechariah and Elizabeth was of the highest order.

**They were both righteous before God** (6) seems to imply both moral and ceremonial religious uprightness according to Old Testament standards. Zechariah, Elizabeth, and their son form a kind of bridge between the Old and the New Testaments.

**Walking in all the commandments and ordinances of the Lord blameless** means living faithfully according to all God's requirements. "Commandments" seems to refer to the Decalogue or to the moral law in general, and "ordinances" to the judicial and ceremonial law.

**And they had no child, . . . Elisabeth was barren, . . . both were now well stricken in years** (7). Verse 6 has made it clear that God was well pleased with Zechariah and Elizabeth. However, those Israelites who knew them could not have suspected this, for it was generally believed that childlessness was a sign of divine disapproval. This childlessness also brought additional humiliation to the couple: they could never realize, so they would feel, the hope which all Jewish married couples felt of being the parents of the Messiah. Both barrenness and old age combined to make parenthood a physical impossibility. It is interesting to note that this was an exact parallel to the case of Abraham and Sarah.

### 2. *The Angel of the Lord Appears* (1:8-12)

**While he executed the priest's office before God** (8) indicates that here was one priest, in an age when the priesthood was often corrupt and secularized, who realized the sacred character of his office and the relation of both his work and his person to God. God not only chooses great men for great tasks but He also picks great parents for them—great as God counts greatness.

**His course** means the course of Abia (see comment on verse 5). At the Passover, at Pentecost, and at the Feast of Tabernacles all of the priests served concurrently, but during the remainder of the year each of the twenty-four courses served for one week every six months. Zechariah was here serving one of these one-week terms in the Temple. After serving the customary term he would return to his home.

The priest's duties were assigned by means of the sacred **lot** (9). The greatest honor that could come to an ordinary priest was that of offering incense, and a priest could not draw another lot during that week of service. The incense was offered before the morning sacrifice and after the evening sacrifice on the altar of incense. This altar stood in the Temple just before the veil which separated the holy place from the holy of holies.

**The whole multitude . . . were praying without at the time of the incense** (10). It was a most sacred occasion. The rising incense symbolized the prayers of the people which at the same time ascended from the women in the Court of the Women, from the men in the Court of Israel, and from the other priests in the Court of the Priests.

**There appeared unto him an angel of the Lord** (11). The divine voice of revelation had not spoken for four centuries. Then suddenly the angel of the Lord appeared. Note that the angel did not "approach"; he *appeared*—suddenly, without warning. The fact that he appeared to a priest in the Temple marks the Old Testament character of this beginning of the New Testament revelation. John was to be a forerunner of the coming Christ and His kingdom. He was also to be a link with the old dispensation which was now drawing to a close.

**The right side of the altar of incense** is the north side, between the altar of incense and the table of shewbread. Note how specific Luke is with seemingly minor details. This is a characteristic throughout the Gospel, and is a further attestation of its authenticity.

**Zacharias . . . was troubled . . . fear fell upon him** (12). This was a natural reaction under these unusual circumstances.

3. *The Angel's Message* (1:13-17)

**The angel said . . . Fear not** (13). Though fear was the natural human reaction, the angel's mission gave cause for rejoicing. His presence was not an indication of God's disfavor but of His approval and of Zechariah's fitness for a most significant divine assignment.

**Thy prayer is heard; . . . Elisabeth shall bear thee a son.** The prayer to which the angel refers must have been prayed at an earlier period in Zechariah's life; his inability to believe the angel's promise shows that he had long since ceased either to pray for or to expect a son. But God does not forget past prayers. What appears to be a delay or oversight on the part of God is often only His perfect timing. Some have suggested that the prayer here referred to was for the coming of the Messiah or the deliverance of Israel, but this would be out of harmony with the context. Zechariah no doubt often prayed for these things, but this prayer was for a son.

**Thou shalt call his name John.** God not only called and sent His prophets, but He often named them as well. "John" means "Jehovah shows grace" or the "mercy" or "grace of Jehovah."[2] This was an appropriate name for one whose ministry so clearly demonstrates God's remembrance of and mercy toward His people.

**Thou shalt have joy and gladness** (14) is literally, "He shall be to thee joy and exultation." Both inward joy and outward honor would come to Zechariah as a result of his son's life and ministry. **Many shall rejoice at his birth.** This phrase does not mean "at the time of" but "because of his birth." His future greatness could not have been appreciated by the multitudes at the time of his birth.

**He shall be great in the sight of the Lord** (15) would imply truly great, "great in the highest sense of the word." There might also be an implied contrast intended here between John's greatness and earthly greatness—a radical difference in kind.

**Shall drink neither wine nor strong drink** is literally "neither wine nor intoxicating beverages." This prohibition plainly marks John as a Nazarite.[3] It puts him in a class with Samson and Samuel.

**Shall be filled with the Holy Ghost, . . . from his mother's womb.** In this particular John is to be more like an Old Testament prophet than a New Testament minister. Being filled with the Holy Spirit from birth is different from the individual choice which is involved in personal sanctification. Here it includes the setting apart to, and the fitting for, the prophetic office.

---

[2]See Adam Clarke, *The New Testament of Our Lord and Savior Jesus Christ* (New York: Methodist Book Concern, n.d.), I, 289 f.; also F. Godet, *A Commentary on the New Testament* (Edinburgh: T. and T. Clark, n.d.), I, 77.

[3]For rules concerning Nazarites see Numbers 6:1-21.

**Many of the children of Israel shall he turn** (16). This prophecy was literally fulfilled (Luke 3:10-18).

**He shall go before him in the spirit and power of Elias** (17) is a reference to Mal. 3:1 and 4:5-6. It clearly points to John as the promised forerunner of the Messiah, the fulfillment of Malachi's prophecy. **Him,** here, refers back to "the Lord their God" in verse 16, but the obvious representation of John as the forerunner of the Messiah gives this pronoun the implied antecedent of "the Lord" in the person of Jesus Christ. John was not actually Elijah, as some have thought, but was to resemble him in "spirit" and in "power." There are also other remarkable resemblances between John and his Old Testament counterpart—his dress, his living habits, his zeal, and his peculiar responsibility to denounce the sins of a wicked king and queen.

**To turn the hearts of the fathers to the children, . . . to make ready a people . . . for the Lord.** The task which Malachi had foreseen, and which the angel repeats, is that John would prepare a people for the Messiah's ministry. This would involve adjustments in domestic relations—**the fathers to the children**—and in moral conduct and attitudes—**the disobedient to the wisdom of the just.**

Though John has many things in common with the Old Testament prophets, he is much more. His relationship to Christ's work unites him with a new dispensation. He marks the dawning of a new day.

### 4. *Zechariah's Unbelief* (1:18-23)

**Whereby shall I know this?** (18) Zechariah seems to have overlooked completely the divine source of the promise and the character of the angelic messenger. He can see only one thing: **I am an old man, and my wife well stricken in years.** Normally this was reason enough for disbelief, but now God has spoken; His angel stands before Zechariah; what more attestation could he want?

But God had given signs in the past—to Abraham, Gideon, and Hezekiah (Genesis 15; Judges 6; II Kings 20)—when they were requested, and without blame. God looks at men's hearts, and He knows the difference between objections of unbelief and natural questionings. God also judges in such cases on the basis of the degree of light and understanding and the character of the divine manifestation. God did not reject Zechariah for this question but He disciplined him because of his lack of faith. The

431

principle which Zechariah violated is this: God deserves to be believed on the basis of His word alone.

**I am Gabriel, that stand in the presence of God** (19). Here the angel emphasizes the source of the promise and the nature of the messenger. The angel had brought a message from God himself.

**And, behold, thou shalt be dumb** (20). It is interesting and revealing to note that here the angel is both reprimanding Zechariah and giving him a sign. This punishment was especially appropriate; since it was with his speech that he had erred, his punishment would be the inability to speak for a time. As always, God's judgment upon the living was tempered with mercy, and the punishment became a means of instruction and of grace.

**The people waited . . . and marvelled that he tarried** (21). Zechariah had stayed in the Temple longer than was necessary for the offering of the incense. Such a delay was not a normal occurrence. Perhaps the people feared that the priest had offended God and had been struck down, or perhaps they suspected what actually happened. This was a most sacred occasion, and Zechariah was in the holy Temple. It would not be difficult for these Temple-loving Jews to expect something out of the ordinary.

**They perceived that he had seen a vision** (22). He was unable to speak to the people when he came out of the Temple. They supposed from this fact that he had seen a vision, or perhaps they readily understood the meaning of his gestures.

**As soon as the days of his ministration were accomplished** (23). Despite his handicap Zechariah finished his week of priestly ministration in the Temple and then went back to his home in the hill country of Judea. He did not use this handicap as an excuse to cut short his service. Rather, his every thought and action must have borne the imprint of this remarkable experience. The vision and the promise must have been continually in his mind.

5. *Elizabeth Conceives* (1:24-25)

After the return of Zechariah, **Elisabeth conceived** (24). The conception and birth of her child were in every way normal except for the divine enablement which healed her barrenness and made possible conception at her advanced age.

**Hid herself five months.** This action has been explained in many ways. The two major questions are: (a) why she hid herself at all and (b) why the time should be five months. She did not hide to conceal her pregnancy, for it was precisely at the period when this was not evident that she concealed herself from the public. The best explanation seems to be that she was waiting until her pregnancy was sufficiently advanced to serve as an unmistakable evidence that God had indeed taken away her reproach. This also explains why she chose a period of five months. In the light of this interpretation the meaning of verse 25 is clear: **Thus** (referring to her condition after five months) **hath the Lord dealt with me in the days wherein he looked on me** (the time of conception and the five months during which the evidence had become unmistakable), **to take away my reproach among men.**[4]

G. Campbell Morgan develops this whole section (1:5-25) under the theme "Our God Is Marching On!" He finds a central text in verse 17, and outlines the thought as follows: (1) The time, in the days of Herod, 5; (2) The place—the Temple, 8-9; (3) The person—a priest, 5-7; (4) The message of hope, 15-17; (5) Human uncertainty and divine assurance, 18-20.

### B. The Annunciation to Mary, 1:26-38

#### 1. *The Angel's Message* (1:26-33)

**In the sixth month** after Elizabeth's conception, **the angel Gabriel . . . unto . . . Nazareth** (26). It is obvious that Luke is writing to non-Jews, for no Jew would need to be told that Nazareth was a city of Galilee. Though, as descendants of David, Joseph and Mary both called Bethlehem their ancestral home, they were at present residing in Nazareth, located about eighty miles northeast of Jerusalem on a mountain plateau on the northern side of the Valley of Esdraelon.

**To a virgin espoused to . . . Joseph** (27). Mary was still a virgin though engaged to Joseph. Betrothals among Israelites in Bible times were more significant and more binding than engagements in our time. The Mosaic law regarded sexual infidelity on the part of a betrothed maiden as adultery and punished it as such (Deut. 22:23-24). Months often intervened between betrothal and marriage, yet the engagement remained binding and could be broken only by divorce.[5] This latter fact is illustrated

[4]For further discussion of this question see Clarke, *op. cit.*, I, 359; Godet, *op. cit.*, I, 85.
[5]For further discussion of this subject see Alfred Edersheim, *The Life and Times of Jesus the Messiah* (Grand Rapids: Wm. B. Eerdmans Publishing Company, 1943), I, 149 f.

by Joseph's intention to divorce Mary before he realized the nature of her conception (Matt. 1:19), though he and Mary were not yet married.

At this point it is well to remember that Luke's narrative of the annunciation and nativity of Jesus are from the viewpoint of Mary. The story differs in this respect from Matthew's account, which is from Joseph's point of view. It is likely that Luke secured his information either directly or indirectly from Mary when he spent the two years in Palestine while Paul was in prison in Caesarea. Luke was also more interested in showing Jesus' relation to mankind through His mother than His legal relation to the Davidic throne through Joseph, his legal, though not actual, father.

**Of the house of David** refers to Joseph rather than to Mary. The grammar of both the original Greek and the English requires this interpretation. But this does not mean that Mary was not descended from David, for verses 32 and 69 of this same chapter imply strongly that she was of David's lineage.

**The angel came in unto her** (28). This was not a dream nor a vision but the actual visit of an angel. **Hail.** This is a joyous greeting. The word in the original is the imperative of a verb which means "to rejoice" or "to be glad." The form used here is a common greeting. It would be the equivalent of "joy be with thee."

**Thou that art highly favoured** (literally, "favored one") **... blessed art thou among women.** She was honored by the angel for what she was to become before she learned the substance of the good news. It is right that Mary should be honored, and the angel set us the example. But worship of Mary is completely uncalled for. Mary, a mere human being, was to be **highly favoured.** Surely no higher favor could have been shown to a mortal. She was indeed **blessed,** or "praised," among women; that is, more than all other women.

**She was troubled at his saying** (29) is literally, "She was greatly agitated." But the verse clearly indicates that it was the salutation rather than the angelic presence which troubled her. What he had said to her was more difficult to understand than the fact of his appearance and, seemingly, more unexpected. **She ... cast in her mind** is literally, "She was reasoning." This is proof of her presence of mind at this critical moment in her life.

**Thou shalt conceive . . . and bring forth a son, . . . Jesus** (31). Here we have the announcement of the Incarnation. God's Son would indeed become flesh, conceived and born of a virgin. In this Son divinity and humanity would be joined in an inseparable union. His name, **Jesus,** means, "Saviour" or, more literally, "Jehovah saves." It is the Greek equivalent of the Hebrew "Joshua." Luke does not make a play on the etymology of the name "Jesus," as Matthew does. His readers, being Gentiles, would have missed the point of the words "for he shall save his people from their sins" of Matt. 1:21, not knowing the etymological relation between the words "Jesus" and "save."

**He shall be great** (32), in the highest and true sense. God is great, and all true greatness comes from Him and is recognized by Him. Barnes thinks this clause is a direct reference to Isa. 9:5-6.[6]

**Shall be called the Son of the Highest** does not mean that He shall merely "be called" the Son of God. It is equivalent to "He shall not only *be* the son of God, but will be recognized as such." He will have the marks of Deity. This Hebraism was in common use. It was literally equivalent to "He shall be the Son of the Highest."

**The throne of his father David.** This evidently implies that Mary was a descendant of David. It is true, as many argue, that Jesus' right to the throne would come through Joseph, even though the latter was not His actual father. But here sonship is referred to, and Joseph is not mentioned. It should be noted, further, that Luke is writing from Mary's viewpoint; also that his interest in Jesus' human relations has to do with the actual, not with what is considered legal among the Jews.[7]

**He shall reign over the house of Jacob for ever** (33). This is practically equivalent to the next clause, **of his kingdom there shall be no end,** except that the former emphasizes the Jewish aspect of the reign. Luke very clearly emphasizes in his Gospel the universality of the kingdom of Christ; but Paul, who was Luke's teacher, emphasized the continuity of the kingdom of

---

[6]Albert Barnes, *Notes on the New Testament* (Grand Rapids: Baker Book House, 1949 [reprint]), p. 7.

[7]For further discussion of this point see Norval Geldenhuys, *Commentary on the Gospel of Luke* ("The International Commentary on the New Testament," Grand Rapids: Wm. B. Eerdmans Publishing Co., 1951), p. 79, note 2.

Israel—and the seed of Abraham—in the kingdom of Christ.[8] The latter is the blossom and the fruit; the former is the vine.

### 2. *Mary's Question* (1:34)

**How shall this be?** (34) is not the product of doubt but of the perplexity of innocence. She is not saying, "It cannot be," but she is asking for an explanation of how it can and will be done. A superficial comparison of Mary's question with Zechariah's expression of doubt (1:18) might make them appear very similar. A close look at these two questions will show conclusively that they are not the same in either meaning or spirit. Zechariah asked, "Whereby shall I know this?" meaning, "What sign will you give me as evidence that this will happen?" But Mary asked, "How shall this be?" or, What means will bring it about?

There is another difference which should be noted. The miracle which was promised to Zechariah was an ordinary case of divine healing plus a divine enablement for a woman to give birth when she was past age. This was indeed a miracle. But the wonder which was promised to Mary is one which has continued to stagger the imaginations of the greatest thinkers of the Church in every generation. It is nothing less than the mystery of the divine Incarnation—God became flesh.

### 3. *The Angel's Answer* (1:35-38)

**The Holy Ghost shall come upon thee** (35). The angel courteously answered the question which was innocently asked. The answer does not clarify the mystery; it only indicates the agency. The Holy Spirit, as Agent of the Godhead, takes the place of a husband in some unexplained—and perhaps unexplainable—way. The sacred purity of this answer can be seen in its fullness only when it is compared with some of the lewd stories of the romantic escapades of the Greek gods. Here, in the angel's answer, we see the procreative power of womanhood in its utmost purity united with the omnipotence of a holy and loving God. We see delicacy, meaning, and mystery united in the words **the power of the Highest shall overshadow thee.** This "overshadowing" of the Holy Spirit possibly includes both the miracle of conception and the continued supervision, care, and protection of Mary by the Divine Spirit.

[8]See Romans, cc. 9—11.

**Shall be called the Son of God** does not refer to the eternal sonship of the preincarnate Christ but to the miracle of the Incarnation. Since God took the place of an earthly father, Jesus can be called the Son of God in the same way that a child is called the son of his father.

**Thy cousin**—Greek, "kinswoman" (36). The angel both encourages and inspires Mary with an account of Elizabeth's great good fortune. He specifically calls attention to the miraculous character of Elizabeth's conception; **her, who was called barren.**

But how could Mary and Elizabeth be cousins, since Mary was of the tribe of Judah (1:32) and Elizabeth was of the tribe of Levi (1:5)? The kinship would have to be on the mother's side. Either Mary's mother was a Levite or Elizabeth's mother was of the tribe of Judah. Edersheim thinks the former alternative is the correct one. This would harmonize with the rabbinic belief that the tribes of Judah and Levi would be united in the Messiah. It would also prove that Mary, though poor at the time of her marriage and the birth of Jesus, was really not a peasant, but came from a family of some standing. Priests were not to marry outside their tribe except into families of high rank, and then particularly with members of the tribe of Judah.[9]

**With God nothing shall be impossible** (37). The Incarnation is the ultimate proof and example of this truth. For Mary these words both supported and inspired faith.

**Be it unto me according to thy word** (39). Never was there a humbler or more complete consecration to God. Even the knowledge of the damage that slandering tongues could do to her reputation did not cool the ardor of her commitment. She left this, as everything else, to God, and He took care of her as only God can.

## C. MARY'S VISIT TO ELIZABETH, 1:39-56

### 1. *The Meeting and Greeting* (1:39-45)

**The hill country . . . a city of Juda** (39). It was no doubt the angel's mention of Elizabeth's conception that gave Mary the idea of visiting her cousin. She must have gone very soon after the angel's visit, for he had told her that Elizabeth was in the sixth month of her pregnancy; then we are told that Mary stayed with Elizabeth three months and left just before the birth of John.

---

[9]Edersheim, *op. cit.*, p. 149.

The city where Zechariah and Elizabeth lived is thought by some to have been Hebron. It was undoubtedly a Levitical city, and this Hebron was, though there are other possibilities.

**Saluted Elisabeth** (40). The haste of this journey (v. 39) no doubt was continued in the entrance into the house and the salutation. Mary was thrilled; she had good news—great news—to tell, and it was reflected in her every action.

**The babe leaped in her womb** (41). This was the unborn babe's response to the salutation of Mary. Such a response testifies to the spiritual sensitivity and prophetic character of Elizabeth's child. God was here and spiritually sensitive beings could detect His presence. This action on the part of the unborn John is in line with the angel's prediction to Zechariah that the promised child would be filled with the Holy Spirit from his mother's womb (1:15).

**Elisabeth was filled with the Holy Ghost: and she spake** (41-42). This was divine unction, and prophetic utterance. The prophetic Spirit seized her, and she spoke inspired eulogy. **Blessed art thou among women.** The Spirit-inspired Elizabeth honors Mary with almost the same eulogy as that used by the angel. **The mother of my Lord** (43). She is guided unerringly by the Spirit, and she correctly identifies Mary's Child.

**The babe leaped in my womb for joy** (44). The Holy Spirit had revealed to Elizabeth not only that it was joy that caused her babe to "leap," but she was also enabled to know the cause of his joy—the presence of God's Son.

**Blessed is she that believed: ... there shall be a performance** (45). Elizabeth seems to be contrasting Mary's faith with Zechariah's doubt. Probably both she and her husband had thought often of that moment of doubt in the Temple, and they had learned some valuable lessons as a result of the experience. Now, inspired by the Holy Spirit, she encourages Mary's faith with the promise of certain fulfillment of the angel's promise.

### 2. The Magnificat (1:46-56)

Here under the inspiration of the Holy Spirit, Mary becomes both poetess and prophetess. This passage is at once one of the world's great poems and one of the greatest hymns of the Church. However, as one commentator points out, "The 'Magnificat' is evidently no carefully composed ode, but the unpremeditated

outpouring of deep emotion, the improvisation of a happy faith."[10]
This song of Mary is very similar to Hannah's song of praise in
I Sam. 2:1-10. It is filled with Old Testament allusions, especially
echoes of the Psalms. The name "Magnificat" comes from the
first word of this hymn in the Vulgate Latin translation.

**My soul doth magnify the Lord, and my spirit hath re-
joiced in God my Saviour** (46-47). These two verses form a
typical couplet, which is the simplest stanza form of Hebrew
poetry. It is composed of two parallel lines, the second of which
restates the approximate meaning of the first with different
words. This same verse form can be seen in the remainder of the
poem. These two verses express Mary's feeling of exultation,
while the succeeding verses of the hymn name the specific works
of God for which He deserves praise.

Though the primary meaning of the Greek word translated
**magnify** is "to make great," here it means to "declare one great"
or "to extol one's greatness." The expression **God my Saviour**
shows that Mary was especially concerned with the saving aspect
of God's relations with mankind.

**He hath regarded the low estate of his handmaiden** (48).
Mary has reference to her own state of poverty and lack of social
or political distinction. **All generations shall call me blessed.**
She has been changed from an insignificant and poor Hebrew
maiden to the most highly honored woman in the history of the
world. Through the Spirit of prophecy she sees her future universal exaltation, but her humility is present to prompt genuine
praise and thanksgiving.

**He that is mighty** (49). Mary sees the relationship of the
almighty power of God to the conception of her Son. The omnipotence of God was required for the accomplishment of the Incarnation. **Holy is his name.** This is both an expression of praise and
a recognition of the holiness of God, which is so deeply involved
in redemption.

God's **mercy** (50) is another divine attribute clearly revealed
in the Incarnation. It has been shown from generation to generation to those who **fear him;** that is, trust Him. But it is now
especially manifested in God's Gift to man, and to the world.

[10]J. J. Van Oosterzee, "The Gospel According to Luke," *Commentary
on the Holy Scriptures,* ed. J. P. Lange (Grand Rapids: Zondervan Publishing House, n.d.), p. 25.

**Put down the mighty . . . exalted them of low degree** (52). God judges men righteously and justly. He exalts those who honor Him and "puts down" even "the mighty" who oppose Him. Mary could have given many Old Testament illustrations of God's putting down the mighty; she herself was the best example of His exalting those of low degree.

**Filled the hungry . . . the rich . . . sent empty away** (53). Another aspect of God's righteous dealing with mankind and of His wise judgments. God is the benevolent Provider, the Feeder of the hungry. The words might also be prophetic of Jesus' compassion and care for the hungry—both physically and spiritually. This reflection of sympathy for the downtrodden is a characteristic of Luke's Gospel. **His servant Israel** (54). God was remembering His promise to Israel. Here we see the divine faithfulness. He has helped Israel in her weakest moments. The word translated **holpen** means "to take hold of and support when one is falling." **As he spake to our fathers** (55). The covenant with Abraham was renewed with Jacob (Gen. 22:17-18; 28:13-22).

**Mary abode with her about three months** (56). This accords with the fact that she came to Elizabeth's home when the latter was in her sixth month of pregnancy (1:36), and she left just before John's birth.

## D. THE BIRTH OF JOHN, 1:57-80

### 1. *His Name Is John* (1:57-66)

When Elizabeth gave birth to her son, her neighbors and cousins came to see the child and to rejoice with her. Her age and previous barrenness made the rejoicing more intense than usual.

**The eighth day they came to circumcise the child** (59). This was in accord with the Levitical law and goes back to God's command to Abraham (Gen. 17:9-14; 21:3-4). The name was customarily given to the child at the time of circumcision—that is, on the eighth day. It was also customary to name the firstborn son after the father. In accord with this custom, those who came to circumcise the child named him Zechariah. When Elizabeth objected and insisted on the name John, they were perplexed and said that he had no relative by that name. Obviously they were not in the habit of breaking custom.

**They made signs to his father** (62). This would imply that Zechariah was deaf as well as dumb. **His name is John.** Zechariah wrote the name which the angel had given. He did not say, "His name shall be," but, "His name *is* John." This shows determination and finality on the part of the father, but there is more. It shows also that he had considered the naming of the child an accomplished fact since the time the angel uttered the name "John."

**His mouth was opened** (64). The angel had told him he would be dumb "until the day that these things shall be performed" (1:20); the performance of "these things" was complete with the naming of the child. Zechariah's praise to God is understandable, being prompted by so many unmistakable evidences of God's activity in his behalf.

**Fear came on all them that dwelt round about** (65). They could not doubt that the hand of God was directing the affairs of this child. Their question, **What manner of child shall this be?** (66) is perfectly understandable. They knew their Scriptures well enough to anticipate a man of prophetic dimensions.

2. *Zechariah's Hymn of Praise—the "Benedictus"* (1:67-80)

The moment Zechariah regained the use of his organs of speech, he burst forth in this hymn of praise which usually bears the title "Benedictus," from the first word in the Vulgate Latin translation.

While Mary's song resembles the song of Hannah, that of Zechariah resembles the utterances of the Old Testament prophets.[11]

**Zechariah . . . prophesied** (67). The priest becomes the prophet. The word "prophesy" describes three kinds of utterances: (*a*) foretelling future events, (*b*) forthtelling truth—ethical, theological, etc.—and (*c*) rhapsodies of praise. A close look at Zechariah's song will reveal all three aspects. The expression **filled with the Holy Ghost** is used in its prophetic sense, but it could also be considered one of the first instances of the fulfillment of Joel's prophecy of the outpouring of the Spirit in the last days, resulting in prophesying (Joel 2:28).

**Blessed be the Lord . . . he hath visited and redeemed his people** (68). Zechariah sees the glories which he is witnessing and the greater glories soon to come in the light of God's relation to Israel—His past dealings and His promises. The Greek word

---

[11]See Geldenhuys, *op. cit.*, pp. 19 f.

translated **visited** means "looked upon." The word **redeemed** is translated from a phrase of three Greek words which literally mean "worked redemption for." We see that Zechariah is not just thinking of the prophetic ministry of his son but of the redemptive ministry of Christ, whom his son is to herald. As a father he exults in his son, but as a priest and an Israelite he goes beyond his son to God's Son, Israel's long-looked-for Redeemer.

**Raised up an horn of salvation . . . in the house of . . . David** (69). Horns were biblical symbols of strength. Zechariah sees through the eye of prophecy a mighty Saviour, a strong Deliverer. His association of this Saviour with the house of David seems to make two things clear: first, the Saviour is the long-promised Messiah; and second, He is identified with Mary's unborn Child whom Elizabeth, aided by the Holy Spirit, has already identified as "my Lord" (1:43).

**By the mouth of his holy prophets** (70). He sees the dispensation which is beginning as the fulfillment of a veritable stream of prophecy from the beginning of the world. His expression **since the world began** no doubt refers to the protevangelium (Gen. 3:15), the first prophecy of the Saviour.

**That we should be saved from our enemies** (71). Zechariah no doubt felt strongly the political and social implications of these words. He would not have been a normal, patriotic Israelite if he had not. But the Spirit who inspired the words did not intend them in that narrow sense alone. Sin and Satan are man's greatest enemies, and Christ came, as we know, to save us from these two enemies. Perhaps Zechariah had some understanding of this aspect of the truth which he uttered.

**To perform the mercy promised . . . to remember his holy covenant; the oath . . . to . . . Abraham** (72-73). Here Zechariah is referring to the Messianic promises of the Old Covenant. God was now demonstrating His faithfulness in fulfilling His promises, in honoring His oath.[12] The word **promised** is not in the original. Literally it says "to fulfill (or do) mercy with our fathers." "Mercy" here has the sense of "kindness." A kindness to the present generation is a kindness to their fathers on the ground that a favor shown to a child is regarded by the child's parents as a kindness to them.

**We being delivered . . . might serve him** (74). God's deliverance entails obligations to serve Him. This service is ren-

---

[12]For the oath referred to, see Gen. 22:16-17.

dered to God without fear on our part. He has delivered us from
those whom we might otherwise fear. Furthermore, we have no
slavish or tormenting fear of God—only a fear which includes
reverence and respect, coupled with love.

**In holiness and righteousness** (75). God's promises and the
fulfillment of those promises in the redeeming work of Christ
include personal holiness and righteousness for His children. In
these two terms we have the Godward and manward aspects of
the Christian life. To serve God in holiness is to serve with an
inward nature conformed to God's nature and will; to serve Him
in righteousness is to serve in uprightness in all human and
earthly relationships. Acceptable devotion to God includes not
only religious fervor but sound ethics.

The possibility of such inward and outward rectitude constitutes the core of the gospel. Anything less is unthinkable,
being contradictory to both the character and the commands of
God. Also the love of God is not consistent with a plan of salvation which would leave man below the plane of personal freedom
from both the acts and the principle of sin. **All the days of our
lives.** Here is the answer to any quibble over the divine time-
table for holy living. These are not only future heavenly blessings in store for God's people, but privileges which we may enjoy
now. Nor does this inward grace need to be spasmodic; it is intended to be an established mode of life.

Verses 73-75 have been called "God's Gospel Grant." Here
may be found (1) Deliverance, 74; (2) Dedication, **serve him**
74; (3) Disposition, **holiness and righteousness,** 75; (4) Duration, **all the days of our life, 75.**

**And thou, child** (76). Zechariah's hymn has continued for
eight verses before he mentions his own son. His priestly and
prophetic spirit put first things first. **Prophet of the highest.**
He is not only content that his son should be subordinate to
Mary's Child, but he glories in the fact that John is to be a
prophet of the Highest and a forerunner of the Lord Jesus.

**To give knowledge of salvation . . . by the remission of their
sins** (77). The theme of his message as a teacher (giving "knowledge") will be "repentance unto salvation." This remission of
sins is through **the tender mercy of God** (78). For man, who is a
rebel against God, deserves death, not life.

**The dayspring . . . hath visited us** (78) is literally "the sunrise from on high has visited us." Zechariah has turned his attention again to Christ. These words are an echo of the prophecy of

Malachi (4:2) that "unto you that fear my name shall the Sun of righteousness arise with healing in his wings." The coming of the Messiah, then, will be a sunrise which will **give light to them that sit in darkness and in the shadow of death** (79). And this light will **guide our feet into the way of peace** (79). Those travelers who had lost their way in the darkness of the night may find the way of peace, now that sunrise has come.

Charles Simeon suggests this topic for verses 78-79: "The Causes of Our Saviour's Incarnation." His three main points are: (1) The advent of our Lord—symbolized by the sun; (2) The end of His advent—to dispel the darkness; (3) The unbounded mercy of God.

**The child grew, and waxed strong . . . till the day of his shewing unto Israel** (80). Here we have about thirty years of John's biography in one sentence. During those years his physical development was normal, he became strong in spirit, and he waited behind the scene for the signal from the Lord that the day had come for his great work to begin. Here we see one of the most important, though one of the rarest, of all Christian virtues— patience.

### E. The Birth of Jesus, 2:1-20

#### 1. *No Room in the Inn* (2:1-7)

(**A decree from Caesar Augustus, that all the world should be taxed** (1). The word translated **taxed** literally means "registered" or "enrolled.") Octavian, the grandnephew of Julius Caesar, became Roman emperor in 29 B.C. **Augustus** was a title rather than a name. The registration here referred to was made for the purpose of taxation. (**All the world** refers to the Roman Empire.)

The fact that Luke is the only writer of the period whose extant work mentions this decree does not prove him in error. Many such omissions have been noted in the works of the Roman historians. Furthermore, not one of the opponents of the Church in the ancient period ever charged Luke with an error at this point. If they had known of such an inaccuracy it would have been to their advantage to expose it. There is, on the other hand, much indirect evidence to prove that Luke was historically accurate.[13] The charge which is sometimes made that Judea would

---

[13]For a full and masterful treatment of this matter, see Godet, *op. cit.*, I, 119-29.

not have been included in such a registration is unrealistic. Since Herod owed his throne to the emperor, he certainly would not have refused to cooperate in such an empire-wide undertaking.

**This taxing was first made when Cyrenius was governor of Syria** (2). Insofar as the divisions of the Roman Empire were concerned, Judea was a part of Syria and subservient to the governor of Syria. Cyrenius, or Quirinius, was governor of Syria twice—at the time of the registration to which Luke refers and again A.D. 6-9.[14] This answers the charge of some critics that he was not governor at the time of Jesus' birth because he held the office at the later date. The expression **was first made** seems to be Luke's way of differentiating between this registration and the more noted one in A.D. 6.

**Every one into his own city;** that is, his ancestral city (3). Though this registration was the result of a Roman imperial decree, it was not Roman but Jewish custom that each person should go to his ancestral city. It seems that some freedom was permitted in the choice of the manner in which the registration was carried out.

**Joseph . . . went . . . unto the city of David . . . Bethlehem** (4). In accordance with the method indicated in verse 3, since Joseph **was of the house and lineage of David.**

**With Mary his espoused wife** (5). See comment on 1:27. Neither Roman nor Jewish law required Mary to accompany Joseph for this registration. Her reasons for accompanying him were probably (a) her love for Joseph, (b) her love for Bethlehem, (c) her desire to have Joseph with her at the birth of her Son, and most important of all, (d) the leading of the Holy Spirit.

**While they were there, . . . the days were accomplished that she should be delivered** (6). The time of year is not given, but the date December 25 was generally received by the Greek and Latin Church Fathers from the fourth century. Edersheim makes a strong case for the traditional date,[15] but there is no ground for certainty at this point.

[14]*Ibid.* See also H. D. M. Spence, "Luke," *The Pulpit Commentary,* ed. H. D. M. Spence (Grand Rapids: Wm. B. Eerdmans Publishing Co., 1950), I, 37.

[15]Edersheim, *op. cit.,* I, 186-87. For opposite view see Clarke, *op. cit.,* I, 370-71.

**She brought forth her firstborn** (7). Commentators who accept the Roman Catholic view that Mary had no other children deny that the term **firstborn** indicates later births by her, but it seems clear to this writer that they are denying fact to support doctrine. The term clearly implies that Mary had at least one other child, and elsewhere the brothers of Jesus are specifically mentioned and named (Matt. 13:55; Mark 3:31-35). Once we see that later and natural births by Mary in no way lessened her dignity or sanctity as the mother of our Lord, we no longer feel any necessity to explain away the facts. We see that they harmonize perfectly with the nature of the Incarnation. The truth of this doctrine demands that Mary be solely and completely human, and later births only demonstrate this fact more clearly.[16]

**Laid him in a manger; because there was no room for them in the inn.** The manger was probably in a cave or stone grotto which was used for cattle. The inn, or khan, was already filled; and the implication is that, had there been room for them, Joseph and Mary would have welcomed the hospitality. However, the fact that there was much noise and confusion and little or no privacy in such inns makes one feel that perhaps the privacy of the stable might have been an advantage to Mary in her present condition. We believe that God in His infinite love and wisdom planned matters this way.

So, while mortals slept or carried on their mundane affairs, and immortals watched the place which was at the same time most lowly and most sacred, the Son of God was born in Bethlehem as the holy prophet had predicted. This is the central fact in all history.

### 2. *Shepherds Hear the Heavenly Announcement* (2:8-14)

**The same country** (8) means the high pastureland near Bethlehem. A millennium earlier David kept his father's sheep in these same pastures. **Shepherds abiding in the field.** Among the Jews the shepherd's occupation was one of the lowest, and it was probably for this reason that God chose to reveal the Saviour's birth first to shepherds. This is in keeping with the choice of a stable for the place of birth. The Greek word translated **abiding** has the sense of dwelling rather than merely spending a day or night with the sheep. These shepherds lived— perhaps in tents or booths—where they tended their flocks.

---

[16]For further discussion of this point see Godet, *op. cit.*, I, 130.

The question of the time of year when Jesus was born (see comment on verse 6) depends a great deal on the question of what part of the year the shepherds kept their flocks in the open field. Three theories have been put forward. One view is that, because sheep in Palestine were generally kept in the field from the Passover (in the spring) until the first rains (early in October), the Nativity could not have taken place in December. A second view is based on stories from travelers that the climate is so mild in December that flocks are taken out into the fields again at that time. A third view (that of Edersheim) is that the shepherds in the Nativity story were in charge of Temple flocks, and that these were kept in the field the year round. He bases his view on a passage in the Mishnah.[17]

This question has seemed very important to scholars and to many Christians who are not scholars, but we should take our cue from the obvious lack of divine interest in the question. God in His revelation remained silent at this point. However, if Edersheim is correct in his contention that these shepherds kept sacrificial sheep for the Temple, another reason for God's choice of shepherds to hear the first announcement of the Saviour's birth appears. There would be an obvious symbolic relation to the Lamb of God, who became man's sacrificial Lamb.

**Keeping watch . . . by night.** The Greek word translated **watch** seems to imply a system of watch. The term is the one used for the guard duty of military sentinels.

**The angel of the Lord came upon them** (9) is literally, "An angel of the Lord stood by them." **The glory of the Lord shone round about them.** The word translated **glory**, when it refers to God or the Lord, often has the sense of "brightness" or "light." The word **shone** suggests the same idea. Thus it was the light of God which suddenly illuminated the countryside as the angel appeared. **They were sore afraid** is literally "They feared a great fear." This was a natural reaction to the suddenness, the splendor, and the divine manifestation in this heavenly appearance.

**The angel said . . . Fear not: . . . I bring good tidings of great joy, . . . to all people** (10). Though fear was a natural re-action, shouts of joy were far more appropriate. The news which this angel brought was the best news man had ever heard. Angels rejoiced that night for man's good fortune, because redemption was not for holy angels but for fallen humanity. This news was for **all people.** The application (potentially) of redemption to human personalities was to be as broad as the race and as enduring as time, and its benefits were to be everlasting.

**Unto you is born . . . a Saviour** (11). The word is a favorite with both Luke and his companion Paul. The terms "Saviour" and "salvation" appear more than forty times in their writings, while they seldom appear in the other New Testament books. It is not only the fact of the Saviour's arrival that constitutes the good news of the angel's message, but the nature of His salvation. (Although the shepherds would probably have interpreted that salvation as being material and political, the entire New Testament is unmistakable in interpreting it as moral and spiritual.) The Babe announced by the angels would be a Saviour from sin.

That the angel intended for the shepherds to go and see the Saviour is seen in the fact that he told them the place—the city of David, their own city. Also, in order that they might be able to identify this Saviour, the angel gave them a sign.

**Ye shall find the babe wrapped in swaddling clothes, lying in a manger** (12). This sign not only made identification easy—for surely they would not find two such infants that night in Bethlehem—but it no doubt also encouraged them to believe that One so humble would not turn even a shepherd away.

**A multitude of the heavenly host praising God** (13). This was the normal function and delight of angels. The choir which so suddenly joined the angelic messenger sang heavenly music about the Prince of Heaven. He had come to earth to set up the kingdom of Heaven and to prepare a way so that earthly creatures could become heaven's citizens.

**Glory to God in the highest** (14). This was not only a continuation on earth of the perpetual praise to God which angels sing in heaven. It was praise to God for His redemptive program and especially for the Redeemer. It is also prophetic of the glory which will accrue to God through Christ's redemptive ministry.

**On earth peace, good will toward men.** "Among men of good will" is the more likely reading, though there is room for argument.[18] Christ is the true Prince of Peace. He came to bring peace to men's hearts, and He is the only hope of world peace.

---

[18]A bare majority of ancient manuscripts favor this reading. The correct meaning seems to be: "among men of His favor" (*Berkeley Version*).

Peace between man and God is an essential prerequisite to peace between man and his fellowmen.

### 3. *Shepherds Visit the Saviour and Publish the News* (2:15-20)

**Let us now go . . unto Bethlehem, and see this thing which is come to pass** (15). There was not a shadow of doubt in these shepherds' minds that what they had been told had indeed "come to pass." This decision to go to Bethlehem was both spontaneous and immediate. **Which the Lord hath made known unto us.** The source of the announcement was unmistakable.

**They came with haste** (16). Belief kindled enthusiasm; hope induced zeal. **Found Mary, and Joseph, and the babe lying in a manger.** The first picture of the Holy Family. The shepherds found the Babe just as He was described by the angel. The wonderful condescension which the humble scene revealed no doubt only increased its significance in the eyes of these shepherds. As we reflect on this scene we are reminded that in our own time men can become personally acquainted with the Saviour if they, like the shepherds, seek Him with genuine faith and with humble and complete devotion. It is also worthy of note that often today the Saviour is found by the poor, the humble, and the unlearned, while the rich and the intellectually elite are completely unaware of His gracious presence.

**They made known abroad the saying which was told them concerning this child** (17). To these shepherds the angelic message, the anthem, and the visit to the Child in the manger formed one unified and complete picture, and thus they preached it—a Babe whom angels had proclaimed as the Saviour of the world. Perhaps the shepherds received additional information about the Child from Mary and Joseph. If so, they surely added this to what they **made known abroad** about the Child. The influence of these shepherds was probably not great enough to be felt far beyond their own circle, but they did enjoy the honor of being the first evangelists of the Saviour.

**They that heard it wondered** (18). Wherever the shepherds told their wondrous story, they left their hearers in deep thought. These hearers did not, and could not, understand the full significance of the story. The interest of many was no doubt temporary, but no hearer was unmoved, and all caught at least a glimmer of the dawn of the new day.

**Mary kept all these things, and pondered them in her heart** (19). Mary knew more about her Child at that time than was known by any other mortal. Even so, there was much that she did not know and more that she did not understand. But the things she did not understand did not stagger her faith. She simply stored them up as precious memories to be prayerfully pondered during the mysterious but challenging years ahead.

**The shepherds returned, . . . praising God** (20). Back to their vocation, back to the old and familiar routine of life they went, but in their hearts they could never be the same again. In our last glimpse of them they are still praising God for what they had seen and heard.

This well-known passage Maclaren titles, "Shepherds and Angels." He notes: (1) The miraculous announcement, 10-12; (2) The humble received the message, 8-9; (3) Titles of the Infant, 9; (4) The song of the angels, 13-14; (5) The hastening shepherds, 15-16; (6) The responses of those who heard, 18-19.

### F. The Infancy and Boyhood of Jesus, 2:21-52

#### 1. *Jesus Named and Presented to the Lord* (2:21-24)

**His name was called JESUS, which was so named of the angel** (21). According to Jewish custom He was both circumcised and named on the eighth day. This is one of many instances where Jesus is shown in complete harmony with the Mosaic law and with the religious customs of His people. It was in the environment of Jewish life that Jesus was born and grew up. There is nothing said about any opposition to the choice of the name **JESUS**—as there was concerning the name "John" for His forerunner. See comments on 1:31 for significance of the name Jesus.

The circumcision of the child and the purification of the mother were enjoined by the Mosaic law. These rites were a perpetual reminder of the taint of sin which was passed on from one generation to another. Thus this rite points to the reality of inherited depravity. Since Jesus was born without inherited sin, these rites were not necessary for Him. But as in the case of baptism later, there was perfect submission to the way that other mortals must take.

**When the days of her purification . . . were accomplished** (22). This was thirty-three days after the seven days of her

450

"uncleanness" or forty days after the birth of her child.[19] The ancient manuscripts differ as to the proper personal pronoun here. Some read "her purification"; some read "their." The best authorities have "their" (Gr. *auton*). This would mean that both the mother and the Child needed purification. Evidently the implication that Jesus was even ceremonially unclean was more than some of the manuscript copyists could accept. But Jesus came both to live among men and to live the life of man. His whole life shows that He identified himself with this sinful race—though He was sinless. Jesus always submitted to religious rites which were necessary for sinful man, even though they were not really necessary for Him. He came not to destroy the law but to fulfill it.

**They brought him to Jerusalem, to present him to the Lord.** Mary could not enter the Temple nor take part in religious services until the forty days had expired. This period having expired, she went to Jerusalem for her own ritual of purification and to present her Child to the Lord. Verse 23 explains that the law required a ransom price be paid for every firstborn son.[20] This was to redeem him from consecration to priestly or religious service—the tribe of Levi had been chosen in place of the firstborn, but God wanted a perpetual reminder of His right of claim on the firstborn.

**And to offer a sacrifice . . . A pair of turtledoves, or two young pigeons** (24). One bird was for a burnt offering, and the other was for a sin offering.[21] The general requirement for this offering was a lamb, but the turtledoves or pigeons was a concession to the poor. This fact identifies Joseph and Mary with the poor.

### 2. *Simeon Gets His Wish* (2: 25-33)

**Simeon . . . just and devout . . . waiting for the consolation of Israel** (25). It is heartening to note that in times of spiritual degeneracy and apostasy on the part of the priesthood, God has always had His devout followers—His Simeons. This **just and devout** man was no doubt only one of many such men who looked for (literally "waited") and prayed for **the consolation**

[19]See Lev. 12:2-6.
[20]See Exod. 13:2; Num. 8:16; 18:15.
[21]See Lev. 12:8.

451

**of Israel.** This expression referred to the Messianic kingdom.[22]
**The Holy Ghost was upon him.** The prophetic impulse was given
to him so that he was aware of the nearness of the coming of the
Christ. He was divinely inspired.

**He came by the Spirit into the temple** (27). The same Spirit
who had told him he would see the Christ led him to the Temple
at the exact time that the Christ child was there. Whether he
had heard the shepherds' story we do not know, but he felt a
divine impulse to go to the Temple at this precise day and hour.

Verses 29 through 32 contain Simeon's song of praise. Compared with the songs of Mary (1:46-55) and Zechariah (1:68-79)
it is less aesthetic and more concentrated on a particular theological truth. It is also shorter.

**Now lettest thou thy servant depart in peace** (29). Though
nothing is said about the age of Simeon, this clause seems to imply
that he was old. He seems to be only waiting for this one great
promise to be fulfilled before he dies. In this statement we sense
complete satisfaction. He seems to say, "Life is now complete;
I have nothing more to hold me in this world."

**Mine eyes have seen thy salvation** (30). Though his physical
eyes saw only a helpless Babe, his prophetic insight saw the
salvation of the world. The average Jew was looking for a political Messiah who would bring independence and greatness to
Israel, but this devout man saw the Messiah as a Saviour. He
realized that man's greatest need was salvation. This was a
universal salvation prepared by God for all men.

**Light to lighten the Gentiles** (32) is literally "a light for
revelation to the Gentiles." **And the glory of thy people Israel.**
Here we see salvation presented under two aspects, as it is applied to the heathen and to the Israelites. To the first, salvation is
a light; to the second, it is a glory. The Gentiles, living in darkness and ignorance, need light; the Jews, living in a state of
humiliation and reproach, need glory.[23] Simeon was more farsighted and broad-minded than other Jews of his day; in this insight he was also more in harmony with Old Testament Messianic
prophecy than they.[24]

**Joseph and his mother . . . marveled** (33). Note the obvious
implication that Joseph was not Jesus' father. Simeon was not

[22]See Isa. 49:13; 52:9; 66:13.
[23]See Godet, *op. cit.*, I, 139 f.
[24]See Isa. 11:10; 52:10; 60:3; 62:2.

telling Joseph and Mary anything they had not previously
learned about Jesus. They marveled, rather, that these truths
should come to them from a stranger and under such circumstances. The marvel to them, and to us, is that everything that
was said by all of God's messengers harmonized so perfectly.

### 3. *Simeon's Blessing and Prediction* (2:34-35)

**And Simeon blessed them, and said unto Mary . . . this
child . . .** (34). After the ecstasy of the song which was addressed to God, Simeon turned again to the Holy Family. His
blessing was evidently for Mary and Joseph rather than for the
Child. The grammar of the sentence seems to require this.[25]
Recognizing the identity of the Child, Simeon refrained from
blessing Him. After the blessing he turned to Mary and gave her
(and us) the first intimation found in Luke's Gospel of the opposition which Christ's kingdom would face.

**The fall and rising again of many in Israel.** The word **again**
is not in the original. When this word is included it gives the
impression that the same persons fall and rise. This is not the
intent of the original. Christ will be the Rock on which believers
find refuge and against which rejecters will be broken.[26] Many
will fall because of their attitude toward Him. This prediction
concerns Israel, and it is indeed an accurate prophecy, for Christ
was the occasion of a mighty sifting of the Jewish people. But
this is more than a prediction of the religious destiny of the
Jewish people; it is a statement of a universal principle, for the
most important decision any man will ever make is what he will
do with Jesus Christ.

**A sign which shall be spoken against.** Isaiah referred to
the Lord as a Sign (Isa. 8:18); and John, throughout his Gospel,
refers to the miracles of Jesus as signs. Here Simeon, guided by
the Holy Spirit, speaks of Jesus as a Sign, but a Sign that shall be
spoken against. There is a contrast in this statement. A sign implies that there will be sufficient evidence to convince all. Yet this
Sign, this Evidence, will be slandered and rejected. A casual reading of the Gospels will amply illustrate how Jesus was slandered
by His own people.

**A sword shall pierce through thy own soul** (35). Sorrow
as well as joy is to come to Mary through her relation to this

[25]See Godet, *op. cit.*, I, 141.
[26]This reflects the truth of Isa. 8:14.

unusual Child. It was not her body but her soul that would be
pierced. Mary was not crucified or pierced with the sword, but
no martyr suffered more than she. Yet the abiding reaction was
joy unspeakable. Godet rightly rejects Bleek's inference that the
sword that was to pierce Mary's soul was doubt.[27] The sword was
the pain of seeing her Son die.

**That the thoughts of many hearts may be revealed.** Because
of the acceptance or rejection of Christ the thoughts and motives
of many, whether good or bad, will be made known.

### 4. *Anna and the Christ Child* (2:36-38)

**And there was one Anna, a prophetess** (36). We know her
fathers' name, the tribe of Israel to which she belonged, her age,
and that she lived in the Temple. We also know that she was a
widow, and we know how long she had been married when her
husband died—all of this in addition to her devout life and
prophetic ministry. This is quite a contrast to the almost complete lack of information about Simeon.

**And she coming in that instant gave thanks likewise** (38).
Simeon was probably still holding the Child when Anna entered.
Her giving thanks immediately, testified to her prophetic insight.
**Spake of him to all them that looked for redemption in Jeru-
salem.** The substance of her message is not given, but the implication is that she spoke of His Messianic ministry. As in the
case of Simeon, redemption—salvation—was her chief emphasis.

Through Zechariah, Elizabeth, the shepherds, Simeon, Anna,
and others the good news about the Saviour was spreading. It
is significant that God revealed this good news only to those who
had the spiritual qualifications for such an exalted revelation.

Barclay finds in this passage a moving story of "One of the
Quiet in the Land." Here was a woman to whom God revealed
himself. What kind of person was she? (1) Though she had
known sorrow, she had not grown bitter; (2) Though she was
old, she had never ceased to hope; (3) She never ceased to worship in the house of God; (4) She never ceased to pray.

### 5. *The Boy Jesus* (2:39-52)

**And when they had performed all things . . . they returned
into Galilee** (39). We are not to understand from this that they
went immediately to Nazareth, for Matthew tells us that the visit

[27]Godet, *op. cit.*, I, 141 f.

of the wise men, the slaughter of the children of Bethlehem by Herod, and the stay in Egypt preceded the return to Nazareth (Matthew 2). This is not a contradiction but a customary kind of omission. The same sort of writing occurs in Acts 9:25-26. Here it appears that Paul returned to Jerusalem shortly after his conversion, but in Gal. 1:17-18 we learn that three years elapsed before his return. Such omissions are common in the Scriptures and in other ancient writings. It did not suit the author's purpose to include the omitted material, and ancient writers did not feel the necessity of notifying their readers of such gaps in their accounts. Since this was the custom, the readers understood and made the proper allowance in their interpretations.

A period of twelve years is spanned in verse 40. During that time Jesus grew physically, He waxed strong in spirit, He was filled with wisdom, and the grace of God was upon Him. He developed physically, mentally, and spiritually. We see here the true humanity of Jesus. One of the basic truths of the Scriptures is that the divine nature never interfered with nor made unnecessary the normal development of Jesus' humanity.

**His parents went to Jerusalem every year at the feast of the passover** (41). Such a practice was required of every male adult (Deut. 16:16). Though women were not required by law to attend, it was considered religiously advantageous for them to go. Here again we see the careful conformity of Joseph and Mary to the ritual of the Mosaic law. Perfect devotion begets perfect obedience.

**When he was twelve years old** (42). This is the one single event in the life of Jesus from His infancy to His adulthood of which we have any specific information. The fantastic stories recorded in the spurious gospels are obviously out of harmony with the life of Jesus as it is given in the inspired Gospels.

It has been assumed by many commentators that this was Jesus' first visit to the Temple since His presentation to the Lord. But this is only conjecture, since there is no evidence in the passage which could serve as proof. The opposite would appear to be more likely. We know that Mary attended the feasts at Jerusalem with Joseph, though her attendance was not required by the Law. Furthermore, Talmudic tradition asserts that even boys of tender years were required to attend the festivals. Luke seems to have recorded this particular journey because of the bearing of the events which transpired in the Temple on the plan and purpose of his Gospel.

Another common misconception is that Jesus attended this particular feast because at twelve years of age Jewish boys become "sons of the Law," but this took place at age thirteen. If this particular visit to the Temple was in any way related to Jesus' becoming "a son of the Law," it was preparatory.

**The child Jesus tarried behind in Jerusalem** (43). The feast lasted seven days. Evidently Jesus was given a considerable amount of liberty during these days. He must have known of the departure plans. So His parents might have supposed that He was somewhere in the vast concourse of people who, with them, had started for home. Two things could account for His being given this much liberty. The first is the fact that boys—as well as girls—in Palestine would be more mature at twelve than in northern or western Europe or in the United States. The second is the confidence that Joseph and Mary undoubtedly had in His dependability and judgment. Their assurance was great enough to permit them to go a full day's journey before they became disturbed.

**After three days they found him in the temple** (46). Having become alarmed, they first sought Him among the kinsfolk and others who were journeying in the same direction. It was not until this proved futile that they returned to Jerusalem seeking Him. **After three days** means "on the third day." The first day was spent going from Jerusalem before Jesus' absence was known; the second day they retraced their steps, arriving at Jerusalem late in the day. The next day—the third day—they found Him in the Temple. Preachers often assert that the parents sought everywhere else first before thinking of the Temple, but this is not stated.

**Sitting in the midst of the doctors, . . . hearing . . . and asking . . . questions** (46). These were not physicians but doctors of the Law. They were rabbis or teachers. Famous rabbis like Shammai and Hillel might have been present. Such discussion groups were common, and perhaps boys would sometimes listen. But here Jesus was not an interested bystander; He was a Participant.

**All that heard him were astonished at his understanding and answers** (47). He was not only asking questions, as a disciple might do, but He was giving answers (as an authority).

These questions and answers astonished those who heard—including the rabbis—by the unusual depth of insight which they revealed. It often requires as much insight and understanding to ask intelligent questions as it does to give informing answers.

This passage, however, must be interpreted in harmony with Jesus' normal growth and development. We must not fall into the error of the writers of the spurious gospels and ascribe to Jesus a manifestation of divinity out of harmony with the progressive unfolding of His Messianic character. At age twelve Jesus could manifest development in every area of His life and person, including His consciousness of His mission and His relation to the Father. This balanced development would continue throughout His earthly life.

**And when they saw him, they were amazed (48)** is literally, "And seeing Him, they were astonished." They were astounded at the whole set of circumstances surrounding Jesus at this moment. **His mother said unto him, Son, why hast thou thus dealt with us? behold, thy father and I have sought thee sorrowing.** Mary here betrayed frustration and a certain amount of exasperation, as well as motherly concern. She had been alarmed; she was tired, and she was confused. She was at the same time startled at His wisdom and upset at His action. Her plea seemed also to betray a sense of helplessness as she faced another mystery in the life of this unusual Child.

**How is it that ye sought me? (49)** Jesus answered a question with a question, and He opposed Mary's astonishment with an amazement of His own. Why should she sorrow, and why should she seek? **Wist ye not that I must be about my Father's business?** is literally, "Did you not know that it is necessary for Me to be in the things of My Father?"[28] Jesus seems to have assumed that His mother understood His mission better than she really did. Note the contrast between Mary's **thy father and I** and Jesus' **my Father's business.** Mary thought He was forgetful of His parents; Jesus indicates that He had a higher responsibility to a higher Parent.

But the surprise of Mary at Jesus' apparent thoughtlessness shows how faithful had been His obedience and consideration up to this point. It also proves that Jesus' childhood had been

[28]*The New English Bible* has, "Did you not know that I was bound to be in my Father's house?"

natural and normal and not marked by frequent indications of supernatural abilities.

**And they understood not the saying (50).** Jesus' question, which is relatively clear to us, only served to puzzle Mary further. Godet is probably right when he implies that Mary did not understand His use of the term **Father** as a reference to God.[29] If she did so understand it, it is very unlikely that the bystanders did. In any case she did not get the meaning of the statement. However, we must not blame Mary for not understanding her Son. This lack of understanding was necessary if He was to have a normal human life. If she had fully realized His divinity, such knowledge might have interfered with her normal treatment of Him—it would have changed a mother into a worshiper.[30]

**He went down with them, and came to Nazareth, and was subject unto them (51).** After this episode in the Temple in which the great mission of Jesus was seen (at least vaguely) He resumed His position of a normal, obedient Son. It was the Father's will that His Son should walk the same path of life as those whom He came to save.

**His mother kept all these sayings in her heart.** What she could not understand she stored up for further thought and prayer. She was patient enough to wait for a clearer understanding, yet interested enough not to be able to dismiss these important matters from her mind.

Under the title "The Boy in the Temple," Alexander Maclaren has these divisions: (1) The consciousness of Sonship; (2) The sweet "must" of filial duty—**I must be about my Father's business;** (3) The meek acceptance of the lowliest duties—**He went down with them . . . and was subject unto them.**

**Jesus increased in wisdom and stature, and in favour with God and man (52).** This is normal development of the whole man—intellectual, physical, spiritual, and social.

---

[29]Godet, *op. cit.,* I, 149.

[30]For further light on this point see Edersheim, *op. cit.,* I, 191 f.

# Section III The Preparation for Christ's Ministry

Luke 3:1—4:13

## A. THE PREACHING JOHN, 3:1-20

### 1. John Begins His Ministry (3:1-6)

All three of the Synoptic Gospels deal with the ministry of John. For a detailed discussion, see comments on Matt. 3:1-12. Comments here will be confined to the differences between Luke's account and those of the other two. Luke gives a fuller treatment of this subject. His account contains twenty verses, Matthew's twelve verses, and Mark's eight verses. Also Luke has some specific additions of facts.

**In the fifteenth year of the reign of Tiberius Caesar** (1). Luke alone attempts to date the beginning of John's ministry, and he does so in considerable detail. He not only gives the specific year of the reign of the current Roman emperor, but also names the incumbent governors or tetrarchs of all of the divisions of the Palestinian region. Though he includes the high priests, it is clear that this dating is for Gentile rather than Jewish readers. This specific and elaborate dating is also a mark of the Greek historian[1]—one of many evidences that Luke was Greek rather than Jewish.

The date given marks the beginning of John's ministry, but to Luke this ministry was simply the preface or introduction to the ministry of Jesus. It was the opening episode of the Great Adventure. Mark considered John's ministry to be "The beginning of the gospel of Jesus Christ, . . ." (Mark 1:1).

Just when this fifteenth year of the reign of Tiberius was is a matter of dispute. Tiberius became emperor at the death of Augustus in A.D. 14-15. If the fifteenth year is counted from this date it would correspond to A.D. 28-29. But this would mean that either Jesus was older than Luke said he was (3:23) or He was born two years later than He is generally believed to have been born (about 4 B.C.). Some scholars contend that Luke is reckoning Tiberius' reign from A.D. 11-12, when he became joint ruler

[1]Compare Thucydides, Polybius, et al.

459

with his stepfather, Augustus. This contention has been challenged on the ground that it is out of harmony with the way Roman historians date the events in Roman history—the custom being to date from the beginning of an emperor's reign as sole ruler. However, Luke was not a Roman historian and there is evidence to show that the custom of dating from the beginning of a joint rule was followed in the East.[2] Since Luke lived, was educated, and wrote in the East, it is most reasonable to suppose that he followed the Eastern custom of dating events in his writings. In the present instance, then, he is dating from the beginning of the joint rule of Tiberius and Augustus—A.D. 11-12— and thus John's ministry began in A.D. 26-27.[3]

**Pontius Pilate being governor of Judaea.** His exact title was "procurator." He held this office from A.D. 26 to 36. He was subordinate to the governor of Syria. **Herod being tetrarch of Galilee.** This was Herod Antipas, son of Herod the Great and brother of Archelaus. He ruled over Galilee and Perea from 4 B.C. to A.D. 39. **Tetrarch** means "ruler of a fourth." Originally the term was used to designate a subordinate ruler who ruled one-fourth of his lord's dominion. By the time of Luke's story the exact mathematical division was no longer strictly adhered to.

Herod the Great in his will divided his kingdom. Judea was given to Archelaus, whose title was "ethnarch" ("ruler of a people or nation"), a somewhat higher title than "tetrarch," the title given to those who ruled the other divisions of Herod's former kingdom. After only six years of rule, Archelaus was removed and Judea was joined to the empire.

**His brother Philip tetrarch of Ituraea and of the region of Trachonitis.** Philip was the best of the Herod family. He ruled from 4 B.C. to A.D. 34. His tetrarchy lay east of the Jordan and north of Perea. **Lysanias the tetrarch of Abilene,** which lay immediately north of Ituraea and southwest of Damascus (see map). Lysanius is not mentioned in secular history.[4]

**Annas and Caiaphas being the high priests (2).** This seemingly strange phenomenon of having two high priests at the same

---

[2]See Godet, *op. cit.*, I, 166 f.

[3]For further discussion of this point see Alexander Balmain Bruce, "The Synoptic Gospels," *The Expositer's Greek New Testament* (Grand Rapids: Wm. B. Eerdmans Publishing Company, n.d.), I, 480 f.; see also Godet, *op. cit.*, I, 166-67.

[4]For a discussion of this problem, see Bruce, *op. cit.*, I, 481; see also Godet, *op. cit.*, I, 168 f.

time is explained by the fact that Annas, the legitimate high priest, had been deposed about fifteen years earlier by Valerius Gratus, Pilate's predecessor, but continued to be regarded as high priest by a majority of his countrymen. During this period four others had been officially in office, the last being Caiaphas, the son-in-law of Annas. He served from A.D. 17 to 36.

The unwillingness of the people to recognize the deposition of Annas was no doubt based upon the fact that in the Mosaic system high priests were supposed to serve for life. It also must be remembered that they would not be expected to recognize an act of a pagan (Gentile) Roman official who removed a Jewish religious official. No orthodox Jew could acknowledge that a Roman had such authority. It is also quite possible that Annas, while unofficially high priest, was filling the important position of nasi, or president, of the Sanhedrin.

**As it is written in the book ... of Esaias,** or Isaiah (4). This passage from Isaiah, chapter 40, is quoted in all three Synoptic Gospels, but Luke quotes farther—the portion in verse 5 not being given by the other two Evangelists. Luke also follows more closely the Septuagint than do the other Synoptists.

**Every valley shall be filled, and every mountain and hill shall be brought low** (5). From Isa. 40:4. This and the succeeding clauses of this verse suggest adjustments which man must make to meet God. The figure in this whole passage is that of pioneers or road builders going ahead of the king to prepare the way over which his procession is to travel. John is the pioneer of the King of Kings, who is about to make His appearance. (1) The valleys of low living must be filled; (2) the hills and mountains of pride and hypocrisy must be brought down to the plane of true humility; (3) the crooked and rough ways must be brought into conformity to the wishes of the King.

**All flesh shall see the salvation of God** (6). This is not a part of the passage in Isaiah 40 but is a free rendering of Isa. 52:10. God's salvation in the form of His incarnate Son will be revealed so that all flesh might know and partake. Also, at Christ's second coming and at the Judgment every eye shall see Him—including those who have rejected Him.

This passage suggests the thought of "How to Prepare for Revival." The text would be **Prepare ye the way of the Lord,** 4, The "how" is found in 5, which gives God's prescription: (1) **Every valley shall be filled;** (2) **Every mountain ... shall** be brought low; (3) **The crooked shall be made straight; (4) The rough ways shall be made smooth.** Verse 6 gives the result of doing this: **All flesh shall see the salvation of God.** This is what happens when real revival comes.

### 2. *A Fearless Preacher* (3:7-9)

For discussion of the material in this passage see comments on Matt. 3:7-10. The only important variation between Matthew and Luke in these verses is that Matthew specifies **the generation of vipers** as "many of the Pharisees and Sadducees" while Luke simply calls them **the multitude.** Luke's Gentile readers would not have gotten the full significance of Matthew's mention of these Jewish sects. It is also probable that Luke wanted to make a wider (a universal) application of these pointed and searching words.

### 3. *What Shall I Do?* (3:10-14)

In these verses John is more the counselor than the evangelist. He here handles characteristic problems of specific groups—problems which might prevent or hinder spiritual life on the part of those confronted by them.

**The people asked ... What shall we do ... ? He answereth ... He that hath two coats, let him impart to him that hath none ...** (10-11). **The people** means literally "the crowd." They represented a cross section of the populace, so John's answer was generally applicable—it was a universal principle. This is the principle we now call Christian charity or brotherly love. The Apostle John gives the same truth negatively when he says, "But whoso hath this world's good, and seeth his brother have need, and shutteth up his bowels of compassion from him, how dwelleth the love of God in him?" (I John 3:17) The opposite of this principle is selfishness and is both God-dishonoring and self-destroying. **He that hath meat, let him do likewise. Meat** (food) and clothing are man's most basic material needs, and Christian love cannot be unmoved in the presence of those who lack them.

**Then came also publicans ... and said ... what shall we do?** (12) Here was a specific homogeneous group which had a characteristic weakness. This is the earliest mention of the publicans in the gospel story, but Luke brings them into his narrative often in the remainder of his Gospel. These tax collectors for the Romans were generally disliked for the double reason that they collected taxes for an unwelcome foreign power and they were often dishonest, collecting more than was due. Their question and their desire to be baptized indicated that they were sincere seekers. The fact that John does not condemn them as he did the Pharisees and Sadducees confirms this interpretation.

**Exact no more than that which is appointed you** (13). John gave the perfect answer, for it was the perfect antidote for their characteristic weakness. Here we have the demand for personal honesty in all official relations.

**The soldiers likewise . . . saying, And what shall we do?** (14) Again John's answer is most appropriate: **Do violence to no man, neither accuse any falsely; and be content with your wages.** This covers the areas of the soldiers' three most common temptations. In John's answers to the publicans and soldiers we see one of many New Testament evidences of the fact that God purposes to revolutionize society, not by a sudden change of the outward social structure, but by a personal and inward revolution and renovation of the individuals who make up society. Outward social changes would be the result of the inward change of the individuals.

### 4. *Who Is John?* (3:15-17)

For a complete discussion of these verses see comments on Matt. 3:11-12. The only significant difference between Luke's account of this material and that of Matthew is that Luke adds an introductory statement (15) which makes a smoother and more literary transition to the next speech of John. It also gives the reason for what follows. Luke tells us that John's reference to Jesus' ministry and baptism and to his own inferiority to Jesus was prompted by the **expectation** and musing (or reasoning) of the people **whether he were the Christ, or not** (15).

In verses 16-17 we see "The Two Baptisms." Here the Bible shows: (1) Comparison: both were baptisms—acts, not processes; (2) Contrast: water vs. fire; repentance vs. Spirit; (3) Consequence: **throughly purge.**

### 5. *John and Herod* (3:18-20)

Verse 18 is another one of those literary links between episodes which characterize Luke's Gospel and mark its literary superiority to the other two Synoptics. Luke brings together all of the remainder of John's preaching into the **many other things** which he preached to the people.

**But Herod the tetrarch, being reproved by him . . . added yet this above all, that he shut up John in prison** (19-20). Matthew gives this information much later[5]—after John's death—and only in order to explain Herod's belief that Jesus was John risen from the dead. Luke, again being more literary, uses this information as the conclusion of his narration of John's ministry, thus presenting it as a unit.

## B. The Baptism of Jesus, 3: 21-22

In his narration of the Baptism, Luke is much briefer than Matthew and even slightly briefer than Mark. For discussion see comments on Matt. 3: 13-17. Luke's only contribution is his assertion that Jesus prayed following His baptism and preceding the descent of the Holy Spirit. Jesus' prayer on this occasion must have been brief—as was His prayer at the tomb of Lazarus (John 11: 41-42), but prayer was so significant to Him that even this brief one must be mentioned and its relation to the descent of the Holy Spirit suggested.

## C. The Lineage of Jesus, 3: 23-38

**Jesus . . . began to be about thirty years of age** (23). This was the age at which priests and Levites entered upon their work and also that at which it was lawful for scribes to teach. Jesus had reached the age when He might enter upon His public ministry.

**Being (as was supposed) the son of Joseph, which was the son of Heli . . .** (23). Here we have Luke's genealogy of Jesus. Matthew's Gospel begins with a genealogy, while Luke places his here at the beginning of the public ministry of Jesus. This is the point where Jesus becomes the chief Character of Luke's narrative. Both writers trace the lineage through David, but Matthew goes back to Abraham, being interested in the relation of Jesus to the nation of Israel, while Luke traces Christ's lineage back to Adam. He was presenting Christ not merely as the promised Jewish Messiah, the Son of David, but as the Saviour of the world and the Son of Adam. Another contrast between these two accounts is that Matthew begins with Abraham and ends with

---

[5]Matt. 14:3. Matthew twice mentions John's imprisonment in earlier chapters but without comment—4; 12; 11: 2-3.

Jesus, while Luke begins with Jesus and moves backward to Adam and God.

In addition to these three differences, there is another which is more difficult to explain: the names in the two tables differ for the period between David and Christ. Many scholars claim that both tables give the lineage of Joseph. Others believe that while Matthew's genealogy gives the lineage of Joseph, Luke's gives that of Mary. Godet would translate the last half of verse 23: "being the son—as was thought, of Joseph—of Heli." That is, Jesus is identified as the "son" of His maternal grandfather, Heli.[6] Thus this is the genealogy of Mary.

## D. THE TEMPTATION OF JESUS, 4:1-13

For full discussion of the temptations of Jesus see comments on Matt. 4:1-11. Both Matthew and Luke give the account of the Temptation in detail while Mark only mentions it (Mark 1:12-13). In the main the accounts given by Matthew and Luke furnish the same information, but they differ in the following respects:

(1) They do not give the second and third temptations in the same order. Matthew lists the temptation to jump from the Temple in second place while Luke lists it third. The temptation to accept the kingdoms of the world, then, is third in Matthew's list and second in Luke's.

(2) Luke says that Jesus was tempted during the forty days of fasting as well as afterwards; Matthew makes no mention of the earlier temptations.

(3) According to Matthew, after Satan shows Jesus the kingdom of this world he says, "All these things will I give thee." Luke emphasizes the authority and glory of these kingdoms. According to Luke, Satan says, **All this power** (literally "authority") **will I give thee, and the glory of them** (6).

(4) In the same temptation, Luke has Satan add to what Matthew reports the follows: **for that is delivered unto me; and to whomsoever I will I give it** (6).

(5) In the temptation to jump from the Temple, Matthew calls the city "the holy city," while Luke calls it by its name,

---

[6]Godet, *op. cit.*, I, 195-207; see also Geldenhuys, *op. cit.*, pp. 150-55; Spence, *op. cit.*, I, 70-72; Clarke, *op. cit.*, I, 385, 394.

**Jerusalem.** (9). Here Luke's reason is obviously clarity to Gentile readers.

These differences do nothing to change materially the teaching concerning the temptation of Jesus.

Barclay titles this section "The Battle with Temptation." He outlines it thus: (1) The temptation to bribe people with material gifts, 2-4; (2) The temptation to compromise, 5-8; (3) The temptation to give people sensations, 9-12. We may add (4) The rewards of victory over temptation, 13-14.

Section **IV** *The Galilean Ministry*

Luke 4:14—9:50

## A. THE FIRST PERIOD, 4:14-44

### 1. *Jesus' Rejection at Nazareth* (4:14-30)

Luke's treatment of this episode is an example of logical rather than chronological arrangement. If this is the same incident as that in the other Synoptic Gospels,[1] the event did not occur at the beginning of Jesus' ministry. Luke is using this episode as his first in the public ministry of Jesus because of its logical significance. For the same reason he includes Jesus' reading of the passage from Isaiah 61 and the application of this passage to His own mission.

Luke does not imply that this is the actual beginning of Jesus' ministry. He states that Jesus had already entered sufficiently into public life that **there went out a fame of him throughout all the region round about. And he taught in their synagogues (14-15).** Also Jesus' prediction (in v. 23) that they would say, **Whatsoever we have heard done in Capernaum, do also here in thy country,** not only makes the truth apparent with regard to chronology, but helps set the stage for the action at Nazareth. From all of this it is clear that Luke begins his narrative of Jesus' ministry at Nazareth because it seemed to be the logical place to begin—Jesus of Nazareth, preaching in Nazareth and proclaiming himself to be the Fulfillment of Isaiah's prediction of the preaching of the gospel.

Luke makes this episode more significant than do the other Synoptics, as can be seen from the fact that he devotes sixteen verses to it, while Matthew gives his version in five verses and Mark in six.

**And Jesus returned in the power of the Spirit into Galilee (14).** This passage, following immediately the Temptation narrative, reminds us that all three Synoptic Gospels connect the account of the return into Galilee with the Temptation story. But both Matthew and Mark imply that the reason for the return

---

[1]See Matt. 13:54-58 and Mark 6:1-6.

467

was Jesus' reception of the news of John's imprisonment.[2] The **power of the Spirit** was the power of the Holy Spirit, who was seen descending upon Jesus at His baptism.

**He came to Nazareth, where he had been brought up** (16). Luke connects this episode with the early life of Jesus which he has just finished narrating. **As his custom was, he went into the synagogue on the sabbath day.** Jesus had been preaching long enough to have established customs. **Stood up for to read.** This was the customary posture for reading the Scriptures in the synagogue. Any other posture would have shown disrespect for the Sacred Writings. The reader was not even permitted to lean on anything for support while he read.

**There was delivered unto him the book of the prophet Esaias** (17). In the synagogue services prominent visitors were often asked to read the scripture and give whatever comments or introduction they might wish, or they were asked to speak after someone else had read.[3] In each service a portion from the Law and one from the Prophets were read. On this occasion the portion from the Law had been read before Jesus was given the Book of Isaiah.

**He found the place where it was written** . . . The passage referred to is Isa. 61:1-2*b*. This was the portion specially appointed to be read on the morning of the Day of Atonement.[4] Some think that the portion which Jesus read was the lesson for the day and that it was providential that Jesus was present that very day; but this is uncertain. It seems more likely that Jesus selected the passage.

**The Spirit of the Lord is upon me** . . . (18). Luke's quotation is from the Septuagint with some variations. This is a Messianic passage and points out the functions of the Messianic ministry. These functions are carried out under the anointing and direction of the Holy Spirit. Here our Lord himself gives us the nature of the gospel message. It may be outlined as follows:

(1) **To preach the gospel to the poor** (18). **Gospel** means "good news" or "glad tidings." The **poor** seemed more ready to hear Jesus. Their need turned them toward the Saviour. No one,

---

[2]See Matt. 4:12 and Mark 1:14. For further comments on this question see Godet, *op. cit.*, I, 227.

[3]See Acts 13:15.

[4]Van Oosterzee, *op. cit.*, p. 73.

rich or poor, can find Jesus until he realizes his spiritual destitution, seeks Christ, and confesses His need.

(2) **To heal the brokenhearted** (18). To console those whom calamities or distressing circumstances or sin have caused heartbreak.

(3) **To preach deliverance to the captives** (18), especially those who are captives of sin and Satan. The expression is reminiscent of Babylonian captivity.

(4) **And recovering of sight to the blind** (18)—both the physically and spiritually blind. A moment's reflection will reveal Christ in both aspects of His light-giving ministry.

(5) **To set at liberty them that are bruised** (18)—those who are bruised by calamity or sin. Freedom from sin is certain and complete; freedom from calamity or hardships means either freedom from the cause or grace to bear it.

(6) **To preach the acceptable year of the Lord** (19). The term **acceptable year** is reminiscent of the year of jubilee—the fiftieth year. Here it implies the season of man's acceptability with God—that God will accept those who turn to Him in true contrition and surrender. This fact is to be preached in the Messianic ministry and in the dispensation of which it is the beginning.

**He closed the book, . . . gave it again to the minister, and sat down** (20) is literally, "Having rolled up the book (or scroll) and having delivered it to the attendant, he sat down." Jewish preachers usually preached sitting down. **The eyes of all . . . were fastened on him**—both in readiness for His message and, possibly, with some slight sense of the uniqueness of the present situation, though the sequel shows they were not ready in heart for what He was to say.

**This day is this scripture fulfilled in your ears** (21). Here we have the official proclamation that the Messiah has arrived and His ministry is under way. This proclamation reveals Luke's major reason for beginning his narrative of Christ's ministry with this episode. Literally it makes an excellent point of beginning, and Luke's Gospel is the most literary of the four.

**And all bare him witness, and wondered at the gracious words** (22). **Gracious words** means literally "words of grace." They no doubt admired His speaking ability and the beauty of

His language, but they also wondered at the marvel of what He was saying and who He was. **Is not this Joseph's son?** This was the stumbling block. To them He was only Joseph's son; how could He be the Fulfillment of this great Messianic passage?

**Ye will surely say . . . Physician, heal thyself** (23). Here Jesus understands their thoughts and anticipates their further comments. But His succeeding remarks are not calculated to win their confidence or persuade them to accept Him as Messiah. Most of what He said on this occasion cut diametrically across some of their blindest and most bitter prejudices.

**No prophet is accepted in his own country** (24). Such proverbs as this are not intended to imply a situation or fact that can have no possible exception. Rather, they are statements of great and general principles. Note further that this proverb would not apply to the great men of this world whose hometowns share in their glory. It applies to prophets who represent God and preach truth—often embarrassing and incriminating truth.

**But I tell you of a truth** (25). The truth which He is about to tell is something they will not like and will refuse to accept.

**Many widows were in Israel . . .** (25). Jesus cites two Old Testament incidents where Gentiles seemed to get preferential treatment by God and His prophets while Jews with the same needs were bypassed. These were the widow of Sarepta (or Zarephath) whom Elijah befriended (I Kings 17:8-24) and Naaman the Syrian, who was cleansed of leprosy (II Kings 5:1-19). This is one of several instances where Luke presents episodes and teachings of Jesus which show Him to have been interested equally in all men and not bound by the narrow prejudices of the Jews.

**And all they in the synagogue . . . were filled with wrath** (28). No wrath is either so fierce or so blind as that which prejudice kindles, particularly religious prejudice.

**Thrust him out of the city, and led him unto the brow of the hill . . . that they might cast him down** (29). Nazareth is located on a high plateau a short distance north of the Valley of Esdraelon. The city is built on a slope from 400 to 500 feet high overlooking a small valley. The traditional site of this attempt to destroy Jesus is about two miles from Nazareth. It is known as the Mount of Precipitation. But a more likely place is a rock wall 40 to 50 feet high on the west side of the town.

**But he passing through the midst of them went his way** (30). This escape was probably due to the Master's agility rather than to a miracle, for Jesus followed the principle of never using His miraculous power for His own personal need of safety. However, this is not to say that Providence and the assistance of the Holy Spirit were not involved. Any assistance which He received was not miraculous in the usual sense of this word, but such as is available to all God's children if the need arises and God wills to interfere.

### 2. *Jesus Goes to Capernaum; a Demon Cast Out* (4:31-37)

This material is not found in Matthew but is given in some detail by Mark. Luke here almost duplicates Mark in substance.

**Capernaum, . . . a city of Galilee** (31). This is another indication that Luke's Gospel was written for Gentiles, for no Jew would need to be told that Capernaum was in Galilee. If any city can be said to be Jesus' home during His public ministry, it was Capernaum. His first disciples were found in and near this city, and many of the incidents reported in the Gospels took place here.

**He . . . taught them on the sabbath.** This was evidently a usual practice of Jesus. He shared in the synagogue services regularly on the Sabbath, taking part in the official reading of the Law or Prophets or both and adding His own comments, as well as preaching the good news of His unique ministry.

**They were astonished at his doctrine: for his word was with power** (32). **Doctrine** here means literally "teaching," and **power** means "authority." The thing that was astonishing about His teaching was that, unlike the scribes, He based His pronouncements on His own authority rather than that of some noted rabbi. In fact we see many instances where He set His own authority in direct opposition to the teachings of the rabbis or "traditions of the elders."

**In the synagogue . . . a man, which had a spirit of an unclean devil**—literally, "demon" (33). Notice that Jesus' typical Sabbath day's work went beyond His teaching and preaching. It was often these "other" activities which brought Him into conflict with the Jewish leaders. To them law was more important than men, and precepts were more significant than principles. Jesus opposed them on both counts.

**471**

It is clear from both the Scriptures and the Talmud that the ancient Jews ascribed as the work of demons much that is not so regarded today, even by conservative Christian scholars. It is also undeniable that the Scriptures teach that demon possession is a reality. No doubt many who were deformed or mentally ill were commonly called demon-possessed. However, if we believe in the divine inspiration of the Scriptures, we must acknowledge that the plain narrative facts in the Gospels reveal the dominion of demons in the lives of many persons.

**Let us alone; what have we to do with thee . . . ? art thou come to destroy us? I know thee who thou art; the Holy One of God** (34). The skeptic would call this the erratic ravings of a demented mind. But in this statement there is perfect sanity and superhuman insight. The shift from the plural to the singular number of the personal pronouns (**us** and **we** to **I**) is not a breach of grammatical principle by the demon. When he uses the pronouns **us** and **we** he is referring to the whole demonic kingdom of which he is a part and in whose punishment he will share. When he says, **I know thee,** he is revealing his own personal insight into the person and nature of Jesus.

Note what the demon knows: (*a*) he knows who Jesus is; (*b*) he knows destruction (eternal punishment) is his portion. But he is limited in his knowledge; he does not know whether or not Jesus has come to destroy him and his kind—God's plans are hidden from Satan and his cohorts except as they are revealed to man.

**Jesus rebuked him, saying, Hold thy peace, and come out** (35). Jesus did not want the testimony of the demonic world to His divinity even though demons know His identity. **When the devil had thrown him . . . he came out . . . and hurt him not.** The demon could neither successfully resist Jesus' command nor seriously hurt the man whom He had chosen to defend.

**They were all amazed, and spake . . . saying, What a word is this!** (36) The last clause is not a question but an exclamation. **With authority and power he commandeth the unclean spirits, and they come out.** Both of the most common Greek words which the King James scholars often translate "power" are used here and they are correctly translated. The congregation of the synagogue recognized that Jesus had both authority to command demons and power (dynamic) to force them to obey.

**And the fame of him went out into every place . . .** (37). Such a miracle could not be kept secret, and Jesus' fame was greatly enhanced as a result of uncontrollable emotions and un-controllable tongues.

### 3. *Healing of Peter's Mother-in-law* (4:38-39)

For discussion of this passage see comments on Matt. 8:14-15 (cf. also Mark 1:29-31). Luke follows Mark more closely than he does Matthew.

Luke calls the fever of Peter's mother-in-law a **great fever.** The other two Synoptics do not use this adjective. The original word here was a medical term used by physicians to describe a serious fever. Galen also uses this term in the same sense. Here is another indication that the author of this Gospel was a physician, and it is added proof that Luke was the author.

### 4. *Miracles After Sunset at Capernaum* (4:40-41)

For discussion of this material see comments on Matt. 8:16-17. Luke omits Matthew's citations of Isaiah and his implication that these miracles are the fulfillment of Isaiah's prophecy. On the other hand Luke tells us that many demons, before being cast out, cried out, saying, **Thou art Christ the Son of God,** (41) and that Jesus rebuked them and suffered them not to speak because they knew He was the Christ. (See comment on Luke 4:35.) Mark contains a part of this addition (Mark 1:34).

### 5. *Jesus Expands His Ministry* (4:42-44)

The material in verses 42-44 is not in Matthew, but it is given in Mark 1:35-38. For full discussion see comments on this passage in Mark.

**And when it was day** (Mark says "a great while before day"), **he departed and went into a desert place** (42). It is usually Luke who records Jesus' seasons of prayer but in this incident it is Mark who tells us that Jesus prayed.

**And the people sought him . . . and stayed him, that he should not depart . . .** They wanted to keep Jesus for themselves. This was better by far than the treatment He received at Nazareth, but Jesus had other plans, and other men needed Him.

**I must preach the kingdom of God to other cities also: for therefore am I sent** (43). Mark says "the next towns" instead of **other cities.** It is easy to see that Luke is giving this material a wider application and thus a greater appeal to the Gentiles. Jesus makes it clear that He is sent, not to a few or to one town, but to others and eventually to all men.

**And he preached in the synagogues of Galilee** (44). A comprehensive statement which shows His ministry expanded to the whole of Galilee. See comments on Matt. 4:23.

## B. THE SECOND PERIOD, 5:1—6:11

### 1. *Jesus Teaches and Calls Fishers of Men* (5:1-11)

Luke's treatment of this episode in Jesus' ministry is much more extensive than that of Matthew or Mark. These briefer accounts are limited to the more immediate details of the call of the four. See comments on Matt. 4:18-22.

**As the people pressed upon him** (1). His popularity had reached the point where the crowds were large enough to create problems for Jesus. There was even danger of His being crushed or trampled by them. **He stood by the lake of Gennesaret.** Luke is the only one of the four Evangelists who calls this body of water by its proper designation of **lake.** The other three use the popular designation "sea." Note that Luke here describes Jesus as standing by the lake, while in Matthew and Mark He is walking. Furthermore, the latter two Gospels say that Peter and Andrew were casting a net into the sea, while Luke says they were washing their nets. A close look at these facts will show that Matthew and Mark began the narrative earlier—while the fishermen were still fishing; Luke begins after Jesus has already arrived (so that He is no longer walking), the fishermen have ceased fishing, and the crowd has gathered.

**Saw two ships** (2). The English word "ship" no longer applies to this kind and size of boat. A better translation would be "little boats." **Standing by the lake.** The boats were drawn up on the shore. **The fishermen ... were washing their nets.** They had finished their fishing for this time and were cleaning their nets.

**He entered into one of the ships ... Simon's, and prayed him that he would thrust out a little from the land** (3). This is the first time that Luke introduces any of the disciples of Jesus into His narrative.[5] The boat was on the beach; Peter pushed it out into the lake—probably wading out some few yards, pulling or pushing the boat.

---

[5]Simon's mother-in-law is mentioned in 4:38, but Simon is not mentioned at that time.

474

**He sat down, and taught the people out of the ship.** Matt. 13:1-3 records a similar experience of Jesus, but it seems to have been a different occasion from the one which Luke records here. The substance of Jesus' teaching on this occasion is not given. Luke is interested here only in what influenced these four men to become disciples of Jesus.

**He said unto Simon, Launch out into the deep, and let down your net for a draught** (4). The word translated **draught** means a "haul" or a "catch," and as it is used here it implies a very large catch. Jesus was instructing experienced fishermen but His authority and knowledge rested on His divinity, not on his experience as a fisherman. He had superhuman knowledge of where the fish were. Jesus' advice that they **launch out into the deep** would imply that these fishermen had been engaging in shore fishing. In this kind of fishing one end of the long net was attached to the shore while the other end was fastened to the boat. The fishermen would then row the boat in semicircles beginning and ending at the shore, keeping the net stretched tight between the boat and the shore. The fact that Matthew and Mark say that Jesus saw them casting a net into the sea (Matt. 4:18; Mark 1:16) would imply the same method of fishing. The words **Launch out into the deep** have an obvious spiritual application.

**Master, we have toiled all the night, . . . nevertheless at thy word** (5). Here we see mixed emotions and reactions. Peter's experience as a fisherman told him that, having fished all night without success, it would be useless to try again now. But he seems already to have known Jesus well enough that the Lord's command made a major difference in the circumstances. Faith said that if Jesus commanded or requested action it would be successful. Such faith begets obedience.

**Their net brake** (6) is literally "Their net was breaking." The "breaking" or tearing did not prevent them from landing the fish.

**They beckoned unto their partners** (7). These were James and John, the sons of Zebedee. We see that James and John were more than just fellow fishermen or neighbors. The fact that there were two boats and four fishermen working as partners would enable them to fish farther from the shore—the net could be attached to both boats.

**Depart from me; for I am a sinful man, O Lord** (8). The tremendous success of their efforts and the obvious reason for their sudden success gave Peter a twofold vision. He saw the Lord—His power, His wisdom and knowledge, His sinlessness—and Peter also saw himself, a sinful creature. He was sinful in contrast to the holiness of Christ, and he was actually sinful. This experience produced a conviction of sin which made him uncomfortable in Christ's presence, and the first impulse was to ask Jesus to depart. Peter always spoke his first impulse. But Jesus knew that his deeper wish was salvation from sin and likeness to himself.

**For he was astonished** (9) is literally "For astonishment laid hold on him." This was his reason for speaking out. It was always a sufficient reason for impulsive Peter to speak out. But the same astonishment laid hold of **all that were with him,** and they did not speak up, although they no doubt felt the same conviction for sin. We sometimes criticize Peter for his impulsiveness, but we should take our cue from the fact that obviously Jesus felt He needed one impulsive disciple.

**And so was also James and John** (10); that is, "and so were they astonished." **Jesus said unto Simon, Fear not; from henceforth thou shalt catch men.** Jesus' attitude toward Peter's outburst is seen in the fact that Peter was singled out for these encouraging words. It was Peter who had said, "Nevertheless at thy word I will let down the net" (v. 5). Peter had caught the fish, and as a result Jesus caught Peter and put him to work catching men for the Kingdom.

**They forsook all, and followed him** (11). As soon as they reached the shore they forsook the fishing trade and followed Jesus to become fishers of men. All four fishermen were of the same mind. Peter differed from the other three in his reactions but not in his basic attitudes and desires. Jesus now has His first four disciples.

For this incident Alexander Maclaren gives these points: (1) The law of service, 4; (2) The response, 5; (3) The result, 6-8.

### 2. *Jesus Heals a Leper* (5:12-16)

Matthew puts this incident immediately after the Sermon on the Mount. Luke merely says that it took place **when he was in a certain city** (12). For full discussion see comments on Matt. 8:1-4. Luke, the physician, adds to Mark's account the observa-

476

tion that the leper was **full of leprosy** (12); that is, the disease had reached a very advanced stage—it was no longer localized.

**He withdrew himself into the wilderness, and prayed** (16). It is not easy to resist the pull of popularity, but it is often wisest —even essential—to leave the crowd and retreat to the place of prayer. When we return to the crowd we shall be far better able to minister to them after our precious session in the wilderness of prayer. Here, as always, Jesus set a wonderful example. Luke alone records this item.

### 3. The Healing of the Paralytic (5:17-26)

All three Synoptics give this episode. Matthew and Mark give Capernaum as the site of the miracle; Luke does not tell where it took place. Mark and Luke tell us that the paralytic was let down through the roof, while Matthew does not mention this fact. For discussion see comments on Matt. 9:2-8.

### 4. The Calling of Levi—Matthew (5:27-32)

This incident is given by all three Synoptics. For discussion see comments on Matt. 9:9-13. Luke's only significant variation from Matthew's is his use of the name **Levi** instead of Matthew. Mark also calls him Levi. Perhaps Jesus gave him the surname Matthew, which means "gift of God."[6]

### 5. The Question About Fasting (5:33-39)

This material is found in all three Synoptics. For discussion see Matt. 9:14-17. Luke's only significant addition is verse 39. Here Luke reports the Master as saying that no man, after having drunk old wine, will want the new, for he says that the old is better. In the parable itself Jesus is using the new wine and new wineskins to represent His kingdom and His teaching. Verse 39 would seem to contradict this unless we see that Jesus is trying to show the slowness of men—especially the Jewish leaders—to accept the new. They insist that the old is better. It has been this insistence which has kept the Jews out of the kingdom of Christ. Note that it is not Jesus who says, **The old is better,** but the hypothetical **man** in the illustration.

### 6. Lord of the Sabbath (6:1-5)

This episode is found in all three Synoptics, and Luke's account is the briefest of the three. For discussion see **comments**

[6]See Godet, *op. cit.,* I, 271.

on Matt. 12:1-8 (cf. also Mark 2:23-38). Luke's only significant addition is his mention of the fact that they rubbed the grain in their hands (to remove the husks) as they ate it. **The second sabbath after the first** probably means the next one after the Passover Sabbath, called "first."

### 7. *Healing on the Sabbath* (6:6-11)

The account of this miracle is found in all three Synoptics. For discussion see comments on Matt. 12:9-14 (cf. also Mark 3:1-6). Luke's only significant addition is his statement that the enemies of Jesus **were filled with madness** (11) at Jesus' healing on the Sabbath. This shows the extent of their discontent, but it also stands out in bold contrast to the joyousness which is the normal human reaction under such circumstances.

The *Pulpit Commentary* suggests the following divisions for this incident: (1) Sin disables us, 6; (2) Christ comes to restore us, 8-10; (3) Christ demands of us an immediate, practical response, 10; (4) Practical kindness is a principal manifestation of renewed power—that is, the man should use his restored hand to help others.

## C. THE THIRD PERIOD, 6:12—8:56

### 1. *The Choosing of the Twelve* (6:12-16)

All three Synoptics give the account of the choosing of the Twelve. For discussion of the material in verses 14-16, see comments on Matt. 10:2-4 (cf. also Mark 3:13-19). Luke adds to the account as found in Matthew the material in verses 12 and 13.

**Went out into a mountain to pray** (12). Luke shows Jesus in prayer before every major undertaking in His life. The calling of the Twelve was so important that Jesus not only prayed, but **He continued all night in prayer to God.** The Master is setting an example for us to follow. We must never make any important move without a season of earnest prayer.

**When it was day, he called unto him his disciples** (13). A disciple is a learner, student, apprentice. Every follower of Jesus was a disciple. Having ended His night of prayer, He was now ready to choose the leaders of His kingdom and of His kingdom work. From among these disciples **he chose twelve, whom also he named apostles.** The apostles were "the sent-out ones," sent with a message. They were messengers, but they were more; they were representatives and ambassadors of Christ.

## 2. The Sermon on the Plain (6:17-49)

This is evidently the same sermon as the one given in Matthew which is generally called the Sermon on the Mount. There are several differences between the two accounts, and these have caused some to conclude that they are two separate sermons on two different occasions. But the similarities outweigh the differences, and these differences can be accounted for. The similarities are as follows: (a) both versions begin with a series of beatitudes; (b) both include Jesus' teachings on loving one's enemies; and (c) both accounts end with the parable of the two builders.

The differences are as follows: (a) Matthew's version is much longer; (b) in Matthew the sermon was preached on a mountain, while in Luke it was on a **plain** or "level place"; (c) Luke includes some material not in Matthew; and (d) Luke has only four beatitudes while Matthew has nine. However the four which Luke gives are the same in substance, though slightly different in form, as the corresponding four in Matthew.

Luke's omissions are in harmony with the plan and purposes of his book—the passages omitted deal with matters which Luke customarily omitted. These are generally matters which would interest, either chiefly or solely, Jewish readers.

The seeming conflict between the so called **plain** and the mountain as the place where the discourse was given is not a conflict in reality. The Greek word translated **plain** in Luke's account literally means a "level place," or a plateau.

That Luke includes material not in Matthew only demonstrates that even Matthew did not report all that Jesus said on this occasion. For a full discussion see comments on Matthew, chapters 5—7.[7] Luke's additions deserve further comment. Luke adds a personal note to his beatitudes by giving them in the second person rather than the third person, as they are in Matthew.

Luke's first important addition is found in verses 24-26. This is a series of woes which follow the beatitudes. It is both interesting and significant that these four woes are the exact antitheses of the four beatitudes. The first beatitude says, **Blessed be ye poor** (20). The first woe says, **But woe unto you that are rich** (24). The second beatitude says, **Blessed are ye that hunger now** (21). The second woe says, **Woe unto you that are full** (25).

[7]See also Godet, op. cit., I, 294 ff.

The third beatitude says, **Blessed are ye that weep now** (21). The third woe says, **Woe unto you that laugh now** (25). The fourth beatitude says, **Blessed are ye, when men shall hate you** (22). The fourth woe says, **Woe unto you, when all men shall speak well of you** (26).

Thus in every case Luke has quoted Jesus as blessing those whom we usually call the unfortunate ones and has pronounced woes upon those whom we generally consider fortunate. **Jesus is not saying that one who is rich or who has friends cannot be saved and go to heaven.** He is pointing out the danger of being too firmly tied to this world. He is also showing us that misfortune is often the angel of the Lord in disguise.

The passage found in verses 33 and 34 is another addition not found in Matthew. This is a part of the discussion on loving enemies. Luke omitted Matt. 5:47, which says, "and if ye salute your brethren only, what do ye more than others? do not even the publicans so?" This has Jewish overtones which Luke evidently felt would not be in place in "the Gospel for the Gentiles." But Luke adds (vv. 33-34) an illustration by Jesus which teaches the same lessons without the Jewish implication. These are as follows:

**If ye do good to them which do good to you, what thank have ye? for sinners also do even the same** (33). *Your brethren* and *publicans,* terms which are Jewish in their connotation, do not appear here.

**And if ye lend to them of whom you hope to receive, what thank have ye? for sinners ... lend ... to receive as much again** (34). Here again we see no term which has a Jewish connotation, though we see the same great eternal principle as that found in the illustration quoted in Matthew. Once more, in verse 35, Luke quotes Jesus' admonition to lend without hope of return. This is an excellent illustration of how these two Evangelists selected the parts of the sermon which best suited their individual purposes of writing.

Verse 38 is another passage not found in Matthew's version: **Give, and it shall be given unto you; good measure, pressed down, and shaken together, and running over.** Though we are not to give or lend in order to get returns, we are assured that giving does bring returns. However, Jesus does not say that we shall always be paid in kind or that the pay will necessarily be material. We are much better paid if the reward is in things spiritual and eternal. There are also many mental and emotional rewards. But still our chief interest must be in giving, not in receiving.

Luke's literary form in describing the four levels of this good measure is excellent. Note the rising force of the descriptive terms: **good measure;** then an increase of this good measure, **pressed down** (so that more can be put in the container); then it is increased again, **shaken together** (so it will hold still more). Then when it will hold no more we see it **running over.** Luke appears to have exhausted the possibilities of increase which his figure could carry.

The material in verse 40 is not in Matthew's rendering of the Sermon on the Mount, but he does give it elsewhere (Matt. 10: 24-25).

In verses 40-45 are found "The Four Goods of the Gospel": (1) Good teacher, 40; (2) Good tree, 43; (3) Good treasure, 45a; (4) Good testimony, 45b.

### 3. *The Centurion's Servant Healed* (7:1-10)

This episode is found also in Matthew. For discussion see comments on Matt. 8:5-13. Luke omits the material found in verses 11 and 12 in Matthew. This is the passage where Jesus says, "Many shall come from the east and the west, and shall sit down with Abraham, and Isaac, and Jacob . . . but the children of the kingdom shall be cast into outer darkness." This is a characteristic omission, for Luke rarely includes the passages which exclusively concern the Jews.

Luke also makes a significant contribution to the story. In Matthew's account we are *not* told that the centurion did not himself come to the Master but contacted him through intermediaries. In fact, if we had the Matthew account alone we would conclude that the centurion came directly to Jesus. Luke tells us that the first contact on this occasion was made through the elders of the Jews who went to Jesus with the centurion's request and also pronounced him worthy of the Lord's consideration. Their high estimate of the centurion was based upon the latter's having built them a synagogue. Luke also informs us that when Jesus approached the house, and the centurion saw Him coming, he sent servants to advise the Master of his own unworthiness to have Him in his house. In Luke's account Jesus and the centurion never come into direct contact. This is not a contradiction of Matthew's account. Matthew is simply following the ancient custom of omitting without comment all material that does not serve his purpose.

### 4. *The Raising of the Widow's Son at Nain* (7:11-17)

This episode is given only by Luke. Nain is situated in the Plain of Esdraelon, about two miles from Mount Tabor, some twenty miles south-southwest of Capernaum and about six miles south of Nazareth. It belonged to the tribe of Issachar. **Nain** means "fair" or "lovely."

This miracle is one of three instances of Jesus' raising the dead which are recorded in the New Testament, though there is clear evidence that some others, not reported, were raised.[8] Two of these three miracles are reported in only one of the Gospels. The raising of Lazarus is found only in John (11:44). The incident now under discussion is found only in Luke. The raising of Jairus' daughter is found in all three Synoptics.[9]

**He went into . . . Nain; and many of his disciples went with him, and much people** (11). Crowds not only gathered around Him in the cities, but they followed Him from one city to another. This crowd was composed of three groups: the Twelve, **many of his disciples,** and **much people.**

**A dead man carried out, the only son of his mother, . . . a widow** (12). Luke's Gospel is the Gospel of the poor, the downtrodden, the unfortunate. The son was an only son and the woman was a widow. Thus he was her only support as well as her pride and joy. Jesus showed an interest in man's economic needs as well as his physical and spiritual needs.

**The Lord** is an appellation found frequently in Luke and peculiar to this Gospel. **He had compassion on her.** Note, first, that the motive of this miracle was compassion. No doubt Jesus did perform miracles to attest His divinity. But His wonderful compassion was never absent when the miracle had to do with human problems or human suffering, and sometimes this compassion appears to be the only motive. Note, further, that this compassion was on the widow. There is no indication that the state of the dead son moved Jesus except as his death brought hardship and heartache to the mother. Christ could not look on death as a tragedy unless it was the death of a sinner. **Weep not.**

---

[8]See Matt. 10:8; 11:5; Luke 7:22.
[9]Matt. 9:22-26; Mark 5:22-43; Luke 8:41-56.

These kind words, coming from the great loving heart of Jesus, would of themselves bring a measure of comfort to the woman.

**He . . . touched the bier: and they that bare him stood still** (14). The bier was not a coffin such as was used by the Egyptians, but a flat, bedlike structure on which the corpse lay wrapped in cloth.[10] The touch of Jesus on the bier brought an instant response from those who carried it. Jesus' fame was so great that they no doubt knew who He was, and they were not altogether unprepared for a miracle.

**Young man, I say unto thee, Arise.** When Jesus spoke these words they seemed to be a simple command or request which would certainly be followed by instant results. The Creator, the Giver of life, is here speaking, and His life-giving power is clearly demonstrated; for **he that was dead sat up, and began to speak** (15).

**There came a fear on all** (16). The effect of the miracle upon the crowd was tremendous. Literally "fear seized all." Such an unmistakable evidence of the presence and power of God does produce a fear on all—on the saint it brings a reverential fear; on the sinner it brings a fear of punishment. But all of them **glorified God.** They accounted for the miracle in two ways: (*a*) **a great prophet is risen among us, and** (*b*) **God hath visited his people.** This second explanation seems to imply the Messiah. Like those who heard the Nativity story or saw the Christ child, they knew that God was at work even though they did not fully understand the evidence at hand.

**And this rumour** (literally, "this report") **of him went forth throughout all Judaea, and throughout all the region round about** (17). Nothing which Jesus is known to have done up to this time would have created such excitement, and no story would have been spread so enthusiastically and so far.

5. *John the Baptist Seeks Assurance* (7:18-23)
See comments on Matt. 11:2-6.

6. *Jesus Discourses About John* (7:24-30)

For full discussion see comments on Matt. 11:7-15. Though Luke omits some material which Matthew includes, he makes one significant addition, found in verses 29 and 30. A casual reading

---

[10]Compare Lazarus' burial, John 11:41-44.

might suggest that this passage is comment by Luke rather than a part of Jesus' discourse. Some scholars have taken this position, but the bulk of New Testament scholarship rejects the view. This passage seems definitely to be a part of the Master's discourse on John. If this were a comment by Luke it would have no precedent in his writings; nowhere else does he break into a discourse with his comments. Note that the next verse (31) continues Jesus' discourse without any introduction or any other indication that the discourse has been interrupted.

**The people . . . and the publicans, justified God, being baptized with the baptism of John** (29). In the preceding verses (24-28) Jesus has been commenting on the person of John the Baptist. Now He points to the varied reception of his teachings by the two major groups of Israelites. To justify God is to declare by word and action the justness, rightness, and excellence of God's acts and words. The common people and the publicans, who were more easily convinced of their sinfulness and their spiritual need, accepted John's message, repented, received baptism, and supported his work.

**But the Pharisees and lawyers rejected the counsel of God against themselves, being not baptized of him** (30). Literally, "have annulled" or "set aside for themselves the counsel or decree of God." They could not frustrate the plan of God, but by their rejection and rebellion they could annul or set aside its benefits as far as they themselves were concerned. Thus we see that anyone who opposes God is only cutting off the flow of divine blessings from himself.

### 7. *A Childish Generation* (7:31-35)
See comments on Matt. 11:16-19.

### 8. *Jesus, a Penitent Woman, and a Pharisee* (7:36-50)
This episode is given only by Luke. It is similar to the accounts of Jesus' eating in the house of "Simon the leper" in Bethany,[11] but the differences are too great to allow for their being the same incident. Among other things the attitudes of the two Pharisees toward Jesus were different; the two women were different—the one in Bethany not having a shadow of shame upon her; the time is different—the present one being early in Jesus' ministry, the other one near the end; and the locations

[11]Matt. 26:6-13; Mark 14:3-9; John 12:1-9.

484

are different—the present one being in Galilee while the other one was in Judea (Bethany).

**One of the Pharisees desired him that he would eat with him** (36). Though many of the Pharisees were growing more and more bitter toward Jesus, the open break had not yet come. It was not surprising, therefore, that a Pharisee should invite Him to dinner. He probably still had many friends or well-wishers among this sect.

**A woman in the city, which was a sinner** (37). Such an expression as this, in New Testament terminology, means a prostitute. The word **sinner** had far more stigma attached to it in New Testament times than it does today. This is due to three causes: (a) the Pharisees used the term in a very restrictive and condemnatory sense to refer to those whom they considered the very lowest persons (morally and spiritually); (b) Jesus removed much of the hate and sarcasm from the word in His beautiful stories of compassion for sinners; and (c) modern usage has tended to remove from the word most of the sense of shame and wrong and rebellion which the word rightly denotes.

**When she knew that Jesus sat at meat.** She had heard much about Jesus, as had everyone else in Galilee. Conscious of her weight of sin and hungry for relief, she came to the house. It was customary for those who were not invited to a feast or dinner to come and stand around the wall and talk to the guests. But such a woman as this would certainly not be expected to enter the house of a Pharisee. She **brought an alabaster box of ointment.** Alabaster is a very fine species of gypsum, usually white, but not as hard as marble, and thus can be more easily hollowed out for containers. Perfumes were commonly transported in such alabaster "boxes."

**Stood at his feet behind him weeping** (38). In Palestine in Jesus' day the custom was to recline at a table across a couch. The feet were extended in the opposite direction from the table. Thus it was easy for the woman to get to the feet of Jesus. Her tears could have been tears of repentance prompted by the remembrance of her past shameful life brought into contrast with the holiness which was evident in the character of Jesus. But our Lord's statements about her in verses 44-50 seem to suggest strongly that she had already been converted in an earlier contact with Him; that these tears were tears of joy, and the ointment was to show gratitude. In her shameful business she was accustomed to buying perfumes, and it is possible that this was originally purchased for sinful purposes. But now her heart was turned from sin and shame and toward the Saviour. As were her body and soul, this ointment was dedicated to Christ.

Her intention was to anoint Jesus. But as she stood at His feet her heart was overwhelmed, tears began to flow and to drop onto Jesus' feet. Having nothing else with which to wipe them, she undid her hair and used it for that purpose.

**This man, if he were a prophet, would have known . . . (39).** The whole scene was shameful to Simon the Pharisee. He no doubt had had some inclination toward Jesus and some love for Him, but Jesus' failure to rebuke this sinful woman seemed to prove that He was unaware of the kind of woman she was. Simon was not speaking aloud; **he spake within himself.** But it is interesting to note that while Simon was musing about the limitation of Jesus' prophetic insight—His supposed unawareness of the true character of this woman—Jesus was also reading Simon's thoughts. He soon revealed that He had not only a perfect insight into the woman's character but into Simon's as well.

**Simon, I have somewhat to say unto thee (40).** Here Jesus gives His parable of the two debtors. In this parable and its application we see an excellent example of the overwhelming force and persuasiveness of the Master's arguments. Jesus is not merely trying to convince Simon that He knows and understands him; He wants to help Simon to know and understand himself. Simon is courteous to Jesus and says, **Master** (literally, "Teacher"), **say on.**

**A certain creditor . . . had two debtors (41).** Jesus knew what most of us overlook: that we can often see ourselves better when we are looking at someone else. One of the debtors of whom Jesus spoke was Simon. He was soon to know which one and to know much more about himself. **One owed five hundred pence, and the other fifty.** The term **pence** is British; the proper name of this coin is "denarius" (pl., denarii). Fifty denarii would equal about $10.00 in U.S. money, and 500 denarii would amount to about $100.00.

**When they had nothing to pay, he frankly forgave them both** (42). In the spiritual realm all men are in this plight, for no man is able to pay his moral and spiritual debt. In Jesus' day there were two courses open to a debtor who could not pay his debt: forgiveness or slavery. Thus, forgiveness would entail a great debt of gratitude. **Which of them will love him most?** The answer is obvious.

When Simon says, **I suppose that he, to whom he forgave most,** (43) he is hesitating, not because he is not quite sure of the answer to Jesus' question, but because he already sees the direction which Jesus is leading him. Accepting Simon's answer as correct, Jesus begins a clear and most effective personal application of the parable to Simon and the woman.

**Seest thou this woman?** (4) He wants Simon to see what he has not yet seen. **I entered into thine house, thou gavest me no water for my feet: but she . . .** He had neglected a common courtesy expected of all hosts in that land. The heat and dust of Palestine and the fact that shoes or sandals were merely soles bound to the feet with leather thongs made the washing of feet on entering a home both a courtesy and a necessity. The woman made up for Simon's thoughtlessness by washing Jesus' feet with her tears.

**Thou gavest me no kiss: but this woman . . .** (45). Another custom had been broken by Simon; but the woman, with purity and true humility, had more than supplied the lack—she had not ceased to kiss His feet.

**My head with oil thou didst not anoint: but this woman . . .** (46). It seems that Simon had neglected all of the courtesies which were the custom and even the delight of a thoughtful host. But the woman had anointed His feet. Simon had proven by his own treatment of his Guest—and a Guest toward whom he seems to have had no antagonism—that he was thoughtless and almost, if not quite, loveless.

**Wherefore I say unto thee, Her sins, which are many, are forgiven** (47). These are among the most precious words Jesus has ever spoken—words which many a sinner has heard and in which many a redeemed soul has rejoiced.

**Thy sins are forgiven** (48). The words in the preceding verse were spoken *about* the woman, but Jesus now turned *to* her. The literal translation here is, "Thy sins have been forgiven." This may imply that the woman had met the Lord earlier and had been converted, and on this occasion she was merely showing gratitude. This is also in harmony with the parable and its application; for in the parable love followed forgiveness, and in the application the woman demonstrated love before these assurances of forgiveness were spoken. It seems that Jesus is reassuring the woman.

**Who is this that forgiveth sins?** (49) To some of these questioners Jesus' forgiveness of sins was possibly a demonstration of His divine nature, and to others it was no doubt a stumbling block. But Jesus never permitted the danger of being misunderstood to keep Him from showing mercy or expressing His love.

**Thy faith hath saved thee** (50). If, as has been suggested, this woman was converted earlier, the faith to which Jesus refers was also earlier. But just as the woman had confirmed her repentance and her love on this occasion, and just as Jesus had confirmed His forgiveness, the woman had demonstrated anew her living faith in Christ. Certainly the courage which her actions demonstrated, and her deep sincerity, testify to a strong faith without which these could not have been possible.

Under the heading, "The Sinner's Faith" (text, 50), Charles Simeon offers this outline: *First,* The marks and evidences of her faith: (1) Her zeal; (2) Her humility; (3) Her contrition; (4) Her love; (5) Her confidence. *Second,* The fruits and consequences of her faith: (1) The pardon of her sins; (2) An assurance of her acceptance; (3) Everlasting happiness and glory.

9. *Jesus on Tour* (8:1-3)

This portion is found only in Luke.

**It came to pass afterward** (1). This marks a change in the Master's method of procedure. It seems that He ceased to use Capernaum as a headquarters and began to move in wider circles. **He went throughout every city and village** is literally "He journeyed through city by city and village by village." This was a planned, concerted campaign to reach the whole of Galilee. **Preaching and shewing the glad tidings of the kingdom of God.** The single Greek word which is translated **shewing the glad tidings** means literally "evangelizing" or "announcing (or proclaiming) the good tidings (or gospel)." This was to be an evangelistic tour; the purpose was to spread the good news and urge men to accept it. The twelve apostles were with Him on this tour.

**And certain women** (2). It has been noted in the Introduction that Luke's Gospel is "The Gospel of Women." Here we see an illustration of this fact. Luke informs us that these **certain women** had a vital part in the evangelistic ministry of Jesus. Each one had a special reason to be very grateful to Christ and to feel indebted to Him. They **had been healed of evil spirits and infirmities.**

488

**Mary called Magdalene** means Mary of the town of Magdala. She is described as one **out of whom went seven devils.** She is commonly thought to have been a prostitute who had repented and became a sainted disciple of Jesus. She is generally so represented by painters and some older historians. But there is not the least bit of evidence, either here or anywhere else in the New Testament, that she ever was an immoral woman. That she was one of Jesus' most devoted disciples is clearly shown. **Seven devils** means many demons, the figure seven often being used to indicate an indefinite number. She had doubtless been so possessed with demons as to be in a state of insanity.

**Joanna the wife of Chuza Herod's steward** (3). The Herod referred to is Herod Antipas, ruler of Galilee. The record does not say just what was the infirmity of which Joanna was healed —whether demon possession or a physical disease. Her rank shows that prominent persons were being drawn to Christ. It is believed that she was a widow at this time. About **Susanna** nothing but her name is known. **Many others.** Only these three names are given—no doubt because of their prominence. But there were many more, constituting a large following of women who made it their business to minister **unto him of their substance.** This would imply that they were all women of some means, perhaps all members of the upper class.

### 10. *The Parable of the Sower* (8:4-15)

This episode is given by all three Synoptists. For discussion see Matt. 13:1-9, 18-23 (cf. Mark 4:1-20).

Here may be found "God's Soil Analysis." Note (1) The wayside soil—hardened hearts, 5; (2) The rock-top soil—shallow hearts, 6; (3) Thorn-infested soil—unsanctified hearts, 7; (4) The good soil—fruitful hearts, 8.

### 11. *Hidden Light* (8:16-18)

This lesson is found in Mark, but Matthew omits it. For full discussion see comments on Mark 4:21-25.

**No man, when he hath lighted a candle** (16); literally, "a lamp." Mark puts this statement in the form of a question. The purpose of light is to reveal. Hidden light is unthinkable.

**Nothing is secret, that shall not be made manifest** (17). God's revealing light cannot be hidden and nothing can be hidden from it. One is foolish to try to keep secrets from God.

**Take heed therefore how ye hear** (18). Not only what we hear, as Mark (4:24) has it, but how we hear is important. We have an obligation to hear—to listen. Then we have an added obligation to act in accordance with the new light which comes from hearing. Light, which comes from the Word and from the Holy Spirit, becomes darkness when it is not heeded.

**Whosoever hath, to him shall be given; and whosoever hath not, from him shall be taken . . .** Whoever has, as a result of right hearing and recognition of obligation, to him can be trusted more. **That which he seemeth to have**—Mark has simply "that which he hath" (4:25). The spiritual laggard and cheat will never have true riches, but even the semblance will finally be lost. Sometimes it is difficult for the onlooker to tell the difference between the real and the appearance, but God knows the difference and deals with men accordingly.

Barclay calls this paragraph "Laws for Life." He notes three of them: (1) The essential conspicuousness of the Christian life, 16; (2) The impossibility of secrecy, 17; and (3) The man who has, will get more—the seeker will always find.

### 12. *Jesus' Mother and Brothers* (8:19-21)

Luke's account of this episode is briefer than that of either Matthew or Mark.[12] It is especially interesting to note that Luke omits the questions, "Who is my mother? and who are my brethren?" which are found in the other accounts. He possibly felt that this might be taken by his Gentile readers as at least a hint of disrespect for Mary, who has been given a place of prominence in this Gospel. Also, as has been seen earlier, Luke gives a higher place to women than was customary in Palestine in his day. For full discussion see Matt. 12:46-50.

### 13. *The Master of the Tempest* (8:22-25)

This account is found in all three Synoptics. For discussion see Matt. 8:18, 23-27 (cf. Mark 4:35-41).

### 14. *The Demoniac Healed* (8:26-39)

The record of this miracle is found in all three Synoptics. The most extensive coverage is in Mark and the briefest treatment is in Matthew. Luke follows Mark rather closely, differing

---

[12]See Matt. 12:46-50; Mark 3:31-35.

somewhat in wording but quite similar in fact. For discussion see Mark 5:1-20 (cf. Matt. 8:28-34).

15. *The Raising of a Girl and the Healing of a Woman* (8:40-56)

These two miracles form a single episode, for one was performed en route to the other. All three Synoptics include both miracles, and all three give the healing of the woman as a sort of interruption in the procession to raise the girl. Mark gives the most detailed account, and Matthew gives the briefest. Luke again follows Mark rather closely. For detailed discussion see comments on Mark 5:21-43 (cf. also Matt. 9:1, 18-26).

Luke gives the age of the girl as twelve, while Matthew omits her age and Mark gives it at the end. Matthew does not mention the woman's failure to get help from physicians. But it is interesting to note how differently this matter is stated by Luke, the physician, and by Mark. Mark says the woman "had suffered many things of many physicians, and had spent all that she had, and was nothing bettered, but rather grew worse" (Mark 5:26). Luke is not quite so critical of the doctors. He says she **had spent all her living upon physicians, neither could be healed of any** (43).

In connection with the healing of Jairus' daughter, Maclaren notes these three points: (1) A word of encouragement which sustains a feeble faith—**Fear not: believe only, and she shall be made whole,** 50; (2) A word of revelation which smooths the grimness of death—**She is not dead, but sleepeth,** 52; (3) A word of power which brings back the child—**Maid, arise,** 54.

D. THE FOURTH PERIOD, 9:1-50

1. *The Mission of the Twelve* (9:1-6)

Of the four periods of Jesus' Galilean ministry, all but the first begin with an episode related to the disciples (or part of them)—of course He had no regular disciples at the beginning of the first period. The second period begins with the call of four disciples—Peter, Andrew, James, and John. The third period begins with the choosing of the Twelve. Now the fourth period begins with the mission of the Twelve. This episode is found in all three Synoptics. Matthew gives a detailed account with accompanying admonitions to the Twelve. For discussion see Matt. 9:36—11:1.

### 2. *Herod Is Disturbed* (9:7-9)

Luke's account at this point is much briefer than that of the other two Synoptists. He deals only with Herod's question as to the identity of Jesus, while the other two Evangelists discuss the death of John in connection with this question. At this point Luke merely mentions John's death. He had mentioned the imprisonment of John as a conclusion to his narration of John's ministry (see comments on Luke 3:18-20). For full discussion see comments on Matt. 14:1-12.

### 3. *The Five Thousand Fed* (9:10-17)

This account is found in all four Gospels.[13] For discussion see comments on Matt. 14:13-23.

### 4. *The Great Confession* (9:18-21)

This episode is found in all three Synoptics. For discussion see comments on Matt. 16:13-20 (cf. also Mark 8:27-30).

### 5. *Jesus Teaches Total Commitment* (9:22-27)

This record is given by all three Synoptics. For discussion see comments on Matt. 16:21-28 (cf. also Mark 8:31—9:1).

### 6. *The Transfiguration* (9:28-36)

This episode is given by all three Synoptics. For full discussion see Matt. 17:1-13 (cf. also Mark 9:2-13). Luke makes three contributions to the story:

(1) He tells us that Jesus went up into this mountain to pray and that it was while He was praying that He was transfigured (28-29).

(2) He informs us that Moses and Elijah talked of Jesus' coming death, which was soon to be accomplished at Jerusalem (30).

(3) He reports that Peter, James, and John slept through a part of the happenings on the mountain and awoke to see the visitors from heaven (32).

These are details which do not materially change the story, yet they are significant. The first is certainly characteristic of Luke. He, more than any other Gospel writer, reports on the significant instances of prayer in Jesus' life. The knowledge of this fact deepens the devotional value of the story.

---

[13]Cf. Matt. 14:13-23; Mark 6:30-46; John 6:1-15.

Since the Transfiguration is obviously related to the mission of Christ on earth, its significance is clarified by Luke's report that the subject for discussion was Christ's atoning death. Knowing this, it is appropriate that Moses and Elijah were there to represent the Law and the Prophets in a last consultation with the Redeemer before the payment of the redemptive price.

Luke's third addition to the account injects the human element into the story. We must always remember that these three energetic and devoted followers of Jesus were intensely human. Sleep, fear, and frustration characterized their reactions on this occasion.

### 7. *An Evil Spirit Cast Out of a Child* (9:37-43a)

Mark gives this episode in detail while the accounts of the other two Synoptists are shorter. Where Luke differs from Matthew he generally follows Mark rather closely. For discussion see comments on Mark 9:14-29 (cf. also Matt. 17:14-20).

### 8. *Jesus Foretells His Passion* (9:43b-45)

All three Synoptics contain this prophecy. Again Luke follows Mark more closely on details than he does Matthew. For discussion see comments on Mark 9:30-32 (cf. Matt. 17:22-23).

### 9. *An Unchristlike Spirit* (9:46-50)

All three Synoptists report this episode. Mark's account is more detailed than the others and it more nearly parallels Luke's than it does Matthew's. For discussion see comments on Mark 9:33-50 (cf. Matt. 18:1-6).

## Section V

# The Journey to Jerusalem—
# The Perean Ministry

### Luke 9:51—19:27

To call this great division of Luke's Gospel "The Journey to Jerusalem" is an oversimplification, for it was not a single and continuous journey toward that city. Rather it was a complex evangelistic and teaching ministry, the final destination of which was Jerusalem. At least once during this ministry the Master took a brief trip there (10:38-42).

The general course which Jesus pursued was as follows: He began this period in Galilee west of the Jordan River. He crossed the Jordan south of the Sea of Galilee and north of Samaria. He then moved through Perea from north to south (with many side trips) until He reached the point on the east side of Jordan opposite Jericho. There He crossed Jordan, went through Jericho, and on up to Jerusalem. Part of the evangelization of this area seems to have been accomplished by sending out bands of disciples. This ministry seems to have filled up the last six or seven months before the Lord's passion.

The major part of the material in this division of Luke's account is not in any other Gospel. Some of the best-known and best-loved stories in all of the Gospels are found here—"The Good Samaritan," "The Prodigal Son," "The Rich Man and Lazarus," and many others.

### A. THE FIRST STAGE, 9:51—13:21

#### 1. A Samaritan Rejection (9:51-56)

**And it came to pass, when the time was come that he should be received up, he stedfastly set his face to go to Jerusalem** (51). Here is Luke's introduction to this entire division, and it sets the tone for all that follows. From this point the shadow of the Cross falls upon everything that is said or done. But note that the emphasis is not upon death or the Cross but the Ascension **(received up)**. Jesus has not lost sight of the Cross, but His attention is focused beyond it.

The phrase **stedfastly set his face** implies a determined and concerted fixing of His attention upon the sacrifice of himself, which was the chief purpose of His incarnation. From this point

494

until Calvary, He was recognized as one with a "set face" and a set purpose. Even the Samaritans noticed it (cf. v. 53).

**Sent messengers . . . into a village of the Samaritans** (52). It would seem that, if the Samaritans had been willing, the final stage of Jesus' ministry before His last days in Jerusalem might have been in Samaria. At least the Samaritans would have shared in this ministry.

The Samaritans were half-breeds in race and semi-pagans in religion. When the Assyrians conquered Israel (the ten tribes) they carried away captive many of the Israelites and brought back pagans from the East to fill their places in Palestine. Thus the race became mixed, and in process of time the religion also became a hybrid with a rival temple and a claim that Mount Gerizim was the proper place to worship.[1] The intense rivalry between Samaria and Judea began in the division of Solomon's kingdom,[2] and was intensified after the mixing of the race by the Assyrians—especially as a result of the conflict between Sanballat and the Jews at the return from Babylonian captivity.[3] In Jesus' time the Jews hated the Samaritans and considered them to be on a level with dogs; the Samaritans reciprocated in kind, so that Jews had two reasons for avoiding Samaria: hatred and fear.

**They did not receive him, because his face was as though he would go to Jerusalem** (53). The Samaritans had no doubt heard about Jesus—His works and His teachings. This verse implies that they might have received Him if He had not been set on going to Jerusalem. They no doubt saw much in Him to be desired, and they knew that the Jewish hierarchy did not like Him. This made Him more attractive to them. But His determination to go to Jerusalem made Him unacceptable.

**Wilt thou that we command fire to come down from heaven, and consume them, even as Elias did?** (54) The Lord knew what He was doing when He surnamed James and John the "Sons of Thunder." Here their natural fiery dispositions, their typical Jewish dislike for Samaritans, and the fact that their Lord had been slighted were enough to make them favor annihilation as a punishment. And they had an Old Testament precedent.

---

[1]See II Kings 17:24-34. See also John 4:30-37.
[2]There was actually tribal rivalry between Judah and Ephraim earlier than this.
[3]Neh. 4:1-2.

**Ye know not what manner of spirit ye are of** (55) is literally "Ye know not of what spirit ye are." Jesus did not condemn Elijah, but He wanted His disciples to know that they were to have a different spirit.[4] They needed to learn that they were entering the dispensation of love, mercy, forgiveness, and forbearance. Jesus had not come to destroy sinners but to give them the gospel and an opportunity to repent. **For the Son of man is not come to destroy men's lives, but to save them** (56). **And they went into another village.** Here is an example of forbearance. It is always better to go to another village than to call down fire. But this other village was a Jewish village, and this marks the turn away from a possible evangelization of Samaria. It also marks the turn toward Perea.

### 2. The Cost of Discipleship (9:57-62)

**A certain man said . . . Lord, I will follow thee whithersoever thou goest. And Jesus said . . . Foxes have holes, and birds of the air have nests; but the Son of man hath not where to lay his head** (57-58). A shallow commitment is easily made, but behind it there is often a selfish motive. Here Jesus made it clear that anyone who wanted to follow Him for earthly gain would be disappointed. For further discussion see comments on Matt. 8:18-22.

**He said unto another, Follow me. But he said, Lord, suffer me first to go and bury my father. Jesus said . . . Let the dead bury their dead: but go thou and preach the kingdom of God** (59-60). The man in verse 57 offered his services and was discouraged. This man (59) received a special call from Jesus **(Follow me)**. He planned to obey the call but wanted to do something else first. Jesus informed him that his present call was more important than anything else.

**Another also said, Lord, I will follow thee; but let me first go bid them farewell, which are at home . . . Jesus said . . . No man, having put his hand to the plough, and looking back, is fit for the kingdom of God** (61-62). This man volunteered his services to the Master but wanted to postpone his religious duties until his social obligations had been performed. Jesus is saying here, as in the two preceding instances, that service for Christ and

---

[4]Though Elijah lived in an earlier and different age, yet it may be there is a hint here that even Elijah was moved by purer motives than were James and John, who were motivated at least partly by race prejudice. **Even as Elias did** is not in the oldest manuscripts.

His kingdom must come first. If we do not put them above everything else, no matter how important, we cannot be His disciples. Once we put our hands to the plow in the Master's field there must be no looking back. Jesus seems to imply that this volunteer disciple is already beginning to look back longingly to the things he is leaving behind.

It must be remembered that Jesus saw deeper into these three commitments or responses than we can see. He saw the heart attitude which prompted them. He knew whether the commitments were complete or halfhearted, and He simply will not have halfhearted disciples. His work and His person are too important for such shallow discipleship.

Charles Simeon describes the three characters here. The first (57-58) professes the utmost willingness to follow Christ. The second (59-60) manifests a great degree of unwillingness. The third (61-62) professes a willingness to follow Christ, but pleads for permission to delay it. To the first, Christ shows the difficulties of discipleship. To the second, He declares that every consideration must give way. To the third, He administers a solemn caution.

### 3. *The Mission of the Seventy* (10:1-20)

**The Lord appointed other seventy also** (1). Literally, "seventy others." Luke does not mean that Christ had sent seventy before, but that the seventy were in addition to the twelve who were sent out. Luke is the only Gospel writer who records this episode, but he is also the only one to treat (in any detail) the Perean ministry, of which it is a part.

The number seventy appears to have had special significance among the Jews. There were seventy elders appointed by Moses, seventy members of the Sanhedrin (seventy-one including the president or nasi), and according to Jewish legend the seventy peoples or nations of the earth other than the Jews. The very fact that Jesus had this many trustworthy disciples is significant. We often forget that He had many loyal followers.

**Sent them two and two.** For mutual help and encouragement. **Into every city and place, whither he himself would come.** They were to make preparations for His own visits to these towns. At this time the twelve apostles were *with* Him; the seventy *went before* Him. It is quite possible that each of these pairs of disciples went to only one town and stayed there, preaching, teaching, and in other ways preparing for Jesus' visit. This would make thirty-five towns and villages visited by Jesus in His Perean ministry, and He could hardly have visited many more in six or seven months' time unless His visits were very brief.

From verse 2 through 16 Jesus is giving instructions and admonitions to the seventy. Much of this is either the same as or similar to instruction given at various times to the twelve apostles. Some critics stumble at such similarity between passages. But it is most reasonable that Jesus would give the same or similar admonition twice if the demands of the situations were the same. Any church leader admonishing groups of ministers would inevitably repeat himself, for all ministers would need much the same instruction.

**The harvest truly is great, but the labourers are few** (2). The harvest metaphor seems to have been a favorite one for Jesus. The harvest of human souls has always been great, and the laborers have always been tragically few. It is man's fatal lack of concern for his fellowmen that keeps the number so small. But the Master makes it clear throughout His gospel that this concern is a test of discipleship. His disciples *are* laboring in the harvest. Those who are not so laboring are not worthy to be called disciples.

**Pray ye therefore the Lord of the harvest, that he will send forth labourers into his harvest.** Getting the harvest into the garner is our responsibility, and even getting the needed laborers is partly our responsibility. We are to see the need, and we are to work and pray for additional workers, but no man has a right to pray for help in the harvest field until he is doing his best. God will not send workers to help a laggard—he does not need help to do what he is doing.

**I send you forth as lambs among wolves** (3). What a paradox: Lambs going out to rescue sheep from wolves! Here is simplicity united with defenselessness: no carnal weapons for defense. But God has a way of making strength out of weakness and using even death as a weapon of victory and life. Here we see the uniqueness of Christ. He is the world's greatest Conqueror, yet His forces have been utterly defenseless insofar as carnal and earthly defense is concerned. Christians have been slain by the thousands, but the triumphant advance has continued. We need to stop and meditate at this point and gain new light and inspiration for the task and the battle of today. We are not without protection, for Christ is with us. When death itself does not defeat us, we are undefeatable. But once we begin to arm ourselves with carnal armor we are headed toward defeat.

**Neither purse, nor scrip, nor shoes** (4) is literally "neither purse nor provision bag nor sandals." The seventy were not to be burdened with baggage nor puzzled about provisions. They had a most important mission, and the King's business required haste. See also comments on Matt. 10: 9 ff.

**Salute no man by the way.** This refers particularly to the long and tedious salutations customary in the East. They were not to waste precious time, but they were to be so absorbed in their mission that their single-hearted devotion would be seen by all whom they should meet.

**If the son of peace be there** (6). **Son of peace** is an Aramaic expression for "a peaceful man," or "one of good report," "reputable." These messengers of Christ were to stay in homes that were reputable. They were not to injure the name of Christ by residing with the base or unworthy.

**In the same house remain, eating and drinking such things as they give: for the labourer is worthy of his hire** (7). They were not to be demanding, but they were to be grateful for anything which was given to them; yet they were not to consider themselves (or be considered by others) as beggars, but laborers receiving their wages. **Go not from house to house.** The house where they are originally taken in should be their abode throughout their stay in a town.

For discussion of material in verses 8-12, see comments on Matt. 10:14-15; for verses 13-15 see comments on Matt. 11: 21-24; for notes on verse 16 see Matt. 10: 40.

**And the seventy returned with joy, saying, Lord, even the devils are subject unto us** (17). They were astonished at the miraculous power they were enabled to exercise. They were joyous at the remembrance of their accomplishments. But Jesus showed them (20) that their joy was misplaced because their emphasis was misplaced. However He did not reprimand them for their delight at seeing Satan's kingdom suffer loss.

**I beheld Satan as lightning fall from heaven** (18). Here Jesus was both reminiscing and prophesying. Satan had suffered some major defeats—especially in connection with Christ's temptation. But Jesus was looking forward to Satan's final fall, his complete defeat at Christ's own hands.

**Behold, I give unto you power to tread on serpents and scorpions, and over all the power of the enemy (19)**. This scripture does have a literal application,[5] but the context seems to demand that the primary meaning is spiritual. Note how Jesus parallels **serpents, scorpions,** and **all the power of the enemy.** Both the preceding and succeeding verses refer to Satanic powers. Also the grammar of this verse implies that these **serpents and scorpions** are included in the powers of the enemy. The symbolism is common for Satanic powers or demons, or for Satan himself. The primary meaning is that they had power to tread triumphantly over Satan's host through Jesus' help and grace.

**Notwithstanding (20)** shows that the foregoing was not a reprimand. **In this rejoice not, that the spirits are subject unto you; but rather rejoice, because your names are written in heaven.** Here is the proper emphasis, the proper ground for rejoicing. Power and its manifestation is more glamorous, but eternal life is more essential. Citizenship in heaven is more important than the ability to produce dread in hell.

### 4. *Jesus' Moment of Exultation* (10:21-24)

**Jesus rejoiced in spirit, and said, I thank thee, O Father, . . . that thou hast hid these things from the wise and prudent, and hast revealed them unto babes (21)**. This is one of those occasions when gladness filled the heart of the Man of Sorrows, and He **rejoiced** (exulted) **in spirit.** He had a twofold reason for rejoicing: victory had crowned the efforts of the seventy, and divine truth had been imparted to these babes in Christ—truths which the wise and prudent of this world had missed. Through the help of God, these untrained men had penetrated more deeply into truth than the philosophers of all ages, unaided by divine revelation. Note that the Father had **revealed** these things to them.[6]

On this passage the *Pulpit Commentary* offers this threefold outline: (1) The gladness of gratitude, 20; (2) The heritage of the humble-hearted, 21; (3) The refuge of the perplexed—**so it seemed good in thy sight,** 21.

[5]See Acts 28:3-5.
[6]For additional light on this and the following verse see comments on Matt. 11:25-27.

**All things are delivered to me of my Father** (22). Two truths are couched in these words. On the one hand, all the power of heaven is at Jesus' disposal, should He choose to use it in His war with Satan. On the other hand, these words show the complete subjection of the Son to the Father during Jesus' earthly sojourn. This subjection or subordination of the Son to the Father is both voluntary and temporary.

**No man knoweth who the Son is, but the Father.** Only the divine Father can comprehend the divine person of the Son. **And who the Father is, but the Son.** Only the divine Son can comprehend the divine person of the Father. Only Deity can comprehend Deity. **And he to whom the Son will reveal him.** Man can have a very hazy and fragmentary comprehension of the Father, but even this is possible only as the Father is revealed to man by the Son. It is the Son who chooses ("wills") those to whom He will reveal the Father. On this occasion he has chosen these **babes** in preference to the **wise and prudent.** Revelation is "from" the Father but "through" the Son.

**He turned him unto his disciples, and said privately** (23). Jesus had a private message for them that He did not want the worldlings to hear. God often shares private messages with His children—messages of which others around them may be completely unaware. **Blessed are the eyes which see the things that ye see.** These words could be remembered with profit in the dark days to come—when the blessedness of their lot would not be so apparent. They were seeing the beginning of the mighty advance of the kingdom of God on earth. These disciples would not soon comprehend the full significance of these words—perhaps never in this world. But as disciples they were to have a progressive unfolding and comprehension of the gracious privilege that was theirs as ambassadors for Christ.[7]

**For . . . prophets and kings have desired to see . . . and . . . hear those things** (24). Men in the old dispensation saw these things dimly through the eye of prophecy. They were destined never to see (in this world) the things which they predicted. No king or prophet in Israel's great past had been so blessed as these humble men. Though picked from the lower ranks of society, they went out to proclaim the establishing of the kingdom of Christ— the good news of salvation.

[7]For additional light on this and the following verse see comments on Matt. 13:16-17.

### 5. *The Good Samaritan* (10: 25-37)

This is one of the best-loved stories of the New Testament. We are indebted to Luke for giving it to us, for no other New Testament writer records it. The occasion for telling the story evidently took place in or near Jerusalem—possibly in Bethany at the house of Lazarus when Jesus made His brief trip to Jerusalem for the Feast of the Dedication. Note that in the next events (38-42) He is at Bethany.

**A certain lawyer** (25). These men are often referred to as scribes—learned in the law of Moses and in Jewish tradition. **Stood up.** He was evidently seated among those who were listening to Jesus' teaching. He stood up to get the Master's attention in order to ask a question. **Tempted him.** His question was not a sincere search for truth but a trick question designed to involve the Master in one of the frequent Jewish disputes. **What shall I do to inherit eternal life?** This apparently innocent search for spiritual guidance was recognized by the Master for the trick that it was. He avoided the expected answer by asking a question of the lawyer, thus putting him on the defensive. **What is written in the law? how readest thou?** (26) If the law had the answer, a lawyer should know what it was.

**Thou shalt love the Lord thy God . . . and thy neighbour** (27). The lawyer went to two texts which are among the best Old Testament expressions of New Testament attitudes. For a discussion of the significance of these texts see comments on Matt. 22: 37-40.[8]

**Thou hast answered right** (28). Jesus commended his answer and added, **this do, and thou shalt live.** Love for God and for one's fellowmen is the very essence of true religion. If the lawyer could live up to this standard, he had assurance that he would live eternally.

**But he, willing to justify himself** (29). He obviously felt condemned by the second rule, even though no accusation was made by anyone. His love for God was sadly lacking also. But his relation to and attitude toward his fellowman could be more easily detected and gauged than his love for God. He condemned himself—at least revealed his sense of condemnation—by trying to justify himself. **And who is my neighbour?** Evidently there were many whom he did not love, but he was asking (and at the same time he was satisfied that he knew the answer), "Are these

[8]See also comments on Matt. 19:19.

whom I do not love my neighbors?" Jesus answered him by giving a significant parable meaningful as a story, memorable as an abiding portion of divine revelation, and strikingly appropriate for the situation and for the man. In this story instruction is given, not by precept, but by example.

**A certain man went down from Jerusalem to Jericho** (30). We are given no information about the man other than the events in his journey. His name is not given, and even his race is not stated. This would be to Luke's liking, since he is presenting Jesus as the Saviour of all men. However, the implication of the story is that he was a Jew—much of the point and force of the story depends upon this fact.

Jericho was situated about seventeen miles to the northeast of Jerusalem and about five miles west of the Jordan River. The elevation of Jericho is about thirty-two hundred feet below that of Jerusalem, so that a journey like the one this man took would be a rather steep descent. The land between these two cities was rugged and in places uninhabited, though the road between them was frequently traveled—one of the more important roads in Palestine. The ruggedness of the country and the number of travelers made it a haven for bandits.

This story might have been an actual incident on the Jericho road rather than an ordinary parable. If so, it was certainly well chosen by the Master, for everything in the story fits perfectly the lesson He is trying to teach.

**He fell among thieves**—literally "robbers" or "bandits." Thieves are interested only in stealing one's property. Robbers or bandits often wound or kill. This traveler was not only robbed of his possessions but was left **half dead** (30).

**A certain priest** (31). A large number of priests and Levites lived in Jericho and went up to Jerusalem whenever their course of service at the Temple was due. It is interesting to note that this is the only time Jesus ever spoke in any way against the priests. Their position as guardians of God's house seems to have been respected by Jesus even though they were often personally deserving of His censure. This particular priest might have been going at this time to the Temple to begin serving his one-week term. If so, he probably passed by on the other side of the road to avoid ceremonial defilement, which would have interfered with his priestly functions. At any rate something else was more important to him than a man's life—even the life of a fellow Jew.

**And likewise a Levite** (32). Levites assisted the priests by doing the necessary labor around the Temple grounds. This Levite did show some pity—or was it curiosity? He came and looked at the man. But he was no better than the priest, because he disregarded what little compassion he felt. He too **passed by on the other side.** Whatever the motive which prompted both the priest and the Levite to pass by without helping their fellow Jew, the point is the same: it is what they lacked that is important, not their reason for failing to act. They were almost (if not entirely) devoid of love for their fellowman. The lawyer for whose benefit Jesus was telling the story would surely have counted this unfortunate man a neighbor.

**A certain Samaritan** (33). His name and rank are unimportant here, for all Samaritans were hated by the Jews, and evidently most Samaritans had a like feeling for Jews. The point is that a man who had no special reason for helping this Jew and almost every racial reason for not helping him was moved by his compassion for a suffering fellow human being. Even though his fellow human being belonged to a hated race, he stopped and aided him to the full extent of his ability.

Note the extent to which the Samaritan helped the Jew: (a) he gave him immediate emergency help; (b) he took him to an inn where he could be cared for while he convalesced; (c) he paid the bill in advance; and (d) he offered further assistance if it should prove necessary. He neglected no kind of service which was in his power to perform.

**Which ... of these three, ... was neighbour unto him that fell among the thieves?** (36) Notice how Jesus has reversed the order and the relationship. The lawyer had said, "Who is my neighbour?" But in Jesus' story and in His question it is, Which one was neighbor to him? That is, To whom can I (must I) be a neighbor? The lawyer's question had no sense of human obligation in it. Jesus' question stresses obligation strongly. So Jesus did not really answer the lawyer's question; He showed him that he had asked the wrong question because his attitudes were wrong and his love for his neighbors was sadly lacking. The man saw the point, for he answered the Lord's question correctly: **He that shewed mercy on him** (37). The application was clear and simple. The lawyer could see this before the Master pointed it out: **Go, and do thou likewise.**

William Barclay notes three significant truths in the story:
(1) We must help a man even when he has brought his trouble
on himself, 30; (2) Any man of any nation who is in need is our
neighbor, 31-33; (3) Our help must be practical, and must not
consist merely in *feeling* sorry.

### 6. *A Visit to Martha and Mary* (10:38-42).

**He entered into a certain village** (38). This village was
Bethany, for this was obviously the Martha and Mary about
whom John wrote (John 11:1 ff.). The descriptions of the sisters
given in these two Gospels clearly point to the same persons. This
incident probably took place when Jesus made His brief visit to
Jerusalem for the Feast of the Dedication during the December
preceding His passion.

A beautiful friendship existed between Jesus and these two
sisters and their brother, Lazarus. In His associations with them
we get one of the best pictures of the human side of Christ found
in the New Testament. Jesus must have known them from very
early in His ministry. He might have met them on one of His
many trips to Jerusalem.

In view of the obvious warmth and closeness of this friendship, it is a puzzling fact that none of the Synoptic Gospels mentions Lazarus, and the only account of the sisters outside John's
Gospel is the one here under consideration. The best answer
available seems to be that it did not suit the purpose of the
Gospel writers or the Holy Spirit to say more.

Many attempts have been made to identify Mary, Martha,
and Lazarus with other known persons. One suggestion is that
Martha was the wife of Simon the Leper. Lazarus has been
identified with the Rabbi Eliezer (or Lazarus) of the Talmud.
But these and other speculations are without proof and must be
treated as mere conjecture.

**Martha** is Aramaic and means "lady"; it is the equivalent of
the Greek *kyria*. It has been suggested that Martha was the
"elect lady" to whom John wrote his Second Epistle. She **received him into her house.** Martha was either married (or a
widow) and Mary and Lazarus were living with her or she was
recognized as the mistress of the house because she was older
than they. In this latter case they might have been living together as a family since the death of their parents.

**She had a sister called Mary** (39). Mary is obviously subordinate to her sister. Her only relationship to the house or to the

present social event is that she is the sister of Martha. **Which also sat at Jesus' feet, and heard his word**—literally, "who also having sat down at the feet of Jesus was listening to (or hearing) His word." It has been suggested that the word **also** implies that she at first helped with the serving; then she sat down to listen to Jesus' words. The expression **sat at Jesus' feet** has a twofold meaning. It would literally imply that she sat beneath Him (on a lower seat), but it also has a figurative or metaphorical meaning of listening as a disciple would listen to his teacher. It implies teacher-pupil relationship. Disciples are generally said to sit at the rabbi's feet as Paul sat at the feet of Gamaliel (Acts 22:3).

**Martha was cumbered about much serving** (40) is literally "Martha was distracted about much service." **And came to him.** The Greek behind this phrase indicates a sudden cessation of her feverish activity—in a mood of desperation or exasperation. **Lord, dost thou not care that my sister hath left me to serve alone?** This clause also bears the marks of exasperation and agitation. A literal translation would be, "Lord, is it no concern to Thee that my sister hath left me to serve alone?" She not only blamed her sister, but she was agitated and somewhat impatient with the Lord for permitting her sister to forsake her. In fact, she seemed to suggest that the Lord was encouraging Mary to neglect her duty. The word translated **left** means "to go away from." This also suggests that Mary had been helping her sister but had stopped and had gone to listen to Jesus.

**Bid her therefore that she help me**—literally "tell her" or "speak to her." The word **therefore** implies that Martha is sure that her previous statements have fully justified her cause and condemned Mary. The implication is, Since my cause has been irrefutably demonstrated, bid her. Martha is obviously confident that she is in the right—that she has been wronged.

**Martha, Martha** (41). Spence points out that "there are several notable instances of this repetition of the name by the Master in the New Testament story, and in each case apparently in pitying love."[9] He has reference to "Simon, Simon," in Luke 22:31; "Saul, Saul," in Acts 9:4; etc. **Thou art careful and troubled about many things.** The Greek word translated **thou art careful** means "anxious" or "troubled with care." Jesus is saying that she is too much disturbed about too many things which are not that important.

[9]Spence, *op. cit.*, I, 278.

**One thing is needful** (42). Note the contrast between the **many things** about which Martha was troubled and the **one thing** that was needful. Martha's "many things" were material, physical, and social; Mary's "one thing" was spiritual and of eternal significance. Martha was not choosing the wrong in place of the right, but the incidental in place of the all-important, the temporal instead of the eternal.

Jesus had come into this home as a Guest. Martha was feverishly going about many things in order to please and properly entertain. But these things were not needful. He was not primarily interested in being received with open arms and a well-filled table but with open hearts and an opportunity to spread His table for them.

This clause could have a secondary application. Martha was preparing a sumptuous meal, and the extra work was harming her more than the additional food would help the Master.

**That good part** was a common expression meaning the portion of honor at a feast. Mary had chosen wisely. She knew what portion was the most desirable and the most honorable, and she chose it. There is a finality suggested in connection with this thought. Jesus guarantees this finality by supporting her choice: **it shall not be taken away from her.** The pervading figure throughout the passage is that of a feast, and the Master makes His point by setting the spiritual feast over against the material.

### 7. *A Discourse on Prayer* (11:1-13)

This discourse is found only in Luke, though certain portions of it are very similar to Jesus' teachings in the other Synoptic Gospels—especially Matthew's version of the Sermon on the Mount (Matt. 6:9-13; 7:7-11).

**As he was praying in a certain place** (1). The place is unknown. Evidently the subject matter alone concerned Luke. **When he ceased, one of his disciples said unto him, Lord, teach us to pray.** He was deeply moved by Jesus' prayer, which he seems to have overheard. It was so different from the prayers to which he had listened in the synagogue and in the Temple. Perhaps it was personal intimacy and simple faith which moved him. Such a prayer as Jesus must have prayed could not help moving any truly pious soul.

**As John also taught his disciples.** This disciple might have been a former disciple of John. If so, though he evidently felt that John's prayers were far above the average, he saw and

507

heard something in Jesus' prayer that marked an advance which his soul wanted to follow. It is also possible that he had heard of John's practices with regard to prayer but had not been taught by him.

Maclaren suggests for this verse: (1) The praying Christ teaches us to pray as a rest after service; (2) The praying Christ teaches us to pray as a preparation for important steps; (3) The praying Christ teaches us to pray as the condition of receiving the Spirit and the brightness of God (cf. 3:21-22; 9:29).

**When ye pray, say, Our Father** (2). For discussion of this prayer see comments on Matt. 6:9-13. The prayer as Jesus gave it here differs in two respects from this prayer as He taught it in the Sermon on the Mount. First, it has **forgive us our sins** where in the earlier form the petition was "forgive us our debts." We who believe strongly that Christians do not commit sin and remain Christians sometimes avoid this form of the prayer. To say **forgive us our sins** seems an admission that we voluntarily commit sin—which we do not believe is in harmony with the Bible standard for Christian living.

But the prayer, in this form, does have some significant lessons for us. Some of them are as follows: (*a*) our past forgiveness was conditioned by our willingness to forgive; (*b*) sin is still possible, and if we should sin, our forgiveness is conditioned by our willingness to forgive; (*c*) our unintentional wrongs, when we are made aware of them, ought to be confessed; and (*d*) God's forgiveness will be conditioned by our own spirit of forgiveness.

**A friend . . . at midnight** (5). Here Jesus uses a parable to illustrate an important aspect of prayer and an important truth about prayer. Night travel in Palestine was common because of the intense heat of the day, so that this friend's arrival at midnight is by no means unusual.

**Lend me three loaves.** Godet points out that one loaf was for the guest, one for the host, who must seat himself at the table and eat with his guest, and the third is a reserve loaf.[10] The reserve loaf would give the impression of a plentiful supply and so prevent embarrassing the guest with the thought that he was eating the last of his host's bread.

**A friend of mine . . . is come . . . and I have nothing to set before him** (6). Here we see both the poverty of the host and the demands of courtesy. He had no bread, but he could not let

---

[10]Godet, *op. cit.*, II, 56.

his guest go to bed hungry. Both the rules of courtesy and his love for his friend demanded that bread be secured. His one hope was to borrow the needed loaves from a neighbor.

**He from within shall answer and say, Trouble me not . . . (7).** The neighbor is unneighborly; the friend does not exhibit friendship. Love and the rules of courtesy demand from him what his needy neighbor asks but he does not acknowledge these demands. **The door is now shut.** No one would knock at a closed door in ancient Palestine unless his reason was very important—in this case, unless need was very pressing. **My children are with me in bed.** The **bed** was actually but a raised place in this one-room home, and the man did not want to disturb the children.

**Though he will not rise and give him, because he is his friend, yet because of his importunity he will rise and give him as many as he needeth (8).** Now we come to the point of the parable. Even where friendship is weak, importunity produces results. The application is obvious: If importunity brings results from a lukewarm friend, how much more will persistent prayer bring results from an all-loving God! Persistence in prayer is not an act of discourtesy toward God. Such resolute and continued seeking shows faith in God and a clear realization that our only hope is in Him.

**Ask, and it shall be given you,** etc. **(9-13).** For discussion see comments on Matt. 7:7-11. The present passage in Luke differs from the earlier discourse cited in Matthew in two particulars: (*a*) Luke's account adds the question in verse 12, "If he shall ask an egg, will he offer him a scorpion?" The meaning here is the same as in the two preceding questions. (*b*) In Matthew the passage closes with the words, "how much more shall your Father which is in heaven give good things to them that ask him?" In the passage in Luke the Master changes "good things" to "the Holy Spirit." Here we see that the Holy Spirit is given in answer to prayer and that the Father is anxious to give Him to us. He is the best of all "good things," and the wise Christian will ask for Him before and in preference to all else. We need the Holy Spirit in His sanctifying fullness, and we need Him as our abiding Paraclete or Advocate. This discourse in Luke comes later in Jesus' ministry and nearer to Pentecost than does the Sermon on the Mount, in which the passage cited in Matthew appears. Therefore Jesus can be more specific in His references to the needs of His disciples.

Verses 1-13 have been called "The Lessons of Prayer." The text would be in verse one, "Teach us to pray." There follow: (1) Pattern, 2-4; (2) Persistence, 5-9; (3) Promise, 10-13.

Verses 9-13 show us "The Father's Gift." (1) For whom? Based on sonship to God; (2) What? The Holy Spirit; (3) How? Ask.

### 8. *By Whom Did He Cast Out Demons?* (11:14-23)

This episode is recorded in all three Synoptic Gospels. For discussion see comments on Matt. 12:22-32 (cf. also Mark 3:22-30).

### 9. *When the Evil Spirit Returns* (11:24-26)

For discussion see comments on Matt. 12:43-45.

Barclay titles this section "The Peril of the Empty Soul." He notes: (1) You cannot leave a man's soul empty, 24-26; (2) We can never erect a real religion on negatives, 24-26; (3) The best way to avoid evil is to do good (27-28).

### 10. *Who Is Most Blessed?* (11:27-28)

**Blessed is the womb that bare thee** (27). This **certain woman of the company** was no doubt overwhelmed by the wisdom and power which were manifested in the words and works of Jesus. She might have been one of those who had experienced the healing from demon possession which Jesus had just finished discussing. Her reaction here is a type of hero worship more or less peculiar to mothers, who characteristically see great men as the fulfillment of mothers' hopes, dreams, and prayers. This woman was probably putting herself in Mary's place and was vicariously enjoying the ecstasy of a mother's pride in the accomplishments of her son. But she was also shortsighted, as the next verse reveals.

Her exclamation by no means implied actual worship of Mary. It is not even certain that she knew Jesus' mother. The word **blessed** combines the meaning of our two words "happy" and "fortunate." In the present instance it also carries at least a suggestion of the idea of "hallowed" or "sacred." This praise of Mary might be considered the first New Testament fulfillment of the prediction in the **Magnificat:** "All generations shall call me blessed" (Luke 1:48).

**Yea rather, blessed are they that hear the word of God, and keep it** (28). The word **yea** would seem to imply approval of

510

what the woman said, but the Greek does not clearly indicate either approval or disapproval. However it is clear that, whatever can be said for the blessedness of Mary as Jesus' mother, it is far more blessed to hear His words and to order one's life in accord with them. Thus, even for Mary herself the relationship of disciple is more blessed than that of mother. The Master did not miss any opportunity to make it clear that the primary and significant relationship of anyone to himself is the spiritual relationship, based upon obedience and oneness of will and purpose. This relationship has its origin in the spiritual experiences of conversion and entire sanctification, with continued fellowship in the Spirit.

## 11. *An Evil Generation Seeking a Sign* (11:29-32)

For discussion see comments on Matt. 12:38-42. Matthew's and Luke's accounts of this discourse are the same in substance, though the order of the statements differs somewhat.

## 12. *Light and Darkness* (11:33-36)

The substance of verses 33-35 is paralleled (either directly or by implication) elsewhere in the Synoptic Gospels. But this does not mean that Luke is incorrect in recording the discourse here and in its present order. What it does mean is that Jesus used that most effective pedagogical device known as repetition. Since the principles which Jesus taught were generally new either in content, spirit, or emphasis, it was most important that He should often repeat himself; otherwise His disciples would never have remembered or comprehended them. When Jesus repeated His sayings He seldom used the same words. It was the principle, not the wording, which He wanted to stress.

Verses 33 and 34 are close parallels of two portions of the Sermon on the Mount as recorded in Matthew. For discussion see comments on Matt. 5:15; 6:22-23.

**If thy whole body . . . be full of light** (36). In verse 34, Jesus said, ". . . when thine eye is single, thy whole body also is full of light." A "single" eye is a sound or healthy eye, and when the eye is sound every part of the body and mind shares the enjoyment of the light—no part is in darkness. It is the same with the soul; the healthy soul receives the light, and as a result every facet, every faculty, of our personality shares the benefits of the light. The emphasis in this verse seems to be on the word **whole**. The central idea is that there must be a healthy soul if health is going to be diffused throughout the whole personality. A lack of unity in one's basic loyalty to God will result in tension, confusion, and darkness in all other relationships. It is just such spiritual and moral soundness which constitutes New Testament holiness. There is no hint here of conflicting natures or any remaining double-mindedness in the New Testament norm for the Christian.

13. *What Is Wrong with the Pharisees and Lawyers?* (11: 37-54)

Many of Jesus' statements concerning the Pharisees and lawyers in this passage closely parallel His denunciation of these same groups in Matthew 23. However these are not two accounts of the same discourse, but two discourses given by the Master on different occasions. The events and teachings recorded in Matthew 23 took place in Jerusalem during Passion Week; the incident now under consideration in Luke took place while Jesus was in Perea on His way to Jerusalem. Also the occasion for the discourse in Luke and other surrounding circumstances were quite different from those of the Matthew account. A careful comparison will make this quite evident.

**A certain Pharisee besought him to dine with him** (37). Since by this time the Pharisees were generally at enmity with Jesus, it is quite possible that this invitation was part of a plan to trap the Master. Since they knew His habits and those of His disciples, they no doubt felt that this would not be hard to accomplish; He could easily be put in a position where some Pharisaic rule or custom would be violated. They could then use this information as ammunition against Him.

**And he went in, and sat down to meat.** The word translated **sat down** means literally "reclined." They did not use chairs; they reclined across couches. Jesus readily accepted the invitation. He would not compromise with the Pharisees; neither would He be in any way discourteous to them.

**The Pharisee . . . marvelled that he had not first washed before dinner** (38). The Pharisees' interest in washing before dinner was not a matter of cleanliness. They followed rigidly an elaborate system of ceremonial washings handed down to them by many generations of rabbis. The simple precepts in the Levitical Law which demanded cleanliness and ceremonial purity had been so completely covered over with rabbinical interpretations and ritual requirements that the original precepts were overlooked.

There is a strong implication here that Jesus purposely avoided washing before dinner. Verse 37 pictures Him coming in and immediately reclining to eat. The attitude which He shows in His discussion of the matter (39 ff.) strengthens the impression of deliberate failure to wash. If Jesus' action was deliberate, He must have had two motives: (*a*) He was expressing His disapproval of a rule which was not only meaningless but which obscured an important principle and gave rise to hypocritical sham; (*b*) He was probably trying to provoke a discussion with the Pharisees about these very matters. Thus both Jesus and the Pharisee (or Pharisees, if others were working through this one) were trying to precipitate the verbal conflict. Of course Jesus was in no sense vindictive; He was trying to help the Pharisees to see the truth, and at the same time He was attempting to save others from the corrupting influence of Pharisaism.

**The Lord said . . . ye Pharisees make clean the outside of the cup and platter; but your inward part is full of ravening and wickedness** (39). The word translated **ravening** means literally "plunder" or "robbery." These were strong words but true and necessary. The Pharisees had been very careful to cleanse the outside but overlooked a cesspool of wickedness in their souls. It was like washing the dishes carefully and then serving polluted food on them. The Pharisees were careful about appearances but careless about reality.

**Ye fools** (40). Certainly their actions and standard of values proved them to be just this. **Did not he that made that which is without make that which is within also?** These various washings were for religious purposes. Then, if religion be their motive, why neglect the inner, the vital man? Why be concerned with the outward, the perishing and overlook the permanent when they are supposed to be dealing with matters eternal? These so-called religious people never even attempted to deal with the source of sin.

**But rather give alms of such things as ye have** (41). The literal translation is much clearer: "But of the things which are within give alms." There is a twofold meaning in these words. First, He is saying that they should unselfishly and lovingly give alms, and in this they would be doing a far greater service than by ceremonial cleansing. The deeper meaning is that they should give unselfishly and lovingly of their inmost being—their love, their sympathy, their devotion, their very selves. Verse 39 implies that these Pharisees were robbing the poor. Here Jesus is telling them that the exact opposite should be their practice and attitude —they should give alms, and do so with no thought of returns.

**All things are clean unto you.** When one acts as Jesus has just admonished—out of pure, unselfish love—then all things will be clean to him. Sin, selfishness, rebellion, pride—these are the things which defile. Such moral defilement can be found only in personalities. Sin begins and is really committed in the will of a *person*—a being who has freedom to make moral choices.

**Woe unto you, Pharisees! for ye tithe . . . and pass over judgment and the love of God** (42). For discussion see comments on Matt. 23:23. In the discourse on this subject recorded in Matthew **the love of God** is not included. It is obvious that love was one of the Pharisees' weakest points, and the one point where they were farthest from Jesus and His teachings.

**Woe unto you, Pharisees! for ye love the uppermost seats . . . and greetings in the markets** (43). For discussion see comments on Matt. 23:6-7.

**Woe unto you, scribes and Pharisees, . . . ye are as graves** (44). Here we have a significant difference from the closest parallel in Jesus' later discourse (Matt. 23:27). In Matthew the scribes and Pharisees are compared to "whited sepulchres, which . . . appear beautiful outward, but are within full of dead men's bones, and of all uncleanness." The contrast in Matthew is between the beautiful exterior and the putrid interior.

Here in Luke the graves are not beautiful whited sepulchres, but simple, unmarked graves which one may tread upon without knowing it. Thus he would contract ceremonial defilement without being aware of it.[11] All graves were supposed to be whitewashed to warn passersby of their location. But these graves had been neglected. The Pharisees had buried their hypocrisy and wickedness so that their fellowmen were not aware of what was really hidden beneath their pious exterior.

There is also at least a suggestion of a secondary meaning in this verse. Just as one could walk over an unmarked grave and be ceremonially defiled without knowing it, so one could be guilty of breaking one of the multitude of intricate and often insignificant rules which made up the tradition of the elders and be ceremonially defiled (in the eyes of the Pharisees) without knowing it.

---

[11]Under the Levitical law all contact with sepulchres brought ceremonial defilement.

**Then answered one of the lawyers, . . . thus saying thou reproachest us also** (45). The word translated **reproachest** means literally "insult." In the preceding verse Jesus had included the scribes in His denunciation. The close similarity between lawyers and scribes, and the added fact that lawyers were usually Pharisees, gave these lawyers in Jesus' congregation the impression that they too were included. At least they felt that they also were insulted.

**Woe unto you also, ye lawyers!** (46) Jesus makes it clear that His judgment of the lawyers is the same as of the Pharisees. They are alike in their weakness and wickedness, and they should share in the condemnation. **Ye lade men with burdens . . . and ye yourselves touch not the burdens with one of your fingers.** For discussion see comments on Matt. 23:4.

**Ye build the sepulchres of the prophets, and your fathers killed them** (47). For discussion see comments on Matt. 23:29-31. In the passage cited in Matthew from Jesus' later controversy with the Pharisees and lawyers, the denunciation is directed at "the scribes and Pharisees." Here it is spoken specifically to the lawyers. Verse 48 indicated that by building the tombs of the prophets the Jews called attention to the fact that they were the children of the murderers. Phillips renders the verse, "You show clearly enough how you approve your fathers' actions. They did the actual killing and you put up a memorial to it."

**Therefore also said the wisdom of God, I will send them prophets and apostles, and some of them they shall slay . . .** (49-51). For discussion see comments on Matt. 23:34-36.

**Woe unto you, lawyers! for ye have taken away the key of knowledge** (52). **The key of knowledge,** the Key which unlocks the door of the kingdom of God, is the Scriptures. The Pharisees and lawyers had so confused and twisted the Scriptures in their maze of meaningless ceremonies and prohibitions that they were lost to the people as an effective means of entering the kingdom of God. **Ye entered not in yourselves, and them that were entering in ye hindered.** Both by their example and by their direct interference they shut the kingdom of God against men. For further discussion see comments on Matt. 23:13.

**And as he said these things unto them** (53). The best manuscripts read "and when he was come out from thence"; that is, from the house of the Pharisee. This reading is also in harmony with the fact that there seems to be a sudden increase in the number of His enemies—a group of Pharisees and scribes seem to have accosted Him when He came out of the house. This latter reading also harmonizes with the fact that two verses later (12:1) a great crowd had already gathered—apparently around Him.

**The scribes and the Pharisees began to urge him vehemently, and to provoke him to speak of many things: laying wait . . . to catch something out of his mouth, that they might accuse him** (53-54). They were evidently feigning a deep and enthusiastic interest in the Master's teaching. They asked many questions about many things as eager seekers after truth might do, but in actuality they were trying to trap the Master into saying something which might incriminate Him. In such cases, however, Jesus always knew what His enemies were about. Whenever He gave them ammunition that could be used against Him, He knew what He was doing.

### 14. *A Serious Look at Christian Discipleship* (12:1-12)

**In the mean time** (1), that is, during the time that Jesus spent in the house of the Pharisee (11:37 f.), **there were gathered together an innumerable multitude of people**—literally, "the myriads of the crowd." Evidently the multitude which had been following Jesus at the time of His invitation to eat with the Pharisee remained in the street or marketplace near the house. By the time He left the house His presence in the city became generally known, and consequently the crowd was greatly increased by a great concourse of people from the town and its vicinity. The size of this multitude is a clear indication that Jesus' fame was very great, even though His popularity was by this time on the wane. The people who made up this crowd undoubtedly represented all of the prevalent attitudes toward Jesus. Some were His friends. Many were the enemies of Jesus, and many more were influenced by the bitter, negative attitude of His enemies toward Him. The time had come when the extremes of love and hatred for Jesus were nearing their peaks.

**He began to say unto his disciples first of all.** The words **of all** do not appear in the original. The whole of chapter 12 seems to have been addressed chiefly to the disciples, but in the presence and the hearing of the multitude. What He had to say to His disciples was no secret, though it was chiefly for their benefit. In fact it might well be that Jesus particularly wanted these outsiders, and even His enemies, to hear these things. As we consider the following serious admonitions which the Master directs to His disciples, we must keep in mind the presence of these enemies in the crowd and the bitterness which they felt as a result of His very recent denunciations of them.

There has been some dispute among biblical scholars as to the proper relation and application of the words **first of all** (literally, "first"). Most authorities, in harmony with the King James Version, connect this phrase to the preceding clause. Thus the meaning would be that Jesus was addressing "first," or primarily, the disciples. This would imply that secondarily He was also speaking to the multitude.

A few scholars relate the phrase **first of all** to the following clause. This would require the meaning that the disciples should first of all, or "primarily," beware of the **leaven of the Pharisees;** that is, of the many things which they must guard against, the most important was the leaven of the Pharisees.

It is not easy to settle this argument from the Greek, since in the original there were no punctuation marks, but the King James reading is probably the correct one; however, either reading would harmonize with the context and with the principles of Jesus' teaching.

**Beware ye of the leaven of the Pharisees, which is hypocrisy** (1). "Leaven," to use Godet's definition, "is the emblem of every active principle, good or bad, which possesses the power of assimilation."[12] The leaven of the Pharisees would be their teaching and practices as they affected the lives of the people. This "devotion of the Pharisees had given a false direction to the whole of Israelitish piety."[13]

Jesus' statement would imply that the one characteristic of the Pharisees which wielded the most dangerous influence over their fellowmen was hypocrisy. Our word **hypocrisy** came to us directly from the Greek. It was a literary term used in connection with Greek drama and meant "play-acting." As Jesus applied it to the Pharisees, the word meant "insincerely acting the part of religious devotion without the reality."

Fairness, however, demands that we take note of the fact that Jesus did not oppose everything about the Pharisees. In theology Jesus was nearer to their position than to that of any other sect of His day. His major quarrel with them, and His major divergence from them, had to do with their hypocrisy, their legalistic attitude, and their lack of the essentials of a vital

[12]Godet, *op. cit.,* II, 89.
[13]*Ibid.*

inner religious experience. However, Jesus' strong denunciations against them show us that these matters weighed more heavily in the scales of divine wisdom than all of the points on which He and the Pharisees agreed. The most tragic fact was that they were lost spiritually and that they were influencing thousands of Israelites to take the same broad road to destruction as they were traveling. See also comments on Matt. 16: 6, 11.

**For there is nothing covered, that shall not be revealed; neither hid, that shall not be known** (2). This shows how utterly foolish are those who practice hypocrisy and sham. Religion has to do with man's relationship to God. Since God knows all and will ultimately reveal all, how foolish it is for one to be content with the form and shadow without the reality! How utterly stupid it is for one to hope to bypass the infinite knowledge and justice of God! See also comments on Matt. 10: 26.

**Whatsoever ye have spoken in darkness shall be heard in the light; and that which ye have spoken in the ear in closets shall be proclaimed upon the housetops** (3). The literary structure of this and the preceding verse is that of the Hebrew couplet, which is the simplest form of the Hebrew poetic stanza. There are two parallel clauses; the second repeats the meaning of the first with different words. Nothing is added to the meaning by the second line of the stanza, but the emphasis is greatly increased. The meaning of this verse is simple: It is an utter impossibility to keep secrets from God, and ultimately God will reveal our evil secrets to all men. The wise man will live with this fact in view.

**Be not afraid of them that kill the body, and after that have no more that they can do** (4). The materialist and secularist—those who see only this world—will say that mortal life is their most valuable possession. To such persons this verse sounds naive. The common expression, "They cannot do more than kill me," is intended as a bit of ironic humor, and even the irony is of a very light variety. But Jesus makes it clear that mortal life is by no means man's most valuable possession. Some of the wisest of men have forfeited life rather than sacrifice a greater treasure. We never see this life in its true perspective until we see it against the backdrop of eternity.

The early history of the Church reveals just how important this bit of wisdom was to the followers of Jesus. Persecution began with the crucifixion of Jesus and did not end, except temporarily, for nearly three centuries. During those years the martyrs tested the truth of these words and found them faultless. They set for all men examples of true courage and a proper subordination of this life to eternity.

**Fear him, which after he hath killed hath power to cast into hell** (5). That is, fear God, for our eternity is in His hands. The word translated **hell** is "Gehenna," originally referring to the Valley of Hinnom, near Jerusalem, where refuse was burned. But it is used metaphorically for hell, where the wicked are punished with fire. The power to cast into hell belongs to God, not to Satan, for Satan himself will be incarcerated there.

**Are not five sparrows sold for two farthings?** (6) The farthing is an old English coin worth one-fifth of an English penny (slightly more than one-fifth of an American one-cent piece). The actual coin referred to by Jesus was the *assarion*—worth one-tenth of a denarius—which in Jesus' day seems to have been worth about one penny. **And not one of them is forgotten before God.** If God shows interest in sparrows, how great must His interest be in man—the crown of His earthly creation! What a consolation to know that God never forgets us! Even the very hairs of our heads are all numbered.

**Fear not therefore** (7). Nothing, no matter how insignificant, escapes God's notice. Thus nothing can possibly happen to us without God's permission. Fear of circumstances or fear of the future is unnecessary; it betrays a lack of faith in God.

**Whosoever shall confess me before men, him shall the Son of man also confess before the angels of God: but he that denieth me before men shall be denied before the angels of God** (8-9). It is not enough simply to fear God. The test of discipleship is our love. And the test of love is our willingness to confess our relationship to Him before all men. One who denies his parents before his friends is not worthy of the home of which he is a part. And he who denies his relationship to the Saviour severs that relationship, or testifies by his action that he did not have a vital spiritual relationship to Christ. God's denial, in heaven and at the judgment, is not the result of a vindictive spirit on His part. It is rather the recognition of a fact. Sonship to God and citizenship in heaven cannot exist where lovelessness, selfishness, and cowardice characterize the human attitude toward God.

For further light on verses 4-9 see comments on Matt. 10: 27-32.

**Whosoever shall speak a word against the Son of man, it shall be forgiven** (10). See comments on Matt. 12:31-32.

**And when they bring you unto the synagogues, and unto magistrates, and powers** (11). The word translated **powers** literally means "authorities." Three levels of authority are indicated here. The **synagogue** refers to the lower ecclesiastical courts; the **magistrates** literally are "rulers," Jewish authorities of a higher level; **powers** or "authorities" probably refers to such rulers as Herod and Felix. **Take no thought how or what thing ye shall answer.** They did not need to prepare speeches and have them ready in case of arrest by the authorities. They should leave such matters to the future and to God. In the meantime they must center their attention on doing faithfully the work of spreading the good news of the Kingdom.

**The Holy Ghost shall teach you in the same hour what ye ought to say** (12). To be burdened with thought of what to say in case of arrest would be wrong because it would interfere with the work of preaching Christ; it would also be worse than wasted time. The Holy Ghost could supply better testimonies and arguments, and He would give them on the spot and at the instant that they were needed. For further light on verses 11 and 12 see comments on Matt. 10:17-20.

This section (1-12) has been called "The Creed of Courage and of Trust." In it we see (1) The forbidden sin, *hypocrisy*, 1-3; (2) The correct attitude to life, *fearlessness*, 4-7; (3) The unforgivable sin, *blasphemy*, 9-10; (4) The reward of *loyalty*, 8; (5) The help of the Holy Spirit, 11-12 (William Barclay).

### 15. *The Parable of the Rich Fool* (12:13-21)

This parable was a part of Jesus' answer to a request made by **one of the company** (13). His parables were generally called forth by the circumstances of the moment, and they were given to illustrate some important principle which the Master was trying to get across. The following request was probably made in a lull in Jesus' teaching—after He had finished His preceding discourse and before He had opportunity to introduce a new subject.

**Master, speak to my brother, that he divide the inheritance with me** (13). There are two possible explanations of the substance of, and motive for, this man's request. In either situation he would have been a younger brother. He might have been one whose legal inheritance had been forcibly withheld from him by his older brother, who was the legal heir to the double portion of the estate. On the other hand he might have gotten his legal share but was opposed to the custom of giving the elder brother the double portion. In this latter case he would be asking Jesus to help him break the custom or at least overturn it in this particular case.

The latter explanation is probably the correct one, for if his legal share had been withheld, he could have gone to the authorities, who would have adjusted the matter. This probability is greatly strengthened by the fact that the Master accused him (by implication, v. 15) of being covetous, which He surely would not have done if the young man had had a just grievance. This young man seems to have been one who had heard Jesus' teachings concerning human relations. But instead of interpreting them in terms of what he could do for his fellowmen, he selfishly interpreted the Master's words in terms of what such attitudes and practices on the part of others would bring to him.

**Man, who made me a judge or a divider over you?** (14) Jesus would probably have taken this stand even if the man's civil rights had been violated, for He consistently refused to try to change the political and social structure of His day. His plan was first to change men, and these changed men would inevitably produce a better world. But the Master knew that a changed world would not solve man's problems as long as his biggest problem was within—sin in the heart.

**Take heed, and beware of covetousness (15).** Translated literally this passage reads, "See and keep yourselves from covetousness." Here Jesus put His finger on this man's real motive. He seems to be saying, particularly to the disciples, "Let this man's experience be a lesson to you to keep yourselves from covetousness." Then follows a statement of one of the greatest principles in the Christian philosophy of life: **for a man's life consisteth not in the abundance of the things which he possesseth.** The world in every age has consistently bypassed or refused to acknowledge the truth of this principle, and yet every age has abounded with proofs of its truth. Every man sooner or later comes to realize just how unimportant **things** are, though many realize it only after a misspent life.

**Things** do not produce a rich and full life, neither do they bring happiness. When we study the lives of those who have lived rich and useful lives, it is remarkable how unimportant "things" were to them. The abundance of things produces anxieties and discontent more often than it produces happiness. Often those who have the most of this world's goods have never once known the thrill of lasting accomplishment. What really counts in life is, first of all, God; then such spiritual treasures as love, contentment, peace, a clear conscience, a feeling of accomplishment, a sense of mission, and a hope of heaven.

It is the principle stated in verse 15 that the parable of the rich fool is given to illustrate. The rich man in the parable disregarded this principle. As a result he not only lost his soul but became, for all time to come, the very personification of the fool and one of the world's best illustrations of how not to live.

**The ground of a certain rich man brought forth plentifully** (16). The abundant harvest was the gift of God to this man. It represented riches, power, and influence, but it was more. Here was an occasion which demanded important decisions; it was a test of the man, the consequences of which were eternal.

**He thought within himself, saying, What shall I do . . . ?** (17) This was the logical question to ask on such an occasion, but his comprehension of its significance was far too narrow. He was thinking only of how he could preserve his harvest; he should have been thinking of the expanded opportunities for service which this harvest presented to him. He said, **I have no room where to bestow my fruits;** but if his heart had been big enough to include God and mankind, perhaps his barns would have held what love would have let him keep.

**This will I do: I will pull down my barns, and build greater; and there will I bestow all my fruits and my goods** (18). Notice the use of first person pronouns. In verses 17-19 he uses some form of the first person singular pronoun eleven times. He is a completely selfish man. He had no thoughts for either man or God. The building of greater barns was not so wrong in itself; it was his reason for wanting them that was wrong. He wanted them so he could keep everything for himself.

**I will say to my soul, . . . thou hast much goods . . . take thine ease, . . . But God said . . . Thou fool** (19-20). In the two preceding verses the rich man was a selfish, inconsiderate miser; in these verses he is a fool. Perhaps we should say that a selfish man is always a fool, for only a fool would leave both God and man out of his life. In the present verse he betrays his utter folly by supposing that riches could bring ease of soul and that he could feed his soul on oats and wheat and barley. A fool, in the biblical usage of the term, is one devoid of reason, "stupid." This man had acted like one who was completely without reason.

The man was a fool: (1) Because he forgot God; (2) Because he forgot his immortal spirit; (3) Because he forgot others.

**This night thy soul shall be required of thee.** He made another foolish and tragic mistake. He seemed to think he had a lease on life—that he would certainly live long enough to work out his plans and enjoy his abundance. He was soon to realize his folly. He had failed to realize that even his soul was not his own, and God, the true Owner, was calling an immediate reckoning. He now realized that in terms of true riches he was a pauper.

**Then whose shall those things be . . . ?** The rich man made another fatal mistake in disregarding an important principle of stewardship. He would now own nothing. But in reality he had never owned anything. None of us owns anything. God is Owner; we are stewards.

**So is he that layeth up treasure for himself, and is not rich toward God** (21). The Master broadens the point of the parable into a universal principle. God calls men "stupid" and "fools" who spend all their time and interest laying up treasures in this world, completely disregarding the interest of their souls. There is nothing quite so foolish as to live for time and forget eternity, to live for self and forget God.

### 16. *Faith Versus Anxiety* (12:22-31)

For a full discussion of this passage see comments on Matt. 6:25-33. Though the language in Matthew is almost identical in substance, the two passages are not from the same address of the Master. The Matthew passage is from the Sermon on the Mount, delivered earlier during the Galilean ministry; the present address reported by Luke was delivered in Perea during the last six months of Jesus' life. It was the custom of the Master to repeat the same or similar teachings whenever the need was the same. Jesus also knew, what educational authorities have since learned, that repetition is an excellent, an almost indispensable, teaching device.

Two clauses in Luke's account deserve special comment. The first is: **neither be ye of doubtful mind** (29)—literally, "neither be ye anxious" or "waver not between hope and fear." There is a similar statement in Matt. 6:31. It is translated in the King James Version "take no thought." The Greek is not the same in these two passages. Matthew uses a verb which means simply "to be anxious," or "to seek to promote one's interest." The verb which

Luke uses includes, in addition to these meanings, the idea of shifting from elation to despair, from hope to fear. Matthew's term comes nearer to expressing selfishness; Luke's is closer to agitation and frustration. In either case the attitude is the opposite of faith in God's providential care and is unworthy of the highest Christian character.

**For all these things do the nations of the world seek after** (30). The word translated **seek after** has the added denotation of earnestness or intensity, so that a better translation would be "earnestly seek after." The corresponding passage in Matthew (6:32) does not have the phrase **of the world,** thus making the Greek word *ethnos* equivalent to "Gentiles." Luke's wording bears the mark of a Gentile writing to Gentiles, while Matthew's statement is typically Jewish. In both instances the meaning is that to be anxious or frustrated or selfishly concerned for those daily physical and temporal needs is to follow the example of the pagans who know not God. However Jesus is by no means suggesting that faith should make work for a livelihood unnecessary. Honest toil and the fulfillment of one's temporal obligation are not only consistent with faith; they are prerequisite to faith (cf. II Thess. 3:10; I Tim. 5:8).

### 17. *True Riches* (12:32-34)

**Fear not, little flock; for it is your Father's good pleasure to give you the kingdom** (32). It should be remembered here that Jesus is still speaking to His disciples in the presence of an immense multitude (see 12:1, 22). With this picture in mind we can see a double application of the expression **little flock.** The group of disciples is very small in comparison with the multitudes; also the total number of Jesus' followers is extremely small in comparison with the world to whom they are to represent Him and preach His gospel.

Note also that He is representing them as a **flock.** Sheep and shepherds were very common in Palestine, and the terms are often applied figuratively to show the relation between Jesus and His followers—His Church. The terms, particularly when used by Jesus, connote an especially close and loving relationship between the Master and His own. The Church has always been touched by the tender connotation of the rustic biblical representation of the "good shepherd" and His "flock," and it has devoted some of its best-loved sermons, hymns, and paintings to this subject.

But the central teaching of this verse is not the representation of the Church as a flock, nor its smallness. The central idea is forward-looking, optimistic, and potentially triumphant. Jesus is saying that their smallness is no reason for fear or pessimism, for it is the Father's **good pleasure to give** . . . (them) **the kingdom.** The Greek words translated **it is your Father's good pleasure** mean literally "your Father took delight." The Father is not only willing, but happy and delighted, to give this little band the Kingdom.

The **kingdom** which His disciples are promised in this verse is the "kingdom of God," which in verse 31 they are admonished to seek. It is first of all a spiritual Kingdom to whose citizenship we are admitted through the new birth; it becomes a heavenly Kingdom of disembodied spirits to those who through death join the present Church Triumphant; it will become a literal, eternal Kingdom at the second coming of our Lord.

The implied promise to give them (and us) the Kingdom includes more than citizenship and the enjoyment of Kingdom privileges. It is also a promise of victory for our militant efforts toward the advancement of God's work in this world. It is a promise that the Church will succeed in its mighty, worldwide task. This promise is ours today, but we must remember that God's promises are conditional—consecration, obedience, and faith being the conditions.

**Sell that ye have, and give alms** (33). Some have given an extremely literal interpretation of this and other similar scriptures. This has taken various forms, but the two most prominent are asceticism and the so-called Christian communism. Both of these views are out of harmony with the life and teachings of Jesus. He nowhere commands all men to give up all material possessions, and He refused to take the side of a man who was interested in overthrowing the accepted custom of property inheritance, accusing this man, by implication, of covetousness.[14] It should also be noted that asceticism has never characterized a vital, militant, evangelistic Church. And so-called Christian communism was tried by the Church but once. This was only in Jerusalem, and even there it was non-compulsory and temporary.[15]

[14]See comments on Luke 12:13-15.

[15]See comments on Acts 2:44; 4:34—5:11.

While these literal interpretations are wrong, we must not overlook the fact that the verse does have a literal application. But this depends upon the individual calling. Many, including the apostles and the Christian missionaries down through the centuries, have had to forsake all worldly possessions to follow the Master. Others have been permitted to retain their possessions and sometimes even to gain great wealth. But one thing is demanded of all: a clear recognition of the principle of Christian stewardship. We own nothing. If God has allowed us to hold some of this world's goods, we are but His stewards; God is still the Owner, and we must use wealth as He directs. This does not apply merely to the tithe. All is God's, and all must be used as He wishes.

The injunction to give alms reminds us of both the duty and the joy of Christian charity. Love is the essence of the Christian spirit, and this love has an outreach as well as an upreach. A calloused heart which can be unmoved in the presence of either human need or the need of the Kingdom is inconsistent with a Christian profession.

**Provide yourselves bags which wax not old, a treasure in the heavens that faileth not, where no thief approacheth, neither moth corrupteth.** It is while we are following sincerely the principles of Christian stewardship and Christian love that we are making the wisest preparation and provision for our own future. This, like so many Christian principles, is a paradox. Following this way of life we are putting our wealth, not in **bags** (literally "purses") which grow old and wear out, but in heavenly purses which are indestructible. We are exchanging the earthly for the heavenly, the transient for the permanent, that which can be destroyed or stolen for that which is indestructible and in every sense nontransferable.

**For where your treasure is, there will your heart be also** (34). This is more than a prediction. It is the statement of a universal principle. Whoever we are, whatever our condition or station in life, whether we are saints or sinners, our hearts are where our treasures are, and our treasures will be put where our hearts are. Thus if we love God we will deposit our treasures in heaven by using both our talents and our possessions for the glory of God. Then as we lay up more and more treasures on the other side, our interest in heaven and heavenly things will increase, and our hearts will be more firmly anchored in the heavenly world.

This verse is a measuring rod by which we can determine the depth of our devotion. It can also serve as a warning. Whenever we see ourselves becoming more interested in earthly possessions than in heavenly treasures, it is time for a serious soul examination; it is time for a transfer of deposits from the earthly to the heavenly bank.

### 18. *Ready for the Master's Return* (12:35-40)

Jesus is still addressing His disciples in the presence of the multitude, and He is still thinking of the danger of covetousness— of being too strongly attached to things material and temporal. In the present passage He is giving another reason why this attachment to the material is dangerous. If one is to be ready at all times for the Master's return, he must have both his treasure and his interest in things spiritual and eternal. Strong attachment to the material would be the chain which would hold him down when the saints are taken up in the rapture.

**Let your loins be girded about** (35). The long oriental robes could hinder both walking and working unless they were gathered up above the girdle to give the feet and legs freedom of movement. The girdle thus served a purpose similar to that of the sleeve garter which some men wear to hold their shirt cuffs off their wrists. The servant thus girded was ready for instant action, like the Christian who has removed all hindrances to service for God and favor with God.

**And your lights** (literally, "lamps") **burning.** The lamp used in ancient Palestine was very simple. It was a small pitcher-shaped bowl with a wick. The wick had to be trimmed and the lamp filled with oil if light was to be provided. The Christian must never neglect his light; he must never permit his wick to be charred or his oil supply to run out. Personal devotion—prayer and Bible reading—and faithful service will keep the lamp of the soul burning brightly.

**And ye yourselves like unto men that wait for their lord, when he will return from the wedding** (36). With gathered robes and brightly burning lamps, these servants wait for the return of their lord from the wedding. They are not asleep; they are on duty, and faithful servants never sleep on the job. No matter how long the lord's return might be delayed, they remain on duty and keep themselves in readiness. **That when he cometh and knocketh, they may open unto him immediately.** No lamps to trim at the last minute, no neglected task to perform before they are ready to meet their master. They are always ready, so they can **open ... immediately.**

**Blessed are those servants, whom the lord shall find watching ... he shall gird himself, and ... serve them.** Such faithfulness on the part of the servants calls forth generosity on the part of the lord. He is so pleased that, instead of his own customary meal at which they serve, he will serve while they eat.

**And if he shall come in the second watch, or ... the third ... and find them so, blessed are those servants** (38). The night was divided into watches.[16] These watches corresponded to our time as follows: first watch, six to nine; second watch, nine to midnight; third watch, midnight to three; and fourth watch, three to six. The later the hour of the lord's return, the more was his gratitude at finding his servants faithful. Spence points out that the second and third watches—those referred to in this parable— are the period of the night when it would be hardest to stay awake and alert.[17]

Since this passage is obviously referring to the Lord's second coming, there is a strong hint here that His return will be delayed and that this delay will be a means of testing the faithfulness of His servants.

**And this know, that if the goodman of the house had known ...** (39). **This know** is imperative here in King James Version but it can also be translated "ye know this" (indicative). The intent of the Master seems to be equivalent to "remember." The **goodman** of the house is literally the "master" or "ruler" of the house.

Note that the emphasis of the figure is shifted from the household servants (in 36-38) to the master of the house. The master would be prepared for a thief if he knew he was coming. The thief succeeds only because the master is unprepared.

**Be ye therefore ready also: for the Son of man cometh at an hour when ye think not** (40). This verse amplifies and completes the preceding one. The master is unprepared for the thief because he does not "know." But when the Son of Man comes, it is completely unnecessary for His professed followers to be

---

[16]The ancient Jews had only three watches, or divisions of the night (Judg. 7:19), but during the Roman occupation a fourth was added, probably as a result of the practice of the Roman soldiers.

[17]Spence, *op. cit.,* I, 337.

caught unprepared, for they can and do "know." They do not know the time of His coming, but they do know the fact that He will come.

The solution is: Be always ready. Thus the very secrecy of His coming is an added incentive to a perpetual high level of discipleship. For further discussion of verses 39-40 see comments on Matt. 24: 43-44.

Barclay succinctly titles this passage, "Be Prepared." Maclaren notes the nature of this preparation: (1) The girded loins, 35; (2) The burning lamps, 35; (3) The waiting hearts, 36.

### 19. *A Steward Must Be Faithful* (12: 41-48)

**Then Peter said . . . speakest thou this parable unto us, or even to all?** (41) Peter is evidently referring to the parable in verses 36-38, in which the servants are rewarded for their faithfulness. This question is perfectly in harmony with the character of Peter as portrayed elsewhere in the New Testament. The fact that in a similar account in Matthew (24: 43-51) this same material is given as a continuous discourse, without Peter's interruption, does not prove that Peter's question is an interpolation, as some have suggested. For not only is it like Peter, but also the present discourse is given during the Perean ministry, while Matthew's account is given during Passion Week at Jerusalem.

**And the Lord said, Who then is that faithful and wise steward . . . ?** (42) Apparently Jesus had ignored Peter's question. But in reality He not only answers the question but goes beyond it, giving additional material not asked for by Peter. The fact that Jesus shifts His subject back to faithful servants not only shows that He is answering Peter, but it also identifies the "parable" to which Peter's question refers.

This **steward** is referred to as a **servant** in the remainder of the parable. Matthew's account uses the word "servant" throughout, but this slave (literal Greek) was obviously a steward. A **steward** (Greek, *oikonomos*) was usually a superior servant (slave) of proven character who looked after the accounts of the household.

Verses 42-44 show the rewards for faithful stewards, and verses 45-46 give the punishment which is meted out to unfaithful stewards. For a full discussion of this material see comments on Matt. 24: 45-51.

**Appoint him his portion with the unbelievers** (46). Matthew's account has "hypocrites" instead of **unbelievers.** These servants must be seen in two lights: first, as judged by Old Testament law; and second, in the light of the Kingdom responsibilities in the Christian dispensation.

**And that servant, which knew his lord's will, and prepared not himself . . . shall be beaten with many stripes. But he that knew not . . . shall be beaten with few stripes (47-48).** For crimes which were punishable by whipping, forty stripes was the maximum for a single offense, but the Jews were known to give as few as four or five stripes for minor offenses.[18] The punishment varied with the crime.

Greater light, ability, and opportunity mean greater responsibility. Greater opportunity for honor, position, and accomplishment carries with it greater culpability in case of unfaithfulness. To know God's will is indeed a great blessing, but knowledge of God's will which is disregarded or perverted only increases the guilt and the consequent punishment.

The principle of degrees of rewards and punishments is clearly taught here as elsewhere in the New Testament, but just how God will apply the principle is not always apparent. One thing is clear, however: The degree of faithfulness or unfaithfulness will determine the degree of reward or punishment, and this faithfulness is judged in the light of the knowledge of the will of God and the opportunities which one possesses.

### 20. *Christ a Divider* (12:49-53)

**I am come to send fire on the earth (49).** Literally, "I am come to cast a firebrand into the earth." Jesus has not changed the subject here; He has merely come to a new division of His discourse. Since verse 14 He has been discussing the danger of a selfish regard for the things of this world. Now He goes on to say that His coming to earth was not intended to smooth the way for a peaceful enjoyment of this world's good. Rather, His coming would of necessity bring division and conflict. How could it be otherwise? Selfish, sinful man would not naturally and willingly submit to such an unselfish and self-giving way of life as that which Christ represented.

Jesus is making it clear to His disciples, and to those who anticipate becoming disciples, that if their motives in following Him are selfish they will be disappointed. He has no material wealth, power, honor, or ease to offer. But if they wish to follow Him

---

[18]See Adam Clarke, *op. cit.*, p. 445.

from pure, unselfish love, He has spiritual and eternal rewards which will far outweigh the cost of discipleship.

Some commentators have suggested that the **fire** referred to here is the fire of the Holy Spirit or the fire of a new faith.[19] But most authorities agree that the context and the meaning of the verse favor the interpretation given above—that it is a fire of conflict. We must not overlook the fact, however, that the end result of the conflict—or the fire—is good. It will be victory for Christ and His kingdom. Only evil will be destroyed. Fire has a purifying effect, even if it is the fire of conflict.

**And what will I, if it be already kindled?** Literally, "and what I wish if already it be kindled?" As this awkward translation shows, the meaning of the Greek is vague, but most authorities are in accord with *The New English Bible*, which renders it: "and how I wish it were already kindled!" Both His natural human distaste for suffering and His anxiety to launch a victorious campaign prompt Jesus in His desire to have this experience accomplished and done with. But the conflict and the victory must be postponed until His death and resurrection.

**But I have a baptism to be baptized with** (50). His soon-coming suffering and death. **And how am I straitened till it be accomplished.** Weymouth has the true meaning of the Greek when he renders this passage, "and how am I pent up till it is accomplished!" The Master is fully aware of both the fact and the necessity of His suffering. He knows that victory over sin and Satan is impossible until the conflict and victory which are His death and resurrection. He is "pent up," anxious to meet and defeat the foe. Also, as suggested in connection with verse 49, He has a natural recoil from suffering, and He desires to have this disagreeable but necessary task over. This passage has been called "a prelude of Gethsemane."

**Suppose ye that I am come to give peace on earth? I tell you, Nay; but rather division** (51). Jesus quickly turns from himself and His coming suffering and returns to His discourse: Not peace but division. Jesus saw prophetically what history now reveals to us: the conflict through the ages between the kingdom of God and the kingdom of Satan. This conflict was to divide nations, cities, tribes, and families according to the personal allegiances of the individuals who make up these groups.

[19]See Bruce, *op. cit.*, p. 562.

The painful nature of some of these divisions is graphically pictured in verses 52 and 53: families divided—fathers against sons, sons against fathers, mothers against daughters. The whole race will be divided into two camps. For further discussion of material in verses 51-53 see comments on Matt. 10:34-36.

21. *The Signs of the Times* (12:54-56)

**And he said also to the people** (54). Godet points out that the expression **He said also** is "the formula which Luke uses when Jesus at the close of a doctrinal discourse adds a last word of more gravity which raises the question to its full height, and is intended to leave on the mind of the hearer an impression never to be effaced."[20] It should also be noted that Jesus is now turning His attention more directly to **the people.** The preceding verses seem to have been addressed more to His disciples.

The sternness and sharpness of the Master in these verses would seem to imply that some of the people had shown disfavor or hostility toward what He had been saying. Perhaps the Pharisees were again stirring up opposition to His teaching.

**When ye see a cloud rise out of the west.** The Mediterranean Sea lay to the west of Palestine, while to the East was a semi-desert region. Thus, all rain must come from the west. These people evidently prided themselves on being able to predict the weather, as is usual with country people or those whose life is largely in contact with the out-of-doors. Yet, wise as they were in reading signs, they showed no ability to read the signs of the time, though these signs were glaringly evident all around them.

**When ye see the south wind blow** (55). To the south and southeast lay the great Arabian Desert, so that a wind from that direction would bring oppressive heat.

**Ye hypocrites** (56). A hypocrite was a playactor. These people who boasted of their ability to read signs were involved in a contradiction. And even though they were well versed in the Old Testament prophecies concerning Christ, they were completely blind to the obvious fulfillment of these prophecies. Professing to be the ones who could see, they were actually blind, as they were deaf to the voice of God.

**Ye can discern the face of the sky and of the earth; but how is it that ye do not discern this time?** The answer to this question is that they had discernment where they had interest. They were interested in rain and the crops which the rain made possible;

[20]Godet, *op. cit.,* II, 115.

they were interested in heat and the damage it could do to crops; but they had little interest in moral and spiritual matters. They were materialistic and grossly selfish.

Spence points out three signs of the time which were completely ignored by the Jewish leaders. They were: (1) the low state of morality among public men, (2) the political situation, and (3) heavenly warnings.[21] Volumes have been written on these subjects, but the Pharisees and other Jewish leaders either ignored them or dealt with them in a purely selfish and materialistic manner. See also comments on Matt. 16:2-3.

### 22. *The Necessity of Reconciliation* (12:57-59)

**Yea, and why even of yourselves judge ye not what is right?** (57) Why is it that you are not able (or willing) to take the initiative in judging rightly? Why do you have to be prodded, prompted, or forced to make righteous judgments; or, because these pressures are lacking, never judge rightly? Jesus follows this question with an illustration.

**When thou goest with thine adversary to the magistrate, as thou art in the way, give diligence that thou mayest be delivered from him** (58). This is just common sense. Be reconciled before you reach the judgment hall, for it is certain that you will find no mercy there, only the full force of a broken law. Any settlement short of this is mercy, and the seeking of such settlement is wisdom. It is obvious here that it is the **adversary** who is on the side of the law and that the **thou** is the transgressor. In the illustration given, it is either reconciliation or prison, and only a fool would choose the latter.

The full force of this truth is felt when we realize that the Master's real concern is with the spiritual application of this parable. The suggested reconciliation is between man and God, and it is man who must agree to terms. The only alternative is to suffer the sentence of the Great Judge, and that sentence is eternal punishment.

We can see now the full meaning of the Master's question in verse 57. He is saying, "Why can you not be wise enough to humble yourselves and be reconciled to God—be converted—instead of risking the inevitable consequences of coming to the Judgment as an incorrigible adversary of God?"

[21]Spence, *op. cit.,* I, 339-40.

**I tell thee, thou shalt not depart thence, till thou hast paid the very last mite** (59). If one rejects repentance, humility, mercy, and grace, then he must expect to pay all that the law demands. The judgment must operate according to law; mercy has no place there.

Some have suggested that hope of ultimate salvation is implied in the phrase **till thou hast paid the very last mite.** However, it is only in the literal story of the parable that such hope is possible. The criminal in prison has hope of release. There is always a chance that in some way he can pay **the very last mite.** But there is no such hope for the sinner in hell. These totally bankrupt souls can never pay even the smallest part of their inestimable debt. See also comments on Matt. 5:25-26.

### 23. *Except You Repent* (13:1-5)

**There were present at that season** (1). Literally, "at that time." This evidently refers to the time of the discourse recorded in chapter 12. Some of those who had been listening to His solemn teaching concerning preparedness, faithfulness, conflict, and the judgment spoke up during a pause in the Master's discourse, or perhaps at the end of it.

**The Galilaeans, whose blood Pilate had mingled with their sacrifices.** This occurrence is not recorded by Josephus or any other authority besides Luke; however it fits perfectly the character of Pilate, the turbulence of the times, and the character of the Galileans.

The facts of the story seem to be as follows: The Galileans were in Jerusalem offering sacrifices at the Temple. While they were thus engaged, Pilate sent his soldiers to slay them, and in the process their own blood was mixed with the blood of the animals they were offering as sacrifices. These Galileans were probably guilty of breaking some Roman law. It should also be noted that they were Herod's subjects and that this action might have been either a cause or a consequence of the bad feeling between Pilate and Herod referred to in Luke 23:12.

**Suppose ye that these Galilaeans were sinners above all the Galilaeans, because they suffered such things?** (2) This gruesome occurrence was evidently related, not to point out the cruelty of the Roman, but to imply that these Galileans were permitted by Providence to be slaughtered because they were great sinners. At least as far back as Job's time it was believed that misfortune

534

came only as a punishment for sin, and therefore calamity of any kind was a sign of prior sin.

It is possible that the report was given at this time to illustrate what Jesus had just said in 12:58-59—thus implying that the calamity of these Galileans was the result of their failure to be reconciled to God. One thing is certain, however: The reporters of this slaughter considered themselves so different from these **sinners** that they were in no danger of a like fate.

**I tell you, Nay: but, except ye repent, ye shall all likewise perish** (3). On the one hand Jesus was at least implying that calamity was not necessarily a direct punishment for sin. On the other hand He was specifically pointing out that, apart from the grace of God, all are sinners and that all sinners will perish unless they repent.

The Jews reserved the word "sinner" for a specific class of offenders whom they considered particularly "unclean." They felt sure that those who were performing regularly their religious function, as prescribed by their leaders, were not sinners.

Even in our day it is easy, especially for church people, to point out others as sinners and in need of God's saving grace. It is not easy for one to look within and acknowledge the sin in his own heart. To all who have sinned (and *all* have sinned) Jesus says, **Except ye repent, ye shall all likewise perish.** And the calamity of these Galileans cannot be compared with the calamity of hell.

**Or those eighteen, upon whom the tower in Siloam fell . . .** (4). The tower of Siloam was probably connected with the pool of Siloam, situated outside the wall at the southeast corner of the city of Jerusalem. The purpose for which the tower was erected is not known. The time is also unknown, but it probably occurred not very long before Jesus' reference to it.

The fact that Jesus uses this event to strengthen His argument would strongly imply that the people knew well the particulars of the case and that the men who were killed in the fall of the tower were not notably wicked men but average Jewish workmen.

**I tell you, Nay: but except ye repent, ye shall all likewise perish** (5). Jesus repeats verse 3 verbatim for emphasis. The truth He was teaching was most significant—important enough to call forth this repetition.

### 24. *Parable of the Fig Tree in the Vineyard* (13:6-9)

**A certain man had a fig tree planted in his vineyard** (6). It was a custom in ancient Palestine, as it is today, to plant fig trees and other trees in vineyards.[22] It was a means of utilizing every available spot of good ground. The fig tree here, as elsewhere in biblical symbolism, refers to Israel.

The Jews' racial and national pride would not permit them to think of themselves as anything less than God's chosen people, the one nation which rightfully belonged to God's domain. Therefore Jesus' use of the fig tree in a vineyard to represent Israel is most interesting. This parable seems to represent the Jews as occupying only a corner of God's great vineyard of the world.

**And he came and sought fruit thereon, and found none.** Though the fig tree was in a vineyard it still had but one purpose: to bear fruit, and Israel had but one reason to occupy either first place or any place; this was to fulfill its God-given mission. Since the fig tree was fruitless, it had no right to exist; and since Israel refused to fulfill its divinely appointed mission, it had no right to continue.

**Then said he unto the dresser of his vineyard** (7). The owner of the vineyard in the parable represents God the Father; the dresser represents Christ, or the Holy Spirit. The dresser of a vineyard is the man whose task it is to trim the vines and take care of the vineyard.

**Behold, these three years I come seeking fruit on this fig tree, and find none: cut it down.** Some have sought to give the figure "three" here some special spiritual or mystical significance. It is referred to (1) the Law, (2) the prophets, or (3) Christ. Some find an allusion to the three years of Christ's ministry. It seems wiser not to attempt to give any such forced meaning. The figure is simply a literal detail in a parable, and it means that ample opportunity has been given to the tree to bear fruit. Thus the order is given to cut it down.

**Why cumbereth it the ground?** Literally, "Why does it even render the ground useless?" To the owner of the vineyard the case is simple: It ought to bear fruit; it is not bearing fruit; therefore it is a waste of good soil to permit it to remain.

**And he . . . said . . . Lord, let it alone this year also, till I shall dig about it, and dung it** (8). The dresser of the vineyard is asking for mercy for the tree, but not for sentimental reasons.

[22]See Geldenhuys, *op. cit.*, p. 372; also Spence, *op. cit.*, II, 2.

He has no more use for a fruitless tree than does the owner of the vineyard. He is asking for more time in the hope that more cultivation and more fertilizer will stimulate fruit bearing.

Under the veil of this parable Jesus is expressing His willingness to bestow additional labor on Israel that He might stimulate fruit bearing—restore His people to their former place as God's special people—and that He might avert the catastrophe which otherwise is inevitable.

**And if it bear fruit, well: and if not, then after that thou shalt cut it down** (9). Success would be well worth the efforts, but this was a last chance. That Israel did not take advantage of this last chance, and that the Master's prediction of national catastrophe was graphically fulfilled, are well known.

Though this parable was especially directed at the Jewish race and nation, it is a solemn warning which all must take to heart. It is either God's way or no way. We must either fill our God-ordained place or forfeit our right to any place. This, as was shown in the previous passage, demands repentance and the salvation which Christ alone can give.

Matthew Henry treats this parable under three heads: (1) The advantages which this fig tree had—**planted in his vineyard** (better soil); (2) The owner's expectation from it—**he came and sought fruit thereon;** (3) The disappointment of his expectation—**found none.**

### 25. *Healing on a Sabbath—Love vs. Legalism* (13:10-17)

**He was teaching in one of the synagogues on the sabbath** (10). Literally "on the sabbaths." Bruce thinks this meant a series of instruction in one synagogue which lasted for several weeks.[23] However the wording in the original Greek would seem to favor the interpretation that a custom of Sabbath teaching in the synagogues is meant. Teaching in the synagogues on the Sabbath was a habit of Jesus during the early months of His ministry, but there is little recorded evidence of this practice during His Perean ministry. This verse, however, would seem to indicate that, though it might have been curtailed due to the opposition of the Jewish leaders, it had not been discontinued. The miracle which follows is recorded only by Luke.

**A woman which had a spirit of infirmity eighteen years, and was bowed together** (11). Note the precise and detailed

[23]See Bruce, *op. cit.*, p. 566.

manner in which Luke, the physician, describes this woman's malady. This seems to have been an extreme case of curvature of the spine, and the case is made more pathetic by the fact that she had been suffering thus for eighteen years.

The expression **spirit of infirmity** strongly implies that the infirmity was caused by an evil spirit or that its basic cause was spiritual. This inference is supported in verse 16, where Jesus says that it was Satan who had bound her. Godet says that the expression **spirit of infirmity** refers to "a physical weakness, which in turn arose from a higher cause, by which the sufferer's will was bound."[24] This "higher cause" to which he refers is obviously spiritual; that is, a Satanic affliction. Thus the afflicted woman had a double malady. The physical difficulty was an outward manifestation of the inner spiritual bondage.

**And could in no wise lift up herself.** Literally, "and was not able to lift up herself wholly." The Greek would permit either of two meanings. They are (1) "was wholly unable to lift up herself," or (2) "was not able to lift up herself completely." The former rendering is preferred, both by the Greek grammar and by the context of the passage.[25]

**Thou art loosed from thine infirmity (12). Thou art loosed** translates a Greek perfect tense verb which indicates that the loosing is an accomplished fact.

**He laid his hands on her: and immediately she was made straight (13).** Here she experienced the miracle. She was "made straight" by the touch of the Master's hand.

**The ruler of the synagogue (14).** Probably the head of the council of ten Jewish men who controlled this synagogue. **Answered with indignation, because that Jesus had healed on the sabbath day.** He was so angry at an apparent desecration of the Sabbath that he missed entirely the meaning and value of the miracle. The Law, as interpreted by the rabbis at that time, permitted physicians to handle only cases of emergency on the Sabbath. The present case was chronic and thus, according to the interpretations of the rabbis, could not be legally healed on this holy day.

**Said unto the people.** He did not have the courage to attack the Master directly, but chided the people—the woman and those who were with her—in a voice loud enough for Jesus to hear.

[24]Godet, *op. cit.*, p. 120.
[25]See Bruce, *op. cit.*, p. 566.

**There are six days in which men ought to work.** The rabbis had so exaggerated the prohibitions of the fourth commandment that such an act of mercy as Jesus' healing of this afflicted woman was interpreted as labor and thus prohibited on the Sabbath.

**Thou hypocrite, doth not each one of you on the sabbath loose his ox or his ass from the stall, and lead him away to watering?** (15) The rulers of the synagogues and the leaders of the Jews would all perform this humane act on the Sabbath. Yet this woman must be left to suffer until the next day. This gross inconsistency makes the Master's appellation **hypocrite** most appropriate. When we remember that these animals represented property—wealth—we see the utter selfishness of these hypocrites. Spence puts it thus: "Every possible indulgence was to be shown in cases where their own interests were involved; no mercy or indulgence was to be thought of, though, where the sick poor only were concerned."[26]

**And ought not this woman, being a daughter of Abraham, . . . be loosed from this bond on the sabbath day?** (16) To anyone who is not blind with prejudice the answer is not only obvious, but it is more forceful when thus implied than when actually stated. Jesus' reference to her being a daughter of Abraham suggests that she has a double claim on the mercy and assistance of all Jews—as a human being and as a fellow Israelite.

**And when he had said these things, all his adversaries were ashamed** (17). The word **all** implies that the ruler of the synagogue had some active supporters in his attack on the Master. But Jesus' reply was so relevant and so adequate that even these self-centered men were made ashamed. They made no rebuttal—there was none to be made.

**And all the people rejoiced for all the glorious things that were done by him.** The people recognized and appreciated what the rulers blindly overlooked: that God had worked in their midst and demonstrated His boundless compassion as well as His mighty power. What they saw forced them to associate this Jesus with the God of heaven. No doubt Jesus' answer to the rebuke of the ruler of the synagogue enlarged their understanding and appreciation of the miracle which they had just seen.

Three reflections on this incident are given by Charles Simeon: (1) What blindness and hypocrisy are there in the human heart! (2) How desirable is it to embrace every oppor-

[26]Spence, *op. cit.,* II, 3.

tunity of waiting upon God!—this woman received healing because she was faithful in attending the synagogue services; (3) With what comfortable hope may we look to Jesus in all our troubles!

## 26. *Two Brief Parables on the Kingdom of God* (13:18-21)

**Unto what is the kingdom of God like? and whereunto shall I resemble it?** (18) The idea of the kingdom of God seems to have been suggested to our Lord by the people's response in verse 17. His miracle and His effective answer of His enemies' challenge brought enthusiastic praise and rejoicing from the people. He saw in the attitudes of these people a beginning of the Kingdom. Note how both of the parables trace the kingdom of God from a small beginning.

The question with which Jesus introduces these parables does not denote hesitation or uncertainty as to what He should say. Rather it is a dramatic, stylistic device used by the Master and quite in keeping with His form of teaching.

Jesus is seeking in nature for analogies to spiritual truth. Spiritual things can never be fully depicted or understood by man in this life. The only language we know is earthly and as such has its fundamental meanings in the realm of the material. Such earthly language can only approximate spiritual truth. Because of this absence of a spiritual language, analogies are used to help describe the indescribable.

It should be noted that Matthew uses the term "kingdom of heaven" while Mark and Luke use "kingdom of God."

It is **like a grain of mustard seed** (19). For full discussion see comments on Matt. 13:31-32.[27] Luke's version of this parable is briefer than either Matthew's or Mark's. The first and second Gospels both add the explanation that, though the mustard seed is the smallest of seeds, the plant which springs from it becomes larger than all herbs.

Luke's version of these two Kingdom parables is not taken from the same discourse of the Master as are those in the other two Synoptics. In Matthew and Mark these parables are reported as a part of Jesus' Galilean ministry, teaching from a boat in the Sea of Galilee to a multitude on the shore. Luke, on the other hand, is reporting another and later telling of these parables by the Master during His Perean ministry.

[27]See also Mark 4:30-32.

**And again he said, Whereunto shall I liken the kingdom of God?** (20) Jesus here repeats the substance of the two questions in verse 18. By means of this repetition He is seeking to maintain and strengthen the dramatic effect of the rhetorical device introduced earlier.

**It is like leaven** (21). For full discussion see comments on Matt. 13:33.

B. THE SECOND STAGE, 13:22—17:10

**And he went through the cities and villages, teaching, and journeying toward Jerusalem** (22). This verse serves both as an introduction to the second stage of the Perean ministry—the "Journey to Jerusalem"—and as a reminder that Jesus still has Jerusalem as His destination. Though His movements are by no means in a straight line, He is moving ever nearer that goal.

As we have seen earlier,[28] this "Journey to Jerusalem" is not simply a traveling to Jerusalem in a physical and geographical sense, but a movement ever nearer to our Lord's great appointment with the Cross. Jesus is moving in that direction in a double sense: (1) He is systematically completing His necessary evangelistic ministry, with every town and village, and (2) He is moving forward in time—time is running out. This is not inconsistent with the fact that during this "Journey to Jerusalem" He took occasional trips to Jerusalem.[29]

This portion of Jesus' ministry (13:23—17:10) seems to follow immediately after His presence at Jerusalem at the feast of the purification of the Temple given in John 10:22-39. After leaving Jerusalem on that occasion He went to Perea—the land beyond Jordan, "where John at first baptized" (John 10:40). He remained there until after He received the message concerning the sickness of Lazarus (John 11:3-7).[30]

1. *"Are There Few That Be Saved?"* (13:23-30)

**Then said one** (23). The vagueness of Luke's reference to this **one,** coupled with the implication in the succeeding context that he is outside the Kingdom, would indicate that he was not one of the apostles but one of the crowd which followed Jesus.

**Are there few that be saved?** We do not know what prompted this question, nor do we know the mood or attitude of the questioner. John P. Lange seems convinced that this anonymous ques-

---

[28]See comments on Luke 9:51 ff.
[29]See comments on Luke 10:38 ff., and 13:22 (below).
[30]See Van Oosterzee, *op. cit.,* p. 217.

tioner was implying, possibly in a tone of ridicule, that a professed Saviour with such a pitifully small following could not be the Lord He claimed to be.[31] Spence sees a reflection of the prevailing Jewish exclusiveness—the Jews being the **few** that would be saved.[32] Whatever the motive or preconception back of the question, the Master gave an objective and serious answer.

**Strive to enter in at the strait gate** (24). The Greek word here translated **strive** is our word "agonize" (Anglicized from the Greek). **Strait** is an archaic English word meaning "narrow." With a narrow gate restricting entrance, forcing the enterer to unload, and with opposing forces hindering his entrance, he must strive earnestly (agonize) to enter. The whole passage is saying, "Whatever the obstacles, you must enter, for the cost of failure is too great." **Many . . . will seek to enter in,** (when it is too late) **and shall not be able.** This has reference either to the second coming of Christ, the end of the day of grace, or to death as ending the period of probation.

**When once the master of the house is risen up, and hath shut to the door** (25). The change of imagery from the narrow gate to the closed door is anticipated in the last clause of verse 24. The narrow gate makes entrance difficult; the closed door makes entrance impossible. When, at the appropriate time at the close of the day, the master of the house would close and lock the door, all of the members of the household were expected to be inside, and if they were loyal and obedient they were inside.

**And ye begin to stand without, and to knock.** Two sins are probably responsible for such late arrivals: revelry and presumption. Love of sin would hold them, and a false hope that the master's love and kindness would force him to make an exception in their case would prevent their acting on the promptings of conscience.

**He shall answer . . . I know you not.** At this point the physical image begins to fade and the Master's words become more literal. We lose sight of the oriental master of the house, and we see in his place the Lord of earth and heaven.

The Greek word translated **know** has a much broader and deeper significance than its English counterpart. In addition to

---

[31]John Peter Lange, *The Life of the Lord Jesus Christ,* ed. Marcus Dods, trans. J. E. Ryland (Grand Rapids: Zondervan Publishing House, 1958) II, 414 f.

[32]Spence, *op. cit.,* II, 4.

the idea of "knowing," as we use the term, it contains the ideas of experience and commitment. To know someone in this broader sense is to have an intimate relationship with him and to be deeply committed to him.[33] But note that the responsibility for God's "knowing" us is not with Him but with us. It is our fault if God does not "know us."

**Then shall ye begin to say, We have eaten and drunk in thy presence, and thou hast taught in our streets (26).** Note again that the image has faded and the Master himself is unmistakably present in His parable. The surface acquaintance which would result from eating at the same banquet with the Master and of being present when He taught in their streets was far from "knowing" the Master or of being "known" by Him in the full and proper sense of the Greek word. Such surface acquaintance was far from sufficient to justify their plea for entrance.

**I tell you, I know you not (27).** The plea for entrance is firmly and finally rejected by a repetition of His significant charge, **I know you not.** The heart of the matter is seen in the Master's characterization of these late seekers as workers of iniquity. Excuses and explanations for estrangement from God are legion, but sin is always the real cause.

**There shall be weeping and gnashing of teeth, when ye shall see Abraham, and Isaac, and Jacob, and all the prophets, in the kingdom of God, and you yourselves thrust out (28).** Here we have the primary application of the parable. The Jews, who fondly and dutifully accepted Abraham, Isaac, Jacob, and the prophets, and rejected Jesus, would someday see these revered ancestors in Christ's kingdom. They themselves would be thrust out as unfit for such holy habitation and association.

The **weeping and gnashing of teeth,** which is the strongest Hebraic formula to express intense suffering, is a gauge of the Master's mood. It portrays the seriousness of His subject and the tragic finality of His sentence.

**They shall come from the east . . . and from the west, and from the north, and from the south (29).** From every race and nation will come citizens of the Kingdom—persons whom the Master "knows" in truth and who know Him.

**There are last which shall be first, and there are first which shall be last (30).** The **first** are evidently the Jews (in the primary application of this verse), and the **last** are the Gentiles.

[33]See also comments on Matt. 7:23.

543

Note, however, that not all Gentiles will be truly first nor will all Jews be really last. As a nation, the Jews of Jesus' day rejected Him; but many individual Jews accepted Him, and many others have accepted Him down through the centuries since. On the other hand the Gentiles have often been far from good examples in their attitude toward Christ.

The permanent truth found in the formula in this verse is that position, heritage, race, or anything else which makes a man **first** in the eyes of men is insufficient to make him first with God. In the final analysis, he only is **first** who gives God first place in his heart and life, and he only is **last** who rejects or neglects God and spiritual things.

### 2. *Opposition and Compassion* (13:31-35)

**The same day.** The best Greek manuscripts read, "the same hour." **Came certain of the Pharisees, saying . . . Get thee out, . . . for Herod will kill thee** (31). We do not know whether the Pharisees were accurately reporting Herod's expressed intention or had invented the story to force Jesus to depart from His present location. Two things seem clear in view of what is known about Herod and the Pharisees. In the first place the Pharisees were hostile enough to use either the truth or a falsehood against Jesus, and they were by no means above collaborating with an enemy. In the second place Herod had shown by murdering John the Baptist that he was capable of killing a religious leader. It is also evident that both Herod and the Pharisees could hope to gain from the result of such a report. Since Herod seemed to be bothered with superstitious fears as a result of his murder of John,[34] he might have sent the Pharisees to Jesus with this report. Perhaps he hoped the Master would depart, and he would be rid of Him without the necessity of repeating a crime which was distasteful to him.

The place from which Jesus was advised to depart was evidently in Perea, a part of Herod's kingdom, where most of the ministry of Jesus recorded in this part of Luke's Gospel took place.

**Go ye, and tell that fox** (32). Herod was cruel and bold, and might be expected to have been represented as a lion rather than a fox. But he was also crafty and contemptible, and it was this aspect of his character which Jesus had in mind. If, as was sug-

---

[34]See Matt. 14:1-2; Mark 6:14; Luke 9:7.

gested above, Herod was purposely sending the Pharisees to Jesus with Herod's warning against Him, the reason for the designation of **fox** is evident.

Spence declares that Jesus is literally saying "she-fox."[35] And from this he concludes that Herodias, the power behind the throne, is probably intended by Jesus' appellation. Spence is undoubtedly basing this judgment on the fact that the Greek word used is feminine. But the Greek word for **fox** is feminine in its basic form, so that we cannot know certainly that the female sex is intended here. However, the fact that "fox" is feminine in Greek shows clearly that Greek-speaking peoples regarded a fox as the opposite of bold and courageous. Thus Jesus was by no means complimenting Herod.

Some have questioned Jesus' use of such an uncompliment-ary term in reference to a king. But the exaggerated courtly address of the Middle Ages and the period immediately follow-ing was not then customary. The further fact that the term fits Herod perfectly is ample justification of the Master. It should also be remembered that Herod was not a legitimate Jewish ruler but a tool of Caesar.

**Behold, I cast out devils, and I do cures to day and to mor-row, and the third day I shall be perfected.** Jesus is saying, first, that He has work to do, and He will accomplish that work in spite of everything—including Herod. In the second place, the kind of work He is doing is in no way a threat to Herod's king-dom—except as sin is threatened by righteousness and holiness. We see also a veiled prediction of the Resurrection (**perfected on the third day**) in the near future. Basically **I shall be per-fected** means that His work would then be ended.

**I must walk** (literally "go" or "proceed") **to day, and to mor-row, and the day following** (33). The time is short. But until His work is finished neither Herod nor anyone else will be able to stop Him. **For it cannot be that a prophet perish out of Jeru-salem.** Van Oosterzee calls this "holy irony united with deep melancholy."[36] And just how ironic these words are can be seen either by looking back to bloody scenes in Jerusalem in the past or by looking forward to that soon-coming Crucifixion.

[35]Spence, *op. cit.,* II, 6.
[36]Van Oosterzee, *op. cit.,* p. 221.

**O Jerusalem, Jerusalem, which killest the prophets . . . how often would I have gathered thy children together . . .** (34-35). Here Jesus pours out the bitter agony of rejected love. The bitterness of His sorrow shows that, though His love has not been requited and His offer of help has not been accepted, His love is unchanged. Jerusalem is hopeless, not because Christ has turned away, but because they **would not**—literally, they "wished not," they "willed not," they "did not want" what He offered. God will not force His attention upon anybody. For further discussion see comments on Matt. 23:37-39.

### 3. *Healing on the Sabbath* (14:1-6)

**As he went into the house of one of the chief Pharisees** (1). This **chief** was one of the highest-ranking Pharisees. He was possibly a member of the Sanhedrin, or held some other high position in the Jewish state which gave him power and influence. **To eat bread on the sabbath day.** Such feasts on the Sabbath day were common, and Jesus was invited to several of them.[37] The only restriction placed upon these feasts was that the food had to be cooked the day before.

**They watched him.** This is the first hint we have that His host had an ulterior motive in inviting Him, and it explains why a high-ranking Pharisee would invite Jesus to eat with him at such a time. The prejudice and hatred of the members of that sect toward Jesus had reached the point where they sought His destruction. This is but one of many occasions when the Pharisees acted the hypocrite—often posing as Jesus' friends to gain their evil ends. They even collaborated with traditional enemies in their campaigns against Him. Jesus' acceptance of such an invitation demonstrated both courage and love. He knew from experience the danger to himself, but His love for all men— including Pharisees—would not let Him pass up this opportunity. There might be a chance to help His host even at this late date.

**And, behold, there was a certain man before him which had the dropsy** (2). These words imply a rather sudden appearance— or at least a sudden recognition of the situation on the part of Jesus. The man was obviously brought by the host to trap Jesus. Without any preparation or introduction he appeared before the Master. That this man's presence was part of a plot against Jesus

---

[37]Lange calls these feasts "perilous entertainments." See Lange, *Life of Jesus*, p. 419.

546

is strongly implied by the "watching" on the part of the Pharisees (2). It is further evidenced by Jesus' immediate defense of His practice of healing on the Sabbath (3-6).

**Jesus . . . spake unto the lawyers and Pharisees, saying, Is it lawful to heal on the sabbath day?** (3) Like birds waiting for their prey these human vultures were waiting for Jesus to fall into their power. But Jesus shifted the responsibility to them by His question. They considered themselves authorities on the Law. But did the Law condemn such acts of mercy? It did not, and they undoubtedly saw the point of the Master's question. But their prejudice and their evil purpose prevented them from acknowledging it.

**They held their peace. And he took him, and healed him** (4). Under normal circumstances the Pharisees would have answered Jesus' question, both to make clear their teaching at this point and to condemn Jesus. But here their sinister designs could best be served by silence. They evidently did not want to do or say anything that would prevent the healing of this man. They wanted to use what they considered Jesus' disregard for the Sabbath as ammunition in their campaign to destroy Him. Jesus was well aware of their designs, but there were two things more important to Him at this time than His own safety: a principle of righteousness and a suffering human being. The man with the dropsy was not a party to the plot but an innocent sufferer who was being used by this scheming host. A wise and loving Master healed him and sent him on his way.

**Which of you shall have an ass or an ox fallen into a pit, and will not straightway pull him out on the sabbath day?** (5) All of these Pharisees knew that the Master was right. They would immediately rescue a trapped animal on the Sabbath. Then why should not a suffering man be healed? The only explanation for their inconsistency is that prejudice and greed prompted their actions. Prejudice for their religious doctrines made them disregard the urgent need of human beings. Greed for the wealth represented by the trapped animal made them eager to pull the ox or the ass out of the pit. In neither case were love and kindness their motives.

**And they could not answer him again to these things** (6). In verse 4 they **held their peace** because silence was in harmony with their evil designs. Here they **could not answer** because they had no reply which would not incriminate them. The

547

Master had healed the man and silenced His enemies. But in so doing He had widened the breach between himself and His enemies and increased their determination to destroy Him.

### 4. *Rules for Guests* (14: 7-11)

**He put forth a parable to those which were bidden, when he marked how they chose out the chief rooms**—literally "first" or "chief reclining-places" (7). The incident of the healing of the man with dropsy occurred immediately after the arrival of the guests, before they had taken their places at the table. The healed man having left the house, and the Master having silenced His critics, the guests began to choose their places. Their selfishness immediately showed itself as they each, like undisciplined children, tried to get the place of highest honor. The Master saw their complete disregard for both etiquette and the feelings of others. So He made their actions the occasion for teaching them, by means of **a parable** (more correctly, parabolic discourse) the proper attitude and conduct of guests. Through these rules for guests He teaches a basic attitude which we are to maintain in all of our human relationships.

**When thou art bidden . . . sit not down in the highest room; lest a more honourable man than thou be bidden** (8). The highest seats are for the most honorable, not for the most egotistical. The fact that honor should be reserved for true merit is so generally recognized that the statement itself is trite. Yet men often seek and give honor with little or no regard for merit. The Pharisees were notorious place-seekers; yet they knew little of the kind of character which deserves the place of honor. In fact, their very place-seeking demonstrated their basic unworthiness and canceled what merit they might otherwise have had.

**And he that bade thee and him come and say to thee, Give this man place; and thou begin with shame to take the lowest room . . .** (9-10). Intelligent self-interest as well as regard for merit would dictate the more humble attitude. For the shame of abasement would more than cancel both the pleasure and the honor of the moment in the chief seat.

The humble attitude not only avoids the danger of abasement, but is often the way to exaltation. If one takes the lowest seat he will probably be promoted—if he has any merit. This promotion will bring honor beyond the intrinsic honor of the place given to him. But the humble attitude should be taken, not because it works—brings honor—but because it is right. The best way for one to keep himself sincerely humble is to keep his eyes upon Jesus. If this is done, the true merit of the Master will so far eclipse any paltry merit which one might feel is his that a genuine humility will be the natural result.

**For whosoever exalteth himself shall be abased; and he that humbleth himself shall be exalted (11).** Here Jesus expands His teaching concerning the attitude and conduct of guests into a universal principle. The way up is down, and the way down is up —a paradox but a most significant truth. Since self-exaltation is evil, it cannot but abase. And since true humility is in perfect harmony with the creature-Creator relationship, it cannot but exalt one in character and in relation to God. Also it often brings exaltation before one's fellowmen.

### 5. *Rules of Hosts* (14:12-14)

**Then said he also to him that bade him (12).** After His discourse to the guests, Jesus saw that something needed to be said to the host. He could see that His host was as selfish in his choice of guests as the guests were in their choices of reclining places.

**When thou makest a dinner or a supper, call not thy friends, nor thy brethren, neither thy kinsmen, nor thy rich neighbours; lest . . . a recompence be made thee.** This is not to be interpreted as prohibiting the practice of entertaining friends and relatives. But it does make it clear that such entertaining has no heavenly reward. It has its compensation here—in the pleasure one receives from the occasion and in the recompense of the return invitation. Jesus is, however, condemning selfish motives in any host. And He is condemning the self-righteous and selfish exclusiveness of the Pharisees which prevented them from being kind and helpful to all men in need—regardless of race, sect, or station in life. Perhaps the worst thing about this attitude of the Pharisees is that it was encouraged, even demanded, by their religion.

**But when thou makest a feast, call the poor, the maimed, the lame, the blind: and thou shalt be blessed; for they cannot recompense thee (13-14).** In view of the attitude and the practice of the Pharisees, this suggestion sounds revolutionary. But in reality it was not new. The Israelites had been commanded in the law of Moses to include the poor, the stranger, the fatherless, and the widows in their feasts (Deut. 14:28-29; 16:11; 26:11-13). The advance Jesus makes here over God's command through Moses is in the stress which He puts upon physical handicaps—the crippled, the lame, the blind.

Since the motive of such unselfish helpfulness is love, and there is no chance of earthly recompense, **thou shalt be recompensed at the resurrection of the just.**

### 6. *The Parable of the Great Supper* (14: 15-24)

This parable is quite similar to that of the marriage of the king's son in Matt. 22:1-10. But the two are not the same. The facts in the stories and the geography and circumstances of the narration are different. Matthew's story was related in Jerusalem as one among a number of "Kingdom Parables." Luke's story was told in Perea in the house of the "chief Pharisee," where Jesus was being entertained. Also, Matthew's story is about the marriage of a king's son and the accompanying feast; Luke's story is about a **great supper** given by **a certain man.** If these parables were based upon historical fact, it is possible that both were based upon the same episode. However it seems obvious that the Master used them differently and on separate occasions.

**When one of them that sat at meat . . . heard these things, he said . . . Blessed is he that shall eat bread in the kingdom of God** (15). This fellow guest was impressed with what the Master had been saying about unselfish giving to those who have the greatest need, and also about the heavenly recompense. He seems sincere, and even wistful, when he comments on the blessedness of this divine recompense—eating bread in the kingdom of God.

If the guest was a Pharisee, as he probably was, he reminds us that not all Pharisees were unresponsive to the gospel message. However it is quite possible, even probable, that he was still thinking that those who would **eat bread in the kingdom of God** would be Jews. This probability is made almost a certainty when Jesus takes his statement as a point of departure for a parable which condemns the attitude of exclusiveness and false security.

**A certain man made a great supper** (16). The use of the imagery of a feast to represent the kingdom of God was common among the Jews in Jesus' day. His fellow guests, being influential Jews, would easily catch His meaning. Jesus was, in effect, saying to the guest who had remarked on the blessedness of eating bread in the kingdom of God, "Yes, it is blessed to take part in the heavenly feast; but you and other Jews might be entirely too confident of your own inevitable part in that feast."

The man in the parable **bade many.** This first invitation was broad but exclusive. The poor, maimed, halt, and blind were not included. In the application of the parable, those who were bidden were the Jews. This was discriminative. But the Pharisees had, in effect, narrowed the invitation still more by their negative legalism and selfish exclusivism.

**And sent his servant at supper time to say to them that were bidden, Come; for all things are now ready. And they all with one consent began to make excuse**—"to excuse themselves" (17-18). This host had every reason and every right to expect those who were invited to be present at the feast. Though they begged to be excused, their conduct was inexcusable, and their excuses were ridiculous. We get the distinct impression that these features of the story are purposely exaggerated to make them fit the spiritual application, which is Jesus' whole purpose for giving the parable.

Both the fact of refusal and the absurd excuses show that these invited guests were showing contempt for the lord of the feast. No one could mistake their disdain. Their action was taken as a personal insult and it was undoubtedly so intended.

Under the topic "Excuses Not Reasons," Maclaren has these three points: (1) The strangely unanimous refusal; (2) The flimsy excuses; (3) The real reason—they did not want to go.

**Then the master of the house being angry said to his servant, Go out quickly into the streets and lanes of the city, and bring . . . the poor, and the maimed, and the halt, and the blind** (21). The ones in the second group invited were still in **the city,** which would imply that they represent Jews. But their location in **the streets and lanes** and their low physical and economic state would point to the outcast Jews—"publicans and sinners"—as well as to those who were literally poor and handicapped. The Pharisees would consider all of these to be beneath themselves and far less deserving of God's attention and invitation. It was this group, however, including the Galilean peasants, that heard Jesus "gladly."

**And the servant said, Lord, it is done . . . and yet there is room** (22). Publicans and "sinners," Galilean peasants and handicapped Jews were not enough to fill the invitation list. The banquet room had still many empty places. Here the imagery grows dim and we see through to the actual conditions of the Kingdom. We see its vast size; we see the unlimited opportunity for all who have the proper regard for the invitation of **the master of the house.**

**Go out into the highways and hedges** (23). The third invitation list extended beyond the city—beyond Israel to the Gentiles. Those who were dogs and outcasts to the Jews were included in the final and universal invitation.

**And compel them to come in.** In the literal setting of the parable this simply implies that these last were pressed into accepting the invitation, **that my house may be filled.** But in its spiritual application we see the evangelistic zeal of the Church as well as the pressure of Holy Spirit conviction for sin which has "pressed" millions of Gentiles into the Kingdom. The injunction in the parable by no means authorizes or justifies the autocratic and wholesale conversion by force of whole nations or tribes by ancient and medieval kings. This pressure must be that of logic, love, and the drawing power of the Holy Spirit.

**For I say unto you, That none of those men which were bidden shall taste of my supper** (24). Contempt and insult have brought their appropriate reward: complete and final exclusion. The imagery of the great supper is almost forgotten here, and the Master's application is brought plainly before us. This is seen in the Greek where the **you** addressed in verse 24 is plural, while the lord of the feast has been addressing his servant in the singular. The **you** cannot be the slave; the word obviously refers to those whom Jesus is addressing. **My supper** becomes more than an oriental feast; it becomes the feast in the heavenly Kingdom. For further discussion, see comments on Matt. 22:1-10.

### 7. *The Conditions of Discipleship* (14:25-33)

**And there went great multitudes with him** (25). As Jesus drew nearer to Jerusalem, the crowds that followed Him increased. Among this vast concourse of people were sincere disciples; selfish hangers-on, interested in any advantage He could bring to them; and enemies, bent on His destruction. The sequel clearly demonstrates that the first group was very small in comparison with the other two. As Jesus' demands of complete renunciation and total commitment became more clearly understood, His band of disciples grew smaller; and as His popularity decreased, His enemies increased both in number and in the vigor of their opposition.

**If any man come to me, and hate not his father, and mother, and wife, and children, and brethren, and sisters, yea, and his**

**own life also, he cannot be my disciple** (26). Jesus recognized the threefold division of the multitude. He further clarified the demands of discipleship and, undoubtedly, further restricted the group of sincere disciples. Of course He did not mean literally that we should hate our relatives. This would be totally out of harmony with His teaching elsewhere. He is using this strong language to say that no other love, no other obligation, no other relationship can be allowed to stand between the Master and His disciples. Anything which comes between man and God severs his relationship with the Lord.[38] Christ will have first place or no place in our hearts and lives.

**And whosoever doth not bear his cross, and come after me, cannot be my disciple** (27). See comments on Matt. 10:38; 16:24.

**For which of you, intending to build a tower, sitteth not down first, and counteth the cost . . . ?** (28) The Greek word translated **tower** is *purgon*, cognate with the German *Burg* (which in ancient times was *purg*), and means "a fortified place." Jesus probably had reference to the towers which were built in vineyards and on country estates for observation and defense. The phrase **which of you** would seem to imply that the tower referred to is one which Jesus' listeners would be likely to build. Some think He had in mind such palaces as were built by the Herods, and by others who tried to imitate them[39] but often were not financially able to complete their pretentious plans. But this distinction as to the kind of building Jesus had in mind is unimportant, for the point He was making was the importance of counting the cost before building. The alternatives to counting the cost are embarrassment, loss of time, loss of material and money.

To begin building an edifice without first checking to see if sufficient funds are available to finish it would be folly indeed. But to take lightly and presumptuously the vow of discipleship is to play the fool in a much deeper and far more tragic sense. Such flippant acceptance of sacred vows and responsibilities betrays either a lack of understanding or a disregard for the seriousness of the step. It could reflect the spirit of self-righteous exclusivism which was so characteristic of the Pharisees.

---

[38]See comments on Matt. 10:37.

[39]This interpretation fits the idea of the parable, but it does not harmonize with the basic meaning of the word *purgon* unless this "palace" is a fortified palace or castle.

The penalty for failure to count the cost of discipleship is not mere temporary loss or personal embarrassment. It involves possible eternal loss for the one involved and embarrassment for the whole Christian Church. It gives the enemy occasion to blaspheme. It makes it easier for non-Christians to doubt the truths of the gospel, and increases the probability that many will be lost.

**Or what king, going to make war . . . sitteth not down first, and consulteth whether he be able with ten thousand to meet him that cometh against him with twenty thousand? Or else, . . . he sendeth an ambassage . . . (31-32).** Jesus is enforcing the truth which He has been stressing by giving another parable with the same meaning. No king worthy of the title would go to war without first taking full stock of his war potential. Counting the cost in temporal matters is done to determine whether one can pay the price. But in the matter of discipleship its purpose is to determine one's willingness. God has seen to it that we *can* if we *will.*

**So likewise, whosoever he be of you that forsaketh not all that he hath, he cannot be my disciple (33).** Here Jesus is repeating the idea contained in verses 26 and 27. There He gave the cost of discipleship. Then (vv. 28-32) He gave two parables to demonstrate the importance of counting the cost. Now He repeats, in different words, just what is the cost of discipleship. This form of discourse is a common Hebraic device used in both poetry and prose. First the proposition is given; then it is demonstrated or developed; then the original proposition is repeated in slightly different words.

This radical passage does not imply that the imperfect discipleship of many of Jesus' followers was not valid at all. He is stating in absolute terms the implications of discipleship, implications which are not always seen at conversion. But as men sincerely follow Jesus, sooner or later He will bring these full claims into sharp focus. Then a man must make a fresh decision: either he confirms and seeks to perfect his discipleship by paying the full price, or he begins to hedge and dodge, and ultimately walks "no more with him" (John 6:66). All believers reach, sooner or later, a second major crisis of decision. This is the crossroad of the call to entire sanctification—not doctrinally stated in this passage, but inescapably implied by the absolute terms of discipleship.

554

### 8. *Savourless Salt* (14:34-35)

**Salt is good: but if the salt have lost its savour, wherewith shall it be seasoned? It is neither fit for the land, nor yet for the dunghill** (34-35). Salt was one of the most important food items in ancient days. Its chief use was for preserving foods. Since refrigeration and modern canning methods were unknown, it performed an extremely important function. But salt is good, either for seasoning or preserving food, only if it is salty. If it loses this quality it is one of the most worthless of materials.

So, too, religion is worthless if it loses the vital element. This essential element cannot be present without self-sacrifice and total commitment to Christ. (For further discussion see comments on Matt. 5:13).

### 9. *Love and Hatred for Sinners* (15:1-2)

These two verses form an introduction to the fifteenth chapter of Luke. An appropriate title to the section would be "Seeking the Lost." The chapter is composed of the three parables: "The Lost Sheep," "The Lost Coin," and "The Lost Son."

**Then drew near unto him all the publicans and sinners for to hear him. And the Pharisees and scribes murmured, saying, This man receiveth sinners, and eateth with them** (1-2). The Greek words translated **then drew near** are more correctly translated "And were drawing near." This implies, not an isolated incident, but a general tendency of publicans and "sinners" to draw nearer to Jesus toward the end of His ministry. This interpretation harmonizes with Luke's statement that **all the publicans and sinners** were drawing near. Such a phrase could hardly imply single occurrence. Also the charge by Jesus' enemies that He **receiveth sinners, and eateth with them** must refer to Jesus' general practice or to earlier incidents. There is no indication that Jesus was at this time eating with sinners or with anyone else.

But since the murmuring of the Pharisees and scribes was Jesus' occasion for giving the following parables, it seems likely that something transpired at this time to remind Jesus' enemies of His affinity for publicans and "sinners." This might, however, have been nothing more than the fact that members of these despised groups were present in the crowd that surrounded Jesus at the moment.

The hatred of the Pharisees and scribes for publicans and "sinners" is well known. They felt that anyone who associated with these despised persons did so because he was of a similar character. They could not conceive of the kind of love that would seek out the sinners, the outcasts, the unlovely for their own sake to lift them to a higher life.

It was such love on the part of Jesus which attracted these despised people. They easily saw the contrast between the attitude of Jesus and that of the Pharisees, and it was natural that they should draw near One who loved them so. The three parables in this chapter all illustrate such regard for the lost. In each case, that which was lost was considered precious. It was worth seeking, and worth rejoicing over when found.

### 10. *The Lost Sheep* (15:3-7)

**And he spake this parable unto them** (3). This and the next item form a pair of brief parables, which give the same truth under different figures. In comparison with the parable of the prodigal son they are minor.

For discussion of verses 4-6 see comments on Matt. 18:12-13.

**I say unto you, that likewise joy shall be in heaven over one sinner that repenteth, more than over ninety and nine just persons, which need no repentance** (7). This verse is the application of the parable or the conclusion of the argument. Jesus is saying that His attitude toward the lost, illustrated by that of the shepherd, is a reflection of the reactions in heaven—more rejoicing over the one who repents than over ninety-nine who **need no repentance.**

But who are these righteous or just ones who need no repentance? Luther and others think Jesus refers to those who have been made righteous by God's grace as the result of a former repentance. Van Oosterzee is convinced that Jesus is referring to those who consider themselves righteous—the Pharisees, for example, who were a part of the crowd to whom He was speaking.[40] It is also possible that these **just persons** might be angels.[41]

Since Jesus was answering the criticism of Pharisees and scribes, it is most likely that He was borrowing their terminology. They divided the Jewish population into sinners and righteous or

[40]Van Oosterzee, *op. cit.,* p. 235.
[41]See Barnes, *op. cit.,* p. 101.

**just persons.** The latter, in their opinion, did not need to repent. They put themselves in this category. Jesus was saying, in effect: "You despise those whom you call 'publicans and sinners,' but heaven rejoices more over the repentance of one of these than over ninety-nine of you who, in your biased opinion, need no repentance."

In interpreting any parable, we should be careful to avoid trying to make every point fit the application.

### 11. *The Lost Coin* (15:8-10)

**Either what woman having ten pieces of silver** (or drachmas)**, if she lose one piece, doth not light a candle, and sweep the house, and seek diligently until she find it?** (8-9) This parable repeats the meaning of the first with a different figure. Here a woman who had only ten drachmas lost one coin, and she sought until she found it. Her joy was so great at having found it that she called her friends and neighbors to help her celebrate.

Verse 10 is practically a repetition of verse 7. The woman's joy at finding the lost coin illustrates the attitude and reaction in heaven when one sinner repents.

Charles Simeon makes three good points on this parable: (1) There are none so worthless but the Lord is deeply concerned about them; (2) There are no exertions, however great, which He will not use for their recovery; (3) There is nothing so pleasing to Him as the recovery of one from his lost estate.

### 12. *The Lost Son* (15:11-24)

The parable of the prodigal son, as the following narrative is usually called, is one of the world's best-loved stories. It is longer and more complex than the two preceding parables, and it has a wider application. But the major point of the story is the same as those which precede it. The complete parable includes verses 11-32, but it is treated here in two parts, the first dealing with the prodigal (the younger) son, and the second dealing with the elder son. This parable is found only in Luke.

**A certain man had two sons: and the younger of them said to his father, Father, give me the portion that falleth to me** (11-12). The characters in the two preceding parables were from the low class of Jewish society; the family in the present story is from the upper class, with considerable wealth, prestige, and influence.

That the father should give the younger son his inheritance before his own death was by no means uncommon in Jewish history. Abraham gave Isaac and his other sons their inheritance before his own death (Gen. 25:5-6). But it was highly irregular for the son to ask for it. Whenever such a favor was shown, it was a free gift of the father.

**And not many days after the younger son . . . took his journey into a far country, and there wasted his substance (13).** This was the son's reason for asking for his inheritance. He wanted his "fling"; he wanted to "sow his wild oats." He had not yet learned that what we sow we reap. Godet points out that two things impelled the boy to leave home: he was repelled by the paternal restraints, and he was attracted by the world with the enjoyment which it offered.[42]

Just where the far country was is not known. It was undoubtedly a foreign country beyond Israel's borders, and it might have been Rome. Wherever it was, it was indeed a "far" country morally—quite different from the atmosphere of home. The wasting of his substance implies that his money was both misused and used up. Riotous living is wrong and it is expensive.

**And when he had spent all, there arose a mighty famine . . . and he began to be in want (14).** Famines were common in Eastern lands, but in a very real sense this was the young man's own personal famine. Its effect on him was increased by his own prodigality and sin. Note the close grammatical relation between his having **spent all** and the coming of the famine. He was destitute: moneyless, jobless, and friendless. He was friendless because he had no money; the kind of friends he chose had loved his money rather than him.

**He . . . joined himself to a citizen of that country; and he sent him into his fields to feed swine. And he would fain have filled his belly with the husks . . . and no man gave unto him (15-16).** He had nothing; he was given nothing; and the only job he could get was contrary to both his social position and his religion. Jews were forbidden to eat swine. They were permitted to raise them and sell them to Gentiles, but the job of tending them was one of the lowest on the social scale. The boy not only took the job but he was at the point of eating with the swine, though the husks which they ate had very little nourishment in them. Having left home in search of freedom, he found instead bondage and destitution—or rather they found him.

---

[42]Godet, *op. cit.*, II, 150.

**He came to himself** (17)—like one awaking from a nightmare. He had been morally and spiritually blind; he had not been able to see things as they were; his sense of values had been out of balance. Now he saw many things more clearly and from a right perspective, but most of all he saw himself for what he really was. He saw not only that he was destitute but that sin—his sin—was to blame.

**How many hired servants of my father's have bread enough and to spare, and I perish with hunger!** How inconsistent! Yet he had cut himself off from the abundance at the father's house. This he sees clearly.

**I will arise and go to my father, and will say unto him, Father, I have sinned . . .** (18). His vision now being clear, the remedy which he chose was the right one: to return, and to repent. Both return and repentance were necessary for him, and the same is true with regard to every sinner.

**And am no more worthy to be called thy son: make me as one of thy hired servants** (19). A clear view of one's sinfulness begets the conviction of unworthiness. When he had asked his father for his portion of the family goods, his request had been based on a sense of merit. Now a consciousness of sin has convinced him that he no longer has any merit; all that he can rely upon is mercy and forgiveness. This is an excellent picture of the proper attitude of a sinner who is seeking salvation.

The prodigal son did not ask to be made a servant, but to be made **as one of thy hired servants.** He knows the father cannot completely forget his former relation to the family, but he is fully convinced that he no longer deserves to be called a son. He requests his former task, but he does not ask to be reinstated into sonship with its privileges and honors.

**And he arose, and came . . . But when he was a great way off, his father saw him, and had compassion, and ran, and fell on his neck, and kissed him** (20). The boy put feet to his resolve— he arose and went. But he had completely underestimated his father's love: love which impelled the father to watch for his return, to run to meet him, and to break into the young man's confession and begin granting more than was requested before the request was complete. He was fully restored to sonship with its privileges and honors, and his return was celebrated with a feast of the best that the father had to offer.

**This my son was dead, and is alive again; he was lost, and is found** (24). Love had covered the past with a blanket of forgiveness when the son had returned and repented. Now the father could think of but one thing: My son who was lost is found; my son who was dead—morally and before the law as well as in the heart of the father—is alive.

Reference to the son as being **found** implies a seeking on the part of the father. But this was a different kind of seeking from that which is found in the two preceding parables. The father did not physically go out in search of his son. He knew this would be useless. The son had left because he wanted to go and would not return simply because the father asked him to do so. The son would never return until he had a change of mind—until he **came to himself.**

It was the father's love and influence which sought the son, which followed every step he took. This love was present the moment the boy came to himself—it was the first thing the son thought of. Thus God seeks the sinner; He follows him with His providence, He attracts him with love, and He woos him through His blessed Holy Spirit.

Maclaren has a good treatment of "Gifts to the Prodigal," of which he lists four: (1) The robe; (2) The ring; (3) Shoes on his feet; (4) The feast.

A simple outline for this parable is: (1) The possessor, 11-12; (2) The prodigal, 13-14; (3) The pauper, 15-16; (4) The penitent, 17-19. Another development has also been used: (1) The sin of this son, 11-16; (2) Returning sanity, 17-20a; (3) The father's welcome, 20b-24.

### 13. *The Prodigal's Selfish Brother* (15:25-32)

**Now his elder son . . . as he . . . drew nigh . . . heard music and dancing . . . and asked what these things meant** (25-26). It is this second part of the parable which gives it point for the immediate situation. The prodigal son represents the sinner, the outcast of the Jewish race. The elder son represents the religious Jew—Pharisees, scribes, and other professed devout persons. They were the ones, according to their claims, who had never gone astray, who had remained faithful.

**And he was angry, and would not go in: therefore came his father out, and entreated him** (28). The father's love for the elder son had not been diminished by the return of the younger. The elder son **would not go in** but the father **came out.**

There were two reasons for the elder son's anger. The first was a legalistic spirit which carried the demand for punishment to the point where there was no room for mercy. Thus to forgive and receive and honor the younger son, no matter what the mitigating circumstances were, was considered weakness and a lack of concern for justice. The second cause of the elder brother's anger, and no doubt the basic one, was selfishness. He wanted everything for himself—all of the honor as well as all of the property.

**Lo, these many years do I serve thee, neither transgressed I at any time thy commandment: and yet thou never gavest me a kid . . . But as soon as this thy son was come . . . thou hast killed for him the fatted calf** (29-30). Here we see the elder brother's two major character traits: self-righteousness and selfishness.

Note the complaint of the elder son. He makes a double contrast. First, he says he has never been feasted at his father's expense while his brother is now being so honored. In the second place he contrasts the **kid** which he has not received with the **fatted calf** that has been prepared for his brother.

Note also that the elder son has lost all brotherly feeling for the prodigal. He refers to him, not as "my brother," but **thy son.**

**Son, thou art ever with me, and all that I have is thine** (31). How blind this elder son was! He was complaining about never having been given a kid, while in reality everything his father had was his. It was his both because he was the eldest son and because the younger son had already received his inheritance.

The one thing for which he should have been most grateful, and which he completely overlooked or ignored, was the fact that **thou art ever with me.** The love, honor, respect, and fellowship of his father should have been cherished above everything else.

**It was meet that we should make merry . . . for this thy brother was dead, and is alive again; and was lost, and is found** (32). The father's love enabled him to see a responsibility which the elder son's legalism, materialism, and selfishness had kept him from seeing. The father kindly reminded the latter that the prodigal was not merely his son but **thy brother.**

The application of this parable is clear. Publicans and "sinners," represented by the prodigal, though their sins are many and grievous, will find forgiveness when they return to the Heavenly Father in true repentance. On the other hand the Pharisees and scribes, represented by the elder brother, are not only devoid of love for sinners, but they try to prevent God's operation in others. They do nothing to restore the lost, and they use their influence to oppose anyone who seeks to do so. This was one of the major reasons for their opposition to Jesus.

### 14. *The Parable of the Unjust Steward* (16:1-9)

This parable was probably given shortly after those found in chapter 15 but on a different occasion. It might have been given later the same day.

**And he said also unto his disciples** (1). The word **disciples** is used in a broad sense, including all sympathetic followers of Christ. Even though He addressed the parable to His disciples, Jesus was still in the presence of the multitude. This is evident in verse 14, where we find the Pharisees opposing His message.

**There was a certain rich man, which had a steward; and the same was accused unto him that he had wasted his goods.** This steward was the manager of the rich man's household, or estate. He evidently had been given broad powers in controlling and dispensing his master's wealth, and he therefore had opportunities to be dishonest. He was accused of wasting the master's goods. The Greek word translated **wasted** means literally "scattering," "laying waste" as in a military campaign. It seems that the steward was actually stealing his master's goods or at least administering them for his own interest. The master evidently did not live on the estate but in the city, and thus he would not know of the steward's dishonest dealing.

**And he called him, and said . . . give an account of thy stewardship; for thou mayest be no longer steward** (2). To **give an account** means literally "render the account." His master demanded that a complete financial statement be prepared. This account was not to be given to prove the steward innocent or guilty. The master was already sure of his guilt and had informed him, **Thou mayest be no longer steward.**

**Then the steward said within himself, What shall I do? . . . I cannot dig; to beg I am ashamed. I am resolved what to do, that, when I am put out of the stewardship, they may receive me into their houses** (3-4). Dr. J. B. Chapman once wrote a brief article in the *Herald of Holiness* on this parable, and he entitled it "Dig, Beg, or Steal." He says that the steward was too lazy to dig and ashamed to beg, so he decided to steal. The man resolved to use the few remaining hours in his office to win the friendship of some of his master's debtors, so that after his dismissal he would have friends who would take him in.

**How much owest thou unto my lord?** (5) This crafty and dishonest steward secretly called in **every one of his lord's debtors,** and decreased the amount of the debt which each one owed to his master. He changed one bill from a hundred measures of oil (a thousand gallons of olive oil) to fifty; he reduced another bill from a hundred measures (one thousand bushels) of wheat to eighty.

**And the lord commended the unjust steward, because he had done wisely** (8). The **lord** who commended the steward was, of course, the master in the story, not Jesus. The word translated **wisely** should here be translated "prudently" or "mindful of his own interests." Though the rich man had been robbed, he admired this unusual display of prudence in managing money to make friends.

**For the children of this world are in their generation wiser than the children of light.** Or, "For, in dealing with their fellows, the men of this world are shrewder than the sons of light" (Weymouth). Christians often use less prudence in handling money than do the men of the world.

**And I say unto you, Make to yourselves friends of the mammon of unrighteousness; that, when ye fail, they may receive you into everlasting habitations** (9). Jesus is by no means approving of the dishonesty of the steward. Rather, He says: "Use your worldly wealth to win friends for yourselves, so that when money is a thing of the past you may be received into an eternal home" (NEB). This verse is unnecessarily difficult in the King James Version. **Mammon of unrighteousness** means "worldly wealth." **When ye fail** is in the best Greek text "when it fails." Jesus is saying: "Use your worldly wealth in such a way as to gain the higher values." He also urges His disciples to use as much diligence and prudence in preparing for their eternal future as the unjust steward used to prepare for his temporal affairs. Trench writes: "I am persuaded that we have here simply a parable of Christian prudence,—Christ exhorting us to use the world and the world's goods, so to speak, *against* the world, and *for* God.[43]

---

[43]R. C. Trench, *Notes on the Parables of Our Lord* (Philadelphia: William Syckelmoore, 1878), p. 324.

Never has better advice been given on the subject of this verse than in John Wesley's sermon "The Use of Money." The three points he makes are simple, but superb: (1) "Gain all you can"; (2) "Save all you can"; (3) "Give all you can." The sermon should be read in its entirety.

### 15. *Wholehearted Faithfulness* (16: 10-13)

The message of these verses is a continuation of the thought and application of the parable of the unjust steward.

**He that is faithful in that which is least is faithful also in much: and he that is unjust in the least is unjust also in much** (10). This is a universal truth. Faithfulness and unfaithfulness are not matters of mathematics. They spring from the moral and spiritual condition of the inner man. Thus a man's faithfulness or unfaithfulness in small matters is an index to his character. On the basis of this index one can determine whether he is to be trusted in matters that are of major importance.

**If therefore ye have not been faithful in the unrighteous mammon, who will commit to your trust the true riches?** (11) Here is a contrast between temporal and eternal riches, the temporal being no more than a shadow when compared with the eternally real. Unfaithfulness in relation to the temporal is a clear indication of one's unworthiness to be trusted with the real and eternal.

**And if ye have not been faithful in that which is another man's, who shall give you that which is your own?** (12) Untrustworthiness as a steward makes one unworthy to be an owner of wealth. The truth veiled behind the figure is that in this life we own nothing; God owns all, and we are His stewards. This verse has the implied promise that in the next world we shall be given true riches for our very own. But if we are unfaithful in our present relationship of stewards, God will not trust us with our own wealth—He will not give us that true wealth for our own in the next world.

**No servant can serve two masters** (13). True allegiance cannot be divided in any realm, and this is especially true in the spiritual realm. **For either he will hate the one, and love the other; or else he will hold to the one, and despise the other.** (See comments on Matt. 6: 24.)

16. *Self-justification and Divine Condemnation* (16:14-15)

**And the Pharisees also, who were covetous, heard all these things: and they derided him**—"scoffed at him" (14). The selfish, perverted man will turn to ridicule when he has no argument to support his conduct. Since the Pharisees were notoriously covetous, they suffered a double sting from Jesus' denunciation: the sting of conscience and the sting of an injured reputation. It is natural that on both of these grounds they would feel that Jesus' teaching was directed against them, as it no doubt was—at least in part.

**And he said unto them, Ye are they which justify yourselves before men; but God knoweth your heart** (15). The reputation which the Pharisees had for piety and their mastery both of the Mosaic law and of logic made it easy for them to impose upon the people their ideas and to justify their conduct when any of their inconsistencies were exposed to public view. But Jesus makes it clear that, even though they might convince men that they were pious and holy, they could not fool God. He knows the truth about all men.

**For that which is highly esteemed among men is abomination in the sight of God.** Men's judgments are misled both by their ignorance and by their perverted, carnal natures. Men esteem temporal possessions more than heavenly riches. They are tricked into believing that Pharisaic hypocrisy is true religion and that true saintliness is heresy. But God cannot be misled. His knowledge is perfect, and His judgments are always true and just.

17. *Pressing into the Kingdom* (16:16-17)

**The law and the prophets were until John: since that time the kingdom of God is preached, and every man presseth into it** (16). See comments on Matt. 11:12-13.

**And it is easier for heaven and earth to pass, than one tittle of the law to fail** (17). See comments on Matt. 5:18.

18. *Jesus' Rule on Divorce* (16:18)

**Whosoever putteth away his wife, and marrieth another, committeth adultery: and whosoever marrieth her that is put away from her husband committeth adultery** (18). See comments on Matt. 5:32; 19:9; and Mark 10:11. Matthew adds the phrase "except for fornication," but Mark and Luke make no exception.

### 19. *The Parable of the Rich Man and Lazarus* (16:19-31)

**There was a certain rich man** (19). In the parables of the prodigal son and the unjust steward a rich man represented God. In this story a rich man is seen only as a man in the light of his responsibilities to God and to his fellowman.

Many have claimed that this story is an account of an actual event and not merely a parable. They think the phrase **a certain rich man** implies a historical person. Whether parable or true story, one thing is clear: Jesus gave an account of what could happen.

**Which was clothed in purple and fine linen, and fared sumptuously every day.** This pictures a life of magnificent luxury and splendor. Everything the world could offer which would minister to the ease, splendor, or worldly happiness of this man was his in abundance. His clothes were princely; his house was a palace; his meals were banquets.

**And there was a certain beggar named Lazarus, which was laid at his gate, full of sores, and desiring to be fed with the crumbs which fell from the rich man's table** (20-21). This beggar was a complete contrast to the rich man. He was the very embodiment of poverty, disease, and want, as the rich man was of wealth, ease, and health. Lazarus was **laid** at the gate of the rich man, no doubt by friends. There he hoped to be given a chance to get the crumbs, or bread morsels which were used as finger wipers and then were thrown to the dogs under the table. But this boon was evidently denied him. The rich man had neither sympathy nor pity. **Moreover the dogs came and licked his sores.** These were probably not the rich man's dogs. They were the wild pariah dogs which roamed the streets and ate the refuse that was thrown there.

**The beggar died, and was carried by the angels into Abraham's bosom** (22). Nothing is said of his funeral, but he probably received the usual pauper's burial. This was really unimportant, for death marked the end of suffering and privation and the beginning of celestial joy. The phrase **Abraham's bosom** is figurative language, borrowed from the custom of reclining at the table. Each one was said to be on the bosom of the one behind him, for his head was adjacent to the other's chest. The phrase was used to signify paradise or the dwelling place of God. Note the Old Testament and rabbinical imagery and terminology in

this parable. Jesus was directing it to those who were expert in
such usage.

**The rich man also died, and was buried.** Specific mention of
his burial reminds us of the pageantry and ceremony associated
with the funerals of the rich in Jesus' day. But there is a dreadful and tragic irony here when we realize where the rich man
was—all that was alive of him—while this costly ceremony of
mourning and commemoration was in progress. The contrast between the conditions of these two men does not end at death, but
it is reversed.

**And in hell he lift up his eyes, being in torments (23).**
There was no sleep of the soul, no intermediate state. He died,
and instantly he was in hell, as Lazarus was carried immediately
to heaven by the angels. This heartless rich man closed his eyes
on his earthly riches and he opened his eyes in hell. The word
translated **hell** is hades, which is a broad term equivalent to "the
land of departed spirits" or the "hereafter." Thus it does not
always refer to a place of punishment. But in this parable it was
unquestionably such a place; the rich man opened his eyes **in
torments.** Note that the word is plural. The fire was only one
of the many causes of suffering for the lost man. There were
memory, conscience, the sight of Lazarus in bliss, and many more.

**And seeth Abraham afar off, and Lazarus in his bosom.
And he cried and said, Father Abraham, have mercy on me, and
send Lazarus, that he may dip the tip of his finger in water, and
cool my tongue; for I am tormented in this flame (23b-24).** For
the first time the man realizes that he is desperately in need of
help, and help is so far away—too far to do him any good. He is
not only in torment in the flame, but he is also helpless. He
wants Lazarus to bring one drop of water to cool his tongue. His
desolation is emphasized when we remember that on earth he
had every earthly comfort. Now he begs for a drop of water. As
he does so, he surely remembers Lazarus' begging for crumbs;
and he remembers, too, that Lazarus begged in vain.

**But Abraham said, Son, remember . . . (25).** It was not a life
of vice or crime which the rich man was asked to remember. It
was only a life of selfish indulgence, a life so crowded with self-
centered concerns that there was no room and no time for others
or for God. **But now he is comforted, and thou art tormented.**
There is a poetic justice here, a balancing of accounts. Yet the
rich man was not tormented because he was rich, nor was Lazarus
in Abraham's bosom because he was poor. In the two preceding

parables the rich man represented God. This parable makes it clear why the rich man went to hell. In the case of Lazarus, though the facts are not given, we must assume that he was a righteous man.

**And beside all this, between us and you there is a great gulf fixed** (26). God has set a gulf between heaven and hell which no man can cross. This life is the time for repentance; this world is the place for soul preparation for eternity. Beyond that line which is marked by death no man can change his spiritual state or place of abode.

**Then he said, I pray thee therefore, father, that thou wouldest send him to my father's house: for I have five brethren . . .** (27-28). Having been refused assistance in his own behalf, the rich man requests that Lazarus be sent back to earth as a missionary to his five brothers. These brothers were evidently following the same path of selfishness and sin that had brought him to hell. Since there was no help for himself, he at least wanted to spare them the torments he was suffering. But this missionary spirit, this interest in the salvation of his family, should have come sooner—when he was still with them.

**They have Moses and the prophets** (29). They have the God-ordained agency and means of salvation, and anyone whose heart is submissive can find the way. God does not make an exception for hardhearted people.

**Nay, father Abraham: but if one went unto them from the dead, they will repent. . . . If they hear not Moses and the prophets, neither will they be persuaded, though one rose from the dead** (30-31). The rich man, like people in every generation, thought that supernatural occurrences would turn men to God. He assumed that the reappearance of those who have died, with an eyewitness account of hell's torments, would make men repent. But God does not use this method. God does not propose to accept those who turn to Him out of fear of hell alone. A completely selfish desire to escape hell and enjoy heaven is not the sort of motive which leads to salvation. God accepts those who serve Him because they now hate sin as God does and want God for what He is, rather than simply for what He can do to prevent an eternal catastrophe for them. The regular God-ordained agencies and means of salvation are fully sufficient for all whose motives are right; and there is no other way of salvation.

### 20. Teaching Concerning Offenses (17:1-4)

**Then said he unto the disciples (1).** Not the twelve apostles, but the wider circle of His followers. It is not certain whether the multitudes were present at this time. But whether they were or not, Jesus directed the following remarks to His disciples. The subject matter has a broad applicability, but it has a special relevance to the Christian who needs guidance concerning his relationship to, and responsibility for, his fellowman.

**It is impossible but that offences will come: but woe unto him, through whom they come!** See comments on Matt. 18:7.

**It were better for him that a millstone were hanged about his neck, and he cast into the sea, than that he should offend one of these little ones (2).** See comments on Matt. 18:6.

**Take heed to yourselves (3).** "Keep watch on yourselves" (NEB). **If thy brother trespass against thee, rebuke him; and if he repent, forgive him.** See comments on Matt. 18:15. Luke's language is somewhat stronger than Matthew's. Luke says, **Rebuke him.** Matthew says, "Go and tell him his fault between thee and him alone." Also Luke says, **If he repent, forgive him.** Matthew says, "If he shall hear thee, thou hast gained thy brother."

**And if he trespass against thee seven times in a day, and seven times in a day turn again to thee, saying, I repent; thou shalt forgive him.** Jesus is not meaning to be mathematical here. By **seven times** He implies infinity—that is, forgive as often as he repents. See also comment on Matt. 18:21-22.

### 21. The Power of Faith (17:5-6)

**And the apostles said unto the Lord, Increase our faith (5).** The Master's stern teaching concerning offenses both startled and depressed the apostles. They did not feel equal to this new demand which, on the one hand, threatened them with an unspeakable punishment if they should be the cause of stumbling on the part of the "little ones" in the Kingdom, and, on the other hand, required them to forgive offenders against themselves as often as they should ask forgiveness. The sense of weakness and need which resulted impelled the apostles to ask the Lord to give them more faith. They felt that they could never meet such standards without something more than they now possessed of spiritual strength; and they felt that a stronger faith would meet this need. Actually their need was not fully met until Pentecost, when they were baptized with the Holy Spirit.

**And the Lord said, If ye had faith as a grain of mustard seed
(6).** See comments on Matt. 17:20; 21:21. **Ye might say unto
this sycamine tree, Be thou plucked up by the root, and be thou
planted in the sea; and it should obey you.** Jesus also gives this
comparison of faith with a mustard seed in Matt. 17:20. But the
demonstration of the power of faith there is the moving of a
mountain rather than a **sycamine tree.** This is the sort of teaching which Jesus would naturally have repeated whenever the
need arose. At the time of the incident referred to here the
Master was probably standing near such a tree, and it was just
like the Master to find His objects for comparison close at hand.
This **sycamine tree** was not the same as the "sycomore tree" mentioned often in the Bible; it was rather the black mulberry.[44]

### 22. *Unprofitable Servants* (17:7-10)

This brief parable, though not directly related to what pre-
cedes it in Luke's Gospel, is related to the general theme Jesus
has been developing since chapter 13. It might be called "anti-
Phariseeism." An excellent title for the present parable and its
application is the one given by Godet, "The non-meritoriousness
of works."[45]

**But which of you, having a servant plowing or feeding
cattle, will say unto him . . . when he is come from the field, Go
and sit down to meat? And will not rather say . . . Make ready
wherewith I may sup . . . and afterward thou shalt eat and
drink? (7-8)** Though the occasion which prompted this parable
is not given, it answers questions which were in the minds of the
disciples, and sometimes were expressed, such as: "What will I
get as a reward for serving Christ?"

The parable reminds Jesus' audience that a servant does not
by working all day in the field earn the right to eat before his
master eats. It is still a part of his duty to serve his master's
evening meal before he serves himself. He is a bond slave, and
as such he has no "rights." He belongs to his master, and his
duties have been assigned by the master. When he has fulfilled
them he has done only his duty. Merit comes only when duty has
been surpassed.

[44]Spence, *op. cit.,* II, 87.

[45]Godet, *op. cit.,* II, 188.

We must not make the mistake of interpreting this parable in terms of present-day standards of ethics. Modern labor laws and Christian ethical standards with regard to the proper treatment of laborers were unknown in Jesus' day. There were sixty million slaves in the Roman Empire, and the right of the system of slavery to exist was almost unchallenged.

**So likewise ye, when ye shall have done all those things which are commanded you, say, We are unprofitable servants: we have done that which was our duty to do** (10). The word translated **unprofitable** here signifies "one who has rendered no service beyond his duty." We are so much indebted to God that we could never go beyond duty into the realm of merit in our Christian service. Thus works cannot be meritorious, for we can never fully do our duty. We can never do all, or even a sizable fraction, of what we actually owe to God.

Verses 1-10 have been titled "Spiritual Inventory." The text is in verse 3, "Take heed to yourselves." (1) To your motives, 1-2; (2) To your spirit, 3-4; (3) To your faith, 5-6; (4) To your service, 7-10.

### C. THE THIRD STAGE, 17:11—19:27

**And it came to pass, as he went to Jerusalem, that he passed through the midst of Samaria and Galilee** (11). This is an editorial note used by Luke to remind his readers that the journey to Jerusalem was still in progress, a fact which the reader might easily forget in the midst of the great number of the deeds and words of Jesus which he is recording. **Through the midst of Samaria and Galilee** could be better rendered "along the border between Samaria and Galilee," the latter place being "Galilee beyond the Jordan," or Perea.[46] There were two regular routes to Jerusalem from Galilee, one through Samaria and the other through Perea. At this time Jesus was following neither route but was between the two.

### 1. Ten Lepers Cleansed (17:12-19)

**And as he entered into a certain village, there met him ten men that were lepers, which stood afar off** (12). He met these lepers before He reached the village. In accordance with Mosaic law lepers were required to live away from populated places in isolation from all but their fellow sufferers (Lev. 13:46). They

---

[46]For an excellent treatment and support of this rendering, see Godet, *op. cit.*, II, 190-91.

were also required to announce their infection to all who came near them by calling, "Unclean, unclean!"

**And they lifted up their voices, and said, Jesus, Master, have mercy on us. And when he saw them, he said unto them, Go shew yourselves unto the priests (13-14).** They no doubt knew Jesus both by sight and by reputation. It is quite possible that they were acquainted with persons whom He had cleansed of leprosy earlier in His ministry. The instruction, which Jesus gave, to show themselves to the priests was in accord with the Levitical law regarding the treatment of leprosy.[47]

**And one of them . . . turned back, and . . . glorified God (15-16).** This man was fully conscious of the miracle which had been wrought, and deeply grateful for the cure. With great emotion and with loud voice he expressed his gratitude. **And he was a Samaritan.** This is not what a Jew would have expected from a Samaritan "dog." The disciples could learn a lesson from the experience: that gratitude and goodness are the result of personal character and not of race or nationality.

**Were there not ten cleansed? but where are the nine? There are not found that returned to give glory to God, save this stranger (17-18).** We do not know that all the nine were Jews, but we do know that none of the nine returned to express gratitude. Why were they unanimous in this failure? Why is there so little of the spirit of gratitude in the human heart?

**And he said unto him, Arise, go thy way (19). Go thy way** probably means, at least in part, "Go to the priests." Even though he had been miraculously healed, the law still required him to get a certificate from the priests before he could resume his normal life. **Thy faith hath made thee whole.** Did he receive something which the others did not? They were all cleansed. If he received nothing more than the Master's commendation, he received a priceless gift. But he also received an inner blessing and enlargement of soul. The commendation implies that he had more faith or a higher quality of faith than the other nine.

Using the topic "Where Are the Nine?" Maclaren has four points: (1) The lepers' cry and the Lord's strange reply; (2) The healing granted to obedient faith; (3) The solitary instance of thankfulness; (4) Christ's sad wonder and man's ingratitude.

---

[47]See Leviticus, chapters 13—14.

## 2. *The Spirituality of the Kingdom* (17:20-21)

**And when he was demanded of the Pharisees, when the kingdom of God should come (20).** The Pharisees had heard and felt His sharp rebukes. They had heard His teaching and noted the many implications that He was the Messiah. And they had seen the manifestation of His miraculous power. But He had not fulfilled their expectation of the Messiah, and that was proof positive to them that He was not this One. The great rabbinical schools in which the Pharisees had received their training, and from which they received their theological views, connected the coming of the Messiah with the ushering in of the kingdom of God. This, they believed, would be a literal kingdom which would revive Jewish political power, throw off the Roman yoke, and make the Jews the masters of the world.

The question which the Pharisees asked was evidently put in a belligerent spirit, with confidence that it could not be rightly answered by Jesus. It has the force of a rhetorical question, the purpose of which was to compel Jesus to admit that He was not the Messiah since He was unable to produce the Messianic kingdom.

**The kingdom of God cometh not with observation.** This is a contradiction of the Pharisees' doctrine of the kingdom of God, an outright denial that it was to be a literal, earthly kingdom.

**Neither shall they say, Lo here! or, lo there! for, behold, the kingdom of God is within you (21).** Many modern commentators have rendered the last phrase "among you," or "in the midst of you," though the wording in the KJV is a literal translation of the Greek. These interpreters insist that to translate the Greek as "within you" would imply that the kingdom of God was within these Pharisees, since Jesus was directing His remarks to them. It seems more reasonable to interpret the **you** as impersonal. Therefore the meaning would be, "The kingdom of God is within men's hearts." The **you** would then not necessarily refer to the Pharisees.

Actually both of these meanings would be in harmony with facts. The kingdom of God, having already come in the person and work of Jesus, was indeed "among" them. Yet it is also true that God's kingdom is within men's hearts and is not external and material. There is, however, a future literal kingdom of God, but the Master chose not to deal with this aspect of the Kingdom at the moment. The major truth which Jesus is teaching in these verses is that the kingaom of God, in the present dispensation, is not an earthly kingdom but a spiritual reign of God in the hearts of those who will submit to the kingship of Christ.[48]

### 3. *Jesus Speaks About the Future* (17:22-37)

**And he said unto the disciples** (22). Having answered the Pharisees' question, Jesus turns again to His disciples with truth which is particularly for them. **The days will come, when ye shall desire to see one of the days of the Son of man, and ye shall not see it.** The Master is here warning His disciples that dark days lie ahead for them—days of persecution, and toil—when their minds will turn back in blessed reminiscence of the time when He was with them. They will long for His physical presence again, but their wish will not be granted. Jesus is also speaking to those yet unborn disciples, down to our own day and beyond, who, in days of suffering and frustration, will long for the physical presence of Christ.

**And they shall say to you, See here; or, see there: go not after them** . . . (23). See comments on Matt. 24:23, 26.

**For as the lightning** . . . **so shall also the Son of man be in his day** (24). See comments on Matt. 24:27.

**But first must he suffer many things, and be rejected of this generation** (25). See comments on Matt. 16:21 and Luke 9:22.

**And as it was in the days of Noe, so shall it be also in the days of the Son of man** . . . (26-27). See comments on Matt. 24:37-39.

**Likewise also as it was in the days of Lot** . . . **Even thus shall it be in the day when the Son of man is revealed** (28-30). The meaning here is the same as that of verses 26 and 27. The suddenness, the unexpectedness, and the certainty of Christ's coming are the points that Jesus is stressing.

**In that day, he which shall be upon the housetop** . . . **let him not come down** . . . **and he that is in the field, let him likewise not return back** (31). See comments on Matt. 24:17-18.

**Remember Lot's wife** (32). The tragic end of Lot's wife is an excellent illustration of what Jesus has just been warning His disciples not to do. Lot and his family had been given a chance to escape from Sodom before its destruction. The angel's command

---

[48]For further discussion of this point see Spence, *op. cit.,* p. 89; and Godet, *op. cit.,* II, 193-94.

was: "Escape for thy life; look not behind thee, neither stay thou in all the plain" (Gen. 19:17). But Lot's wife disobeyed this command and looked back, evidently longing to go back, and was turned into a pillar of salt. She had been taken out of Sodom but Sodom had not been taken out of her. She is thus a perpetual warning that salvation is incomplete unless the heart is purged from the love of the world.

In the verses immediately preceding 32, Jesus is predicting the destruction of Jerusalem. He is warning His disciples to take full advantage of the opportunity which will be given to escape. To be dilatory at that time would be to repeat the tragic mistake of Lot's wife.

Jesus' admonition was taken literally. After Vespasian and the Roman army began the siege of Jerusalem, it was lifted for a short time as a result of the strife at Rome over the succession to the imperial throne, left vacant by the suicide of Nero. During this lull in the siege the Christians in Jerusalem took advantage of the opportunity to escape. They fled to Pella on the east side of the Jordan River.

**Whosoever shall seek to save his life shall lose it; and whosoever shall lose his life shall preserve it (33).** See comments on Matt. 10:39; 16:25.

**In that night there shall be two men in one bed; the one shall be taken, and the other shall be left. Two women shall be grinding . . . Two men shall be in the field . . . (34-36).** See comments on Matt. 24:40-41. The material in verse 34 is not paralleled in Matthew; but its meaning is the same as that of the other two verses. The Master has put two persons in each of three sets of circumstances to show how such persons could be engaged in the same activity or rest and one would be taken and the other left at the Lord's coming.

**And they answered and said . . . Where, Lord? (37)** This question had already been answered in verse 24. But the disciples could not conceive of any event which was not local—they could not conceive of the worldwide aspect of Christ's coming. **Wheresoever the body is, thither will the eagles be gathered together.** These **eagles** are literally vultures. See comments on Matt. 24:28.

William Barclay treats this paragraph under "The Signs of His Coming." He notes: (1) There will be times when the Christian will long for the coming of Christ, but he will need to be patient, 22; (2) The coming of Christ is certain, but the time is unknown, 23-30; (3) When Christ comes, the judgments of God will operate, 31-36; (4) Christ will come when the necessary conditions are fulfilled—when the causes are right. This is the meaning of the proverb in 37.

### 4. *The Parable of the Unjust Judge* (18:1-8)

**And he spake a parable unto them to this end, that men ought always to pray, and not to faint** (1). Literally, "And he spake also a parable, etc." The "also" indicates that this parable is a part of the preceding discourse. Thus we see that prayer is prescribed as a remedy for fainting in the difficult days ahead— the days of the siege of Jerusalem, the days preceding the second coming of Jesus, and all other distressing times. When Jesus is taken from the earth, the Church will be like the widow in the parable. But prayer will be her means of support and redress.

**There was in a city a judge, which feared not God, neither regarded man: and there was a widow . . . and she came unto him, saying, Avenge me of mine adversary** (2-3). The word translated **avenge** does not mean to get revenge but to secure justice. But what chance would a helpless widow have of getting justice from a judge who has no fear of God and no regard for man? There is one way, and this is the one she takes.

**And he would not for a while: but afterwards he said . . . because this widow troubleth me, I will avenge her, lest by her continual coming she weary me** (4-5). Her one weapon was importunity, persistence. The judge's reference to **her continual coming** indicates that he was convinced that she would never cease to come until her request was granted. There is nothing profound here. She simply would not quit seeking until she received a just handling of her case.

**Hear what the unjust judge saith. And shall not God avenge his own elect, which cry day and night unto him . . . ? I tell you that he will avenge them speedily** (6-8). The application is clear and simple. A widow can get justice from a judge who has no fear of God and no regard for man simply by "her continual coming." How much more should a Christian have faith to believe that a good and loving God will answer his prayers, even though He might **bear long with them**—that is, appear at times to be delaying the answer! He will **avenge them speedily**; that is, suddenly, unexpectedly, but not necessarily when they think the answer should come.

**Nevertheless when the Son of man cometh, shall he find faith on the earth?** In view of the teaching of the parable, faith ought to be easy. Yet in spite of the fact that Christians have every reason to have an unshakable faith in God, it is often difficult to believe. Jesus' question was not to be answered. It cannot be answered now by anyone but God. It was given as a warning lest the apparent delay of the return of the Lord should be made an occasion for doubt. The ultimate answer will be given by Christians. The answer can be, "Yes, there will be faith," if we determine to resist Satan's suggestions of doubt. We can stay close enough to our Lord so that faith becomes the natural result of our intimate relationship with Him.

Thomson, in the *Pulpit Commentary,* points out three contrasts in this parable: (1) God in contrast with the human avenger; (2) God's people in contrast with the widow; (3) The long-suffering of God in contrast with the long-suffering of man.

5. *The Parable of the Pharisee and the Publican at Prayer* (18:9-14)

Having taught the need and power of prayer by means of the preceding parable, the Master gives a second to teach the proper attitude. Here we are taught that mere persistence in prayer is not enough.

**And he spake this parable unto certain which trusted in themselves that they were righteous, and despised others** (9). They did not trust in the grace of God for their righteousness, but relied on their own good works. They considered themselves to be justified by good deeds.

**Two men went up into the temple to pray; the one a Pharisee, and the other a publican** (10). They did not go into the sanctuary but into one of the courts of the Temple where prayer was customarily offered. This was the Court of the Women. In choosing a Pharisee and a publican for this illustration, Jesus chose two extremes. The Pharisees were the strictest, narrowest, most legalistic of the Jewish sects. The publicans were Jewish officers of the Roman government, whose job was to collect taxes for Rome. They were hated by the Jews both because they collected taxes for the foreign conquerors and because they were often dishonest. They collected more tax than was due, thus making themselves rich by their odious business. For further information concerning Pharisees and publicans, see comments on Matt. 3: 7; 5: 46.

**The Pharisee stood and prayed thus with himself, God, I thank thee, that I am not as other men . . . (11).** This is the prime example of the prayer of a self-righteous man. It really does not deserve to be called a prayer. It is scarcely more than a recitation of the Pharisee's supposed good qualities and deeds, an attempt to demonstrate to God that he deserved divine consideration. The Pharisee did not, however, take the full credit for his supposed lofty state of grace. His **God, I thank thee** was a recognition of the fact that God was at least partly responsible for his being one of the righteous. But the phrase **prayed thus with himself**—literally, "prayed these things to himself"—indicates that his chief attention was directed toward himself. The most significant word in his prayer is the personal pronoun *I*: **I am not as other men, I fast, I give tithes** (12). He was probably more conscious of being heard by man than by God. His eulogy on himself contains only one reference to his fellow worshiper. Even this reference to the publican was made so that the Pharisee would appear better by contrast.

**And the publican, standing afar off (13).** **Afar off** from the Temple, the symbol of God's presence. The Pharisee evidently stood on the side of the court nearest to the Temple, whereas the publican stood on the side farthest from the Temple. It is possible, also, that Jesus means that he was not even in the Court of the Women, the customary place of prayer, but farther away in the Court of the Gentiles (see p. 624).

**Would not lift up so much as his eyes unto heaven, but smote upon his breast, saying, God be merciful to me a sinner**—literally "the sinner." Both his attitude and the contents of his prayer were opposite to those of the Pharisee. He was deeply conscious of his sins, and he was almost overwhelmed by the sense of his own unworthiness. He had nothing to say in his favor; his only plea was mercy.

**I tell you, this man went down to his house justified rather than the other (14).** The word *justify* means to declare or treat as righteous. This publican was both forgiven and approved of God, though he had been a sinner and acknowledged it. On the other hand the Pharisee, who was glad he was not like this publican, was not forgiven. He acknowledged no sin and sought no forgiveness, though in fact he was in God's sight one of the worst of sinners. His sin was that of self-righteous egotism.

**For every one that exalteth himself shall be abased; and he that humbleth himself shall be exalted.** See comments on Luke 14:11.

From this parable of Jesus, Barclay notes three universal truths: (1) No man who is proud can pray, 11-12; (2) No man who despises his fellowmen can pray, 12; (3) True prayer comes from setting our lives beside the life of God, 13-14.

### 6. *Jesus and the Children* (18:15-17)

**And they brought unto him also infants . . . but when . . . his disciples saw it, they rebuked them. But Jesus . . . said, Suffer little children to come unto me** (15-16). See comments on Matt. 1:13-14. Luke differs from Matthew only in the word which he uses for children. Luke's term denotes older children.

**Whosoever shall not receive the kingdom of God as a little child shall in no wise enter therein** (17). See comments on Mark 10:15.

### 7. *The Rich Young Ruler* (18:18-30)

For discussion of this incident see comments on Matt. 19: 16-22. Luke refers to him simply as a **ruler.** Matthew tells us he was young, and all three Synoptics say he was rich.

### 8. *Jesus Foretells His Suffering* (18:31-34)

For discussion of verses 31-33 see comments on Matt. 20: 17-19. See also Mark 10:32-34. Matthew and Mark both omit the material in verse 34.

**And they understood none of these things: and this saying was hid from them, neither knew they the things which were spoken** (34). The three clauses of the verse all say the same thing. Undoubtedly Luke used this method to emphasize what he was saying. The disciples heard Jesus' words, but they were so contradictory to everything they believed about the kingdom of the Messiah that they were completely at a loss for an explanation. The suffering and death of the Messiah were unthinkable; yet Jesus seemed to be referring clearly to himself. The contradiction was, of course, in their own concept of Christ's work on earth.

### 9. *A Blind Man Healed* (18:35-43)

See comments on Matt. 20:29-34; see also Mark 10:46-52. The miracle is found in all three Synoptic Gospels. But there are two significant differences between the three accounts. Matthew says there were two blind men, while Mark and Luke refer to only one. Luke says the miracle took place as Jesus was drawing near to Jericho, while the other two Synoptists say that it took place as He was leaving Jericho. The problem concerning the number of blind men is not difficult. Undoubtedly there were two, but Luke and Mark are concerned with only one of them—perhaps the more striking or more significant of the two men.

The problem as to when the miracle took place is more difficult but not significant. Many solutions have been proposed. The most likely one is that the first contact with the blind man, or men, was made as Jesus drew near Jericho. However, due to the size of the accompanying multitude and perhaps to Jesus' effort to test the sincerity of the sufferer, the case was not finally disposed of until He was leaving the city. There is also a distinct possibility that one of the Evangelists was referring to Old Jericho and the others to New Jericho, or vice versa. A third possible solution is that one blind man might have been healed while Jesus entered Jericho and another as He left.[49]

### 10. *The Conversion of Zacchaeus* (19:1-10)

**And Jesus entered and passed through Jericho** (1). He was on His way to Jerusalem just before His passion. Jericho was a prosperous trade city on the road from Perea to Jerusalem and Egypt. It was located in the Jordan valley about five miles from the Jordan and seventeen miles from Jerusalem.[50]

**And, behold, there was a man named Zacchaeus, which was the chief among the publicans, and he was rich** (2). Because of the considerable trade which passed through Jericho, due to its strategic location on an important trade route and the fact that it was the center of the worldwide traffic in balm, there must have been located there one of the principal custom houses in that part of the Roman Empire. Zacchaeus was the chief of the customs collectors at Jericho, with an income that made him a rich man. The name Zacchaeus is of Hebrew origin and means "pure."

**And he sought to see Jesus, who he was** (3). These words suggest curiosity as the reason for his desire. But the sequel shows that he either had a deeper motive or that after he saw Jesus he was so deeply impressed that his motives changed. It is

[49]For further discussion of these problems see Spence, *op. cit.*, II, 114, and Godet, *op. cit.*, II, 213 f.

[50]See note on Luke 10:30.

very likely that at least a part of his interest sprang from having
heard of some of Jesus' kind remarks concerning publicans.

**And he ran before, and climbed up into a sycomore tree
(4).** Being too small of stature to see over the heads of those who
made up the crowd which surrounded Jesus, he ran down the
street which he knew Jesus must take en route to Jerusalem.
There he sought and found a vantage point from which he could
see Jesus. The sycamore tree which he climbed was the *ficus-
sycomorus,* the fig-mulberry. Its low horizontal limbs made
climbing easy, and its foliage was sufficient to hide him from the
multitude.

**And when Jesus came to the place, he ... said ... Zacchaeus,
make haste, and come down; for to day I must abide at thy house
(5)**—literally, "it is necessary for me to abide at thy house." This
implies that there was in the heart of the Master an inner compulsion to go home with Zacchaeus. Such compulsion was inspired and motivated by Zacchaeus' eagerness to see Jesus. Our
Lord always responds sympathetically to those who seek to know
Him.

Jericho was one of the cities of the priests, but Jesus chose
the house of the chief of the publicans instead of that of a priest
in which to rest and to dine. He knew that He was choosing the
man most worthy of His presence to be His host, but who else
would have expected Him to choose Zacchaeus?

**And when they saw it, they all murmured (7).** The multitude must have been almost unanimous in their disapproval of
Jesus' choice. His action, they felt, was an affront to the priests
and other religious leaders whose houses and whose persons He
passed by. His choice was an overt approval of this man who
was so generally regarded as a "sinner." Two things kept them
from recognizing Jesus' true motive. One was their blind exclusiveness which refused to see any good in a publican. The
other was their inability to understand how Jesus could associate
with sinners without defiling himself.

**And Zacchaeus ... said ... Behold, Lord, the half of my
goods I give to the poor; and if I have taken any thing from any
man by false accusation, I restore him fourfold (8).** Here we
see both a truly generous spirit and a genuine desire to make right
any past wrong. Both attitudes reflect a change of heart. The
speech of Zacchaeus was not addressed to the crowd but to Jesus.
It was not an effort to convince the people that he was sincere.

Rather it was the unpremeditated, spontaneous response of a heart made clean and a spirit given new and eternal life.

Just how generous Zacchaeus was can be seen in the offer of half of his wealth to feed those who were less fortunate than he. How willing he was to right his wrongs is seen in the offer of four-fold restitution. Zacchaeus was undoubtedly guilty of some injustices in his collections of customs—his bringing up the subject seems to imply as much. It is unlikely, however, that he was as wicked or had gotten as much of his wealth dishonestly as either the Jews of his day or many preachers of our day have accused him of. If he had gotten as much of his wealth through dishonesty as some have suggested, he would not have had enough money to make a fourfold restitution.

**And Jesus said unto him, This day is salvation come to this house** (9). A seeking sinner had met a seeking Saviour. In true repentance, the man had found personal salvation. These gracious words of the Master were an assurance of salvation to Zacchaeus, a proclamation in his behalf to the multitude, and a promise to all men in every land in every age that Jesus Christ saves sinners.

**Forsomuch as he also is a son of Abraham.** This was a reminder to those self-righteous Jews that Zacchaeus, too, was a Jew, a descendant of Abraham. The words were also an announcement that Zacchaeus had now, in a new and living way, become a son of Abraham, the "father of the faithful." Through the new birth he was now a spiritual son of Abraham and a member of the new Israel.

**For the Son of man is come to seek and to save that which was lost** (10). Here we have Jesus' own statement of His major purpose for coming to this world. The truth of this universal statement is the ground of the assurance given to Zacchaeus in the preceding verse.

Bishop Ryle, in his *Expository Thoughts on the Gospels*, suggests several lessons to be learned from this incident: (1) No one is too bad to be saved, or beyond the power of Christ's grace; (2) How little and insignificant are the things on which a soul's salvation often turns; (3) Christ's free compassion towards sinners, and Christ's power to change hearts; (4) Converted sinners will always give evidence of their conversion.

## 11. *The Parable of the Pounds* (19:11-27)

**And as they heard these things, he added and spake a parable (11).** These words show the relation between the episode involving Zacchaeus and the following parable. Jesus' statement in verse 10 seems to have increased interest in the subject which was ever present in these last days of our Lord's ministry. Both the disciples and Jesus' antagonists had shown interest in the kingdom of God.

**Because he was nigh to Jerusalem, and because they thought that the kingdom of God should immediately appear.** This interest increased as Jesus neared Jerusalem. There was an excitement, an air of expectancy, which finally exploded into open praise and acclaim at Christ's triumphal entry. But the excitement was due largely to a mistaken notion—the universal belief, on the part of those who considered Jesus the Messiah, that the Kingdom would immediately appear. Jerusalem was the place where Messiah would be expected to set up His kingdom, and many evidently believed that now was the time. It was to correct this notion that Jesus gave the parable.

**. . . A certain nobleman went into a far country to receive for himself a kingdom, and to return (12).** Notice that the story is not about a nobleman who *set up* a kingdom, but about one who went into a far country to **receive** one. Two noblemen, Herod and his son Archelaus, had left this very city of Jericho to go into a far country—Rome—to secure kingdoms,[51] and it was no doubt one of these whom Jesus had in mind.

The inference here is that Christ would not immediately set up a kingdom, but would go away to heaven to secure one. He would **return** for those who were fitted for citizenship in His kingdom.

**And he called his ten servants, and delivered them ten pounds, and said unto them, Occupy till I come (13).** The nobleman had a dual purpose when he made this distribution. He wanted to multiply his wealth, and he wanted to test his servants to determine their fitness for places of responsibility in his coming kingdom.

The **pounds** were literally "minas," worth one hundred drachmas ($20.00). The word translated **occupy** means literally "gain by trading." Thus they were to multiply their lord's money

---

[51]Josephus *Antiquities* 14. 14; 17.9.

through using it in trade. In like manner Jesus was to go away to heaven and leave His disciples in charge of His work on earth.

**But his citizens hated him, and sent a message after him, saying, We will not have this man to reign over us** (14). This **message** was not sent to the nobleman but to the one from whom he was to receive the kingdom. Evidently Jesus was drawing parallels from events in the Roman Empire, from which the Herods received their authority. The Jews sent such an accusing message—along with a delegation of citizens—when Archelaus was seeking his kingdom. In its application, this part of the parable refers to the fact that the Jews refused to acknowledge Jesus as their King. They were ready to destroy Him to prevent Him from "ruling over them."

**When he was returned, having received the kingdom, . . . he commanded these servants to be called unto him** (15). He demanded an immediate and complete reckoning. This is a picture of the judgment at the return of our Lord.

**Then came the first, saying, Lord, thy pound hath gained ten pounds. And he said unto him, Well, thou good servant . . . have thou authority over ten cities** (16-17). The servant had proved both his loyalty and his ability. As a reward he was given a place of major responsibility in the new kingdom.

**And the second came, saying, Lord, thy pound hath gained five pounds . . . Be thou also over five cities** (18-19). The principle and the formula are the same as in the case of the first servant.

**And another came, saying, Lord, behold, here is thy pound, which I have kept laid up in a napkin:** (or "handkerchief") **for I feared thee, because thou art an austere man** (20-21). The story relates the reckoning with only three of the ten servants. The other seven are not important to the point of the parable. It is in the reckoning with this third servant that we find the real meaning and purpose of the story.

The last servant seemed to feel that he had fulfilled his obligation to his lord when he returned the money, even though he had disregarded the express command, **Occupy** (trade) **till I come.** The word translated **austere** means "hard," "severe," "oppressive," "harsh."

The servant explained his meaning by saying, **thou takest up that which thou layedst not down, and reapest that thou didst not sow.** Here he implies dishonesty, accusing his master of taking what was not his own. A spirit of love coupled with the realization that both he and the money he possessed belonged to his lord would have given him a different outlook; it would have led him to follow the example of the other two servants.

**Out of thine own mouth will I judge thee, thou wicked servant** (22). He had confessed that he knew exactly what his lord would expect of him, yet he used this very expectation as a reason for his failure to obey the master's command. If this had indeed been his lord's disposition and expectation, there would have been only one sensible and safe course. He should have done such a good job of trading that even an **austere** master could find no fault.

Spence puts the nobleman's words thus, "The more thou knowest that I am austere, the more thou shouldest have tried to satisfy me."[52]

**And he said . . . Take from him the pound, and give to him that hath ten pounds** (24). Thus loyalty and love are paid with a bonus, while legalistic dodging of responsibility is rewarded with deprivation.

**For I say unto you, That unto every one which hath shall be given; and from him that hath not, even that he hath shall be taken away from him** (26). These are not the words of Jesus but of the nobleman stating the principle upon which he has judged his servants. Those who had gained by trading—those who "have"—would receive additional benefits; those who had failed to do so—those who "have not"—would lose even the original pound.

In its spiritual application, this means that those who have made Christian opportunity a means of spiritual enlargement and blessing will receive a divine bonus. Those who excuse their failures by legalistic reflections upon their assignments will lose both the bonus and the principal.

This servant represents the man who has allowed a spirit of resentment and bitterness to displace love and loyalty. He has become a self-appointed judge of his lord's methods; because he does not like the way his lord does things, he lies down on the job. He also represents the man who thinks that stewardship consists solely in not stealing his lord's money. His "goodness" is negative, not positive. He does no harm (so he thinks), but neither does he do any good. In reality he is a thief in spite of

[52]Spence, *op. cit.*, II, 137.

his illusion of self-righteousness, for in being useless he has robbed his lord of the gain he might have had. By the time his lord returns, he is a backslider and a confirmed cynic. In both his unfair criticism and in his unfulfilled stewardship he typifies the carnal Christian who fusses and whines instead of producing. When such a struggle first develops in a Christian's mind, if he will yield completely even to what seems like divine "austerity," and trust without further questions, the tension will be resolved, and the outcome will be different .

**But those mine enemies, which would not that I should reign over them, bring hither, and slay them before me (27).** These are, of course, the words of the nobleman and part of the story. In the application, which is Jesus' reason for telling the story, they predict the loss, by the Jews, of the favored position which they have enjoyed. The ruin of the Jewish nation is prophesied because of their rejection of the Messiah.

A. THE ENTRY INTO JERUSALEM AND THE CLEANSING OF THE
TEMPLE, 19:28-48

**And when he had thus spoken, he went before, ascending
up to Jerusalem** (28). This one verse spans the time between
the giving of the parable of the pounds at Jericho or shortly after
leaving that city and the Triumphal Entry.

After leaving Jericho, Jesus and His disciples climbed the
fifteen steep miles to Bethany, where they spent the time from
Friday evening until Sunday morning, the multitude having gone
to Jerusalem.[1] Luke omits the story of the feast at the house of
Simon the Leper, at which time Mary anointed Jesus with spike-
nard.

### 1. The Entry into Jerusalem (19:29-40)

For discussion of verses 29-38 see comments on Matt. 21:
1-11; see also Mark 11:1-11. The material in verses 39 and 40
is found only in Luke.

**And some of the Pharisees from among the multitude said
unto him, Master, rebuke thy disciples** (39). That is, rebuke
them for their shouting and for their use of Messianic expressions. The Pharisees had two reasons for raising these objections.
First, they considered such Messianic expressions a kind of blasphemy when used in praise of one whom they considered a mere
man. Second, the Romans' chief Jerusalem garrison, the Tower
of Antonia, was in sight while this demonstration was in progress.
The leaders of the Jews were afraid that such demonstrations
might arouse the Romans to use repressive measures.

**And he answered . . . if these should hold their peace, the
stones would immediately cry out** (40). The terms used in
Jesus' answer seem to be proverbial. Godet's dramatic comment
on the verse is worth quoting. He says: "The answer of Jesus

---

[1]See Matt. 26:6-13; Mark 14:3-9; John 11:55—12:11.

has terrible majesty: 'If I should silence all these mouths, you would hear the same acclamations proceeding from the ground.' So impossible is it that an appearance like this should not be, once at least, saluted on the earth as it deserves to be."[2]

It is quite possible that Jesus had in mind the words of Habakkuk, "For the stone shall cry out of the wall, and the beam out of the timber shall answer it" (Hab. 2:11).

### 2. Jesus Weeping over Jerusalem (19:41-44)

**And when he was come near, he beheld the city, and wept over it** (41). The view of Jerusalem from the Mount of Olives was in sharp contrast to the Master's mood of lamentation. The magnificent Temple, the palaces and gardens of the wealthy Jews, and the great wall encircling the city made the view one of beauty and splendor. Add to this the memories associated with more than a thousand years of sacred history, and one envisions a sight which would all but overwhelm the pious Jew seeing Jerusalem for the first time.

But all of this moved Jesus only to tears. He saw something which others did not see. He saw the coming destruction of the city. He knew that all of His efforts to avert the tragedy had been repulsed and rejected.

**If thou hadst known . . . the things which belong unto thy peace! but now they are hid from thine eyes** (42). If they had only known, if they could even now learn, the conditions upon which peace could be had! These conditions were repentance and acceptance of Jesus as Saviour and Lord. There is still a little time. Yet their case is all but hopeless, because sin, prejudice, self-will, and self-righteousness have hidden from their eyes these basic conditions of peace.

**For the days shall come upon thee, that thine enemies shall cast a trench about thee, and compass thee round** (43). These graphic words describe, as though from actual sight, the siege of Jerusalem and the ultimate destruction of the city by the Romans.[3]

### 3. Jesus Cleanses the Temple (19:45-46)

For discussion of this incident see comments on Matt. 21: 12-13.

---

[2]Godet, *op. cit.,* II, 230-31.

[3]For a detailed, eyewitness account of the siege and destruction of Jerusalem, see Josephus *Wars* 5. 12.

4. *Opposition to His Teaching in the Temple* (19:47-48)

**And he taught daily in the temple. But the chief priests and the scribes and the chief of the people sought to destroy him** (47). This teaching was not an isolated event but refers to the activity of Jesus during His last week (cf. 21:37). The opposition also was a continuing and concerted effort on the part of the Jewish leaders to destroy Him.

**And could not find what they might do: for all the people were very attentive to hear him** (48). Their plans were temporarily fruitless because Jesus still maintained a considerable amount of popularity with the masses. But this popularity did not amount to true devotion on the part of the people. This fact was soon demonstrated when they were so easily led to take sides against Jesus at His trial before Pilate.

B. TEACHING DAILY IN THE TEMPLE, 20:1—21:4

1. *Jesus' Authority Questioned* (20:1-8)

For discussion of this incident see comments on Matt. 21: 23-27.

2. *The Parable of the Wicked Husbandmen* (20:9-18)

For discussion of this parable see comments on Matt. 21: 33-45.

3. *"Render . . . unto Caesar . . . and unto God"* (20:19-26)

For discussion of the teaching in verse 19 see comments on Mark 12:12. For verses 20-26 see comments on Matt. 22:15-22.

Maclaren has an excellent outline on the question of 24: "Whose Image and Superscription?" Emphasizing the thought that man has stamped on his soul the image of God, he makes these three points: (1) The image stamped upon man, and the consequent obligation; (2) The defacement of the image and the wrong expenditure of the coin; (3) The restoration and perfecting of the defaced image.

4. *The Seven Husbands and the Resurrection* (20:27-40)

See comments on Matt. 22:23-33. Luke makes a slight addition to Matthew's account in verse 36: **Neither can they die any more: for they are equal unto the angels; and are the children of God, being the children of the resurrection.** Parallel to this full statement, Matthew simply says "but are as the angels of God in heaven." Marriage will not be needed after the resurrection, for all men will be immortal. The purpose of marriage is to re-

589

populate the earth, to replace those who die; after the resurrection people will no more die, so they will not need to be replaced. **Equal unto the angels** means equally immortal.

**Then certain of the scribes answering said, Master, thou hast well said** (39). See comments on Mark 12:32-34a. Luke's statement is an abbreviation of the incident which Mark gives in more detail.

**And after that they durst not ask him any question at all** (40). See comment on Mark 12:34b.

　　5. *Son or Lord of David?* (20:41-44)

See comments on Matt. 22:41-45.

　　6. *"Beware of the Scribes"* (20:45-47)

These three verses in Luke are a very brief abridgment of the discourse of Jesus from which Matthew composed his "chapter of woes." See comments on Matthew 23.

　　7. *The Greatest Gift* (21:1-4)

See comments on Mark 12:41-44.

C. REVELATION OF THE FUTURE, 21:5-38

　　1. *"When Shall These Things Be?"* (21:5-9)

See comments on Matt. 24:1-6. Luke makes one addition to Matthew's account. In the reference to the Temple, in verse 5, which led to the discourse on the future, Luke is more specific than Matthew. In Matthew's account we are told simply that the disciples showed him "the buildings of the temple." But Luke says they **spake of the temple, how it was adorned with goodly stones and gifts**—literally, "consecrated gifts."

**Goodly stones** probably refers to the beauty and to the enormous size of the blocks of marble with which the Temple was constructed. Josephus says that some of the stones were as much as forty cubits long and ten high. This would be about sixty feet long and fifteen feet high.

It is also possible that these **goodly stones** referred, not to blocks of marble, but to precious stones with which the Temple was decorated. The use of the word **adorned** would lend weight to this interpretation. However, Jesus' answer that there would **not be left one stone upon another** would seem to make the first interpretation the correct one.

The **gifts** were evidently the many costly ornaments which were given to the Temple by important personages, such as Herod's gift of the golden vine.

## 2. *Hardships to Come* (21:10-19)

See comments on Matt. 24:7-14. See also comments on Matt. 10:17-22, 30. In verse 15, Luke gives a most beautiful and comforting addition to Matthew's account: **For I will give you a mouth and wisdom, which all your adversaries shall not be able to gainsay nor resist.** As Mark reminds us, it is the Holy Spirit who will speak through the Christian's mouth at such times (Mark 13:11). Instances of the fulfillment of this promise are Stephen's defense before the Sanhedrin (Acts 7) and Paul's defenses before Felix (Acts 25) and King Agrippa (Acts 26).

**In your patience possess ye your souls** (19). Patient bearing of persecution and hardships, and trust in the power of an all-wise, all-loving, and all-powerful God is the way to victory.

On 17-19, Ryle has this threefold outline: (1) An alarming declaration—**Ye shall be hated of all men;** (2) A consoling promise—**There shall not an hair of your head perish;** (3) An encouraging direction—**In your patience possess ye your souls.**

## 3. *The Siege of Jerusalem* (21:20-24)

See comments on Matt. 24:15-28. Luke's account is briefer than Matthew's but its reference to the destruction of Jerusalem by the Romans in A.D. 70 can be seen more clearly. Where Matthew uses the vague language of Daniel's prophecy, "the abomination which makes desolate" (24:15), Luke states clearly that they will see **Jerusalem compassed with armies** (21:20). Again, where Matthew refers to "great tribulation" and in rather vague terms suggests the destruction of Jerusalem (24:21-28), Luke uses clear and direct language. He says **they shall fall by the edge of the sword, and shall be led away captive into all nations** (21:24).

At this point we find in Luke a significant bit of prophecy which the other two Synoptics omit: **And Jerusalem shall be trodden down of the Gentiles, until the times of the Gentiles be fulfilled** (24). Here Jesus clearly announced that Jerusalem would be dominated by Gentile conquerors. The **times of the Gentiles** may mean the Gentile "day of grace";[4] that is, the Church age.

## 4. *Signs of Christ's Second Coming* (21:25-28)

See comments on Matt. 24:29-31. In verses 26 and 28, Luke gives us bits of the Master's prophecy omitted by the other two

[4]EGT, I, 621.

Synoptics: **Men's hearts failing them for fear, and for looking after those things which are coming . . . for the powers of heaven shall be shaken** (26). This expresses the terror which will seize the unconverted when these predicted calamities come to pass. **Men's hearts failing** is literally "men fainting at heart," and suggests a willingness to die rather than to face these terrible judgments.

**And when these things begin to come to pass, then look up, and lift up your heads; for your redemption draweth nigh** (28). The same unusual occurrences which will produce terror in the hearts of the unconverted will be signs to Christ's true disciples that their final and eternal redemption is drawing near. It is interesting to note how often Luke includes the encouraging statements of the Master which the other Synoptists omit.

5. *The Parable of the Fig Tree* (21: 29-33)

See comments on Matt. 24: 33-41.

6. *The Importance of Watchfulness* (21: 34-36)

**And take heed to yourselves, lest at any time your hearts be overcharged with surfeiting,** (or "do not let your minds be dulled by dissipation" [NEB] **and drunkenness . . . and so that day come upon you unawares** (34). The Master ends the discourse with a stern and vivid warning to His disciples never to become careless so that the day of the Lord would find them unprepared. There is here the definite intimation that the return of the Lord cannot be dated. It may occur at any time.

**For as a snare shall it** (the day of the Lord's coming) **come on all them that dwell on the face of the whole earth** (35). The sudden coming of the Lord will be to those who are unprepared like the sudden closing of a trap upon an unsuspecting animal. In that day there will be only two classes of people: those who are ready, for whom Christ's coming will be a supreme pleasure; and those who are not ready, for whom His return will be as the stroke of doom.

**Watch ye therefore, and pray always, that ye may be accounted worthy to escape all these things . . . and to stand before the Son of man** (36). Prayer and never-ending watchfulness are the key to constant readiness. This demands our own efforts plus the help of God obtained through prayer. To **stand** means to stand acquitted, to stand approved.

### 7. How Jesus Spent His Time at Jerusalem (21:37-38)

**And in the day time he was teaching in the temple; and at night he went out, and abode in the mount . . . of Olives (37).** This refers, not to a specific occasion, but to the practice of Jesus during the last day before His death. The Greek words translated **in the day** mean literally "of the day" or "daily." Luke had omitted many events of Passion Week, and he covers the omission with this general statement.

Adam Clarke thinks that the assertion that Jesus spent His nights on the Mount of Olives refers to Bethany, where He often visited with His friends, Bethany being "a town at the foot, or on the declivity of the Mount of Olives."[5] But the Greek word translated **abode** in this verse means literally to lodge in the open.[6] Thus it seems that Jesus spent the nights in the open on the Mount of Olives.

**And all the people came early in the morning to him in the temple, for to hear him (38).** This too refers to His practice during those last days rather than to an isolated event. Here is evidence of Jesus' continued popularity with the masses. They could hardly wait to hear Him; they would rise early and hurry to the Temple, where it was His custom to be in the early morning.

---

[5]Clarke, *op. cit.*, p. 485.

[6]See Godet, *op. cit.*, II, 276. See also Thayer's *Greek-English Lexicon of the New Testament*.

Section **VII** *The Passion of Christ*

Luke 22:1—23:56

A. THE FINAL PREPARATION, 22:1-13

1. *The Plotting of His Enemies* (22:1-2)

See comments on Matt. 26:1-5. See also Mark 14:1-2.

2. *Judas Makes a Bargain* (22:3-6)

See comments on Matt. 26:14-16. Luke adds the detail that **then entered Satan into Judas.** This is more than a mere instance of the use of strong and graphic language; it shows the relation of Satan to the drama of the Crucifixion. Satan, and not merely Judas and the chief priests, plotted the death of Christ. When he had gained his purpose he doubtless thought he had dealt a mortal blow to God's kingdom on earth. But, on the contrary, he had helped to bring about his own ruin, for this "defeat" of Christ was the world's greatest victory.

3. *Preparation for the Passover* (22:7-13)

See comments on Matt. 26:17-19 and Mark 14:12-16. Mark's account of this episode is much more detailed than is that of Matthew. Luke follows Mark closely.

B. THE LAST SUPPER, 22:14-38

1. *The Lord's Supper Instituted and the Betrayal Predicted* (22:14-23)

**And when the hour was come** (14) refers to the hour of the Passover—the eating of the paschal lamb, which was in the evening, at sundown. **He sat down** (literally "reclined"), **and the twelve with him.** He and His twelve apostles reclined together around the table where the Passover feast was spread.

**And he said . . . With desire I have desired to eat this passover with you before I suffer** (15). This is a Hebrew form of expression that means, "I have greatly desired to eat the Passover with you, etc." Note how closely Luke is translating into Greek the exact words of Jesus as they appear in his Aramaic source.

This great desire sprang from two sources. Jesus had the normal human yearning for those last precious moments of communion with the companions whom He loved before death should

594

separate Him from them. Also He knew the religious significance which this evening would have for the Church in the coming centuries.

**For . . . I will not any more eat thereof, until it be fulfilled in the kingdom of God** (16). This prediction points to a double fulfillment. First to the spiritual blessing that Christ and His people will have together as a result of His coming death. This is the spiritual heritage of every true follower of Jesus Christ. The second and ultimate fulfillment of this prediction is what we might call "The Great Messianic Banquet" at our Lord's second coming. The Lord's Supper typifies both the spiritual feast and the Messianic banquet.

**And he took the cup** (literally "having received the cup"), **and gave thanks, and said, Take this, and divide it among yourselves** (17). The Master is here officiating in the celebration of the Passover feast rather than in the Communion service. Barnes is correct in asserting that this was not the sacramental cup but one of the cups partaken of as a part of the Passover feast.[1] The sacramental cup is the one referred to in verse 20. Jesus here gave the whole contents of this paschal cup to His disciples.

**For . . . I will not drink of the fruit of the vine, until the kingdom of God shall come** (18). This is figurative language. Jesus is for the last time eating the Jewish Passover. Before another such feast His redeeming death, His resurrection, and the descent of the Holy Spirit at Pentecost will have taken place. The Passover will have been replaced with the Lord's Supper, and the kingdom of God will have come in a new and glorious sense. See also comments on verse 16.

For discussion of verses 19 and 20, see comments on Matt. 26: 26-29. For discussion of verses 21-23, see comments on Matt. 26: 21-25.

### 2. Who Shall Be Greatest (22: 24-30)

**And there was also a strife among them, which of them should be accounted the greatest** (24). This was evidently a debate about which of the disciples would have the highest position in the kingdom which they still expected Jesus to establish in the not too distant future. Almost three years of proximity to Jesus had not purified their hearts of self-seeking. This would be the ministry of the sanctifying Holy Spirit. Neither Jesus' spirit nor

[1]Barnes, *op. cit.*, p. 147.

His explanations of the nature of the Kingdom had been fully comprehended by the disciples. Nor had His prophecies of the destruction of Jerusalem and of the hardships which His followers would be called upon to endure been sufficient to change their notion of the Kingdom or dampen their ardor for places of prominence.

Though the account of this particular **strife** over the relative greatness of the apostles is peculiar to Luke, there is no sufficient justification for supposing, as Adam Clarke does, that Luke has gotten this episode out of place in his Gospel. Clarke agrees that this could not have been the dispute recorded by Luke earlier (9:46), so he concludes that Luke must have had in mind the episode recorded by Matthew (20:20 ff.) and Mark (10:35 ff.).[2] This conjecture would be reasonable only if the episode were out of harmony with either the context into which Luke inserts it or the attitude and level of comprehension of the apostles at the time. Neither of these necessary conditions is true.[3]

**And he said . . . The kings of the Gentiles exercise lordship over them** (25). In the kingdoms of the Gentiles greatness was synonymous with authority. **And they that exercise authority upon them are called benefactors.** Such tyrants as Egypt's Ptolemy Euergetes chose the title "Benefactor." It was also applied to several of the Roman emperors. In some instances the rulers deserved the title, but they were more often a curse or a scourge.

**But ye shall not be so** (26). In Christ's kingdom greatness is more than a title and more than position or authority. **But he that is greatest among you, let him be as the younger.** Youth was expected to show deference for those who were older. This same deference, or humility, is shown by the "great" in the kingdom of God. Humility is one of the major qualities of true greatness. **And he that is chief, as he that doth serve.** Service is to be a mark of distinction: the greater the service rendered, the greater the man. All Christians are to be servants—to God and to their fellowmen.

**For whether is greater, he that sitteth at meat, or he that serveth?** (27) In Jesus' day the almost universal answer to this

---

[2]Clarke, *op. cit.*, p. 448.

[3]Spence, Barnes, Godet, Geldenhuys, and Van Oosterzee all support Luke at this point.

question would have been that the one who sat at meat was the greater. The servant was a mere slave. So Jesus answers His own question in terms of the prevailing concept of greatness: **Is not he that sitteth at meat?** It is almost as though He is agreeing with this popular notion, and it is against this hypothetical background that He says, **But I am among you as he that serveth.** Jesus is saying that service is a necessary element of true greatness. He is also saying that even in a world where the opposite view is held, where authority and position are the badges of greatness and where a servant is next to nothing, the Christian must take the path of service. When he takes that path, the divine footprints will show that the Master has taken it before him.

**Ye are they which have continued with me in my temptations** (28). After the gentle rebuke, and after His corrective instructions on the subject of true greatness, Jesus tenderly reminds the disciples that they had been loyal to Him in His hours of trial. Insofar as they have been able and have understood, they have taken the path of service. The Master knew that the one remaining obstacle, carnality, would be removed at Pentecost.

**And I appoint unto you a kingdom, as my Father hath appointed me** (29). This verse refers to the present spiritual Kingdom, the Church, in which the apostles would soon be the leaders. The word translated **appoint** has in it the idea of a covenant. Christ makes a covenant with His disciples as the Father has made with Him. Thus the disciples are to get places of prominence in the Kingdom, but with a difference which they had not anticipated. Service to God and to mankind is to be joined with privation, persecution, and a martyr's death. But they would not be forgotten by the Master, for whom their service would be gladly given.

**That ye may eat and drink at my table in my kingdom, and sit on thrones judging the twelve tribes of Israel** (30). This refers to the heavenly Kingdom, which will include as citizens those who have been faithful to their spiritual responsibilities in this life. The Master uses two figures to picture the honor and the reward of His disciples in the heavenly reign. The first figure is the Messianic banquet, a favorite metaphor among the Jews. At that banquet they will eat at the Lord's table the good things of heaven. The second figure is that of kingship: they will sit on *thrones* judging the twelve tribes of Israel. This is figurative language, but it seems to imply that, though like their Master they will be rejected by the Jews, they will ultimately be the highest ranking of all Israelites.

### 3. Peter's Denial Foretold (22:31-34)

**And the Lord said, Simon, Simon, behold, Satan hath desired to have you, that he may sift you as wheat (31).** This is reminiscent of Satan's efforts to get Job by his "sifting" process. The sequel shows, however, that he was more successful with Peter than with Job, though his success with Peter was only temporary. Perhaps Satan was emboldened by his success in tempting Judas away from the Master.

Satan desires to **sift** all of God's children, and he will do his best to prove them unworthy of the Master's garner. There is need of constant prayer to be delivered "from the evil one."[4] This figure of sifting as wheat is a metaphor which would have been easily understood by Jesus' listeners. Sifting is for the purpose of removing chaff or foreign substances. Satan sifts by means of temptation that he might remove us from the Lord's **wheat.**

**But I have prayed for thee, that thy faith fail not (32).** The Master prays thus for all of His disciples. The prayer is answered as our faith is strengthened. Satan was not forbidden to tempt Peter, nor is he prevented from tempting us. In these temptations the final decision for victory or defeat must be made by the one tempted. But Christ is not an idle spectator to the combat. We have His intercession and we have heavenly assistance.

**And when thou art converted, strengthen thy brethren.** "When thou art recovered," or "when you return" from the conflict with Satan, then help to establish your brethren. Jesus knew what Peter would soon go through. Humiliating as the outcome would be, He also knew that Peter would be wiser as a result of the experience, and he would be able to help his brethren and prevent their falling victim to a similar temptation.

For discussion of verses 33 and 34, see comments on Matt. 26:31-35.

### 4. Changed Orders (22:35-38)

**When I sent you forth without purse, and scrip** (literally, "provision bag") **and shoes** (literally, "sandals"), **lacked ye any thing? (35)** When Jesus had sent out the Twelve early in His

---

[4]This is the literal translation of the part of the Lord's Prayer which is translated "deliver us from evil" in KJV (Matt. 6:13).

ministry,[5] they were enjoying the benefits of their Master's popularity. They lacked nothing, though they took no provisions with them; all was provided by a generous and favorable populace.

**But now (36).** A major change is taking place. Instead of popular acclaim the Master sees the Cross, and His disciples will share His disgrace as they have shared His popularity. Furthermore, He will soon no longer be with them. They must go out to carry a message which is not always popular to a people who are **often far from kind.** And this time they will go, not merely to the "lost sheep of the house of Israel" (Matt. 10:6). Their commission will be to go "into all the world, and preach the gospel to every creature" (Mark 16:15).

**He that hath a purse, let him take it, and likewise his scrip** (provision bag). Though the workmen are worthy of their hire, they will often not receive their due. They must be prepared to provide for themselves. The phrase **He that hath a purse** reminds us that there will be inequality of worldly possessions among the messengers of the Cross. Some will be able to provide for themselves and for others, as Barnabas, for example. Others will be without earthly substance.

**And he that hath no sword, let him sell his garment, and buy one.** This is a difficult passage. Some have suggested that the word **sword** was not in the original autograph of Luke's Gospel but is an interpolation.[6] Others think the word should be understood figuratively, implying the difficult days which lie ahead—the general unfriendliness of the world to those who carry the gospel message.[7] Still others think the word should be understood literally, but that the sword was to be used only in case of self-defense (as against robbers, etc.).[8] Upon one thing the scholars agree: that Jesus is not advocating the use of force either to propagate or to defend the gospel. Jesus himself set the example in this regard by giving himself without opposition to those who came to arrest Him. The blood of hundreds of thousands of Christian martyrs speaks eloquently of how others have followed the Master's example.

[5]Matt. 10:2-15; Mark 6:7-11; Luke 9:1-5.
[6]See Clarke, *op. cit.*, II, 489.
[7]See Spence, *op. cit.*, II, 201.
[8]See Van Oosterzee, *op. cit.*, pp. 342 f.

**For I say unto you, that this that is written must yet be accomplished in me, And he was reckoned among the transgressors (37).** Jesus is saying two things here. He is saying, first, that Isaiah's prophecy of His death as a malefactor (Isa. 53:12) must be fulfilled. He is saying, further, that since He is to be treated thus, His followers need not expect preferential treatment. **For the things concerning me have an end.** His present, earthly ministry is a thing of time, and thus must come to an end, and that end is near at hand. Isaiah's prophecy had implied as much.

**And they said, Lord, behold, here are two swords (38).** The material and earthly bent of the minds of the disciples is evident. Jesus' reference to the need for swords, coupled with their awakening sense of the present danger, made them more concerned with finding these two swords than with the great truth which the Master was expounding. **And he said . . . It is enough.** This does not seem to refer to the swords, but is equivalent to saying, "It is time to go," or, "We have tarried long enough," or, "He need say no more." Jesus seems to have ignored their reference to the swords.

Godet suggests another possible meaning of the Master's remark, **It is enough.** He thinks it might have been given as an ironic reaction to the disciples' physical- and material-mindedness. Thus He would mean, "Yes, for the use which you shall have to make of arms of this kind, those two swords are enough"—meaning, of course, that for such as they the fewer swords they have the better.[9] Interesting as this suggested meaning is, the grammar of the Master's words seems to favor the former interpretation.

## C. Gethsemane, 22:39-53

### 1. *Prayer in the Garden* (22:39-46)

See comments on Matt. 26:30, 36-46. Luke gives two bits of information not reported by the other two Synoptists. They are found in verses 43 and 44.

**And there appeared an angel . . . from heaven, strengthening him (43).** His need of this strengthening testifies to the intensity of the mental anguish of the struggle going on in His soul. The strength received was probably necessary to prevent His dying before the time for His sacrifice for sin on Calvary.

[9]Godet, *op. cit.*, II, 302.

**And being in an agony he prayed more earnestly: and his sweat was as it were great drops of blood falling down to the ground** (44). Some have interpreted this verse as indicating only the great size of the drops of **sweat,** but conservative church authorities from Athanasius to the present day have insisted on the literalness of the blood. The meaning seems to be that the **sweat** was mingled with **blood,** thus giving the impression of pure blood coming through the pores of Jesus' skin. Many authorities testify that great suffering or mental agony can cause blood to mingle with the perspiration of the human body.

### 2. The Betrayal and Arrest (22:47-53)

See comments on Matt. 26:47-56. Luke adds two bits of information not found in the other Synoptics. In verse 48 he reports Jesus' saying to Judas, **Betrayest thou the Son of man with a kiss?**

A more significant addition is found in verse 51. There Luke reports that Jesus healed the servant of the high priest whose ear had been cut off. This is not only another fact about the life of Jesus; it also gives us one of the few glimpses of the special interest of Luke. As a physician it is natural that he would take note of this miracle, which is not a duplication of any other recorded miracle of Jesus. This special interest of Luke lends weight to the traditional belief that he was a physician.[10]

For **This is your hour, and the power of darkness** (53), Maclaren suggests: (1) The cross of Jesus Christ is the center and the meeting point for the energies of three worlds; (2) The Cross is the high-water mark of man's sin; (3) The temporary triumph of the darkness is the eternal victory of light.

### D. The Jewish Trial, 22:54-71

#### 1. Peter's Denial (22:54-62)

See comments on Matt. 26:57-75. Luke makes one significant contribution in relating this event. It is found in verse 61. **And the Lord turned, and looked upon Peter.** This probably took place as Jesus was being taken from His examination before Annas to His trial before Caiaphas and the Sanhedrin. John refers to this change of location when he says, *Now Annas had sent him bound unto Caiaphas* (John 18:24). Jesus was taken across the courtyard just as Peter was vehemently engaged in his

---

[10]See Introduction to this commentary on Luke's Gospel.

third denial. The sudden and unexpected appearance of the Master, the look of kind and gentle reproof which he saw on Jesus' face, and the memory of the warning that he would do just what he was now doing, all tremendously reinforced the effect produced by the crowing of the cock. The result was bitter remorse and sincere repentance.

### 2. *Jesus Condemned by the Sanhedrin* (22:63-71)

For discussion of verses 63-65, see comments on Matt. 26:67-68. For discussion of verse 66, see comments on Matt. 27:1.

**Art thou the Christ? tell us. And he said unto them, If I tell you, ye will not believe** (67). Caiaphas and the Sanhedrin had fully decided on what they intended to do. Though the question asked, evidently by Caiaphas, has the appearance of sincerity, it was in reality a subtle attempt to get Jesus to say something that would incriminate Him. His answer shows how well He understood them.

**And if I also ask you, ye will not answer me, nor let me go** (68). The Greek word translated **ask** is a broad term and can be translated "ask," "question," "request," "entreat," "beseech." So Jesus' statement could have two different meanings. It could mean, "If I question you concerning the Christ, you will not answer Me, and therefore I cannot convince you that I am correct in My claim, and I cannot hope to be acquitted." Or the statement could mean, "If I beseech or entreat you to let Me go, you will ignore Me and will refuse to give Me My freedom." The fact that either of these meanings is in harmony with the context makes the choice between them more difficult. However the exact wording of the sentence, especially the insertion of the clause, **ye will not answer me,** seems to favor the former interpretation. Godet, who is in harmony with this view, paraphrases the Master's words thus: "I cannot address you either as judges whom I am seeking to convince, for you are already determined to put no faith in my declarations, nor as disciples whom I am endeavoring to instruct, for you would not enter into a fair discussion with me."[11]

**Hereafter shall the Son of man sit on the right hand of the power of God** (69). Jesus goes beyond their question with His claim and prediction. This was a daring step, for the statement

[11]Godet, *op. cit.*, II, 317.

could be more easily construed as blasphemy than an affirmative answer to the question, "Art thou the Christ?" The Jewish concept of the Christ, or Messiah, was not so high—it did not include divine sonship. Jesus seems to have had two reasons for making His bold claim and prediction: to put an end to the useless trial and to leave a final pronouncement of the truth about himself.

**Then said they all, Art thou then the Son of God?** (70) They wanted Jesus to clarify the implications of His statement in verse 69. They doubtless understood what this implied; but they wanted His categorical claim to be the Son of God, for with this they could condemn Him. **And he said . . . Ye say that I am.** This is a Hebrew form of affirmation. It not only satisfied the Sanhedrin that Jesus had blasphemed, but it can be taken by us as a clear claim by our Lord of His deity.

**What need we further witness? for we ourselves have heard of his own mouth** (71). They accepted the affirmation, they interpreted it as blasphemy, they condemned our Lord. But this is what they had been determined to do from the start.

### E. The Roman Trial, 23:1-25

#### 1. *First Appearance Before Pilate* (23:1-5)

For discussion of verse 1 see comments on Matt. 27:2. See also Mark 15:1.

**And they began to accuse him, saying, We found this fellow perverting the nation, and forbidding to give tribute to Caesar, saying that he himself is Christ a King** (2). Not a thing is said about the charge of blasphemy for which He was condemned by the Sanhedrin. They did not mention this because it was not a crime under Roman law, and they were determined to put Him to death. Therefore they invented new charges that were criminal.

The extent of their hypocrisy is seen in the fact that the "evils" which they charged against Jesus were the positions which they themselves (except for the Herodians) strongly held under normal circumstances. Conservative Jews in Christ's day despised Rome and hoped for someone to throw off the foreign yoke. They could not, on the other hand, have been sincere in their charge that He was a danger to Rome. He had always resisted every effort calculated to move Him to do or say something which could be interpreted as anti-Roman.

For discussion of verse 3 see comments on Matt. 27:11.

**Then said Pilate . . . I find no fault in this man. And they were the more fierce** (4-5). Pilate was aware of their motives and he saw nothing in Jesus that was a threat to Rome. Their fierceness attested their determination and their intense hatred. Since Pilate was not disturbed at their insinuation that Jesus was guilty of treason, they invented a new charge. This time they came nearer to Pilate's own personal interest: **He stirreth up the people, teaching throughout all Jewry, beginning from Galilee to this place.** They undoubtedly knew that Pilate lived in fear of Jewish uprisings, for he could not hope to hold his position unless he could control these unruly people. Jesus' accusers felt that Pilate must act if there was danger of a popular revolt. But their mention of Galilee gave Pilate an idea which they had not anticipated.

### 2. *Jesus Brought Before Herod* (23:6-12)

This episode is peculiar to Luke. **When Pilate heard of Galilee, he asked whether the man were a Galilean. And . . . he sent him to Herod, who himself also was at Jerusalem** (6-7). This seemed to Pilate an excellent opportunity to turn a knotty and potentially dangerous problem over to someone else. He probably hoped that Herod would either handle the case for him or at least render a supporting judgment. This would both help him in his decision and lessen his own responsibility for the fate of Jesus and the reactions of the Jewish leaders. See verse 12 for a second motive which was undoubtedly present in Pilate's mind when he sent Jesus to Herod.

**And when Herod saw Jesus, he was exceeding glad: for he was desirous to see him of a long season, because he had heard many things of him; and he hoped to have seen some miracle done by him** (8). This was Herod Antipas, infamous for his adultery with Herodias and for his murder of John the Baptist. His only interest in Jesus was curiosity—he wanted to see, and be entertained by, the famous Miracle Worker.

**Then he questioned with him in many words; but he answered him nothing** (9). Herod's efforts were extensive but fruitless. Jesus refused to be made an entertainer for this incestuous, royal murderer whom He neither feared nor respected.

**And the chief priests and scribes stood and vehemently accused him** (10). Jesus was the only passive Figure in the judgment hall. Though His accusers did their utmost to make their accusations effective, Jesus was unmoved. Herod had no interest in the case except curiosity.

**And Herod with his men of war set him at nought, and mocked him (11),** or "made light of him and ridiculed him" (Goodspeed). In the words of Spence, "He treated him, not as a criminal, but as a mischievous religious enthusiast, worthy only of contempt and scorn."[12] This attitude was undoubtedly heightened by Jesus' failure to satisfy Herod's curiosity.

**And the same day Pilate and Herod were made friends . . . for before they were at enmity (12).** This was probably one reason Pilate sent Jesus to Herod. The cause of their enmity is not known, but it is commonly believed to have been Pilate's slaying of the Galileans mentioned in Luke 13:1-2. It was Pilate's civility and deference to Herod which healed the breach.

### 3. *Second Appearance Before Pilate* (23:13-17)

**And Pilate, when he had called together the chief priests and the rulers . . . Said . . . ye have brought this man unto me, as one that perverteth the people: and . . . I . . . have found no fault in . . . him (13-14).** They had utterly failed to establish even a reasonable suspicion of seditious tendencies on the part of Jesus or of any danger of a popular uprising.

**Nor yet Herod (15).** Pilate is using Herod's failure to condemn Jesus as support for his own judgment that Jesus should be released. **And . . . nothing worthy of death is done unto him.** More correctly "nothing worthy of death is done by him." Though He had been tried twice by the Jews, once by Herod and now twice by Pilate, no charge had been proved.

**I will therefore chastise him, and release him (16).** If Pilate had been less the coward than he was, this would have been the end of the trial. But this verdict, though far more favorable to Jesus than the final one, was nevertheless both unjust and cruel. To scourge a man whom he had publicly declared to be innocent was most unjust. Pilate hoped by this concession to Jesus' enemies to keep them from their purpose. He underestimated both these enemies and the extent of his own cowardice.

**For of necessity he must release one unto them at the feast (17).** The **necessity** here was that of custom. It seems that the

---

[12]Spence, *op. cit.*, II, 236.

practice had arisen of releasing a prisoner, perhaps usually a political prisoner, each year at the time of the Passover feast. Verse 17 thus reminds us that the offer to release Jesus, made in verse 16, was not to be an acquittal. Pilate was saying in effect, "I have found no fault in Jesus and therefore He deserves to be acquitted, but I will treat Him as guilty, by scourging Him and then releasing Him in line with our annual custom." Thus, he hoped, Jesus would be free and at the same time he would have succeeded in appeasing the Jewish leaders.

### 4. Jesus or Barabbas? (23:18-25)

See comments on Matt. 27:15-26. Though Luke adds little to Matthew in fact or interpretation, he expresses excellently, in verse 25, the irony, the injustice, and the contradiction in Pilate's actions and final verdict.

### F. The Crucifixion and Burial, 23:26-56

#### 1. Teaching on the Road to Calvary (23:26-31).

The material from verses 27-31 is peculiar to Luke. For discussion of verse 26 see comments on Matt. 27:32.

**And there followed him a great company of people, and of women, which also bewailed and lamented him** (27). Luke has been called "The Gospel of Women" because women have a larger place in this Gospel than in any of the others.[13] The lamentation of these women was a demonstration of true sympathy for Jesus and a reminder that not all Jewish hearts were hardened toward Him.

**But Jesus turning unto them said, Daughters of Jerusalem** (28). This speech would have taken more time than a condemned man would likely be allowed on the way to his execution. Since the forcing of Simon the Cyrenian to bear the Cross is mentioned in verse 16, immediately preceding, it is reasonable to suppose that this speech was given during the pause which took place while the Cross was being transferred to Simon. The appellation **Daughters of Jerusalem** would indicate that at least the major part of these women were residents of Jerusalem, thus distinguishing them from the women who followed Him from Galilee.

**Weep not for me, but weep for yourselves, and for your children.** His tragedy, if it be so called, is far less than theirs. His soon coming death will be followed by a glorious resurrection,

---

[13]See Introduction to Luke in this commentary.

while they are to suffer one of the great calamities of history in the destruction of Jerusalem.[14]

**For, behold, the days are coming, in the which they shall say, Blessed are the barren** (29)—because those who have children must see them starve in a besieged city or be slaughtered by the enemy or sold into slavery. The tragic connotation of this strange beatitude, **Blessed are the barren,** can be fully grasped only when we realize the passionate desire of Jewish women to bear children, and the shame which was suffered when they learned that they could not give birth to them.

**Then shall they begin to say to the mountains, Fall on us; and to the hills, Cover us** (30). Here Jesus refers to the almost unmentionable suffering during the siege of Jerusalem and following (A.D. 68-70).[15] In those days to be suddenly crushed under a mountain of earth would be a welcome relief.

**For if they do these things in a green tree, what shall be done in the dry?** (31) This proverbial expression compares what is now being done to Christ with what will be done to the Jews when Jerusalem is destroyed. The green wood refers to Jesus' loyalty to the Romans; the dry wood refers to the Jews' chronic disloyalty. If the Romans are cruel enough to do what they are now doing to One whom even their governor considers to be innocent and loyal, how much more cruelly will they treat these disloyal and provocative Jews when the break in relations comes!

### 2. *Christ Crucified* (23:32-38)

For discussion of verse 32 see comments on Matt. 27:38. Matthew and Mark call these two fellow sufferers robbers, while Luke calls them **malefactors**—"evildoers" or "bad men."

For discussion of verses 33-38 see comments on Matt. 27:33-44. Luke alone reports the intercessory prayer of Jesus: **Father, forgive them; for they know not what they do** (34). This prayer, which is the first of the seven sayings of Jesus from the Cross, seems to be for the soldiers and was possibly uttered while they were nailing Him to the Cross. The expression **they know not what they do** could hardly apply to those Jews who had plotted His death; nor could they fully apply to Pilate, though Jesus bore no ill will to either the Jews or Pilate.

[14]See Josephus *Wars* 5. 10—6. 10.
[15]*Ibid.*

### 3. *A Dying Thief Converted* (23:39-43)

This episode is peculiar to Luke. **And one of the malefactors which were hanged railed on him, saying, If thou be the Christ, save thyself and us** (39). The Greek word translated **railed** is literally "blasphemed" and means here to use injurious and insulting language. The other two Synoptics say that both of the robbers reproached or reviled Jesus. But the words used in the original there are not as strong as the one used here by Luke; they do not indicate anything blasphemous. Putting the three accounts together we see that both of the malefactors reproached Him but only one of them used insulting and blasphemous language.[16]

**But the other answering rebuked him** (40). Having become aware of what and who Jesus was, he ceased to reproach Him and even chided his fellow robber for his blasphemy. By this time he had seen Jesus' reactions to suffering and to reproach; he had heard Him pray for His executioners. He had heard Him referred to as the Christ, and probably had had some previous knowledge of Jesus. He must also have seen the superscription above Jesus' head. Now his true manhood rises, perhaps for the first time in many years.

**Dost not thou fear God, seeing thou art in the same condemnation?** This is no time to blaspheme. At such a time as this any thinking man should be seriously concerned about his relationship to God.

**And we indeed justly . . . but this man hath done nothing amiss** (41). He is thinking rightly now. He sees the innocence of Jesus and the injustice of His suffering. He sees his own sin and the justice of the condemnation of himself and of his fellow robber. But He saw more, as the next verse shows.

**And he said unto Jesus, Lord, remember me when thou comest into thy kingdom** (42). He has sufficient understanding and faith to recognize Jesus as the Messiah. When Jesus comes into His kingdom, he wants the Master to remember one who died by the side of His cross. This man's knowledge was incomplete and his prayer did not fully reveal the yearning and cry of his soul. But what he was really asking was salvation from sin and a place in Christ's coming kingdom.

**To day shalt thou be with me in paradise** (43). Not "someday in My kingdom" but **to day . . . in paradise.** Jesus heard

[16]See also comments on Matt. 27:44.

the cry of this man's heart as well as the prayer of his lips, and, disregarding the gap in his knowledge and understanding, gave him instant salvation and a promise of paradise. The word **paradise** came originally from Persia and denoted a beautiful pleasure garden. It came to mean a place of happiness, and here it refers to heaven.[17]

### 4. The Sinless One Dies for Sin (23:44-49)

See comments on Matt. 27:45-56. Luke relates two items which are not in the other Synoptics. In verse 46 he gives the last of the seven sayings of Jesus from the Cross. Spence says that Christ's words, "It is finished" (John 19:30), were His "farewell to earth," and that this one in Luke, **Father, into thy hands I commend my spirit,** is His "entrance greeting to heaven."[18]

The second bit of information peculiar to this Gospel is found in verse 48. Luke tells us that, in addition to those witnesses to the death of Jesus mentioned in the other Gospels, there was a multitude that **came together to that sight,** and that when they saw, they **smote their breasts, and returned.** The multitude had had a share in the crucifixion of Jesus, but it was not their idea. They were used by their leaders; they were the subjects of mob psychology and demagoguery. Now they were experiencing an unexpressible revulsion of feelings.

For these verses (44-49) Ryle points out: (1) The miraculous signs which accompanied our Lord's death on the Cross; (2) The remarkable words which our Lord spoke when He died; (3) The power of conscience in the case of the centurion and the people who saw Christ die.

### 5. The Burial (23:50-56)

See comments on Matt. 27:57-61. See also comments on Mark 15:42-47.

---

[17]For a fuller treatment of the word "paradise," see Barnes, *op. cit.*, p. 158.

[18]Spence, *op. cit.*, II, 243.

A. THE RESURRECTION, 24:1-12

For discussion of verses 1-6a see comments on Matt. 28:1-10. See also Mark 16:1-8.

**Remember how he spake unto you when he was yet in Galilee, Saying, The Son of man must be delivered into the hands of sinful men, and be crucified, and the third day rise again** (6-7). Not having understood the words of Jesus to which the angel refers, the women might have all but forgotten them. The angel refreshes their memory at a time when they can understand the prophecy in the light of its recent fulfillment. Thus, both their understanding of Jesus' ministry on earth and their faith in His deity would be enhanced.

Matthew and Mark omit the angelic reminder of this prophecy. In its place they relate the angel's charge to the women to tell the apostles they were to go before Jesus into Galilee.

**And returned from the sepulchre, and told all these things unto the eleven, and to all the rest** (9). See comments on Matt. 28:8.

For discussion of verse 10 see comments on Mark 16:1. The name of Joanna is omitted from Mark's account. She was the wife of Chuza, Herod's steward, mentioned in Luke 8:3.

**And their words seemed to them as idle tales** (11). Though Jesus had clearly foretold His death and resurrection to His disciples, their conception of the Messianic kingdom had no place for such an idea. Now that it had come to pass, they were as doubtful and as surprised as if they had never heard the Master's prophecies. They must have dismissed these predictions from their minds completely as incomprehensible, or else they interpreted them spiritually. The disciples' forgetfulness is in sharp contrast to the memories of the members of the Sanhedrin in this regard. These Jewish leaders remembered that Jesus had predicted His resurrection after three days, and it was for this reason that they petitioned Pilate to set a watch.[1]

For discussion of verse 12 see comments on John 20:2-10.

## B. Appearances of the Risen Lord, 24:13-49

### 1. *Jesus' Appearance on the Road to Emmaus* (24:13-27)

Godet calls this "one of the most admirable pieces in Luke's Gospel."[2] The account is peculiar to Luke, though Mark does make a brief reference to the event (Mark 16:12-13).

**And, behold, two of them** (13). Not of the Twelve but two of Jesus' wider circle of disciples. They might have been a man and his wife. One is named in verse 18. The other one has been the subject of considerable conjecture, Luke himself being named by some, but there is no real evidence which would enable us to determine the person of this unnamed disciple. Concerning the one whom Luke names Cleopas, an abbreviation of "Cleophatros," nothing beyond his name is known.[3] **That same day.** Resurrection day, the first day of the week. **To a village called Emmaus.** The village is now called Kolonieh, so called from the emperor Titus' having made of it a colony for some of his veterans. It is located, as Luke says, about sixty **furlongs** or *stadia* from Jerusalem. A *stadion* is 606.75 feet. Thus the village was about six and three-fourths miles from Jerusalem.

**And they talked together of all these things which had happened** (14). The events connected with the death of Christ, and the very incomplete report that He had risen from the dead.

**And ... while they ... reasoned** (15). They were trying to make sense out of a jumble of confused facts, reports, preconceived notions of the Messianic kingdom, and their own personal feelings toward Jesus. It was like a jigsaw puzzle that appeared to have some pieces which did not belong to it and other pieces which were missing.

**Jesus himself drew near, and went with them. But their eyes were holden that they should not know him** (15-16). That is, something "held" their eyes so that they could not recognize Him.

One thing which prevented these disciples from recognizing Jesus was the fact that, as Mark puts it, "he appeared in another

---

[1]See Matt. 27:62-66.

[2]Godet, *op. cit.*, II, 352.

[3]For further discussion see Godet, *op. cit.*, II, 352 ff.

form" (Mark 16:12). In some way His personal appearance was
changed. Mary Magdalene had seen the risen Lord without recognizing Him, though she met Him in the vicinity of His tomb
(John 20:15). The disguise of Jesus was here made more effective by the incredulity of the disciples with regard to the Resurrection, and also by the suddenness of His appearance on the
Emmaus road.

**And he said . . . What manner of communications are these
that ye have one to another, as ye walk, and are sad? (17)** The
Master did not need to be told the subject of their conversation.
This was merely His way of joining in the discussion, which He
did in order to teach them some valuable truths.

**And . . . one of them . . . said . . . Art thou only a stranger
in Jerusalem? (18)**—literally, "Dost thou only sojourn in Jerusalem?" This question implies that they knew He had overheard
at least a part of their conversation. Perhaps He had walked
with them for a short time in silence before He joined the discussion. Anyone but a stranger in Jerusalem on that morning
would have known the import as well as the contents of a **conversation** about Jesus of Nazareth.

**And he said . . . What things? (19)** He wanted them to give
Him enough information to permit Him to teach His truths from
their subject. And He wanted to do this without revealing His
identity—at least for the present. He was also giving them an
opportunity to open their hearts to Him. **And they said . . . Concerning Jesus of Nazareth.** Taking it for granted that He is a
Stranger, they relate briefly, but graphically and with deep emotion, the story of Jesus: that He was a prophet **mighty in deed
and word,** that He was condemned through the efforts of the
Jewish leaders, and that He was **crucified.** They probably included other details which are not related by Luke.

**But we trusted that it had been he which should have re-
deemed Israel (21).** They still love Him; they are deeply grieved
for Him, but can a dead Messiah redeem Israel? They are thinking of the Messiah-king, the one who would drive out the Romans
and make Israel a great nation again.

**And beside all this, to day is the third day . . . and certain
women . . . made us astonished, which were early at the sepulchre; and when they found not his body, they came, saying, that
they had also seen a vision of angels, which said that he was alive
(21-23).** This report by the women seems to have confused these
two disciples more than it encouraged them. They are still **sad**

612

(verse 17), and their hope that Jesus would be the Messiah is still past tense. They have two problems: first, Is the report true? and second, What does it all mean in terms of Jesus' Messiahship and their own happiness? At the moment they seem to be suspended midway between hope and despair.

**And certain of them which were with us went to the sepulchre, and found it even so as the women had said; but him they saw not (24).** This investigation had resulted in partial corroboration but no explanation. They saw the empty tomb, but they did not see Jesus. The empty tomb will be valuable supporting evidence, but only the presence of the risen Lord will satisfy these disciples.

**Then he said unto them, O fools, and slow of heart to believe (25).** The word translated **fools** means "lacking in understanding." It does not have the evil connotation which our English word has in its everyday usage. This is not the same word as the one used in Matt. 5:22, where we are forbidden to say, "Thou fool," to our brother. Godet points out that this word **fools** refers to the understanding, while the word translated **slow** refers to the heart.[4] Jesus is saying to them that they had misunderstood the prophetic prediction concerning the Messianic ministry, and that this failure was due to both an intellectual lack of comprehension and a spiritual slowness. More intellectual application coupled with a deeper and more intense devotion to God and to truth would have gone far toward solving their problem.

**Ought not Christ to have suffered these things, and to enter into his glory? (26)** The word **ought** signifies the necessity of the suffering of Christ. His sufferings were necessary for the redemption of man, and they were the way by which He would **enter into his glory**—the glory which begins with His resurrection.

**And beginning at Moses ... he expounded unto them in all the scriptures the things concerning himself (27).** This was their first extensive and correct lesson on the Messianic teachings of the Old Testament Scriptures. What a lesson it must have been, taught as it was by the risen Lord! In this panorama of the Hebrew Scriptures, Jesus drew an unmistakable likeness to himself as He had lived, taught, and suffered and as He was now— the risen Lord. Though they had never seen it before, this

[4]Godet, *op. cit.*, II, 354.

picture is as clearly drawn in the Old Testament as is the picture of the Messianic king.[5]

### 2. *The Master Recognized* (24:28-35)

**And they drew nigh unto the village . . . and he made as though he would have gone further. But they constrained him, saying, Abide with us** (28-29). Evidently these two disciples, possibly man and wife, lived in the village of Emmaus and were returning to their home from Jerusalem. Jesus' movement to pass on, as they stopped at their home, was not deceptive. As Spence points out, He would have gone on if they had not invited Him to stay.[6] Their invitation testifies to both their courteous hospitality and their interest in this Stranger—an interest and regard which must have grown to considerable proportions during the short time they had walked together.

**And . . . as he sat at meat with them, he took bread, and blessed it, and brake, and gave to them. And their eyes were opened, and they knew him** (30-31). This was almost a reenactment of the Lord's Supper, which had been instituted only a few days before, and it spoke to them of a blessed and holy fellowship. No wonder their eyes were opened; no wonder they knew Him! The Stranger with whom they had offered to share their bread was the Saviour, who was ready and able to break for them the Bread of Life. This Stranger at their table suddenly became the Head of the house, the Master of the feast, and so will He be in every home and in every heart where He is invited to **abide.**

**And he vanished out of their sight.** We cannot understand the nature of the resurrected body which would permit such unhampered movement as we see here and elsewhere in the story of the risen Christ. Our Lord's body was real and not just apparent. Yet it was exempt from the common limitations of the human body.

In these two verses (30-31) describing the meal at Emmaus, Maclaren notes that the three points of the narrative are: (1) The distribution of the bread; (2) The discovery; (3) The disappearance.

---

[5]For a list of the Old Testament passages to which Jesus might have called attention in this discourse, see Spence, *op. cit.,* II, 271 f.

[6]*Ibid.,* p. 272.

**And they said one to another, Did not our heart burn within us, while he talked . . . and . . . opened to us the scriptures?** (32) Now that they recognized Him as their Lord, they understood why their hearts burned as He taught them by the way. These were not the last disciples of the Lord who have known the experience of the burning heart. The Living Word, the Revelation of God, had communicated divine truth, and their redeemed spirits responded naturally to His voice—which was indeed God's voice.

**And they rose up the same hour, and returned to Jerusalem, and found the eleven . . . saying, The Lord is risen indeed, and hath appeared to Simon** (33-34). Their thrill and optimism were in stark contrast to the pessimism of these disciples when they began their walk to Emmaus. Completely oblivious to the dangers which lurked on that semi-wilderness road at night, they literally bounded back to Jerusalem. But their joyous news must wait until a second appearance of the risen Lord has been related. As they entered the abode of the Eleven they heard the jubilant words of an excited disciple saying, **The Lord is risen indeed, and hath appeared to Simon.** The evidence was beginning to multiply.

**And they told what things were done in the way, and how he was known of them in breaking of bread** (35). They related the whole episode, from the sad conversation to the glorious realization of the Lord's presence. The expression **breaking of bread** has definite sacramental implications, especially when we remember that at the time Luke was writing his Gospel this expression was the common name for the sacrament of the Lord's Supper.

### 3. *The Risen Lord Visits His Disciples* (24:36-43)

**And as they thus spake, Jesus himself stood in the midst of them** (36). Both John and Luke place this appearance on the evening of the day of Christ's resurrection. John informs us that "the doors were shut . . . for fear of the Jews" (John 20:19). The expression **Jesus . . . stood in the midst of them** implies a sudden appearance rather than an observable entrance. **And saith . . . Peace be unto you.** This was the ordinary Jewish greeting. But it had more than the ordinary significance for Jesus' disciples at this time. It spoke a message of comfort, courage, and hope. For additional information on this and the following verses of the section see comments on John 20:19-23.

**But they were terrified and affrighted, and supposed that they had seen a spirit.** They had been jubilantly discussing the reports of His post-Resurrection appearances, and they must have been hoping He would reappear to all of them. But despite their joy and their hope, His sudden appearance—when all the doors were shut—terrified them. Despite the seeming contradiction of feelings here, we must all confess that their reaction was very human and very normal. The only explanation that seemed at all reasonable to them at the moment was that this was a spirit. How else could He appear in this manner?

At this point there appears to be a contradiction between Luke and John, for John says, "The disciples . . . were glad, when they saw the Lord" (John 20:20). However John evidently refers to the situation a few moments later, after they had recovered from the fright of the sudden and supernatural appearance, and after Jesus had reassured them with His precious words.

**And he said unto them, Why are ye troubled? . . . Behold my hands and my feet . . . handle me, and see; for a spirit hath not flesh and bone** (38-39). Jesus proceeds to show them that their fears are groundless and that their notion that He was a disembodied spirit was incorrect. He first shows them His hands and feet—the scars of the recent Crucifixion. Spirits do not have scars from earthly wounds. He then invites them to handle Him —to feel the solid flesh of a material body. Spirits do not have materiality; they do not have flesh and bone.

**And while they yet believed not for joy, and wondered** (41); this is equivalent to our modern expression, "It is too good to be true." It was so wonderful that they feared it might not be true. They were happy and fearful at the same time, like someone who suddenly gets what he has wanted more than anything else in the world.

**He said unto them, Have ye here any meat? And they gave him a piece of a broiled fish, and of an honeycomb. And he took it, and did eat** (41-43). This is a third demonstration of His materiality. Spirits do not eat fish and honey. In all of these demonstrations our Lord is trying to show that what the disciples see before them is not the disembodied spirit of a dead Jesus of Nazareth, but the risen body of the incarnate Son of God. He is really before them—body, soul, and spirit. His resurrection is in every sense a glorious reality.

### 4. *The Commission and the Promise* (24:44-49)

From this point to the end of the Gospel the reader must be aware of a passage of time that Luke does not make particularly evident in the narration. If this Gospel were the only source of information concerning the period between the resurrection and the ascension of Jesus, the reader might get the impression that not more than twenty-four hours of time passed. But Luke himself informs us in Acts 1:3 that the period was forty days long. It is not certain whether the instruction related in the present section was given to the disciples on the evening of the Lord's resurrection, on the same occasion as the preceding verse, or later. But this lack of information does not affect the interpretation.

**These are the words which I spake unto you, while I was yet with you** (44). Jesus refers to His ministry up to the time of His crucifixion as something in the past. The words **while I was yet with you** not only predict His ascension, but they also indicate that even at the moment He is speaking He is not "with them" in the same sense as before. His death and resurrection have changed the mortal to the immortal and put a difference between them which only their own deaths and resurrections can enable them to transcend.

**That all things must be fulfilled, which were written in the law of Moses, and in the prophets, and in the psalms, concerning me.** The **law,** the **prophets,** and the **psalms** are the three major divisions of the Hebrew Scriptures. Thus Jesus is referring to the full gamut of Messianic prophecy, from the first promise in Gen. 3:15 to the Book of Malachi. He makes clear an unbreakable tie between himself and this Old Testament prophecy. He reminds His disciples that He made this point clear while He was yet with them. Before His death the emphasis was that **all things must be fulfilled,** insofar as His earthly ministry is concerned.

**Then opened he their understanding, that they might understand the scriptures** (45). Just how Jesus **opened . . . their understanding** is not stated. It is possible that He did this by explanation of the Messianic prophecies just referred to. But Spence suggests what is probably the true meaning of this verse. He believes that these words were spoken on the evening of the first Easter. If this be so, Luke's **then opened he their understanding** is equivalent to John's declaration that Jesus "breathed on them, and saith unto them, Receive ye the Holy Ghost" (John 20:22). When we remember that "inspiration" means "in-

617

breathed," we see the logic of Spence's suggestion. Jesus was here giving His disciples the inspiration necessary to understand the Scriptures.[7]

**Thus it is written, and thus it behoved Christ to suffer, and to rise from the dead . . . and that repentance and remission of sins should be preached in his name among all nations, beginning at Jerusalem (46-47).** Here we see the necessity of the atonement related, in the past, to the Old Testament Scriptures, and, in the future, to the worldwide and agelong evangelistic crusade of the Church. The negative and positive aspects of the message can be stated thus: No salvation for anyone without the atonement; full salvation available for all men through the atonement.

**And ye are witnesses of these things (48).** The disciples of Jesus had seen His acts and heard His words; they had been given the gift of interpretation of Scripture by the "in-breathing" of Christ. After Pentecost they would have the required purity and power. All of this must be crystallized in a divinely appointed mission, **ye are witnesses.** Jesus was depending upon them to carry His message—the news of Blood-bought redemption. If they failed, He had no other way to send the word. But they would not have to go alone; the Holy Ghost would witness both *to* them and *through* them.

**Behold, I send the promise of my Father upon you:**[8] **but tarry ye in the city of Jerusalem, until ye be endued with power from on high (49).** This was a divine command which, until its fulfillment, must take precedence over the divine commission. Until they received their Pentecost they were not qualified to carry out the commission. The fulfillment of both the promise and the command contained in this verse came on the Day of Pentecost, when the 120 disciples were sanctified, baptized with the Holy Ghost.

The words of verse 49 were probably spoken by Jesus on the day of His ascension, ten days before their fulfillment, and forty days after the Resurrection.

C. The Ascension, 24:50-53

**And he led them out as far as to Bethany (50)**—meaning a part of the Mount of Olives which overlooks Bethany. For in

[7]See Spence, *op. cit.,* II, 275.
[8]See John 14:16-26; 15:26-27; 16:7.

Acts 1:12, Luke tells us that Jesus ascended from the Mount of Olives. **And he lifted up his hands, and blessed them**—a high priestly blessing and a parting benediction.

**And . . . while he blessed them, he was parted from them, and carried up into heaven (51).** Only Luke, of the four Gospel writers, tells us of the ascension of Jesus, though it is taken for granted throughout the remainder of the New Testament. Luke gives a fuller treatment in Acts 1:9-11.

**And they worshipped him, and returned to Jerusalem with great joy (52).** Their worship is an act of homage to an ascended but ever-present Saviour. Their joy shows how much they now understand their new relation to Jesus. They know they have not lost Him, but in some mysterious way He will be closer to them than before.

**And were continually in the temple, praising and blessing God (53).** This statement is amplified in the Acts of the Apostles. Luke thus summarized the latter lives of the apostles with this brief statement, knowing that he intended to cover the material in detail in another treatise.

# BIBLIOGRAPHY

## I. INTRODUCTIONS AND NEW TESTAMENT SURVEYS

BARNETT, ALBERT E. *The New Testament: Its Making and Meaning.* Nashville: Abingdon Press, 1958.

CAMBRON, MARK G. *The New Testament: A Book-by-Book Survey.* Grand Rapids: Zondervan Publishing House, 1958.

EARLE, RALPH (ed.), BLANEY, HARVEY J. S., HANSON, CARL. *Exploring the New Testament.* Kansas City: Beacon Hill Press, 1955.

FARRAR, F. W. *The Messages of the Books.* New York: The Macmillan Co., 1927.

FRANZMANN, MARTIN H. *The Word of the Lord Grows.* St. Louis: Concordia Publishing House, 1961.

GOODSPEED, EDGAR J. *An Introduction to the New Testament.* Chicago: University of Chicago Press, 1937.

MILLER, ADAM W. *An Introduction to the New Testament.* Anderson, Ind.: Gospel Trumpet Co., 1943.

PRICE, JAMES L. *Interpreting the New Testament.* New York: Holt, Rinehart and Winston, 1961.

TENNEY, MERRILL C. *New Testament Survey.* Grand Rapids: Wm. B. Eerdmans Publishing Co., 1961.

THIESSEN, HENRY C. *Introduction to the New Testament.* Grand Rapids: Wm. B. Eerdmans Publishing Co., 1943.

## II. SPECIAL WORKS

HOBART, WILLIAM KIRK. *The Medical Language of St. Luke.* Grand Rapids: Baker Book House, 1954 (reprint).

RAMSAY, WILLIAM M. *Luke the Physician and Other Studies.* Grand Rapids: Baker Book House, 1956 (reprint).

## III. GENERAL WORKS

EDERSHEIM, ALFRED. *The Life and Times of Jesus the Messiah,* 2 vols. Grand Rapids: Wm. B. Eerdmans Publishing Company, 1943.

GEIKIE, CUNNINGHAM. *New Testament Hours,* 4 vols. New York: James Pott & Company, 1897.

JOSEPHUS, FLAVIUS. *The Life and Works of Flavius Josephus.* Translated by WILLIAM WHISTON. Edited by REV. H. STEBBING. Philadelphia: The John C. Winston Company, n.d.

LANGE, PETER JOHN. *The Life of the Lord Jesus Christ.* Translated by SOPHIA TAYLOR and J. E. RYLAND. Edited by MARCUS DODDS. Grand Rapids: Zondervan Publishing House, 1952 (reproduction of 1872 edition published by T. & T. Clark).

# IV. COMMENTARIES

BARCLAY, WILLIAM. *The Gospel of Luke.* Philadelphia: The Westminster Press, 1956.

BARNES, ALBERT. *Notes on the New Testament.* Grand Rapids: Baker Book House, 1949.

BRUCE, ALEXANDER BALMAIN. "The Synoptic Gospels," *The Expositor's Greek Testament.* Edited by W. ROBERTSON NICOLL, Vol. I. Grand Rapids: Wm. B. Eerdmans Publishing Company, n.d.

CLARKE, ADAM. *The New Testament of Our Lord and Saviour Jesus Christ.* New York-Nashville: Abingdon-Cokesbury Press, n.d.

DAVIDSON, F. (ed.). *New Bible Commentary.* Grand Rapids: Wm. B. Eerdmans Publishing Company, 1960.

GELDENHUYS, NORVAL. *Commentary on the Gospel of Luke.* "The New International Commentary on the New Testament." Grand Rapids: Wm. B. Eerdmans Publishing Company, 1951.

GILMORE, S. MACLEAN. "The Gospel According to St. Luke" (Exegesis). *The Interpreter's Bible.* Edited by GEORGE A. BUTTRICK, *et al.,* Vol. VIII. New York: Abingdon-Cokesbury Press, 1952.

GODET, F. *A Commentary on the Gospel of St. Luke.* Translated by E. W. SHALDERS. Edinburgh: T. & T. Clark, n.d.

GRAY, JAMES COMPER, and ADAMS, GEORGE W. *Bible Commentary,* Vol. IV. Grand Rapids: Zondervan Publishing House, n.d.

HENRY, MATTHEW. *Commentary on the Whole Bible,* Vol. V. New York: Fleming H. Revell Company, n.d.

MACLAREN, ALEXANDER. *Expositions of Holy Scriptures,* Vol. VI. Grand Rapids: Wm. B. Eerdmans Publishing Company, 1959.

SPENCE, H. D. M. "St. Luke" (Exposition). *The Pulpit Commentary.* Edited by H. D. M. SPENCE, Vol. XVI. Grand Rapids: Wm. B. Eerdmans Publishing Company, 1958.

VAN OOSTERZEE, J. J. "The Gospel According to St. Luke." *Commentary on the Holy Scriptures.* Edited by J. P. LANGE. Grand Rapids: Zondervan Publishing House, n.d.

# HEROD'S TEMPLE

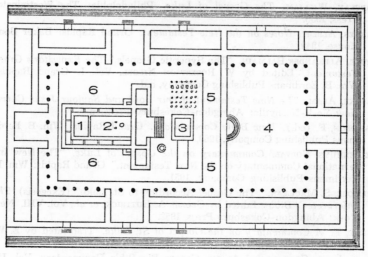

Tower of
Antonia

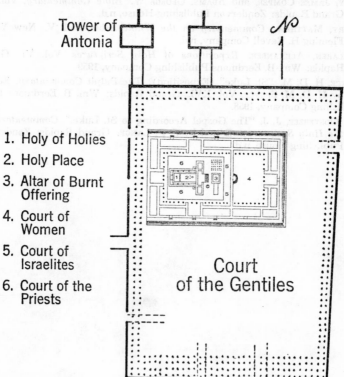

1. Holy of Holies
2. Holy Place
3. Altar of Burnt
   Offering
4. Court of
   Women
5. Court of
   Israelites
6. Court of the
   Priests

Court
of the Gentiles

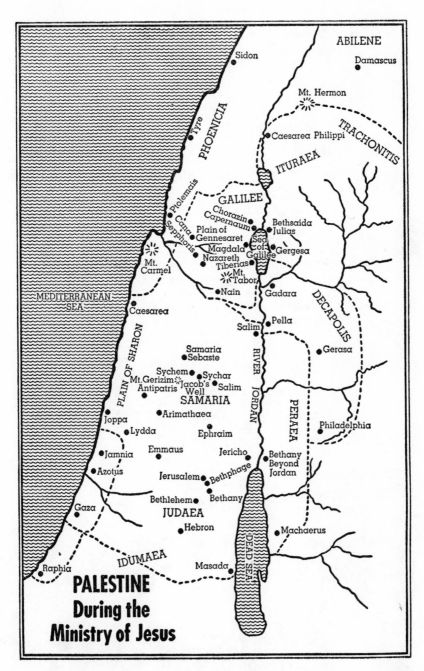

ABILENE

Sidon

Damascus

Mt. Hermon

PHOENICIA

Tyre

TRACHONITIS

Caesarea Philippi

ITURAEA

Ptolemais

GALILEE

Cana

Chorazin

Capernaum

Bethsaida
Julias

Plain of
Gennesaret

Sepphoris

Magdala

Sea
of
Galilee

Gergesa

Nazareth

Tiberias

Mt.
Carmel

Mt.
Tabor

MEDITERRANEAN
SEA

Nain

Gadara

DECAPOLIS

Caesarea

Salim

Pella

RIVER JORDAN

Gerasa

PLAIN OF SHARON

Samaria
Sebaste

Sychem

Sychar

Mt. Gerizim

Jacob's
Well

Antipatris

Salim

SAMARIA

Joppa

Arimathaea

Lydda

Ephraim

PERAEA

Philadelphia

Jamnia

Emmaus

Jericho

Bethany
Beyond
Jordan

Azotus

Jerusalem

Bethphage

Bethlehem

Bethany

Gaza

JUDAEA

Hebron

DEAD SEA

Machaerus

Raphia

IDUMAEA

Masada

**PALESTINE**
**During the**
**Ministry of Jesus**